More praise for *Shame and Pride:*

"This is a remarkable and stimulating treatment of two important human experiences, shame and pride, which have been on the whole surprisingly neglected. The book is full of human examples as well as solid clinical material and is characterized by a good deal of personal charm and wit. I found it the kind of book that one can enjoy reading and rereading because it generates interesting skeins of association to one's own life and experiences as well as to issues of theory and clinical practice."

—Jerome L. Singer, Ph.D.
Professor and Director of Graduate Studies in Psychology,
Yale University

"Shame: what is it, what brings it about, how may one avoid or compensate for it, and why is it so important in the conduct of our lives? Donald Nathanson, an expert psychotherapist, gives us the answers to these and other questions about shame and its centrality for relationships in this comprehensive but eminently readable book. *Shame and Pride* is essential not only for the practicing psycho-therapist, but also for every reader who has an interest in understanding human nature."

—Michael Franz Basch, M.D.
Professor of Psychiatry, Rush Medical College, Chicago

"Donald Nathanson's lucid writing and in-depth knowledge of Tomkins's affect theory bring the emotion of shame out of the shadows and into the light of understanding. He enables us to see that shame is both biology and biography. This book is a benchmark in the literature of shame; all future discussions of shame will need to be measured against Nathanson's work. And besides all that, the book makes great reading."

—David R. Cook, Ed.D.
Professor, Department of Counseling and Psychological Services,
University of Wisconsin-Stout

By the same author

The Many Faces of Shame

SHAME AND PRIDE

AFFECT, SEX, AND THE BIRTH OF THE SELF

Donald L. Nathanson

W.W. Norton & Company   New York   London

Copyright © 1992 by Donald L. Nathanson
All rights reserved
Printed in the United States of America
First published as a Norton paperback 1994

The text of this book is composed in Palatino with the display set in Gill Sans.
Manufacturing by The Haddon Craftsmen, Inc.
Book design by Ruth Mandel

Library of Congress Cataloging in Publication Data
Nathanson, Donald L.
    Shame and pride : affect, sex, and the birth of the self / Donald L. Nathanson.
        p.   cm.
    Includes bibliographical references and index.
    1. Shame.   2. Pride and vanity.   3. Affect (Psychology)   4. Self psychology.   I. Title.
    [DNLM: 1. Ego.   2. Psychoanalytic Theory.   3. Self Concept.
    4. Shame.   BF 575.S45 N275s]
    BF575.S45N375   1992
    152.4—dc20
    DNLM/DLC
    for Library of Congress   91-29112

ISBN 0-393-31109-0

W. W. Norton & Company, Inc.
500 Fifth Avenue, New York, N.Y. 10110
www.wwnorton.com

W. W. Norton & Company Ltd.
Castle House, 75/76 Wells Street, London W1T 3QT

6.

Show my stories → pull away from people for feel

good vibes, when it's not warm = affectionate

Beyond the white picket fence:

website true stories → TRUTH

what's really going on in these homes?

To Silvan S. Tomkins

Let go, let flow → see where it goes, let it roll . . . .

On talk shows at end mention website +

What I am doing → share your experiences!!

First 50, win copy of my book to send to favorite Republican.

Nick & I polar opposites → I'm connected to my

insight + intuition, N not, But he is

connected to the pure emotion of it + I'm not.

This is what we can help each other with. He knows

joy + love

add "a work in progress" at bottom of my title

I'm the publisher, I can do whatever I want.

Also in preface discuss the px with citations.

discuss it being a quilt.

up until now, I've created energetic friction

kept me in control, kept the joy + freedom

down as well. That is scary to me. I never

experienced it.

I have concerns of N. communication. what I need →

a man committed to personal growth.

With my brand, Truthsayers Unite
\ fill my soul - experience

My journey To feeling

I would like To explore more p̄ my "in progress"
      shame, soul, grace.
   * The "Anti - Kardashian" -> is my life's work.

CONTENTS

ACKNOWLEDGMENTS

This book introduces an entirely new way of thinking about shame and pride. The ideas involved lead inescapably to new theories about love, about sexuality, and about the emotional intensity of our present era. The reader will find novel explanations of rape, police brutality, and a wide range of violent behavior. We live in times made more dangerous by our misunderstanding of shame.

For many, it will be a first presentation of the new theories of emotion made possible by two generations of research. Even the word "emotion" will be replaced by the more versatile term "affect." Since the midpoint of this century there has been an avalanche of experimental data about the nature of feelings and mood. Our cupboards are filled with medications capable of turning off and on a wide range of affects as if by a switch; daily, the physician sees people with medical illnesses characterized by specific alterations of affect. Psychotherapists, novelists, and filmmakers have observed, described, and depicted the effects and range of affect. Yet this is the first book that connects into one coherent system all of this information. Without such an approach, both shame and pride remain mysterious and confusing.

One does not attempt such a synthesis lightly. Many friends and colleagues have protected and supported me during these years of study and deliberation. Early in this work, feeling overwhelmed by the amount of information requiring assimilation, I asked some of them to join me in a study group. Psychiatrist Vernon C. Kelly, Jr., came to my assistance and has remained a powerful ally throughout. Our teaching efforts have been materially assisted by Robert E. Desmond, Karen Miura, Andrew M. Stone, James Pfrommer, and Shelley Milestone.

A small coterie of friends devoted so much of their time and energy to my project that I am, in retrospect, embarrassed to have asked so much of them. Michael Franz Basch, whose attempt to bring to psychoanalysis a new understanding of emotion proved of great importance to my own, has been essential to my work. Not only did he read and offer critical comment on every chapter, but he also made it possible for me to speak at a number of public gatherings where I would learn to handle the equally daunting experiences of criticism and praise. Psychoanalytic psychologist Johanna Krout Tabin also went over every line from her perspective, helping me explain the older theories and making sure my own ideas were clearly stated. Psychiatrist and lifelong friend Joseph M. Dubey also contributed a tremendous amount of time to my project. Robert J. Stoller discussed my new theory of sexuality and made many cogent suggestions.

Most new scientific ideas are presented first at professional meetings. Often my own budget was inadequate to support extended travel to the meetings that counted. At critical moments I was helped by Layton McCurdy, then psychiatrist-in-chief of the Institute of Pennsylvania Hospital, and now dean of the Medical University of South Carolina. Everybody's ideas seem a little easier to express in the company of this great educator.

The serious writer on shame joins a club filled with kind, gentle, helpful colleagues. It was Léon Wurmser who first declared that my singular approach deserved attention; he has been unstinting in his support and assistance. Francis J. Broucek, Gershen Kaufman, Andrew P. Morrison, and Carl D. Schneider have helped at every turn, both by their important writings and by their personal attention to the myriad of questions I raised at odd moments and in peculiar locales. The death of Helen Block Lewis robbed all of us of her friendship, wisdom, and guidance. David Cook and I have spent innumerable hours discussing the fine points of theory and their application to his highly original test for "internalized shame."

Some friends helped make other parts of life easier during this period of writing. I mention them in a rush rather than embarrass them more specifically: Stefanie and L. Donald Tashjian, Diane and Alan Chase, Ileen and Gilbert Abramson, and many, many more. Ronda Throne and D. Craig Althouse conspired to keep to a minimum the distraction provided by an aching back; it is far easier to think when free from pain. Others, like James Hinz and Christopher Wolfe of F. Thomas Heller, Inc.; Joseph, Madelaine, and Michael Fox of the Joseph Fox Bookshop; John Gach of John Gach Books; Sue Davis; and Walter Bacon McDaniel, showed me books that made a difference. Paul J. Sherman, as both lawyer and agent for Buddy Hackett, made possible my work with that great but busy entertainer. I would not have dared to offer some of the linguistic speculations that appear herein without the assistance of Patricia Furey. Werner Gundersheimer, director of the Folger Shakespeare Library, opened to me that vast treasure house of Renaissance literature and advised my historical survey with his characteristic kindness and erudition.

There is a section in every preface where the writer expresses gratitude to the secretaries who turned scribbles and dictation into typescript. In my case, however, the "secretary" is a bunch of electronic marvels—computers, word-processing software, printers, and other machines that make writing possible for me. David Rothschild has made sure my equipment is current and choice. But it is Jeff Goldberg I must thank most, the astute and patient technician who makes house calls day and night, teaches me the arcane new software he insists I learn, and who turns these mysterious machines into household friends.

The relationship between writer and editor is dynamic and tenuous; no one knows the tender art of criticism better than the great editors. If you read psychology books then you know about W. W. Norton's Susan Barrows Munro. Everybody thanks her all the time, few of us really communicating how good it feels to have an empathic editor who is truly capable of making us better writers. Candace Watt's gentle assistance toward clarity has been most welcome. Books also require a link between the worlds of scholarship and commerce. Anyone who has had the opportunity of working with John A. Ware knows how important it is to have so intuitive and capable an agent act as interface between the two worlds.

A little girl some years ago when I began to study shame, my daughter Julie has not only read and studied every page of this book but also tested many of its ideas on her then high school cronies. Some of them have accosted me on the lacrosse field or at play rehearsal to ask the kind of intelligent questions that reveal remarkable understanding. Her love and support have buoyed me greatly during these years of struggle.

Empathy, support, love? No one could ask for more than what I have always received from my beloved wife, Rosalind. Time to write this book was carved, stolen, from our shared life, making more precious each moment we spent together. Rarely did she complain when speaking engagements pulled us away from home during the busiest parts of her real estate season. Whoever writes on shame knows as much about pain and failure as about the healing balm of love. How lucky I am to have her beside me!

But of all those whose efforts have assisted my work, one stands so far above the others that it is to him I dedicate this book. Silvan S. Tomkins, to whom so many refer as "the American Einstein," developed his affect theory nearly 40 years ago. Only now is the scholarly world beginning to understand what was to him obvious long ago. (Nothing places greater demand on our mental equipment than the need to unlearn what we have always taken for granted.) In a lifetime of exposure to the greatest and most celebrated minds in many areas of science, never have I met his equal. Tomkins made available to me unlimited amounts of time—at his home in Strathmere, New Jersey, over the telephone, and in his meticulous attention to every page of this book. Every aspect of his theory discussed or described here has been negotiated to our mutual satisfaction. I am honored that he accepted the many additions to his work described herein. That Tomkins did not receive the kind of national or international award that might have saluted appropriately his contribution and its genius is the shame of our era.

Those who have come to understand Tomkins's contribution ask again and again why, in this era of rapid dissemination of scientific knowledge, it has taken so long for his ideas to "catch on." A recent meeting of my local astronomy club provided some intriguing answers:

A group of astronomers noticed that certain basic concepts, no matter how carefully taught, never got integrated into the minds of their students. Funded by a grant from the National Science Foundation, they caught on film some of the reasons for the persistence of incorrect science. Resplendent in caps and gowns, twenty graduating Harvard College seniors were asked why it is cold in winter and warm in summer. Nineteen replied that the earth is further from the sun in winter and closer in summer.

To us as audience, the astronomers explained that heat and light do, indeed, vary in proportion to distance from their source. That is why Mercury and Venus are too hot to sustain human life, Neptune and Pluto too cold. But even though the Earth's orbit around the sun is slightly elliptical, the alterations in distance involved are relatively trivial and insufficient to account for our weather. (The Earth is actually *nearest* the sun during the first week of January, and *furthest* during the first week of July!) Our planet just happens to be tilted $23\frac{1}{2}°$ from true vertical (from the plane of its orbit around the sun), and it carries that orientation in space no matter where it happens to be. As a result, the slant of the Earth–sun line changes as the Earth obeys its orbit. The energy contained in a beam of light will be distributed most compactly, most efficiently, during summer, while the same amount of energy will be spread over a much wider swatch of ground during winter. There is more than one way to control the amount of energy reaching a target.

That sounds easy enough, doesn't it? Next, the astronomers were shown teaching this material to a group of talented high school students, each of whom had also believed that seasonal variation in weather depends on distance from the sun. As you might expect, all of them were fascinated to learn about the tilted earth, and all of them did well on the quiz that followed. Only a couple of weeks later, when asked to explain the seasons, the brightest among them drew the solar system correctly—earth tilted just right, our moon placed appropriately—and discussed the way heat varies in proportion to distance from its source. It is extraordinarily difficult to teach the simple geo-metric truths on which our weather is based because nearly all of us formed our own homemade theories about the seasons when we were children. We are incapable of learning anything new until we give up the old.

One is reminded of the Zen teaching story in which a European professor asked a Zen master for instruction into his philosophy. Before each man was a full cup of tea. Picking up the teapot, the Japanese sage poured more tea into the cup of his guest until so much had spilled onto his lap that the astonished European exclaimed for his host to stop. Replied his teacher: "You must empty your cup before it can accept anything new."

Tomkins deserves honor both for the incisiveness of his thinking and the willingness to open his mind to the implications of those observations. Let us try to do the same.

INTRODUCTION

One spring day, not so many years ago, I ventured forth from the safety and sanctuary of my office and my study to share with some colleagues my growing conviction that we were all pretty much ignorant about the nature of shame. I said that we might help our patients better if we remedied this situation. A lifetime of painful shyness had made it difficult for me to speak in public, even though I had by that time spent more than 20 years studying the biology and the phenomenology of emotion. This was my first professional presentation in psychiatry.

I knew that shame was considered the ignored emotion, "the Cinderella of the unpleasant emotions," according to Rycroft's *Critical Dictionary of Psychoanalysis.* It didn't seem possible to me that any one paper would change this, so I had organized an entire symposium on shame to take place under the umbrella of the American Psychiatric Association. Co-sponsored by the American Psychoanalytic Association, it turned out to be the first meeting in the history of psychiatry or psychoanalysis, either here in America or over in Europe where psychoanalysis got its start, to focus on the nature of shame.

Afterwards, a friend took me aside and said, "That was really nice. But don't do anything more on shame. You wouldn't want to get a reputation for that." A kind and thoughtful man, he was truly concerned about my public image. Better to hide new ideas in obscurity than risk exposure and humiliation, especially ideas about an unpopular subject.

It was in that moment that I learned that the very *idea* of shame is embarrassing to most people.

So much discomfort does shame produce that people will go to great lengths to avoid it. Many of us who have studied shame in depth believe that it is a primary force in social and political evolution. Shame—our reaction to it and our avoidance of it—becomes the emotion of politics and conformity. It guides and creates fashion; its influence in human civilization is paramount.

In the opening scene of George Bernard Shaw's *Man and Superman*, John Tanner tells us that "we live in an atmosphere of shame. We are ashamed of everything that is real about us; ashamed of ourselves, of our relatives, of our incomes, of our accents, of our opinions, of our experience, just as we are ashamed of our naked skins." For one interested in shame the problem is not that it is difficult to find examples worth study. Rather, the more significant puzzle is how it has managed to elude us until now. This most common of unpleasant experiences is also the least discussed.

Who among us has not at some time been paralyzed by shame? As a boy, poring over the *Reader's Digest* anecdotes called "My Most Embarrassing Moment," I wondered whether I could ever tell anybody about those moments when I had goofed, or made a fool of myself, or said precisely the wrong thing to someone I wanted to impress. Since we all tend to place ourselves in the position of the person telling a story, were I to tell you any of them right now I am afraid you might shudder with discomfort and stop reading. I have never mastered the clown's art of turning my own misfortune into comedy.

Perhaps laughter is the best defense against the pain of shame. The clown makes a trade. Dressed in his traditional costume (the classical clown is always male), he behaves with all the foolishness of a small child pretending to be an adult. Although people are laughing at him (which is embarrassing) the laughter is under his own control, which makes him feel powerful and proud of himself rather than helpless and ashamed.

Most of us work hard to present ourselves to the world as competent and "cool." Any time people laugh at us our self-esteem is reduced and we are embarrassed. Any moment of embarrassment is guaranteed to interrupt the flow of our day and reduce our ability to live comfortably among others, let alone feel comfortable within ourselves. The clown gives up this very important piece of self-esteem in order to gain whatever sense of personal pride comes from his success in getting us to laugh at his command.

Most clowns, and certainly all comedians, are quick to admit that they are basically shy people, terribly afraid of being laughed at. One comic told me privately, "The only time in my life I really feel comfortable with myself is when I'm on stage working and the audience is laughing. Going out socially is a trap because I'm too shy to talk to people as myself, and if I start to tell jokes or do my routine I'm working and not going out to relax like ordinary people. So I tend to stay home a lot."

The circus clown strikes a good deal. It is only his garish costume and heavy makeup that identify him as the object of our laughter. Dressed in civilian clothes, he merges quietly, imperceptibly, into the crowd, his power and his frailties held privately within him. Throughout this book we will see everywhere how we adults balance our private selves and our public presentation, and how intricately these are tied up with what for each of us becomes our personal definitions of shame and pride.

The easiest way to start the study of shame is to observe the fine points of this linkage between embarrassment and laughter. All the equipment you need is in your own living room. Make a videotape of your favorite situation comedy and, after you've enjoyed it once or twice, watch it again to see why you laughed. Pick, if possible, a show without a fake audience, one that does not resort to a phony laugh track to force us into synchrony or conformity by telling us when to laugh. The conventional wisdom of the television industry dictates that a successful show must have a certain number of laughs per minute, whether or not something "funny" is happening. What we are after here are the moments in which you laugh.

Notice how often what you found amusing involved somebody's embarrassment. Examples may range from pratfalls or clear, obvious flashes of unexpected stupidity to subtle comments or allusions that made you think of something stupid you yourself had once done but that you didn't know anyone else had ever experienced.

Next, try to figure out why there was embarrassment associated with the action within the show. Pretty soon you will see that shame seems always to involve a more-or-less sudden decrease in self-esteem, a moment in which we are revealed as somewhat less than we want to believe. On a sitcom most people are friendly to each other, so whoever has been exposed is in an atmosphere of interpersonal safety. When our frailties or foibles are exposed before those in whose presence we do not feel safe or loved, this mild, humorous embarrassment gives way to the deeper forms of shame like humiliation or mortification. Comedy, however, rarely does more than hint at the darker side of shame; perhaps some of its success lies in the delicacy with which it plays around the edges of what is hidden within each of us. We all live on some line between shame and pride. The work of comedy is to make this border a bit safer.

The comedian stands alongside us, pointing at others, exposing the falseness of their self-esteem and so allowing us the safety of laughing at them, while the clown focuses our attention on himself and asks us to laugh at him. The only remaining performers who make us laugh are the jesters, who (to the extent they are given permission) can expose our secrets and make us laugh at ourselves. They live at the greatest risk, for the slightest slip will move them past the boundary of "good taste" into a realm where they incur only wrath. In the medieval court the jester alone could tell the truth about the king. Usually a deformed and therefore already "defective" and shameworthy creature, his humor came from this ability to expose and embarrass within strictly defined limits. There are a lot of jokes about jesters sentenced to death for "going too far."

There is, of course, much more to comedy than its relation to shame. Bill Cosby, who is gifted as clown, comedian, and jester, brings an additional talent I haven't seen since Jimmy Durante, whose contagious happiness made audiences laugh because they just plain felt good. (All of the affects are capable of "infecting" others.) With the sound turned off, watch an early videotape of Cosby and you will often see him shaking with silent mirth, the most potent form of infectious laughter. When he does that, we observers tend to laugh, even though we aren't laughing "about" anything. Robert Culp, who starred with Cosby in their 1960s detective sitcom "I Spy," said that there were many times they had to do a number of "takes" of a scene because both he and the other members of the cast were laughing unaccountably when Cosby was involved.

If you take the trouble to study videotapes of television shows from previous decades, I think you will see that Red Skelton, Lucille Ball, Carol Burnett, and Jackie Gleason are great clowns; stand-up comics like Bob Hope and Johnny Carson fit my definition of comedians (even though they often clown); while the tradition of the jester is upheld by Buddy Hackett (who can poke fun at anybody safely) and Don Rickles, whose insults are so focused and piercing that the object of his attack must ever be on the edge of fighting back—shame experienced as an uncertain balance between laughter and rage. Watching Rickles insult others on a television show has become a form of spectator sport. Merely to attend his nightclub act places one at risk of assault by jest.

The work of these masters of comedy has stood the test of time because it touches on themes of shame and pride important to major segments of the population. Comics come and go, each with an idea or a gimmick that may or may not attract a secure following. Steve Martin worked as a clown who allowed us to laugh at his exaggerated narcissism; when this maneuver wore thin he became a screen actor. Bobcat Goldthwaite is a clown in the realm of fear. When he screams we see an adult exposed as a little boy forced to live in the terrifying world of grownups. The talented young Rita Rudner uses her considerable intelligence to appear naive and a bit stupid, her grace and poise operating in stark (and often hilarious) contrast to the embarrassed incoordination we would expect in one who is aware of what she is saying. Check out the current crop of entertainers (while they are available) to see how each of them uses shame.

In societies that do not foster the work of the jester we see the emergence of satire, which exposes to bitter laughter what has been hidden. Shame can power all forms of humor. Of course I know that there is more to humor than shame, and more to happiness than liberation from shame. Nevertheless, few experiences in life are so pleasant as the moment of release from shame or the realization that our foibles are accepted with love.

A FEW TERMS DEFINED

People use a wide range of words to describe their personal experience of shame. Any simple definition will be influenced by an individual's life experience, including the family, neighborhood, nation, or era in which one grew up. I suggest that we follow the lead of the psychoanalyst Léon Wurmser, who speaks of the shame experience as a family of emotions. These are uncomfortable feelings, ranging from the mildest twinge of embarrassment to the searing pain of mortification, the Latin roots of which imply that shame can strike one dead. Shame often follows a moment of exposure; what has been exposed is something that we would have preferred kept hidden, usually something of an intimate and personal nature. Although it can be handled or diminished by laughter, anger, or withdrawal, shame always speaks about our inner self rather than our actions.

Often shame is confused with guilt, a related but quite different discomfort. Whereas shame is about the *quality* of our person or self, guilt is the painful emotion triggered when we become aware that we have acted in a way to bring harm to another person or to violate some important code. Guilt is about *action* and laws. Whenever we feel guilty, we can pay for the damage inflicted. The confessional is a system of release from guilt, for it allows us to do penance for sins we know we have committed—a simple trade of one action for another.

Sometimes we are accused of wrongdoing and brought to public trial. The legal proceedings themselves are a source of shame, even though by them we are adjudged "guilty" or "not guilty." If guilty, we are punished within the system of laws that governs us. No such easy system exists to facilitate our return from shame.

Whether our good works have been occasioned by priestly instruction or by personal choice, when we do something well we usually feel good about ourselves. Just as we will use the word shame to indicate the family of negative emotions associated with incompetence, failure, or inadequacy, "pride" will define a whole family of positive emotions. The basic feeling of pride stems from the pleasure we achieve in a moment of competence.

All too often our self-esteem has been reduced by a myriad of circumstances far out of our control, and the only way we can get a quick pick-me-up is to do something that makes us feel good. Throughout this book I will talk about the balance between shame and pride, between the sort of hoped-for *personal best* that hovers as an unreachable image within most of us and the terribly feared *personal worst* that, when revealed, will trigger an avalanche of deadly shame. This *shame/pride axis* will occupy much of our attention, for it is against this yardstick that we evaluate all of our actions, and along which is strung our fragile and precarious sense of self.

Such concepts are easy to understand when we study people who are more or less like us—who take pride in accomplishments we favor, are guilty about actions we consider wrong, and are embarrassed at the disclosure of personal qualities we do not fancy. Yet at the level of the emotion itself, can there be any real difference between the pride of a hunter bagging his quarry, the pride of a soldier who kills his enemy in battle, and the pride experienced by a terrorist when his bomb kills a busload of schoolchildren? I think not. In each situation the same emotion has been triggered by a different source.

Consider, too, the fact that the driver of a bank robber's getaway car may feel guilty when a maneuver executed to avoid killing an innocent passerby results in the arrest of a partner. Can we also suspend our own sense of morality enough to understand the possibility that a Nazi officer working in a death camp might feel humiliated when his superiors saw that he was unable to kill his quota of Jews that day? Our adult experiences of shame and pride are linked inextricably to the culture in which we live, the interpersonal milieu within which our personalities are formed. We must be careful to avoid the trap of saying that our understanding of any emotion is better or more valid than that of one who grew up differently.

Some years ago I read in *Newsweek* that scholars had translated a medieval literary work loaded with meticulous descriptions of the personal habits of rather commonplace people. Neither the quality of observation nor the importance of the subjects seemed to have warranted publication of the original book. After much study it was determined that this was a book of humor, little or none of which was funny today. Comedy involves exposure that triggers embarrassment capable of being handled as amusement. Those personal attributes we wish to keep hidden serve as the resource, the reservoir for shame.

Remember when we read in school the comedies of Shakespeare and dutifully studied the dour scholarly footnotes telling us what was probably funny around 1600? Whatever is contained in the reservoir changes from one era to another; thus the reasons for embarrassed laughter vary over time. But no matter what type of embarrassment forms the basis of humor, it is discussed and presented and experienced as humor, rather than anything primarily related to shame. Shame is the hidden power behind much of what occupies us in everyday life.

One might think that shame, this most deeply personal of emotional experiences, would be a common subject in the world of psychotherapy. It is, after all, in our personal therapy that most of us learn to overcome the shame associated with the revelation of our most cherished and painful secrets. The general reader may be surprised to learn that until quite recently shame has been almost totally ignored by the various schools of psychotherapy.

Whenever a patient tried to talk about an embarrassing experience, the therapist was likely to nod sympathetically or laugh tolerantly to indicate that the embarrassment was probably deserved. A deeper experience of shame was handled by addressing the anger or fear that accompanied it or by confusing it with guilt. Highly competent therapists had been trained neither to treat nor even to recognize shame, but were immediately attentive to those other emotions, which they understood quite well. Certainly the world of psychotherapy has acknowledged the existence of shame, but as a "primitive" emotion worthy of less serious attention than guilt.

A CLUE: SHAME AND DEPRESSION

It happens that both shame and guilt are important symptoms of the group of illnesses now called "depression." When someone is filled with guilt unrelieved by confession and penance, by recollection and interpretation, or by the intentional restructuring of thought patterns, a modern psychiatrist offers antidepressant prescriptions. Such symptoms are typical of a biological depression and often easily relieved by proper medication.

But it also happens that some people seem depressed but complain more that there is something wrong that makes them shy away from and fear contact with others or that makes them seek hedonistic experiences which offer transient relief. Interestingly enough, this sort of discomfort has always been difficult to treat by any means, and it has come to be known as "atypical depression." More recently, it has been shown that these patients respond to a group of medications entirely different from that which works with classical depression. Like my colleagues, I am pleased that we are now able to help a greater number of patients. Nevertheless, it seems to me incorrect to ignore a basic emotion.

In 1984 I suggested that classical depression involved the thinking, the feeling, and the chemistry of guilt, and that the atypical depressions were about shame. Many of my associates were startled by the idea that there was a chemistry for any individual emotion and astonished at the idea that shame and guilt might have different biological origins. Suddenly, the very fact that we had a "treatment" for persistent and unremitting shame made it worthwhile for many people to contemplate shame, a subject about which they had almost no information.

THE STUDY OF SHAME

Paradoxically, many fine, well-written books and journal articles about shame had been available for years, although none had ever found its way into the mainstream of psychotherapeutic education. I know of no textbook in general psychology or psychiatry that allots more than a few sentences to shame. Many fail to mention it at all.

It is axiomatic that therapists treat their own patients in a manner and style somewhat akin to the way they themselves were treated. In part, we therapists base our personal style—the way we "do therapy"—on what we learned from our teachers and from our reading. The overwhelming majority of psychotherapists has had some experience of personal therapy, for it really is very difficult for anyone to understand the deeper layers of another's personality unless one has had some experience dealing with one's own. This period of personal therapy is so important to a growing therapist that, for better or worse, it is stamped indelibly onto that therapist as a major piece of his or her personal style. And therapists who have never been trained or treated in the area of shame can neither recognize nor treat the shame of another.

In an attempt to change this situation, as I mentioned above, I organized the symposium "Shame—New Clinical and Theoretical Aspects" for the May 1984 national meeting of the American Psychiatric Association. Four of the papers presented there became the core of a book called *The Many Faces of Shame*, in which I attempted to bring together and call attention to the work of every living scholar known for either theoretical or clinical work in this area. The enormous interest generated by that meeting has produced a flood of books and articles on shame, making it today more trendy than ignored.

THE NATURE OF EMOTION

Such shifts in both the public and private perceptions of an emotion have been a central interest of mine for many decades. From early childhood I have asked three questions: What is emotion? Why does the human have so much of it? and What can be done about it? It is neither desirable nor even possible to write sensibly about any emotion without addressing these three questions. Any attempt to study shame and pride will be flawed and misleading unless these emotions are placed in the context of a general theory of emotion. This is more true for shame than for any other emotion. As I will demonstrate in a later chapter, the reasons it has been hidden and ignored are both intrinsic to its biologic nature and implicit in the general theories of emotion prevalent until recently.

Many of us treat emotion merely as something that interferes with thinking. We demean arguments by calling them emotional, discredit people who seem emotionally involved in whatever bothers them, trust feelings less than cognition. Our culture even has code words that allow us to pretend we are talking about thinking rather than feeling. Rather than admit that our concern is emotional, we will say, "I have a *problem* with that," or "Don't *bother* me with such ideas," or "That *upsets* me."

Whenever we place somebody on the inherently pejorative axis of rational versus irrational we have implied a judgment about the degree to which reason has been impaired by emotion. Our concept of maturity is related to the observation that children are more likely to be overwhelmed by emotion than adults. An adult does not merely cry when distressed—one is *reduced* to tears. (Even to express certain emotions is shameful.) The champion of my high school debating team won a great victory arguing that any decision made with passion was intrinsically flawed, an attitude equally prevalent these forty years later.

Some complex emotions, like love and loyalty, are valued when kept within limits; others, like cold hatred and murderous rage, are generally viewed as inhuman or beyond the range of acceptability. But despite our attitudes toward one or another emotion, we rarely think about emotion as such or try to place a particular emotion within a coherent scheme for all emotion. Pretty much, we take for granted that emotion exists, for better or worse, and that we have to live with it.

Even more perplexing is the fact that every one of us has a personal system of definitions for each emotion. Somewhere in the initial series of interviews through which a prospective new patient and I evaluate each other, I have always asked this stranger certain questions about his or her experience of anger. I want to know how each parent behaved when angry, what anger feels like to my patient, and how he or she behaves when angry. One man may shout, yell, and pound his fist on the table; another throw small objects around the room; another may treat people with similar violence; still others may curl the lip in contempt and sneer at the object of their anger; while another group of adults may grow cold, withdraw, and become silent until the storm of emotion has passed. And if I ask the man who shouts what he thinks of anger expressed by icy withdrawal, he may tell me that such behavior is not anger but "meanness," which (to him) is an entirely different emotion.

Until recently there has been neither language nor science capable of explaining everything we do and do not know about emotion. Just as each of us has arrived at our current age and station in life by treading a path of experiences on the soil of time, so have the various schools of medicine, psychology, and philosophy traveled through time accumulating language and tradition.

The general thrust of medical research has been to study and treat the human body. In their search for causes and cures, physicians have asked questions about the physiological and biochemical systems of the body. The medically trained practitioner is likely to think about emotion in terms of biology.

Although the field of psychology is broad and its interests varied, for many years academic psychology favored scientific experimentation in the areas of perception, cognition, memory, and learning. Until quite recently, in neither medicine nor psychology had the study of emotion as such been of great interest. And, although there have been many philosophers who discussed specific emotions in detail and considered the idea of emotion itself as a worthy discourse, none of their work fits well with that of scholars in the other fields.

For the greatest part of this century psychoanalysis has been the dominant philosophical/psychological system attempting to explain all human mental and emotional processes. Freud began as a medical scientist, the early papers documenting his study of nerve tissue with dissecting knife and microscope and of the effects on neural mechanisms of such complex chemicals as cocaine. As a practicing neurologist, it was natural for him to study patients with hysterical paralysis. A century ago it was quite difficult to determine whether a limp and useless limb had been weakened by injury to the nerves leading to its muscles or was evidence of an affliction of the mind. Among the great contributions in this formative period of his work was the development of a method of analysis that allowed new understanding of the latter such cases. It turned out that these patients had learned to handle intense emotion by focusing attention on some part of the body little related to the source of that emotion.

Thus, psychoanalysis was initially a method of studying the effects of emotion on cognition and bodily function.

There was a red thread woven through all the cases Freud studied. In each patient the dangerously intense emotions that led to the illness had been associated with thoughts and feelings about sex; consequently, the founder of psychoanalysis turned his attention to the nature of sexuality.

No matter how great the mental equipment of a scientist, he or she is still a product of an era. Freud grew up in that explosive period of scientific thinking during which the greatest minds were searching for basic forces, for unitary solutions to complex problems. This was the time when Einstein was looking for a unified field theory that would explain all matter and energy in terms of their relation to some basic substance or force. Sir William Osler, the reigning medical genius, was only seven years older than Freud. He changed medicine by teaching physicians a new method of diagnosis in which one tried to attribute all the symptoms of the patient to one illness. Before Osler a patient might be diagnosed and treated for many illnesses at the same time; after Osler the clinician would search for the single disease that could produce all the symptoms observed. It was an epoch that fostered the condensation of forces.

There is no question that Freud was one of the great thinkers of all time. Many of his contributions hold up even today, when our science is advanced enough to provide the technology needed to test his theories. Nevertheless, most of those who study emotion have discarded his basic idea that all human mental and emotional functions are powered by the sexual force he called libido. Too much work has been done in too many other areas of science for this brilliant synthesis to remain acceptable.

Of course I believe that there is a sexual drive and that it has a powerful influence on human development. But it is neither the basic motivating force for which Freud searched nor the source of emotion itself. As a matter of fact, the new work on emotion (around which this book is woven) allows us to present an entirely new theory for the nature of human sexuality, as well as the relation between sex and shame.

Such statements are taken for granted when I lecture in settings that favor the study of physiology or other medical sciences. It has been said that 95 percent of what is known about the human brain was learned in the past decade. Pouring in daily as research reports from the great laboratories of medicine and neurobiology, often popularized by newspaper accounts of this research offered to the public as filtered through the bias of reporters with deeply personal predjudices, are data undreamed of at the other end of this century.

Often I am asked to speak before psychoanalytic groups, who are of course deeply interested in anything concerning the nature of emotion. But time and time again I will be thanked for my efforts and told, "What you say is very interesting, but it is too soon. We do not yet know enough about the brain. For the moment we will stick with the ideas given us by Freud." Then someone will ask me to reread one of his papers from 1924, as if to say that had I really understood his work I would not have needed to ask the questions that always hover around me.

When, however, I discuss these ideas about shame and the entire spectrum of emotion before audiences whose training has led them to evaluate patients in terms of their need for medication, I am told with equal vigor, "We are tired of all this psychoanalytic language. You are nothing but a psychoanalyst with a laboratory coat. You want us to ignore biology and think about things for which we cannot test."

Needed most is some method of integration, some system of thought that pulls into one coherent system all known data on the nature of human emotion. In the chapters that follow I will try to explain one such logical approach, showing how it has developed and giving credit to the scientists responsible. Rather than overload the reader who neither has nor wants a technical education, this material will be presented in language accessible to all, while the bibiliography will allow one to check my sources either for further edification or for later dispute.

HARDWARE, FIRMWARE, AND SOFTWARE

One central theme underlies every aspect of this book. I ask you to look at the total picture of human emotion influenced by your experience of the contemporary desktop electronic computer. Imagine for a moment that you have just switched on all the components of your personal computer. Immediately it begins to whir and buzz, while across the viewscreen flicker a number of messages. Soon, however, the device comes to rest and lets you know that it is prepared to operate as a writing device or a spreadsheet or a dictionary or a printing machine.

You are, of course, well aware that the electrical contraptions involved are known to us as *hardware* and that these machines know how to assist our work with numbers or words because they have been programmed to do so by *software* instructions. Frankly, all the digital computer really does is handle various assortments of the numbers "1" and "0." It is the software that makes a computer useful, that manipulates the handling of those two numbers in such a way that we seem to be writing or doing mathematical tasks.

Yet no computer can work without the interposition of yet another technical wonder. As the machine was warming up, you may have noticed on its screen some indication that it was manufactured by one or another company. It "knew" to do this neither because of any software program nor because of anything intrinsic to the hardware itself, but by virtue of a specific form of prewritten instructions locked in tiny devices called "chips." We call this form of instruction *firmware*; it is neither "soft" nor "hard." Computer firmware was once written by some remarkably intelligent human, but now has become "part of the machine."

Humans, too, have hardware, firmware, and software. All the parts we call "the body"—bones, joints, hair, skin, blood and all the chemicals transported by it, central nervous system—may be thought of as our hardware. How we grow up, how we are influenced by parents, peers, school, government, advertising—all this may be considered analogous to software. But the way the fetus grows within the uterus and develops from a one-celled organism to a squalling baby, the way baby grows into full biological maturity, how the menstrual cycle knows its monthly responsibilities—all that is directed by firmware programs written permanently into the biological structure called the human genetic code.

One name will recur throughout this book, that of the late psychologist

---

Table I
COMPUTER MODEL
FOR THE HUMAN EMOTIONAL SYSTEM

HARDWARE

Central nervous system, including biochemical environment, neurotransmitters, structural "wiring," data handling capacity, information storage and retrieval.

Striated muscles controlling face, posture, vocalization.

Endocrine and exocrine systems.

FIRMWARE

Affects
Drives

SOFTWARE

Learning
Social conditioning
Experience

Silvan S. Tomkins. Right at the midpoint of this century he recognized in a flash the nature of the firmware programs responsible for normal emotion. He called this group of mechanisms the affect system, and described it in a series of books called *Affect/Imagery/Consciousness*. For reasons peculiar only to him, the first two volumes appeared in 1961 and 1962, and the third in 1991. The final volume will probably emerge contemporaneous with my own.

Tomkins is the American Einstein, that sort of genius whose work was so far ahead of its time that it simply could not be understood when it first appeared. Slowly, quietly, affect theory has come to influence thinkers all over the world, many of whom do not even know where and how it originated. Others, truly unaware of Tomkins's work, have unwittingly duplicated parts of it and thought their work original. *Affect/Imagery/Consciousness* is written in a dense prose style requiring far deeper study and an attention span far longer than that usually required by even the most difficult theoretical work.

Many scholars have taken advantage of the relative inaccessibility of this unique and demanding theoretical system, cribbing from it one chunk at a time and passing off as their own what they have stolen from Tomkins. On occasion, corrupt editors, journalists, colleagues, and competitors have actually conspired to erase his name from textbooks and journals. An astonishingly tiny fraction of the current crop of honest, well-trained psychologists and psychiatrists is aware of Tomkins and his life work. Here is one of the most fascinating stories in the history of science, some of which will become apparent from these pages, but much of it yet to be told by others.

I am interested in the hardware, firmware, and software of emotion. I want you to share my fascination with the idea that we can be frightened when accosted by a thief in the night, by an otherwise inaccessible memory hidden within the unconscious, by an inborn error in metabolism that produces "fear chemicals," and by any number of medications taken into the body for other purposes. In each case, we experience fear that differs only in respect to its source; only one firmware program, one affect, is necessary to produce each type of fear. Each of the affects can be triggered by hardware, firmware, or software. Shame can occur when our secrets are exposed, when an aberration of biology produces an atypical depression, or when we ingest certain chemicals.

To my knowledge, all previous books about the nature of any specific emotion—or about emotion itself—have ignored this simple observation. This is a book about the many and varied interactions made possible by the extraordinary flexibility of our biochemical hardware system, the remarkable group of firmware systems we call the drives and the affects, and the intricate medley of experiences that is the software of human life. We begin the book talking about emotion; soon we will give up that overly inclusive term in favor of the more precise language made possible by affect theory.

A gripe: Most theories work not because of the information, the data they describe, but because of what they ignore. I have spent my life studying emotion. We simply dare no longer to maintain psychoanalytic or cognitive theories about emotion that ignore what we know about brain function and neurotransmitters or to insist on biological theories that ignore the vast body of psychoanalytic experience. Incorporated here is all the information needed to bridge the widening schism separating what have been caricatured as "mindless" biology, "brainless" psychoanalysis, "unfeeling" cognitive theory, and social psychology that ignores the internal. To the best of my knowledge, the theories introduced here ignore or are incompatible with no realm of current knowledge.

A challenge: Theory is meant to be revised in favor of new information. If this synthesis of old and new ideas is successful, it will provoke research that confirms or disconfirms these new arguments for the nature of emotion. Should information emerge that demands alteration in the system introduced herein, I will openly and gladly add it to future editions.

THE PLAN OF THIS BOOK

Here, then, is a map of the book. It is divided into five sections, the argument of each dependent on what has been discussed in the preceding one.

New theory demands new language. In the first section I will describe the biology of emotion so that the reader will be able to understand in this context the groups of emotions called shame and pride, as well as all the illnesses in which they figure. But there is far more involved here than biology. In each adult experience of shame and pride these biological mechanisms are called into play somewhat differently, producing what we may call the psychology of shame. Although the action of these firmware affect mechanisms can be demonstrated in the newborn infant, it is clear that the adult experience of emotion is greatly influenced by the way our personality has developed over time. I will try to explain how the brain of the newborn becomes the mind of the adult and the role in this development played by shame and pride.

The next section takes up the theme with which I began this introductory :er—the scope of the shame experience. We will look at shame and pride l their aspects, surveying both their public and private appearances. In order to understand the wide range of shame emotions and the broad array of painful thoughts accompanying any moment of embarrassment, we will study each and every realm of human function in which the firmware for shame can be involved. Furthermore, any experience of shame calls forth the sense of a defective self. We will show how the concept of self evolves and how shame comes to be associated with it.

In the third section we discuss love and sex. Shame produces a terrible sense of alienation, a sense of being shorn from the herd. The more one knows about the affect system, the easier it is to understand the nature of attachment. Love and hate are the most profound forms of attachment; redefined in terms of affect theory, their relation to shame will be elucidated.

One of the best-known group of firmware programs, perhaps the cluster most visibly associated with shame, involves what has come to be known as sexuality. Most of us have taken for granted that the work of Freud, focusing as it did on the relation between sexuality and the development of the personality, answered nearly all the questions one might ask about the psychology of sex. Much to my surprise, the more I began to investigate shame in the manner described above, the more it appeared necessary to offer a new theory for the sexual drive. I had no intention of entering that particular thicket of psychological theory; once you approach the subject of shame in an orderly fashion many things must change. From this new work we begin to understand why so much embarrassment hovers around gender identity and sexual experience.

Both the length of this book and the wide range of subjects covered can be blamed on the genius of Tomkins rather than the tenacity of the author. One who comes to understand affect theory feels something like a scientist handed a totally new instrument—like the early microscopists, or Gallileo suddenly empowered to look deeper into the night sky.

All possible sources of shame are brought to mind any time shame affect is triggered. What happens next, presented in the fourth section, is much more complicated. Each time something triggers an episode of shame we tend to act in a very predictable fashion. There are four basic patterns of behavior that govern our reactions to this complex emotion; these I have grouped as "the compass of shame." It is the four poles of the compass that house all the scripts we know as shameful withdrawal, masochistic submission, narcissistic avoidance of shame, and the rage of wounded pride. For each of us, this group of reaction patterns has a great deal to do with the nature of our personality. Character formation, the essence of self-definition, is immutably linked to shame.

Anything that can cause pain may be used to hurt people, so we must study shame as some have used it in a weapon system. We take for granted that wars have been excused on the basis of national honor; yet this is but another way of saying that our species will fight to avoid the sting of shame.

Where there is a natural source of pain one might expect a natural form of solace. Throughout history, comedy has offered its own balm; from the work of the comedic masters we can learn much about shame. We will examine in detail the work of Buddy Hackett, a great comedian whose art not only informs us about shame but offers its own style of solace. The more you know about shame, the less trivial seems comedy.

I am concerned not just with the range of affect experienced during normal existence but also with that experienced at levels of intensity far beyond anything for which the human has evolved. What is a rampage? What is a killing frenzy? How are these states related to shame? Of those who can avoid the experience of shame neither in their relationships with others nor in the privacy of their innermost selves, many turn to drugs, alcohol, and sexual excess. In the final section we will also study the ease with which such activities bind up unbearable amounts of shame, as well as the ease with which shame itself can freeze or bind an entire personality.

It may come as a surprise to many that, although the basic biological mechanisms involved seem to have existed relatively unchanged for thousands of years, there is good evidence to suggest that the conscious adult experience of affect has undergone many shifts. We will learn something about shame and pride throughout Western history and see how much these two emotions have themselves been responsible for major changes in culture and society. Were I only to demonstrate the ubiquity of shame in our present world or its central position in the group of discomforts that plague modern man, I would mislead you by ignoring the history surrounding shame.

All this is necessary if we are to understand the nature of shame today. Changes in the experience of shame, in the realm over which it holds sway, have caused drastic alterations in civilization itself. The book ends with some suggestions about the role of shame in this dangerous modern culture of emotional explosion.

This book may well define a paradox. If it is successful, all of us will know more about the nature of shame and its place in the panoply of emotions. The work of Freud changed—indeed may be said to have formed—the civilization that followed it. From the contributions of classical psychoanalysis it became permissible to investigate the realm of unconscious life, to study and enjoy our sexual selves in a new way, to disavow the shame that had protected our private and secret thoughts from public view. Now, thanks to the clues granted us by the work of Tomkins, shame and all the emotions related to it become capable of study in an entirely new mode.

Who will we be next, what sort of society will follow from a thorough and general understanding of human emotion? How will shame change when it is no longer so secret? What will happen to us as we become aware of this powerful force that has done so much to bring us into the present?

But I rush too quickly to the end of my book. Let us start by investigating the biology of emotion, the hardware required in order for us to have emotions.

THE NATURE OF

HUMAN EMOTION

WHAT IS EMOTION?

A former patient dropped in for a session the other day. Head of his own immensely successful business, pillar of his synagogue, widely known for his work on a number of charitable boards, and justly celebrated for his remarkable ability to march into battles shunned by competitors, this man, for the better part of a week, had been troubled by anxiety. "I am afraid of everything," he said. "Wherever I look I see danger."

A decade earlier the sudden, unexpected, serious illness of his 12-year-old son had triggered more anxiety than even that crisis might have been expected to produce. Our work in psychotherapy had uncovered an earlier terror related to the death of his own mother. This tragedy, combined with a host of other childhood experiences, had led him to the decision that he must never let anything get out of control—his adult personality had been built around an ironclad attitude of self-control and the control of every situation in which he found himself. His extraordinary intelligence, energy, and talents had provided the tools that allowed success in business; an unquestionable ability to make those around him feel good had contributed to enormous popularity. He sought and enjoyed competition in a number of sports, and excelled at many. Anyone willing to accept his leadership profited by joining him; rarely did his actions inspire jealousy and envy in his peers. But he could no more control, cajole, or intimidate the virus that had reduced his son to temporary incapacity than as a boy he had been able to stave off the cancer that had plucked his mother from a happy home.

Therapy had been quite successful. He was able to see the link between these two experiences. It was reasonable for him to remain concerned and perhaps somewhat frightened until his son achieved full recovery. What had clouded his vision and made him far more fearful than appropriate to the situation was this overlooked piece of his own much earlier emotional reaction to an analogous experience. At the termination of his formal therapy I joined the long list of consultants to whom he maintained regular access in the course of his professional and charitable work. Now he came with a new and uncharacteristic complaint.

"What I learned when we worked together was that any time I'm overwhelmed by an emotion it is because I have been overlooking something that either I do not want to look at or I never knew how to examine. After a while I learned to internalize this process and take it over myself, so I really haven't needed you to do this. But this one has me buffaloed. There have been very few times in my life I have been this anxious, and even then I knew what caused it. How can I be having a nervous breakdown when everything seems to be going well?" He sketched the current structure of his business life—complex matters requiring skill, daring, and tremendous financial resources, all of which would have daunted me but none particularly unusual for him. Personal life? Marriage, children, charitable work all ticking away with the required degree of intensity. Little here for our investigation.

I commented on his somewhat nasal speech. "Goddamned cold. Been taking cold pills all week. At least I can breathe, but I hate to take pills." The "cold pills" turned out to contain *pseudoephedrine*, a synthetic compound that affects the body much in the same way as adrenalin, the naturally occurring substance that prepares the body for flight, fright, or fight. Whenever the adrenal gland releases its stored adrenalin we are ready for action with an alerted mind, tightened muscles, racing heart, cold sweaty skin, an instant surge of energy from the glucose reserves stored in the liver, and a peculiar type of breathing characterized by flared nostrils and widening of all the tubes in the respiratory system. Whatever else it does to our psyche, danger (by triggering the release of adrenalin) really clears the respiratory tree. Pseudoephedrine duplicates the effect of adrenalin on nasal stuffiness more than it affects the heart, but in high doses this difference is minimal. In his desire to control and suppress the normal symptoms of his upper respiratory infection, my friend had bought an adrenergic experience. Amused by my suggestion that he risk buying calm for the expense of sniffle, he discarded the medication. Within a few hours he was no longer frightened.

A host of chemicals can produce a similar picture. Too much thyroid hormone can make one anxious, whether this occurs naturally in the disease called *hyperthyroidism* or when too much is given as medication for the symptoms caused by an underactive thyroid gland. More than half of those later diagnosed as being hyperthyroid present to their physicians for complaints related to anxiety. Too much caffeine can produce a similar picture, even though most people who are chronically or even acutely anxious from overuse of coffee are completely unaware of the connection between what they drink to increase alertness and the discomfort they call anxiety. The chemistry and the psychology of these common aberrations can teach us a great deal about normal emotion.

Each emotion is characterized by some combination of thoughts and *somatic feelings*. The machine called a "lie detector" allows the examiner to know when an apparently calm subject has produced enough sweat (salty water) to allow better conduction of electricity on the surface of the skin; it also informs about variations in heart rate and breathing. It is, therefore, a machine for the detection of hidden fear, of the physiological activity associated with and perhaps responsible for the feelings associated with fear. What we *think* when we are afraid is a little different for each of us; that depends on our previous experience of fear. Someone who has been terrified in battle is likely to think about that earlier group of experiences when frightened years later, no matter what has triggered the current fear.

What we have been discussing so far involves hardware and software, two of the three factors responsible for adult emotion. The way we sweat, the manner in which the heart pounds, the sudden alteration in breathing: all that is dependent on hardware. I know a woman who found herself shaking unaccountably, shivering in fear, immediately after hearing a melody from her childhood. Certainly that particular trigger for fear qualifies as software—it is a perfect example of a situation for which no animal is likely to have a genetic program.

There are lots of times that a computer program fails, and skilled technicians can often locate the error that has caused breakdown. In the world of human software, the art of locating errors in programming is called psychotherapy. Much of what we know about both normal and abnormal psychological function comes from data provided by psychotherapeutic sleuths. The gentleman discussed above is always susceptible to anxiety when anything threatens him with loss of control. In treating such patients one can use "uncovering therapy" to demonstrate the linkage between the current danger (one easily seen and understood) and the analogous trigger for fear that he might well have preferred to keep out of awareness.

The archaic fear carries all the terrible power and intensity one might expect in a small child. Reevaluating such experiences in the company of a trusted adviser allows the patient to reduce their power and thus to diminish their ability to magnify current fear. Such an approach is central to what is now called psychodynamic psychiatry—a method correctly traced to the work of Freud.

Quite in contrast is another (perhaps equally effective) school of therapy that helps people deal with their fears by outlining and then altering the thoughts or *cognitions* associated with fear without ever dealing with their *significance* in terms of prior experience. Rather than unlink the many experiences of fear that have occurred in the life of a patient, *cognitive therapy*, as developed by Aaron T. Beck and his colleagues, revises how an individual experiences fear. This may be regarded as alteration, rather than repair, of preexisting software.

Just as there are chemicals that simulate or trigger fear, there are many medications that can block the physiological mechanisms that produce fear. Some of these impede the effects of adrenalin itself (like the so-called β-adrenergic blocker *propranolol*). Others, like the tranquilizers, work on brain mechanisms related to the circuitry specific for fear. Such treatment involves manipulation of the hardware system.

WHAT DO WE KNOW ABOUT EMOTION?

No matter how you try to study emotion you run into problems. First of all, emotion is by definition a subjective experience, somewhat different for each person. It is not enough to ask people what makes them embarrassed, angry, or frightened, or even to describe their subjective experience of these emotions. This approach yields a great deal of information about the psychological range of emotional experience but nothing about its mechanics, about what is happening at the level of cells and synapses.

We have now accumulated a huge amount of information about the structure of the brain as well as its chemistry and physiology. For example, sudden bursts of anger, even to the point of murderous rage, have been traced to tumors in a region called the *amygdala*. The most celebrated such case is that of Charles Whitman. One evening he wrote a note describing his inability to control or understand sudden bursts of feelings that threatened to take over his personality and that interfered with his ability to think clearly and perform routine tasks. In this letter he stated that the world was no longer a place in which he could live, that he did not want to leave his beloved wife alone in such a terrible place, and that he planned to kill her in some way that would cause her the least amount of pain. He asked that after his own death an autopsy be performed to see if there was any physical cause for these unbearable emotional experiences. That night he killed his wife and his mother; the next morning he ascended a tower on the campus of the University of Texas, from which he shot 38 people, 14 of whom died. At autopsy the pathologists found a walnut-sized tumor near the amygdala.* In experiments on laboratory animals, stimulation of the amygdala can trigger astonishing degrees of rage-like behavior.

From this sort of data we can guess that anger has something to do with the amygdala. What it does not tell us is why Mr. Whitman decided to kill people as an expression of his rage, why people vary so much in the types and patterns of thoughts they experience when angry, or even the function of anger in the normal organism. And there are other people who have slaughtered similar numbers of innocent bystanders but in whom no abnormality of the amygdala was found. It is not enough to study only the pathways within the brain associated with emotion.

Infants cry, rage, and smile. Is this emotion? Can we really say that babies are distressed, or angry, or happy when we cannot prove that they know what they are feeling? Most attempts to study emotion in small children have been limited by the communication block—it is difficult to get information from a subject who cannot yet talk. And if this inability of infants to communicate about their feelings presents problems for such research, how much more difficult would it be to find an animal model for the study of emotion! Many people believe that it is impossible for "lower" animals even to have emotions, despite the fact that they seem to exhibit many of the same emotion-related behaviors as do adult humans.

THEORIES OF EMOTION

Charles Darwin

It was Darwin who first noted that the display of emotion in nonverbal creatures was similar, and often identical, to that seen in man. He realized, for instance, that the artless and untrained expressions of emotion easily visible on the face of the newborn infant were the same expressions observable on the face of the sophisticated and more highly controlled adult. Since many of these expressions could be seen in animals, Darwin was able to trace an evolutionary progression for the display of emotion. (Everything he saw was evaluated for its importance to the theory of evolution.) Although he did not incorporate his work on emotion in *The Origin of Species*, which was published in 1859, these

*As reported by Ross Buck in *The Communication of Emotion.*

ideas were beginning to occupy his attention as part of the specific consideration of human evolution. By 1871, when he published *The Descent of Man*, his
research on emotion had grown too much for incorporation in that book, and
so it was released the following year as *The Expression of Emotions in Man and
Animals*.

In 1867 Darwin sent a questionnaire to missionaries and others who lived
among "primitive" peoples or in cultures vastly different from his own Victorian England. He wanted to know whether certain expressions were universal.
In your country, in the people you see, he asked, "Is astonishment expressed
by the eyes and mouth being opened wide, and by the eyebrows being raised?
. . . Does shame excite a blush when the colour of the skin allows it to be
visible? and especially how low down the body does the blush extend? . . .
When a man is indignant or defiant does he frown, hold his body and head
erect, square his shoulders and clench his fists? . . . When considering deeply on
any subject, or trying to understand any puzzle, does he frown, or wrinkle the
skin beneath the lower eyelids? . . . Is extreme fear expressed in the same
general manner as with Europeans? . . . Is laughter ever carried to such an
extreme as to bring tears into the eyes? . . . Is the head nodded vertically in
affirmation, and shaken laterally in negation?"* and so on. From 36 correspon-
dents all over the world he learned that the expression of emotion is essentially universal.

Oscar Reglander, the celebrated photographer whose portraits of Lewis
Carroll and his Alice remain icons of their era, collaborated with Darwin to
produce a series of pictures of actors posed to show these expressions. Wherever these photographs were shown, Darwin found agreement with his basic
premise.

He interpreted emotion in three ways. (1) Part of the emotional response
was habit—"generally inherited" but little different from reflex actions. "When
certain actions are carried out in order to relieve or gratify certain states of
mind," he said, "there is a tendency for them to become habitual and to be
evoked whenever the same state of mind is once again experienced" even
though "they may not then be of the least use." Emotional habits were ves-
tiges of behavior once useful to our remote ancestors but now only useless
reflexes.

(2) Next, Darwin offered the principle of "antithesis," the idea that certain

---

*Darwin (1872), 15–16. The great surgeon George W. Crile (1915), whose interest in these
matters was initiated by his experience operating on the thyroid gland, devoted many years to a
study of the biological mechanisms underlying Darwin's observations.

postures are designed as opposites to whatever the organism is really feeling. He noted that when a stranger approached, a dog might assume the posture of threat, with tail held high, head stiffly erect with a threatening scowl. But when the stranger turned out to be friendly, the dog might communicate the gestures of affection with wagging tail—the body crouched, supple, and relaxed. These latter expressions of affection, thought Darwin, had little biological significance other than their existence as opposites to the initial display of threat. (3) And finally, he believed that most of the facial expressions he had described resulted from the direct action of the nervous system, independent of habit or will.

No matter how trenchant his observations, Darwin's attempts at theory were doomed to failure simply because they could not be linked with what we now know to be the normal development of the child. He had discovered the group of mechanisms I call firmware, understood intuitively their dependence on hardware, but had no concept of software!

Although it is true that these facial and bodily expressions remain consistent throughout life, the mind of the infant is not the mind of the adult. Ignored completely in his work was the question of the inner experience of the organism gripped by these patterns of expression. We cannot know what the dog or the infant "feels," simply because both are unable to communicate with us in words. Similarly, we may not merely assume that these emotional expressions maintain the same significance throughout life. It is difficult to imagine that such complex emotional states as love, scorn, contempt, and humiliation can be experienced by the infant; yet each of these is associated with characteristic external expressions that may be seen in babies. His theory depended on the organism's ability to perceive and to understand what then triggered emotion and what next triggered these habitual and autonomic reactions.

Darwin's immense contribution to the study of emotion was his discovery that the expression of emotion remains consistent throughout life. What prevented him from forming a useful theory, capable of providing a valid explanation of all emotional phenomena, was his ignorance of human development. Adults differ from children partly because the body itself, including the brain, changes during the first decade or so of extrauterine life, and also because the layering of experience makes for vast changes in our inner makeup.

The James–Lange Hypothesis

Like Darwin, most investigators also assumed that what we experience as adults is pretty much what we experienced as children, that emotion is consistent throughout life. Ignoring completely this work by Darwin, many authors have tried to build theory from their understanding of the adult. One of the earliest and most important of these was offered independently by William James in America (1884) and Carl Lange in Denmark (1887) and is still known today as the James–Lange hypothesis. They felt that the mind, which they saw as an apparatus for perception and cognition, *perceived* and assessed something that then triggered a group of physical manifestations, following which the thinking brain assessed the *pattern* of these bodily changes and labeled it as an emotion.

In the James–Lange system I know I am frightened because I see myself running away; I know I am happy because I laugh. Perception and assessment (hardware and software) have triggered a somatic reaction (firmware) that is interpreted and labeled as an emotion (software).

This system requires an intact and highly developed group of organs that allow one to acquire information and to process it—a functioning computer. With it, emotional life is seen as secondary to advanced cognitive life, to the processing of information. Babies, then, who have no verbal language, cannot know names for their emotions and therefore cannot be said to have emotions, even though they make all the facial expressions, gestures, and noises we associate with adult emotion.

Developed in the days when we didn't know much about the circuitry of the brain—the intricate connections between individual neurons and groups of neurons—the James–Lange theory depended on the ebb and flow of "humoral substances," of chemical compounds coursing through the bloodstream. It can never explain the rapid shifts in emotion that occur in ordinary day-to-day living. Some emotional experiences last only a few hundredths of a second. Often we find ourselves gripped by emotions that oscillate far too swiftly for any substance that must flow through something as sluggish as the circulatory system.

Sigmund Freud

Another major system for understanding emotion was offered by Freud, whose work spanned the decades between 1895 and 1938. In keeping with the science of his time, Freud postulated the existence of a life force he called *libido*, energy that traveled throughout the brain to power or drive the mental apparatus. Freud thought he had found a concept around which he could organize all our knowledge of the human mental and emotional systems. In the fully developed adult, this libido energy was seen as normal sexuality. While the terms libido and sexuality are not precisely interchangeable, for practical purposes they are taken to be so.

His original statement of this theory was elegant, poetic, and beautiful. Infants, of course, were by no stretch of the imagination viewed as sexual beings; libido energy was first expressed as activity around the locus of the mouth and called *orality*, or oral sexuality. Somewhere in the second year of life, right about the time we adults begin to ask the child to take control of excretion, Freud said that the libido shifts to the rectum and ushers in the anal phase of development. A year or so later, babies become more interested in their genitals, and the libido energy comes to be attached to them. Freud believed that children from birth through this so-called *phallic* period remained more involved with themselves than others—this genital expression of libido is not yet the same as interpersonal sexuality. Occurring between ages three and five is the family romance, the passionate attraction little girls feel for their fathers and little boys for their mother. Named the *oedipal phase* in honor of the classic Greek play *Oedipus Rex* from which Freud deduced the importance of this developmental process, it is declared the period during which libido energy becomes truly sexual.

All of Freud's conclusions were derived from his meticulous study of those disturbed adults who came to him for relief of their symptoms. The brilliant scheme described above was a marvel of deduction assembled by him from bits of data gleaned in his analysis of adults. Freud never studied infants—his own children had grown up well before he developed these theories.

The more disturbed a patient, the more likely was that person to experience emotions with the uncontrolled ferocity of an infant. Freud understood the symptoms of mental illness to be caused by patterns of improperly or incompletely channeled libido energy. Children were by nature more emotional than adults, and infants by nature more emotional than children. In 1915* he suggested that it seemed logical to assume that emotion itself occurred whenever libido energy was prevented from achieving its natural aim of sexual congress. What powered emotion was the same energy that drove every other mental function.

Always looking for a simple unifying structure around which could be arranged a complex group of observations, Freud divided all emotions on the basis of their pleasant or their unpleasant quality. In his clinical work he had noticed early that anxiety could often be traced to certain sexual practices. For instance, it was common for men to engage in intercourse to a point just short

*Charles Brenner (1955) gives an excellent summary of Freud's theories in this area.

of ejaculation—this was a form of contraception. Masturbation, a possible outlet for sexual energy, was widely regarded as a sin, a religious and social concept that went far deeper than a modern reader might think. Richard von Krafft-Ebing, a non-psychoanalytic contemporary of Freud, had a passionate interest in sex, sexual crime, and the forms of madness associated with sexuality. Many of his case reports begin with statements like "This 20-year old confessed masturbator. . . ." Reading Krafft-Ebing—a psychiatrist purporting to liberate emotionally disturbed patients from their troubles—one contemplates masturbation with gravity and trepidation. One early benefit brought by the psychoanalytic movement was a tremendous reduction in the guilt associated with the feeling of sexual release.

How exciting this must have been for the discoverer of psychoanalysis! The logical equation, the syllogism, was simple: (1) The sexual drive (by his definition) was the basic force that powered all human activity; (2) when this drive was prevented from achieving its goal, people complained of anxiety; (3) therefore, all anxiety was caused by sexual tension. It is a flawed syllogism, actually (as any college student knows), a classic example of the error called "the undistributed middle." There are lots of causes for anxiety, not just sexual tension. But it served an important purpose for Freud—it focused attention on sexuality, and it answered his need to find a theory for emotion. Not just painful emotion, either, for clearly the achievement of libido's goal produced pleasure.

Here, indeed, was a neat system to explain all emotion. All positive feelings were created by the satisfaction of libidinous needs; all negative feelings by the denial of those needs. In the language of classical psychoanalysis, all unpleasant emotions are considered to be subdivisions of anxiety, the primary negative emotion. Thus, *guilt* is the anxiety caused by the two-year-old child's recognition that certain sexual wishes are wrong and may be punished by the parent. And *shame* cannot appear until the child understands guilt and knows he or she should not use nakedness (or other forms of what psychoanalysis called *sexual exhibitionism*) to attract the parent of the opposite gender into some sort of fantasized sexual liaison. Shame, then, is seen as a specific form of anxiety, a learned behavior acquired by the three-year-old.

This elegant scheme was destined to survive neither the onrush of information provided by the psychoanalytic revolution itself nor that provided by other branches of science. Freud himself made frequent alterations in theory to handle data pouring in from many sources. From the constant observation that some people seem determined to destroy themselves and those they love, it proved necessary to add a life-destroying force called *aggression* to the life-affirming force he had earlier called libido. Anger and certain destructive forms of sexuality were attributed to this new driving force, and the language of psychoanalysis shifted from discussion of libido to an even more vaguely defined form of energy called *the drives.*

The problem grew even worse. No other science was able to find evidence for drive energy or to detect structures that might resemble the little channels through which Freud thought this energy traveled to make emotion. The failure of these theories to find scientific confirmation became even more significant as the physical sciences discovered more and more forms of energy and as the biological sciences demonstrated the actual channels along which information traveled.

Psychoanalysis was faced with a major crisis. Psychoanalytic treatment benefited a great many people, and within every case each clinician could always find data that confirmed these theories. This consistent internal validation of the Freudian system convinced the overwhelming majority of psychoanalysts that drive theory was essentially correct, that science would one day demonstrate what they knew in their hearts was really true. From the death of Freud in 1938 up to the present time, psychoanalytic theory has become increasingly defensive about this position.

Central to the idea of science itself is the search for the errors and inconsistencies that force us to reappraise any theory. It is through this honorable process that new science evolves from and replaces the old. To the extent that psychoanalysis continues to claim that its critics are enemies rather than colleagues, and rejects as irrelevant the data of other sciences, it retires to the status of a system of belief—a religion rather than a science. Sober scientists and clinicians are always astonished when their papers are summarily rejected by the leading psychoanalytic journals with the criticism that the data are not from the psychoanalytic investigation of adults. While psychoanalysis remains a valid—and often wonderful—form of treatment for many emotional disorders, its theoretical base in drive theory is simply outdated, a relic of a physiology long ago disconfirmed. We must look far beyond the invisible drives in our search for the nature of emotion.

Transformation of Energy Theories

There is another group of theories for emotion, also involving various types of *transformation of energy.* Updated in 1961 by James Hillman, but introduced earlier by the Swiss psychologist Carl Jung (1923), is the idea that emotion is instigated when the conscious and unconscious selves are united by a symbol, thus releasing psychic energy and transforming it into experienced emotion. Philosopher Jean-Paul Sartre (1948) said that emotion occurs when a person discovers that he or she cannot act in the experienced world, thus transforming consciousness to the more primitive attitude of a magical world. Karl Pribram (1969) said that emotion arises when some stimulus unbalances the plan by which the neural system has organized behavior. He said that there are two basic types of emotion, one which operates to adjust the stimulus to make it conform to our plans, and another which adjusts our internal plan to conform to the stimulus input. Lastly, Joseph DeRivera (1977) believes that emotions are instructions that tell the organism how to behave in relation to the situation that triggered them—toward or away from self, or toward or away from the other.

All of these theories share similar defects. No one has found anything even vaguely resembling psychic energy, making the Jung–Hillman theory obsolete. Sartre's theory depends on the idea of "discovery," which is a cognitive act, and speaks more about the unpleasant emotions than about pleasure and excitement. Neither Sartre nor DeRivera can explain the type of emotion we see in the infant. By none of these theories can we explain the type of emotion experienced by the patient described in the beginning of this chapter—there is no room for variations in emotional experience caused by alterations in biology.

The trick is to use all the data. Each of these theories explains some of what we know about emotion; none explains everything we know about emotion. One path remains, and that is the system we will discuss in the next chapter. It starts with what we can observe in the infant, takes into account what we have learned from the physiologists and biochemists, and offers an opportunity to integrate all known systems of psychology and psychotherapy. I know of no information that must be ignored in order for it to be useful. Best of all, it explains shame and pride.

2

THE AFFECT SYSTEM

Despite our view of ourselves as thinking beings, cognition is but a frail craft floating on a sea of emotion. Wondering how I might convey to you some sense of how thinking is influenced by affect, I found myself pausing, then distracted by something immediately past my left shoulder. What follows is an attempt to put into words my experience of the next few minutes, phrased as it felt while it was happening:

Dawn has just begun to declare the shape of this winter day. Seen from the window of my study, the pinkish ice cream cone of light glowing from the roof of my neighbor turns general blackness into the texture of earliest morning. The brief beauty of this always unexpected sky-painting is my reward for the decision to trade the comfort of sleep for the work of writing. I stop briefly as the window garners more attention than the viewscreen of my writing device. Backlit, the black walnut tree is revealed in perfect outline and I am reminded of its beauty. Delight is short-lived. Quickly I remember that in spring I must decide whether to replace the two dwarf apple trees that succumbed to last summer's drought. Garden thoughts tumble around in my mind as I scan to see what else promises trouble. The pleasure of dawn has been replaced by a myriad of concerns. With conscious effort I pull the shade and return to writing.

I cannot tell you how long I stared at the winter sky, for until the period of discomfort for which I wrenched myself away, fascination had made me un-aware of time. Yet when distressed I moved swiftly to regain control of my mood and to reorganize my thinking for the task at hand. Each scene described above came and went with its own metronomic indication, its own distinct temporality. Each scene felt different, each experienced with singular intensity.

This was an ordinary morning, and the scenes perhaps too trivial and commonplace to warrant attention in a book on shame and pride. Nevertheless, even the emotions attending an ordinary dawn deserve investigation, for until we share a common language by which all emotion can be explained, we will risk confusion where I want to bring clarity. It is the internal circuitry responsible for certain qualities of thought and feeling that will be the subject of this chapter.

It is easier to focus on scenes with heightened drama, like the humiliation of a defeated pugilist or the terror of a patient whose crushing chest pain signals the death of some portion of his heart. Yet fear can follow the ingestion of medication taken to reduce the volume of a sniffle, while guilt or shame is a common companion of medication taken to reduce high blood pressure. One can easily be overwhelmed by the sheer volume of information available to the student of emotion.

Imagine, for the moment, a device operating in more than the conventional three dimensions, one that allows us to study human emotion from every conceivable vantage point at the same time. An adult in the moment of emotion will exhibit certain characteristic actions: when angry, one may yell; when embarrassed, turn away; when frightened, flee. Alterations in internal biological function accompany these outward displays of emotion—the heart, for example, beats faster during the moment of fear or anger. In order for these large-scale events to occur, a host of tiny events must take place at the microscopic and submicroscopic level; electrochemical messages must travel along pathways within the central nervous system. Yet nothing recorded so far by our hypothetical device quite resembles the experience of emotion—what this emotion feels like to the individual being observed.

Emotions, which are themselves events in the life of an individual, are triggered by events. Whatever resides in our memory is stored with its accompanying emotion; thus each of us has a highly personal "information bank" of emotion-related data. This storehouse provides the coloration of an event— that which is personal for each of us. Our hypothetical machine must be able to detect, sample, and sort each and every life experience as held in memory and to determine the influence of memory on our perception of the emotion of the moment. It must separate the biological from the biographical.

THE VOCABULARY OF EMOTION

We have no such mechanical wonder, but we can approximate it by introducing and defining a few terms that allow us to speak with greater precision. For an exact science we need an exact language. The basic words that I will be using in the remainder of this book form a new vocabulary of emotion. Most important within this new system are the concepts called *affect, feeling, emotion, mood,* and *disorder.*

Affect

From now on I will use the word *affect* to describe the strictly biological portion of emotion. Affect is the root of such words as *affection,* our warm-toned feelings for those people who are particularly special in our lives. When we have been *affected* by something we have experienced an emotion because of it; when *disaffected* we are indifferent and have little emotional involvement.

The word affect has been part of the language of emotion for a long time. Once broad and vague, its meaning has been made highly specific by the work of Silvan Tomkins, the psychologist most responsible for the revolution in our understanding of emotion. What is now called *affect theory* first appeared in his book *Affect/Imagery/Consciousness,* the first two volumes of which were published in 1962 and 1963.

When we say that an affect has been *triggered,* we mean expressly that some definable stimulus has activated a mechanism which then releases a *known pattern of biological events.* Each of the innate affects unfolds according to its own precisely written program. Each one lasts a strictly determined period of time, ranging from a few hundredths of a second to a couple of seconds. There is good evidence that these patterns, now genetically transmitted and part of the biological heritage called evolution, appeared first in life forms as primitive as the reptile. In the human, then, we say that the circuitry for the affects is stored in that primitive portion of our equipment which Paul D. MacLean (1975) has called the reptile brain. The argument of my book depends on an understanding of affect; however, before we get too involved in the nature of affect we must define the remainder of the terms listed above.

Feeling

Michael Franz Basch, the psychoanalyst who has done the most to integrate affect theory into the main body of modern psychotherapy, has suggested that we use the word *feeling* to indicate that the organism has become *aware* of an affect. Many animals will look startled when exposed to an unexpected loud noise, like a gunshot or a thunderclap. But only to the extent that a life form has the advanced brain mechanisms needed to produce the degree of consciousness we call *awareness* will it be able to recognize that it has been gripped by an affect. Feeling implies the presence of higher order mechanisms or components that allow knowledge and understanding. It is, of course, possible for us to be so occupied by something else going on at the moment that we may be unaware an affect has been triggered. Alternatively, people may be raised in a culture or an environment that denies the existence of certain feelings; even when an affect is triggered they may not feel it because the ability to perceive it has been extinguished. From now on, wherever we use the word feeling, it will imply that a person has some level of awareness that an affect has been triggered.

Emotion

The move from affect to feeling involves a leap from biology to psychology. How much more difficult, then, is our concept of *emotion*, for it requires still another level of complexity! Each affect has been triggered time and time again over the life span of every individual, and on every occasion this has happened in the context of some situation, interaction, or scene. As an adult, for instance, I am not merely embarrassed. I am embarrassed in a situation that resembles one in which I was embarrassed last month, or last year, or frequently in a way I cannot alter, or in a relationship that resembles the one in which I find myself today. Very quickly, as the growing child accumulates experience, affects become intertwined with memory. To the extent that an organism has an intact system for the storage and retrieval of information, it will be able to call upon this storehouse for memories of previous experiences of an affect. *An emotion,* suggests Basch, *is the complex combination of an affect with these memories and with the affects they also trigger.* Whereas affect is biology, emotion is biography.

Affect is about unvarying physiological mechanisms. To fit our definition of emotion an affect must be placed within a script or a story. Prior to the work of Tomkins, most people neglected the biology of affect in favor of the historical path along which that affect had traveled. We have spent too much time studying biography and far too little on the biology that makes it possible!

Everybody has pretty much the same built-in affect mechanisms; the affect anger, when triggered, is identical in both you and me. Where we differ as individuals, how we diverge in the process of development to achieve different personalities, is in the unique way each of us understands or "remembers" our experiences of innate affect. If you are to understand how I experience the emotion I call anger, you must know something about how we got angry in my family when I was a boy, how anger was socialized in the culture of my peers, and what particular incidents trigger anger in my personal world. For me to understand your anger you must tell me something about the *history* of your affective experiences.

An affect lasts but a few seconds, a feeling only long enough for us to make the flash of recognition, and an emotion as long as we keep finding memories that continue to trigger that affect. Often an emotion lasts quite a while. When something triggers the particular combination of feelings we call *nostalgia*, our ability to retrieve memory and to form associative linkages between memories has produced an emotion that will continue as long as new memories enter awareness. But when our storehouse of such memories is exhausted, the emotion wanes and our attention shifts to whatever next triggers an affect.

Mood

What happens if some of these memories bring to current attention an unsolved problem from the past or the emotions hovering around a relationship we never managed to resolve? What if the now-triggered combination of thoughts and feelings places us squarely in the middle of some part of our emotional life we had hoped to escape by the magic of ignoring? What if the sheer weight of current sadness compounded by sadness past is more than can be dissipated? Emotion then gives way to mood, a persistent state of emotion in which we can remain stuck for hours or days.

Not long ago I experienced profound distress at the untimely and unexpected death of a colleague, my discomfort all the more intense because of the number of levels at which we were connected. Over the next few days this mood of grief waned and I was able to concentrate on a number of other matters. It happened that about this time one of my cherished Renaissance clocks, long resting on the workbench of a London clockmaker, was finally ready to be picked up. Too delicate for conventional shipping, it had to be carried by hand on the airplane. Unable to find a friend or colleague who might add this chore to an already scheduled vacation, I hired the 25-year-old son of a friend.

The deal was simple—I traded airfare for his agreement to convince the airline personnel that this strange parcel should travel upright and on his lap. Suddenly, however, the deal became less simple, for not a day after my purchase of these tickets came word that an airplane bound here from London had been destroyed in flight by a terrorist's bomb. Again I began to think about and mourn my late colleague, while also I grieved for the 260 strangers who had died in flight. Worst of all was a persistent anticipatory grief as I fantasized what might happen if my suddenly frivolous desire to get back this old clock should result in the death of another friend. This mood lasted until a conversation with both father and son convinced me that neither shared my terrible concern for the safety of the latter. After all, they had not just lost a colleague. Affect acts to magnify the scenes with which it is linked. Directly proportional to the number of layers included in my musing was the severity of my mood.

There are times when a mood simply won't go away, when nothing we can do will disperse it. In times like these one tries everything, from the distraction or diversion offered by an entertainment or a vacation to a major reorganization of life like a shift in career. Often such a mood will precipitate a person into psychotherapy, for each therapeutic system offers its own method for the alteration of mood. The uncovering therapies work by demonstrating the links between current mood and previous life experience. Had not the death of my colleague occurred so close in time to the purchase of those airline tickets, I might have been unable to recognize the influence of one set of scenes on another. Therapy might have assisted my recall and helped me deal with what had been placed in some hidden compartment of my memory. When the door to that compartment has long been bricked over and access permanently denied, the techniques of cognitive therapy can work to alter the conscious experience of emotion by changing the thoughts that accompany affect and so relieving one's mood.

Disorders of Mood

But even the most persistent psychoanalytic sleuth can sometimes fail to find any information secretly responsible for mood, and the best-designed exercises set up by the most doggedly determined cognitive therapist and practiced by the most devoted patient can fail to decrease the morbidity of mood. Even when the patient learns to visualize the scenes suggested by the hypnotist, or act out what is suggested in psychodrama, or work through what can be encountered in Gestalt therapy, sometimes all methods of therapy fail to alter the ongoing, day-to-day emotional experience for which one sought assistance.

I treasure a New Yorker cartoon showing a village scene with an African tribal dance in the background, the magnificently costumed sorcerer and his apprentice walking through a clearing in the midground. "I danced the best I could," says the sorcerer, "but what that guy has is an iron-deficiency anemia." Sometimes the problem isn't where you are trained to treat. These are the *disorders* of mood caused by interference with the biology of the person.

Medical biology is not biology. In biology, said the great French scientist Claude Bernard, we ask the cell a question. We alter the conditions in which a cell, or an organism, or a cluster of organisms, lives, and observe what changes. The charm of medical biology is that everything we know was learned because something "went wrong" with someone. It is the study of the abnormal that came to our attention only because some person, or some system within an individual person, failed to operate as we have come to expect. Biology is the study of life for its own sake. Medicine is the art of returning people to their expected norm.

Much of what we know about the biology of emotion has been learned from the study of people whose uncomfortable moods were incapable of alteration by the techniques described above. We know that lithium salts normalize the emotional world of someone with manic-depressive illness, and that people who do not manufacture enough thyroid hormone tend to be depressed. I have been fortunate to grow up in psychiatry during the era when the tools and techniques of biochemistry and neurophysiology have been informed by data from computer-assisted radiologic probes that allow us to peep within the brain with enormous sophistication and perfect safety. Great scientists have discovered one neurotransmitter after another, deducing the sequence of their action and their role in normal as well as abnormal mood. For each of these messenger molecules we can find some chemical capable of altering its manufacture or utilization, some method of making better or worse the mood of an afflicted person. Charles Whitman's tumor produced a disorder of mood, just as did the pseudoephedrine taken by my otherwise self-controlled patient. Perhaps the most dramatic and exciting field of study within contemporary psychiatry is this search for biological circuit diagrams.

Will the magic of pharmacology replace the hard work of psychotherapy? Are we entering an era when any bad feeling can be dispelled by medication which produces permanent and positive change in one's life? Hardly. To take this position is as silly as to claim that the repair of a computer is the same as its intelligent use, or that the repair of an automobile is the same as the use to which that car is put by its driver, or that the music emanating from the loudspeakers is the same as the tubes or transistors that turn electrical impulses into sound. Intuitively we know that some people will be returned to normal on relief of their disorders of mood, while others will need a considerable amount of psychotherapy to permit integration into their personality of their new range of possible emotions.

Why this should be will become evident as we learn more about the relation

---

Table 2

COMPONENTS OF THE AFFECT SYSTEM

SITES OF ACTION
Places where affect can be recognized as feeling.

STRUCTURAL EFFECTORS
Nerve trunks that carry messages to the sites of action.

MEDIATORS
Chemicals that also trigger effects at the sites of action.

RECEPTORS
Detect affect-related information that is transmitted back to the affect system
to cause more affect.

ORGANIZERS
Prewritten programs that organize these mechanisms into coherent scripts.
The innate affects of Silvan Tomkins.

---

between affect and emotion. It is time to study affect itself, to learn the components of the affect system.

COMPONENTS OF THE AFFECT SYSTEM

Sites of Action

One of the reasons each affect feels different from the others is that it triggers a separate group of bodily reactions. I use the term *site of action* to describe the places in the body where an affect can become a feeling. In fear, individual hairs stand on end because some mechanism has stimulated the *erector pili* muscles attached to the hair root. In distress, we cry—the lacrimal apparatus is another *target* or *end organ* of the affect system. Affect can alter patterns of secretion and movement in the gut, for in fear some are cotton-mouthed while others have diarrhea or nausea. Affect can make us sweat just as it can make us shake and shiver.

Clearly, the primary function of tearing is protection of the eyes from dryness or noxious chemical stimuli, just as the evaporation of sweat from the skin cools the body, and secretion within the gut varies normally in response to the needs of digestion under the control of the autonomic nervous system. Nonetheless, we can cry because such preexisting mechanisms are available to be triggered during affect; we can sweat or experience diarrhea when frightened because the mechanisms for sweating and gut function can also be taken over temporarily by affect.

Crying is more than tearing, for sobbing involves a vocal expression of distress. The voice, independent of its use in the production of words, is a major instrument of the affect system. Whereas the baby can utter communications only in the language of affect (by using such wordless expressions as cooing, laughing, screaming, or grunting), the adult can use the same affect-based expressions to produce the emotional tonality that adds delicate shades of meaning to words. Perhaps the voice evolved because the additional power it gave to the expression of affect increased the organism's ability to survive.

The circulatory system is intimately involved in the experience of affect. Just as the heart speeds in fear and in excitement, blood vessels in the hands and feet may constrict to give the cold feeling associated with fear. The anger of the "redneck," the flush of sexual excitement, the blush of shame, and the blanched face of terror are other examples of the changes in circulation triggered during affect. Similarly, the respiratory apparatus may be a target of affect when we breathe faster during excitement, suspend our breathing in fear, or make the sudden intake of breath associated with surprise. Affect is posture also—we may stand erect when proud, droop in shame, adopt a "fighting stance," jut the head forward in anger or disgust, and cringe in fear.

But by far the most important site of action for affect display is the face. Nowhere else in the body can the anatomist demonstrate so many perfectly developed muscle groups packed together so well, each group served by its own specific nerve trunk. As Darwin pointed out, human facial expression remains the same from cradle to grave, and the closer a life form to us in looks, the more the range and type of its facial expression resembles ours. Many of the muscles of expression seem to have no function other than their relation to affect. There is a great deal more to say about the face, which Tomkins considers the display board for the affect system, but for the moment I wish only to include it among the bodily sites capable of displaying affect. The face alone can provide enough information to determine the nature of a feeling.

Effectors and Mediators

In order for an end organ of affect expression to be triggered, it must either be served by nerve trunks carrying a message acceptable to that organ or be stimulated directly by chemicals brought through circulation. I call the anatomical structures that carry such messages the *effectors* and the stimulating chemicals the *mediators* of affect. An example of the structural effectors would be the primitive section of the brain called the *reticular activating system*, which seems to be responsible for varying levels of arousal. Also, we know that certain regions in the hypothalamus are involved in the production of anger, "sexual aggression," fear, and pleasure. If the tips of the temporal lobes of the brain are removed on both sides, an organism (person or experimental animal) develops the Kluver–Bucy syndrome, with blunted affect and inappropriate responses to stimulation. I can list literally hundreds of similar brain structures with the clinical disorder known to be related to each; my only point here is to fix in your mind the idea that a great many pieces of equipment must be choreographed in some very precise manner for us to get the specific patterns of action we call innate affect.

The brain is more than a large instrument built to handle electrical impulses like a telephone switching office. It is also an endocrine organ—a hormone factory—and some investigators believe that fully a third of its bulk serves this function. It is known to manufacture the major neurotransmitters *norepinephrine* and *serotonin*, messenger substances which are necessary for the maintenance of normal mood and to provide the chemistry for a wide variety of secondary messenger systems. Compounds taken into the body for other reasons can become mediators of affect, as when depression is caused by drugs given for high blood pressure or to prevent pregnancy, or when medication used for the control of asthma causes anxiety.

Receptors

A moment ago I mentioned that hair, made to stand on end by the *erector pili* muscles, is a site of action for affect. Calm, limp hair, tousled by a passing breeze, sends one kind of message to the brain; stiffly erect hair transmits something different when disturbed. In this sense, structures all over the body are capable of conveying information about the presence or absence of affect. Affect, which causes all sorts of things to happen at its various sites of action, also turns those sites of action into secondary sources of data capable of analysis by central brain structures and capable of triggering more affect.

Tomkins and the Organizers of Affect

Here, then, are all the basic ingredients needed to produce an affect—the structural *effectors* and chemical *mediators* that will carry messages to specific *sites of action* where *receptors* allow recognition of the patterns of activity we call affect. All we need is some system to organize them. The final portion of the affect system is the group of internal scripts that we may call the *organizers* of affect. These are the innate affects first described by Silvan Tomkins.

How Tomkins first came to recognize the nature of innate affect, of a group of "hard-wired" commands operating much as today we would describe a computer program, is one of the most charming stories in the history of science. As a boy I used to read books about the lives of the great scientists who were my heroes. Every bacteriologist, for instance, had been forced to throw away culture plates contaminated with mold. The green and crusted mold so often found on stale bread would get into bacterial cultures and eat up all the food left for the bacteria, ruining whatever experiment had been in progress. But Andrew Fleming noticed a halo, a ring of clear, bacteria-free culture medium around each little island of bread mold, and guessed that the mold *Penicillium* manufactured some substance that prevented the growth of bacteria. He was able to extract that substance, the first antibiotic, and named it penicillin for the mold from which it had been derived. From Fleming's "chance observation" came the beginning of the antibiotic era.

There are dozens, hundreds, of such stories in the history of science, all characterized by certain unchanging features. In general, an event available to many was witnessed by someone with a mind prepared to see it differently and the skill and training to evaluate that observation in some novel and useful way. What is not recorded in the novelistic treatments of great scientific discovery are the tens of thousands of similar observations made by excellent scientists with superb training and equipment that produced nothing but reams of useless data and unproductive speculation. Either much in history depends on luck or luck is a label used by those who have not discovered anything significant. Little has been written about what I would consider one of the attributes of genius—the specific quality of mind that allows some to assess, comprehend, and ignore the trivial but concentrate on what is truly significant.

Prior to his discovery in the mid-1940s of the affect system, Silvan Tomkins was a successful experimental psychologist who had developed (with his colleague, the statistician Daniel Horn) the Tomkins–Horn Picture Arrangement Test, still used to evaluate certain parts of the thinking apparatus. His great friend and mentor was the psychiatrist Henry Murray, who developed the Thematic Apperception Test, known as the TAT, in which subjects are asked to make up a story that explains the drawing being shown them by the testing psychologist. (The TAT is a good tool by which to learn about the emotional life of an individual without seeming to ask personal questions.) The early papers of Norbert Weiner, the mathematician whose theoretical work made modern computer science possible, had entranced Tomkins. It was a time of ferment, of novelty, of excitement. Something new was in every wind.

Tomkins and his wife, having decided it was time to raise a family, took advantage of a scheduled sabbatical year to plan for their first child. So a great and prepared mind witnessed the birth of a baby in a period when little else but the magic of a new life needed to occupy attention. The baby, of course, cried at birth. To Tomkins, this was a miracle. In a flash he saw a critical similarity between the cry of an adult and the wail of a newborn. Clearly, he thought, the infant does not appraise the world as a vale of tears (1982). Notwithstanding the "reasons" that an adult might cry, the newborn baby does not know why it cries—it merely cries.

Crying is a very complex series of behaviors. The eyes pour forth tears. The laryngeal apparatus must sound the cry. The face gets red and the mouth takes on the peculiar shape called "the *omega* of melancholy." No newborn infant is capable of *deciding* to organize all these activities in order to cry. Most likely there was a script for crying, a program that could be set off (unleashed, released, triggered) by some "button." Adult and infant alike merely pushed the button for the cry. *There was no reason to suspect the existence of more than one button!* Tomkins had seen the halo around the island of bread mold.

This was the burst of insight that ushered in a new science of emotion. Tomkins knew, just as well as you and I, that both the infant and the adult cry. He recognized that the cry is an organized behavior with a precise form— every cry resembles every other cry. But the cry itself, this very complex series of behaviors, *produced* so much information that it seemed unlikely to him that the infant could remain "unaware" of it, that the organism "wasted" this information, allowed it to unfold without making further use of it. Just as whatever allows an infant to cry must somehow trigger something that allows this organized behavior to start and then to unfold in its own particular way, and just as whatever allows an adult to cry must somehow involve the same switch and the same script, despite whatever else is going on in the far more educated mind of the adult, the cry itself must become a source of information. Now Tomkins began to extract penicillin from the halo.

Anybody who cries, whether an organism as naive and untrained as the infant or a personage as sophisticated and learned as the professor, must engage this switch and then permit the expression of the program we call the cry. The secret to the nature of emotion was suddenly available. Tomkins had discovered the affects, the group of "hard-wired," preprogrammed, genetically transmitted mechanisms that exist in each of us and are responsible for the earliest form of emotional life. What remained for him was to see how many affect programs could be found in the newborn and to discover the connections between these innate affects and the highly complex mental formations we call adult emotion.

How many affects are there, how many of these prewritten scripts that appear equally available to newborn and adult? Perhaps a better question would be how few—we want to find the smallest number of building blocks necessary to make our structure. Remember the problem we studied in school: what is the smallest number of colors needed to draw a map on which no two countries would share both a boundary and a color? (That answer, according to the mathematical discipline called topology, is four.) How sparse an alphabet of affects is needed from which to assemble every possible emotion? At the moment, it seems as if the magic number is nine. To the best of our knowledge, every known emotion and emotion-laden situation can be explained on the basis of the nine innate affects described by Tomkins. They come in three types or categories—two affects that are basically pleasant or *positive*, one that is neutral, and six others that are basically unpleasant or *negative*.

With only a couple of exceptions, each innate affect is given a two-word group name, the first indicating the mildest form in which it may be seen, the second representing its most intense presentation. The positive affects are *interest–excitement* and *enjoyment–joy;* the neutral affect is called *surprise–startle;* and the negative affects are *fear–terror, distress–anguish, anger–rage, dissmell, disgust,* and *shame–humiliation.* Each may be regarded as a pattern of expression, a specific package of information triggered in response to a particular type of stimulus. Much of the information in this package involves the skin and muscles of the face, just as Darwin had observed a century earlier, but affect does vastly more than operate as display at its various visible sites of action.

By far the most important idea for me to convey—indeed, the concept that is so central to the argument of my book that one might say the book pivots around it—is Tomkins's idea that the function of any affect is to amplify the highly specific stimulus that set it in motion. A stimulus involving an increase in brain activity will trigger an affect that increases brain activity, while a stimulus that involves a decrease in brain activity will trigger an affect that further decreases brain activity. No matter whether that stimulus has come from what the infant has just seen, heard, smelled, tasted, or remembered, if the stimulus triggers an affect, the stimulus will now become important in the way typical of that affect. Affect, says Tomkins, makes good things better and bad things worse. Affect makes us care about different things in different ways. The reason that emotion is so important to a thinking being is that affect controls or acts upon the way we use thought, just as it takes over or influences bodily actions at the sites specific for it. Whenever we are said to be *motivated*, it is because an affect has made us so, and we are motivated in the direction and form characteristic of that affect. Whatever is important to us is made so by affect. Affect is the engine that drives us.

Is there anything really revolutionary in this definition of affect? We have always known that an excited person thinks and talks excitedly, that a startled person is jumpy and unlikely to think calmly until the moment of surprise has passed, that anxious people are skittish in everything they do, and that someone suffused with contentment is likely to be calm and complacent. The problem is that we were brought up to understand emotion as some sort of climate that interfered with or only hindered intellectual function. We have been so charmed by our own ability to store and retrieve memory or to handle numbers that we have overlooked the fact that our affects were what gave these attributes importance.

Before this contribution of Tomkins we said that affect, behavior, and cognition represented three separate functions of the human brain. Such distinctions are not only arbitrary but incorrect. Affect causes behaviors all over the body. Not only does affect influence and often control the thinking made possible by the most advanced structures of the new brain (what we call the neocortex), but it is a form of thinking—the action thinking of the old brain.

Take, for instance, the affect Tomkins calls interest–excitement. In the presence of any novel stimulus, a baby will furrow its brow and begin to track with eyes and ears the source of information that attracted its attention. Instantly alert and attentive, it is in the grip of the affect interest; the more interested the baby gets, more will its affective response resemble what we call excitement. Yet it is clear that the baby does not "understand" why it is excited or even know that it is excited, let alone know who it is that has become excited.

Consider, then, the nature of novelty, of a stimulus capable of triggering interest. Tomkins suggests that interest is a patterned response to an optimal increase in the rate and intensity of *whatever* is going on within the brain. Thus, an optimal increase in brain activity triggers an affect program that causes an amplification of this optimal state of brain function. The triggering of affect takes what might be interesting and now makes it very interesting. As E. Virginia Demos has pointed out on the basis of her meticulous observations of infants studied with the aid of videotape, an affect converts what is essentially a quantitative occurrence (these meaning-free shifts in brain physiology) into the kind of qualitative experience we can call a feeling.

In the case of the affect interest, a meaning-free increase in the activity of the brain has occurred, enough of an increase to trigger the affect program. The affect program now makes things happen all over the body, the effect of which is to add urgency to this increase. No matter when an affect is triggered, it is neither a trivial nor a casual event. The triggering of an affect program initiates a mechanism that is urgent as soon as it begins.

Lots more is happening to the excited infant than this optimal increase in brain function, for among the functions amplified are the bodily motions available at the sites of action of this particular affect script. Again, observe the infant, who is not merely "somewhat" stirred by affect. The entire infant, suddenly alert and visibly more alive, is *taken over* by affect. Affective responses are immensely important events in the life of an infant, whose entire being is now under the control of the affect.

Swiftly the growing organism learns to associate the experience of affect with what triggered it, to form the linkages that, as its powers of memory and higher cognition improve with age, will become adult emotion. And, since it is on the display board formed by the skin and muscles of the face that affect is primarily expressed, it is awareness of its own facial display that tells the infant what affect has been triggered. Do not for a moment think that we are talking about the relatively mild facial displays of affect seen in the adult, who has learned to modulate or mute what he or she shows the outside world. When an affect hits an infant, that affect is the only game in town!

So the infant grows up with its affects, learning to identify each affect by its mode of facial display, learning to handle and live with the alterations in function caused by affect. The affects are perhaps the most frequently recurring experiences in the life of the baby because they are responses to physiological conditions (variations in the level of internal activity) that must occur merely in the process of living. Since the facial expression of affect involves voluntary muscles momentarily taken over by an involuntary mechanism, the infant gets used to feeling these muscles being captured by the affect programs and sooner or later begins to play with these muscles of expression.

By this normal activity of imitation the baby now learns how to perform all the displays associated with emotion, whether or not an innate affect mechanism has been triggered. Affect display, initially an involuntary mechanism representing the quality of a physiological experience, begins to operate also as voluntary activity. For the rest of its life, the growing organism will know how to mimic intentionally the expressions that originally occurred involuntarily as the result of innate affect. Tomkins describes this form of self-mimicry as *autosimulation*—the intentional simulation of one's own unintentional movements.

Still more is happening. The fact that each of these powerful physiological experiences is displayed on the face and also in a definable group of distinctive bodily motions makes them quite visible to anybody who spends much time taking care of an infant. Naturally we are talking about the baby's mother, but nowadays this mothering job is more and more a shared effort, so we therapists and theoreticians have begun to substitute the term *caregiver* to indicate that we know fathers, siblings, other family members, nurses, and a host of other people may take over some or most of this job. Although I will follow conventional usage and refer to the mothering person as the caregiver in most of this section, please understand that this is pretty much a code word for mother. A big part of taking care of a baby involves watching and responding to its affect display. Although we call this interplay "babytalk" because it is accompanied by a great deal of vocalization, most of what the caregiver really seems to be doing is mirroring or imitating the facial display of the infant.

A moment ago I mentioned that the baby is learning to recognize its own affective states by connecting the inner changes caused by affect to the bodily feelings generated when the face is rearranged in the patterns specific for each affect. The sensory equipment involved here is the kinesthetic apparatus, the same system of nerves that tells us the location of our arms and legs no matter where they are moved. Recently, a group of psychologists led by Paul Ekman asked actors to arrange their facial muscles in certain patterns (1983). The instructions were given in a way that the subjects of this experiment could not have known that they were being asked to mimic the display of innate affect—yet to these actors it *felt* as if they were experiencing affects, even to the point that other sites of action (like pulse and respiration) were affected. It seems that simulated affect expressions are themselves a real (even if somewhat weak) stimulus for affect.

If mere simulated affect can produce real affect, then we must look a bit more carefully at what is going on between caregiver and infant. Affect is extremely contagious. Something about it—one of its inherent qualities—makes affect infectious. That, of course, is one of the main reasons all societies teach their children to mute or dam up the expression of innate affect. It just won't do to have people walking around infecting each other with laughter, anger, excitement, sobbing, or surprise.

But our current definition of normal parenting not only accepts but more or less requires that mothers remain available to the contagious quality of their babies' affect. Not that this is an entirely onerous task—another quality of affect is that by and large it feels good to resonate with another person's affect. Whether a mother, intensely focused on her child's smile or frown, is unintentionally swept up into its contagious quality or purposefully imitates a facial expression, instantly she begins to experience the same affect as the child. Suddenly they are in communication, for by either the simple process of imitation or the acceptance of contagion, the caregiver has entered the internal system of the baby.

Basch, whose definition of affect, feeling, and emotion we discussed earlier, indicates that this is the beginning of empathy, the highly sophisticated system through which adults learn to share and perhaps understand each other's feelings (1983a). What we do during empathy, Basch explains, is try out each other's affect display, which triggers a weak experience of innate affect, following which we bring to this affect our own lifetime of remembered emotional experience in an attempt to appreciate the world of the other person. Although the affect system of the baby is far more primitive than the sophisticated language of specific words that will be available to the three-year-old, affect provides the infant with a powerful link to the outside world, one that remains part of our equipment throughout life.

THE AFFECT SYSTEM

We need to discuss a few more of Tomkins's ideas about the nature of affect and the affect system itself before going on to present the alphabet of nine specific affect programs he describes. Let's tackle the idea of an affect *system* first.

Although, as a biology major, I took courses in college that were not specifically designed as preparation for the study of medicine, they provided a pretty good link to it. As has been known for centuries, the best way to learn how the human body is put together is to take one apart. In an atmosphere of reverence, awe, fear, disgust, and curiosity, medical students dissect human corpses. This experience is made less gruesome for us by virtue of the fact that we all dissected frogs in high school biology, guinea pigs in college biology, and cats in college comparative anatomy courses. Each of these four life forms differs from the others in many ways, but they are alike in many others. Each experience of dissection—of disassembly—prepares one for the next.

The four animals we dissected had many organs in common. Each had a circulatory system which took blood through the lungs to cleanse it of carbon dioxide and replenish its store of oxygen, following which this blood was pumped all over the body. The student of biology begins each dissection with the sure and certain knowledge that the circulatory system exists, and that it conforms to charts long ago established for each life form. Similarly, dissection confirms what may be learned from the study of texts and drawings in other areas. We humans also have a central nervous system (a brain, housed in the head, linked to nerve trunks coursing all over the body) and a skeletal system (bones which are linked by joints and moved by muscles connected to tendons and ligaments).

I suspect that our species has "always" known about the skeletal system, at least from prehistoric times. After all, we have always eaten meat, which comes from bones (archaeological sites often contain piles of animal bones as evidence of this), so primitive man must have studied the skeletal system to some extent. And, through injury, early humans must have occasionally lost limbs and come to understand the relation between normal function and normal anatomy.

We did not so easily understand the circulatory system. In fact, the relation between the heart, the great vessels, the lungs, and the blood that travels along these conduits was not discovered until the pioneering work of William Harvey, physician to Kings James I and Charles I of England. The results of his meticulous studies of circulation were published in 1628. What most of us do not know is that his work was neither accepted nor fully substantiated for 200 years! Similarly, the idea of a central nervous system, and its importance as the seat of consciousness and the source of the personality, has come to our culture only within the past century or so.

Someone pointed out to me that science involves pattern-finding, while art involves pattern-making. I think the border between great science and great art is perhaps a bit more blurred than that simple dichotomy might indicate, but for our purposes it will do to suggest that the scientist is one who attempts to find linkages between seemingly unrelated bits of information in order to form useful patterns from which we can make accurate predictions. Recent science has demonstrated the existence of systems undreamed of in older times. Today we take for granted the existence of an *immune system* that guards the boundary of what is us and what is alien to our very cells. We accept the idea of *biochemical systems* working at the submicroscopic level within our cells and of complex systems of interconnected hormonal processes that allow the *reproductive system* to function. Every few years another system is discovered.

So it should surprise us neither that Silvan Tomkins should have discovered the affect system nor that it has taken a generation or so for the scientists who study human emotion to take it seriously. The volume of data Tomkins assembled is literally staggering, and the breadth of the conclusions he drew from those data is astonishing. Furthermore, as I have indicated elsewhere, he presented these ideas in books so densely packed with ideas, observations, and theories that they are extraordinarily difficult to read. Worse still, especially for those who might try to study his work, Tomkins, for a host of personal reasons, delayed for a generation the publication of the last section of what was planned as a three-volume work. And this was the section with both the index and the bibliography! So the developer of the system did not make it easy for us to understand.

Luckily, others took up small, selected sections of the work he started.

Table 3
QUALITIES OF THE AFFECT SYSTEM

The innate affects are:

URGENT

ABSTRACT

ANALOGIC

INTERACTIVE WITH THEIR RECEPTORS

MATCHING IN PROFILE TO THEIR STIMULUS

CORRELATING OF STIMULUS AND RESPONSE

GENERAL

Ekman, in California, has devoted his extremely productive career to the study of facial affect display, writing a number of books that have influenced many. With his colleague Wallace Friesen he has produced *The Facial Affect Coding System*, used by psychologists all over the world to provide an easily replicated method of assessment. Others, like Carroll Izard, have more or less taken Tomkins's system, renamed it according to their own preference, and allowed it to be taken as their own. Scientists like Demos have devoted years to the observation of infants in an attempt to demonstrate how the innate affect displays of newborns come to evolve into the sophisticated emotions of adults. Psychoanalysts, like Basch, have brought Tomkins's ideas into the mainstream of modern psychotherapy. In addition to my work on shame, I have attempted to sketch a few of the links between affect theory and the world of psychopharmacology, as well as some of the methods by which adults manage to become somewhat immune to the emotions of others. But the concept of affect as part of a system is rarely discussed.

THE QUALITIES OF AFFECT

Urgency

The full dimensions of the affect system will become more apparent as we discuss the individual affects, but perhaps a presentation of some characteristics of affect itself will assist our study. I mentioned above that the affects are always *urgent*, that wherever in human experience we see any sort of urgency, it has been provided by an affect. It must also be mentioned that the kind of urgency they provide is quite nonspecific.

Are you interested in coins, in cars, in carpets, in costumes; are you fascinated by corruption, by cats, by callousness? In each case something has triggered the affect program for interest: That which a moment ago excited neural firing at a rate capable of triggering the quite abstract affect called interest has now become urgently much more interesting. Are you afraid of snakes, of rapists, of thugs, of the Internal Revenue Service, of lady wrestlers, of computers, of hats? In each case something has triggered the affect program for fear. What we understand, what we experience as *fear of* some entity or *fear during* some event, is only the linkage we ourselves have formed between this particular entity or event and the quite abstract innate affect called fear. No matter what has frightened us, no matter what has triggered fear, the affect fear is identical in each situation. That which is *too much* is now *urgently* too much.

Abstractness

Note that the affect bears no intrinsic relation to any particular triggering source. The presence of the affect fear–terror can never by itself offer a clue to its source. If we are frightened, *some other mechanism will have to tell us* what *has become not just too much but more too much.* Tomkins describes this characteristic of the affect system by noting that the affects are completely *abstract,* completely free of inherent meaning or association to their triggering source. There is nothing about sobbing that tells us anything about the steady-state stimulus that has triggered it; sobbing itself has nothing to do with hunger or cold or loneliness. Only the fact that we grow up with an increasing experience of sobbing lets us form some ideas about its meaning.

It appears that animals lower in the evolutionary tree do have affects that are linked to specific sources. Mice, squirrels, and other ground-dwelling animals are inherently afraid of shapes flying above them. There doesn't seem to be any evidence of innate fears in the human.

Analogues

Now we come to the most difficult concept in the bunch. Each affect is *analogic.* It resembles what triggered it. An affect is in some way similar to what triggered it.

There are other psychobiological systems in which the triggered program resembles in some way the stimulus that acted as a switch for it. Take, for instance, the resemblance between sexual arousal and the orgasm. Sexual arousal, whether we administer it to ourselves or experience it in the company of another person, has a definite quality. Part of an optimal sexual experience is conferred by the affect Tomkins calls interest–excitement, but the specifically sexual quality is brought by the sexual drive system. And the orgasm, the specific form of release triggered when the requirements for it have been met, is itself a highly amplified form of arousal. In this special connotation, says Tomkins, orgasm is an analogue of sexual arousal.

Take the relation between pain and injury. In a way I find difficult to express, but which I think you can grasp intuitively, pain itself has some of the qualities of injury. Pain feels like ripping, or tearing, or breaking—but more so. We do not experience anything as thrilling as an orgasm when we break a leg. I doubt that a life form with such circuitry could survive very long or continue to evolve, for it might seek constantly to crash into walls, jump over cliffs, and fight desperately in order to break limbs and be rewarded by the equivalent of an orgasm. Pain is a useful mechanism in that it amplifies our awareness of an injury and focuses our attention on the location of that injury. Thus it appears that pain is an analogue of injury.

So the body is wired to respond to a number of situations with genetically programmed mechanisms that act as analogues of their triggering stimulus. Thus it is for affect. Each affect is an analogue of its triggering stimulus in that it more or less *feels like* the situation that incited it. Equally important, each affect feels different from the others. The *felt quality* of each is unique, recurrent, reproducible, and consistent. A rush of ideas triggers an affect that makes the mind rush more; the analogy is the *feeling* of "rush." Affects that are responses to increases in the rate of neural firing will themselves feel like an increased activity. Affects that respond to intense, constant levels of neural firing will themselves feel like an intense, constant but highly amplified level of activity. We will discuss the nature of the individual affect programs later, but for now it is important to understand that in addition to their urgency and their neutrality or abstractness, affects are analogues of their stimuli.

Receptors

Recall what I said about the original flash of insight that allowed Tomkins to deduce the existence of the affect system. He had observed the crying of his newborn son and realized that this complex group of behaviors activated so many parts of the body that crying itself must provide a great deal of information to the organism. In a very special sense, then, each time an affect is triggered, it creates information. How this information is picked up, where it is received, and the nature of the sensory *receptors* for that information are matters of great interest.

The affect program for fear does something to the hairs that changes them from their quiescent state to an erect state; "relaxed" hair feels quite different from erect hair. As I mentioned earlier, a breath of air wafting over the erect hair of a frightened animal will call further attention to the fact that it is frightened. The hair follicles, just a moment ago the target of the affect program, now act as a sensory device transmitting to the brain the information that the organism is frightened. Hair becomes both the site of action of an affect program and a receptor site for information about the affect.

The affect system seems to have receptor sites all over the body. I suggested that some chemicals act as messenger molecules for the affect system, as chemical mediators of affect. Recently discovered compounds, like the body's own morphinelike *endorphins*, are now known to influence receptors located throughout the body. It seems likely that the affect Tomkins calls enjoyment–joy can release endorphins, which then go into the circulation and cause some reaction at their receptor sites. This reaction itself feeds more information back to the brain and acts as a further trigger to the initiating affect.

Just as we keep on discovering new mediator substances, Tomkins suspects that there are more receptors to discover, especially receptors for the affect system. Some of these will turn out to be very tiny, like the sites on cell membranes where specific molecules like peptides will localize. (Much of the research being done today in the field of biological psychiatry involves the search for receptors and mediators, although their relevance to the affect system has not been suggested before.) Others will be found in the skin and subcutaneous structures of the face, where alterations in the microcirculation of blood seem to be such an important part of the affect mechanisms.

The face blanches in fear; the neck reddens in anger; the face, neck, and entire upper body can blush in shame; there is a recognizable flush of excitement. What if there were a series of receptors activated by the circulatory effects of these affect programs, each receptor capable of transmitting back to the brain further information about the affect program currently in progress? There is evidence that an analogous type of receptor exists in a region of the body where you might most expect it—the genital apparatus.

In 1950, Frank A. Beach and Gilbert Levinson published a study of the sexual mechanism in rats. Using a microscope, they found that the skin of the flaccid, unengorged penis folded into tiny creases which, in cross section, resembled a cog wheel. Within the creases were even smaller hairlike *papillae* surrounded at the base by *touch corpuscules*. Thus, the unit made up of "hair" and neurofibrils could function as a receptor for touch. When the penis was limp and flaccid, these sensitive receptors were completely encased—protected from contact. But when the skin of the rat penis was fully stretched by the engorgement normally accompanying mild, early sexual arousal, the creases were smoothed and these hair receptors rose to the surface, where even the lightest of touches might produce maximal stimulation.

Here was a situation in which a minor alteration in blood flow altered the effective sensitivity of a receptor mechanism. The limp penis is only slightly affected by stroking, while the erect penis is in a state of exquisite sensitivity. The change in blood flow readied a receptor that was otherwise quiescent. Might not we find, asked Tomkins, other such receptors—most likely in the face, but also all over the body—brought into similar states of readiness or availability by the circulatory changes known to accompany innate affect? When fatigued we can get a moment of relief by splashing the face with cold water; inappropriate or unwanted sexual arousal can be quenched by a cold shower. These truisms depend on poorly understood interactions between temperature-sensitive receptors and bodily systems quite remote from them.

Here, I believe, is a clue to the extraordinary contagious quality of af- fect—which, incidentally, is the characteristic that so fascinated me that it drew me into a lifetime of study. I don't think there is any difference between the internal contagion that makes each affect trigger more of the same affect within us and contagion from the outside, from other people. Likely it is the receptors for internally derived affect that "pick up" the "music" of affect from other people. Alternatively (as my colleague Francis J. Broucek has suggested), the mechanisms for the appreciation of "broadcast" affect may have evolved as receptors separate and quite distinct from those sensitive to one's own innate affect. I think it is unnecessary to postulate the existence of two types of receptors for the same information, but Broucek's idea is as valid as mine until someone does the necessary research.

Profile

We have discussed four facets of affect—its inherent urgency, its abstract quality, its operation as an analogue of whatever triggered it, and how it interacts with its receptors both to stimulate more affect and to provide the information from which we come to know that an affect has been triggered. Yet each stimulus for affect has a particular shape in time, a *profile*. The affect Tomkins calls surprise–startle is triggered by a hand clap or a pistol shot. In either case, a very brief event is followed by a very brief affect. Distress, the crying affect, is triggered by a steady-state type of stimulus, and sobbing is a steady-state affect. Each affect matches the "temporal profile" of its triggering stimulus. This concept is similar to the idea that affect is an analogue of its trigger, but differs in that it carries implications in terms of the quality of time.

Correlation

Two more qualities remain to be discussed before we can get to the affects themselves. Tomkins points out that the affect programs stamp their effects on body systems other than the normal sites of action we have been discussing. If I am angry, my voice will be angry, my fist will move angrily, my walk and my posture will be stamped or imprinted by my anger, no matter what made me angry. When I am in the calm state of contentment, the affect Tomkins calls enjoyment–joy, my voice will be mellow, my hand move gracefully, my walk and my posture relaxed, and ideas will float in and out of my mind easily, no matter what made me happy. Affect imprints itself on all bodily function in such a way as to make the stimulus for that affect into something that *correlates* the stimulus with its eventual response. Whatever triggered the affect now becomes linked in memory with whatever followed it. In other words, we have a correlation of stimulus and response that is forged by the interposition of an affect program.

Generality

The last feature of the affect system is one that may by now seem obvious to most readers, but for historical reasons it is important to mention it here. The system is inherently *general*. It has no built-in links to any other system of the body or mind. Affect can amplify cognitive activity like the storage and re-trieval of memory; it can alter body mobility, as when we fight angrily or romp gaily; it can be linked with sexuality, or with pain, or with hunger, or with thirst. Like a wonderful kind of building block, affect can be assembled with any drive, with any voluntary action, with any function of the mind, even with other affects. It is entirely and perfectly general. Using the language of this era, we might say that affect is modular, capable of infinite assembly. There is no inherent limitation on the ways affect can be used by the human.

Limitations appear soon enough in development—much of the process of socialization involves affect control, and much of the process of fitting into a culture involves learned displays of affect and styles of affective expression. But Freud was wrong when he thought that all excitement derived from sexual excitement and that all curiosity was "desexualized libido."

Each of the nine affect programs contains instructions for a wide range of activity. Mild interest, which calls into play only a few muscles, differs greatly from passionate excitement—even though both are expressions of the same innate mechanism. No one has attempted to figure out the specific triggers for what Tomkins calls *the range of affective expression*, even though it is obvious that such a range exists.

WORKING WITH THE AFFECT SYSTEM

Look, for a moment, at the various ways we can study individual people—alone or in an interaction: Think what happens when we try to watch someone while we are with that person. Next, consider how much easier it is to stand aside and watch his or her interaction with somebody else. Now imagine that you are watching such an interchange using binoculars and hidden microphones, or through a one-way mirror. Next, think what might be different when you saw the same scene on the screen of a color television set. What if the videotape had been made in black and white? What if you merely heard the interaction on audiotape? Suppose someone translated the spoken word to typescript which was then read aloud by a computer-driven voice simulator? And what if you were given the typescript and could read it to yourself, silently? How about a summary, or an abstract of the conversation in question? And, finally, what if you were given a description of the people involved, one written by somebody else?

Each of these ways of studying the human involves a different stance in relation to affect. Personal involvement brings the greatest immersion in affect—our own, and that of others. Each of the other modes I have outlined filters out one or another moiety of innate affect. Our empathic involvement (affective resonance) is diminished by standing aside and reduced further by physical distance or the relative "safety" of the mirror room. Color television removes the sense of immediacy brought by smell and reduces the quality, the fidelity of affect-related information transmitted. When color is removed we filter out most of the facial data produced by circulatory change. When we filter out all visual stimuli our awareness of affect is limited to cues from tone of voice and the words themselves. And the remaining filters remove more and more of the affect that was so much a part of the original scene. We really do own and operate a lot of systems that help us avoid affect.

Now that I have given you some idea of the general theory of affect, let's go back to the innate affects themselves and discuss all of them in terms of the structure I introduced in the previous chapter. I will describe each affect and the related feelings, emotions, moods, and disorders known to be associated with it. Difficult as it may seem, we will try to keep in mind all the features of the affect system discussed above. Surprisingly enough, in order to understand the astonishingly broad and far-reaching impact of shame, the importance of pride as a force in human life, and the emotional system I have called the *shame/pride axis*, all of this information is necessary.

Think of it as a figure-ground problem. Any attempt to understand shame that ignores the entire affect system must provide a limited and flawed explanation.

We've just gone over the structure of the affect system. Now it is time to present the actors themselves, the cast of nine that make up the repertory theater of the emotional world.

3

FEELING GOOD:

THE POSITIVE AFFECTS

Once Tomkins figured out the basic nature of the affect system it became necessary to study adult emotion in an entirely new way. Everything we thought we knew about emotion turns out to be at least slightly wrong. Some of the experiences we have called "shame" turn out to be combinations of shame affect with other affects, stored and remembered in their own particular way, while many, perhaps most, of the uncomfortable moments made so by shame affect—emotional experiences every bit as miserable as the ones we know so well—never achieve the recognition of a label or name. I can assure you of one thing: The affect Tomkins calls shame–humiliation is utterly and completely involved with the positive affects of interest–excitement and enjoyment–joy. Shame feels so miserable because it interrupts what feels best in life. But there is no way of *understanding* shame until you learn about excitement and contentment, about the pleasures with which it interferes.

INTEREST—EXCITEMENT

Whatever causes an optimal increase in the intensity and rate of activity of anything going on in the brain will trigger the affect interest. The information capable of providing such a stimulus for the infant may come from situations we can figure out, like a chance sound in the room, a bright object above the infant's crib, or the smell of mother, but interest may be triggered by a slight increase in hunger, by an image remembered, or by other internal sources of stimulation we may never discern. Nonetheless, when the proper conditions are met, the affect is triggered: The infant's eyebrows lower, the face takes on the attitude of rapt attention, and the entire child seems to be tracking something.

The affect interest makes us more interested in whatever is going on, and, if interest has been triggered by the face of another person, these two people will now be locked in the highly pleasant state of mutual interest that is the forerunner of social interaction. Whatever has triggered this degree of interest is now linked or assembled with it, making it interesting by amplifying it in an optimal fashion. Interest can make us pleasantly hungry, excited to see an old friend when memory presents the proper cascade of neural stimulation, fascinated by a puzzle with problems that create stimulation within a certain range of neural activity.

The more mature the child, the more memory can be "brought to mind" when interest is triggered. Early in development memory seems to be stored as groups of images, rather than words, so we believe the interested infant is comparing the focus of its interest to whatever is already in storage or, when necessary, making new categories of memory. With increased maturity comes

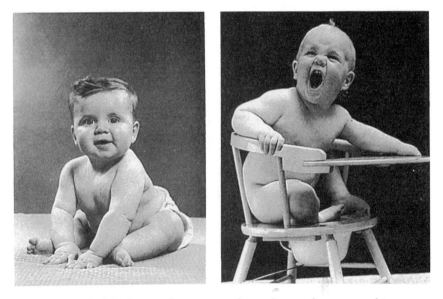

Fig. 3.1. Brow slightly furrowed, gaze riveted on whatever has triggered **interest–excitement**, mouth partially open. Often the tongue is thrust to the corner of the mouth.

Fig. 3.2. Ready to spring out of his potty chair in excitement, this little boy demonstrates the same affect at the upper end of its range.

vast expansion of memory and, therefore, the potential for growing complexity of affect–experience linkages. Whereas each episode of affect is an identical, short-lived event, the addition of related memories defines the more complicated and longer-lasting phenomenon we call an emotion.

An excited mood can be sustained when some external situation like an entertainment provides constant novelty or some internal source produces new thinking, as in the case of creativity. Anybody who writes, paints, composes, dances, or invents will gladly tell you how life can be taken over by the excitement generated in the wake of such novel thoughts. So alien to one's normal life can be the excitement of creativity that the ancient Greeks believed new ideas and the emotionality associated with them were the gift of an external being called the Muse. When we say that someone has been "struck by the muse" we mean to indicate that this person is "helplessly" excited by the new ideas constantly triggering the affect interest–excitement.

Are there disorders of this mood, situations when excitement or interest have been triggered in the absence of real novelty? Often, as a psychiatrist, I have treated people with what we used to call manic-depressive illness, nowadays labeled *bipolar affective illness*. When these patients are depressed, they complain that nothing interests them, that they are incapable of becoming excited about anything. And in the manic phase of the illness, they experience an opposite reaction—everything is interesting, everything that occurs to them can be exciting. When manic, they think with extraordinary speed; when depressed, thoughts flow like molasses in January. Affects are contagious. Just being around someone with an intense affect will make us share that part of his or her experience. Anyone who has ever been around even mildly manic or moderately depressed people will tell you how quickly we are drawn into their mood.

In this illness, both the decreased ability to be interested and the increased ability to be interested are part of a biological disorder of mood now thought to be caused by interference with the metabolism of one of the neurochemical messenger systems, a disorder often normalized by the addition of lithium salts to one's diet. So far as I can determine, since the innate affects provide the vocabulary for all normal emotion, no matter what interferes with or triggers inappropriately our experience of emotion, it is interpreted by us as some sort of affect. And this affect feels to us as if it were normal innate affect. What I find fascinating is that a problem in the circuitry of the brain, perhaps in the manufacture of a single chemical, leads to a distortion of normal mental experience that the patient can interpret only in terms of his or her lifetime experience of innate affect.

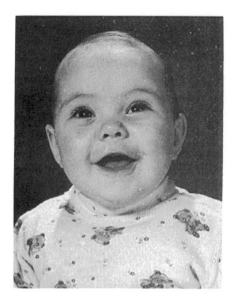

Fig. 3.3. The face of **enjoyment–joy** is always described as bright, or shining, muscles relaxed, lips open and widened. You wouldn't be surprised if this child laughed a moment after the picture was taken.

Is there a difference between the excitement felt and exhibited by an inventor rushing toward discovery and the excitement felt and exhibited by someone who, through a disorder of neurotransmitter function, has been made hypomanic? Not at the level of innate affect mechanisms, for the identical affect has been triggered in each case. For the inventor, interest has been stimulated by the onrush of ideas. Occasionally these novel ideas, when amplified by interest, trigger more and more novel ideas, leading to intense excitement and the quite pleasant "high" of discovery. However, we call hypomania an illness because the intense interest and excitement are brought on by alterations in neurotransmitter function—the ideas expressed by the individual are the result of the excitement rather than the source of it. Rarely are they truly creative or truly useful, and the more severely manic the individual, the less clearly reasonable will be the ideas involved.

You will recall that one of the cardinal features of affect is that by its ability to amplify anything with which it is linked, affect is responsible for attention. Anything that may be said to occupy our attention has taken center stage and become the subject of consciousness simply because it now has affective amplification. So far, we have only considered the type of attention produced by one affect, interest–excitement; but it is intuitively perceptible that each of the other affects we have yet to discuss also produces its own quite specific form of attention and therefore its own form of consciousness.

Once thought to be only a disorder of childhood, the spectrum of conditions called *attention deficit hyperactivity disorder* (ADD or ADHD) may be reconceptualized in terms of the affect system. These children seem unable to focus attention on anything for more than a moment. We adults know *boredom* as a state in which there is an insufficient amount of novelty to trigger ongoing interest–excitement. When bored, we search for the sort of stimulus, of data flow that we call distraction. Children with ADHD seem distracted by stimuli most of us would fail to notice, and are unable to maintain interest–excitement in situations the rest of us would find compelling.

The hypomanic patient's excitement seems to devolve from a constant and ongoing excess of the chemicals normally released only when the affect has been triggered by data flow—the conditions of stimulus gradient described by Tomkins. Manic hyperactivity is the result of the correlative function of affect; anybody is physically active when excited, no matter what the source of the excitement. Children with ADHD are hyperactive because affect has been triggered for some other reason. They are hyperactive simply because their attention shifts rapidly from one source to another and because the correlative function of interest–excitement raises their activity level.

Anything characterized as a problem with attention must somehow involve the affect system. All of the medications used to treat these children involve the neurotransmitters associated with the maintenance of normal affect mechanisms. Most of those who work with ADHD are pediatricians, pediatric neurologists, child psychiatrists, or child psychologists—all of whom tend to stop working with patients beyond early adolescence. Now we are beginning to consider the possibility that certain conduct disorders of adolescence and young adult life may represent the adult manifestations of ADHD. And those who treat this group of patients tend to prescribe the same group of medications as is used for the childhood disorder.

Most investigators approached ADHD as if it were analogous to the pediatric disorder known as *infantile colic.* Colicky babies cry constantly, distress–anguish apparently triggered by some failure of gastrointestinal development. Kids grow out of colic—indeed, the treatment consists mostly of calming the parents who are locked to a baby for whom solace seems so woefully inadequate. Colic usually disappears after a few months; we think it simply takes that long for some pattern of neural or digestive maturation to be completed. And there is no evidence that colicky babies grow up to be colicky adults. Since most children with ADHD seem to get better as they grow older, we have until recently paid little attention to the adult manifestations of this condition.

My own guess is that ADHD represents a genetic disorder of firmware, of the internal scripts responsible for normal affect. Although we treat these children and adolescents by making alterations in hardware function (using one or another form of artificial chemical mediator substance), it may be that the real source of the disorder is in the circuitry for affect stability. Tomkins introduced the concept of the central assembly, the parts of the brain responsible for affect utilization and the maintenance of attention. I suspect that ADHD may be linked to this locus of neurological function.

All through the history of medicine we have been able to learn about normal function through the analysis of disease. (Our earliest understanding of glucose metabolism and the role of insulin was made possible by the study of diabetes mellitus.) ADHD may be the sort of condition that allows us to peer into the circuitry for normal affect in a way offered by no other clinical entity. I have begun to discuss such research at a number of clinical centers.

Normal interest and excitement are always around us. Whether or not you have any interest in astronomy, it is hard not to be caught up in the exhilaration generated by an impending solar eclipse. Magazines, television, and newspapers all carry instructional material that can let even the least scientific among us get some understanding of the factors involved in this monumental exercise in space geometry. The total eclipse of 11 July 1991 was the longest in our lifetime, and its path over some of the most heavily populated regions of our planet let millions see it.

Reports from those who have seen such spectacles often contain information about the emotional reaction of observers. Almost universally, eclipse-watchers mention a rising tide of excitement as totality approaches. In the December 1991 issue of *Sky and Telescope*, columnist Dennis diCicco quotes one amateur astronomer: "The shadow came down on us over the ridge of mountains to the west enveloping everything in a single indrawn breath. The diamond ring flashed, followed by unbelievably delicate and gossamer coronal streamers stretching, stretching everywhere. Now everyone was yelling, hollering, screaming, pointing. 'Look at that!' 'Look at this!' 'Look there!' Just look! LOOK! . . . No grammatical gymnastics of mine can begin to describe what I saw in those precious, fleeting minutes" (p. 589).

But another astronomer, equally sensitive to the onrush of excitement felt by observers, pointed out something different: "We watched as a huge double sunspot group, perhaps 20,000 miles long, swam toward the Moon's black rim (perceptibly wrinkled by mountains) and was swallowed, followed by two single tiny spots and another great group . . . I realized more clearly than ever before that it is the *acceleration* of the dimming daylight that drives the excitement" (p. 594, emphasis in original). Tomkins himself could not have said it better.

ENJOYMENT—JOY

From its name you might think that Tomkins's label for this affect is synonymous with such vaguely defined conventional terms as "happiness." Far from
it. It is a technical term, like interest—excitement in that it is a name for another
highly specific biological condition. I ask you to accept the idea that anything
capable of causing a decrease in the rate and intensity of neural firing in the
brain of infant or adult will trigger the response of a smile, with the lips slightly
opened and widened—a pattern Tomkins calls the affect enjoyment—joy. Perhaps a better term for the weaker forms of this affect would be *contentment*,
which is less likely to be confused with the social phenomenon also (and more
conventionally) called "enjoyment."

I ran across a Latin proverb in an early 19th-century medical dictionary that
conveys some of the sense of this affect: *Omne animalium languo post coitum*—
all animals are calmed after intercourse. Do we need such a complex theory of
emotion to tell us that an orgasm can leave us with a feeling of contentment?
Surely not. But this theory does help explain in what way all feelings of calm
resemble each other. Again, observe the infant and note that every time distress is relieved, the baby smiles and becomes calm. No matter what the source
of distress, relief produces contentment. Similarly, the reduction in stimulus
level accompanying the relief of any high-density experience will trigger the
smiling face of enjoyment—joy and the calm spirit of contentment.

At times this experience of affective response to stimulus decrease will
range from tinkling laughter to uproarious guffaw, while at other times we will
barely smile. Darwin commented that monkeys also laugh and that they exhibit something like a smile; both he and other investigators have suggested
that the smile is a milder or attenuated form of laughter. Tomkins believes that
our ability to smile is the result of further evolution of this affect, and that the
more sudden and dramatic the decrease in stimulus level, the more likely we
are to laugh.

The laughing, smiling face of enjoyment functions to enhance social relatedness, much as does interest—excitement. Again, if you watch mothers and
babies playing at face-to-face interaction, you will notice that they spend a
great deal of their time oscillating between these two affects. Tomkins has
commented that shared interocular contact—people merely gazing at each
other—is the most intimate of human activities. How easy is this to understand when we recognize that the wonderful process of empathy depends
entirely on the fact that each of us shares with the other this identical group of
affect mechanisms.

Even though mothers and babies play at bouncing affect-based messages back and forth between them and thus learning a great deal about the feeling states going on in each other, their interaction is not limited to affective communication. The game of "making faces" at each other is quite complex. It seems that babies are true artists and experimenters—from the moment of birth on they seem to enjoy making up new combinations of facial expressions and bodily motions. Some of these expressions may involve the intentional display of an affect (used more in the spirit of a game than to indicate the presence of a feeling), while others will be quite unrelated to the facial displays of innate affect. Each mother-infant couple develops its own thesaurus of non-affect expressions, a shared vocabulary of meaningful looks and glances that grows in complexity and importance as the child matures. The interpretation of these expressions will depend on the history shared by this twosome—but whenever an innate affect is experienced and expressed by one, its meaning will be known unequivocally to the other.

What we as individuals call "having fun," or an entertainment, usually involves something quite different from the affect Tomkins calls enjoyment–joy. Good times are characterized by frequent shifts between stimulus increases and stimulus decreases, producing sequences of excitement and contentment. When we watch a sporting event our attention is captured by the action on the field, which triggers interest by its novelty. Although it is true that by the time we are old enough to watch games we have a pretty good idea of the range of possible happenings (so that very little goes on outside an expected frame of reference), what does occur is unpredictable within certain limits. And it is that degree of unpredictability which triggers interest. Similarly, when an action is completed to our satisfaction (the outfielder catches a ball, the hitter does well, the goal is achieved, etc.), the immediate reduction in stimulus level produces the affect of enjoyment.

At the level of innate affect it really does not matter whether a splinter has been removed from one's finger, or a burp has reduced the pressure in baby's tummy, or a chiropractic manipulation has clicked something back in place, or a patient recovering from anesthesia realizes both that he or she has survived the procedure and that the surgeon has removed the source of terrible pain, or the punch line of a joke has caught us off guard and suddenly reduced the intensity of our attention. Each is an example of stimulus decrease; each a source of enjoyment affect.

Have you ever had a prolonged massage administered by a trained professional? Apparently my vertebrae never quite learned to hang in a straight line, and I endure a significant degree of chronic muscular discomfort. At regular intervals I will treat myself to a massage, and such treatment dissolves for a while the constant, low-grade pain with which I live. "Low-grade pain" is a fine example of what in Tomkins's language would be called a constant level of stimulus density, and the relief of this pain triggers such a profound degree of "relaxation" that it takes me hours to return to my normal level of activity and alertness! The degree to which we are affected by enjoyment–joy is directly proportional to the intensity and prior duration of the preexisting level of stimulus. Does enjoyment–joy involve endorphins? Maybe so. I doubt morphine itself could have affected me more profoundly than the feeling of the first massage from which I arose completely relaxed and without pain.

This might be a good moment to repeat something I said earlier. Each of these first six affects is described by Tomkins as an *analogue* of its stimulus condition. Thus, enjoyment–joy is triggered by reduction in the level of intensity of any stimulus, and the affect itself produces a further reduction in all brain activity. It was easy to accept that interest–excitement *amplified* the condition of stimulus increase, but we have to bend our understanding of the concept of amplification to accept that enjoyment–joy can amplify a *decrease* in neural stimulation. This is the reason Tomkins describes the innate affects as *analogic amplifiers* of their stimulus conditions. Admittedly, this is a complex language. But what I like about it, and the reason I keep bringing it up from time to time, is that it seems to explain every single phenomenon ever observed in the realm of emotion. The importance of this will become increasingly clear as we proceed.

All of the examples noted above feature situations in which the decrease in stimulus level triggers enjoyment–joy, even though each one of these pleasant experiences will feel somewhat different. This is because each of these experiences represents the assembly of the affect with different sources and in different adventures. Emotion is defined by its context and its history, while affect is not.

As an affect, of course, joy is short-lived; recognition of the affect produces a somewhat longer feeling of pleasure, which is expanded into a pleasant emotion as we reflect upon similar experiences in our lives. When we muse about a whole group of such events, this pleasant emotion can give way to a prolonged mood of contentment sometimes called happiness. In such situations, the affect program, triggered continuously, provides a stable experience of stimulus decrease. There are those who, like the Puritans, avoid joy in fear that an unguarded moment might lead to danger (Leites 1986).

Can there be a disorder of this mood? Perhaps one such situation involves the type of drugs known as euphoriants, narcotics that can give one an experience of no feeling, which is interpreted by the individual as pleasant because it triggers contentment. Every drug user I have interviewed has convinced me that nobody resorts to these substances unless already in the grip of a chronically unpleasant mood, for chemical reduction of stimulus level only works to relieve misery. If you take a euphoriant when you're already in a good mood it will "bring you down" to an unpleasantly low level of mental activity. These drugs rarely produce a pleasant experience for someone with a normal range of affective freedom.

I have heard clinical anecdotes about people in whom a chronic state of euphoria was traced to a brain tumor. Although most patients with multiple sclerosis are depressed, some will exhibit a degree of happiness singularly inappropriate for the extent of their neurological damage, which is probably due to the destruction of specific groups of brain cells. But by and large I think that disorders of mood characterized by steady and continued decreases in the intensity of stimuli must be quite rare, if only because there is a finite limit to the amount to which neural firing within the brain can decrease and life continue. We joke about feeling so calm that we might slip into coma, but I do not think such a thing really happens.

What about such common emotion labels as happiness and elation? Once again, it is almost impossible to know what another person means when using these words. As far as I can tell, elation seems to be a pleasant mood that follows a period of unpleasant mood; this pleasant mood contains elements of excitement and contentment. There is nothing wrong with using such words, but unless we can get a look at the face of the person who claims to be happy or elated, it is difficult to know what affects are involved. This is the difference between a theory of emotion based on adult experience and one built from what seems to go on in the brain of the infant. Later on, when we start talking about the affect we call shame—humiliation, you will see why these distinctions are important. Nevertheless, what little we have now said about the positive affects is enough to derive a theory about the nature of pride.

4

PRIDE

Even babies look happy when they accomplish what they set out to do. You can watch infant Johnny in his high chair, banging a metal cup, enthralled by the sound, ecstatically happy at his ability to make noise. Despite our opinion of the quality of the music produced by this little composer, we must recognize this particular expression of joy as the face of pride. Look again at our noisy little citizen and watch how his chest seems to swell in the moment of pleasure; how the child looks around with an exultant expression, as if certain that the world shares his joy; how the cup seems to linger at the top of its journey almost in the gesture of triumph we have come to associate with the raised arm of the triumphant adult.

This exultation involves the affect enjoyment–joy and should properly be considered as one of the named emotions in which that affect figures prominently. I define this feeling as one form of healthy pride—a normal emotion occurring in a rather specific situation, one that can be seen naturally and reproduced experimentally from earliest infancy throughout adult life. There are three conditions necessary for one to experience this sort of pride: (1) A purposeful, goal-directed, intentional activity is undertaken while under the influence of the affect interest–excitement; (2) this activity must be successful in achieving its goal; following which (3) the achievement of the goal suddenly releases the individual from the preceding effort and the affect that accompanies and amplifies it, thus triggering enjoyment–joy. In short, healthy pride involves what Broucek (1979) calls *competence pleasure* when our competence has been tested in an atmosphere of excitement. We can see it easily in three- or four-month-old infants. A baby old enough to try something "on purpose" is capable of feeling proud of its accomplishment.

How early does pride figure into human development? Tomkins points out that, as soon as the infant begins to imitate its own displays of innate affect by the process of autosimulation, it is performing actions intentionally. So powerful is the infant's ability to sense, store, and match patterns that, when the child recognizes the correspondence between the feel of innately triggered affect display and its own self-mimicry, we can assume that it is rewarded by a burst of competence pleasure.

It is fascinating to watch how this competence or efficacy becomes integrated into our self-image, our personal identity. The self that can do things is my best self simply because it is the "me" most associated with excitement and joy. The competent self is the one that evokes the happiest memories. Later (once we have defined shame as rigorously as we now have identified interest and excitement), we will start to figure out *how* incompetence triggers shame, but already we know intuitively that failure is embarrassing. Since our memory of each experience is stored with the affects that accompanied it, the part of our identity associated with pride is the part we wish to show the world. That portion of us which is associated with shame must always be hidden. The joy in pride makes us public; for reasons we have yet to determine, shame makes us private.

Pride itself is infectious, both to the one who has suddenly experienced efficacy and to those watching. In the latter case, we tend to smile happily with the victor, thrilling at the victory, while in the former pride and the joy of conquest act as spurs to further action. A woman once confided that she had yielded to her husband's entreaty to join him at skeet shooting, an activity she had earlier derided as violent and disgraceful. But after demonstrating a remarkable talent for the art of shattering clay discs with shotgun pellets, she said of this self-discovery, "I shot it right in the middle and now I'm hooked!" Throughout life, any experience in which personal efficacy is linked with a positive affect will produce healthy pride.

As most of us have experienced or observed, added to the adult sense of pride is a pleasant feeling of uniqueness and social distinction. Not only are we aware of having met or surpassed the standards we set for ourselves, but we feel that others share our pride and are happy for us. Somehow, then, pride moves from an individual experience, a solitary assessment *of* the self *by* the self, to a statement *about* the self-in-comparison-to-others. In the moment of pride I am willing to be—indeed, I want to be—seen and judged by my peers. This spirit of exultation is captured by the song from *Sweet Charity*, "If they could see me now . . . if my friends could see me now." It is the song of justifiable, healthy pride.

Partly this happens because the positive innate affects form the basis for all socialization. Humans are built so that the intrinsically pleasant experiences of interest and contentment feel even better when shared. From the earliest moments of infancy we have enjoyed the mutualization of positive affect; efficacy is only one of many triggers to shareable joy. We look forward to sharing joy, and when we have a great deal of joy we look forward even more to sharing it. I suspect that family attitudes have a great deal to do with our expectations in such matters. Some parents maximize the display of joy by resonating with it and thus amplifying the experience, while others are embarrassed by it and stifle its expression. The healthier the family, the more likely it is that the child will anticipate a positive reaction to joy.

But there is a turning point in the life of the infant, a developmental milestone initially described by Amsterdam and Levitt in 1980, that has a great deal to do with the way pride and shame help us define ourselves in relation to others. All of a sudden, somewhere during the period from 18 to 24 months of age, the child will begin to behave in a way that makes us observers believe it has formed a new appreciation of its reflection in a mirror. Up to this time the child shows nothing more than interest in its reflection—whatever is mirrored there exists only as a source of novelty. Even if the baby recognizes this image as a representation of itself, it is a pleasant sort of recognition. But what happens next is quite another matter.

If you watch the child who is beginning to make this transition you notice that he or she studies the mirrored image with more care than before. An arm is moved, and its reflection analyzed. One has the feeling that the baby is saying, "Yes. This is my arm." I have watched these children making faces in the mirror and then turning away with a look of perplexity. Often they turn away with the look of shame—eyes averted, head hung low as if all power had left the muscles of the neck. Some observers have called this the look of "painful self-awareness." Broucek (1982) points out that this form of self-awareness is no more than shame, triggered now by the awareness that others see us much as we see ourselves. In a sense, it heralds the awareness that we are less private than we might have thought. Now the child knows that other people look at her just as attentively as she looks at them. Now the child becomes capable of true self-consciousness, an attribute that will influence the further development of the very public emotion of pride.

Success, especially success in an exciting venture, triggers joy; the pattern or sequence of these events is known to us as healthy pride. Along with this joy will come our memory of previous experiences of competence pleasure, making for some of the complex emotionality of pride. But accompanying it will also be our memory of how much we admired others who were successful at their goals, as well as a sense of triumph at having achieved a new level of competence by which we come closer to matching those we held dear as models for ourselves. We know also that others now admire us just as we once admired those who could do what we could not. At best, we will expect others to love us and to want contact with us just as we once wanted contact with those we admired. Pride is affiliative—it allows us to hoist the victors on our shoulders and share their triumph.

One of my patients entered a psychotherapy session brimming with pride over a recent accomplishment of her husband. "You're proud of him, aren't you," I said. Her face relaxed into the smile of pure joy. Others can become a source of positive affect for us and, by our affiliation with them, a source of personal pride. We love it when our cherished teams or political candidates do well in their competitions. The increase in self-esteem granted us by their performance is another realm of pride.

Shame, of course, is the polar opposite of pride. Where pride allows us to affiliate with others, shame makes us isolate ourselves from them. All our actions are capable of being viewed along a shame/pride axis, a yardstick along which we measure our every activity. By this shame/pride axis we decide whether we have come closer to our hoped-for personal best or to our dreaded personal worst. Few of us have grown up with the habit of perpetual success, of easygoing self-assurance and uncomplicated personal pride. To the extent that we have grown to maturity in an atmosphere of incompetence and failure or have come to believe that our true self is a defective self, we have formed a personal identity based more on shame than pride. When this happens, anything that can give us a moment of pride is capable of acting as an antidote for what amounts to a chronic sense of shame.

What happens when our best efforts produce a result far better than we had any "right" to expect? In my youth an avid and quite mediocre golfer, I remember the day I hit a drive 314 yards—far, far longer than ever before or since. Immediately after this uncharacteristically athletic achievement I ran out to purchase an extremely expensive set of clubs, with which I never again hit the ball nearly as well. Contrast this anecdote with the story told me by a patient in therapy not long ago, an excellent golfer who hit a hole-in-one during a tournament. "God had blessed me," he said. Whereas my youthful response to a moment of remarkable effectiveness had been to pretend that this unique event defined a more accomplished me, his solution was to attribute the event to divine intervention only little related to his own abilities.*

---

*Henry Murray, the great psychiatrist and founder of the discipline called *Personology*, referred to this tendency of humans to overvalue certain accomplishments as the *Icarus effect*.

Arrogance, haughtiness, disdain for the accomplishments of others, jealousy, envy, and greed are only a few of the defensive attitudes and emotions that characterize those for whom self-awareness is more painful than pleasant. For those whose lives are ruled by shame, anything that can reduce the self-esteem of others can assist them to feel better about themselves in relation to those others.

Shame is not the only unpleasant emotion; it is not the only negative affect. We have much to take in before we can address shame and consider it as we have the two positive affects of interest–excitement and enjoyment–joy. We have yet to study the brief, inherently neutral affect Tomkins calls surprise–startle, and then the inherently negative innate affects of fear, distress, and anger. Then we will discuss the three "attenuators" of the affect system: dissmell and disgust, which limit our appetites, and shame, the built-in mechanism that attenuates the other affects. Let us turn first to the mechanism of surprise.

5

SURPRISE–STARTLE:

THE NEUTRAL AFFECT

Any loud noise can startle a baby, and in the moment of surprise that child will always blink and raise its eyebrows. The general characteristic of a stimulus capable of triggering surprise–startle is what the mathematician calls a "square wave," something that rises and falls very suddenly. The affect thus triggered lasts only a few hundredths of a second, again quite analogous to its triggering stimulus and conforming to Tomkins's rule that an affect not only amplifies its triggering stimulus but is an analogue of it. Startle and surprise are brief because they amplify a fleeting experience. The affect is so brief that it cannot be said to have either a pleasant or an unpleasant quality, for which reason I have called it a neutral affect, even though Tomkins originally considered it a positive affect.

I might point out that the guffaw—the sudden burst of laughter accompanying a sudden and unexpected decrease in stimulus density—resembles surprise–startle in some respects. The guffaw is a short-lived affective reaction, not unlike a pleasant form of startle. My own guess is that surprise–startle appeared earlier in the evolution of the affects; after the organism was able to respond to the combination of sudden rise and sudden fall in stimulus density, it developed the ability to respond to sudden fall alone. The ability to respond to more gentle rates of decrease would be an even later acquisition. It seems reasonable to suggest that the mild, polite laughter we consider more urbane than raucous hilarity is the result of systems of modulation not possible for the first life forms that learned how to laugh. (The flow of evolution seems to foster an increasing range of expression.) This would correspond with Dar-

Fig. 5.1. Eyebrows up, eyes wide open, mouth open. **Surprise–startle** stops everything and allows us to reset, to prepare for new sources of information.

win's observation that monkeys are better at laughing than at smiling and expand Tomkins's surmise that the capacity to smile evolved later than the ability to laugh.

The real function of the innate affect surprise–startle is to clear the mental apparatus so that the organism can remove attention from whatever else might have been occupying it and focus on whatever startled it. Usually we forget to think about the moment of surprise and remember only what caused it (the thunderclap or the scream or the explosion), so that the affect is usually confused with its trigger. We said earlier that any bodily function, whether memory, perception, cognition, the need created by a drive, or anything else, can be assembled with an affect to make that function more urgent and give it motivation. Similarly, we believe that the affect surprise–startle clears or empties out whatever was previously assembled, leaving the central assembly system available to take on new data—which of course will then trigger whatever affect is appropriate to it. Surprise–startle is the affect of instant readiness.

Surprise–startle is the affect involved when we stop someone's world, when we create a situation that requires an immediate fresh start. It is all the forms of information that have "shock value," moments in which we are prodded or precipitated into sudden awareness.

In the Japanese language, the word *hai* is usually translated as our word *yes*, but if you listen to its use in ordinary Japanese conversation you will appreciate a level of meaning quite unrelated to our simple term of affirmation. It is pronounced not as a long syllable, like our friendly greeting "Hi," but barked

"Hai!" as a sudden burst of sound. It indicates not only the speaker's affirmation but his instant availability to the command of the person to whom it is addressed. The initial sound of a ceremonial gong produces a similar effect, drawing our attention to the long tone that follows. Americans new to Italy are often confused when Italians answer the telephone by barking "Pronto!" "It has the effect," said one friend, "of clearing my mind of carefully phrased questions."

You might think that an affect which operates so rapidly offers little opportunity for the range of expression Tomkins implies by calling it surprise–startle. Something that operates so swiftly must be studied by techniques of even greater temporal sensitivity. During one era of his research, Tomkins observed this affect using a motion picture camera capable of taking 5,000 photographs each second!* It turns out that as the sudden, brief stimulus is increased in intensity, more and more minute facial muscle movements may be identified. But such a direct correlation between stimulus and response cannot go on indefinitely, especially when the reaction itself is an analogue of brevity. When the pistol shot was repeated more frequently, and/or the intervals between stimuli reduced, fewer and fewer structures were triggered during the affective expression. So even in this most brief of affects, the concept of range may be understood clearly as long as it is studied properly.

It is easy to see that one can recognize the affect and know that one feels surprised, and, further, that we can form an emotion by recalling previous experiences of surprise. An adult who remembers with great displeasure a parent who was forever saying "Boo!" or disturbing his or her peace of mind with unexpected bursts of anger is unlikely to treat any surprise with pleasure or look forward to surprise parties. If our life expectation of surprise is of specific affect-loaded situations to follow, then we have an emotional attitude toward surprise that colors our experience of all surprise.

Surprise–startle does create a mood when we have experienced enough unpleasant surprises that our memory of them begins to trigger further unpleasant surprises beyond our capacity to reset or calm ourselves. Such, I believe, is the case in the post-traumatic stress disorder (years ago called shell shock), in which war veterans are incapacitated for years by their experiences of battle. The conditions for the establishment of this illness are relatively simple to understand: A person is exposed to repeated sequences of a stimulus

---

*"It went off like a cannon," he told me ruefully. "You had to isolate the subject from the camera completely or else it could be a source of affect. Sometimes the camera itself would sort of explode. Very dangerous. But lots of good pictures."

capable of producing surprise—startle, such as bursts of gunfire, the noise of bombs, or attacks by snipers; each time (or most of the time), this is followed by a group of events triggering terror and helplessness. Recurrent episodes of the sequence startle–terror–helplessness produce a family of memories that recur in toto whenever the affected individual is startled, even when this new experience of surprise occurs in a benign situation. It is now more than a generation since the end of the Viet Nam War, and the psychotherapy profession is still dealing with the enormous number of former servicemen seriously afflicted by it. The condition can be treated by a number of methods, all of which change the patient's attitude toward, or experience of, startle. I am, of course, aware that the label of post-traumatic stress disorder is now applied to symptom complexes unrelated to startle; my comments apply only to this older use of the term.

Although I have, on rare occasion, seen hospitalized schizophrenic patients who seem regularly to be startled by hallucinated voices or other inner events, I do not know of any proven biological disorder characterized by an excessive amount of surprise—startle. Severely depressed patients and some epileptics do seem to have a decreased ability to be startled, and this would fit in my flow chart as a biological disorder of this affect.

6

FEELING BAD:

THE NEGATIVE AFFECTS

Just as we are "wired" or "constructed" so that certain experiences are intrinsically pleasant, our genetic programming causes us to develop into creatures who experience other stimulus conditions as inherently unpleasant. Our ability to govern and control our actions is influenced markedly by this fact of life. We seek out the pleasant and avoid the unpleasant. The innate affects of fear–terror, distress–anguish, and anger–rage are produced by yet another group of stimulus conditions. These three affects are alike in that they are responses to what we have earlier called "overmuch." There are three types of overmuch, and three distinct affects triggered by these three distinct stimulus profiles.

FEAR–TERROR

Watch the face of an infant when too much seems to be going on at once, when information is pouring in to that central assembly system at a rate less than what is needed to produce surprise but greater than that optimal level capable of triggering interest. Quickly the baby begins to stare with fixed gaze at or just to the side of (a bit away from) whatever might be the source of the stimulus. All over the body individual hairs may begin to stand on end. While the face becomes cold, pale, sweaty, and uncharacteristically immobile, much more is going on inside. Fear will race the engine, speeding up pulse and respiration, amplifying attention and cognition at a fearful rate. Nearer the upper range of terror will appear additional somatic experiences, such as a gripping sensation in the chest. The more adult the individual, the more knowledge and experience are brought into play to become part of fearful thinking—yet always accompanied by the staring face of fear.

Where interest itself might trigger our memory of novelties past and enjoyment–joy remind us of contentments past, fear brings reminiscences of frightening scenes, which cascade upon our consciousness at a rate guaranteed to produce increasing amounts of fear. Too many memories of too many dreadful situations may shift us from the discomfort of a scare to a direful mood, especially when some of these images represent unsolved terrors of the past.

The affect we call fear, which at its height might be seen as terror, is (like all affects) initially only a physiological reaction—in this case to a rapid increase in data acquisition. Growing and developing, we fill a storage bin with remembered incidents of fear and their triggers. This process will both shape and color the emotion each of us calls fear—and it will make the experience of fear quite different for each of us.

You will notice that so far I have avoided the word *anxiety*, the form of fear most important in current texts of psychiatry and psychology. Freud thought it important to distinguish between the fear triggered by an external event and that produced by something kept hidden from conscious awareness. When we knew the source, Freud called it fear, but when the source was unknown, fear became anxiety. Nearly a century later this distinction seems a bit antique, for it is unlikely that the process of evolution has given us different mechanisms to

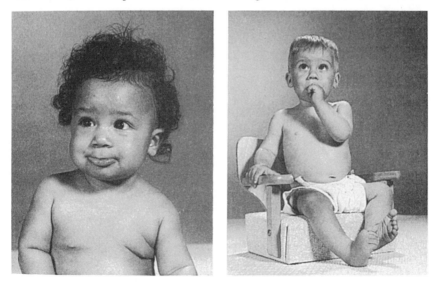

Figs. 6.1. and 6.2. Note the fixed stare and the frozen face of **fear–terror**.

produce the same experience. Yet Freud was right to call our attention to the existence of the unconscious, to focus us on the mental world pushed out of awareness by mechanisms his genius revealed with clarity.

At the level of innate affect it does not matter what triggered fear—all fearful emotion is at its core merely fear. Nevertheless, in psychoanalysis it is correct, even essential, to learn the relation between anxiety and the unconscious. I mentioned earlier that we can no longer use anxiety as the family name for all negative affects. In this book we will use it to represent the specific group of emotions in which the affect fear is triggered by a source whose origin lies in that portion of our memory kept hidden from us by a number of mechanisms.

There are so many marvelous expressions that capture the essence of anxiety. In Elizabethan prose a character might describe a sudden burst of anxiety with the expression, "Someone is walking on my grave." I think that phrase describes the following sequence: (1) Some thought or memory peeps out from its hiding place in the unconscious, probably brought forth as an association to whatever was going on at the moment; (2) because of its intrinsic nature, this thought triggers the affect fear; (3) since the source of the fear is invisible to the individual, the memory bank is consulted to see if it contains any previous experience known to be capable of producing that type and degree of fear; (4) no real experience being found, the fear is declared equivalent to the colorful, fantasized situation then described.

In other eras this type of fear has been called "the heebie jeebies" or "the willies." Always it is described with a sense of mystery because its source is occult.

When fear is preceded by startle, we say we were "scared by" whatever surprised us. When fear is mixed with shame, we are "caught unawares." We can be frightened stiff, scared to death, aghast, panic-stricken, terrorized, apprehensive, timorous, or leery. But all of these emotions or attitudes bear some relation to the innate affect fear, assembled with its triggering experience in ways that make for the poetry of emotional life.

Panic, of course, is only another name for fear, and what are popularly called *panic disorders* today are nothing more than biological illnesses predisposing us to the experience of fear. We are beginning to learn a great deal about the biological circuitry for fear, or at least what circuit defects can produce inappropriate bursts of fear. As I mentioned in an earlier chapter, some of the sites of action normally stimulated by the affect fear–terror may also be triggered when our blood contains too much thyroid hormone, too much caffeine, or too much of the nasal decongestant pseudoephedrine.

It is fascinating that whenever these sites of action are triggered in a pattern resembling an innate affect, the brain assesses this pattern of responses as if it really had been caused by an innate affect. After all, since infancy we have been exposed to the patterns of muscular contraction, circulatory changes, odors, postures, and noises associated with innate affect, and we have learned to associate certain mental phenomena (which we call our feelings or our emotions) with those patterns. We have no such precedent for nasal decongestants. There is no intrinsic, prewritten script or program associated with hyperthyroidism, one that allows us to recognize it as such when it occurs. So biological malfunctions that affect any of the same sites of action that are triggered during innate affect can only be "understood" by us as peculiar episodes of ordinary innate affect.

This aspect of mental function is what we call *pattern matching*, and it is apparently one of the earliest attributes of the human brain. It seems that one of the basic characteristics of brain function is this activity of comparing current experience to the stored representations of previous experience. Time and again, in our study of human emotion, we run into this phenomenon. Everything that goes on, everything we do (or see, or remember, or in any way experience), is compared to what has been amassed as memory. Imagine how difficult would be our path through life were every situation always to be novel! The ability to compare immediate experience to past experience is the basis of all learning.

One of the great gifts brought by the psychoanalytic movement is the understanding that when people seem unable to learn from their experience one should consider the possibility that something has gone wrong with this mechanism of comparison. Empirically, it turns out that some life events accumulate too much negative affect. When even the memory of such an event brings with it a surfeit of unpleasant emotion, the event can be forced out of awareness by a group of mental mechanisms. By the time we reach adulthood we have accumulated enough such hidden uncomfortable memories and ideas that we give their warehouse a special name—"the unconscious."

Since what is kept in this treasury is not available for normal business, it cannot be accessed for normal learning. As Freud taught us, some of it may leak out in dreams or those peculiar errors called "slips of the tongue." But for general purposes, what has been restricted to the world of the unconscious is unavailable for the work of healthy comparison or pattern matching. Thus we believe that those who seem unable to learn from their experiences, to use failure or success as a guide to future behavior, may be blocked by their inability to make reference to certain memories that have been kept hidden within the unconscious. Part of psychoanalytic therapy or psychodynamic treatment is to use the special tools of psychoanalysis to investigate what is held as unconscious and to reduce the amount of negative affect bound with it. There are lots of ways to diminish the family of emotions called anxiety.

Yet recall the experience of fear described by people unprepared for the "side effects" of substances like the commonly available nasal decongestant I have mentioned so often. One of the concepts that will recur throughout this book derives from my observation of people in whom the emotion of the moment was triggered neither by current nor past events, but by an aberration of biochemistry and physiology. Whenever someone complains that an emotion seems inappropriate to the lived moment, we must first identify the affect involved and then search for the source of the affect. The system works in both directions—events trigger the neurobiology of affect, and disturbances of neurobiology that resemble the biology of normal affect can make us think of the kind of event that normally triggers affect. Particularly is this true for fear and for the myriad ills that can mimic the experience of anxiety.

Occasionally we meet patients in whom many or all of the sites of action normally associated with fear have been stimulated, but who seem unable to recognize these patterns of activity as an affect. Somewhat concretely, they describe the pounding of the heart as if it could mean nothing other than an affliction of that organ, appearing in one emergency room after another until referred to a psychiatrist by cardiologists who have exhausted their entire stock of test procedures.

John C. Nemiah and Peter E. Sifneos described a group of patients who had no language for emotion, coining the term *alexithymia.** In my experience, these people fail to organize the subtle *patterns* of activity seen at the various sites of action I have described as associated with affect. They do not recognize its presence until affect reaches the upper limits of its range, at which time the heart does indeed pound as if it wished to leap from one's chest, and thoughts of imminent death appear quite logical. Effective treatment often requires pharmacological suppression of extraordinary activity at these sites of action, and an intense, prolonged period of education leading to the recognition of affect as such. One critical characteristic of the patient with such forms of panic disorder is this inability to "know" the milder presentations of innate affect.

Nevertheless, no matter what quickens the pulse, pales the cheek, and arrests the freedom of gaze, it will be understood by us as some form of fear. It will be accompanied by an unpleasantly rapid increase in speed of thought and access to memory. And anybody looking at us will know we are afraid.

*See Nemiah et al. (1976) for a brief review of this fascinating concept.

DISTRESS—ANGUISH

So far we have discussed only those situations in which the infant is programmed to respond to increases or decreases in the level of neural firing
going on at any particular moment. Surely there must be periods of constancy,
occasions when everything just goes along at the same speed. As you might
guess, there are certain levels of stimulus density to which the affect system
does not respond, levels which are acceptable to the system. This corresponds
to those comfortable adult experiences we call *periods of calm*, moments in
which a fair amount may be happening but with no augmentation by affect. So
long sections of our day may be characterized by relatively constant levels of
stimulus density accompanied by the phenomenon of no affect or very little
affect. Not every moment is amplified by affect; not every moment is emotional.

The affect system contains a group of mechanisms responsive to a special
range of such constant stimulus levels. What if some life situation immerses the
infant in a batch of stimuli that remain constant but at a higher than optimal
level? When the baby is cold, or hungry, or lonely, or wet, some organ of
perception transmits data about these conditions to the central assembly system. For example, if the baby's blanket falls off and the heat generated by its
body is no longer kept within its tiny ecosystem, the temperature sensors of
the infant's skin report this as a constant stream of information. When this data
stream is recognized by the central assembly system as a constant and higher
than optimal level of stimulation, an affect is triggered in which the corners of
the mouth are pulled downward, the eyebrows arched upward, and the infant
begins to cry with tears and rhythmic sobbing. Distress—anguish produces
varying levels of sobbing or crying, *an activity that in itself is a constant-density
experience*, and that calls to the attention of the organism and its caregiver that
some constant stimulus demands attention.

What the caregiver witnesses and experiences is the infant's display of
distress, after which this adult will react in a variety of ways to its sobbing or
crying. The experienced mother will look over at her child, checking to make
sure it is not exposed and cold, and next pick it up by slipping her hand under
its buttocks, which will tell her immediately whether the baby is wet. If a dry,
warm baby quiets immediately on being picked up, distress had been triggered
by loneliness; if not, the mother checks for signs of pain or hunger. In a couple
of seconds the caregiver has, without "thinking" about it, checked for all the
common causes of a constant and higher than optimal level of stimulus density. If these maneuvers don't work, she will look for other sources of distress.

It does not matter what organ of perception has transmitted information to

Fig. 6.3. Here is "the *omega* of melancholy"—corners of the lips pulled down in the unmistakable face of **distress–anguish**.

the central assembly system of the baby. Distress can be triggered by data from memory, from a drive, from perception, from cognition. The affect we call distress is completely neutral with respect to its trigger. Any constant and unpleasant stimulus will activate the constant and unpleasant affect of distress. All this has something to do with the remarkable ability of distress to infect others—the contagion of crying that can take over an infant nursery or drive mad the parents of an inconsolable child.

Anything that produces steady-state neural density within a certain range will make us feel like crying, and we can become distressed in a number of situations. We can sob, whimper, cry, or gulp for a moment when distress affect is triggered; and we can easily recognize it as a feeling. We can remember a couple of similar episodes and have the emotion of sadness, or our biography may contain so many tearful scenes that distressing memory can overwhelm and dominate our mood. One mood associated with distress is *grief,* a term that should be reserved only for prolonged periods of distress precipitated by the experience of personal loss. Grief requires distress, but not all distress is grief. *Mourning* and *melancholy* are other common moods involving the affect distress–anguish. There may be a great deal of distress in the wide variety of clinical conditions characterized by the "wastebasket term" *depression,* but depression is far more than distress.

By the way, since affect is independent of its source, anything that can cause even a minor degree of constant-density experience is capable of being added together with one or more low-grade stimuli that, when taken together, finally achieve the level necessary to trigger distress. We can handle a certain number of minor annoyances, but when the group of aches and pains that get to make up our day becomes large enough, we can unaccountably feel like crying. This is why the sort of thing that would never bother you on a good day is capable of driving you crazy when you are mildly ill. It probably is part of the reason women are more likely to cry when they are premenstrual. Some alteration of hormones, some change in the biochemical environment of the brain, may be producing the equivalent of a steady-state stimulus or decreasing the threshold for distress; with the addition of some "minor" pressure we can cry. Much that people call "stress" or being "stressed out" is the affect distress either in pure form or with a little bit of the affect fear thrown in for good measure.

Many of us slightly obese chronic overachievers eat when we are more tired than hungry. Just like hunger, fatigue is also a steady-state noxious stimulus. If we are the driven sort of personality that must ignore or disavow exhaustion in order to conclude what we declare to be the "more important" business of the day, we will pretend we are not tired. Since the trick of disavowal has prevented us from "knowing" that we are sleepy, we search for another common source of distress. The result is a culture of adiposity—paradoxically linked with our culture-wide embarrassment that we are not modishly slim—and our energetic attempts to lose weight.

Why don't adults cry as much as infants? Indeed, why are children so much more "emotional" than adults? In the case of distress we can see how social training alters and perhaps suppresses the expression of innate affect. Children learn very early that it is childish to cry—those who cry are babies. If you want to humiliate a child into not crying, you need merely call him or her a *crybaby*. The British tradition of the "stiff upper lip" is related to this system of affect control. The first thing that happens when distress is initiated is that the corners of both lips are drawn downward. But the act of crying is preceded by a wrinkling and trembling of the upper lip, which itself then becomes a constant density stimulus. Training a child to focus on the upper lip distracts attention away from the experience of distress, and any interference with the affect decreases its ability to create more distress. Throughout our lives we are encouraged to do nearly anything that will prevent us from crying in public.

"TEARS OF JOY"

I should mention one other situation in which people cry. Most of us have been embarrassed to find ourselves crying at weddings or other similarly happy events. There used to be a series of television advertisements for a popular brand of instant coffee in which a happy or loving scene (usually involving the resolution of loneliness) was assembled with information suggesting that the coffee tasted good. ("Times like these were meant for *Taster's Choice.*") Many, many people cried during these commercials, weeping in response to the deeply moving interpersonal scenes. I don't know whether they sold a lot of coffee, but they sure affected people! Yet had you observed their faces as they reached for a handkerchief to dab a suddenly moist eye, you would have seen no other evidence of distress. Tearing was independent of the facial display of distress—no downturned mouth, no wrinkled and trembling upper lip.

Tomkins believes that in this very special case tears are triggered by the sheer density of memory brought to mind by the event being witnessed. In the case of the *Taster's Choice* commercials, the scenes depicted by the advertiser are assessed by the central assembly system on the basis of their resemblance to our lifetime of powerfully affecting experiences of loneliness and coming together, of love lost and love redeemed, of social failure and healing success. The utter volume of such data suddenly brought into awareness is thought to be another specific trigger for tearing. In a letter to me, Basch referred to it as a form of "emotional sweating." I believe that the human capacity for the storage and retrieval of memory has evolved more rapidly than has the integration of this power with the subcortical mechanisms that produce affect.

Recently, Mike Schmidt, Philadelphia's lone baseball hero, retired after a generation of literally spectacular athletic achievement. Like Julius Erving, the superstar of the Philadelphia basketball team who had retired not long before, Schmidt decided to quit not when he was no longer able to play, but rather when his body could no longer allow him to work at a world-class level of performance. As befitting his stature within the world of sport, he announced this decision at a press conference—before an immense assembly of reporters, microphones, and cameras. Doubtless what he had planned to say was clear, cogent, and pithy, well in keeping with his character. "I felt lucky enough just to be able to make it into the major leagues," he said, continuing as if to say what it had meant to him to have played so well for so long. Yet he was "overwhelmed with emotion" and nearly unable to speak for the tears that welled up. Embarrassed by this "lack of self-control," Schmidt turned away and terminated the conference.

This sequence of events can be observed no matter whether the triggering scenes are pleasant or unpleasant. (Those of us who cry at weddings are rarely experiencing true sadness. And I doubt that the newly crowned Miss America is sad when, each year, she bursts into tears on learning of her victory.) As is typical of all situations involving innate affect, there does not seem to be any connection between the quality or meaning of the stimulus and the affective response. I suppose that this should be given the status of another innate affect, but the situation is uncommon enough that it is considered to be an oddity of the affect system. It makes sense, though. The bodily mechanisms that can be taken over by innate affect range from the involuntary to the voluntary systems. We are used to the fact that tearing (which certainly must have evolved as a method of protecting the eyes from physical danger) can be taken over by distress. So, at least until a better answer comes along, I suspect that we can accept Tomkins's answer for the puzzle that in certain peculiar situations our eyes leak tears when we are not sad.

In the final chapters of this book I suggest some of the reasons modern life has become so complex, and, for many, so overwhelming. Evolution has "conferred" on us the ability to store and retrieve memories with a facility impossible for prior life forms. With such structural potential comes the proclivity for avalanche. Only of the human can it be said that memory is capable of overloading our circuitry. The enormous amount of information made available to us by so many channels of data acquisition, as well as the huge and growing number of ways that the activities, interests, and accomplishments of individual humans can be brought into public consciousness, all encourage the likelihood for overload. The tearful response to such overload may very well be a major affective experience for the humans of our future.

ANGER–RAGE

A man stands in front of me at an airline counter. Nothing he can do will affect the inalterable rules of the airline. By his side is a package a few inches too tall to be brought on board as carry-on luggage and containing porcelain too delicate to be placed in the baggage hold where it will be thumped, bumped, and tumbled until it is returned to him. I observe the man, whose face is red, whose whole body is shaking with increasing intensity, and who begins to pound the ticket counter with his tightly clenched fist. His voice begins to rise in volume, as if the reason he is not being heard is that people cannot hear him.

Having checked in and received my boarding pass, I grab a bite of food at an airport restaurant. Ordering a meal and a bottle of wine at the table to my left is a young woman. Although she is smiling as she gives her order, everything about her seems tight. The hand clutching her menu is white-knuckled. When she pauses to listen to the waitress I can see from the rhythmic bulging of her cheek muscles that she is clenching and unclenching her jaw. She taps her foot impatiently while waiting for service. As luck would have it, the food that finally arrives is unacceptable, and she explodes in rage, denouncing the waitress, the airport, and the city she is leaving.

So many things can make us angry, and so many things can happen when we get angry. One problem for the student of emotion is that people vary so much in their expression of anger. Early in my career as a psychiatrist I saw a great many people for diagnostic evaluation. Disappointed with what I had been taught, I developed a new kind of standardized interview that allowed me to figure out not only what was wrong but what needed to be done next. I ask a lot of questions that will tell me how this stranger experiences each of the innate affects. Especially am I interested in the way he or she handles anger and the way each parent behaved when angry. Having now interviewed over a thousand adults, I have learned a great deal about the expression of anger.

Some people are never angry. Others are always angry. Some people explode like a summer thunderstorm—raging for moments and sunny thereafter. Others simmer and burn for hours. Some yell or hit, others clam up and withdraw. Some will never forgive, others forget immediately. Each of these people is experiencing the same affect, assembled in ways developed over a lifetime, magnified or damped by virtue of their having grown up in a particular family, neighborhood, and era—and, despite all these differences, perceived by them as real anger. Naturally, when I tell them about the ways other people get angry, they act surprised that anybody would behave in such a manner.

If we are going to understand anger, we had better return to our study of the newborn and ask how and where anger fits into the affect theory we have been discussing. Is there a red thread that connects everything we know about anger?

Everybody knows that a crying infant can become a screaming infant. Sobs of distress give way to the face of rage—the clenched jaw, furrowed brow, reddened cheek, and scream of anger. Why? How can an infant "know" what to be angry about? Tomkins draws an analogy to our understanding of the affects discussed above.

Just as certain low, steady levels of stimulus density are acceptable to the system and do not trigger any affect, and other steady-state but higher than optimal levels of stimulus density trigger distress–anguish, there is an even higher range of steady-state stimulus density that triggers the innate affect we call anger–rage. Again, the innate affect is not a state in which the organism is *angry at* somebody or *angry about* something. It is merely a state in which the affect anger is expressed because the program for it has been activated.

The affect anger is another of those circumstances in which we are dealing

Fig. 6.4. Mouth and chin tight, eyes narrowed, legs planted firmly, right hand about to make a fist—this is the isometric muscularity of **anger–rage** at the milder end of its spectrum.

initially with *quantities* of stimulation, with what might on an oscilloscope screen be seen as the number and the height of little green blips. And these little green blips achieve a pattern that is recognized by a system that does not "care" what they "mean," and which then sets in motion a series of events that becomes for us the *qualitative* experience we call anger. This is the implacable logic of the affect system. The newborn infant, squalling and raging on its changing table, fists and feet clenched, jaw alternately clenched and screaming, brow intensely furrowed—this infant does not know that it is angry and does not know what made it angry. "All" that has happened is that some group of stimuli has achieved a level of density adequate to trigger anger. Stated another way, some noxious steady-state stimulus has triggered an affect that tenses the muscles of the face and other parts of the body in a manner analogous to this triggering stimulus.

Once you get the idea that anger in the infant is associated with muscular contraction and an intensification of all activity, you can see fascinating variants of the affect. A friend asked me to observe her infant, saying that she was frightened by one of his gestures. Whenever this two-month-old boy was unable to get what he wanted, he would clasp his hands and push them against each other as hard and as steadily as he could. Within a few moments his face and upper body became red with effort, and quickly enough the entire picture of anger–rage had been triggered. It was a perfect example of Tomkins's observation that autosimulation of innate affect is one of the earliest realms of learning. I suspect that, having learned the association of anger and muscular contraction, he now knew how to make himself angry when he wanted to, to amplify intentionally whatever degree of anger he was then experiencing. He looked for all the world like someone practicing isometric exercises. I wondered whether that had anything to do with my observation that so many chronically angry people seem to be extremely strong.

Infants learn quickly. Just as we group by the pattern of their occurrence all the situations in which we have become excited or all the situations in which we cried, we begin to group the situations in which we became angry. From the massing of such memories comes our understanding of what it means to be angry. And from such experiences each of us develops our own private emotion, what we as individuals know as "our" anger.

Like all affects, anger calls to the attention of the organism and to its caregiver that something needs to change in order for the infant to be released from its discomfort. In the case of anger, the affect system says that change has to be damn quick so that the stimulus density will be reduced enough for the child to recover its composure. Anger, in the language of the psychologist, is *instrumental*. It makes things happen. Anger, with its tremendous expenditure of energy, can be the instrument of change.

Dr. Joseph Lichtenberg,* a psychoanalyst who studies child behavior, asked me to "watch a nine-month-old child pushing a toy around the room. He gets to a point where the toy won't budge, and after pushing it for a little while, he gets angry at it and gives it a whack. Suddenly the toy goes flying. Now the child goes around the room happily whacking the toy." Anger, which had perhaps in this instance been an affective response to the child's experience of futility, turned out to provide the needed change in technique. Anger had taught the child just how much force and what kind of force was required to move the toy past an obstacle. The affect became the instrument of change. You can see something like this operating in the theater of professional sports, where anger and intensity of play often run hand in hand.

You will recall that one of the major features of the affect system is that, once it is triggered, each innate affect exerts its influence on any bodily action occurring concurrently. This is what Tomkins calls the *correlative* action of affect—it imprints its pattern of action on whatever is linked to it. That helps explain why a whining child is so irritating to us. In whining, a child speaks with great intensity and draws out each syllable as long as possible. Whin-

*Lichtenberg's text (1983) was the first to join the disciplines of infant observation and psychoanalysis.

ing is a perfect example of an activity influenced by an affect that is both a response to constant-density stimulus and an amplified analogue of this constant-density stimulus.

Anger communicates broadly and rapidly. Just by looking at someone who is angry we can tell a lot about what is going on inside. So vividly does anger communicate that we learn to mask its display in order to retain some sense of privacy when we are angry. In some people the display of anger becomes so refined and contained that only tiny remnants remain, like the bulging jaw muscles or whitened knuckles of the woman I described a moment ago. Once I saw in consultation a young lawyer who professed to be the least angry of men. We smiled pleasantly at each other as we discussed both his needs and his biography. Later, when I thought that by my attentiveness I had earned enough of his respect for him to be willing to look at something he had not expected, I asked this calm, pleasant man to glance over at his right hand, which was clenched in as tight a fist as I had ever seen. "Huh. What d'ya know?" he said. "I'm angry."

Nowadays most American cities have strict rules about when one is allowed to use an automobile horn. When you toot the horn in one or two short bursts you have activated the resetting affect of surprise–startle. But when you "lean" on the horn, maintaining its noise for a prolonged period of time, you have mimicked the profile of anger–rage, which indeed gets the attention of others but is capable of getting them quite angry. You might think of the ordinances that prohibit promiscuous horn honking as a public health measure aimed at the modulation of the affect anger–rage. In normal interpersonal life the most prominent stimulus to anger is humiliation. What makes the slings and arrows of everyday life into fortune that we find outrageous is some as-yet-unexplained link between shame and anger.

Anger as affect can be the fleeting tension of a moment, or it can be recognized as an angry feeling. To the extent that any particular episode of anger recalls to mind previous similar experiences, we are experiencing anger as an emotion. Too many angry thoughts about too many issues left too long unsolved can produce an angry mood capable of lasting until something brings relief. I have seen patients with brain tumors whose raging anger always seemed inappropriate to the situation at hand, and there are many documented cases of people in whom attacks of rage are caused by the kind of electrical discharge called an epileptic seizure. Cocaine and the amphetamines can arouse people to states of rage. Everybody who has any degree of manic-depressive illness is likely to have attacks of rage secondary to this biochemical condition, and the intensity of these bursts or periods of rage are a good measure of the seriousness of the illness itself. I cite these examples to remind you that the affect anger—rage can be seen as affect, feeling, emotion, mood, and disorder. We all have to deal with angry people from time to time, and it helps to know both the source and the meaning of their anger.

7

EMPATHY: AFFECTIVE RESONANCE

AND THE EMPATHIC WALL

Just for a moment, let's go back to watching babies. Sneak a look at a little person who doesn't know you're there. Watch how a baby brightens when looking at its crib mobile, reaching out to touch it, laughing in delight at its colors or at the feel of the brightly colored wood or plastic. As long as the mobile holds its interest, which can be a matter of seconds, the baby's face is alive and shining with interest and enjoyment. When no longer involved the baby may grow quiet, its face reflecting the neutral state of no affect. Should a small noise startle it to full attention, we would see the next series of affective responses to whatever stimuli are perceived or experienced. The qualities we call "alertness" or "aliveness" seem to be due to the innate affects of interest and enjoyment that are triggered in the normal course of the infant's day.

Although most people are fascinated by babies and charmed by their facial expressions (even though they may not know the relation between these movements, colors, or vocalizations and their origin in innate affect display), it is happy babies we like best. There are many reasons for this commonplace observation. The positive affects of interest–excitement and enjoyment–joy are so intrinsically rewarding that when we see an infant express them we are drawn into an interaction because happy babies make us feel good. Similarly, the basic wiring pattern of the human, the circuit design of the affect system, makes babies and adults alike enjoy the experience of sharing positive affect.

I have mentioned that each of these innate mechanisms becomes a powerful communication device. A baby in the throes of an affect is a *broadcaster* of affect, and we observers *resonate* with their transmission. The contagious (

ity of broadcast affect literally drags the observer into resonance. The intensity or effectiveness of this broadcast is decreased to the extent that this organism learns to modulate the display of innate affect. Babies, with their nearly pure, unmodulated display, are the most powerful broadcasters and the most compelling partners in affective interaction or "conversation."

This is, of course, the physiological basis for what later will be called empathy, the sharing of emotion that accounts for much of the quality of adult interpersonal relationships. Around strangers we control our affective display more than with our intimate friends—we share our feelings in proportion to how safe we feel in the company of another. Nevertheless, we are lightning-quick to sense minuscule variations in the degree of resonance, the "fit" between ourselves and the other. This learned, adult achievement—the ability to exhibit affect over a wide range of display, from the most subtle and sophisticated to the most broad and infantile—allows us a wide variety of styles of interpersonal behavior. We "know" when it is permissible to "let it all hang out" or when we must be "contained." Social awareness makes us take care to vary the extent to which we ask the other to handle our affective output.

I keep repeating that each affect is analogous to whatever has triggered it. Fear, which is triggered by an unpleasant cascade of data, makes that experience even more unpleasant when affect and source are joined; the calming affect of enjoyment–joy reduces brain activity in a manner parallel to what has triggered it; distress makes us more distressed because it is a constant-density experience quite capable of triggering further distress; and so on. As I have mentioned, Tomkins feels that it is from our awareness of the way the skin and muscles of the face have been "rearranged" or "distorted" by the affect as it "hits" us that we figure out what we are feeling. Most likely a host of tiny alterations in the microcirculation of the face increases the sensitivity of other receptors that in turn carry still more information back to the brain. These facial displays are capable of changing rapidly—some of them in tenths or hundredths of a second—and our awareness of what we feel is also capable of such rapid shifts.

Since such a significant portion of each affect is expressed as external display (always on the face but also over the entire body), the affects are as much social phenomena as they are internal experiences. Anyone who is "tuned in" to someone with a visible display of innate affect is looking at a face that has been "arranged" by the contraction and relaxation of specific groups of voluntary muscles. To the extent that we are willing to mimic the operation of these muscle groups, we can share the affect just triggered in the other person.

It does not matter whether the face we imitate is one projected on the giant silver screen of the motion picture theater, or our beloved beside us, or the newborn infant cradled in our arms. Whatever the source of the affect we imitate purposively or the contagion we accept passively, it becomes the source of the affect we now experience. This is the basis of empathy, the sharing of emotion that makes for so much of the pleasure of social experience.

Basch (1983a)* has pointed out that there are a number of separate steps in this process of empathic linkage. First, of course, we resonate with each other's affective broadcast. Next, simply because we have agreed to experience an affect broadcast by someone else, we begin to recall previous experiences of that affect, just as if it had been triggered by some experience unrelated to

*An excellent review of some earlier theories for empathy may be found in Max Scheler, 1954.

Fig. 7.1. Faces, hands, and posture all suggest the affects **fear–terror** and **distress–anguish**; the lassitude with which these people are painted suggests also that they may be in an early stage of depersonalization as a defense against intense negative affect. Yet artist George Tooker titled his painting "Birdwatchers," leading us to expect the positive affects of **interest–excitement** and **enjoyment–joy**, therefore setting up a disturbing oscillation between what we feel through affective resonance and what we read.

other people. Now we begin to form an emotion in the sense Basch has described—the assemblage of this affect (which we have just received from someone else) and our associations to our own previous experiences of that affect. For this reason, empathy is nothing like what happens when two computers are wired together. Whereas each of us shares the identical vocabulary of nine innate affects, we differ so greatly on the basis of our life experience that what we think and feel during the period of empathic connection is similar, but actually quite different.

People who are in tune with each other live in a fellowship of feeling. Yet this phenomenon, which I think of as affective resonance, is not always so pleasant an occurrence. Resonating to the broadcast of affect from a demagogue, we can become members of a mob. Taken in by the false display of affection that draws us into the confidence of a scoundrel, we can be fleeced of our earnings or seduced in a way "better judgment" might have prevented.

Affective resonance is so powerful, so distracting a system of interaction, that infancy is the only period of our lives during which we are allowed free range of affective expression. In every society on the planet, children are speedily taught how to mute the display of affect so that they do not take over every situation in which they cry, smile, or become excited.

Many years ago I heard a famous entertainer say that she didn't mind hecklers or even a hostile audience now and then—that was a fair challenge to her. "But," she told us, "never try to work a room with any kid under three. You can't compete with a baby." She knew that the pure and unmodulated expressions of affect transmitted by babies were capable of distracting the most attentive audience. It is okay for mommy and baby to be locked in an interaction based on the interplay of innate affect, but society demands that these interactions become increasingly private as we grow up.

Just as most or all of the affect we broadcast into our environment must be limited by social or cultural forces, we adults are also obliged to learn a number of skills to help us manage the affect broadcast by others. Imagine how difficult it would be to keep your mind on whatever interested you if you were forced to resonate with every burst of affect that came your way from someone else. Suppose, by way of analogy, that no one thought privately about anything, that humans were only capable of talking aloud instead of "thinking." Privacy would depend on our ability to develop some kind of adaptive deafness.

Science fiction writers have tackled this sort of problem in their speculations about telepathy. If all our mental processes were broadcast into the space that surrounds us and experienced with clarity by our neighbors just as by ourselves, we would live not as individuals but as some sort of communal being—

unless we developed some way of shielding our thoughts. Our whole concept of ourselves as private individuals is based on the idea that we can be alone, free from the intrusion of others, just as our concept of society is based on the idea that we can communicate with others. Adult life as we know it requires some balance between privacy and communion.

There are two reasons we do not walk around constantly being taken over by the affective experience of others. On the one hand, as I noted a moment ago, social form dictates that with maturity we will learn to express very little affect. Somewhere around the age of three we learn to trade the powerful language of affect for the more specific but far less compelling language of words and sentences. Affect is damped, suppressed, blocked, by social convention. Our whole concept of what it means to be mature is based on the expectation that adults can "control themselves." Control of affective expression reduces the amount of affect broadcast into the interpersonal environment. It makes life easier for those around us.

This contagious quality of affect is so powerful that the normal adult has built a shield for protection from the affective experience of the other person, a mechanism I call the *empathic wall*. It is a skill, a learned mechanism by which we can tune out the affect display of others. One way of building an empathic wall would be by refusing to mimic the facial or bodily display of affect we see in other people, but there are other ways this can be accomplished, other places to block in the circuitry for the interpretation of innate affect.

One might, for instance, learn to recognize the feeling of contagion, learn to sense the very moment that another person's affect begins to tickle our own receptors. Then we might decide to shift our attention to something else, to manipulate the central assembly system and stop the process of resonance. We can block completely the experience of affective resonance by this mechanism of distraction, or we can limit it over carefully graduated levels of connectedness.

Men, especially, will recognize this as the system most of us use to avoid being taken over prematurely by the sexual excitement of our partners during intercourse. Part of the skill required of a man for effective partnership in sexual intercourse is the ability to monitor his partner's level of arousal. Through experience we learn to recognize the degree of her readiness for orgasm. When we sense that she is on the brink, we allow ourselves full resonance with her excitement, which moves us to the level of excitement and arousal that will trigger our own release. In well-matched couples, a woman will use (join with) this last increment in his broadcast excitement as an amplifier of her own, and the couple can share the pleasure of each other's orgasm.

Often the treatment of premature ejaculation involves little more than training in the modulation of affective resonance—shoring up the empathic wall.

It is this empathic wall that allows us to maintain our own boundaries in the presence of other people when they are experiencing or displaying affect. The empathic wall helps preserve the unity of the self. Adults who do not learn how to shield themselves from the emotional life of others suffer greatly because they fail to develop a secure identity, just as those who are overly "immune" to the affects of others suffer in the closet of emotional isolation. If the empathic wall is too rigid, we will be immune to the feelings of others; if too flimsy, we will tend to be taken over by powerful feelings broadcast from outside ourselves.

In general, then, we adults have learned to mute our own affect display so that we are acceptable to the society in which we live, to shield ourselves from the affect display of others, and to rely on the relatively drab and colorless transmission of data by verbal language. One implication of this developmental tendency is that most adults have to "learn" how to communicate with babies or to become "sensitive" to the feelings of their fellows. Most likely mothers learn to adjust to the affect display of their infants by giving up the empathic wall, by agreeing to allow themselves to be taken over. Doing this, of course, they achieve a degree of connectedness with their babies that is a major part of the complex group of emotions we call love. Despite the importance to each of us of finding a relationship in which our worst feelings are tolerated or accepted, for the vast, overwhelming majority of humans the experience of love implies mutual permission to share the positive affects of excitement and joy. The absence of love is experienced as lonely for those who enjoy such communion.

When we study that remarkable phenomenon called "good mothering," we notice over and over again the caregiver's ability to "tune in" on the affect display of her child. In recent years there has been much research on the transactions of "affective attunement," and many scholars are now providing empirical evidence for the interactions between mother and infant that Tomkins described in detail nearly 30 years ago.

So special is the appearance of a healthy system for the reception and interpretation of innate affect that we tend to think of anybody with this kind of sensitivity as gifted. Mothers, therapists, novelists, actors, and confidence men are usually successful to the degree that they are empathic. Perhaps the reason it has taken so long for our civilization to understand the nature of the affect system is that each of us has grown up working hard to avoid and control our own affects.

Fig. 7.2. No empathic wall here! The child on the left demonstrates **distress–anguish** at the upper end of its scale. Gazing directly at the face of his unhappy companion, the child on the right has begun to resonate with this broadcast affect and shows mild distress.

This is particularly important in the case of the affect distress–anguish, for we adults vary considerably in our attitude toward crying. Every once in a while, in every city, in perhaps every era of recorded history, the murder of an infant can be traced to the mechanism of unwanted and unbearable affective resonance. The stories are all pretty much the same. Recently, here in Philadelphia, a young mother told her husband she couldn't stand the constant crying of her baby, which made her feel like screaming. One day, when the husband called to check in, the mother announced that she had drowned the baby in the bathtub to stop its crying. More often it is the father who kills a baby in such situations, but always the clearly stated reason for the murder is this inability of one parent to handle the constant and inalterable experience of an infant's unmodulated anguish.

That such tragedies are rare speaks for the general observation that by and large people learn to modulate their own affects and to develop the interpersonal affect management system I call the empathic wall. That they can occur at all forces us to acknowledge the power and the nature and the inherent contagiousness of innate affect.

There are, of course, other family situations made unbearable by the presence of unmodulated affect—all characterized by manifest discomfort on the part of the receiver. Although alcohol can act as a calmative agent, many of those who are addicted to it drink until they become quite explosive. Children forced to live in the midst of such affective explosions are often deeply scarred by them. There is a wide variety of clinical syndromes produced by parental affective excess, among which are patterns of personality development characterized by literal terror of high-density affect. As adults, some who have grown up in such families tend to suppress the display of affect in themselves and in their children, to act as if they were allergic to affect itself. This strategy produces offspring with a limited experience of affect modulation, thus predisposing to the use of alcohol (as well as other drugs and diversions) as a modulation device (with the same pattern of noxious effects that started the cycle) or an explosive personality with no relation to alcohol.

The clinical disorder of alcoholism is extraordinarily varied in its presentation, and only a small fraction of alcoholic families develops in this manner. All dysfunctional families are islands, clusters of people with immense walls protecting one or another horrible system of affect modulation, walls that prevent the intrusion of other systems of modulation. The walls are meant to protect the protagonists from the shame of exposure to the outside; actually they immure the family illness.

Recently, on the basis of anecdotal evidence, it has become the fashion to claim that all dysfunctional families share the relation to affect modulation described above—and to claim that the cause lies in the use of alcohol rather than anything to do with affect. The benefit of this therapeutic maneuver has been to allow an immense number of people to group themselves into a supraordinate family within which they can feel a previously unavailable kinship. Unfortunately, in order to take advantage of the love and succor offered by these systems of group treatment, many lonely and distressed adults have been encouraged to redefine their histories in the language of this one specific theme.

There are lots of reasons for violence within the family, for manifest failure of affect modulation. Although shame plays an important role in every aspect of this dysfunction, no treatment method can be effective until it has been placed within a complete understanding of all affect. Even though it is the basis of all empathy, affective resonance can be torture for those forced to live in a system they cannot handle.

It is precisely this ability of broadcast affect to take over consciousness that must call to our attention another of Tomkins's major points: Consciousness itself is a function of affect! Only those bodily or mental activities that achieve affective amplification will realize the degree of significance that makes them conscious. It is only through its assembly with affect that anything becomes important enough to us that it can be called the focus of our attention. Even psychoanalytic exploration, which brings into consciousness long-buried thoughts and memories, is totally dependent on this relation between affect and awareness. The analytic therapist's muted display of affect assists internal reflection by avoiding distraction. Meditation is a system through which we agree similarly to allow affective amplification of thoughts normally left out of awareness.

Broadcast affect can take us over just as surely as that derived from purely internal sources. It is difficult enough for us to pay attention to anything for more than a few moments at a time, simply because our associations to whatever is going on trigger affect that then turns attention to those more internal sources. This is why we so often have to ask people to repeat what they were saying only a moment earlier. We simply cannot "hear" what fails to garner affective amplification, just as we can only hear whatever is currently being amplified by affect.

Once I heard a radio interview with a Walt Disney Studio artist who had worked on *Snow White*, the first full-length feature film done entirely in cartoon. What surprised him most was the degree of audience response to the scene in which the seven dwarfs were huddled around Snow White's funeral bier. "Everybody in the theater was weeping simply because we had drawn the backs of the dwarfs with a certain curve." Anything that signifies innate affect is capable of breaking through the empathic wall and taking us over.

Have you ever encountered someone who smiles at you during a difficult discussion, nodding emphatically and constantly in order to draw you into agreement? Such people are attempting to trick us into positive affective resonance (and therefore agreement) so that we will disregard some potential source of negative affect. It is the adequacy of the empathic wall that protects us from such maneuvers.

8

A BRIEF DIGRESSION:

THE DRIVES

So far, we have been discussing Tomkins's theory that affect amplifies anything with which it is assembled. In this respect it is sort of like the amplifier section in your home audio equipment, which takes relatively weak signals from the radio tuner, the compact disk player, or the tape cassette unit, and changes nothing but the amplitude or intensity of the information. This newly amplified signal is then fed to the loudspeakers or earphones, so that electrical energy is converted to the physical movement of little sheets of paper and plastic, which we experience as sound. Interest–excitement, enjoyment–joy, surprise–startle, fear–terror, distress–anguish, and anger–rage are alike in that they share the ability to amplify variations in the rate of flow or the steady-state density of information coursing through the neurological equipment. Whatever need or information they amplify is altered only in the style or quality intrinsic to that specific affect.

We have not really looked at the types of information available to the affect system, the categories of data that it will amplify. This is easy to do in the adult, for we become interested in, or happy about, or startled by, or frightened of, or stressed by, or angry at, anything we can see, hear, touch, remember, or even hallucinate. We expect this information to come from the various organs of perception, cognition, or memory. But these are pretty sophisticated sources of data, streams of information dependent on knowledge and experience. There is nothing here to explain why an infant cries in distress when it is hungry or screams in terror when it cannot breathe properly. We must ask, what is hunger and how does it work? How does the body know it needs oxygen, and how does it get this information to the affect system so that we become upset enough to do something about our hunger for air? How do these bodily needs fit into a psychological scheme?

We take for granted that the more advanced a life form, the more time it needs to spend in the company of its elders from the moment of birth until ready to take its place as a full adult. Birds stay in the nest until they are able to fly, puppies with their dam until they are able to forage for food by themselves, humans more or less among family until adolescence. What happens during this prolonged period of dependence on elders? Why are the young at so much risk? It turns out that there are two reasons for childhood.

On the one hand, not all the neurological systems that will be present in the adult are fully functional in the newborn. Some experts say that the development of the human nervous system is not complete until early adolescence, for up to about age 13 we can still find nerve tracts in the process of building the protective myelin sheath so important for the conduction of impulses. The Swiss psychologist Jean Piaget (1968) showed that in our move from tiny children to full-fledged adults our ability to think changes greatly. Even a brilliant child does not think like an adult. Despite the eventual or even the intrinsic intelligence of an individual, the thinking processes normal for those who have passed through adolescence are technically impossible for the small child.

On the other hand, as life itself becomes more complex, it is not safe to release a child into the world until he or she is taught the ways of that world. We provide various levels of schooling that teach children what types of information are available, as well as methods for gaining access to that information.

Complicated stuff, and quite labor-intensive. Any mother will tell you how difficult it is to teach anything to an infant. Imagine how much more troublesome our lives would be were we required to figure out when the baby needed food or whether its level of oxygen were high enough. For food, that would necessitate our ownership of gadgets capable of assaying the level of glucose in the baby's muscle tissue; for oxygen, we would need another group of devices. All this equipment would have to be connected to alarm systems informing us about danger points when the levels got too low or too high.

The reason we do not have to purchase, maintain, and keep our attention glued to such equipment is that babies are born with a group of internal mechanisms called the *drives*. Each drive is a separate biological system that informs the organism about the need for a particular substance and the place where that need is to be satisfied. The hunger drive analyzes the level of glucose in the blood, tells us when it is too low and that we need to put food in our mouths. The breathing drive tells us that the level of oxygen is too low and that we need to breathe in the mouth, nose, and chest.

A drive, then, is a prewritten program that acts as an information source by creating a wish or a need. As Tomkins defines the drive system (1962, 31) "The basic nature of this information is of *time*, of *place* and of *response—where* and *when* to do *what*—when the body does not know otherwise how to help itself." These drive mechanisms must be sensitive enough to tell the organism about a need long before the lack they sense is dangerous—if the level of glucose (for example) falls too low, we can become unconscious. And they must be capable of "letting go" before consummation is complete, for we lose our hunger long before food has been digested enough for nutrients to be distributed to the tissues. People who override this mechanism can eat themselves to death.

All drives inform us about bodily systems that are necessary for life; as such, all drives are equally important. But since we can only go without oxygen for a couple of minutes before our brain tissues are irreparably damaged, the need for oxygen is more acute than the need for food. We can fast for days with relative ease, but we dare not hold our breath for more than a minute or so. Our need for air is more frantic than that for water, which is needed more urgently than food, which in turn is needed more insistently than sex, which is needed at least once in the lifetime of an individual if the species is to survive. Though all drives are equally important, they inform us about needs with dramatically different temperaments.

Pretend, for a moment, that we have a kit from which we can assemble any drive with any affect. (That's actually what happens in real life anyway, for each affect can be assembled with any other bodily function to give it "meaning" or motivation.) The assembly of hunger with interest makes for our pleasant anticipation of a good meal; with distress it creates the sobbing hunger of early childhood. One who is hungry and frightened may eat furtively or not at all, while one who has been made ashamed of hunger may avoid food completely. In all of these people the drive called hunger has done its job exactly the same way. It has sensed the level of glucose in the blood and informed us that we must put food in our mouths. The *quality* of each experience is determined by the governing affect.

Everything we have been taught about the sex drive suggests that it is an imperious force demanding urgent satisfaction. But is this really a characteristic of sexuality itself or of the affects with which the sex drive is assembled? When sexual desire (a need just like the other drives) is assembled with interest or excitement, it produces the combination we know so well as lust. Indeed,

Freud misunderstood this one particular union of drive and affect as the source of all excitement! Freud thought that all curiosity was sexual interest with the sexual part neutralized. But desire can be assembled with fear to create, for some, the thrilling sense of taboo and the forbidden, and, for others, the chill of impotence or frigidity. Assembled with anger, sex blends into sadism; assembled with shame, sex can lose all excitement or be accepted as masochistic submission. Linked with disgust, the very idea of sex can produce great displeasure rather than any positive experience.

Very little of Freud's original theoretical system linking sexuality and the mental-emotional organization holds any water today. Most of us in the psychotherapy world have given up the idea that the sex drive is the operating force that runs the human and powers our emotions. This decrease in acceptance for what has come to be called "drive theory" has forced a long hard look at *aggression*, Freud's other drive. Basch, especially in his papers 1975a, 1975b, and 1984, has stressed the need for psychoanalysis to drop this archaic concept. You will recall that I mentioned earlier that Freud was unable to explain everything in human behavior on the basis of a life-giving drive, and was forced to postulate the existence of a life-destroying drive. In classical psychoanalytic theory all anger, hatred, meanness, cruelty—indeed, all the negative passions—are traced to this hypothetical destructive force. Nevertheless, even the brief description of the negative affects offered in the preceding pages should allow the reader to assemble any emotion that previous theorists thought was caused by "aggression."

Even the biologists who study other members of the animal kingdom have been forced to renounce the concept of innate aggression. Aggressive behavior obeys none of the rules common to other instinctive forces—it has no intrinsic periodicity, there are no metabolic changes produced by its absence (as when the organism is deprived of food, water, or air), and animals do not need to attack unless provoked.

So extensive is the modern study of affect in infancy and early childhood, and so damaging for classical psychoanalytic theory are its findings, that many eminent scholars have attempted to force some sort of reconciliation between the new and the old systems. Otto F. Kernberg (1990) calls attention to Freud's early supposition that the affects appeared when drive energy was prevented from reaching its goal, and now suggests that libido and aggression are actually formed from building blocks made up of affects and experiences. It is illogical to assume that "the primary affects themselves are the ultimate motivational systems," he says, because "a theory of motivation based on affects rather than on two drives would be complicated and clinically unsatisfactory" (121). Seeing the affects "as complex psychic structures that are indissolubly

linked to the individual's cognitive appraisals of his immediate situation" (125),
he makes the action of affect quite subordinate to neocortical cognition, despite his apparent rejection of the James-Lange hypothesis.

One wonders how so literate and gifted an observer can so thoroughly
misunderstand the nature of innate affect. One clue may lie in Kernberg's
deeply clinical focus: "Psychoanalytic exploration of intense affect storms in
regressed patients, in my experience, consistently demonstrates that there is
no such thing as 'pure' affect without cognitive content" (123). Such an attitude resembles an attempt to determine the biology and life cycle of chickens
and cows from the study of cake. Eggs and milk are so thoroughly altered by
the baking process that scant clues to their origin remain in the final product.
Yet all psychoanalytic theory is based on Freud's belief that the way things
developed might be discovered by decomposition of their final end product.

Okay. If we discard the "aggression" drive as an unnecessary and nonphysi-
ological creation of the founder of psychoanalysis, and then reject the idea that
the sexual drive is responsible for all the excitement of life, we are left with sex
as just another biological drive shorn of the special characteristics given it by
Freud. These two assumptions remove the mysticism that surrounds psychoanalytic theory and return psychology entirely to biological science. With
these two changes we are able to ask whether there are any special features of
the drives that influence our study of the emotions. Dissmell and disgust—two
affects that Tomkins feels are among the most recent to evolve—are mechanisms that protect the hunger drive.

The six innate affects we have discussed so far are all alike in that they
amplify stimulus conditions that are basically quantitative variations in the
level of brain function. As we discussed earlier, they are ways that relatively
meaningless quantities are given significance through their association with
specific qualities of experience. Three affects remain: Dissmell, disgust, and
shame–humiliation: affects equal in importance to the others, but triggered by
different mechanisms. They are the "attenuators" of the drives and the affects,
acting to limit other functions once they have been turned on. Notwithstanding their physiological basis, these three become the affects of interpersonal
distance. As such, they take on tremendous significance in the realm of social
interaction.

Although shame–humiliation can, like all the affects, be assembled with any
other function to lend its particular kind of urgency to that function, a great
deal of our personal concept of what is shameful comes from our lifetime
response to the affects dissmell and disgust. We will now investigate these two
affects that monitor and protect our intake of food.

9

DISSMELL AND DISGUST

Look again. If you pronounced it like "dismal," you missed Tomkins's point. Just as the word "disease" means "not at ease," and "dissimilar" means "not similar," *dissmell* conveys the sense of some interference with the act of smelling. We are leaping back in evolution to the era when a tremendous part of the information available to an organism was based on what could be smelled.

Odor was much more important to the life forms from which we evolved than it is to us today. On the island of Madagascar live many representative species of the life form called the *prosimians*, the group from which evolved the true apes that Darwin recognized as our more immediate ancestors. Sleeping by day and foraging at night, lemurs and tarsiers communicate not by visual signals from their facial affect display, but by bursts of scent from specialized glands. Anyone who walks a male dog has waited impatiently while this pet goes through the urgent ritual of sniffing communal posts to see who has preceded him that day, for canines identify each other by the specific odors in urine.

So important are the connections between the scent receptors in the nose and the brain centers where smell is analyzed that anatomists used to call a large section of the central nervous system the *rhinencephalon*, or nose-brain. (Later discoveries have led us to discard this label in favor of the more modern term *limbic system*.) Earlier, we discussed the amygdala, a knot of brain cells that seems to analyze information later to be involved in emotion. The amygdala is wired to receive data from all the sensory systems, but, except for smell, these inputs come from parts of the cerebral cortex that have already processed the raw data of sensation into highly refined interpretations of it. Alone of all the sensory reports, olfaction connects directly to the amygdala, placing the raw data of smell on a par with the processed messages of the others.

Data from the olfactory system can be used in many ways. *Pheromones,* scent-borne sexual messenger molecules, are known to transmit information about species, gender, and sexual availability in beings as disparate as gypsy moths, mice, rhinoceroci, and perhaps even man. After only a few months of living together in closed communities, like college dormitories, women note that their menstrual cycles tend to become synchronized. This phenomenon has been attributed to scent-borne information. Olfaction bears an important connection to the sexual drive—it is possible that part of our interest in perfume derives from our biologic relation to pheromones.

It might be suggested that the sense of smell guards the drive system that tells us we need oxygen, for in theory smell can inform us about the presence of bad gases. Nonetheless, there is not much an oxygen-starved organism can do about bad odor—rarely is a life-form offered a choice of gaseous environments. As far as breathing goes, what you smell is what you get.

The drive most intimately associated with the sense of smell is hunger, which is regularly informed about the quality of possible foodstuffs on the basis of their emitted odor. It is thought that the newborn infant moves toward the nipple because of its fragrance. Just as the growing child learns to differentiate between people by their visual characteristics, he or she will learn the smells of freshly baked apple pie and new-mown hay.

Tomkins points out that certain of these airborne molecules trigger a definite and repeatable program or series of actions. Confronted by noxious compounds, the infant wrinkles its nose, raises the upper lip, and withdraws from the offending odor. This is the recurrent pattern of activity, present from birth and visible on the face of the adult throughout life, that he calls dissmell. Dissmell will pull the infant away from whatever has triggered it; we are protected from some harmful foods by this mechanism. Thus dissmell operates to limit the hunger drive; odor can stimulate a protective mechanism that creates in us an immediate requirement for distance from its source.

We can wrinkle our noses at people we dislike and move away from them; at worst we can call them "stinkers" and reject them totally. Somehow, dissmell (which nevertheless continues to monitor food) turns into an affect as it enters our emotional life and especially as it begins to alter our interpersonal behavior. Tomkins calls this type of affect a *drive auxiliary* because it is a programmed mechanism originally operating to limit a drive. However, the more importance a society places on interpersonal closeness, the more emphasis it will place on the odors we ourselves emit and on those we sense arising from the intimate other. The enormous expenditure on underarm deodorants, perfumed soaps, perfumes, "toilet" water, cologne, after-shave lotion, mouth-wash, toothpaste, lozenges to control "bad breath," vaginal deodorants, and sprays to mask bathroom odors is but a casual indicator of the importance to civilized life of dissmell in the name of odor control.

Some years ago a dentist asked me to see a patient who had already consulted half a dozen of his colleagues in an attempt to rid herself of a mouth odor only she could perceive. Claiming with great intensity that her breath smelled like "dragon dung," she had avoided people for over a year rather than be summarily rejected by them. I knew that epileptic seizures involving the *uncus*, the tip of the temporal lobes of the brain (these are called "uncinate fits"), typically involve the hallucination of odor, but this seemed different in that the offending smell was constant rather than episodic. For some years she had been taking the antihypertensive drug *reserpine*, which will often give people a sense of being guilty about something or even produce a full-fledged depression. In cooperation with her treating physician we stopped the medication, and the symptom disappeared. This seems to have been a disorder involving the affect dissmell (she distanced other people in order to protect them from having to do the same to her), with more than a little shame thrown in as a secondary reaction. It is the only biological disorder of dissmell I have ever seen.

Smells, by their associations, can produce a mood, as when incense recalls to mind one's early experiences in church; similarly, one would expect noxious odors and dissmell to do the same. Dissmell figures prominently in the experi-

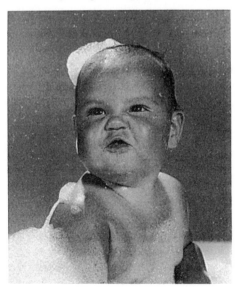

Fig. 9.1. Upper lip wrinkled, head drawn back in the display of mild **dissmell**. We know this is not the beginning of a cry because the corners of the mouth are level. If you simulate this affect with only one side of the mouth you communicate the attitude of contempt.

ence and the phenomenology of interpersonal rejection. It is a primitive mechanism by which we keep something at a distance from us, something or someone we define as too awful or too foul to get near. Whenever one person decides that another person is unacceptable at the level of dissmell, it is very difficult (if not nearly impossible) to get them together, to find a way for them to get to know each other. Dissmell is the cornerstone of prejudice.

Haughtiness, a way of looking down your nose at people, is often accompanied by the face of dissmell. The British custom of making a "stiff upper lip," which we discussed earlier as a learned modulation of distress–anguish, may also be understood as a dissmell response to crying.

"Uggh! Eeeooo! Yucchh!" said Cleo about two years ago when speaking about her estranged husband. All during the session she had been telling me how much she wanted to "put things together again," to restore their marriage to its once-happy state. They did get together every once in a while, mostly to talk about the children; occasionally they hugged. "I can't stand his smell," she said. As a psychotherapist, I have never seen a marriage, a business partnership, or any working relationship survive once dissmell has entered the picture.

One of my patients, an enormously successful entrepreneur who seems always ready and able to turn ideas into lucrative schemes, suggested that there was money to be made from Tomkins's concept of dissmell. "You therapists spend too much time helping patients get close to others. Imagine all those people who just want to be alone. You could market a product called 'Repel' or 'Away!' that allowed someone the peace and quiet of privacy. Yeah, you could even call it 'Privacy.'" I wonder whether some of those who go through life unwashed and unperfumed are trying to achieve the same effect.

An issue of *Science News* carried a story about the possibility that garlic contained a substance capable of reducing high blood pressure and preventing other diseases. Six weeks later, the following letter appeared in response:

In "Garlic medicine: Cures in cloves?" (SN: 9/8/90, p.157) the researchers seem to overlook the obvious. Garlic may not have any direct chemical influence on hypertension, heart disease and cancer. But garlic's ability to repel other human beings may.

For instance, I use at least three cloves of garlic a day. The result is that my boss will not come into my office to abuse me. When I go to a bank or retail store, my transactions are handled quickly and efficiently, even abruptly, and any questions or complaints I have are always granted. Neighbors bid me hello from across the street or not at all.

I am blissfully happy and healthy. The only people with whom I have any real concourse are other garlic eaters, and these are equally blissfully happy and healthy.

Therefore, in my experience, garlic counteracts the stress and morbidity of unnaturally dense human populations. It does so by repelling unhealthy and unhappy individuals and by attracting healthy and happy ones.

Martin Donovan
Salem, Mass.

By inverting normal experience under conscious control, the writer calls attention to our point. Whenever someone treats us as if we smell bad we suffer a profound decrease in self-esteem; therefore, those who are treated with dissmell must experience shame. And when people accept this label, if they are forced to agree that they are so foul as to deserve the innate response of avoidance, henceforth these people will live with chronic shame that becomes a part of the very structure of their personalities. Just as you can see people who walk around turning up their nose at everybody, wrinkling the upper lip and withdrawing from contact with strangers as if they were contaminated with filth, so you will see people who feel that they are indeed the filth that triggers such a response. On occasion I have worked in therapy with adults reared by mothers who expressed dissmell at whatever displeased them; never have I seen one of these people achieve a comfortable, loving interpersonal relationship. The way they withdraw from themselves as well as others will occupy us as we discuss the clinical manifestations of shame.

DISGUST

While the nose may act as the sentinel of the mouth, not every noxious food has a foul odor. Just as the olfactory system operates to detect and identify airborne molecules, the gustatory system evaluates and identifies chemicals in water. Sometimes what smells great tastes simply awful.

Were we investigating only the eating behavior of adults, our study of the reaction to bad tastes might be quite tame. Should some morsel fail to meet our standards for taste, as adults we are capable of putting fork or spoon back to the mouth, discreetly removing the now unwanted food (while covering this transaction from view with a napkin), and placing food and utensil back on the plate. Much of adult eating behavior derives from our awareness of other people and the social mores dictated by custom.

Not so the infant, whose need for food has been initiated by the drive hunger amplified powerfully by distress or perhaps interest. The drive, which "knows" only that blood or tissue levels of glucose are too low, is sending a continuous, insistent signal of hunger. If the gustatory sense is to be granted the ability to protect life by limiting the urgency of the push to omnivorous devouring that we call hunger, taste must trigger a mechanism capable of interfering with the hunger drive when hunger is at its height.

Tomkins points out that there is such a programmed response triggered by the gustatory sense and uses the common word *disgust* to indicate a second powerful auxiliary mechanism that limits the drive hunger. Like dissmell, it is a drive auxiliary that has also evolved to the status of an affect. In disgust, both tongue and lower lip are protruded, and the head thrust forward. As with all the innate affects, the infant is not "mildly" affected by disgust. When the affect hits, it clearly garners the totality of the child's attention. The child is simply "taken over" by disgust, all interest in food temporarily suspended as the offending substance is expelled with vigor.

The affect disgust is as compelling a force as the drive it reduces, and is powerful in direct proportion to the degree of preceding desire for that food. As soon as the noxious substance has been removed from the mouth, the infant is ready to respond to the drive-borne information informing (reminding) it that food is still needed. But not the food just spit out.

This patterned activity may be seen on the face of the newborn and its expression is constant throughout life. Later, of course, as with all affects, its display may be modulated to fit the social structure of the culture to which each person adapts. Yet no matter how refined an individual, the affect retains all its archaic power.

Not only do we react with disgust to any substance that tastes foul or unpleasant, but we can retain memory of our reaction to it and develop an intelligent aversion to that compound. Disgust then becomes part of a system

Fig. 9.2. Head forward, tongue protruded, lower lip pushed down. **Disgust** favors the expulsion of an offending morsel of food.

of aversion, an attitude chosen to avoid this negative affect. Repugnance may be thought of as the assembly of disgust affect with memory to produce a specific realm of learning. It produces a host of associations giving rise to the general group of things believed capable of causing what is called *contamination*.

We can also develop an aversion to things we have never tasted but which for other reasons give us a feeling of repugnance. As Drs. Paul Rozin and April Fallon have pointed out in their meticulous studies of disgust (1987), the overwhelming majority of people will refuse to eat such psychologically "contaminated" things as a cockroach, even if sterilized and even though they have never tasted one. In particular, most American adults have a disgust response to substances that have come from the interior of the body, like saliva, urine, feces, and mucous. Such specific aversions are culture-bound and by no means innate or inherently linked to the human condition. There are, for example, Middle Eastern cultures in which camel dung is regularly used as cooking fuel, and at least one culture in which compressed dung is used as a roofing material. Yet in every culture there are substances commonly considered to be disgusting and to contaminate whatever is associated with them.

Do you find yourself "turned off" by such facts? If so, your avidity for new information has been affected by disgust.

Had disgust remained only a food-centered drive auxiliary, we might not be discussing it here in a book about emotion. The ease with which any affect can be combined with any thought (or indeed any human function) has produced for disgust a wide range of emotion completely unrelated to food and hunger. We have a remarkable ability to understand complex situations as concepts or ideas and a natural tendency to represent these ideas by symbols. Whenever any of these higher-order mental processes bears a resemblance to the process of food ingestion, it is capable of being assembled with food-related affect. Thus, we talk about our beloved as being inside us, and the process of intimacy as incorporating the other person. "I love you so much I could just eat you up." "You look good enough to eat." "You make me feel good in my tummy." "She gave me a delicious smile."

When love turns sour, something that had been taken into us with full confidence in its ability to nurture has now turned foul. In our humiliated rage at the confidence man we say we were "taken in," a defensive reversal of the more accurate observation that we took him in. It was we ourselves who had accepted him into our system as if he were good for us. There is a terrible sense of betrayal, of being made a fool, when the magic is taken from love and the person we held so dear turns out to regard us poorly. In each of these situations we are likely to react with disgust to—spit out with violence—our relationship with this significant other. Alternatively, should we feel unable to regard and reject the other person with disgust, we may accept the idea that we are worthy of such treatment and then regard ourselves with disgust. No matter what happens, when what has previously been "ingested" becomes unpalatable, a violent reaction is triggered—a reaction whose power comes from the affect disgust.

Recall, though, Tomkins's idea that disgust operates to limit the drive hunger when that drive is at its height. Disgust is powerful because it creates intense conflict over our continued desire for what had appeared so tasty and has now become nasty. Disgust, then, is a good model by which to examine the phenomenology of divorce, in which people who have loved now turn against each other. The extraordinary force and tenacity of marital hate is dependent on the power of the preexisting marital bond, of the "drive" to be close, of the need for each other, of the warmth each once gave the other, of the degree of nurturance each represented to the other. In every moment, however brief, that an estranged person thinks of his or her partner, the affect of disgust will now intrude.

In the interpersonal world, wherever there is disgust there will be gross alteration of self-esteem or in our esteem for another person. Divorce can be experienced as victory if we view ourselves as perfect and the other as the pure object of disgust, and as defeat if we must maintain as pure our internal representation of the other. Lurking at the corners of consciousness then will be self-contempt and self-loathing as explanations for such a huge defeat, along with the chronic shame that accompanies the chronic loss of self-esteem.

A generation ago one of my senior colleagues, Reuben Robert Pottash, startled a study group by stating that when a couple divorces and later remarries, "at least one of them is crazy." We pressed him further. "Think about what has gone on in people who divorce. All the love turned to hate, all the fighting through lawyers. Who can go back to someone you have hated so much? Only people who are so crazy that they can ignore hatred or forget their recent history. You have to be pretty crazy to be willing to overlook something like that." Today, thinking of divorce in terms of mutual disgust, and understanding disgust as an affect that protects us by destroying our wish to incorporate something that we used to want, I agree with him all the more. Who can eat what has been spat out in disgust?

Yet often we do hear about such cycles of divorce and remarriage. I suspect that all of us are forced to swallow many things we would like to reject. Apparently there is no limit to our socially constructed ability to disavow or hide our innate reaction of disgust. Often I find that the "suppressed anger" emerging in psychotherapy is a reaction to long-hidden disgust.

Even though affect is far more than facial reaction, you can make some pretty shrewd guesses about what is going on in someone when you watch the face. There are lots of ways to express anger, but someone who yells at another by jutting his head forward with the lower lip protruding is demonstrating the combination of anger and disgust.

Have you ever watched the audience during a horror movie? Turn around in your seat some time and look at the faces people make as the horrific events unfold. Often I see the blanched and frozen face of fear, combined with the upper lip of dissmell and the lower lip of disgust. Most likely, as for all the emotions, each of us has a personal definition of horror, but I think that combination of facial displays appears regularly enough for me to ask you to consider the possibility that, for some people, horror is a combination of those three affects. You can test my observation by mimicking the facial displays yourself. First draw up and wrinkle your upper lip and nose, then draw down and protrude your lower lip, and, finally, stare at something with widened eyes. Doing this you may experience a moment of horror.

Tomkins has pointed out that the sneer of contempt may be a clue to its origins from innate affect—at one corner, the mouth is raised as in dissmell, while at the other corner it is pulled down as in disgust. Contempt is a form of anger in which we declare the other person, this object of our negative affect, as far beneath us and worthy only of rejection. The purpose or function of contempt seems to be to instill in the other person a sense of self-dissmell or self-disgust and therefore shame at self-unworthiness.

There are lots of times you can observe people making strange faces when they don't know we are watching. Sometimes they are at a height of emotion, while at other times they believe their feelings to be invisible. You can draw your own conclusions about the relation between the innate affects and the various styles of anger you see around you. Paying attention to the face can be a rewarding occupation.

Can we carry further the alimentary analogies suggested by Tomkins? Good-tasting food can become toxic after it leaves the mouth and hits the stomach, in which case it triggers nausea and vomiting. If food becomes toxic in the lower intestines, it triggers diarrhea. Often we see people whose reaction to "stress" is of these latter types, and perhaps their gut symptoms are an emotional response related to dissmell and disgust. In the movie *An Unmarried Woman*, Jill Clayburgh portrayed a woman whose husband was involved in an extramarital affair. During a luncheon which she thought might have dealt with their possible reconciliation, he announced his intention to marry his paramour. Moments after leaving the restaurant, she vomited. This is an example of the disgust family of affects operating to extrude something deep inside her—the internalized husband she must now push away. It is the degree of the prior need or wish that determines the violence of the reaction that will be created by disgust.

In the passages above I have sketched some of the feelings and emotions that can accompany the affect disgust. Just as with the other affects, memory can trigger a mood of disgust that lasts until something distracts us from our preoccupation with what was once loved and is now toxic. People with chronic nausea from gastrointestinal illness or from medication experience a chronic feeling of self-disgust. Few people can tolerate such medications for very long.

Is there such a thing as an inborn organic disorder involving the affect disgust? Are there situations in which feelings of disgust and fantasies of contamination may be traced to problems in the biology of affect? On several occasions I have treated or evaluated patients with what is called obsessive-compulsive disorder, more popularly known today as OCD. A common symptom of this illness is an incessant desire to rid one's hands of something dirty, to remove an invisible, fantasized contamination. In addition to compulsive hand-washing, these patients may complain that "dirty words" come to mind, words which, if said aloud, would cause terrible embarrassment.

One of my patients, an otherwise comfortably heterosexual gentleman, experienced bursts of "homosexual thoughts," in which he would think of sucking a penis—an idea he found disgusting. I am, of course, aware that conventional psychoanalytic thinking would dictate that "the wish is father to the fear," and that his symptom represented a covert homosexual wish. Other symptoms of OCD prominent in his case included a desperate need to check literally everything in his apartment that could be a source of danger. Each time he reached the door he was seized by the need to check the stove to make sure the burners were off. He might go back to the bathroom a dozen times to make sure the toilet was not running or the faucets leaking. And he was unable to leave his apartment without returning as many as four or five times to check whether he had locked the door properly. All of these symptoms vanished when he began to take the drug *fluoxetine.*

Some years ago, before the arrival of these new medications for OCD, I saw a distinguished, elderly banker who had been plagued for more than thirty years with a recurring group of thoughts that formed a highly specific obsessional symptom. Whenever he thought about his beloved and mused about the pleasure of their sexual relationship, he was seized by images of her previous lovers and the possibility that they had in some way contaminated her. Each time, he became overpowered with disgust and horrified that he was in a relationship with so filthy a person.

Traditional psychoanalytic lore suggests that such fears derive from the anal phase of psychosexual development, viewing feces as the primary contaminant, the basic precipitant of disgust. Unfortunately, psychoanalytic treatment aimed at the understanding of such issues has rarely proved useful in diminishing either the intensity or the frequency of such recurring clusters of thoughts. Pharmacologic agents capable of increasing the amount of certain neurotransmitters seem more effective.

On the basis of the many years I have spent observing patients with OCD, I believe that some portion of the symptoms described may represent a biological disorder of the affect disgust, interpreted by the central assembly system as the need to avoid a contaminant. How the affect becomes part of such a specific script is not known, but it seems reasonable to consider some forms of OCD as a script disorder in which the impelling or irresistible force to action involves a disorder of affect.

THE LANGUAGE OF AFFECT

A moment ago, in recounting the story of Cleo, the death of whose marriage was foretold by her dissmell response to her husband, I rendered her vocalizations as "Uggh! Eeeooo! Yucchh!" If you say these words in front of a mirror (with all the emphasis they normally carry) you will see the facial display of disgust accompanying *uggh!* and *yucchh!* and the display of dissmell accompanying *eeeooo!* Affect, which itself is not a matter of words, does tend to shape the face in patterns that lend themselves to the pronunciation of certain words.

Every once in a while I have mentioned that the growing child shifts gradually from a communication system based on the display of innate affect to one based securely on verbal language. Much scholarly work has been done on the nature of language, most of which seems to indicate that (just like affect) words, grammar, and syntax seem to come from their own quite specific location within the brain. The science of linguistics has identified some of the earliest forms of language and traced the path of certain words over large sections of our planet. Many linguists have attempted to show that, despite the importance of emotion, it has no connection to the language system except as a modifier of already existing language.

Unfortunately, all of these studies have failed to take into account any aspect of the affect system as described by Tomkins. Even though I am well aware that the overwhelming majority of words derives from the brain mechanisms well known within the field of linguistics, it is important to describe those few that are clearly connected to innate affect.

Take, for instance, surprise–startle, which normally produces the vocalization "OH!" If startle occurs when your mouth is closed, this will be rendered as "wha," the forerunner of "what?" and "wow." We call such words *echoic* or *onomatopoeic*, for they echo sounds found in nature, like the "whoosh" of the wind or the "plop" of something falling into water.

For distress–anguish we have an entire family of long-drawn-out words that mirror the profile of both the affect and its triggering source: whine, wail, weep, whimper. They are onomatopoeic because they evoke both the sound and the feeling of distress. *Growl, roar,* and *arrgh!* are echoic for anger–rage. And for dissmell we have a full range of words that, when uttered, require that the upper lip be drawn back and upward just as it is when we are in the throes of the affect: snide, snot, snivel, snarl (dissmell and anger), snicker (dissmell and enjoyment–joy manifested as contempt), sniff, and snit.

Kids and adults alike say words like *puke, yuccky, icky,* and *york* when they mean to indicate their disgust for something or somebody. And I suspect that there is a connection between the full-blown expression of *Yayyy!* or *Yippee!* and the experience of excitement, just as the relieved outpouring of previously arrested breathing we know as *whew* may be an expression of the relief and release accompanying enjoyment–joy.

All of these words are common in contemporary American culture. I suspect that similar vocalizations may be found in Chinese, Hindi, and all of the Indo-European languages. This realm of linguistics is another realm of study made possible by affect theory.

DISMISSIVES

The study of dissmell and disgust reveals yet another linguistic category, to which I have given the name *dismissives.* This term lends a peculiar potency to our understanding of the affective roots of prejudice and discrimination.

In order to reject individuals it is sometimes easier to declare them to be members of a disgusting or dissmelling group, after which it is more logical to distance them. Thus I may pronounce my unloved neighbor to be Jewish, obese, a warmonger, a coward, a Nazi, *nouveau riche,* stupid, an egghead intellectual, or a member of any one of an endlessly long list of categories that make easier his or her dissmell. In such cases, rejection has actually been based on dissmell or disgust triggered by reasons much more deeply personal, motives more specific to our own relationship with that person but attributed to membership within that category. I have noticed that those who are most likely to place others within dismissive categories are those with the greatest frequency of the facial gestures we might call disgust and dissmell tics.

The history of our African-American subpopulation, for example, is made much more comprehensible by an understanding of dismissive language. The habit of comparison, one of the cardinal features of the human cognitive apparatus, leads us to assess new precepts on the basis of their resemblance to the old. Thus, when Caucasians first encountered African members of their own species, they were struck by such differences as skin color, hair texture, and facial structure. But humans have more skin than hair, and it was their pigmentation (which had allowed these tribes to become so well adapted to tropical life) that formed the basis of categorization. Darkness of skin was described as *blackness*, latinized as *niger*, translated as *negro*, and corrupted in slang to *nigger*. And it was by these pigment-based indicators of difference that this great mass of our fellow humans was organized and dismissed for several centuries.

It was not for reasons of actual odor that bigoted Southern Caucasians claimed that "niggers smell bad." This was always a violent dismissive based on the *affect* dissmell and falsely attributed to smell itself. The affective roots of prejudice *always* involve dissmell and disgust. Enough shame and rage have evolved along with our societal use of the word "nigger" that now, even to use it in a scholarly discussion of affect triggers so much negative affect that an audience becomes unable to think about its affective history and its use as a justification for the socioeconomics of slavery!

Powerful mechanisms, these affects. The more you examine disgust and dissmell, the more you realize the breadth and extent of their power. It is fascinating that some people can be trained to ignore disgust, to accept what they revile. Also can people be made to ignore dissmell, to accept that which might naturally turn them away. One way this can be accomplished is through shame, which can reduce, limit, or even turn off any affect. Now that we have presented Tomkins's idea that dissmell and disgust operate to limit the drives when they are at their height, let us investigate shame—humiliation, for this is the affect that interferes with other *affects* when they are at their height.

10

SHAME–HUMILIATION

There is good evidence to lead us to suspect that the physiological basis of the emotion shame is an inborn script that attenuates affects much in the same way that dissmell and disgust limit hunger. We believe that the affect Tomkins calls *shame–humiliation* is the inherent, internally programmed "innate attenuator circuit" for the positive affects. Since it is the mutualization of interest–excitement and enjoyment–joy that powers sociality, shame affect is therefore an innate modulator of affective communication. Just as dissmell and disgust are auxiliaries to a drive, mechanisms that have evolved to the status of affects, shame–humiliation is an auxiliary to the affects, one that has achieved a status equal to its predecessors.

Recall, asks Tomkins, all those times you have seen an old friend at a distance and waved vigorously to get his or her attention. When that other person gives us the smiling face of recognition we are rewarded by a surge of pleasure. But occasionally it turns out that we had hailed a stranger, having been fooled by an unexpected resemblance.*

The moment we recognize our error something surprising happens to us. Although one might think all we need do is maintain our composure, nod politely, and ask this person to excuse the intrusion, before we can get the words out of our mouths something else has taken place. As soon as we have seen the face of the other person our own head droops, our eyes are cast down, and, blushing, we become briefly incapable of speech. Sometimes a hand goes unbidden to the mouth as if to prevent further communication, and we feel a

---

*Tomkins (1963), 123. This example is used by Izard (1977, 395), to whom it is often attributed incorrectly.

surge of confusion. This series of events is one adult manifestation of the innate mechanism Tomkins calls shame–humiliation. Like all the innate affects, shame–humiliation seems to be a script, a series of events initiated when its button is pushed and terminated when the entire script has been played out.

Shame differs from all the other affects in at least one significant feature. It appears to be triggered neither by variations in the shape and intensity of nonspecific internal neural events (as in the case of the six basic affects) nor by the detection of specific noxious chemicals, as in the case of the attenuators dissmell and disgust. Shame–humiliation is an inborn script, an attenuator system that can be called into operation whenever there is an impediment to the expression of either positive affect. It depends on the remarkable ability of highly organized, advanced life forms to assemble the data of perception into patterns and to compare those patterns to whatever has been stored as memory. In certain situations, as, for instance, when a pattern mismatch is detected while we are in the midst of interest or enjoyment, the affect shame–humiliation attempts to reduce the affect that had held sway a moment before.

I know you are disappointed that I didn't say anything that resembled in any way your own experience of embarrassment, humiliation, shame, mortification, ridicule, put-down, and so on. Just as when I described the difference between the affect enjoyment–joy and the enormous group of adult experi-

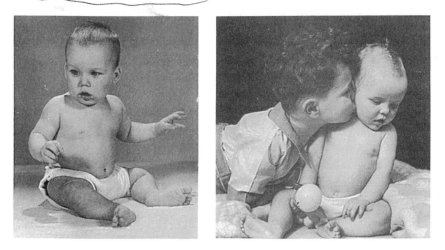

Fig. 10.1. Eyes averted and downcast, neck and shoulders beginning to slump. This is the purest presentation of the affect **shame–humiliation**.

Fig. 10.2. Here shame interferes with this baby's ability to remain interested in the toy. Was the kiss intended to pull the baby out of its slump, or was it the trigger for **shame–humiliation**?

ences we lump together as "fun" or "a good time," there is a world of differ-ence between the meaning-free physiological mechanism Tomkins calls shame–humiliation and the highly meaningful adult assemblages that we know as our own personal emotions.

Trust me. There had to be a good reason that I asked you to learn the entire affect system before presenting the concept of shame. It is the most recent affect to develop through the process of evolution, with the possible exception of the tears leaked when we are "overwhelmed by emotion." Shame requires the presence of other affects. Shame exists only in terms of other affects.

Let's go back to review the positive affects interest–excitement and enjoy-ment–joy for a moment. Interest–excitement is a response to an optimal in-

---

Table 4
THE INNATE AFFECTS

POSITIVE

1. **Interest–Excitement**
Eyebrows down, track, look, listen

2. **Enjoyment–Joy**
Smile, lips widened and out

NEUTRAL

3. **Surprise–Startle**
Eyebrows up, eyes blink

NEGATIVE

4. **Fear–Terror**
Frozen stare, face pale, cold, sweaty, hair erect

5. **Distress–Anguish**
Cry, rhythmic sobbing, arched eyebrows, mouth down

6. **Anger–Rage**
Frown, clenched jaw, red face

7. **Dissmell**
Upper lip raised, head pulled back

8. **Disgust**
Lower lip lowered and protruded, head forward and down

9. **Shame–Humiliation**
Eyes down, head down and averted, blush

---

crease in neural firing, a program triggered when a certain gradient of increase is sensed by the affect system. Interest itself is an intrinsically pleasant amplification of its stimulus. It makes us more interested in whatever is going on, more avid for whatever experience triggered it. Interest has a characteristic feel. We have experienced interest since birth. We know what it feels like, we know to a fare-thee-well every nuance of its rise and fall, its temporal profile.

Enjoyment–joy is a response to any decrease in neural firing. It is a program triggered when a certain gradient of decrease is sensed by the affect system. Enjoyment itself is an intrinsically pleasant amplification of its stimulus. It makes us enjoy more whatever is going on by calming us pleasantly. Enjoyment–joy has a characteristic feel. We have experienced enjoyment–joy since birth. We know what it feels like, we know to a fare-thee-well every nuance of its rise and fall, its temporal profile.

But there are lots of times that something interferes with the operation of either of these intrinsically pleasant affect programs. For instance, take the situation where lovers are communing, sharing the interplay of interest and enjoyment. In such situations we are exquisitely sensitive to tiny alterations in the flow of affective resonance. Should our partner in love but for a moment decrease his or her degree of resonance, instantly there is a shift in the interpersonal field. This need be nothing more than a frown crossing the face of the other, or failure to smile when one said something intended as "funny" but which stimulates an unexpected memory and therefore an unexpected affect, or a slight alteration in the degree of relaxation taken for granted in the relationship. Where, a moment earlier, we could by all means expect a certain flow of affect expression, suddenly there is an impediment to this flow.

This concept of impediment is quite specific. It refers to anything that disturbs the normal, expected flow of the patterns for the positive affects interest or enjoyment. An impediment to positive affect is an interference with the pleasure of everyday life. Do you live in a home with a burglar alarm? Most likely it involves an ultrasonic system (something like radar) in which a signal is broadcast into the environment from one point and received and interpreted at another. Anything that interferes with the normal pattern of broadcast and reception will trigger an alarm mechanism. Affect is like that. We are so used to the normal ebb and flow of our interest and of our enjoyment that any interference with this well-known and oft-experienced sense of flow will be recognized immediately.

Naturally there must be occasions when an impediment to positive affect quite definitely turns off that preexisting state of excitement or enjoyment. One sunny summer afternoon, when my then six-year-old daughter and I were watching television together, the electricity for our neighborhood was knocked out by a local storm. The images that had so entranced her were suddenly replaced by a blank screen, and she screamed in terror. In this case the interruption of what had been maintaining the pleasant state of triggered interest and enjoyment, the interruption itself, had been so sudden as to trigger the affect surprise–startle, which then was followed by the affect fear–terror as she tried unsuccessfully to figure out what had happened to her friends—the characters on the television screen. In adults, such a sudden alteration in stimulus contour will also produce an immediate shift in attention despite our conscious and cognitive "wish" for that stimulus to continue.

The affect program for shame–humiliation is triggered in those common situations when an impediment occurs but whatever had been a competent stimulus for interest or enjoyment *remains* a competent stimulus for those affects. In other words, shame affect is a programmed response to an impediment to preexisting affect when there is every reason for that preexisting affect to continue! Shame affect is a highly painful mechanism that operates to pull the organism away from whatever might interest it or make it content. Shame is painful in direct proportion to the degree of positive affect it limits. As Tomkins has stated, shame will occur whenever desire outruns fulfillment. To the extent that we humans seek pleasure we must experience shame. Indeed, much of the folk wisdom about the nature of heaven seems to be a description of a realm with a better match between desire and fulfillment than that found in nature.

Once, while I was in college, Robert Frost, then poet-in-residence, quipped "Give us the life that the movies show us / That the party in power is keeping from us." He paused for a moment, then said more seriously that we were all looking for "A world where ask is get / And knock is open wide." Embedded in these thoughts of the great poet are some of the concepts to which I refer: Life is full of impediments to positive affect, impediments that cause the acute and the fleeting as well as the chronic and the indwelling experiences of shame that so influence our lives and the development of our personalities. We have yet to open the discussion of how this happens, how this affect gets involved in the specific assemblages by which we know shame; yet intuitively you will grasp the idea that any mechanism capable of causing a painful limitation of what we most enjoy is a mechanism capable of involvement in nearly any aspect of human existence.

But even though shame is an auxiliary to the positive affects, rather than a true innate affect in the sense of the first six we described, it bears all of the properties of the other affects. Shame affect is an analogue of its stimulus.

Triggered by an impediment to positive affect is a highly amplified impediment to further positive affect. The specific "feel" of shame is that of an impediment to something we had wanted or enjoyed or which excited or pleased us. Although the affect is triggered initially by chance occurrence, later we learn new triggers for shame. The more information we can absorb, the more functions that can be handled by the ever-evolving brain of our species, the more triggers for shame can be found.

Notice that Tomkins does not claim shame to be an "off-switch" for interest–excitement and enjoyment–joy, a mechanism strictly analogous to the action of dissmell and disgust in turning off hunger for specific substances when hunger is at its height. Shame affect is a unique biological mechanism. It is called into action when the organism remains fascinated by whatever had triggered its interest or remains desirous of communing with whatever or whoever might next have been a source of the contentment, relaxation, or mirth associated with the affect enjoyment–joy.

So the innate affect shame–humiliation is conceptualized as a mechanism that throws the organism into a painful experience of inner tension by attempting to reduce the possibilities for positive affect in situations when compelling reasons for that positive affect remain. As in the example mentioned above, when we hail a woman who turns out to be a stranger, we remain quite interested in that person, quite fascinated by her appearance for the same reasons that made us hail her a moment earlier. Just because she has turned out to be someone other than we expected does not really make her a bit less interesting. Had she indeed turned out to be who we expected, she would have been someone quite accepting of our rapt attention to her face, body, and costume. But she is not that particular friend, and our searching gaze can be interpreted by her as an unwelcome intrusion. It is shame affect that is triggered to reduce our level of interest in a situation where every other stimulus operates to continue the process of amplifying our interest.

The more excited the organism, the more shame is triggered when this impediment is sensed; the more enduring our interest in the stimulus that triggered our attention, the more shame will be needed to reduce our interest. Similarly, the more we had been in the throes of enjoyment–joy, of the contentment produced by some stimulus capable of producing pleasure by reduction in stimulus level, the more shame affect will operate to *interfere with the ability of the affect program to continue its action of amplifying the decrease in stimulus density!*

A dauntingly difficult concept? You bet. Let's take an example and see how it works. Consider the plight of a small child who sees an interesting stranger as a novel stimulus and is burning with excitement at the prospect of studying his or her face and body. Had the child no machinery for the recognition, storage, retrieval, and comparison of patterns, it might not know that this individual is a stranger. It is these complicated neocortical mechanisms that allow the child to understand the new person as novel and therefore a source of interest. Precisely because the face of the stranger does not conform to any pattern already present in its storehouse of remembered patterns, it becomes a stimulus for the investigation we call interest.

Faces, however, are more than mere sources of interest. They belong to people, and people differ greatly in how they respond to full, unthrottled, push-the-accelerator-pedal-to-the-floor investigation—which, of course, is the normal way small children undertake an investigation. There are rules for the investigation of faces. What starts out as a competent trigger for innate interest is now remembered to be a face, the face of a person who might object to staring, who might get angry—in general, who might not allow the mutualization of interest so important to friendly human interaction. The very pattern that had just a moment ago been the stimulus for interest now can act as an impediment to the further examination of the novel individual.

Suddenly, perhaps providentially, shame affect (the amplification of impediment) is triggered. Eyes that had only a moment earlier been burning with curiosity now are averted, the bodily posture of fervent interest abruptly afflicted by the slumped neck and shoulders of shame. Swiftly the child withdraws behind the safety of mother's leg, peeking out from behind mother, darting a glance now and again, still burning with curiosity but now partially restrained by shame. Active, full-fledged interest has not been thwarted completely. It has been reduced, impeded, painfully constrained for a little while. The natural desire of the child to explore what it finds compelling will eventually win, but at the cost of experiencing shame.

The innate affect shame, like all the other affects, does not start out as anything remotely like an emotion. It is a biological system by which the organism controls its affective output so that it will not remain interested or content when it may not be safe to do so, or so that it will not remain in affective resonance with an organism that fails to match patterns stored in memory. Unlike the other innate mechanisms, the existence of which can be traced as far back in evolution as the reptile, it is quite recent. Shame–humiliation could not appear until life forms had developed powerful tools for the perception, storage, retrieval, and comparison of complex images. It protects an organism from its growing avidity for positive affect.

Let's look at another aspect of this. There are lots of times that an advanced organism is fascinated or delighted and continues to experience that affect as long as the stimulus conditions meet the criteria for fascination or contentment. When the stimulus is no longer novel, interest fades; when there is no more stimulus to reduce, enjoyment fades. These are the conditions for what we call boredom.

But now and again, as mentioned a moment ago, the organism becomes fascinated by, or involved in, or starts sharing laughter with, a quite ordinary source for that affect but hits an impediment to the continuation of that affect. Sometimes what drew our interest remains compelling. Whenever we cannot immediately and voluntarily reduce the intensity of the affect so triggered, some mechanism sends a message to the affect center and an *interrupt* signal is dispatched. The method of interruption is simple—the face is removed from involvement with the fascinating or enjoyable source. It reduces the possibility that new data about this source will be received through perception and tends to limit, attenuate, or impede further affective resonance. It is the physiological mechanism that underlies all of the experiences we come to know as the shame family of emotions.

I think I know how one part of it works, but I haven't as yet been able to get funding or time for the laboratory experiments to prove my theory. My hypothesis is that shame affect involves a neurochemical, a substance secreted in the ancient subcortical portion of the brain, a compound that causes sudden widening or dilatation of the blood vessels in the brain. I think this substance, which we would call a *vasodilator*, sets off the mechanism responsible for the sudden loss of tone in the muscles of the neck, causing the head to droop and the eyes to drop from contact with the shaming other. Sometimes you can see the entire body droop in the moment of shame, as when by defeat an athlete is humiliated in public. Perhaps public situations require more interest and attention, and therefore a larger "dose" of this chemical. We hold ourselves more erect in public and therefore are all the more reduced by shame.

Earlier in evolution, before the development of the "higher centers" of cognition, all that shame affect did was turn off the positive affects. But the more complex the brain became, the more functions came to be influenced by shame. In *The Emotions*, Jean-Paul Sartre described shame as "an immediate shudder which runs through me from head to foot without any discursive preparation" (261), a disruption so powerful that it felt to him like "an internal hemorrhage." Darwin saw this "confusion of mind" as a basic element in shame: "Persons in this condition lose their presence of mind, and utter singularly inappropriate remarks. They are often much distressed, stammer, and make awkward movements or strange grimaces" (1872, 332).

I can't think clearly in the moment of embarrassment, and I don't know anybody else who can. It seems to me that this "cognitive shock" is the sort of thing that could happen if the higher thinking centers were suddenly to be bathed with a substance that dilated blood vessels.

The "time curves" of the other affects seem to fit Tomkins's hypothesis that each is an amplifier of its stimulus conditions, with a "shape in time" just like its trigger. But shame is "a short fuse with a slow burn." It lasts longer than I would expect just on the basis of its resemblance to the detection of an impediment. Perhaps it lasts a bit longer because its function is to limit interest or enjoyment when we don't really want to give up that preceding affect. Continuing interest would then have to be blocked by continuing shame affect, which would make shame last as long as the interesting situation continued to be novel or enjoyable. Similarly, whatever made us experience contentment by reducing stimulus gradient and density might continue to attract our attention and tempt us to allow it to continue making us feel good, which would also make shame last as long as there was a stimulus for us to enjoy. Nevertheless, the other affects seem to be crisper mechanisms. Shame, even at its most fleeting, feels to me like the ebb and flow of a humoral mechanism, something operating over a longer period of time than the others.

Isn't the blush merely a matter of dilated blood vessels? No one has ever explained why so many of the affects are associated with changes in the microcirculation of the face. We suspect that there are nerve fibers coursing from the subcortical brain to the facial blood vessels, just as the subcortical brain sends *bulbofacial* nerves to facilitate the contraction of the facial muscles during affect. (It is nerves from the neocortex, *corticofacial* fibers, that are responsible for voluntary movement of the facial muscles.) But that would not account for the frequent observation that some people blush all over the head and neck, even down to the entire chest! Here, too, I suspect that we are dealing with a chemical substance that dilates blood vessels and that people vary considerably in the amount they manufacture as well as the regions of the body outside the brain that may be affected. It is possible that the vasodilator substance can be manufactured at more than one location, thus accounting for the tremendous variability in individual sensitivity to blushing.

Maybe I'm wrong to postulate a neurohumoral vasodilator. Affect theory, as originally propounded by Tomkins, would suggest that shame affect works by another, equally simple mechanism. All that is needed is for the affect program to reduce tone in the neck muscles and turn the face away from contact with the now problematic situation. That alone would account for much of what we know about shame—whatever had triggered interest or enjoyment would be removed from view. And that movement itself might call attention to the nature of the just-detected impediment, accounting for the moment of confusion associated with shame. Given the wonderful new equipment available to the researcher, my addition to affect theory is easy to disprove. We need only hook up a willing volunteer to one of the harmless new devices that measure circulation inside the brain (by computer analysis of X-ray data) and see if shame causes a transient increase in cerebral blood flow.

Others among my colleagues have suggested that I set up a laboratory capable of detecting the levels of known vasodilator compounds and check the amounts of these substances in the blood of people before, during, and after a shame experience. I look forward to the opportunity to direct such research.

The existence of a "shame chemical" might make a lot of things easier for us psychiatrists. There are many people who are unusually sensitive to embarrassment, who seem always poised at the edge of shame. It might make their lives easier were we able to find and block a chemical system responsible for their discomfort. Such ideas are quite controversial because there is great debate over the very notion of "tampering with the mind." But, for shame as well as all the other innate affects, such debates must be postponed until we start looking for the neurochemical systems that make them work.

For each of the eight preceding affects I have described some of the assemblies by which it is experienced as feeling, emotion, or mood, and the biological disorders in which it may figure. I will outline some of the ways shame figures in this sort of scheme, but it will take the remainder of the book to fill out this sketch to its full dimensions. It is not difficult to imagine that such an affect mechanism might find its way into a great many assemblies.

Consider, for a moment, some of the properties of shame affect that must occupy our attention. It is a painful experience. Shame interrupts affective communication and therefore limits intimacy and empathy. Shame interferes with neocortical cognition. In its basic role as an impediment to interest—excitement and enjoyment—joy, it can interfere with everything on earth that we enjoy, from the thrill of scientific discovery to the joy of sex.

I like to start with the ideas of Léon Wurmser, the psychoanalyst whose powerful book *The Mask of Shame* so affected me when I began the study of what was then called "the ignored emotion." Using affect theory and infant observation, I try to take physiological affect programs that are equally present in all babies and watch them turn into emotions as the growing child accumulates experience. From the opposite vantage point, that of a psychoanalytic archaeologist who searches for the childhood antecedents to adult experience using the uncovering technique pioneered by Freud, Wurmser called shame a layered emotion.

During the moment of shame, he pointed out, certain thoughts are likely to occur—some near the surface, others accessible only by attention to the world of the unconscious as revealed in dreams and free association. "What one is ashamed for or about," he says, "clusters around several issues: (1) I am weak, I am failing in competition; (2) I am dirty, messy, the content of my self is looked at with disdain and disgust; (3) I am defective, I have shortcomings in my physical and mental makeup; (4) I have lost control over my body functions and my feelings; (5) I am sexually excited about suffering, degradation, and distress; (6) watching and self-exposing are dangerous activities and may be punished" (27–28). Like most writers on shame, Wurmser agrees that the emotion usually follows a moment of exposure, and that this uncovering reveals aspects of the self of a peculiarly sensitive, intimate, and vulnerable nature.

One of the most prominent groups within the shame family of emotions consists of the feelings we know as *guilt*. Try as we might, we have been unable to find a physiological mechanism, an innate affect, that would explain guilt in any way other than its relation to shame. Included in the experience of guilt is a moment of discovery or exposure. In some cases the exposure is actual, while in other cases it is fantasized. But since shame follows the exposure of what one would wish hidden, we may be sure that shame is involved in guilt.

Certainly guilt feels different from shame; nevertheless, it appears that guilt involves, at the very least, shame about action. Usually this action is one that has violated some rule or law or that has caused harm to another person. Guilt, however, seems to contain some degree of fear of retaliation on the part of whoever has been wronged by our action, so we might say that it involves a coassembly of the affects shame and fear. Empirically, we know that guilt often involves both the shame that lies latent in hidden action and the fear of retribution. Since fear blanches the face, this might be the reason most people do not blush when guilty, despite how redfaced they get when embarrassed. And the vasoconstriction of fear might alter the ability of facial affect receptors to sense the presence of shame.

Such a definition of guilt fits our experience as adults. The most powerful among us feel the most free to undertake courses of action that violate all sorts of rules. Fear of retribution seems unimportant to those who can afford unlimited legal representation or against whom no one has power. Since lawyers can protect us from real damage, with maturity comes relative disdain for civil retribution. Shame is by far the more commanding affective experience in the life of mature, successful people. It is the fall from grace, the loss of face, the forfeiture of social position accompanying exposure, that we fear most.

Throughout the book I will demonstrate that the shame mechanism is triggered often in situations that we do not recognize as embarrassing, painful circumstances when our attention is drawn from whatever had attracted us and we are momentarily ill at ease. The psychologist Helen Block Lewis called this "bypassed shame," when people experience what she called a "wince" or a "jolt to the self" (1971, 1981), and then begin to worry that the other person is thinking bad thoughts about them. There are many such situations in which we fail to recognize that we are in a moment of shame, so it is important to acknowledge that the affect is not always interpreted as one of the feelings normally associated with shame. In general, what we call "hurt feelings" is caused by shame affect—these are always moments when a positive affect is interrupted by the painful affect of shame.

For the most part, however, shame is known to us in a variety of feeling-states. Even though each of these states carries a different label, each resembles the other in that the core affect is shame. Thus some people might say that they are *shy* around strangers, *embarrassed* when they experience shame in the presence of others, and *humiliated* when this shame is the result of an aggressive attack on them by a valued other.

Later in the book I will show how shame gets to be associated with privacy and the world of the hidden, but for the moment let us look at some of the results of that association. We have noted that shame often attends the exposure of something that we would have preferred kept hidden, of a private part of the self. There are a host of exposure experiences in which we feel a variety of minor shame feelings, and a huge number of circumstances when the betrayal of a confidence leaves us feeling exposed and humiliated. I think that whether we call such experiences shame, embarrassment, humiliation, mortification, discouragement, or by other terms depends mostly on our lifetime experiences of shame affect.

So from my point of view, whenever we realize that our face has turned abruptly from the previously interesting or enjoyable or empathic other, and/or our eyes become downcast, and/or our confusion bad enough that we are unable to talk, we are experiencing some variety of shame. Each member of the shame family of emotions involves, like all the emotions, no more than one or another group of associations to shame—the coassembly of one's memory of previous similar experiences of shame affect with the shame of the moment.

Everybody who writes about shame has his or her own idea of what these names mean, and I don't think one list is any more valid than another. Sure, I would agree that the Latin root *mort* means death, and that the state of mortification implies being shamed to death, but I have no idea what you mean (or what any other individual means) when you differentiate between embarrassment and mortification unless we get to know each other very well and learn about each other's lives. Implicit in the process of getting to know another person is the sharing of whatever information is necessary to enable us to understand each other's emotions.

When memory brings forth an earlier but unresolved experience of shame, like the crushing sense of betrayal and loss that once accompanied the sundering of an important personal relationship, the aftershock of such a recollection may leave us in a shame-filled mood for a long period of time. Shame moods may become so toxic that they are interpreted by us and by others as "depression" and push us to ask for psychotherapy.

Nowhere has this been stated better than in this oft-quoted passage by Tomkins:

> If distress is the affect of suffering, shame is the affect of indignity, of transgression and of alienation. Though terror speaks to life and death and distress makes of the world a vale of tears, yet shame strikes deepest into the heart of man. While terror and distress hurt, they are wounds inflicted from outside which penetrate the smooth surface of the ego; but shame is felt as an inner torment, a sickness of the soul. It does not matter whether the humiliated one has been shamed by derisive laughter or whether he mocks himself. In either event he feels himself naked, defeated, alienated, lacking in dignity or worth. (1963, 118)

Small wonder that the overwhelming majority of people who seek the aid of professional therapists bring complaints in the realm of shame. Of greater wonder is that until recently we failed to understand the many forms in which the pain of shame is disguised.

Can shame occur when there is no shamer, when no one has attempted to attack our integrity, when nothing has happened to expose us to ourselves? I think so. There are biological disorders of shame just as there are biological disorders of every other affect.

People who take medication to reduce high blood pressure, especially those drugs that decrease our sensitivity to the neurotransmitter *norepinephrine*, are likely to complain of "depression." Questioned closely, these patients seem to have a disorder of guilt, telling us that they have done something bad for which they should be punished even when they "know" they have not. Early in the era of experimentation that led to the development of the antihypertensive drugs, patients were given a chemical called *alphamethylparatyrosine*—a compound that resembles the amino acid *tyrosine*, one normally found in the body and which is important in the manufacture of norepinephrine. Although the patients given this compound were described only as "depressed," monkeys given the same medication were seen as socially withdrawn, unable to make facial contact with each other, likely to sit with bowed head and averted gaze. It is commonly said that these chemicals are interfering with the circuitry for normal mood, but I think they do this by producing an internal experience that can only be interpreted by the organism in terms of the innate affect shame.

As I have commented in the case of the other affects whose mechanism of action can be simulated by biological disorders, it seems likely that we interpret certain organic malfunctions in the language of shame. Patients with depression can be divided into two groups on the basis of whether their expressed symptoms are more shame-loaded or guilt-loaded. Those who complain more of guilt seem to respond better to the *tricyclic antidepressants* such as *imipramine*. These people are said to have a "typical" depression because psychiatrists have been trained to look for guilt.

Patients whose depression is characterized by complaints about their self-esteem or self-worth, about their need for the approval of others, their sensitivity to rejection, their sense of themselves as failures, or who say that they are in some way defective or deformed, are said to have an "atypical" form of depression or a "social phobia."[*] Likely this is atypical only because psychiatrists have not yet been trained to recognize the stigmata of shame, the most prominent affect in each of the symptoms described. Nonetheless, in general these patients respond well to the group of medications called the *monoamine-oxidase inhibitor antidepressants*, what we call the "MAOI" drugs, and the relatively new family of antidepressants represented by *fluoxetine* (Prozac). Not long ago one of my patients stopped her MAOI medication more rapidly than I would have liked, and experienced great discomfort. "I'm so embarrassed," she said over and over. "I feel so ashamed of myself." She was astonished to see these feelings of shame disappear when she resumed her medication.

Shame is rarely mentioned in psychopharmacologic studies of depression. It would, however, seem logical to implicate shame in a patient complaining of a morbid fear of being deformed. Michael A. Jenike (1984) reports the case of a young woman who had sought psychotherapy for feelings of shyness, low self-esteem, and inadequacy. Two days before her therapist left for vacation, this patient developed the terrifying feeling that she looked like a "monster." Translating this ideoaffective complex into the language of the body, she claimed that her face had become swollen to monstrous proportions, despite

*Liebowitz et al., 1985

the inability of competent observers to see anything unusual. Tricyclic antidepressants made her feel less depressed but more "crazy," while she
achieved complete resolution of all symptoms within four days of taking her
first MAOI drug.

Still other patients describe what I understand as shame due to interference
with normal affect physiology—occurring not as a steady-state phenomenon,
but all at once, in paralyzing bursts of incapacitating embarrassment or mental
pain interspersed with periods of relative comfort. I view this latter syndrome
as a disorder of shame affect directly analogous to panic disorder, in which the
patient is afflicted by bursts of fear–terror. "Shame panic" usually responds
well to varying doses of MAOI drugs or fluoxetine, either medication prescribed in combination with *alprazolam* (Xanax). Experience with this clinical
condition leads me to suggest that in it, neither type of medication works
adequately without the other.

I mentioned earlier my impression that guilt is a combination of shame and
fear, the two affects fused and hooked together with a wide range of memories
of situations in which we were caught doing forbidden things or breaking
rules. It seems logical to me that there is one form of depression caused by
biological interference with the circuitry for shame, and another form of depression that occurs when the circuitry for fear is affected as well. There are
other affects gone wrong in depression, notably distress (which accounts for
the tearful quality of depression); the term depression itself has become little
more than a wastebasket for a large group of uncomfortable and persistent
moods.

Some people are afflicted with chronic, unremitting shame. This noxious
affective state can be produced by interference with the normal functioning of
hardware or software; yet in either case the individual is equally uncomfortable. On occasion I have studied adults whose character structure was based
on an apparent "decision" to hide shame through the false (and highly exaggerated) display of both interest–excitement and enjoyment–joy. Everything,
everybody interests them; anybody, any situation can provide an opportunity
for the mutualization of laughter. Woe to the unwary other who fails to accept
such a brittle and artificial demand for mutualization, for such refusal of attunement is greeted by suspicion and anger quite resembling a paranoid display.

Tomkins (1963) and Kaufman (1989) have described another device used to
disguise chronic shame: Unable to prevent the lowered lids and averted face of
the innate affect itself, these individuals force themselves into direct gaze by
tipping the head back, jutting the chin forward, and adopting a disdainful look
through which they seem to be observing us as a lower form of life. Several

well-known television interviewers/personalities utilize this system of defense against shame.

There is much more to say about all of these aspects of shame, but for the moment I wish only to remind you that the innate affect is a physiological mechanism, a firmware script that guarantees the operation of functions that take place at a number of sites of action. The script for shame is dependent on the integrity of certain structures in the central nervous system, on many chemical mediators that transmit messages, and on the organizing principle stored in the subcortical brain as the affect program. No matter what shame or any other affect "means" to us, it is essential for us to keep in mind that we are dealing first and foremost with a mechanism that is initially free of meaning.

"Shame," says Tomkins, "strikes deepest into the heart of man." Sota, in the Talmud, says that "humiliation is worse than physical pain." Elsewhere in the Talmud, Baba Metzia says that "shaming another in public is like shedding blood." The poet Vern Rutsala speaks of "the shame of being yourself, of being ashamed of where you live and what your father's paycheck lets you eat and wear. . . . This is the shame of dirty underwear, the shame of pretending your father works in an office as God intended all men to do. This is the shame of asking friends to let you off in front of the one nice house in the neighborhood and waiting in the shadows until they drive away before walking to the gloom of your house."

We have much to do if we are to explain how a physiological mechanism, one that evolved as a modulator of other physiological mechanisms, has evolved further into so potent a source of pain. Shame is intimately tied to our identity, to our very concept of ourselves as human. To the extent that man is a social animal, shame is a shaper of modern life. It may be that shame has built the border between what each of us knows as the outside world and the inner realm we have come to call the unconscious. Some have gone so far as to say that there would be no unconscious were it not for shame! It is to the ubiquity of shame that we will now turn our attention.

II

The Development of Shame and Pride

11

THE FACES OF SHAME

"There's this girl at work," began Casey, "who blushes and turns away every time you look at her. Everybody notices it. And she's real pretty, too. I almost think that she's prettier than she can handle." Embarrassed himself at the apparent irrationality of that statement (after all, isn't she in control of how pretty she looks?), he paused for a moment to check my face to see if I thought he was being silly. I nodded, and he continued. "I mean, she's so pretty that you can't help looking at her. But every time somebody does look at her, she runs away and can't talk for a couple of minutes."

Let's not speculate why this young woman experiences shame when noticed. There are lots of possible reasons, all of them interesting, none of them really important right now. All I want is for you to recognize that shame can be expressed by a gesture—sudden withdrawal of the face from the view of others—accompanied by the autonomic display of blushing and a brief period of apparent confusion. It is neither subtle nor suggestive. Seen in infant or adult, this is the plain, unvarnished, undisguised face of innate affect.

Casey himself demonstrated another form of shame recently. Walking into a session with his usual friendly and polite greeting, he seemed thereafter somewhat remote and inaccessible. None of his statements carried any affective tonality; everything he said, notwithstanding its content, was courteous, pleasant, and lifeless. Some minutes later he broke into his description of a hockey game to mention, as if in passing, that he had goofed at work, but with so little emphasis that when (a few seconds later) he resumed his description of the game I did not think further about it. He was unfailingly pleasant, steadfastly and resolutely proper. Everything he said was clear, cogent, well-phrased. Paradoxically, despite the apparent clarity of his statements, I felt the session becoming more and more vague and unfocused. It was turning out to be one of the most boring psychotherapy sessions I had ever endured.

There are lots of procedures a therapist can follow in such a situation. Usually we call attention to those words or phrases used by the patient that seem to carry a lot of emotion, using displayed affect as a guide to hidden meaning. But in this session every one of his statements seemed just like every other—there was no evident emotion. It was clear that Casey really did want psychotherapy, really wanted to work on some issue that contained intense emotion, but was somehow prevented from discussing it more directly. Sometimes the clue comes from how the therapist feels during the interaction. In this case, I had the weird feeling that I was a Roman Catholic priest receiving confession from a dutiful boy whose behavior was too good to be true.

No matter what I said, he responded only by pausing or nodding politely. I had never seen him so emotionally constricted. Since he wasn't giving me any more clues, I decided to use my own emotional reaction as a guide. Perhaps feeling like a priest in a confessional was a serviceable empathic response to something going on in Casey. Maybe this is how he felt about me—that he had been forced by custom to attend confession when there was a lot he wanted to keep private.

After a moment of hesitation, I conveyed that idea to him. He chuckled briefly at the idea of his Jewish psychiatrist feeling like a priest, and then turned away. I took that gesture as a hint that I was on the right track and pressed further. What might have happened to change our interaction from its more usual free-spirited interchange to this constrained and limited form of discourse? Had he perhaps suffered some insult so severe that the resulting shame had rendered him essentially speechless? Casey mentioned the incident at work I had ignored earlier, and said it had been "pretty difficult" for him.

Even knowing what had happened did not make the session suddenly work well. Although Casey wanted to tell me what had happened to him, the very forces that had made him so uncharacteristically dull and restricted now conspired to prevent him from finding words for his experience. So much was he forced to resist the process of self-revelation that we "joked" occasionally that it seemed "like pulling teeth."

The error itself was simple to understand. From a list of possible entries he had told the computer the wrong interest rate around which a huge list of client bills was then calculated. Swiftly the implacable automata of the business world churned out stacks of paper stuffed automatically into envelopes with immediately metered postage, stopped from programmed delivery to the post office and thence to clients by only the merest of coincidences. Was it a small error, an understandable error, an important error, or an unforgivable error? Had he himself caught the blunder before it came to anybody's attention, Casey's emotional reaction might have been the mixture of fear and relief we all experience when escaping danger. But the boner was spotted when the maximum number of people might find out about it. And it was detected by the rival who stood to profit most from Casey's reduction in public esteem.

Have I sketched in adequate detail the reasons for his humiliation? There is yet more. Casey is young, handsome, single, well-liked, and the youngest of eight brothers—all of whom work in the business founded by their father. Understandably, the women of this firm see themselves at considerable competitive disadvantage relative to those eight heirs apparent. Casey's error was discovered by the woman most senior in his office, the person who feels most thoroughly stigmatized and perhaps victimized by her gender. The broadcast and dissemination of his goof were revenge so sweet that, these many months later, she still smiles knowingly at him whenever they pass in the halls.

Excruciating. Who wouldn't be humiliated in such a situation? But I introduce Casey to demonstrate another, quite specific facet of shame, one that derives clearly from the innate mechanisms discussed in the preceding chapter. The very deadness that characterized Casey's verbal output was a clue to the presence of shame. Shame affect operates to reduce interest–excitement and enjoyment–joy, the affects that make us vital, lively, charming, fun, interesting, enjoyable, exciting, charismatic, thrilling, inspiring, and appealing. If you wonder why someone lacks vitality, look first for nearness to shame.

These two stories illustrate something else. You will notice that not once did I mention the inner experience of shame. I avoided any discussion of how Casey *felt* when his error was discovered, or how he feels each time his supervisor reminds him of this incident, or how it influences his ability to work and flirt with his colleagues. Similarly, I avoided any mention of the inner world, the private feelings of the young woman whose beauty brings more attention than she can handle. What I depicted might be called the visible expressions of shame affect acting as an innate attenuator circuit. These are the places where we outsiders can see the affect at work.

Next, we need to consider how it *feels* to have an attenuator, a limiting device that you can't control, one that simply takes over when you least expect. From what we have presented about the nature of shame as an affect that limits the expression of other affects, it should be clear that shame can interfere with any human activity. But what is the inner experience or, more properly, what is the range of inner experiences that accompany the action of this attenuator? Recall Sartre's comment that shame "runs through me from head to foot without any discursive preparation." No matter how often we have been shamed, the attenuator event is still relatively unexpected.

All this is from the standpoint of an adult, a fully-grown person prowling about the planet in pursuit of life, liberty, and happiness, a mature human in acceptably good command of his or her faculties. Equally interesting is the problem of what it is like to grow up with a limiting device you can't control. I know more about my daily experience as an adult than I can possibly remember about the earliest years after birth. As a mature adult I have come to accept the pattern of powers and limitations typical of the complex system that I recognize as *me*, the system we call "the self." I can walk, read, work, earn, eat, and type at such-and-such a pace; I have come to understand and accept the limits of my ability to store and recall information; there is just so much that I can get done on a particular day; and I know all this from experience. I know when I am happy, I know when I am excited, I know when I am aroused, and I know when I am embarrassed.

Each of these intricate combinations of affects, cognitions, and drives has been experienced by my adult self so often that it has some sort of "name," some label that allows assignment to its proper compartment of my mind. By now, it is rare that anything feels entirely new; everything pretty much resembles something else. It was not thus when I was a child.

Observe, for a moment, the household cat. As a kitten, it lives in a world of constant novelty, to which it responds with curiosity, the playful interest we find so charming. The older it gets, the more our pet sleeps. This is not a mere reduction in activity consequent to bodily aging but the loss of novelty precluding the activation of interest—excitement. Even an ancient feline will act like a kitten in the presence of a totally new stimulus, as (for instance) when it is released into new surroundings. But it is a wise and sedentary old cat because it recognizes what it has already learned and wastes little energy on the process of "discovering" what it already knows.

Like the kitten, the human infant is similarly occupied by novelty. Early enough in development, every adventure is novel—it has not occurred prior to this moment. (True, what has been initiated with interest may be terminated by any negative affect. But new situations normally trigger interest.) By forming associative linkages between each experience and the affect that accompanies it, the baby builds from nothing an increasingly extensive lexicon of emotion. Although we see evidence of the operation of each innate affect from birth, it is obvious that as we age affective experiences take on new realms of meaning. Sometimes a baby is scared by a situation that would not upset the more worldly and experienced toddler. Sometimes the child has neither background nor equipment to comprehend and thus experience danger as might an adult. But, occasionally, what frightens a newborn may yet threaten a toddler, strike fear into the heart of an adolescent, or terrify an adult.

In each case the affect is identical, but at each stage of development the individual will bring to the experience of affect a different level of appreciation. So, too, does the experience of shame shift and change during development. Shame affect is triggered throughout life, but the shame family of emotions develops slowly and somewhat differently for all.

The easiest way I can visualize both the changes in the infant's equipment (including the way the developing brain picks up new abilities) and the way that equipment responds to shame affect is through my appreciation of beginner-level chemistry. To me, solitary things and unitary concepts are like atoms, which, when linked, form combinations like molecules.

Take, for instance, the element chlorine, by itself a noxious (even poisonous) green gas at room temperature. Bubbled through water, chlorine turns into hydrochloric acid. In purified form, the element sodium is a silvery, light, shiny metal. When added to water, sodium combines with it to form the caustic and destructive compound we call lye (sodium hydroxide). Yet sodium and chlorine can combine with each other to make white crystalline sodium chloride—table salt—a chemical necessary for life. Neither element resembles table salt in any way, yet both are necessary for its manufacture. If we combine iron with chlorine we get a green salt called ferric chloride that neither tastes good nor is necessary for life. All chemicals that contain chlorine are alike in that we call them "chlorides," despite how very different they may be.

Now let's see what happens if we view shame affect as if it were an element and try to find out what familiar molecules contain it. Some will turn out to be easily recognizable compounds, emotional states we have always understood to be part of the shame family of emotions. Others will look quite strange in the list of shame-related states, for shame affect turns out to be involved in situations that may surprise you. The shame family of emotions is just as complex and varied as the chloride family of chemicals. In the next few chapters I will identify shame in a great many of its assemblages, demonstrate the sequence of events leading to the development of each assembly, and suggest reasons for the differences in power and impact of each resultant emotion.

Over and over I have stated that people differ both in their descriptions and their apparent experience of shame. Who we are is dependent on how we got to be us—each of us is the product of our development. How we experience and identify shame is contingent on the importance to us of the situation in which the attenuator of shame affect is triggered.

For some, shame is a moment when they wish a hole would open up and swallow them; it makes them want to disappear, for they feel at risk of death. Others experience shame as a failure of such proportion that the entire self is suddenly disvalued—now their whole person is worthless and deserving only of exile. "Attacked" by shame, one can estimate the "damage" over a broad compass, from the total destruction of one's self-esteem to the relatively minor devaluation of a superficial attribute. There are those who seem quite capable of "forgetting" or disavowing a moment of embarrassment—they merely go on as if nothing has happened. Women, more likely than men, tend to experience and describe shame in the language of shame. Men, in our society, are taught to experience shame as an excuse or a stimulus for anger and describe shame in the language of insult and threat. For many men, shame triggers immediate rage and fighting, as in the motion picture cliché called the barroom brawl. And at the opposite end of the activity spectrum sit those who withdraw into depression when humiliated. Children giggle when embarrassed, clowns make sport of shame, satirists and sadists use it as a weapon.

As a boy I was warned to guard my wallet when in crowds. "Be especially careful," said my father, "when somebody announces that there are pickpockets around. Hicks and rubes immediately check to make sure their money is safe. They reach for the pocket where they keep their wallet. And that's how the thieves know where to look!" Sometimes shame does the same sort of thing. No matter what has caused a moment of embarrassment, there are people who tend to think about what they most want to hide, rather than the actual triggering stimulus. Their inner and outer reactions are guided by whatever else they have hidden. "I feel so fat!" says one of my friends whenever she is embarrassed. Another looks automatically at the zipper of his trousers, as if his genitals—rather than his thoughts—had suddenly been exposed.

How does shame mold character? Some folks are brassy and apparently shameless, others are cautious, still others so frightened at the possibility of humiliation that they become paranoid, withdrawing from human contact lest something be exposed. The mere glint of sex will throw some people into paroxysms of shame, while others bask in sensuality. Why should this be? What can make an unvarying affect, a physiological mechanism, into so diverse a spectrum of experienced emotions? How can shame be at one time only a moment of discomfort related to a single special attribute, and at others a feeling of such destructive force that it represents the dissolution of the self? Why is shame sometimes an earthquake but now and then no more than a giggle?

Here is a clue: The mind of the child is not the mind of the adult. Abilities and attributes, all latent and potentially present in the brain and body of the infant, "come on line" in different epochs of development. We take it for granted that every event is stored as a memory linked with the affect that accompanied it, yet we must recognize that the meaning and significance of that memory (its ability to act as an association for later experiences of affect, and therefore as a part of the complex emotionality of shame) will be determined by the special qualities of thinking and the special types of experience characteristic of that era. We can identify certain themes in the progress of the child toward maturity, and an understanding of these vectors will aid considerably our perception of the varied assemblages that include shame affect.

Thus, in order to explain the tremendous variability of the presentations of shame in the adult, the enormous range of subjects about which we may grow embarrassed, and the spectrum of significance to each of us of our shame-based cognitions, it may be helpful to sketch the modern concept of child development. How does the baby differ from the adult, and what happens along the way? What are the changes that take place as newborn becomes baby, baby becomes toddler, toddler a schoolchild, then adolescent, full adult, perhaps spouse and parent, and finally an old and perhaps widowed senior citizen?

The key phrase, of course, is *growth and development*. We clinicians and teachers tend to use these two important words, expressions that reference the governing forces in this transformation from infancy to adulthood, as if they were a unitary pair. Not so. They represent related but different concepts. By *growth* we mean increases in size, certain changes in shape, and increases in strength that characterize the movement through time of the infant. *Development* is the process by which already existing structures change in some manner, altering toward their final function. The tiny infant boy grows into a hulking adult man; by the time his endocrine system has developed to the point where he can sprout a beard, most of his growth has been completed. Girls have achieved their maximum height by the time their endocrine system has developed to the point where they can begin to menstruate. Indeed, manufacture of the hormone responsible for bodily growth is switched off by the process that allows release of the hormones responsible for the development of adult sexual characteristics.

The basic themes of growth and development involve changes in (1) size and strength; (2) dexterity and physical skill; (3) dependence vs. independence; (4) cognitive ability; (5) communication; (6) the sense of self; (7) gender identity and sexuality; and (8) interpersonal skills. Just for a moment, pick any of these eight realms of change and consider the differences between baby and grownup. How tiny and helpless the infant; how stalwart and majestic the adult! How primitive and nonspecific its cry of distress, especially in contrast to the delicacy, nuance, and specificity of complaint available to the adult. No one can detect the gender of a newborn infant without examining its genitals, yet note how clearly gender is signaled by the adult. And so on through the list.

Is it really possible to separate these intertwined vectors of change? Aren't they all immutably connected? Yes, they are linked, but not as solidly as you might believe. Nature distributes its bounty along a bell-shaped curve. The great majority of us grow to the range of height we therefore call normal, while some are midgets and others giants. One can achieve the height of an adult in childhood or become a chronological adult while still partially resembling a child. Usually, age is linked to height, and height thereby associated with other age-determined signs of growth. But occasionally we see ten-year-old boys who are six feet tall, who have adult stature but remain in other respects quite definitely ten years old. The streams of growth and development can run at different rates, suggesting that they are many and separate.

As a matter of fact, we all know people who are big but clumsy, or who have the cognitive equipment of a genius but the interpersonal skills of a toddler, or who demonstrate the dexterity of a watchmaker but the emotional dependence of a tot. If there is a system by which adult attributes are distributed, it is a system with much inequity. There are few guarantees; wish does not control destiny; biology is not a shopper's world.

Over the next few chapters I will make the case that (unless something interferes with the process) pride is attached to the acquisition of each moiety of normal growth and development and shame is attached to any failures along the way. As each way station on the road to maturity is reached, it soon loses its power to trigger pride; while at all stages in development reminders of one's previous (and therefore more primitive) status remain capable of activating shame. We will discuss all of the themes mentioned above, suggest the forms of pride and shame associated with movement along each stream, and draft some sort of blueprint from which we can understand the many faces of shame.

In chapter 4 I introduced one simple schema for pride: The child must have a want or a wish; it must be capable of making some sort of plan to suit and serve that need; it must then be capable of taking some action toward a related goal; successful action must be accompanied by (amplified by) either or both of the positive affects interest–excitement or enjoyment–joy, as, say, interest to power the activity and enjoyment to reward it. The entire sequence of wish/plan/affect/action/affect, the sequence itself, is then recorded as a pattern and labeled as an instance of pride.

As for shame, recall that Tomkins's theory also requires quite a few pieces of equipment. In order to experience shame the organism must have a sophisticated perceptual apparatus capable of registering minute alterations in stimuli generated both from the environment and from within. The data provided by these sensors must be assembled into patterns that the organism can recognize. There must be machinery capable of storing the patterns so generated, systems permitting the retrieval of this stored data, and procedures for the comparison of these retrieved patterns both with each other and with the new images constantly being formed by current perception. It is only when an impediment is detected which disturbs the expected flow of the affects interest or enjoyment that shame affect is triggered to reduce painfully that preceding positive affect. The resulting amalgam of memory, drive, affect (and anything else capable of being assembled with affect) will be recorded as a pattern and labeled as an instance of shame.

Who has such equipment, who can experience shame and pride? Not fish, turtles, earthworms, birds, insects, or snakes. Each of them has enough brain power to form a few patterns; snakes may even have some of the rudimentary equipment necessary for the equivalent of a few innate affects. None of them has enough to make shame affect. That really isn't as silly as you might think, for a mechanism protecting an organism from being locked in interest might protect moths from being killed by their fascination with an open flame and other insects from getting stuck and dying in incandescent light fixtures. Dogs, apes, and man certainly can experience shame.

For better or worse, we have evolved into shame. But the qualities of shame depend on the nature of the patterns involved. Human infants demonstrate a rudimentary form of shame based on the rudimentary patterns made available by whatever parts of their equipment are available for use. The more equipment at one's disposal, the more patterns that can be discerned in the data presented by the organs of perception, and the more these patterns can be stored and retrieved for the purpose of comparison.

How are these patterns formed, and what is the range of knowledge they represent? Experience turns into knowledge only as it gets registered in memory. This is easy enough to accept for the activities of a fully grown or developmentally stable organism. But how is that simple concept affected by the differences in the storage, retrieval, and associative abilities of newborn and adult? Are there patterns specific for, or at least typical of, each era?

Each action we take, each bodily function we use, each effort of psyche or soma helps define us. As I mentioned a moment ago, part of what it means to be an adult is to have a more-or-less defined self. The sense of self changes greatly during development.

From infancy to senescence, as we age and change, each alteration in us must be perceived and understood to the degree possible at that time. Infants, of course, do form patterns—they learn to recognize the patterns that make us caregiving adults uniquely us, and they interact with us on the basis of that information. Similarly, they are learning to recognize themselves by the patterns that define them.

The complexity of these patterns is limited by the level of cognition possible at each stage. But when a new cognitive attribute comes on line, the child's ability to form patterns is enhanced and therefore altered. There are at least two levels of definition associated with developmental changes in cognition: On the one hand, the child now has the ability to perform some new function; on the other, it can recognize itself as the new being defined by these new accomplishments. Both the new ability and the associated new definition of self are patterns that figure into the geometry of shame and pride.

Babies burble, while toddlers talk. The mind that can communicate only in burbles and by the display of affect can handle far less complexity, master fewer patterns, than the mind that can learn and manipulate a vocabulary of words. Yet toddlers have only an elemental sense of grammatical structure. Soon, when they can speak in sentences, they will look down on the monosyllabic toddler as a city dweller looks down on a cave man. And they will do it in the new language appropriate to that phase of development.

The new attributes and abilities that become incorporated into our vocabulary of stored patterns mature into the reference library to which we adults compare any new perception or experience. The name we give to the resulting gestalt, the mixed bag of patterns stored in that reference library, is "the person" or "the self." The characteristics by which we know each other as persons or selves is the gestalt of our experience with those others—their "personality." Generally speaking, I experience me as a self, but I experience your personality. Both personalities, yours and mine, have evolved over time.

It is this process of evolution that will now occupy our attention. I will sketch the paths along which the infant journeys—indeed, the paths all of us have traveled to achieve adult status. Each advance will be shown as a nodal point for the definition of pride. Each bit of forward motion makes the preceding attribute into something slightly backward and archaic—the nidus around which can crystallize the later expression of shame.

12

SIZE AND SHAPE

In 1985 a singer named Randy Newman released an unexpectedly popular song called "Short People," in which he said, "Short people got no reason to smile." Although some listeners got angry at the unremitting string of insults based on size, almost everybody got the joke. Not only is height a source of pride, and lack of it a source of shame, but any time we are stuck for something to feel superior about, we can find people shorter than us and lord it over them. But why? How did size get linked with pride and shame?

As we age, we get larger. Most of us weight between five and ten pounds when born, and between 100 and 200 pounds as adults. We get longer, too. Babies, when uncurled, usually measure about two feet long; by full maturity, most adults more or less triple their birth length. We do not merely grow, we grow "up" because we get bigger in the vertical dimension. These increases in measurable size have tremendous importance to the growing child. Bigness is associated with power—the ability to accomplish tasks—and therefore efficacy. To the child, growing bigger means becoming less helpless and dependent, even though these concepts are not strictly the same. But in the mind of the child they become inextricably linked.

It is not just the child who is focused on size. The growth of children is noted and complimented by adults: "My goodness, what a big girl you are!" "Look how tall you've gotten!" "Hey! Look who's growing up!" There is a clear message, a definite emphasis on the unspoken "Look who's not little anymore!"

"Big" draws compliments—the verbal accompaniment of positive affect—therefore big is better than small. Anything that makes us a source of positive affect to ourselves, and (within certain limits) to others, becomes a source of personal pride. Thus most moves from small to big are sources of pride, while whatever reduces our size is a source of shame. We praise people by calling them "prominent," for a promontory is that which sticks out *above* the rest. Similarly, any reduction in size is likely to trigger shame, as when we *cut up* or *put down* another person, *tear down* a reputation, *diminish* someone's self-esteem. When we accuse a man of being "too big for his britches" we are saying that he is behaving as if he carried more weight than is actually his. A "swelled head" is about having too much of your self-esteem based on fantasy rather than real accomplishment, on wish or assumption rather than deed or fact. We psychiatrists are called "shrinks" because, just as other physicians reduce swelling in a joint or any other part of the body, one of our jobs is to reduce the swelling caused by inflated opinions about the self.

Bigness is about power. When we are little children, every increment in height and weight makes us better able to "stand up to" our peers and reduces the possibility that we will be tormented (and therefore humiliated) by somebody bigger. In the world of children, at least to a certain extent, with size comes strength. Although kids grow larger along a fairly predictable path, it is less easy to foretell increments in brute strength. In this matter of muscular attributes we vary, each to the other, much more than we vary in matters of height and weight. Especially is this important in early childhood, when slight differences in measurements make for huge disparity in power. What we experience as small children carries with us throughout life—big means pride, and small means shame.

We take it for granted that children are reared in the company of adults; thus, it is clear that children are always able to evaluate themselves in terms of these adults as their own likely final form. Pretty much, children know how they are going to turn out, the range of possible goals. Then, too, most are brought up around other children, who become therefore an additional standard of comparison.

All of this is pretty easy to understand when viewed at the level of children and authentic alterations in size and power. To a certain extent we would expect children to want to be larger. Some people from childhood—even into adult life—seem obsessed about size, focused inordinately on attributes relating to the axis of big and small. As we will discuss later, it turns out that they have suffered from other shame-based injury, such as a central feeling of not being loved. We humans are great bargain hunters. A prime characteristic of our internal psychological life is our avidity for deals in which we concentrate our attention on matters that resemble what bothers us most—matters of far less toxicity. Thus, notwithstanding how much discomfort a child feels about being short when she wants to be tall, this particular source of shame is a less undesirable focus of attention than the shame that floods us when we feel unlovable.

We insult people by labeling them as smaller than they really are. When, for his own emotional needs, a policeman must show his power, he examines the driver's licence of the motorist he has stopped and addresses him as James, or in the diminutive as Jim, or (even worse) as Jimmy—ignoring completely whatever status forms this driver's personal identity. Many southern Caucasians still intimidate and control their African-American employees by addressing them as "Boy." The trigonometry of size, the ratio of reduction achieved to preexisting self-image, and the exact degree of reduction in size needed to cause shame in any given individual on any given day will depend on other factors. Wherever a person sees himself as having a certain size, or expects that he will be viewed by others as being that size, he is capable of feeling shame when he is exposed as or treated as being smaller.

I hope this sketch of the relation between whole body size and shame or pride helps to convey the breadth of the problem facing anyone who tries to explain how a couple of relatively simple physiological mechanisms become adult emotions. There is an infinitude of possible patterns that can be made into reasons for pride or shame. If the possession of an attribute can make us proud, the sudden "loss" of that possession will cause shame, no matter what the nature of the attribute. Simple enough when it comes to bulk size, to patterns involving the whole self. What about sections of the body, small parts? Can they, too, be sources of shame and pride?

Do you admire the dancing of Fred Astaire? My wife has pointed out that "Fred Astaire was the essence of Art Deco." He was a master of line as well as movement. Astaire's linearity stands in sharp contrast to the curvier style of previous generations of dancers. Mikhail Baryshnikov, the preeminent male ballet dancer of our era, described him as one of the greatest dancers in history. Even standing still, dressed in the top hat, white tie, and tails that became his emblem, he seemed to be dancing elegantly. Actors, dancers, comedians who worked with him, friends who knew him off stage, everybody recognized his unique grace.

One of the women who danced with him (one of the many beautiful, supple, talented dancers who are remembered more for the fact that they danced with Astaire than for what they actually did on screen) asked why he had gone into the "lowbrow" world of motion picture dance rather than the classical ballet, where his greatness would have been acknowledged in a more conventional forum. His reason was astonishing. Fred Astaire felt that his hands were too big for classical ballet! He was certain that people would laugh at him for trying to appear graceful. The man who set the standard for masculine elegance and grace lived in shame because he had large hands.

Next time you get a chance, slow down a videotape of his dancing and try to see his hands. The number of tricks he used to hide them is remarkable, especially if you then compare his use of his hands to the work of any other male dancer. Sometimes he ducks his thumb under his palm and pulls the other fingers close together; at other times he curls the fingers. Almost never will you see his hands with the fingers spread out—even in the non-dancing dramatic scenes. Often a dancer will end a step or a complex routine in such a way that our focus is on his hands. Never Fred Astaire. But occasionally you can stop the videotape at just the right frame and study his hands. They were literally huge, especially in proportion to his slim, lithe frame.

So what? Why on earth should that have mattered to the greatest dancer America ever produced? The answer is that the person who decided his hands were too big for classical ballet was not the mature, adult Fred Astaire, the motion picture star admired by millions. The person who was so terribly concerned about his hands was probably a small boy to whom they were for some reason a constant source of shame.

Is the size of other body parts associated with shame and pride? Ask the plastic surgeon, whose life work is the repair of perceived defects. Myriads of people spend large amounts of money in an attempt to purchase a smaller nose or to vary the size of their breasts. Why? Men can be so concerned about the size of their penis that one could fill many books with the anecdotes, slurs, jokes, puns, retorts, and rejoinders designed to counteract the embarrassment associated with genital size. Why? "Body building" has become a national obsession, men and women alike struggling to achieve a degree or range of visible muscularity in conformity with ever-more-exotic norms. Some will take illegally prescribed hormones (steroids) in order to appear more muscular— despite the fact that such medication puts them at great risk of diabetes, early heart disease, and some forms of manic-depressive illness. What underlies this strange and often dangerous quest?

The answer is inherent in the way we grow up learning to handle our affects. Since there is relatively little we can do to prevent affects from being triggered (they are called forth by physiological mechanisms over which we have no control), we are forced to draw conclusions, to form ideas and concepts about our experiences of affect in order to gain some control over them. Through most of our years of growth and development, shame and pride are so often experienced over matters of size that for many of us the seesaw of feelings about ourselves (whether we are flustered and chagrined or calmly self-satisfied, our "position" on the oscillating system of the shame/pride axis) leads us to experience shame as if we were little and pride as if we were big.

Neither the surgical augmentation of one's breasts nor the exercise-induced hypertrophy of one's muscles makes one a bigger or a better person—but the sheer mass of people who experience pleasure and pride as a result of these maneuvers forces us to ask why they work to increase self-esteem. Adult humans seem to be able to live in a world of affective barter. We are willing to balance the decrease in self-esteem, the shame that accompanies recognition of one or another less-than-wonderful attribute, against the pride that derives from a completely different, unrelated sort of accomplishment.

Some reductions in size and power are so profound that our only recourse is to humor. The great actor John Barrymore, confined to bed during his final months and forced to accept severe limitations on all aspects of his life, bitterly resented the erosion of his accustomed self-esteem. Alcoholic cirrhosis had destroyed the ability of his liver to synthesize certain substances needed for life and to metabolize the protein in food. Staring at the thimble of wine and the tiny plate of edibles offered him, the Great Profile roused himself briefly, stared at his hapless nurse, and in the voice that had moved audiences for decades said, "And now, would you please bring me a postage stamp. I should like to do some reading."

In the world of shame and pride, size comes to be a metaphor of tremendous importance. The interest and enjoyment accompanying increases in size, and the shame-amplified impediments to these pleasures attending the recognition that we are somehow smaller than we thought, these affective experiences become the nidus around which are crystallized large portions of our personality.

13

DEXTERITY AND SKILL

It is not merely our tiny size that makes us helpless as infants. The long period of childhood, of utter dependence on others for basic care, is one during which we mature from thrashing, squalling little beings into competent adults capable of precise manipulation of complicated equipment. An infant, facing the computer terminal at which I write, would bang the keyboard with open hand—perhaps delighted at its success in hitting whole groups of keys—but it would be simply unable to address them one at a time. Even were the infant able to understand the logic involved in typing, it would be incapable of utilizing the machinery involved.

Newborn monkeys are able to clamber about the body of their mother while searching for her breast and can hold firmly to her fur while nursing. Human babies are less dexterous, for it seems there is a law of inverse ratios in evolution. The more advanced an organism, the less competent it is at birth and the longer it takes to mature into a fully developed adult. In the human, mastery of motor movements occurs over a predictable schedule. First we gain control over the large muscle groups needed for crawling and walking. Some many months afterwards we are capable of learning how to control fine motor movements and integrating the operation of hands and fingers.

Each developmental acquisition is by definition a new ability, each the source of pride for the growing child. Any time the child can plan an activity and accomplish it, that moment of efficacy will be experienced with pride. Parental pleasure at the child's growing competence adds to the storehouse of attributes linked to the pride experienced when we have made others happy.

Similarly, any time the child fails when attempting something he or she feels competent to perform, this failure will trigger shame. We can visualize the "circuitry" for this as follows: In order to anticipate the performance of a task the child must conceptualize it as a pattern. Inability to perform in accordance with this pattern forms a new, non-matching pattern. To the extent that the child remains interested in or excited by the task, involved in the result of its actions, effectively unable to detach its interest from that task, the disparity between the internalized, hoped-for pattern and the actual pattern created by its behavior now acts as an impediment to interest and triggers shame affect. Painfully, for shame is an extremely uncomfortable affective experience, interest is reduced and the child thus encouraged to focus on other activities.

Studying the ability of infants to plan actions and to assess the effects of their actions, one group of investigators set up a clever experiment. The husband and wife team of Papoušek and Papoušek (1975) took a group of three- to four-month-old infants and exposed them to five-second bursts of multicolored light situated off to one side. As we might expect, the babies treated this novel stimulus as a source of interest and turned toward it. Naturally, the novelty soon wore off, and after a while they began to lose interest in the lights.

But the experimenters had built another trick into the system. Any time a baby turned its head toward the light display more than 30 degrees and repeated this motion three times, the exciting display would be turned on. In other words, the experiment rewarded the baby for a specific piece of behavior. Apparently the babies loved it. Their behavior changed dramatically! As soon as they learned that certain repetitive gestures could bring on the light display, they became tremendously interested in this new activity and kept trying to repeat what now became a skill. Accompanying the actual movements of head rotation were squeals of joy when success greeted their efforts. As I have indicated earlier, this "competence pleasure" is what I believe to be one of the major sources of the complex adult emotion we call healthy pride.

Now the Papoušeks added a twist. On occasion they let the infant demonstrate its expertise—three purposeful rotations of the head in quick succession—but followed these actions by no rewarding burst of pretty lights. What happened next was fascinating. Most of the babies exhibited a sudden loss of muscle tone in the head and neck, slumping and turning their faces away from the now problematic situation. They seemed for all the world to be suddenly confused and uncoordinated. Their faces showed discomfort, their breathing intensified, and the blood flow to the skin increased.

The observers who set up the experiment understood that this moment of frustration had upset their subjects. It was Broucek (1982) who reinterpreted this data to explain it as an episode of primitive shame experience. Behavior performed in order to achieve a known pattern of events, an action that might reasonably be expected to produce its usual sequence of interest, effort, efficacy, enjoyment, and pride, now produced an unexpected pattern. This acted as an impediment to both interest and enjoyment, and triggered shame affect, which in turn decreased the infant's interest in further involvement with the experimental situation.

I have described this experiment in some detail in order to make another point that is critically important to our understanding of shame. Throughout the experimental situation these babies were not involved with other people. *This is an example of shame affect triggered in the clear absence of a relationship.* Because the mature, adult emotion of shame is seen predominantly in the context of an interpersonal relationship, and indeed becomes one of the basic monitors of all social functioning, many sober investigators have assumed that shame is at core a social emotion. It is not. The social function of shame is merely one possible assembly of shame affect, even though it is the assembly by which we know it best.

Again, we come back to my analogy to the family of chemicals known as chlorides. Chlorine can bleach clothing whiter than white. If you are going to recycle paper, chlorine bleaches will return even the grubbiest newsprint to shiny white. But the cancer-producing dioxins that leach out of the paper into our environment are also chlorides. Wouldn't we be foolish to restrict our understanding of chlorine to the study of table salt? It is the same for shame. Any time the affect system detects an impediment it is capable of engaging the attenuator called shame affect. The infant who blushes and becomes suddenly disorganized when unable to turn on a display of colored lights is neither embarrassed nor humiliated by this failure. It is in the grip of shame affect pure and simple, an affect mechanism that functions to suppress the excitement and enjoyment normally attending the exercise in progress.

I have come to believe that most of the time people complain that they are "confused" they are really describing an episode of shame affect. Even when we are reading or studying, paying attention to thought-provoking material, we have assembled some advanced neocortical function (a learned skill) with the affect interest–excitement. The very act of studying, or of trying intentionally to master new material, involves us in situations where we know ahead of time we do not understand the material. This sense of "difficultness," of complexity, is an acceptable quality inherent to the task we have taken on. But at the moment we feel *daunted* by this material, even momentarily *unable* to comprehend what we feel certain is within our range of abilities, shame affect is triggered to produce its painful interference with the positive affect that only a moment ago had powered our study.

Shame can attach to the very idea of a task, impeding further attempt at its completion; alternatively, shame can bring with it the resolve to work at a task until the achievement of mastery. Much depends on the way we are brought up and on biological, constitutional factors we understand poorly. But any time we take on something new we court pride and risk shame in the service of comprehension.

Occasionally we are able to break away from this temporary alteration of our mood, to decenter ourselves and pay attention to the emotion accompanying the confusion. (One must be fairly mature and centered to do this.) And on these occasions we may become aware that we are indeed embarrassed by our failure to comprehend the subject of our attention. But more often—indeed, most of the time—all we know is that we feel uncomfortably confused. Check this out the next time somebody comes to you with a question about something perplexing. I'll bet they address you with head somewhat bowed and turned to the side, shaking the head from side to side, saying "I don't get this." Although the stated complaint is about confusion, the broadcast affective message is about shame. Any failure of mastery produces shame.

Then, too, any time we wish to decrease the shame that accompanies our awareness that a task is daunting, we can merely make a (cognitive) decision to reduce the level of our interest in that activity. The ubiquity of this culturally sanctioned method of shame reduction may be adduced by inspection of the classical fable of the fox and the grapes. Daunted each time he attempts to snatch an apparently delectable bunch of grapes, the fox walks away with haughty pride, rather than shame and dejection, saying, "They were sour, anyway."

A patient gave another example of this process recently: Successful in every area of her life except the quest for a new husband, she reported meeting a man whose presentation of self excited her to feverish interest. Swiftly she located a mutual friend, who provided his telephone number, and prepared to call him. In the theater of her mind she previewed each possible outcome of her call, dwelling with terrible intensity on each imaginable form of rejection. The sheer mass of anticipated humiliation proved too daunting, and she decided not to place the call that evening.

Next day she was a bit less excited about the prospect of dating this man, saying, "I was much more in control of myself." Again she devised artistic scenarios of failure, but noticed that the humiliation was of lesser intensity in each. By the third day she noted neither an anticipation of rejection nor any significant interest in calling the man who had innocently sparked this three-day torture. There can be no shame in the absence of interest or enjoyment. To the extent that avoidance of shame is a central issue for any individual, reduction of interest will be a sturdy defense against shame.

Yet without interest life is dull. Adult patients who describe their experience of depression often say that nothing interests them. I understand the job of the clinician as the challenge of figuring out what has caused this decreased ability to trigger interest—excitement. Sometimes we use medication to return toward normal an aberration in neurotransmitter physiology deemed responsible for the perceived alteration of normal mood. But equally often we find that interest has been withdrawn in an effort to diminish the expectation of shame, and therapy is designed around this realm of causation.

In the world of infants, massive withdrawal of interest is called "apathy." The skilled clinician who sees an apathetic baby asks first whether the child has been presented with sources of novelty adequate to trigger interest, and then looks for the kind of disordered affective interaction that an infant might handle by withdrawal. An apathetic infant cannot learn, cannot advance properly in development, for the mastery of any skill will be proportional to the affective charge that makes it urgent.

There are so many skills to master. Children initially unable to grasp objects by any other means than simple reflex action will learn to hold their bottle, grip a cup, bang a cup, drink from a cup, grip a spoon, bang a spoon, eat from a spoon, master the intricacies of knife and fork, punch the buttons of calculators, telephones, and computers, drive a car, operate video games, handle a myriad of sports-related equipment, and even grow up to become neurosurgeons operating on structures so delicate they can only be seen under a microscope. The mastery of every skill involves the affect-driven wish to be more skillful; it means that growing people must not only visualize themselves doing a new task but also deal with the affect generated by the performance of that task. Even when the behavior to be learned is initially a matter of chance or random occurrence, both the desire to emulate it and the actions of autosimulation require some sequence of affects.

Clumsiness is about shame, grace is about pride. Generations of moviegoers loved Fred Astaire because he made grace look easy. For a few moments we could look up at the silver screen and pretend we were Fred and Ginger, dancing on chairs, making the intricate look simple. Right after we saw Fred Astaire we felt like dancing out of the theater. For a moment or so (until, once again, we saw our "real" natural level of skill), we were transformed into creatures beyond our regular selves. You prefer tennis or golf to dancing? Then I am willing to bet that you align your movements to those of the stars you watch on television, and that you play your best game right after seeing a major tournament. For those few moments that we are able to identify with someone more skillful or more graceful, at least until some impediment to positive affect returns us to our accustomed place on the shame/pride axis, we live and operate at a higher level of self-esteem and self-confidence.

Trial and error are not moves made by a logical machine devoid of feeling. The very concept of skill is immutably locked to matters of shame and pride. Throughout life, from infancy to senescence, our dexterity will bring us pride and our incompetence will trigger shame. Indeed, to the extent that the courage to experiment depends on interest and the failure of any undertaking triggers shame, the entire system of learning by trial and error will be limited by our attitude toward shame. As we grow from nurslings to nurses, from crib-bound curiosity seekers to scientists in spaceships, increases and decreases in dexterity and skill will be powerful stimuli for pride and shame.

Nowhere is this as easily seen and studied as in the infant's struggles to develop control over the process of excretion. Standards for the accomplishment of these skills have changed greatly during the past few decades, and the enlightened parent of today places much less pressure on a child than in years past. Nevertheless, so much shame and pride are associated with these activities that it is no wonder that Freud mistook the child's attention to them as a sign that excretion bore some intrinsic relation to the sexual drive system. The link between sexuality and excretion is that both activities trigger or are closely associated with excitement, enjoyment, and shame. But not in the way he thought.

What really happens when the child learns the sociology of excretion? Try, if you can, to visualize the plight of a baby whose otherwise doting caregivers (people who can be counted on for the rewarding mutualization of the calming smile of enjoyment and the increasing energy of excitement) begin to exhibit the rejecting face of dissmell or disgust for no discernible reason. Imagine smiling up to greet mother only to encounter an unexpected distortion of her features. Where only a moment ago the face of mother could be counted on for the pleasure of gestural communion, suddenly she presents a serious impediment to the child's expression of interest or enjoyment. Very little can convince a child to "lose interest" in mother. This is a perfect example of a situation in which shame affect is triggered to produce its painful interference with positive affect.

As the face of the infant turns away from mother and its head droops in shame, the baby becomes momentarily disorganized and uncoordinated. What happens next is fascinating, and I have observed countless variations of this group of scenes. Most often, mother's concern for her child replaces or overrides her dissmell and disgust at its excretions. Usually she smiles at her baby, who now finds no impediment to the resonance of positive affect and returns from the shame experience, although perhaps a bit warily. Occasionally the mother, herself in a "bad mood" and unwilling to let the baby off the hook for its transgression, remains unavailable for pleasurable communion. This amplifies the severity of the preceding rejection; frequently, the now dissmelling or disgusting baby moves from shame to distress and begins to cry.

Earlier, I emphasized the importance of dissmell and disgust as mechanisms that do not turn off the hunger drive but prevent it from allowing us to seek satisfaction from specific substances. Now consider how it might feel to find that you yourself have become the trigger for these affects of total rejection, rejection by the person whose loving attention is necessary for life. Thus, the significance to that child of having been the stimulus for dissmell or disgust will be proportional to the baby's ability to form linkages between events, to store the memories of these events, and to retrieve this information for comparison with new data (in other words, proportional to the child's level of cognitive maturity).

From this point a number of interactions are possible. Mothers, of course, differ greatly in the degree of comfort they feel with each negative affect. Some will scoop up their child and smother it with kisses, attempting to undo the rift in the relationship. Others will take this opportunity to admonish the hapless infant about the sins of soiling, thus reinforcing its distress. For some mothers, it is the very presence of excreta that has precipitated their own negative affect—mother's personal reaction to the substances involved. For other mothers, the presence of feces or urine has a more symbolic meaning. Soiled diapers can tell her, for instance, that the baby is still a baby and not adult enough, thus placing the mother in invidious comparison with whatever standards are important to her. In such a situation, the baby has become a source of shame to the mother, the stimulus for her own personal responses to a source of shame.

The infant is unable at first to understand that it is the presence of feces or urine that has precipitated maternal disfavor. Depending on the age of the child, which will determine the type of thinking process by which it will try to solve the problems thus presented, there are a number of solutions for the now problematic interaction with mother. I will discuss these modes of thinking in a later section; for the moment I wish only to point out that children are not really able to understand the logic of toilet training until somewhere in the third year of life. Their reactions to our concerns about bowel and bladder control are based more on the affective interactions involved than on any real comprehension of the reasons for our concern. Eventually the baby learns to link the process of excretion to its magnetic ability to attract parental negative affect, and excretory control becomes a major realm of competence pleasure and failure shame.

There has been much scholarly debate about the nature of the human dissmell and disgust responses to feces and urine. Most people take for granted that our aversion to these substances is "natural" and biologically programmed. For a long time I have wondered when that particular group of programs was written. I know no other animal with such an aversion—dogs, for example, lower their eyebrows and wag their tails with great interest in the presence of excreta, from which they seem to derive a great deal of information. My pet Gordon Setter, bred as a hunting dog, routinely tastes rabbit droppings unless one of us humans is adequately repulsed by this otherwise normal appetite. Every dog owner knows the avidity with which a male dog sniffs fire hydrants to determine which neighbors have left their olfactory calling cards. There is never a trace of negative affect in the canine response to excreta. I have observed horses, cows, goats, rhinoceri, elephants, giraffes, lions, monkeys, and chimpanzees without finding any evidence of such a prewired aversion.

In the era before modern chemistry, a physician would taste the patient's urine in order to determine the presence or absence of sugar. There was literally no other way to make the diagnosis of diabetes. Actually, there are two groups of illnesses characterized by raging thirst and copious urination—*diabetes mellitus*, with sweet urine, and *diabetes insipidus*, in which urine has no taste. Despite my years of reading ancient medical texts, I have never seen any instruction to the physician that indicates the need to overcome an inherent aversion to the tasting of urine. It would seem that our societal dissmell and disgust for these natural substances are examples of cultivated triggers for innate affect rather than innately programmed triggers.

Often I have heard patients in psychotherapy discuss their attitude toward excretion and their discomfort over the way they were toilet trained. Rarely have I ever heard anybody discuss aversion to fecal odors—either their own or those of others—outside of the context of embarrassment. Rather, it seems that such aversion is learned, and learned as a strategy for the avoidance of shame. Stated more bluntly, I believe that all aversion to excreta is shame related.

One more item of interest: Return again to that fascinating change in the infant that takes place as it passes into the third year, one that we discussed briefly in our section on pride. Somewhere in the period between 18 and 24 months of age, the child develops a radically different reaction to its own reflection in a mirror. Until this remarkable developmental acquisition, the baby it sees in the mirror is only another baby—a competent trigger for interest. But now, somewhere during this six-month period of time, the child begins to respond to the baby-in-the-mirror quite differently. Almost universally, babies of this age begin to act shy around their own reflection!

Amsterdam and Levitt (1980), who first demonstrated this phenomenon, called it "painful self-awareness" and thought it was one of the earliest manifestations of shame. Broucek (1982), using the more sophisticated analysis made possible by Tomkins's affect theory, reevaluated their data. Knowing that the shame affect triggered in the toddler is no different from the shame affect triggered in infants, he pointed out that the two-year-old had developed the ability to understand that it could be the object of other people's awareness. If the person I see in the mirror is me, reasons the child, then other people, any other people who look at me, see me exactly as I am in that mirror.

Broucek's elegant term for this is *objective self-awareness*, by which he means that we are no longer merely the subject of our own musings but the object of the scrutiny of others. This developmental milestone, he reasons, brings with it a shame crisis for every child. Until this moment, the shame that could occur in a host of situations involving impediments to positive affect bore no necessary relation to the eye of another person. Now we become susceptible to another whole realm of situations in which we can experience shame! It is from this moment forth that we are able to be embarrassed because someone else sees us or learns something about us.

You will, of course, have noticed that the period in question, the 18-to-24-month era of child development, is right around the time that (in our culture) most families decide to potty-train their children. So it appears that just when most families concentrate on excretory control, the child is going through the shame crisis of objective self-awareness. This forges an immutable link between excretion and shame. Right at the time children are made aware of the degree to which their families are displeased at their excretory habits, they have newly become aware that much they thought was private, or secret, was really public. This new propensity for shame causes a radical magnification of the importance of toilet training.

In a culture that venerates cleanliness and abhors "filth," toilet training is a condition necessary for membership. To a certain extent, more for some of us than for others, the shame and pride associated with the achievement of the specific skills needed to produce excretory competence come to take on great importance in our definition of ourselves as individuals. A three-year-old might introduce himself to us with pride by saying, "My name is Johnny and I can go to the bathroom all by myself!" No adult would even think of saying aloud so ridiculous a thought—indeed, even the idea itself may be a bit embarrassing to some readers. Put it another way: It is nearly unthinkable for an adult to be incompetent in the arena of excretion.

Actually, loss of excretory control in adults is more common than you might imagine, and just as embarrassing as you might fear. Many women suffer a reduction in bladder control both during and after pregnancy. I remember particularly the agony of a young lawyer in her eighth month of pregnancy who had misjudged the amount of time it would take her to return home from a trip to the shopping mall and found herself unbearably close to losing control of her bladder. Screeching her car to a stop in her own driveway, she ran toward the house only to realize she could not get to the toilet in time. "Just like a dog," she said, covering her face in her hands, "I crouched down on the lawn and peed. And that wasn't the worst of it. I could see my next-door neighbor looking at me from her window. I still haven't been able to face her since that day." We talked at length about her self-disgust and the shame that it has caused.

Often I have lectured and written about the perplexing fact that embarrassment is more and better discussed in the entertainment media than in psychotherapy. It is fascinating to note how much advertising depends on shame. We tend not to "notice" advertisements that have nothing to do with us—or, more properly, that speak to sources of shame we have never encountered in our own lives. Men tend not to remember technical details about brassieres, women have little or no awareness that jockstraps and jockey shorts help reduce the visibility of erections and thus are favored over boxer shorts by younger men.

So unless you are sensitive to the problems associated with the loss of excretory control normal to an aging population, you may not have paid much attention to the ubiquitous television and print advertisements that describe the advantages of diaperlike garments for older folk, or products that help control odor and leakage from colostomy and ileostomy pouches. Every one of these products and every advertisement for each such commodity are about the shame that accompanies loss of excretory control in the adult.

Equally interesting is the fact that these advertisements only attract the attention of people who have experienced shame because of their newfound lack of skill in the management of excretion. Just as shame produces a painful impediment in interest–excitement and enjoyment–joy, anything that reduces or relieves shame becomes suddenly interesting or enjoyable.

So much are we stigmatized by our own failure to control excretion that one way we attempt to create shame in others is to curse at them using language that indicates such lack of self-jurisdiction in them. As a beginning student of psychotherapy, I was taught that the frequency with which "four-letter words" appear in conversation is an index of unconscious anger. It seems much more likely that whatever anger appears in one who curses is some form of reaction to the experience of ridicule or put-down. The investigation of spoken invective is very much the study of shame and pride.

As an indication of this, examine, for a moment, the relation between curse words and shame. "Bad" words are usually related to excretion or to matters of genitals, gender identity, and sexuality. We'll get to the latter in the section about the relation between shame and sex, but for now let's concentrate on the reasons we insult people by using the terms of excretion. Why do we label people with such epithets as "asshole," "shit," "pisser," and so on? Even more interesting, why do people get upset when we fling these terms at them?

By now it should be clear that all of them refer to matters that become part of our system of self-esteem quite early in development. What we have learned so far serves to explain what Wurmser pointed out: in the moment of embarrassment we feel infantile, weak, dirty, and unable to control our bodily functions. Again, this observation serves to demonstrate the differences between affect and emotion as we now define them. No matter what kind of impediment to positive affect triggers shame affect, memory brings forth our history of previous experiences of shame. The self-disgust and self-dissmell associated with excretory dyscontrol are so powerful a stimulus for shame, triggers that come to matter so much to the growing child, that excretory competence becomes a kind of reference point within our construct of shame as an emotion. Shame, of course, is about much more than just excretion, but excretory epithets are about shame.

When you study human development in terms of the affect system, the emotions associated with control of urination and defecation are easily understood as derivatives of the three painful affects of attenuation. The skills involved are hard-won by the growing child. Indeed, it is the shame and pride associated with the achievement of these particular skills that make their accomplishment so important. It is the peculiar timing of the demands we place on the child that give them such unique importance in the formation of these emotions.

Much more happens during this period than the battles of the bathroom. And there are a myriad of skills on which we might lavish similar attention. But it is time to discuss other vectors of development, other systems that change as we mature and that become involved in the complex world of shame and pride.

14

DEPENDENCE/INDEPENDENCE

It is wonderful to be able to rely on others, but the design characteristics of the normal human seem to favor independent action as well as the linked behaviors associated with caregiving and affective interchange. Although babies are born helpless, each system that "comes on line" during the process of growth and development brings them closer to their adult range of abilities and further from the era of dependence.

The "universal" fear of abandonment is a relic from our days of complete dependence on the caregiver. Modern researchers of infancy have observed that the awake, alert baby spends about half its time playing by itself and the other half engaged with the caregiver. When *interested* in self-generated activity, the baby is apparently unconcerned that it is alone. Only when the presence of another person is required to serve some need or wish does it appear that one has been forsaken. The terror linked with the "concept" or the "idea" of abandonment is really a complex assemblage of fantasies colored by our associations to previous, perhaps infantile experience of being *distressed* or *frightened* when alone. The state of being alone is called "independent activity" when we are happy and "abandonment" when we are upset.

Throughout the long period of growth and development one sees change in the systems both of self involvement and of self-other involvement. Any definition of the normal adult must take into account the need for people to handle both solitude and communion.

Infants are fascinated by things they cannot control. They want to touch, taste, smell, and handle objects to which access is denied simply because they are at a distance. It is adults—or at least larger and more skillful children—on whom they must depend for transportation to those desired objects. Fascinated by its odor or color, a child may develop a passionate desire for some special food, but that food is available only if a caregiver provides it. Similarly, whatever the child can visualize and desire is accessible only to the extent that the caregivers are willing to provide that access.

We can't exactly tune in on the thinking process of infants, but, watching them and listening to their mothers, we can conclude that babies sure seem to know what they want and are not shy about telling us. The demands of children, always amplified to urgency by affect, are the wishes of little people who are dependent on others. This is not unimportant to the child. From birth to adolescence, every smidgen of growth and development moves the child from the position of one who needs others for the accomplishment of its aims to one who is self-reliant. An event that represents self-reliance will bring pride, while one that suggests failure to mature (and therefore maintenance of the level of dependence more typical of smaller children) will act as an impediment to excitement or contentment and bring shame.

Each increase in size or power, each developmental acquisition, permits the child new opportunities to test and perhaps savor its growing skills and abilities. Each success brings some measure of pride, while each failure is capable of bringing shame. Every venture is a chance for pride or shame, which will then be linked to each of the three scales we have discussed so far. Success—at any age—tells us something about our size, our skill, and our growing degree of independence from those who previously have performed these tasks on our behalf. In normal development, independence is inextricably linked with pride. It is a measure of competence. Failure—at any age—tells us something about our size, our skill, and our dependence on others. It is a measure of incompetence, and therefore a major stimulus to shame.

This is not to say that independence is by definition good and dependence bad. Most of us enjoy being at least somewhat dependent on somebody; we like having someone to count on. "No man is an island, entire of itself; every man is a piece of the continent, a part of the main," said John Donne. Truth be told, we are all more or less dependent on each other, some more than others. We live, as John F. Kennedy said, in a world of interdependence. The adult must find some balance between the helpless dependence on the whims of others characteristic of infants and slaves and the splendid isolation of the renegade or hermit. These are the decisions of adult life, ruled by the emotions and cognitions of adults.

How each of us adults feels about our position on the axis of dependence and independence is the result of long years of emotional development. Such attitudes are the result of having grown up in a particular family that lived in its distinct neighborhood within one or another city of some country. That family represented some specific culture or confluence of cultures. It lived during an era that valued some styles and attitudes and disvalued others. For each of us, the adult sociopolitical concept of dependence/independence is based on all these factors. I can feel proud of the fact that my corporation houses and feeds me and that all my needs and wants are served by a huge organization. Equally can I feel chronic and deepening shame that, in the words of the song made famous by Tennessee Ernie Ford, "I owe my soul to the company store." In the adult, pride and shame can become attached to qualities and experiences quite opposite to the principles that obtain early in development.

So our progeny are likely to experience pleasure when the application of a newly acquired skill produces a novel burst of independence. A parent who greets with pleasure the burgeoning independence of a child will reinforce the linkage between that group of skills and childhood pride. One who experiences the same skills as a threat, or who sees danger in these new actions, will convey this information to the child in the form of some negative affect, like fear, anger, distress, dissmell, disgust, or even shame. The face of negative affect will be a daunting impediment to the juvenile expectation of the rewarding smile of parental enjoyment. Thus, parents who, for their own personal reasons, are made unhappy by childhood independence will foster the linkage of independence with shame, the painful affect triggered by impediment to ongoing positive affect.

There is, of course, much more than shame involved here, for the child must deal with the specific affect emanating from the caregiver as well as its own shame response. When, for instance, a mother is frightened by the implications of her toddler's ability to wander away, it is her fear or her anger that greet the child. What occurs inside the child is a combination of shame (a response to this unexpected failure of maternal attunement) and fear—for the child must deal with the implications of the specific affect she is exhibiting. Any child who grows up with a mother who is frightened and angry about matters of autonomy will be liable to develop a peculiar emotional state in which the affects of shame and fear are bound together and linked to the idea of independence. In the example I have just given, the child develops a linkage between shame and fear that Tomkins calls a *shame–fear bind*.

These linkages have profound implications for the development of the affect–experience assemblages we term emotion, which characterize what for each of us is called our personality. Since shame affect works to interfere with our ability to commune with the object of our interest or enjoyment, it is an intrinsic instrument of isolation and withdrawal. Shame affect produces an involution into the self. It distances us from the other person—indeed, it punishes us for wanting communion with or connection to the impeding other. The younger the child, the more primitive will be its explanations of this type of shame experience.

The most profound forms of rejection known to the infant are the mechanisms of dissmell, which keeps its trigger at a great distance, and disgust, which sends to a great distance that which had originally been desired and acceptable. Suddenly rejected by the caregiver for behavior the child expected might bring pleasure, the humiliated child often sees itself as a dissmelling or disgusting object. In such manner do our early experiences of socialization, of immersion in the emotional systems of our parents, produce many linkages between the affect auxiliary of shame and the drive auxiliaries of dissmell and disgust.

Just as the child learns to associate maternal dissmell and disgust with the shame of soiling and to link the concepts of self-dissmell and self-disgust to the very idea of shame, the child shamed by its rejection for any behavior will tend to build a lexicon of self-related negative affect states characterized by a fusion of dissmell, disgust, and shame. By the time we get to adult life, shame affect has been so thoroughly fused with these other affects of rejection that, for all practical purposes, what we think of as a deep and abiding sense of personal shame is no longer shame affect as such, but the complex result of such fusion.

It is to this fusion of affects and ideas that the child attaches the label "bad." I know of few emotional experiences more toxic than to feel completely deserving of rejection. Children, whose affective experiences are of vastly greater sophistication and complexity than can be represented in their beginners' verbal language, think and express themselves in more global terms. "Good" is how I feel and what I am when I experience competence pleasure or when I feel loved for some other reason, and "bad" is how I feel and what I am when in this state of shame/dissmell/disgust. We carry these labels into adulthood from our own childhood and teach them to our children. They know what it feels like to be called bad; they know what it feels like to be called good. In the simplest possible terms, "good me" equals pride, and "bad me" equals shame.

Such an understanding of the paths along which children develop brings with it a new opportunity to figure out the root causes and some novel approaches to treatment for a whole group of adult emotional disturbances. The very success of the psychoanalytic method in treating illness stemming from inadequate resolution of the family romance Freud called the oedipal phase of development served to highlight those conditions in which such treatment failed with regularity. Foremost among these are what are now (in the language of Kernberg) called the "borderline illnesses," a cluster of clinical conditions characterized by severe emotional instability, terrible intolerance for loneliness, crippling difficulties in forming close personal relationships, a deep sense of emptiness, and a chronic incapacity to develop a solid sense of self.

They are people who make passionate but brief and unstable relationships, who vary between heartwarming displays of personal openness and spiteful rage at what one might think a minor request for disclosure. Most of us know one or two people whose life history leads us to suspect that they fit into this diagnostic category. Every therapist has been humbled by the attempt to treat these high-energy patients. Clinicians who write about their successful work with borderline illness take for granted that the duration of treatment may be measured in decades rather than years. Although for many of these patients the relationship with a therapist is as unstable as any other, the key issues of abandonment, loneliness, personal disclosure, and the nature of identity are well tolerated within the system of relatedness characteristic of psychotherapy.

It seems obvious to anybody who has studied shame that the so-called "borderline illness" is little more than an exaggerated result of the interference in development to be expected when a child encounters severe impediments to positive affect while learning to be independent. "Borderlines" are shame-bound people loaded with self-dissmell and self-disgust. Often, their entire character structure is so deeply entwined with these complex forms of shame that a large part of the time spent in therapy is devoted to meticulous reconstruction of life events made painful by shame. The importance of shame in these cases is rivaled by few clinical conditions encountered in the practice of psychotherapy.

Most therapists are still unaware of the nature of shame, the importance of shame-based psychopathology, and the modes of treatment that free patients from shame-related complaints, so "borderline" patients frequently go from one therapist to another in search of relief. While I have no intention of minimizing the difficulty of these cases, those of us who understand this new language of affect report far fewer problems in treatment and a considerably shortened duration of psychotherapy.

Not surprisingly, most of the books and articles written about "borderline illness" neglect to mention shame, while few if any of the writers on shame think to group these patients in a special category. "Borderline illness" seems to be a wastebasket term for severely shame-damaged people, an observation

made with especial vigor by Helen Block Lewis (1987). I am supported in this
belief by the frequency with which my colleagues who study psychopharmacology report that depressed "borderlines" respond to the same group of
medications (the MAOI and the fluoxetine group of antidepressants) that I find
effective in shame-based depression. The more we know about affect, the more
we are forced to revise our standards of diagnosis and our methods of treatment.

Families vary in their attitudes toward dependence and independence. A
child whose mother can tolerate with ease the normal interplay of closeness
and distance, who can handle a wide range of oscillation between intimacy and
solitude, may encounter surprising intolerance to his or her wish to achieve the
new level of freedom implied by the right to drive an automobile. Some
families hold their children closely, releasing them only grudgingly into marriage, while others send them off to boarding school or summer camp as soon
as possible. We can fight for independence from a clinging family by using
pregnancy to force marriage, or we can enlist in military service to escape our
milieu.

The range of variation is infinite, the number of styles of personality development immense. Yet throughout the long period of growth and development
we see the importance of shame and pride in determining the meaning of
independence and dependence for each individual person. It is to the nature of
our personal identity that we will turn next, for shame and pride figure prominently in the development of the sense of self. Who is it that has been growing
and developing, and how does the individual establish a sense of a "me" or an
"I"? Instinctively, we know that shame forces us to think about ourselves,
albeit about a defective self. Why should this be? How does the child form a
self-concept, and how does this self-concept get to be so involved with shame
and pride?

15

THE SELF

"Look at me," said the young boxer from Lexington, Kentucky. "I am beautiful. I am the greatest. I float like a butterfly and sting like a bee. Look at this face. Nobody has ever touched this face. I am beautiful." He mocked his opponents in doggerel verse, predicting (correctly) the round in which they would fall.

I was deeply offended by the arrogance, the "narcissism" of Cassius Clay, later Mohammed Ali, and disliked him intensely in those early years. How could anyone ever have the effrontery to say such things aloud? When, for religious reasons, he refused to "fight for his country" I thought him insincere. After all, wasn't fighting in war the same as fighting in the prize ring? What a narcissistic character, I thought. He should be ashamed of himself for such behavior!

A simple, chance observation permanently altered my understanding of this great athlete. Watching one of his fights on television a couple of years later, I saw him make a series of three right jabs in astonishingly quick succession—effortless blows executed with a combination of speed and power no one else could have achieved. I had been studying Okinawan *Kempo Ru* karate at the time and (even as a beginner) knew enough about the martial arts to recognize from his technique what I had disavowed, refused to accept about his person: Mohammed Ali *was* the greatest. He was beautiful. And it was true that nobody touched his face.

It was only his way of speaking about himself that so "turned me off" that I prejudged him, that I was temporarily unable to give him the respect he deserved. What is it about self-praise that offends or alarms the listener?

Clicking through the television dial one day some years ago, running the channels in hope of entertainment, I was arrested by one of the sweet-voiced, ed Hollywood interviewers' asking Alan Alda, "You don't have nasty to say about anybody, you aren't here to push a cause—why come on my show?" He answered with quiet intensity, "I have just ed the two best films of my career. *The Seduction of Joe Tynan* is about a goo man, a senator who falls from grace and has to rethink his life; and *The Four Seasons* is about the changes that take place in the lives of a group of friends. I am very proud of this work and I wanted to tell people about it so they would see it." What impressed me was his quiet pride. Why wasn't he embarrassed to laud his own work? Shouldn't such things only be said by others? All my training had led me to expect that he was bragging, that this was narcissism; yet what I heard sounded healthy and enlightened. I saw both movies and loved them—he was right that they represented his best work, and I was left with admiration for his ability to say that aloud.

In the Hall of History at the Smithsonian Institution in Washington is an exhibit about colonial life. Large and proud, on a plaque in front of a realistic grouping of tools, is this statement, written in 1784 by a New Jersey farmer and tavernkeeper: "I am a mover, a shoemaker, furrier, wheelwright, farmer, gardener, and, when it can't be helped, a soldier. I make my bread, brew my beer, kill my pigs; I grind my axes and knives; I built those stalls and that shed there; I am barber, leech, and doctor." What are we to make of this calm, confident self-appraisal? Is it shameless or arrogant? Does it contain what the Greeks called *hubris*, the sin of pride? Or is it (as I believe) merely healthy self-reflection?

Deems Taylor, a composer who achieved fame in later life as a radio personality, once told the following anecdote about his friend Arturo Toscanini, arguably the greatest orchestral and operatic conductor of their era. "We were standing together after a concert, and a middle-aged woman came up to him and gushed, 'Maestro Toscanini, you looked so *handsome* tonight!' He thanked her politely, and after she left, he turned to me and said, 'That woman made me very happy. No one can tell Toscanini how well he conducted.'" This is another sort of self-appraisal.

Yet here, from the artist Jonathan Borofsky, is a public statement of more negative self-appraisal. Perhaps you have seen an exhibit of his work—paintings and sculptures covered with numbers. Borofsky has filled countless notebooks with numbers, since childhood scribbled numbers in the millions over every scrap of paper available to him. To a psychiatrist it would appear either that he had developed the defense of obsessive counting in order to drive away bad thoughts or that he suffers from some form of obsessive-compulsive disorder. One way or another, he has turned into art what appears to be either madness or a defense against madness.

A lithograph, a print sold in art galleries not long ago, contained no drawings (and no numbers) but only the following hand-lettered words, copied here
exactly as he wrote them: "I don't like where I'm at now (that I'm not perfect)
and instead I want to be there (God state) now. I don't want to work for this
because I know deep down inside that I never can be God-like, so though I
don't give up, I never work really for what I can do—namely MY BEST. And
this way I get into the comparing state which is Death because as soon as I
start to compare myself I loose my uniqueness. I can only do mine and what is
in me and the more I know myself, the self will then come out in my work."

What does Borofsky mean to convey when he says, "And this way I get
into the comparing state which is Death"? Why is "the comparing state" like
death to him? I suspect that he is dealing with the shame that accompanies
invidious comparison. Borofsky's "comparing state" is most likely an emotional state, a mood based on some form of shame—a highly personal bun-
dling of shame affect with his own concept of self. Intuitively we can grasp the
idea that he is aware of a stratification of possible selves, levels of self-value. By
choosing God to represent the highest possible level of personal attainment he
guarantees constant shame, for the Judaeo-Christian God is always defined in
terms of qualities that are unattainable by the human.

A wide range of self-as-identity and self-as-the-subject-of-appraisal appears
in these anecdotes. The great martial artist sees his own ability and proudly,
easily, appraises it as greatness. The competent actor feels pride that his accomplishments measure up to his best hopes for himself. The successful artist
describes a damaged self. The comment made by the world's best conductor
can be viewed either as *authoritative* or *arrogant,* whatever the border between
these two descriptors of competence. All these men show a tendency to rate
themselves on some sort of scale, whether in terms of others, or in comparison
to their own previous efforts, or along some yardstick unavailable to anyone
else. The statements themselves, as well as our own responses to them, reflect
the importance of shame and pride in matters of self-definition.

Earlier I mentioned that usually pride is affiliative and shame alienating. We
love to hoist the victor on our shoulders. "Everybody loves a winner." Alan
Alda's quiet pride drew me into the theater to see his films. Yet I recall quite
well that many people followed the career of Mohammed Ali with prejudice
based on a general attitude of dissmell and disgust attributed (at least in part)
to his African heritage. Publicly they hoped someone might "give him his
comeuppance" and "wipe that arrogant smile off that nigger's face." The great
boxer's pride produced a legion of angry, racist, shaming detractors, as well as
the more expected troupe of admiring, complimentary fans.

Léon Wurmser once defined creativity as "the heroic transcendence of shame" (1981, 291). To the extent that one is the very best at something, or that one strives to be the best, one risks alienation from the remainder of humanity. In some cultures, Wurmser pointed out, anyone who dares to rise above the horde is shamed into emotional exile. Self-definition can be a risky business.

The struggle to define oneself when one is better than others at some task or skill, or when one possesses an attribute valued highly by others, is made more difficult by the reactions of those others. Those who are defeated will usually experience shame and feel estranged from the victor. Most often we hear about the "thrill of victory," the pride or sense of triumph accompanying the success of a competitive venture. Rarely do we consider that one who "wins" may be guilty or embarrassed that s/he has caused the discomfort of another. Victory can "elevate" one right out of a peer group and produce shame!

"Who is that lovely girl?" asked a schoolteacher recently. "And why doesn't she seem to have any friends? Nobody ever talks to her." "Oh, that's Mary-Louise," said one of her classmates. "She was voted Most Popular Girl in the Class last year." Often such recognition creates distance by triggering a sense of inadequacy in one's peers and a compensatory alienating jealousy. Shame can accompany both victory and defeat in the struggle to define a "better" or a more effective self.

One generation of baseball fans was so attached to the work record of Babe Ruth that any athlete whose accomplishments rivaled those of their hero became the target of significant abuse. During the period that Mickey Mantle and Roger Maris eclipsed Ruth's record for the number of home runs hit in a single season, these fans protested with vehemence that no athlete should *dare* to compare himself with Ruth. And as Henry Aaron's lifetime home run record approached that of Babe Ruth, many whites said that "no Negro had the right even to think he was as good as Ruth." It was bad enough that these fans were forced to accept the impermanence of dominance. It was even more difficult for them to accept a new hero whose other attributes made him the object of dissmell.

We seem to need heroes. They form some sort of ideal toward which we can strive. Whenever we approach our ideal we feel pride; whatever pushes us further from this standard causes shame. So important is this mechanism of model-making that people get quite upset when their hero is defeated or threatened with replacement. Of equal importance, and far more rarely discussed, is the fact that we seem to need goats. Most people function better when they know there is someone inferior to them. The internal psychological

structures that surround and support the system of idealization, the very essence of what is ideal, the entire system of best and worst, all of these are
cognitive constructions built to house and perhaps disguise our lifetime of
personal involvement with shame and pride. The very idea of personal identity
seems to be intimately involved with whatever we measure along the shame/
pride axis.

Less clear is a rationale for the powerful linkage between these emotions
and the nature of the self. We take it for granted that in adult life the complex
ideoaffective families we call shame and pride are inextricably intertwined with
the concept of self. But we have come a long way in our study of the process
by which emotions are constructed over time, of how the building blocks of
innate affects are assembled with our recorded and retrieved memories of
situations in which those affects were triggered. We have come too far merely
to accept that shame and pride are the emotions of self-appraisal without
asking how they achieved this particular power. I believe that we have enough
data to sketch the maps and circuit boards for this supremely important group
of connections.

Yet just as we begin to focus our attention on the relation of the concept we
call "self" to both shame and pride, we are forced to notice another range of
problems. There are times that both emotions seem to involve people at what
they experience as "the core of the self" and other times when shame or pride
seem to be attached to a relatively minor attribute. In other words, shame
varies from a global experience to a less wrenching specific happening. In
every one of these experiences of shame it is "I" who am embarrassed, yet in
each I experience myself quite differently. And we can be proud of a specific,
limited ability or attribute, just as we can be proud of our entire being.

Recently, for example, a woman humiliated by a former lover told me, "I
feel as if I can never show my face in public again. No one will ever ask me out.
I am destroyed. I feel like dying. Maybe I really have died and this is hell."
Speaking to one of her students, the protagonist of *The Prime of Miss Jean
Brodie* describes the slur that destroyed her reputation as an "assassination."
Both women link the experience of shame with a profound reduction in the
value of the total self. Still another woman remarks about the time a friend
pointed out a defect in the design of her dress: "I was so embarrassed! I gave
that dress to my sister." Here it was not the self that was reduced in value, but
the dress. How is it that in one case shame reduces the value of the entire
organism, while in another it diminishes the importance of something that can
be discarded?

The same holds true for pride. Does an accomplishment speak for a better self, or about improvement in some minor aspect of the whole? If a small boy hits a home run in sandlot baseball, is he merely more competent at a task or already as good as Henry Aaron? What if I beat you at quoits, table tennis, badminton, handball, squash, bowling, boxing, wrestling, karate, or chess; if my team defeats yours in football, baseball, soccer, field hockey, volleyball, swimming, or lacrosse; if my school ranks higher than yours in the number of graduates placed prestigiously; if my nation explores the moon before yours? Each competition creates order ranked on the basis of some attribute. Neither contestant is changed in totality, neither declared to have a better soul or essence. There is a world of difference between an attribute and a self.

What links together all these different types of experience is, of course, the presence of the ideoaffective complexes we learn to call shame or pride. What makes the wounds of shame and the surge of pride vary along the axis of superficial to deep? How do the basic physiological mechanisms responsible for shame and pride get involved with the notion of "self," and what explains the enormous variation in the depth of self associated with each experience of these powerful affective assemblies?

DEFINING THE SELF IN PSYCHOANALYTIC LANGUAGE

Just as you might expect, in the search for clarity it is the everyday words that give us the most trouble. In order to discuss the relation between the self and either shame or pride we need to agree about what we mean by the very idea of "self." Most readers will be aware that during the past couple of decades my field has witnessed a shift from what Freud and his followers called *ego mechanisms* (the specific mental techniques and skills that differentiate a baby from an adult) to a focus on the nature of the whole person. There are now two major theoretical systems, each of which views the individual somewhat differently. Both are extremely important, both are used by the overwhelming majority of therapists, and both are dead wrong.

It is difficult for the uninitiated reader to understand that all psychoanalytic theory about the nature of infancy must be wrong simply because Freud deduced it by working backwards from the analysis of adults in treatment for emotional illness. It is based on what adults told him about their infancy or what he was able to reconstruct about their early lives from what they could not tell him. He never studied infants!

Freud believed that the infant lived in a completely narcissistic state, unable to distinguish the presence of other people as persons outside itself. In his system, the infant was declared incapable of understanding the concept of "otherness" and seen as experiencing every portion of its perceptual surround as a part of itself. In other words, *all interaction with mother was defined as interaction within parts of this extended self.* Freud maintained that there was no real infant-mother interface. Rather, the infant took for granted that mother was a part of an as-yet-undifferentiated mixture; in the mind of the child, infant and mother were, for all intents and purposes, fused. Emergence from the birth canal, freedom from the confines of the womb, the process of parturition itself did not really separate fetus and mother. Physical birth, thought Freud, was not psychological separation.

Relying again on the sexual life force he saw as the prime mover and the major agent of change in psychological development, Freud claimed for libido the primary responsibility for the differentiation of mother as a separate person. Not until the child became truly sexual (in the commonly accepted adult sense of the word) could the concept of mother emerge from this fusion. And, as the child became capable of seeing mother as a separate person, other people took on their realistic form as supplementary separate beings.

Let me state as succinctly as possible Freud's equation for this complex philosophical position: As long as the libido force is thought to be concentrated in the organ of sustenance, the mouth, the child lives in an *oral phase* of psychosexual development. Mother, then, is merely a synonym for breast, for she is *that which satisfies oral need.* But Freud meant by this not the actual mammary gland of a specific person—the breast of mother—but the breast as a symbol of the food-giving, need-satisfying part of the fused or undifferentiated infant-mother continuum. At this stage, libido may be said to *link* child and mother.

A bit later in this hypothesized psychosexual development of the infant, the libido force is said to move from the oral realm to the anal. It is during this period of time that the child is forced to interact with an outside world that requires the establishment of internal controls previously unimaginable to the infant. Still, within Freudian theory, the mother is not viewed as a separate person, but as a part of the fused, undifferentiated system. Since mother is not viewed as a separate person but part of the inner world of the infant, her requests for the establishment of these inner controls are viewed as causing *inner conflict* within the psyche of the infant.

It is only when the libido force is declared to have made its final shift from the anal apparatus to the purely genital, and libido can finally be said to be a truly sexual force, that mother begins to be defined as a person separate from the child. To Freud, it was the child's growing sexual interest in mother that created in the child a dawning realization of mother's otherness. According to classical psychoanalytic theory, the action of lusting for another person defines that person as an other and defines the one who lusts as an individual, a self. Mother and father, notwithstanding all the ways they have interacted with the child until this moment, are not believed to have had any influence on the internal development of the child. Within classical psychoanalytic theory, *social interaction* cannot be said to exist until self and object are split apart by the forces of libido; the child is defined as living in a state of narcissism until this moment.

There are some holes in this theory, as Freud and other members of his circle were quick to point out and later plug. It requires one to postulate that girls, who have no inherent biological reason to be sexually attracted to mother, achieve full freedom from the state of fusion and its associated narcissism only by recognition that they are different from boys, appreciation that they are boys who lack a full genital apparatus. It is only (says theory) when the girl realizes that her "little phallus," the clitoris, is not a "real penis," that she becomes, on the one hand, envious of the larger male organ and, on the other, capable of libidinous interest in men.

The dawning of sexual interest in father further highlights his otherness and helps define the female self. In our culture, women seem more interested in forming close relationships than men, who seem to favor independence and solitary activity. Many psychoanalysts believe that this pattern of adult behavior derives from the period in time when these supposed gender-linked differences in psychosexual development sent children on vastly different paths. Within this construction, women are seen as inherently more narcissistic than men because they have not detached themselves completely from the early fusion with mother.

So Freud produced a theory that links a postulated psychosexual development of the child (this assumed movement of libido from the oral to the anal to the phallic regions of the body) with the hypothesized shift from narcissism to true interpersonal relatedness. One major problem with this scheme is that it requires us to ignore completely the obvious fact that children from the earliest days of extrauterine life relate to their parents as if they were real people, each quite different from the other, and quite separate from themselves. And, of course, it avoids all the data provided by the affect system and its importance in producing an interpersonal world.

Most of the new developmental theorists, especially those who focus their attention on the affective life of the infant and the interplay between infant and caregiver of affect-related behavior, have long ago discarded libido theory and its restrictively sexual notion about the development of self and other. Although, as we will discuss in a later chapter, the infant derives a great deal of information from its sexual urges, the concepts of self and other are not dependent on genital strivings.

One psychoanalytic writer, Heinz Kohut (1971, 1977), noticed that some adults, while in psychoanalytic treatment, formed powerful transference relationships that could be neither explained nor treated on the basis of this scheme. For these patients, the analyst had come to represent a parent whose function seemed quite different from anything possible within classical theory. Kohut recognized that there were times that the infant needed to be soothed by mother, indeed, could only be soothed by mother. Focusing attention on the interplay between child and mother, but unaware of the existence of the innate affects, Kohut noted that the caregiver tends to mirror back to the infant some reflection of the infant's inner states. Kohut suggested that this soothing function, so essential to normal parenting, was experienced by the infant as *deriving from an extension of the infant's self* rather than from another individual.

Psychoanalytic language has its own unique syntax—the person being studied is referred to as *the subject*, and the other person with whom he or she is involved is called *the object*. Since, in classical psychoanalytic language, mother's "breast" function is the one by which Freud thought she was known to the infant, and since the breast is only a part of her, mother is not considered an object (a whole person) but a *part-object* (a partial person). Kohut suggested that the infant sees in mother neither the presence of another whole person like itself nor a breast-like partial person, but a mirror of its own inner being. Looking at mother, he reasoned, the infant sees only whatever is being reflected back to it. For this reason he coined the term for mother-as-a-special-form-of-other, a particular variant of object that he called *the selfobject*. According to this theory, the selfobject is that part of the self the infant sees when it looks at mother. Mother is not really other because she only mirrors the child's self.

Basch put it best in a recent conversation: "Within self-psychology, the infant is unaware of mother as a separate individual, but only as an extension of his own function. He wants the ball, she moves it to him; she is out of the room, he is angry. She is, therefore, a part of him just like his hand. Think of it like Aladdin and the genie of the lamp. The infant rubs the lamp, mother comes and does his bidding, then she returns to the lamp. It is not as if she is an extension of *me*, for there is no *me*; there is only an experience." Self-psychologists devote a great deal of attention to what are called *selfobject functions*. For the most part, these are what I have discussed throughout this book as the techniques by which the caregiver experiences the affect that is broadcast by the infant and comes to act as an external modulator of displayed infantile affect.

Kohut's work is seen by some as a revolution in theory and by others as only an evolutionary step. Not unlike Harry Stack Sullivan, the founder of American psychiatry, whose *interpersonal psychiatry* claimed that the personality of the individual is molded in a social context, Kohut made some alterations in classical psychoanalytic structure and established (for psychoanalysis) the importance of the caregiver's role in helping to form the identity of the infant. In doing so, he shifted attention away from the preeminence of libido, thus earning the enmity of his more orthodox colleagues. The earlier bitter and often acrimonious debates between the proponents of these two wings of psychoanalysis have mellowed somewhat—everybody is beginning to focus more on the concept of self.

Unfortunately, Kohut believed that the infant was unable to see mother as anything but a selfobject early in development. But just as the mother is more to the child than a breast function (the mechanism that served the libido-based oral need), she is more to the infant than a mirroring selfobject. Simple observation of mother-child interaction reveals that mother is not limited to behavior that mirrors the affective states of the infant—and I think the child sees her as much more than a mirror. One of her attributes is this selfobject function (some sort of extension of the infant's self), but she has other aspects that have nothing at all to do with selfobject functioning and is also therefore a clear example of "other." For this reason I think it is wrong to view mother only as "the selfobject." Mother has selfobject functions, but is always an other. Again, Basch explained it to me quite succinctly: "Only when the self of the infant is threatened does mother enter the picture as a selfobject. Otherwise, she is an independent center of activity and therefore an object."

Why did Kohut make this error? I think he was trying to maintain Freud's understanding of the infant-mother relationship, in which people were thought to emerge slowly from some sort of primordial relational slush into distinctly differentiated groups of self and others. He was unaware of the discriminatory power inherent in the innate affects, separate and highly differentiated scripts that create a host of inner experiences and outer displays that allow infant and mother to understand quite a bit about each other. So Kohut retained much more of Freudian psychology than necessary.

Instead of completely rejecting the idea that infant and mother are fused in some sort of narcissistic relational haze and recognizing that the infant is a separate being from the moment of birth (and perhaps before!), Kohut adopted Freud's concept of normal infantile narcissism and extended it to form a major portion of his new self-psychology. Assuming (with Freud) that the self-concept emerges from a background of basic, inherent narcissism, Kohut called self-development the process of *narcissistic development*. Similarly, he viewed all of the problems that can occur in the development of the sense of self as narcissistic disturbances. Kohut discussed cases in which patients suffered pain from "narcissistic injury" (1972). At times he seemed to understand this as shame, but he clearly misunderstood shame as merely another part of the more general negative state called "anxiety" by Freud.

One of the purposes of this current book is to offer psychology a way out of the terminological quagmire described above. We need a language for the self, but one based on the healthy and normal, on what can be observed in the infant and tested in the relationship between infant and caregiver. Our search for a new language of the self should be aided immeasurably by this review of the innate affects as a biological reality that evolves into a psychological system somewhat different for each person and by our new awareness of the importance of the affect system in the evolution of the sense of self.

Working a century ago, within a biological science truly primitive by our current standards, Freud was an archaeologist who attempted to deduce the nature of normal functioning from the analysis of desperately sick patients. The Freudian infant is a theoretical construction, little pieces of psychopathology glued together to make a strangely limited kind of baby. This "derived" infant can become an adult only after it has developed the ego mechanisms necessary to allow the solution of problems that exist solely within Freudian theory. The Kohutian baby develops a self only after negotiating the stages of "narcissistic development."

These differences in definition are not trivial. Agreement with the Freudian scheme of psychosexual development requires acceptance of two parallel progressions—that of libido energy from mouth to anus to phallus, and that of interpersonal relatedness from narcissism to object-relatedness in the context of this libidinal development. In this system, nearly everything is viewed in a sexual context. Shame is viewed as the failure to renounce sexual exhibitionism—all shame is either vaguely or specifically sexual.

Acceptance of the Kohutian scheme of "narcissistic development" limits one's understanding of shame to those situations in which there has been a "narcissistic injury" or in which the sense of self has been damaged. Andrew Morrison, the self psychologist best known for his writings about shame, commented to me that "shame is an affective response to a perception of the self as flawed, and thus inevitably involves narcissism."

I realize that these few pages of description are neither detailed enough to do justice to the two schools of thought described nor concise enough to satisfy the reader who may wonder why I have devoted so much space to these two particular concepts of self. For the adult, however, shame is almost always defined as the pain associated with some perceived deficiency in the self, and pride as the pleasure associated with an elevation in the sense of self. Not surprisingly, within the psychoanalytic world, it is the self-psychologists who have at last begun to pay attention to shame, although they remain a bit skittish about the nature of pride. (After all, people come to doctors complaining about pain rather than pleasure.) And the pain caused by damage to the self is called shame.

Within either of these highly regarded views of shame it would be unthinkable to consider shame as an innate affect, a physiological mechanism that limits the expression of interest–excitement and enjoyment–joy. Both philosophies ignore the fact that newborn infants show all the facial and bodily manifestations of shame. In these theoretical systems shame *means* narcissism, shame *means* sexual exhibitionism. And now we affect theorists come along suggesting that shame can occur in an organism too young to have enough of a self-concept that it can be damaged in an interpersonal context, and well before the libido force has even reached the level of genital sexuality. How strange it must seem to one trained in these philosophies to read here that shame can exist before the cognitive equipment of the child can allow the mechanism of self-reflection and inner looking!

Some years ago, when I began to write about these matters, I yielded to the pressure of my prior training and used the term "proto-shame" to describe these early experiences of shame affect. This new term helped my colleagues accept the idea that the scripted firmware mechanism Tomkins calls shame–humiliation can affect us long before we have a self-concept, long before we can know enough about our self-system to see it as damaged. But it drew attention away from the far more important issue: Very, very few of the experiences in which any affect is triggered have labels. This whole book represents my attempt to shift our language away from an adult-oriented emotion vocabulary toward one based squarely on the concept and language of innate affect. There is no such thing as "proto-shame." There is only a huge group of experiences in which shame affect plays a role; of these only a tiny fraction is known as the shame family of emotions.

Our next task is to define the self in the new language made possible by affect theory and the recent decades of research in infant observation. We must show how the child's growing self-concept becomes intimately linked with the affect of shame and the emotion of pride. As happens so often, the data have long been available and ready for assembly.

16

SHAME AND THE SELF

Daniel Stern, a psychoanalytically trained infant researcher, has suggested that we think of the hypothetical Freudian baby, derived as it is from the work of those therapists who treat disturbed adults, as "the clinical infant" and of the baby described here as "the observed infant." The clinical infant fits the data reconstructed from classical psychoanalysis and is a useful construction within that discipline.

The Kohutian baby seems to be a little closer to the real thing, even though it too is a construction derived from the psychoanalytic investigation of disturbed adults. Kohut is right to point out that the self is more than a bunch of ego mechanisms, even though his inability to give up the idea of infantile narcissism places rigid limits on the usefulness of his work.

Yet we need to spend a moment or two redefining some of this language. What do we really mean when we use words like "self" or "person"? We talk about character structure, but what is a "character"? These terms are used so much in the world of psychology, and used so differently by so many people, that we are in danger of losing them unless we find some acceptable standard of definition. In the bookshelf flanking one wall of my consultation room sit those texts and novels I use for emphasis during therapy sessions. Nearest to my hand is a dictionary, the book I use more than any other. In my study at home rests a much larger dictionary, which protects me from the confusion that afflicts all writers. Like most of my colleagues, when these otherwise competent references fail me, I dive into the greatest work of scholarship ever assembled, the Oxford English Dictionary, where one can trace the history of a word. The OED is a series of articles about words, scholarly documents explaining—and demonstrating with examples—how a word accumulated the meanings by which we know it today.

Words travel through history accumulating meanings and rarely losing them completely. What the OED does best is draw me backwards in time. A session with the OED is an archaeological expedition showing how a word represented experiences, feelings, and emotions in the cultures that preceded ours. Affect-laden words travel through time collecting culture-bound connotation. That seems very much to me like the definition of emotion itself used throughout this book. I am trying to show how the concepts of shame and pride are derived for each of us over the course of our lives.

How we as a culture know these words today is dependent on the world in which we have grown up as that civilizing tradition has evolved through time. Forgive the analogy that springs naturally to the mind of one trained first in biology—recall the statement that *ontogeny recapitulates phylogeny*. It is a reminder that each human embryo, in its path from zygote to full-term fetus, resembles in its appearance the ancestral life forms from which our species evolved. I believe that our contemporary words for emotion carry with them all the implications that can possibly be derived from their usage through history.

So old is the word *self* that its origins are obscure. It appears in most European languages, from Gothic to Scandinavian, with remarkably little difference in spelling or pronunciation. The root *se* appears in the Latin *ipse*, which conveys the sense of sameness. (In medicine we refer to something on the same side of the body as *ipsilateral* as opposed to something on the other side, which is therefore *contralateral*.) The German form of this root is *selbst*; in Old English it is written *selfa* or *selva*.

From the earliest written uses of the word self we see this concept of sameness. A *self-bow* is a bow made out of one piece of wood, a *self-handle* is one carved into the body of an object. When we refer to somebody as *himself*, or to our own person as *myself*, we acknowledge that an individual has certain attributes or qualities that are invariant. John, or Bill, or Mary can each be said to be or have a self, to be *themselves* because we recognize in them something that makes them unique. Intrinsic to the idea of self is some sort of consistency despite what might also be changed.

This differs somewhat from the word *identity*, which also conveys the idea of sameness—identity is a label that remains attached to a person or thing as long as it is not altered. It conveys the sense of things being the same in substance, nature, composition, or properties. Identity is about absolute or essential sameness, the sense of "oneness." Anyone whose appearance is changed radically by plastic surgery, and who is thus viewed differently by others, is said to have undergone a change in identity. I have assumed a new identity if my "label" has changed so much that you cannot recognize me—even though my "self" has not been remodeled. In current usage, identity refers to those more external or superficial features by which we are known, whereas self refers to all aspects—inner and outer.

The concept of self, then, is an overarching construct. It takes into account that we have good moods and bad moods, that we have successes and failures, that we look good on some days and simply awful on others. The self is an umbrella concept—everything about us fits into it—a system rather than an entity.

We toy with this idea of sameness when we say "I'm not myself today," indicating that we would like to disavow some particular portion of our makeup. Declaring a component piece of us to be not-self is probably a way to escape the implications of some part of our makeup that brings us negative affect.

Such an understanding of self is helpful when we try to understand the concept of other, which the OED defines as "that one of two which remains when one is taken, defined, or specified." In the world of people and their relationships, "other" can only be defined while we are in the process of defining "self." Those who have the greatest difficulty understanding the nature of others are usually those who have the most trouble establishing a sense of self or whose idea of self is the most distorted. Sometimes we therapists discuss this in terms of boundaries—it is necessary for each of us to determine the limits of our self in order for us to know who we are in relation to others.

The sense of self becomes more complex over time, partly because the cognitive equipment available to the infant is far less developed than that available to the adult. It is assembled from the informational matrix formed by experiences accumulated as we develop a personal history. If "other" is what remains when we subtract "self," then we know intuitively that the concept of other must also develop over time, along pathways analogous to those determined by the development of the concept of self.

The word character also has an interesting history. It starts out as the instrument used to make a mark that cannot be erased—an engraving tool. Later, the word comes to mean the mark itself, as in a "character of the alphabet." Whatever has been "characterized" has been marked indelibly. The forehead of bondslaves might be marked with the character of a horse, defining people as the property of their owner, just as modern ranchers still brand their livestock. Individual adults can be characterized by their invariant qualities, which become the hallmarks by which we identify them.

When we say that someone has such-and-such a character, we imply that a simple term can encompass or symbolize all the features of a highly complex individual. Thus, a playwright can give an actor enough information to portray (make a portrait of) the person created for dramatic purpose. When we give a "character reference" for someone we have stated our belief that the interpersonal style of an adult can be sketched fairly simply. It is the fact that so much of an individual falls into a clear pattern, a gestalt, that allows us to treat this gestalt itself as an entity to which we can make reference. "Character" has evolved from the tool that makes a mark, to the pattern of the mark itself, to its present use as a pattern existing only in the mind of the observer.

The idea behind *person* is quite different. Its earliest appearance is in the Latin word *persona*, the mask held by performers in a drama to cover the face and thus give them a different apparent identity. This sense of the word remains in theatrical programs, where the list of characters is still called *Dramatis Personae*. You can see the linkage between the idea of a character played by an actor and the mask by which an actor once signified the nature of the role so assumed. The concept of person, or personality, seems to take into account that we play roles in life. It has to do with roles taken on, offices assumed, characters played out.

Often we hear that nothing in the history of a politician prepares us for what he or she will be like as an elected leader. No matter what someone has been like as a lawyer, judge, or senator, appointment to the Supreme Court brings out qualities previously unpredictable. The personality adapts—it is merely one facet of the larger entity, the self. Given a new role, we tend to change our person both for ourselves and for other people. Professional actors often say that their lives, their careers, their day-to-day character structure are permanently altered by the roles they have played on the stage or screen. Phrases and expressions like "clothes make the man," or "let the marines make a man of you," or "dress for success," or "dressed to kill," convey the idea that roles are costumed much as the mask worn by the Roman actor became his persona.

Each role assumed, each personality essayed, involves (among other things) some specific pattern of affect display. In each role we vary somewhat the range over which we modulate innate affects.

Look what happens if I take on the role of a sophisticated, urbane, upperclass WASP gentleman: Shelved, for the moment, will be my own more characteristic ebullience and the tendency to wave my arms as (with interest–excitement) I warm to my subject. My body will be held in a relaxed and easy-going posture; everything about me will suggest that I am in command. My facial set will be one you might describe as "sensitive"; when upset I will tend to turn away in a mild demonstration of reticence (shame–humiliation). Brought to the fore will be such mannerisms as an air of utter restraint, a debonair and condescending attitude of uninvolvement (mild disgust and dissmell) in the antics of what are now defined as "lesser folk," and a certain highly stylized set of attitudes toward nearly everything, all expressed with considerable economy of gesture. When mildly angry, I will tend to become scornful and raise one corner of my lip in contempt; when very angry I will tend to imbibe alcohol in order to allow myself full expression of temper as massive rejection based on disgust and calculated to produce in the recipient terrible shame. Maturity, for me, will be displayed in terms of relaxed self-confidence.

Quite in contrast will be the schedule of affect regulation posted for certain working-class men of Mediterranean extraction. To play this role I must hold differently my entire body. I am required to accentuate my muscularity, adopt a somewhat truculent attitude, and convey to the outside world that I am ready, willing, and perhaps eager to deal with you as a source of physical danger. I will express interest with large, powerful, and definite movements of my entire upper body—on occasion I will smile broadly to indicate my approval, clench my fist like a boxer and punch upward from the shoulder in emphasis. I will tend to walk on the balls of my feet with a springiness that indicates that I am prepared to greet a new situation with rapid physical activity. When upset I will jut forward my lower jaw or square my shoulders as if in preparation for a fight. On occasion, I may raise my eyebrows in mock surprise at something you have said, tilt my head to the side in the characteristic gesture of a boxer preparing to dip one shoulder in readiness for a blow, and ask you to repeat yourself. Like my upper-class friend, I will use alcohol as a general disinhibiting agent, but the affects released will be more boisterous. Brought up in a macho culture, I will fight rather than exhibit distress or shame. Maturity will be expressed in terms of readiness to fight.

These cultural differences are probably not bred in the genes. I know plenty of Mediterranean gentlemen of extraordinary refinement and lots of truculent WASPs. The overwhelming weight of evidence suggests that such behavior is trained into us during childhood by a culture or subculture with highly specific rules for the display and control of innate affect. (Even in common language we say that someone "affects" a personality.) Each role or cultural stereotype involves a different pattern of affects damped or magnified—what Tomkins calls "the differential magnification of innate affect." And when I, as an actor, mimic these stereotypes for you, I have succeeded in "creating" the character by altering the set of rules for the modulation of innate affect I consider normal and adopting the rule book used by those from another society. But when I, as the actor, "take off my makeup" and say, "Hey guys! It's only me," I have declared the existence of an umbrella under which all of these parts have been performed, a "real" self that is my personal concept of "me."

Few of us have the skill and training to be professional actors. Yet all of us play a variety of roles in everyday life. So much is this true that we tend to mock people who are limited in the range of roles they can assume, saying that they do not know "how to behave" in certain situations. I am not (my "self" is not) a character but rather a range of characters, not a role but an assemblage of roles; my personality varies to fit the immediate situation.

I should point out here that there is a rarely achieved level of maturity, a final form of self-evolution, in which an individual has learned what is called "mastery of self." Zen masters and others who have achieved significant degrees of enlightenment demonstrate a remarkable order of attainment in a wide variety of situations—but their personality seems invariant. (A good mid-nineteenth-century American example of this is the character of Eugene in Nathaniel Hawthorne's short story "The Great Stone Face.") Mastery of anything is unusual enough—given the high visibility in this era of professional sports presented as entertainment, we are more likely to see it in great athletes near the end of their career than anywhere else—and mastery of self an exquisitely rare extension of that realm of development.

In my personal experience, most people who seem to "have it all together" are pretty much fake—enlightenment is for them merely a role to be assumed rather than a state of being. Perhaps you recall the character of Yoda in the Star Wars series of movies—a costly plastic marionette with the facial and bodily display of enlightenment, designed to mimic the lively sameness associated with the rarely achieved real thing. Almost all of us look different when we are required to act differently. We are deferential to our priests, haughty to our servants; we tug our forelocks in the face of authority and act somewhat more discourteously free-spirited as spectators at the stadium. We "gear up" to be daring, seductive, brave, cowardly, truculent, or gracious when occasion demands or permits.

In general, then, merely trying to be different fosters the emergence of a somewhat new personality. It does not matter whether we have learned new behaviors through happenstance or from a script as suggested by an author outside the self. What we have done in one role can be carried over into another. Yet all of the roles I have assumed, all of the characters I have played on the stage of life, all of the personalities I have exhibited in my interpersonal world, all of these are subsumed under the overarching construct of self.

This, incidentally, is why we therapists can assure our patients that no matter how they change in psychotherapy, they retain the right and the ability to go on being whoever they were before they entered. Therapy doesn't commit one to any single role! Successful therapy, however, expands the sum total of roles available to the individual.

Adults are expected, required, to play a certain number of roles. I think it is pretty easy to accept such a role-based concept of the relation between personality and self when we look at grown-ups. Two critical questions leap to mind: Is this true of children (do they play roles)? And, if children develop by learning a series of roles, how do all the roles come to be coalesced into a unitary self?

Maybe the first question is a bit silly. Of course we know that children play roles. They imitate nearly everything and everybody at every stage of their development. To watch a child grow up is to attend the theater of roles assumed, assimilated, and discarded. Increasing maturity does not halt the process of experimentation—it merely allows us to substitute the audience of our peers for the original family of spectators.

By framing the problem in this manner I have called attention to the fact that our mature style of role assumption, of character formation, is only a late derivative (a final form) of the normal process through which children learn to become adults. One cannot understand childhood without comprehension of the enormous number and variety of roles played by growing people. Every bit of business attempted by a child is being tested to see if it is worthy of incorporation into the final form of the self. Roles are shaped and limited by shame, the affect of impediment to excitement and enjoyment.

The second question is a bit more difficult to answer. Early on, it is only when a role achieves importance in the context of the infant–mother relationship that it is rehearsed often enough to be made permanent. What we call "the self" is not an innate internal structure but a composition formed in an interpersonal context. The durability of any new behavior is dependent on the affect it elicits from the caregiver as well as from within. The shape of the self is heavily dependent on the affects generated in a complex interpersonal milieu. And, finally, the cohesiveness of the self system (the integrity of the package into which all these component personal styles are assembled) is completely dependent on the ability and willingness of the caregivers to accept them as part of a whole.

Another pair of questions: How early does the self begin to form? And, how early in self-development does shame begin to get bundled into identity? Since shame will be triggered any time there is an impediment to ongoing interest–excitement or enjoyment–joy, we can assume that shame will be experienced quite early. (Certainly we can demonstrate the visible expression of shame affect in the days-old infant.) It remains for us to determine how early we can link shame to those experiences through which the infant develops its personal identity.

Although there are many theorists, clinicians, and experimenters who have worked on this problem, I will concentrate on the writings of the two who have interested me most, Daniel Stern and Johanna Krout Tabin. Each of them published a book in 1985. Stern summarized his years of research observing babies in *The Interpersonal World of the Infant* and offered a new way of integrating an astonishing amount of scientific data. It is devoted to the problem we have just been discussing, the nature and the development of the self.

Tabin, a psychoanalytic psychologist with a deep and abiding interest in the eating disorders called *anorexia nervosa* and *bulimia,* forces our attention on something all of us thought had been settled by Freud at the other end of the century—the sexual life of the infant. Her book, *On the Way to Self: Ego and Early Oedipal Development,* asks us to recognize that the infant shows signs of sexual arousal from the earliest days of extrauterine life. Just as generations of psychologists said that the facial display of affect seen on the face of the newborn was unimportant because it was "only a reflex," we have always ignored the infant boy's equally visible erections. Most important for our purposes is her conviction that the toddler decides "I'm a girl!" or "I'm a boy!" at least partly on the basis of the way it feels to be sexually aroused. Thus, a significant portion of our identity (the label called gender identity) is conveyed by the sexual drive, a prewritten program as basic to our life form as the affects.

To my disappointment, neither book deals with affect theory and the work of Tomkins. Although Stern recognizes that innate affect is central to the experience of the growing infant, he avoids any attempt to define affect and ignores Tomkins almost completely; the words *sex, gender,* and *shame* do not even appear in his index. Tabin, a classically trained psychoanalyst, was innocent of the work described in this current book. And neither seems to have been aware of the work cited by the other.

Both of these sober and excellent scholar/scientist/clinicians seem to me to have areas of blindness. Stern ignores or finds no significance in what Tabin sees so clearly, that baby boys have highly conspicuous erections in situations that seem interpersonal. Also, although he is aware that affect causes things to happen all over the body, he is singularly uninterested in the face as well as in the search for whatever might trigger affect. Indeed, his misunderstanding of affect forms a deep flaw in an otherwise landmark book. Tabin apparently accepts Freud's theory that the affects come from the drives—she, too, ignores the data available on the face of the infant. She derives most of the sense of self from genital arousal and accepts without question the concepts of infantile narcissism, infant-mother fusion, and the idea that development requires separation from this fused, narcissistic state.

Clearly, if these investigators devoted entire books to their work on the development of the self, I can do justice to neither in these few pages. I will allude to their ideas and recommend both books to my fellow students and clinicians. In the passages and chapters that follow I will describe a theory for the formation of the sense of self and other that takes into account Stern's summary of the data on infant-mother interaction, Tabin's understanding of sexual arousal, Tomkin's work on innate affect, and my own interest in shame. I ask the indulgence of my colleagues for the omission of the host of references from which these ideas have been drawn.

The Ways of Sensing Self

During the first two months after birth, as Stern points out, the infant is occupied with the task of adjustment to extrauterine life. Doubtless it could not live unless protected by certain prewritten programs that organize its behavior to some extent. Drawing on the language of computers for my analogies, I referred earlier to the drives and affects as firmware, analogous to data processing programs that can be written as integrated circuits, installed on "chips," and inserted in computers. Firmware is neither software nor hardware. Although part of our genetic heritage, and therefore not software like the training programs and other learning experiences from which we build a self, neither is it hardware like our bones, muscles, blood vessels, and neurological equipment.

The affects are a group of built-in mechanisms triggered in response to conditions of stimulation that recur constantly throughout life. Every time an affect is triggered, the infant is exposed to a sequence of events that is relatively invariant. Similarly, the drives are responses to needs that recur constantly, responses that inform the organism both that something is needed and the region of the body where that need can be satisfied.

Consider, for a moment, hunger and the transactions associated with eating. The newborn baby is not capable of "deciding" that it is hungry. When the level of glucose in its blood drops within a critical range, the hunger drive triggers a message that begins a sequence of events culminating in feeding behavior. The information provided by the drive system has no inherent urgency, so the way the infant will experience ("receive" or "process") this message depends entirely on the affects that amplify it.

Some of this activity is highly variable. Mother may be right there, smiling at a baby who has just begun to exhibit sucking movements—and she may be quite prepared to offer breast or bottle. Alternatively, mother may be in the next room, taking a much-needed break from her rapt attention to the baby, whose earliest indications of need will go unnoticed. The persistent call of hunger now acts as a competent stimulus for the affect distress–anguish, producing first a couple of sobs and eventually a full spectrum of crying behaviors that blend into anger–rage as the density of stimulation reaches the range set for its release. What the caregiver finds is a hungry infant in a crying rage. What the caregiver must do is modulate (soothe) the baby's affect display, make sure what need (drive) has triggered this highly visible assemblage of affects, and provide what is required. The variable aspects of the situation depend on a great many factors, including the length of time the infant has been hungry and the ability of the caregiver to respond to this need.

Nevertheless, certain parts of this system are invariant: Hunger occurs with regularity; hunger amplified by affect makes the caregiver appear; the appearance of the caregiver means that food will appear; food makes hunger wane; the combination of food and caregiver also modulates negative affect and triggers positive affect. Since our concept of the self focuses on the idea of invariant qualities, any time we find an invariant experience it must be evaluated for its relevance to the self.

Stern says it nicely: "Sense of self is not a cognitive construct. It is an experiential integration" (1985, 71). Initially, the self is not something that is created by conscious thought, but rather the summation of our invariant experiences. The drives, the affects, and the actions of the caregivers in handling the constantly recurring situations triggered by these built-in mechanisms, the very patterns formed by these sequences, are enough of an invariant that they may be said to provide some framework for the experience of self. During the first two months of life, when the job of the caregivers is to act as regulators for the infant, Stern suggests that the baby demonstrates an "emerging sense of self." With the slow, steady emergence of the sense of self comes a matching emerging sense of the caregiving other.

Tomkins has commented that it looks as if there is something genetically given in the infant that makes it elect to imitate its own actions, to improve on what had been initially a reflex. The urge to improve on nature seems to be built into our very equipment! The hungry newborn will make sucking motions, and it is clear that these muscular activities are prewired reflexes—set in motion by a prewritten script. Yet within a few hours of birth the infant can be observed imitating its own previously reflexive sucking movements—taking over, as it were, cultivating happenstance into intentionality. From the moment of birth the infant automatically tracks mother with its eyes; yet within hours the child is capable of substituting voluntary tracking for what had only a moment ago been a reflexive action.

Even though it is initially innate affect that takes over the face of the baby and makes it frown or smile, the child soon learns to "make faces" on purpose. Even though it is the drive hunger that makes the infant produce sucking movements, and the need for oxygen that makes it breathe, the child soon learns to suck when it wants and to alter its breathing "on purpose." The newborn's efforts at the intentional simulation of bodily functions initially produced by the action of prewritten scripts (its autosimulation of affect- and drive-related behavior) are the result of *observations that must be analyzed to whatever extent is necessary to allow conscious imitation.* Whatever behavior the growing child attempts, whatever skills it tries to master, each series of self-directed actions becomes part of the child's definition of self for that epoch of development.

The programmed response, whether a sucking reflex, or a tracking reflex, or an affective reaction, is not necessarily an *I*. But as soon as the infant decides that *I* will do it, the self-concept has begun to form. With the decision to initiate behavior comes the beginning of self-affirmation. Whatever is done voluntarily defines a self.

As soon as the infant learns to recognize that crying brings mother, that infant is capable of using the vocal and facial display of cries and whimpers as a semiotic device to achieve contact with mother. Thus, the visible portion of an innate affect comes to be used intentionally even when the conditions for the triggering of that behavior as a true innate affect have not been met. The sequence of events involved—intentional whimper; mommy runs over to me; mommy picks me up; I am pleased that my trick got mommy to pick me up—this entire sequence of events allows one of the earliest types of self-definition. Nobody but I did that. I intended to whimper, I intended that mommy would react to my whimper. I am a center of intention; conversely, wherever there is intention there is an I.

Developmental theorists argue this point a great deal. How, some ask, can we say that an infant has a sense of self when it is not yet capable of conscious and intentional *internal* reflection, when it is unable to meditate on the nature of the self? Intrinsic to the sense of self, they say, is the ability to think intentionally about the self. The ability to reflect, to understand that others can see us when we do not intend them to see us, that we are the object of the attention of others—these aspects of self-awareness are milestones in development achieved somewhere in the second year of life. And these theorists find it hard to accept the idea that there is any sort of self-concept before there is an inward-reflecting self. They confuse the idea of self with the ability to focus attention on the self.

The answer, of course, is inherent in the definition of self that we established earlier. Any action that can be planned, initiated, carried out from beginning to end and remembered as a personally written script will be subsumed under the umbrella of "me." The knowledge that I did something is equivalent to the knowledge that there is an I who does things. The concept of self travels through development along with every other part of us. The earliest form of self-definition is made of the information associated with the decision to imitate one's own unintentional actions. The more advanced versions constitute an upgrade on the earlier product—they contain the sort of information that accumulates over time and is made possible only by the incremental advances in brain function accompanying biological development. The intricacy of our psychology varies directly with the complexity of the equipment available to it.

Stern proposes that the sense of self develops in fairly discrete jumps. Birth brings emergence from the warm, dark, quiet world of the womb where food is supplied automatically through the umbilical cord—issue into the cold, harshly bright, noisy outside universe. Even hunger must be a novel and somewhat unpleasant experience for the newborn. He suggests that the sense of self begins to emerge during the first two months, during the period when child and caregivers are negotiating the regulation of all these physiological needs that had previously been handled by the intrauterine environment.

During the third through sixth months, infants develop what he calls a "core self," becoming increasingly certain that "they and mother are quite separate physically, are different agents, have different affective experiences, and have separate histories" (27). Over the next couple of months, they discover that the people outside have minds like their own, and that they can relate to others on the basis of shared feelings and experiences. Stern calls this the "sense of a subjective self" (27). At around the age of 15 months, as the infant is developing an ever-increasing vocabulary, it begins to develop a "verbal self" (28). Words confer the ability to render objects by symbols and to negotiate with the caregivers on the basis of these shared symbols. Not long after, noted Stern, the three-year-old demonstrates the emergence of a "narrative self,"* a me who can tell stories about me, and who can therefore create a desired sense of me for you. With the development of Stern's narrative self comes what I interpret as a marked increase in our conscious control over the nature of the self.

Using Stern's schedule for the development of the self, let us see how the infant might experience shame affect during the first three years of life: The conditions for shame affect are simply that the infant must already be experiencing either of the positive affects (interest–excitement or enjoyment–joy), that whatever conditions had triggered positive affect remain operative, and that some impediment to the continuation of positive affect be encountered. Shame, then, is a painful amplification of any impediment to positive affect. It is an auxiliary mechanism, a piece of firmware that limits the operation of other affects. Shame produces a sudden loss of muscle tone in the neck and upper body; increases skin temperature on the face, frequently resulting in a blush; and causes a brief period of incoordination and apparent disorganization. No matter what behavior is in progress when shame affect is triggered, it will be made momentarily impossible. Shame interrupts, halts, takes over, inconveniences, trips up, makes incompetent anything that had previously been interesting or enjoyable.

Have I conveyed enough of the sense of shame affect for you to see it as I do? Shame impedes what until that moment had been most interesting or most enjoyable. When triggered, it interferes with precisely those activities that cause the most pleasure to the infant. Every instance of shame is a moment of painful incapacity. The younger the child, the more dependent the sense of self on the presence of prewired invariant capabilities and the ability to simulate these as learned behavior. And the younger the child who experiences shame affect, the more powerful will be the interference with the sense of self. Shame is the great undoing of whatever had been exciting or pleasurable.

But how early can we see evidence of shame affect? Watching the development of his own son, Tomkins mentioned to me his observation that at three weeks Mark was clearly trying to imitate human speech by mimicking the mouth movements of adults. But the neurological equipment of an infant is unable to handle such sophisticated skills. This is one of those situations where desire outruns ability, where life places natural impediments in the path of a wish. Only failure could reward each of his attempts to make speech, and each

*This concept was introduced at the Basch–Stern course on child development given in August, 1990, at the Cape Cod Institute.

failed attempt was followed by the slump of shame. Demos, studying infants with film and videotape, has recorded many similar examples of neonatal shame. It seems that most observers have ignored the data I would find most significant—that shame affect can be seen in babies long before they can be said to experience embarrassment.

One might think that such an affect would have little to do with the development of a sense of self, that it would even tend to undo whatever experiential integration had already been achieved. Yet to the extent that shame itself is a scripted mechanism, a programmed unfolding of bodily reactions, shame is a relatively invariant experience. I suspect that shame produces a *sense of an incompetent self*, that there is a part of the self created by shame.

Furthermore, I believe that very little in the life experience of the child calls attention to the nature of the self as powerfully as does shame affect. First there is a me who was just beginning to look at, or perhaps do, something interesting. I am used to that self; I know me in that mode of activity; I have certain expectations of that self. But now along comes some impediment, some totally unexpected interference with my interest or enjoyment in looking or doing or communing. Suddenly, even though the activity itself continues to look interesting or pleasing, I am in the throes of shame affect. My neck is no longer under my own control; my eyes cannot look at the object of my desires; my thinking process and all my heretofore confident actions are suddenly scrambled.

So there is a me before the moment of shame and a me who is in the midst of a shame experience. Shame wanes as I withdraw interest or stop trying to commune with whatever had previously been enjoyable. (There is life after shame.) I recover, I come back to my former self, although perhaps with some lesser degree of *aplomb*. (Aplomb is more about shame and pride than you might think. *Plumbum* is the Latin word for lead and refers to the weight on a string used by surveyors to define a perpendicular line. Aplomb means the ability to stand proud and straight, rather than droop in shame.) Shame is so uncomfortable that it can cause a lingering sense of wariness, of unwillingness to trust positive affect quite so easily. A burned child dreads the fire that brought pain, and a shamed child avoids (at least briefly) the full expression of positive affect.

All of the modern students of child behavior, the experts in infant observation, seem to agree that infants are born to make comparisons. They seem always able to weigh one perception against another, whether the information comes from vision, hearing, touch, the sense of body motion (proprioception), temperature, or from the complex sources we call innate affect. I suspect that even the very young child can tell the difference between the self that is competent and the self that is made uncoordinated by shame.

I suggest that the innate affect shame–humiliation, at all ages and in all stages of human development, is a powerful mechanism for the elaboration of the sense of self. The very ability of shame affect to upset all mental activity, to render incompetent our ability to perform intentional activity, to afflict muscle tone in the head and neck, to wrestle gaze away from what might have occupied us only a moment ago—all these powers of shame force us to consider who we were before shame hit and to what we have returned as shame subsides. Shame is the affect most likely to produce attention to the nature of the self. Shame produces a painful self-awareness at every stage in human development simply because of the ability of this affect script to interfere with every pleasant way we know ourselves. Through shame we are forced to know and remember our failures. While it is clear that shame affect is triggered by experiences that have nothing at all to do with competence, shame produces awareness of an incompetent self.

That may not be such a bad deal, after all. If you were going to design a system capable of learning from experience and educating itself, you might as well build in the capacity to magnify failure. Shame augments our memory of failure and protects us from whatever danger might occur, when, in a moment of need, we might try something well beyond our capacity. An intelligent organism will avoid what might produce pain unless there are compelling reasons to accept that noxious reward. Near the end of Shakespeare's Sonnet 64 the speaker comments, "Ruin hath taught me thus to ruminate." So shame is a teacher, often drawing us within ourselves to think deeply about the self.

We should not ignore, even for a moment, the fact that the process of trying out a new character, of learning new functions, of diving into the depths of our soul to find a new way to live or to be, that none of these activities can be accomplished without the amplification of affect. Nothing new is attempted unless affect makes it urgently important. Whenever these new activities are greeted by success, we are likely to experience pride. And whatever acts as an impediment to the completion of an action that involves interest–excitement or the contentment of enjoyment–joy will be afflicted painfully by the amplified analogue of that impediment, shame–humiliation. Therefore it is easy to understand why the coassembly of shame affect with memory is to such a remarkable degree a self-related experience.

DEPTHS AND DEGREES

We have left unanswered one realm of questions set earlier: Why does shame afflict us sometimes to the core of the self and at other times appear as the merest of inconveniences? Why do some people describe shame as "the death of the soul" when others see only a mild insult to be shrugged off? In a Talmudic tractate we are told that to humiliate one in public is worse than shedding blood; anyone who mocked the oversized nose of Cyrano de Bergerac risked death at the hands of the great swordsman. (Real blood exchanged for humiliation—retaliation is indeed talionic!) How can the same affect mechanism account for situations in which we are "embarrassed to death" (mortified) and also those in which we are embarrassed *about* something quite limited, some aspect of the self clearly demarcated from the whole by firm walls and boundaries? Why do shame and pride afflict the self in levels, sizes, grades, intensities, magnitudes, dimensions?

There is a whole range of solutions for this puzzle. We know intuitively that it has something to do with age. With maturity comes the ability to modulate all affects; shame, too, can be tamed and held within limits. The younger a child, the more thoroughly and deeply will shame produce disorganization. The infant whose every muscle slumps suddenly when it has been defeated in the act of will is a muddled mess of a baby until the moment of shame passes and other affects lend their more positive urgency. This is shame affect unmodulated, shame pure but by no means simple.

There is a point in development when we learn to recognize that someone is *trying* to humiliate us. This awareness allows us to bring into play other learned mechanisms, and we become capable of deciding not to let our reactions show. Conscious control of affect display will always mute emotional experience, just as the intentional augmentation of affect *display* will amplify it. Even the "cognitive shock" of shame can be limited by certain learned strategies. Later in this book I will discuss *how* I think this is accomplished, but for the moment I want only to point out that it can be done at all.

The maturation of affect modulation has been little studied. There is a flow, a rhythm to these capacities, which Tomkins describes as "the differential magnification of innate affect." Parents take it for granted that little children must be taught to "keep a stiff upper lip," not to gloat when they win, and to control irrepressible laughter without losing the sense of fun. (I remember how my daughter and her friends used to giggle when I would ask them, "Please scream softly.") Psychiatrists take for granted the matching tasks of first teaching patients the freedom to express anger within the safety of the therapeutic encounter and then helping them learn how to be angry within culturally acceptable limits. As we mellow into adulthood we acquire those skills that make us acceptable to and comfortable within our social networks. Among the rules to be learned are those for the modulated expression and experience of shame and pride.

Intuitively we know that these abilities are learned over a long period of time. Our expectations of teacher and toddler differ because very young children lack some of the cognitive equipment needed to handle the advanced techniques of affect modulation. Babies have only global affects. Their emotional experiences are whole-body states, and they seem to understand these events as relating to the whole self. Only in the second year of life do they develop the ability to make things partial, to assign responsibility to a part of them rather than the whole. Only when a child can understand that he or she has a hand, that the hand is only a part of the whole being, and that something done by that hand can be "blamed" on that hand; only then can that little boy or girl understand that the source of shame can be the hand rather than the whole self.

One researcher who has devoted a great deal of attention to this part of the riddle is psychologist Michael Lewis. I like his explanation of *hubris*, which we mentioned earlier as "the sin of pride." Hubris, says Lewis, is when we lose the idea that there is a difference between an attribute (a small part of us) and our whole self. In hubris, we think of ourselves as elevated in toto—as a better person deserving of different status—simply because we have won a game or a prize. That, of course, is what rankled so many people about the young Cassius Clay, who claimed that his boxing ability made him both beautiful and "the greatest." The label of beauty is usually attached by viewers outside the self, and his pugilistic ability had yet to be tested adequately to justify the label of greatness he professed. It was his hubris, rather than the accuracy of his assertions, that made him obnoxious to some people. In both pride and shame, these most self-related of the emotions, the depth of the emotional experience will be related to the importance-to-the-self of whatever has been magnified or impeded.

For the most part, I have restricted my discussion of the shame experience to situations in which the impediment to positive affect is independent of interpersonal interaction, such as those all-important moments during which the infant is trying out new skills without regard for the presence of others. While it is true that half the infant's waking moments are spent in solitary play, the other half are expended in communion with the caregivers. The infant's perception of the external world is also shaped by social experience, by the way the caregivers respond to the patterns created by the tensions of the drives and the urgency of affects. There is much more we can say about the importance of shame affect in the early months of life, the period during which infant and caregivers are learning how to regulate the physiologic mechanisms made urgent by extrauterine existence. Our concept of the relation between self and other is formed in such a context. To put it another way, the entire self/other matrix is an early organization of the infantile mind—one that will be affected powerfully by shame.

Since we have established that (regardless what triggers it) shame affect causes a momentary disorganization of infantile abilities and self-confidence, indeed producing what I have called the sense of an incompetent self, now we must ask how shame influences our perception of others. Of equal importance will be the attempt to demonstrate how our personal, individual experience of shame is affected by the other in whose presence we are embarrassed. Our understanding of "otherness" must be broad enough to take into account the various classes of other, the variety of others important from infancy through adulthood. Shame affect triggered in the context of social relationships becomes social shame, the realm and range of emotions thought to be shame itself by most people. Such will be our focus in the next chapter.

III

LOVE AND SEX:
GETTING TOGETHER

17

LOVE, EXILE,
EXCOMMUNICATION,
AND DISGRACE:
SHAME AND THE OTHER

My daughter asked me to look at something she was reading for her science class in high school. On the theory that all the sciences are easily interchangeable, the school had assigned to its best physics teacher the task of putting together a course in psychology. Cheerily, uncritically, this amiable young man had assembled a mélange of classical texts to be digested and regurgitated back to him in relatively pristine condition. "Daddy!" she said, "They don't know *anything* about affect! And my whole class knows more about shame than the teacher." My earliest work on the importance of shame in interpersonal relationships had been greatly informed by Julie's reports from school. She and her grade school cronies were among the first to use these new theories "in the field."

Looking over the list of books from which she was to choose one for a report, I had suggested she read Erich Fromm's 1956 work *The Art of Loving*. Nearly two generations of adolescents, consumed as they are with concerns about love and sex, have been exposed to this immensely popular work. I use sections of it in my teaching and in psychotherapy, even though I sort of close my eyes to the parts that no longer make sense. His work is, of course, based on the Freudian logic that dominated psychiatry until recently, even though Fromm himself offered many important revisions of classical psychoanalytic theory. I had always liked his explanation of the different ways we love our parents, our children, our peers, and our partners in erotic play.

Julie drew my attention to Fromm's initial premise—that we are created as beings fused with mother and are terrified of separateness: "The experience of separateness arouses anxiety; it is, indeed, the source of all anxiety. Being separate means being cut off, without any capacity to use my human powers. Hence to be separate means to be helpless, unable to grasp the world—things and people—actively; it means that the world can invade me without my ability to react. Thus, separateness is the source of intense anxiety. Beyond that, it arouses shame and the feeling of guilt. . . . *The awareness of human separation, without reunion by love—is the source of shame*" (8–9). (Italics in original.)

Fromm is not the only scholar to link shame to separation. One of the most influential early investigators of shame, Helen Block Lewis, felt that the human is intrinsically social, that the infant is born social. She believed that shame and guilt are mechanisms built into the firmware of the body, well differentiated and highly specific emotional systems that monitor our involvement with each other. In her system, shame monitors our tendency to be narcissistic, to adopt an opinion about ourselves that does not conform to what is seen by those important to us.

For Lewis, the blush is a flag that tells the other before whom we have been shamed that we are ready to admit our transgression and by which we ask that we be returned to the fold. Guilt is a mechanism that tells us we have violated some rule of the group and punishes us for transgression. Both emotions are viewed only in terms of the way they affect our membership in social net-works, and for this reason her work must now be considered inadequate to explain all the phenomenology of shame. Like Fromm, she is too quick to explain emotion on the basis of the way it appears to a therapist who works with adults.

Fromm continues along this vein, maintaining that the search for "orgiastic pleasure" in drugs or hedonistic activity is an attempt to return to the feeling of fusion with mother—"to escape from separateness" (12). Conformity, too, is evaluated as a means of fooling ourselves into the belief that we are not alone. Even creative activity is described as a mere hedge against separateness: "In any kind of creative work the creating person unites himself with his material, which represents the work outside himself. . . . (I)n all types of creative work the worker and his object become one, man unites himself with the world in the process of creation" (17).

All three solutions—orgiastic fusion, conformity, and productive work—are only transitory, producing what he calls "pseudo-unity."

Hence, they are only partial answers to the problem of existence. The full answer lies in the achievement of interpersonal union, of fusion with another person, in love.

This desire for interpersonal fusion is the most powerful striving in man. It is the most fundamental passion, it is the force which keeps the human race together, the clan, the family, society. The failure to achieve it means insanity or destruction—self-destruction or destruction of others. Without love, humanity could not exist for a day (18).

I think these explanations of love must now be considered incorrect, or at least inadequate to explain what we have learned more recently about the early development of children. In this chapter, and the one that follows, I will discuss some of the major theories about human connectedness and suggest a new way of looking at the relation between love and shame. But it would be unfair to judge *The Art of Loving* as if it had been published today. When a new book (or play or film) is reviewed, both author and reviewer must be citizens of the same culture, creatures of the identical era. Erich Fromm wrote for two audiences. At the superficial level, he aimed this book at his contemporary reader. But at a deeper level, he was fighting with the ghost of Sigmund Freud.

Throughout this book I have mentioned the Freudian concept known as *libido theory.* As you know, it was Freud's view that the psychological life of the human is powered by a basically sexual life force that animates us much as a marionette, or a puppet, or a velveteen rabbit may be "brought to life" in fiction. In classical psychoanalytic theory, this libido force presents itself first as the newborn's insatiable drive to consume the world through its mouth, an *oral drive* that links the infant to the breast of mother with great passion. Fromm repeats this in his lovely, poetic style when he says that to the newborn, mother *is* food, mother *is* warmth, mother *is* safety. What the psychoanalyst calls "oral needs" link infant and mother. But since Freud viewed the infant as quite unable to differentiate between self and other at this time, he taught that even the "need-satisfying" breast of mother was seen by the child as an extension of its own being and not really separate from it. In the Freudian system, the infant is locked in the state he called narcissism, and infantile love is no more than narcissistic self-love.

Within this system of thought, the libido force is believed to move to the anal region as the growing child begins to oppose and disagree with the mother he or she had previously seen only as the source of sustenance. As I mentioned earlier, however much child and mother seem to be in contention, Freudian theory argues that (at least to the child) what we outsiders would see as interpersonal conflict is really a form of inner conflict because it is being viewed by the child as part of a narcissistic system. Their relationship is still not truly interpersonal because mother and infant are thought to be locked in narcissistic fusion, for theory states that the child still does not know that mother is another being.

Only much later, when the libido force is thought to become really sexual, does the small child begin to see the opposite-gender parent as the object of this sexual drive, and thus to define another person as a sexual object. Eventually the child renounces his or her sexual interest in this parent, but the passionate interest that had drawn the child to this object of the sexual drive remains as a nonsexual attraction that is the forerunner of adult love. To Freud, who would not tolerate within his circle any scholar who wished to diminish the primacy of his libido-based theory, love was an inherently sexual force.

Where Freud saw love as the irrational validation of a relationship made powerful by sexual attraction, Fromm saw the need to overcome our terror of separateness. *The Art of Loving* is a wonderful book because it makes us think about the varieties of love, about the need to blend sexuality and human intimacy into a dynamic relationship. Fromm's moving and passionate treatise on love would have been quite different had he been granted the opportunity to study the affect system of Tomkins and to integrate with it the work of Stern, Tabin, and other modern observers of infancy. His book can be understood best in terms of the world it sought to change. Considering the fact that it remains a classic nearly 40 years after its publication, and that an enormous number of adults have grown to maturity with Fromm's book by their side, it would seem that he accomplished his aim. But too much has been learned in those intervening years, and it is time to reevaluate some of the classical assumptions about love and especially about the relation between shame and separateness.

Connections abound. In the moment of shame we feel isolated, terribly alone, shorn from the herd. Equally well can shame make us feel that the eyes of the other—normally the window of friendly human interchange—have become a source or a symbol of oppressive attention. It is then that we wish for the earth to open up and swallow us; shame makes us long for invisibility. When embarrassed, we feel that we are no longer known to the world by our best attributes, but by our worst. Léon Wurmser,* surely the most gifted psychoanalytic writer ever to plumb the depths of the shame experience, has often remarked that at the core of shame is the feeling that we are both unloved and unlovable.

---

*Read, especially, pp. 87–97 of *The Mask of Shame* for his poignant and evocative description of this painful experience.

Intuitively, then, we know that shame affect, when triggered, causes an immediate effect on our place in the social system. Fromm's conclusion is too superficial. He starts out with the theory that physical birth is the most important trauma ever experienced by the individual because it is the moment when the infant is torn from fusion with mother. This wrenching separation becomes, for him, the model of all human woe. As Fromm sees it, we spend the rest of our lives searching for ways to return to this blissful state of union with mother. And, since shame is one of the most painful forms of separation, he links it to his basic theoretical system by defining it as what happens when we become *aware* of our separated state.

His concept of shame, then, derives from the theories popular in the late 19th century (both Darwin and James-Lange), which taught that all emotion depends on an initial cognitive appraisal. It is a system that denies the connection between infantile affect display and adult emotion, one that restricts our understanding of shame to a small part of its spectrum. Fromm's theories were central to his being: So much did he himself long for reunion with the mothering figure that he persuaded his psychoanalyst to marry him and wrote a long series of books about the meaning of separateness.

Fromm's work differs from that of Margaret Mahler and her followers, which also takes for granted that the embryo's presence within the womb means that fetus and mother are a fused being. But even after emergence from intrauterine existence, say these scholars, the baby remains emotionally fused with mother for quite some time. Their theory teaches that fusion is breached only by sequences of attempts at separation and individuation alternating with frequent efforts of *rapprochement* (return to mother on an emotional tether). The infant is seen as unable to separate from mother until it can master the skills that allow it to manipulate the large muscles of locomotion—emotional separation depends on physical distance.

Thus, the ability to link with another person is taken for granted as a biological attribute. Separation, in this system, really implies the ability to walk away from mother. Like the Freudian system from which it evolved, the "separation/individuation" school of child development teaches that we do not become fully individual until completion of the family romance, the oedipal phase of development.

The separation/individuation theory is one of the most popular systems of our current era. It is used to explain nearly all emotional disorders characterized by failures of socialization or problems of intimacy. One who is overly dependent is said to have failed at separation, one who cannot get close to others is seen as having failed at rapprochement, and those who are emotionally unstable are shown to have grown up with mothers who would not let them separate properly from fusion. Love, within this system, requires both the healthy return to this fusion and the presence of mature self-awareness.

Stern and his colleagues in the field of infant observation have presented droves of evidence to unseat this remarkably attractive and tenacious theory, which is based so heavily on our understanding of the adult. Feelings of fusion, of being immersed in the being of our beloved, are so powerful a part of adult life that many people have assumed that fusion itself is a "natural" phenomenon. As we will discuss in the next chapter, there is a great deal of reason to believe that fusion is really a developmental milestone, a developmental acquisition of importance equal to any of the others we have discussed so far.

We have come to understand that infant and caregiver, beginning in the earliest moments of their relationship, communicate through the external display modality of the affect system. It all starts with the infant's unintentional manifestations of innate affect, to which the caregiver responds with empathy. Soon the child learns to use both the intentional broadcast of affect-related movements and sounds, to which the caregiver also responds, and a growing assortment of communications with roots in the affect system but not actually meant to convey information about the broadcaster's affective state. Watching this process of data transfer between infant and mother, Beatrice Beebe* has described the "packages of information" through which they communicate.

This is not a system of communication in which the infant is either passive or helplessly dependent. And most certainly it is not a system in which the baby is unable to declare either its status as a separate person or its complete independence! Stern notes, "During the three- to five-month period, mothers give the infant control—or rather the infant takes control—over the initiations and terminations of direct visual engagement in social activities. . . . It must be remembered that during this period of life the infant cannot walk and has poor control over limb movements and eye–hand coordination. The visual–motor system, however, is virtually mature, so that in gazing behavior the infant is a remarkably interactive partner. When watching the gazing patterns of mother and infant during this life period, one is watching two people with almost equal facility and control over the same social behavior" (1985, 21).

Only by ignoring the facial display of affect and the interplay of facial communication can one defend a theory that says infants are fused with mother until they can walk away from her. Walking away from mother is nothing more than walking away from mother; rapprochement is not return to

*Beebe and Gerstman (1984), Beebe and Lachmann (1988).

fusion but rather a request for a moment of maternal selfobject function, of reassurance through affect mutualization. Children are, of course, attached to their mother; they are obliged by nature to be dependent on her. Part of the job of growing up is to become less dependent on mother. Each of us must find our own way to achieve the fullest development of the self. But we are both separate from mother and quite individual right from the day sperm and egg meet to initiate the process of intrauterine development.

The whole system of separation/individuation theory, attractive as it has been for so many years, is another dinosaur ready for extinction in the new environment of modern infant observation. Perhaps equally deserving of study is the need of adult humans to prove that they are not really created alone, that they are brought into existence with a link to a loving and helping other.

It is easy to understand how primitive science might develop the naturalistic theory that intrauterine existence defines us as a part of mother rather than a boarder living within one of her enclosures. The discipline of infant observation shows us that this old theory is untenable. There remain only two further possibilities, two rationales to explain both separateness and togetherness in terms of human biology.

On the one hand, we might view our species as a vast horde of individuals floating through a void and featureless interpersonal space, each of us bound tightly within our own private enclosure. The universe of stars and galaxies would then provide an analogue for a cosmos of solitary selves who achieve connection by building tenuous bridges from one to another through whatever means of communication might be devised by the mind of man. Our failure to form links to our fellow humans would be only a reflection of whatever might limit our ability to send or receive messages.

Yet this facility with which we communicate, the ease with which most of us seem to form close, meaningful, loving, and intimate relationships, this process itself seems so natural that one is led easily to wonder whether there is something built into the very structure of the human that lends itself to such relatedness. Man is the life form most involved with individual others of its species. Might not the very form and type of this involvement be the result of an evolutionary process leading man from the solitary status more typical of presocial organisms toward the intense interpersonal preoccupation that characterizes the human of our time? Might the individuals of our species be predisposed by nature to be linked to others?

There is a great deal of evidence for both theoretical positions, which, although presented as mutually exclusive, are capable of coalescence into a solid working hypothesis. The evidence for our solitary status is intuitively perceptible. It is to the evolving theme of an evolving predisposition to intimacy that I would next like to turn our attention. Like most realms of scientific thought, it, too, has a history.

In the computer analogy I developed earlier, the human may be viewed as an assemblage of hardware, firmware, and software. In the domain of human development, software is an analogue of all the ways a baby or an adult is instructed about the world in which it lives.

There are, of course, myriad intricate bodily activities that work quite well without any sort of overriding control program. No complex scheme need be imputed to understand what happens when the skin is cut by a knife—the integrity of our integument is disturbed and its component structures leak blood. Yet any physician can tell you that what happens next depends on an immensely complicated group of working parts called the clotting factors. Chemical substances carried in the blood or kept in storage within the skin itself all begin to interact in ways that produce new and highly complex molecules that staunch the flow of blood. Yet there does not seem to be any realm or region of the body where the program for this series of chemical actions is stored. All parts of the body seem equally capable of bleeding and clotting, whether or not they are connected to the brain.

The next level of complexity might be described as simple sequences of reaction to stimuli—like the jerky motion of the lower leg that occurs when the tendon below the knee is tapped suddenly. Programs like this are stored in the spinal column and called "reflexes" because they involve mechanisms as simple as the reflection of light from mirrored surfaces. One can be trained neither to have a reflex nor to avoid having a reflex, although by autosimulation one can imitate the gross aspects of its action pretty well.

There are many types of behavior that seem to be run by scripts stored at levels of the central nervous system that have evolved more recently. Rather than merely mount his pillow, curl up on it, and prepare for sleep, one of our dogs—a Gordon Setter—must place his feet squarely in its center and with great care twirl around three times before lying down. Comments Rapoport, whose studies of the obsessive-compulsive disorder I mentioned earlier, "My collie dog, for example, turns in circles to prepare his bed before lying down. Historically it may have been necessary for some of his ancestors to trample tall grasses or to chase off snakes or insects. But my collie circles the same way whether he is preparing to sleep outside my camping tent in the Shenandoah or on my living room carpet" (189).

What impresses me is that these acts seem to be executed so much the same way each time, as if performed from a script written in the genetic material of certain dogs and stored somewhere in the brain. The script for this particular behavior is a good example of what I am calling firmware. It is the very existence of firmware that has charmed and puzzled the life sciences for generations—systems of action that are neither learned nor merely the results of simple reactions.

As life forms travel through evolution there seems to develop a fascinating balance between prewritten and learned scripts. Prewritten scripts abound in nature, and there is an abundance of firmware to study. More "primitive" organisms, like the bee, can manage enormously complicated routines as soon as they emerge from the egg. Bees fly and they communicate with each other, despite the fact that they have been trained to do neither. The Austrian biologist Karl von Frisch studied the firmware of bees during the first half of this century, explaining the inborn mechanisms that allow such highly social behaviors as the transfer of information about the location of specific sources of nectar, and those that organize proper etiquette within the hive.*

In the second quarter of this century, the biologist Niko Tinbergen noted that each spring the male stickleback fish goes through a highly ordered sequence of behavior relating to the mating process. First it begins to prepare a nest in the sand at the bottom of its tank. As this work nears completion, the fish suddenly changes color from its usual dull gray to a vibrant red. Now the brightly dressed male begins to court any female who happens through his neighborhood, initiating a highly stereotyped mating dance that garners both her interest and her apparent agreement to back into his nest until only her head can be seen peeping out from it. Speedily the male begins to nudge and massage her egg-swollen abdomen. All at once she releases a clutch of eggs and swims away, after which the male drifts a mist of sperm over these eggs. When he has made sure the eggs are safe, he is once again available to make contact with another female stickleback. This sequence of actions is repeated until he has filled his nest with fertilized eggs.

Now the courting male turns into an attendant, expectant father, guarding the eggs with great intensity, "ventilating" them with fresh water every once in a while. When the hatchlings start to swim away, he retrieves each of them by carrying it back to the nest in his mouth. Only when they have reached a degree of maturity adequate to allow them to survive unaided does the watchful father allow them to venture unaccompanied into the wild. And only then does the male stickleback return to his normal patterns of swimming, feeding, and fighting.

The stickleback fish measures two inches or so in length; its brain can be no

*See Krogh (1948).

larger than a grain of corn. Yet contained within this tiny organ of organization is all the firmware needed to produce these marvelously interwoven performances. Tinbergen found ways to interfere with each segment of this system, with what might in computer terms be called the *subroutines* from which is assembled the whole script for mating. He ascertained that some subroutines are triggered by seasonal alterations in hormone levels and others by specific visual stimuli. Sometimes Tinbergen was able to block an entire segment of the mating script, thus forcing the animal to ignore that phase of its program. The experimenters could destroy the nest each time it was built— and the hapless little fish then began the next part of the mating sequence without its nest. No portion of this wonderful sequence of activities proved to be either "conscious" or "intentional." All of it is under the control of specific biological scripts written into the genetic code of the stickleback.

Do you have a favorite play or opera? Buy a ticket to see it. Watch the actors, singers, musicians, stagehands, ushers, and the rest of the crew put on the program as directed by their scripts. Yes, they are competent adult humans capable of other tasks. But for the duration of this entertainment they agree to act under the control of prewritten scripts, and we agree to be charmed by their work. Coleridge said that the mental set necessary for our enjoyment of the drama is "the willing suspension of disbelief." As long as we accept the conventions of the theater we are able to experience what happens on stage as if it were "real" and unfolding "naturally" before our very eyes and ears. The theater of live actors is even more a miracle of programmed behavior than the motion picture, for when we watch a film we can allow ourselves the illusion that a hidden camera has recorded a slice of life, something that "just happened that way." In the legitimate theater, the actors must live out their scripts each and every day that their play draws enough interest to make it commercially viable.

But in each case a group of highly skilled performers has entertained us by its artful presentation of something scripted. For the adult human, such activity is all the more pleasurable because we are free to behave without scripts, to run our lives without direction. That someone would take the trouble to learn a script and perform it for us is all the more exciting because of the range of choices involved. And often we spectators learn new responses because we have seen them onstage and decided to add them to our personal collection of software. Learned behavior is quite different from firmware, the inborn scripts that direct action within a tiny realm of choice.

Might there be internally scripted courting dances in humankind? Does not the male of any species, including our own, dress in his finest garb when undertaking the selection of a mate? Does evolution favor the development of more prewritten scripts, or do life forms grow only more free from internal control as they evolve?

Quite recently, Dr. Wagner Bridger assumed the leadership of the Society for Biological Psychiatry. He caused quite a stir when, in his presidential address, he expressed the belief that perhaps two-thirds of human behavior was directed by firmware little different from that of the stickleback, and that the search for such mechanisms was the legitimate concern of psychiatry. He argued, somewhat pugnaciously, that too much attention had been paid to the psychoanalytic exploration of early experience, to the software dealing with sexual firmware. He stands unfairly accused of psychophobia, the morbid fear of the inner life that has always stood in opposition to the self-examination intrinsic to dynamic psychotherapy. Yet I believe Bridger represents an equally valid approach to the understanding of human interaction, one that must be accorded its rightful place in this pleomorphic realm of study.

The type of firmware studied by von Frisch and Tinbergen is generally known as the *instincts*, patterns of behavior that seem motivated by species-specific needs having mostly to do with food gathering and reproduction. There are many other systems in the central neurologic apparatus, systems that we take for granted in the healthy, functioning adult, but which do not work unless they are "brought on line" in the proper order. One of the most fascinating of these was discovered by the German eye surgeon von Senden,* who developed the first truly safe operation for congenital cataracts. Sometime around 1935, he began to treat a group of children and young adults whose lifetime blindness had been caused only by the presence of an opaque substance that prevented light from getting to an otherwise healthy and well-formed optical apparatus.

Believing that he could now offer the gift of sight to these young people, von Senden removed the offending cataracts and fitted his patients with the same sort of spectacles used by people whose cataracts have developed in later life. Yet not one of these patients was ever able to "see" in the conventional sense. What afflicted and disturbed them was a blur of painfully intense lights and colors, none of which could be understood as the perceptions we normal adults take for granted. Many of these patients expressed the wish that they could return to the state of blindness, which they found far less bothersome. It seems that what we own at birth is a visual apparatus ready to receive stimuli, but still unable to organize them. Only as we grow and develop during the

*Described by René Spitz (1965), 40, 54–64.

first few months of extrauterine life is the visual apparatus tuned properly so that it can become the sort of interface with the world that we normally take for granted. Some scientists believe that the final development of those parts of the brain that handle and process visual information is not completed until these structures have been used for a while.

Here is a situation in which the vagaries of life, the coincidences of illness, have produced an experiment no scientist would dare perform on a human infant. Hundreds of similar studies have been done using laboratory animals more acceptable to our sensibilities, but all with the same result: There are a number of mechanisms that work only if they are triggered just at the correct moment in early development.

Near the middle of this century, Konrad Lorenz studied such patterns of development in the graylag goose and introduced the concept of *imprinting*.* He divided a single clutch of eggs into two groups, one hatched by the mother goose, the other in an incubator. The goslings hatched by the goose immediately followed their mother wherever she waddled. Yet those hatched in the laboratory showed no interest in her. The first living being they encountered was Dr. Lorenz, and they followed him everywhere. Now he placed both groups of goslings under a large box; when released, they returned immediately to the creature they had previously followed.

It is all very reminiscent of the scene in Shakespeare's play *Midsummer Night's Dream*, in which Oberon tells Puck to place in Titania's eyes special drops that will make her fall in love with the first creature she sees when she awakes. Konrad Lorenz is not Bottom with the head of an ass, and hatchling geese are not adult fairy queens; yet there is this lingering feeling in all of us that we love mother because it is she whom we first encounter when we awaken into extrauterine life. Shakespeare suggests that it is the eyes that govern the definition of whom we love, while Lorenz would move from that organ of perception to some point deeper within the structure of the brain.

A great many scientists rushed to duplicate and extend this research. What they learned is that there is, in birds, a group of social conventions that seem to be under the control of firmware scripts, each of which must be triggered at a moment optimal for its imprinting into the permanent behavior of the organism. Hess and Ramsay, for instance, showed that ducklings will form similar attachments to wooden models as long as the imprinting stimulus is presented to them between 13 and 16 hours after hatching. Before the age of 13 hours, imprinting is weak and ineffective; after 16 hours imprinting is considerably

*Ekhard H. Hess (1958) presents an excellent summary of this important work.

impaired. Only during the proper window of opportunity is it easy and "natural" for the hatchling duck to imprint onto its "consciousness" the identity of the "parent" who will lead it until full maturity.

There is a special "wisdom" to this brevity of opportunity. At the 16-hour mark a new behavior pattern takes over. By the beginning of the second full day after hatching, 80 percent of ducklings show a fear or avoidance reaction to moving objects; by 32 hours all ducklings have developed this "emotional" response. Only for a few brief hours is it possible to instruct the fledgling bird that mother is safe to follow.

The biologist of today understands that imprinting is not always so precisely determined a process as it might seem from the experiments described above and that it may be neither reasonable nor useful to extrapolate from the study of birds to the nature of man. Yet it is important for us to recognize the existence of biological systems that, for all intents and purposes, do not really "exist" until and unless their "switch" is "turned on" at the proper moment in development.

Sometimes we really do forget that science itself has a history. Looking back at the work of Harry Harlow, who studied the attachment behavior of monkeys, we tend to forget that his research was conducted at a time when early Freudian theory was dominant. Freud and his circle saw the infant's passionate attachment to its mother as a derivative of the child's need for food, amplified by the forces of libido. The breast, as the organ of sustenance, became an engrossing symbol for infant–mother attachment.

Harlow built one sculpture that contained a fairly standard nursing bottle held firmly in a bare wire frame in the vague shape of a mother monkey, and another that mimicked her form similarly and was clad in soft cloth, but contained no source of nourishment. Although infant monkeys learned to feed at the nipple of the glass bottle, they clung to and vastly preferred the cloth surrogate, much as they might a mother of flesh and fur. Such experiments served to reveal as myth the idea that infant humans have any primary attachment to the maternal breast and that the act of feeding deserved consideration as a primary source of love.

Harlow's work emerged so early in my education that I took it for granted—what came to be called the "cupboard theory of love" was never a part of my world. Even today, as I review the now-classic papers on "Love in Infant Monkeys" by Harlow and his group, I am surprised at the vehemence and evident triumph with which he dismissed this aspect of Freudian theory. To Harlow, mother was what you clung to, not what fed you. Monkeys reared by a cloth mother grew up pretty near normal, he said. And he demonstrated that prolonged periods of maternal deprivation reduced the ability of monkeys to form an affectional tie in later life.

Seymour Levine and other behavioral psychologists showed that laboratory rats handled by friendly experimenters were more likely to form normal affectionate attachments with their peers than those reared in isolation. These investigators presented evidence that there may be critical periods for the development of this response to stimulation. In other words, it appears that the genetic makeup of many life forms may include scripts for the development of attachment, and that those attachment behaviors are "released" only when triggered in the proper sequence.

Perhaps the most important school of psychology owing its origin to this line of experimentation is that founded by John Bowlby, one of the leading psychiatrists at London's Tavistock Clinic. Bowlby's well-known book *Attachment* was first published in 1969. In a 1987 taped interview, Dr. Bowlby remarked that he was led to study attachment behavior by the work on fish and birds of Tinbergen and Lorenz, and that he used the theories they derived from their study of fish and birds as a point of departure for his own work on human love. "In this formulation, it will be noticed," wrote Bowlby, "there is no reference to 'needs' or 'drives'. Instead, attachment behaviour is regarded as what occurs when certain behavioural systems are activated. The behavioural systems themselves are believed to develop within the infant as a result of his interaction with his environment of evolutionary adaptedness, and especially of his interaction with the principal figure in that environment, namely his mother" (1982, 179–80). It is a system that can be assessed or graded from without, a theory that lends itself to evaluation on purely "objective" grounds.

You will note that Bowlby does not mention the feelings that are involved in attachment, only the behavior. It is fascinating to read his rationale for this position: He explains emotion in the language of James and Lange—conscious, cognitive labeling of a visceral response to an initial cognitive appraisal. Whatever role affect might be given in the search for the primary sources of motivation, this role would have to be completely dependent on the organism's ability to make cognitive appraisals.

Might affect be responsible for early infantile behavior, he asks? Not likely, he answers, because affect could only follow a process of assessment not possible for the infant. Certainly affect is capable of altering the behavior of an adult, but not an infant. "We must conclude therefore that the process of interpreting and appraising sensory input must unquestionably be assigned a causal role in producing what behaviour emerges" (from affect) (117). This distinction is critical to his thesis, and to all of attachment theory, for Bowlby intends to demonstrate that attachment itself occurs long before the child can "understand" it and therefore have feelings about it.

Although the word "love" does not appear in the index of *Attachment*, he does refer to the "affectional systems" of Harlow, recording that psychologist's description of five forms of inter-individual attachment. Bowlby remarks: "In the terminology used in this book each affectional system is an integrate of behavioural systems mediating socially directed instinctive behaviour of a particular kind" (232n.). The human is viewed here as if we were recently derived from the stickleback fish or the graylag goose. If we love at all, it is because we have learned to appraise the prewritten attachment behaviors that were set in motion long before we were able to interpret them.

The work of Tomkins was already available to Bowlby, and quite well-known at the Tavistock Clinic, which had already reprinted and distributed in England the first volume of *Affect/Imagery/Consciousness*. To Tomkins, as must by now be quite clear, the affects are a series of prewritten scripts exactly like those studied by Tinbergen and Lorenz. Affect theory states simply that the affects are triggered by meaning-free alterations in biological systems, that they cause changes to occur at sites of action all over the body, and that we learn to appraise these changes with growing sophistication as we grow older. But affects cause external display at the same time they are producing their characteristic alterations of internal function; it is these external displays that allow those outside us to intuit what we are feeling. It is the affects, then, that first link infant and caregiver; attachment behaviors are all derivatives of affective expression. Love is an affective experience because it is based on the experience of affect, not because we become affectively involved in a meaning-free display of attachment!

Astonishingly, immediately after defining affect in terms of cognitive appraisal, Bowlby nods politely at Tomkins in a footnote and dismisses affect theory by misrepresenting it: "The causal role of appraisal processes has led Tomkins in his two-volume work on *Affect/Imagery/Consciousness* (1962–63) to postulate that 'affects constitute the primary motivational system', defining a motive as 'the feedback report of a response' " (117n.). Bowlby then notes, quite correctly, that infants appear to be attached to their mothers long before they are capable of the level of cognition necessary for the intelligent appraisal of the situations in which they find themselves. And, of course, he proceeds to develop a theoretical system that explains attachment without regard for affect.

I hope that I have been able to make clear to the casual reader, to one not steeped in the literature and tradition of my field, just how maddening it is to try and understand how it is that great scientists can stare at the same landscape and see it so differently. Here, on the one hand, is Tomkins, studying the facial display of affect and linking it to the very interactions that so intrigue Bowlby. And on the other hand, here is Bowlby, immersed in the new science that has derived from the study of fish and birds, two life forms that have no facial affect display, seeing everything but the face.

Most theories work not because of the data observed and evaluated, but because what is ignored makes the new theory work better. Had Bowlby only looked at the face he might have come to understand the relation between the external display of affect and the internal experience of feeling, and his theory would not have been so dry and devoid of emotional resonance. Affect theory and attachment theory have traveled along unnecessarily separate paths for too long.

What, then, do students of attachment theory see when looking at a child? Basic to their investigation is a standardized behavioral assessment designed by Mary Salter Ainsworth* and performed when a child is 12 months old. Infant and mother are led into a room they have never seen, thus creating what is called a "strange situation." They are observed for a predetermined amount of time, following which the mother is instructed to leave the child alone with the examiner, who is a stranger. The child's behavior with the examiner is noted, again for a specific amount of time, after which the mother returns to the examination room. The final phase of the study involves an assessment of the child's response to mother's return.

Three patterns of interaction are noted. In Pattern A, called "Anxious/Avoidant Attachment," the child is readily available to separate from the mother, shows little affective sharing with her, seems affiliative with the examiner, shows little preference for mother over the examiner, and is well able to explore independent of her. When mother returns, these babies actively ignore her, even to the point of turning away.

Pattern B is called "Secure Attachment." Infant–mother pairs who demonstrate this type of relationship are quite different in many respects. Here the infant uses the caregiver as a secure basis for exploration, readily separates from her to check out new toys in the room, freely and easily shares with mother on an affective level, and is readily comforted by her when distressed, returning easily to play. Indeed, when distressed, as by her programmed departure, these children actively seek out mother for solace on her return. And

*See also Sroufe (1979) for another excellent discussion of these theories and their application to the study of children and families.

when her departure does not produce distress, for many of these securely attached babies are quite comfortable to be without their mother for a while, they greet her happily and initiate interaction with gusto.

Pattern C, "Anxious/Resistant/Attachment," is characterized by quite another form of infantile response. These babies have great difficulty separating from mother even to explore the novel room in her presence. They are wary of new people and new situations. When she returns, they seem even more upset, mixing contact with resistance—kicking, squirming, rejecting toys—and occasionally showing a striking degree of passivity.

Ignore, for a moment, the obvious parallel between these "attachment behaviors" and the innate affects clearly being described. Ignore, as well, the implications of these excellent and succinct descriptions of three styles of maternal mutualization and regulation of infantile affect. The attachment theorists have developed a simple, elegant, standardized technique for the assessment of affect expression and modulation within the parent–child relationship—even though they disavow the relation of these behaviors to the internal experience of both child and mother.

Even more important, the patterns of attachment described here hold true for each child over many years of follow-up. Anxious/avoidant children show more negative orientation toward peers. Anxious/resistant children are far less competent in developing peer relationships than securely attached children. Bullying, submissiveness, avidity for problem-solving, behavior with teachers, and a host of other, easily observed behaviors have been linked to these three patterns of attachment.

It should be clear from my necessarily overbrief summary of this immensely active area of modern psychology that I have no quarrel with the validity of its observations. Patterns of attachment appear soon after birth, and they remain remarkably stable over the course of life. Yet the attachment theorists and the affect theorists are eons apart in their understanding of the meaning of these data. Some attempt at healing this rift has been made by Carol Malatesta[*] and by David Cook, whose sophisticated studies of the relation between shame and attachment are just beginning to appear in print.

Bowlby sees attachment as the result of specific, inborn systems built for no other reason than to produce attachment. In this respect he follows the work of Tinbergen and Lorenz with great precision. He chooses to ignore the emotional aspects of attachment, to relegate the affective accompaniment of attachment to a period in life far later than infancy. For Bowlby, attachment

[*]Malatesta & Wilson (1988), Malatesta (1990).

occurs merely because it is programmed to occur; our feelings about that attachment are a late acquisition dependent on cognitive appraisal.

The attachment theorist, therefore, sees the human as predisposed by nature to be linked. Where primitive science saw this link only in terms of our origin as a piece of mother's flesh, Bowlby sees all life forms as truly separate except insofar as they are connected through the attachment system. That man is the most social of organisms can be explained by our ownership of the greatest number of built-in attachment mechanisms. Evolution has conferred on us the ability to become more involved with each other than those life forms from which we evolved; the path of evolution is toward increasing society.

Were there no evidence that attachment behaviors have much to do with the broadcast, resonance, and modulation of affect within an interpersonal system, I might be able to accept the existence of an attachment system. I think that the entire fabric of attachment theory is but another example of 19th-century rationalism, a philosophical position that avoids emotion as an interference with proper cognition or as a derivative of proper cognition. The observations of these excellent psychologists are trenchant, and the predictive ability conferred by their attachment test is extremely important. But just as we must reject Freud's idea that love is nothing more than a derivative of sexual longing, and Fromm's idea that love derives from the need to return to the mother from whom we have been shorn by birth, and Mahler's belief that love represents a rapprochement with the mother from whom we have recently learned to separate, we must go beyond Bowlby's narrow and emotionless view of attachment behaviors.

We are back to the matter I raised earlier in this chapter: I see the human as a solitary being, created in the isolated micro-universe of the womb; then delivered as a baby into the outside world as if it still lived within a bubble; and as an adult still floating through life with no connection to those other bubbles that make up its human environment save what bridges it learns to build. In this system of thought we are capable of emotional attachment to others only because the commonality of affective experience allows us to know the world of others as if from their core. Love would be viewed as the name we give the most powerful positive form of this connection. In terms of interpersonal relationships, shame would then be regarded as an affect that returns the individual to its state of primary isolation, but also as a complex emotion retaining whatever other meanings it has accumulated during our individual development.

In the next chapter I will present a theory of love based on the affect system. It takes for granted the relation between affect and attachment described in the preceding sections of this book. It demonstrates the crucial links between shame and love and establishes a logical explanation for Wurmser's observation that at the core of shame is the feeling that we are unlovable. All attachment is, indeed, due to firmware mechanisms, to inborn scripts that govern certain human actions. Love is not, however, simply the type of instinct that causes fish to mate and birds to follow their mothers, not the desexualized remnant of libidinal attachment, not the result of any inborn system of connection.

I propose to show that love develops as a complex set of linkages established for each of us from the experiences of innate affect and of interaffectivity. We have indeed evolved into the ability to love. But it is the innate affects, these highly developed patterns of affective expression, that have made it possible for us to understand each other at the deepest level. Love and hate, those most powerful of the emotions of interpersonal involvement, involve affects. It is affect that makes the heart beat strongly in the presence of our beloved and our gorge rise in the presence of those we hate. And it is specific patterns of interpersonal expression and experience that have made shame so deeply painful and so antithetical to love. The explanation of its relation to interpersonal life is necessary to any understanding of love.

18

TRUE LOVE

There are so many kinds of love. Erich Fromm wrote of mother love, father love, sibling love, love of country, and sexual love. Did the Greeks have a word for it? Not just one, but three: *eros*, the sexual, erotic love of man and woman; *filios*, the love between parent and child; and *agape*, the rich, deep love of good friends, a form of love with neither sexual nor filial component. Scientists and psychoanalysts write of the powerful forces that bind people together in love. Religious leaders speak of the manner in which we are loved by God and of proper ways to love God.

All of these experts declare love to be a positive experience. Look up all the wonders of *love* in that ultimate authority on adjectives, the 1947 Rodale Press book called *The Word Finder.* I skim from a full page of modifiers. Love is: abiding, absorbing, abstract, approving, ardent, artless, blissful, boundless, bounteous, brave, burning, celestial, chivalrous, confiding, deathless, deep-rooted, earnest, endearing, enduring, entrancing, everlasting, genuine, heroic, immoderate, intimate, invincible, lavish, matchless, meritorious, mutual, mystical, nameless, never-wearying, noble, passionate, persistent, pounding, predominating, primal, profound, responsive, reverent, romantic, sentimental, sin-destroying, strong, stupendous, sustaining, tranquil, trusting, unbounded, unchanging, unconquerable, undying, unconscious, unquestioned, valiant, virtuous, visionary, vivid, willing, wondrous, yearning, and zealous. Good stuff, this love.

But I cheated by ignoring a host of negative modifiers. Love is also: adulterous, ambitious, animal, baffled, barbaric, barefaced, betrayed, bleeding, brittle, calculating, casual, changeful, chastising, coerced, common, condescending, condemned, conventional, corrupt, costly, cunning, cutting, debasing, debat-

able, depraved, despised, despiteful, dire, disgusting, embittered, erring, exact-
ing, faddist, faithless, false, feigning, festering, foolish, frustrated, hapless, hol-
low, hopeless, humiliated, illicit, immoderate, jealous, loveless, melancholy,
misguided, obdurate, obsequious, one-sided, painful, palsied, paltry, pathetic,
rending, repudiated, satiated, selfish, sham, shameless, sinful, thwarted, tragic,
transient, transparent, unfashionable, unreasonable, unrelenting, unrequited,
unrestful, unreturned, unruly, unsatisfactory, violent, warped, wasted, weaken-
ing, well-quitted, wilting, and worst. Not good for the soul, this love.

So to the list of authorities we add *lexicographer's love*. I ask your attention to
cultural sources that inform with equal proficiency. I am interested in the forms
of love studied by poets and songwriters, by novelists and moviemakers, by
therapists who work in the theater of intimate revelation, by the civil and
criminal officials who deal firsthand with the mayhem of love.

Lovers: "I'm crazy about him (her)." "I love you so much that you drive me
crazy." "Even hearing his name makes my heart pound like mad." "I love her so
much I think my heart will burst." "I'm so happy I could just die!" "Hubba
hubba, ding ding. Baby, you've got everything!"

Songwriters: "What is this thing called love; this strange, wondrous thing
called love? Just who can explain its mysteries?" "How can I believe you when
you say you love me when I know you've been a liar all your life?" "I give to
you and you give to me, true love, true love, love forevermore . . . Now you
and I have a guardian angel on high with nothing to do/But to give to you and
to give to me, love forevermore." "If this isn't love, then the whole world is
crazy." "My heart goes boom tiddy boom tiddy boom tiddy boom tiddy
boom tiddy boom tiddy boom boom boom." The entire genre of *torch songs*
owes its name to the ubiquitous and quite painful phenomenon of unrequited
love that cannot be quenched, like the glowing embers of a torch that cannot
be extinguished.

Legal experts: Here is a passage from a 1901 English translation of *Passion
and Criminality in France—a Legal and Literary Study*, written by Louis Proal. He
was, according to the title page, "one of the Presiding Judges at the Court of
Appeal of Riom."

How comes it that affection may turn to hate, and lovers become the bitterest
foes,—that the transition is so easy from love to loathing, from the transports of
the most exalted tenderness to the frenzies of the most savage anger? How is it so
fond a feeling may grow so cruel and lead to the commission of so many barbarous
murders by poison and strangulation, and the infliction of such appalling wounds?
Whence comes the cruelty of love and the ferocity of jealousy? Why does the

jealous lover strike the very woman he adores? Why does he pierce with dagger thrusts the very bosom on which he has lain, and disfigure the very features he has just been covering with kisses? Why does the woman whom her lover has deserted burn out the eyes that moved her soul to love, and send a bullet through the heart she was so fain but now to feel beating beneath her hand? How is it love may grow so venomous as to put knife and pistol into the hands of lovers and husbands, who after having sworn eternal affection, tear each other's eyes out at the domestic hearth, and in the very conjugal bed? Why does this passion, capable as it is of producing heroes, so often manufacture only cowards and murderers?

To end our string of questions, why does love if unrequited make people so unhappy that they must needs kill themselves? How is it that lovers, who might well live together, prefer to die together? (preface, 6–7)

Filmmakers: In *Fatal Attraction*, one night of apparently casual intimacy releases from within the female partner a marauding monster whose need and apparent purpose are to own, consume, or destroy the man who entered her script. Similarly, in *Crimes and Misdemeanors*, the murder of a bitter and dependent lover (a woman with a clearly delineated "borderline personality") is excused on the grounds that she had failed to live within the rules of callous and casual "love."

Not enough? I grew up in the world of grand opera (which may have something to do with my lifelong interest in high-density emotion). Opera is not about "singing." It is an excuse for singers to let loose the most powerful emotions known to man at their highest range of intensity. Judge Proal's description of the vagaries of love sounds like the plot summary of any major opera. Death and tragedy hover around romantic love as surely as do the scenes of domestic tranquility with which we prefer to envision it. Sometimes I think that those with the greatest authority about love are the people who have suffered from it the most.

Love varies from one culture to another. It shifts in meaning as we move in one era and out another, changes even within a single relationship as we and it mature. Any definition of love must take into account this inherent variability. My intuition is that love varies so much because it is based on the history of our experiences of innate affect, which will differ in all of the ways I have suggested throughout this book. Whenever we encounter a word with too many layers of meaning it is best to return to the dictionary and find out its history. I rely, as usual, on the OED.

THE LINGUISTS OF LOVE AND HATE

Through all its linguistic travels, *love* has conveyed the sense of something held dear or precious. Key to our understanding of love are both aspects of that definition—what is loved must on the one hand be *experienced* as dear and precious, while on the other hand be *held* so with some degree of constancy. The modern word *love* seems to have come through the Old English form *lufu* on the way from its earliest known origins as the Old High German *luba*. To the sailor, those who prefer land to sea are *landlubbers*. In Germany, *luba* became *liebe*; in Holland it moved to *lieven* and then *liefe*. Our word *belief* originally meant "that which is held dear"; when we "take our leave" of someone we ask that our departure meet with that person's pleasure. Love and *life* share no common derivation—the word *lif* is just as old as the root word *luba*. What also derived from *luba* is *libido*, the Latin word for desire—which became for Freud a biological life force more sexual than loving.

There does not seem to be any accepted linguistic source for the root *luba* (no word or root known to have preceded it) so perhaps I may be forgiven an amateur's guess. I suspect that it is an example of *onomatopoeia*, a vocalization made up to resemble a common sound—like the *woosh* of the wind, or the *tick-tock* of a clock. If you've ever put your ear to someone's chest and heard the normal heart, you know that it beats not with a single sound, but with two notes. Generations of medical students being taught the art of the stethoscope have learned to call the sound of the heart *lub-dub*. Check this out if you don't believe me. *Luba* is a wonderfully descriptive word for the heartbeat.

Romantic love has always made the heart pound. ("Hubba hubba," "Boom tiddy, boom tiddy, boom boom boom.") I believe that the intimate association between the emotional experience of love and the physiological effect on the heartbeat of the innate affects accompanying it led our early ancestors to name the feeling for the vital structure so linked to it. Is it only a coincidence that the heart has always been taken as the organ of love? An infinitude of poetry, prose, greeting cards, love songs, and paintings of lovers clutching the left side of the thorax supports my conclusion.

You need not accept my idea that our word for love derives from the sound of the beating heart. Yet no one would contest the need to explain either the universal association between love and the heart or the real and powerful effect of love on that organ of circulation. My etymological speculation speaks for the former, while the affect theory of Tomkins defines the latter, as we will discuss in a moment.

Look next at the word *hate*. Like love, it has come to mean not mere dislike, but malice held with some degree of constancy. Just as love must be fueled by some source of energy to keep it held constant (the law of entropy suggests that everything runs down eventually), hate, too, must be fueled and maintained. Any dictionary will inform us that hate implies extreme aversion, disgust, or abhorrence. It is a complex emotion in which we wish to destroy or to get some distance from its source while also maintaining a relationship with it. Just as we are never free of thoughts of our beloved, we are always emotionally entangled with what or whom we hate.

Yet hate, like *luba*, has been found in our language as far back as words can be traced, always with the same sort of sound, never associated with any linguistic source other than that sound. Maybe affect theory can offer a clue: Does not the word itself sound much like the noise made when we hawk up phlegm in preparation to spit in disgust or contempt? That association would allow me to define hate as some sort of complex ideoaffective construction in which the cognitive part involved our internal representation of another person and the affective part involved disgust. Romantic hate is a situation in which we remain powerfully drawn to something that must produce an experience of negative affect. Just as the affect (drive auxiliary) called disgust has power directly in relation to the preexisting hunger it must impede, hate has power and durability directly in proportion to the preexisting wish for continued relatedness that it must block.

There are, of course, plenty of situations in which we can hate someone for whom we have never experienced positive affect. Our reaction to any form of severe abuse, to torture or torment, is to hate whomever we define as the perpetuator. We can hate the unknown assailant or the faceless burglar who takes from us by death or stealth that which has given us pleasure. Hate can be associated with a host of invisible unconscious scripts and also with highly visible obvious sources. No matter what examples of hate are chosen for study, always will be found the paired factors of constancy and negative affect.

THE PRECONDITIONS FOR LOVE

I wish to present a new approach to love and a new way to understand the relation between love and shame. Since love is, at core, an emotional experience, my formulation will be based on affect theory. It will take into account the new understanding of child development made possible by this system of thought and discussed throughout this book.

All love is based on the experience of positive affect, of interest–excitement and enjoyment–joy. The part of love that is exciting and makes the heart pound owes its power to interest–excitement; the part of love that makes us feel calm, safe, relaxed, and untroubled owes its power to enjoyment–joy. The pain of love comes from shame affect, for any impediment to either of the positive affects will be amplified as shame and experienced as hurt feelings. Shame always wounds in direct proportion to the degree of preexisting positive affect that it has restrained. It is for this reason that the more we are excited by the person who has become the object of our love, or the more we anticipate the contentment to be achieved from this relationship, so much more are we susceptible to the misery of shame.

It is of interest to enquire why love provides so many examples of the highest levels of excitement and enjoyment to be found in our culture, to ask why love can drive us with such power and intensity. I ask you to understand that it is wrong to think of love only in terms of the positive affects it produces, but to consider the emotional state of the person who is capable of such an intense affective experience.

My definition of love requires attention to the preconditions of love. The greatest of meals prepared by the most enticing of chefs would draw no interest from one with no appetite. Great dining is a dialectic between hunger and the arts involved in the selection, preparation, and presentation of food. What makes us crave love? Who needs love, and why? What is the dialectic of love?

Take, for instance, the nearly universal description of love as the happy "togetherness" that relieves painful loneliness. A patient in therapy confides his experience of falling in love: "Selena causes in me feelings of ecstasy, wonderment, beauty. Merely to think of her brings this combination of happy and exciting feelings. She makes me feel good all over. But when I think that I may never see her again I am filled with terror, anxiety, dread, the feeling that monstrous jaws are grabbing at me. Even worse is the feeling of nothingness, flatness—the idea of life without her."

His disclosure provides an interesting example of that feature of the affect system Tomkins calls its *correlative* property—its ability to imprint other activities with the specific features of whatever affect has been triggered. There is a distinct correlation between the sweetness, beauty, calm, and happiness with which my friend experiences all his perceptions and the affect of enjoyment–joy that has been triggered by love. Equally are all of his actions and thoughts governed by fear–terror when the specter of her absence triggers that realm of affect.

Notice that, like most lovers, he is almost incapable of thinking about love without dreading its absence. Why does romantic love seem always to imply this dialectic between some sort of pain and its relief? In order to answer this question we must once again turn to the modern study of infant observation and to the interplay of affects between caregiver and infant. It is in the way each mother responds to the needs of her baby that we will find the seeds of love.

Stern points out that

> The vast majority of the mother's time during the infant's first two months is spent in regulating and stabilizing sleep-wake, day-night, and hunger-satiation cycles. . . . When the baby first comes home from the hospital, the new parents live from minute to minute, attempting to regulate the newborn. After a few days they may be able to see twenty minutes into the future. By the end of a few weeks, they have the luxury of a future that is predictable for stretches of time as long as an hour or two. And after four to six weeks, regular time clumps of three to four hours are possible. The tasks of eating, getting to sleep, and general homeostasis are generally accompanied by social behaviors by the parents: rocking, touching, soothing, talking, smiling, and gazing. These occur in response to infant behaviors that are also mainly social, such as crying, fretting, smiling, and gazing. A great deal of social interaction goes on in the service of physiological regulation. (1985, 42–43)

This paragraph describes the bare bones of what happens between infant and parents during that frenzied period of their first mutual encounters. It is a very important passage, one which exemplifies the basic difference between the European model of child development and the American. Freud, the exemplar of the European system, ignored the social aspects of physiological regulation and made of the infant's experience a solitary world. Sullivan, the founder of American psychiatry, said that we are born into an interpersonal system, and that right from the beginning of extrauterine life our self system has an interpersonal core. My own recognition of the empathic wall honored Sullivan's observation that we are born into the climate of mother's emotions. Both mother and infant are powerful broadcasters of affect, notwithstanding the particular need that has triggered that affect. Initially, at least, they call to each other in the language of affect.

As a matter of fact, infant and caregiver actually create each other in the language of affect. Most of the time we accept the conceit that we create children. But this primitive and simplistic bit of hubris ignores the fact that we become parents only when we have children and that (despite whatever we thought we knew about child-rearing before their arrival) it is our children who teach us how to be parents. Their needs call forth from us the qualities essential for parenting. They find the parent within us, the latent or precursor parent that does not exist until a child is added to our lives.

Yet each of us responds differently to the needs, requests, and demands of our offspring, from infancy through toddlerhood and on into adolescence. Indeed, often we find ourselves being quite different parents for each child! The infant is not born into the neutral and entirely predictable climate of a laboratory. We parents were once infants with a normal assembly of hardware and firmware, all of which was influenced into an adult personality by the software of experience. We parents have our own history, our own highly specific temperaments. We vary across a wide spectrum of dispositions and proclivities, just as do our children.

So infants are born into a climate that took a long time to evolve, even before they popped into the picture. Even though each of them is equipped with the same basic range of hardware and firmware, they differ remarkably. No two babies seem quite the same in their affective output, and this temperament of theirs touches us in surprisingly specific ways. They vary over a wide range, and we vary over a wide range. The possibilities are endless. The permutations and combinations made possible by the huge degree of variability in both parent and child, the very number of possible relationships, are staggering beyond imagination. It is taken for granted that they have to get used to us—but it is a two-way street. We create each other.

Even if we believe that all babies have pretty much the same spectrum of needs, and all parents have pretty much the same spectrum of abilities, the little differences that make us individuals will foster the emergence of hugely different patterns of interaction. Even if I take for granted the obvious untruth that women are adequately prepared to care for their infants by reason of biology (or any other mysterious undefinable force), the rhythm and style of that care will differ from one mother to another.

I suspect that in the affective interaction between the needy infant and the solacing parent we may find the nidus of love. It is obvious (watch any mother and baby) that children respond with positive affect to the reduction of negative affect, to the relief of their needs. Yet I do not think that love is merely the positive affect that we observe in these situations, but a far more complex formation.

Again I draw my analogy from the world of physics and chemistry. No matter how beautiful a crystal may appear, it is not a "pure" substance. Usually, some chemical compound has formed an intricate latticework of molecules around a central impurity. It is the nature of the impurity that determines the shape of the resulting crystal, even though the "contaminant" and the surrounding chemicals are totally different in composition. A lustrous pearl is no more than an oyster's attempt to smooth away the irritation brought by an intruding grain of sand; without the sand there is no pearl. Love, too, is a beautiful crystal made possible only by its "central impurity." I believe that the nidus of love is the sequence that results when some infantile need has triggered negative affect and the caregiver provides solace by responding to that affect, determining its source, relieving the underlying need, and accepting the resulting positive affect. Love implies not a positive affect but a series of negative and positive affects linked together in sequence to form a scene. Built from the accumulated scenes of urgent need and solacing relief characteristic for each of us are the scripts that we will in adult life call love.

Anybody who studies the affect system comes naturally upon the concept that events are colored by the affects they trigger, and that what is stored in memory is not merely an event but a combination of our perception of that event and the affects that accompanied it. In an attempt to bring order to experience, we humans, from infancy through dotage, link together in memory the sequences of affect that characterize significant and recurrent interactions.

Not surprisingly, since it was he who first recognized the nature of the system, Tomkins has devoted a great deal of attention to this latter phenomenon, which he has described as *script theory* (1979, 1987b, 1991). You will recall that we defined the firmware mechanisms, the drives and the affects, as groups of innate, prewritten scripts involving a number of actions taking place at far-flung sites of action. The process of growth and development creates software scripts, sequences of lived moments characterized by a variety of needs, affects, and responses.

Once again let me interpolate a bit of history. The word *biology* is of more recent origin than you might guess. It was coined in 1802 by the German writer Gottfried Rheinhold and brought into English about a decade later. It was constructed from the Greek root words for life *(bios)* and for scholarly discourse *(logia)*. Central to our understanding of what it means to be alive is the concept of *irritability*, the property of response to a stimulus. Whereas the anatomist might tear apart the remains of a life form in order to determine its structure, and the chemist degrade its tissues in order to ascertain the nature of their components, the biologist kept the organism relatively intact and prodded it into a response. The study of life was initially the study of stimulus and response.

Psychology has always considered itself a "life science." It was in such a philosophical climate that the early psychologists began their study of the psyche. Since the psyche—this soul-like essence that made us human—could not be removed from the body and studied as a part of the anatomy or degraded to find its constituent molecules, it had to be analyzed on the basis of its properties. The brain was considered as a "black box" into which we could never peer, its dauntingly complex mass of circuitry too mysterious for the assignment of specific structures to particular practices. There was no apparent connection between the construction of the brain and the fine points of human behavior. Thus, one wing of psychology was born as a method of analysis based on the evaluation of stimulus and response. This form of early psychology involved the search for discrete events that might act as a stimulus to the psyche, and the analysis of its response.

Freud made a huge leap forward by insisting that the psyche was powered by invisible programs operating out of awareness, and that the language of stimulus and response could not explain the phenomenology of the unconscious. Psychoanalysis has encountered massive resistance for two basic reasons: First, many people were repulsed by Freud's insistence that the basic driving force was sexual in nature, preferring to avoid the data he amassed; and second, psychology has always seen itself as a science like other sciences, with "real" data capable of study from without, rather than the highly suspect subjective feelings of individual humans in analytic treatment.

I suspect that Bowlby, who was initially trained as a psychoanalyst, felt so uncomfortable about psychoanalytic dependence on anecdotal data that he swung the pendulum in the direction of pure external observation in the spirit of stimulus-response psychology. "Science" must be based on replicable experiments. Koch's postulates required that the bacillus you isolated from an animal that died of a disease be capable of causing that disease in another subject. Much of psychological science looked with disfavor on the use of Freudian archaeology to derive ideas about the nature of the inner life. It could not accept psychoanalytic inferences that were incapable of being tested from infancy forward. The arrow of time moves only in one direction, and experimental science depends on that inviolate truth.

LOVE SCRIPTS

Now comes Tomkins, who links the wide range of subjective experiences to what can be observed with ease—the facial and other bodily displays of innate affect. And, further, he points out that affective experiences themselves can be linked into structures held within the mind and remembered as scenes. In this new psychology, a stimulus triggers a mechanism that involves a whole series of responses stored as firmware; sequences of these affective responses become linked together to form a scene; and sequences of scenes are then linked together to form a software script. From a simple psychology of primitive biological stimulus and response we have evolved to a computer-language-based system through which any piece of behavior, feeling, or experience can be understood by analysis of its component scenes.

Stern underscores the importance of our ability to collect experience in the form of remembered scenes. He suggests that the infant is capable of storing them as internal "Representations of Interactions that have been Generalized" (1985, 97–99), for which he creates the acronym RIGS. Through these RIGS the infant assembles a set of rules about the nature of life. Such internal formulations allow it to know what to expect when in situations that resemble but are not precisely identical to those in which they were deduced. Just as Basch defines an emotion as the combination of an affect with our retrieved memories of previous experiences of that affect, Stern defines a RIG not as a specific remembered experience but the summation and integration of a host of experiences—that from which we can make assumptions about a new but related experience.

In his work on script theory, Tomkins explains that scenes are linked to-gether to form a script only when the child has discovered that in its life certain scenes follow each other with such regularity that rules for their association and governance can be determined. Using videotape analysis of mother–infant interaction, Demos (1983, 1988) has been able to demonstrate that individual mothers have highly specific styles of responding to infantile affect display, creating for their children sequences of negative and positive affect conform-ing precisely to Tomkins's predictions. A script is a sequence of RIGS con-nected by rules worked out through experience; it connects past and present to suggest, define, or determine a particular future.

Finally, Tomkins asks us to recall that, although each affect is an amplifier of its stimulus conditions, when groups of affect-based scenes are linked to form a script, these groups or sets of scenes themselves generate affect. He introduces the term *affective magnification* to differentiate between the type of urgency produced by individual innate affects as amplifiers of their stimulus conditions and the higher order of increase in significance conveyed when these scenes are grouped and thus magnified. Each experience of innate affect is a moment of urgency created by amplification. In a script, whole groups of experiences are made incrementally more urgent because they have been magnified by affect. Affective magnification is a higher order of action than affective ampli-fication.

Love, then, is an example of a script in which the most important scenes of need and nurturance have been assembled and magnified with tremendous intensity. For each of us, love will depend on whatever scenes, whatever interpersonal interactions of nurturance, have become generalized. Love is not merely a RIG, but the result of a series of RIGS nested within each other, all magnified by the positive affects of excitement and joy that we anticipate will reward our experience of anguishing loneliness and need.

"The fear that men have of a woman's anger—that unbelievable fear that a man has of a woman's rage—where in hell does it come from?" asked a 49-year-old businessman during a psychotherapy session just the other day. He is *Taipan*, supreme leader of an industry. His next statement reveals more of the script from which this fear derives: "From our earliest moments as boys we are taught that men are superior to women, that we are more powerful and more dangerous. But when a woman screams at me I have no power. All I can do is hope it will end soon." Vaguely, he knows this has something to do with his expectation of love; empirically we know that he is drawn to certain women, all of whom humiliate him similarly and from whom he derives calm and surcease only by escape. He and I wonder together what might be his function in this drama, what role he plays in each woman's script. "Why is it that you can see a little shrimp of a woman hitting her son (who looks like either a mountain or a linebacker) as hard as she pleases, totally knowing he will not hit her back?" asked another patient. Both forms of interaction are based on the scripts for love that have evolved within each of the participants described.

All of the early experiences of need form their own inner representation. The infant's experience of the mother who responds with alacrity, who most easily enables the baby to achieve self-regulation when needy—this feeling forms the core of what it means to be loved. The infant's experience of the mother who does not come, the mother who is unresponsive to the infant's urgency, the mother who responds angrily to its need, forms the nidus of what it means not to be loved. When, with evident relief, lovers say, "At last I've found you," they describe the astonishing degrees to which can be magnified these paired experiences of loneliness and redemption.

EMPATHIC FAILURE

Study, for a moment, this next statement of how it feels to be lonely within a crowd. Born in an upper-class family, to a narcissistic mother whose self-absorption had left him either in the care of servants or (when in her company) bereft of affective communication, the writer tries to tell us what it was like to be an infant with no bridge. He describes what was, to him, the most painful part of his early childhood:

> Little by little I began to realize where I was and to want to make my wishes known to others, who might satisfy them. But this I could not do, because my wishes were inside me, while other people were outside, and they had no faculty which could penetrate my mind. So I would toss my arms and legs about and make noises, hoping that such few signs as I could make would show my meaning, though they were quite unlike what they were meant to mime. And if my wishes were not carried out, either because they had not been understood or because what I wanted would have harmed me, I would get cross with my elders, who were not at my beck and call, and with people who were not my servants, simply because they did not attend to my wishes; and I would take my revenge by bursting into tears. (25–26)

But this poignant description of empathic failure comes from no ordinary child. Speaking is St. Augustine, a child early in the fifth century, who later discovers or recognizes God as the polar opposite of his unempathic mother. The God of Augustine reads him in every pore, fills him with the feeling of being understood. This perfect empathy is the central meaning of love in Christianity. The God of Abraham and Isaac exemplified his love as power over our enemies, as might arrayed on behalf of those who honored him, a paternal God of right and wrong who struck fear into the hearts of those who stood in opposition.

Carl D. Schneider, both a psychologist and an ordained minister, has written about the role of shame and guilt in contemporary religion. He points out that, should we dare to compare ourselves to God, we would recognize immediately the immense disparity in our sizes and realms of power. God is huge, we are tiny. (I have always liked it when friends placed on their boats the plaque that reads, "Oh God, thy sea is so vast and my craft is so small.") The proper relationship between man and God is one of awe, writes Schneider, for awe involves the mature sense of shame relative to one who looms so far above us. You will remember that I define guilt as our label for a specific named group of situations in which shame is triggered along with fear. The God of Christianity creates an atmosphere of awe and shame within the umbrella of love, while the addition of fear within the system attributed to the more warlike God of Judaism adds the dimension of guilt. One is alone with neither realization of God; one is with God quite differently within these two systems of worship.

There are, of course, lots of ways of being alone. Not all aloneness is painful—the infant spends about half its waking time in solitary activity, apparently quite happy to be alone. The shift from "being alone" to "painful isolation" seems to occur when the infant needs something that cannot be provided in the absence of another person. It is then that affect is mobilized to amplify need, and whatever had been desired now becomes urgently needed from another.

Again recall that offhand remark of Robert Frost that so charmed me more than 35 years ago—he said we longed for "A world where ask is get/And knock is open wide." It is an insight meaningless without an understanding of affect, without comprehension of the magnification provided by certain scripts. When there is no gap between "ask" and "get," when no affect is triggered by insufficiency, there need never be pain associated with the state of aloneness. But when need itself becomes defined in terms of the solacing other, aloneness becomes isolation and abandonment.

The number of possible scenes beggars one's imagination. Countless times the infant needs or wants something and mother is right there, attendant and ready and capable of providing whatever is required. But no mother can be eternally available, no caregiving system totally and constantly attentive and always exactly right in its assessment of the infant's needs.

There are so many subtle gradations of maternal unavailability. Sometimes the most sophisticated, competent, and loving of mothers finds it literally impossible to know why a baby is crying; sometimes it just takes time to figure out what will provide solace. Maternal attention can be demanded and received and still actually ineffective—we can feel "alone" and unattended even when someone is there! And mother may be in the next room, or asleep, or out of the house, or depressed and inattentive, or angry for her own reasons and therefore unable to commune with her infant, or mildly ill, or seriously ill, or any of a myriad of perfectly understandable but nevertheless "imperfect" mothers.

Viewed from the vantage point of an infant whose needs are amplified by negative affect, each variant of maternal imperfection is capable of producing the experience of painful isolation and the subsequent group of affect-loaded ideas we call abandonment. The infant really can't understand why its needs have not been met. In a sense, all experiences of unmet need can be interpreted in terms of their similarity to the type of unmet need resulting from abandonment.

Examining carefully the situations described above, it seems clear that there is one group of "abandonments" (states of painful isolation) caused by actual maternal absence and another caused by insensitivity. Using the language of affect theory, we might say that insensitivity is a static word that describes what happens when there is a failure in the dynamic and fluid process of affective resonance. Stern describes this sort of unavailability as a failure of attunement, reserving the term "misattunement" for situations in which the caregiver seems to tune in to the affect display of the infant but then fails to deal sensitively with this information (1985, 148–49, 211–14). Within the system of Kohut's self psychology both types of interaction are described as "empathic failure." All of us are talking about the same problem. Sometimes the caregiving adult is right there, in the immediate vicinity of the needy infant, and that adult is just as unavailable as if he or she did not exist.

So the concept of abandonment must take into account both physical isolation and empathic failure. What else must we add to the picture? What other situations will the infant experience as the absolute or relative absence of human contact?

LOVE AND SHAME

Here is where we begin to think about the role of shame in interpersonal life. Up to now we have concentrated on the internal experience of shame, on what shame does to our self-concept. When shame affect is triggered in an interpersonal context, all of the physiological reactions and all of the steadily increasing number of psychological meanings attached to that affect will now take on a special significance in terms of the relation between self and other.

If *self* is defined by all of the mechanisms described in the previous chapter, and if *other* is defined as what remains in the interpersonal field when the self is subtracted, then to the extent that shame alters the nature of the self it will alter the way we identify the other. If shame creates a sense of a defective self, it therefore creates in us a sense of *an other who sees us as defective*, no matter what that person really thinks of us. Whenever we experience shame in the presence of another person, we experience that person as holding all the beliefs about us that shame has already created within our personal psychology.

It is beyond the scope of this present book for me to suggest the full range of possibilities inherent in that statement. Let me repeat one more time my basic thesis about the adult experience of affect: Each of us grows up in a particular family that lives in a neighborhood as part of a definable culture brought into existence during a specific era. Each individual will form, for shame as well as for each of the other innate affects, a lexicon of ideoaffective complexes based on the interplay of nature and experience, of hardware, firmware, and software. Our lifetime of shame experiences will form our archive of shame and thereby influence for each of us the development of the self. But this schedule for the development of the shame-related self will also create a highly particular catalogue of others.

Of course I am aware that there is much more to the nature of
created by our personal experience of shame. Our sense of other is for...
an immense range of interpersonal experiences. But the idea of an other who
sees us as bad, or defective, or incompetent, or damaged, or small, or stupid;
the idea of an other whose eyes are the symbol of all that is revealed about us
when we are shamed; the idea that a major defect in the self is a just and
reasonable rationale for our exclusion from the society of all previously loving
or accepting others—all these are only constituents of the huge roster of
possible relationships between self and other formed by the sting of shame.

Shame haunts our every dream of love. The more we wish for communion,
so much more are we vulnerable to the painful augmentation of any impediment, however real or fancied. To love grandly is to risk grand pain. Intimacy
with the other validates the value of the self, and any impediment to intimacy
causes severe injury to self-experience.

"Y'know that funny stage when you really start to like someone and you
get all sort of awkward and clumsy?" asked a young woman the other day. She
referred to the fact that with each increase in mutualized positive affect comes
an increasing likelihood of shame. "Remember the yucky feeling you get when
someone you like is with someone else?" asked an adolescent girl. "You
weren't good enough, or something." When in love we tend to disavow any
understanding of our beloved that might become an impediment to interest
and enjoyment. True love will not look at its own diminishment.

Shame becomes the most social of the negative affects because it modulates,
regulates, impedes, contains, the interest and enjoyment that power all sociality. Just as the experience of shame pulls us from social interaction, it calls
attention to and helps define social interaction. If shame is the affect of withdrawal, of sinking down and slumping, of physiological removal from interaction of the face (and therefore the quintessential definition of what it means to
lose face), it is still and always an affect made painful only to the extent that
interest and enjoyment remain. We experience shame only as long as one of
the two positive affects remains active, for shame is only possible in the
context of positive affect. We cannot feel shame where there is nothing to lose.
Whoever feels shame the most is the most desirous of positive affect; whoever
feels shame the least has renounced most successfully the goal of positive
affect.

It is to protect ourselves from the pain of love sought and love refused that
we steel ourselves to withhold interest, to remain aloof and immune to the
entreaties of the possibly loving but possibly shaming other. Social life demands the development of highly ritualized forms of address, social dancing
around issues of trust and safety within relationships all refined to protect us

from the pain of shame. Any time someone says, "You hurt my feelings," that person has experienced shame affect: not embarrassment, humiliation, mortification, or "shame," but an otherwise unnamed assembly of shame affect as an amplified impediment to the mutualization of positive affect expected within a loving relationship. (Only a few of the recurrent and repetitive experiences of affect get to be named.) Most of the bad feelings that accompany social interaction are based on shame affect. And whenever someone seems particularly available for social interaction, remarkably unprotected and unshielded from our intuitively friendly and loving forays into his or her inner world, unusually willing to commune with us on the basis of positive affect without the distancing maneuvers we experience as off-putting defensiveness, we compliment that individual as being "vulnerable."

One of my favorite passages in Erich Fromm's *The Art of Loving* is the section, early in the book, where he asks us to understand the distinction between "falling in love" and "standing in love" (p.3). Most of what I have discussed above relates to the problems of falling in love, of finding and holding within a relationship some person with whom we can hope to stand in love. Freud taught us that central to the ability to stand in love is the willingness to ignore those characteristics of our beloved that might lead us to reduce our investment in each other. But Shakespeare said it best of all in Sonnet 116:

> Let me not to the marriage of true minds
> Admit impediments; love is not love
> Which alters when it alteration finds,
> Or bends with the remover to remove.
> O, no, it is an ever-fixèd mark
> That looks on tempests and is never shaken;
> It is the star to every wand'ring bark,
> Whose worth's unknown, although his height be taken.
> Love's not Time's fool, though rosy lips and cheeks
> Within his bending sickle's compass come;
> Love alters not with his brief hours and weeks,
> But bears it out even to the edge of doom.
>> If this be error, and upon me proved,
>> I never writ, nor no man ever loved.

SHAME AND THE SADNESS OF HOLIDAYS

Shakespeare makes us think about the qualities necessary for the permanence of love. Yet even within a system of permanence, even where there is consistency of relatedness, there is some fluctuation in the climate of our emotion. Look, for a moment, at the mild, seasonal variations of love that occur in our culture. "This must be a difficult time of year for you," dozens of people tell me every year around Christmas. "Isn't this the time when you therapists get the most business?" What are they saying?

Holidays like Christmas, Passover, and Thanksgiving imply that whole families will get together and share their warmth and love. Yet these occasions are really organized for the benefit of children, who (when it is done well) remain blissfully unaware of the stagecraft required to mount such productions. "I created Christmas for 22 years. Every year my children saw Christmas exactly as I hoped they would. Every aspect of it let them know what it meant to be loved, to understand the love of Jesus, and to feel completely safe and secure," said a recently divorced Irish Catholic gentleman the other day. "Now where do I go?"

Around the time for each of these celebrations one can discern a rising tide of nostalgia for holidays past. Yes, we all know that there were always some discomforts associated with each of these historical events, but by and large we recall only the best portions of them. (To me, nostalgia implies the retroactive disavowal and falsification of negative affect. "It was a nice picnic. There were no ants," replied Tomkins instantly when I mentioned this to him some years ago.) For a great many people, holiday-time is a period during which we are flooded with (both real and "adjusted") memories of situations characterized by the mutualization of positive affect.

And the nearness of Christmas makes us uncomfortable because it releases from within us all the ignored and suppressed wishes for love that buzz around inside us. Christmas makes people unhappy because of the disparity between the degree of interest and enjoyment theoretically available and the amount really attainable. It is a perfect and specific example of a situation in which desire outruns fulfillment, in which our wish for the communion of positive affect is impeded by the harsh reality of everyday adult life. The "depression" of Christmas, or Passover, or Easter, or Thanksgiving, the sadness that afflicts so many people, this complex assortment of ideas, memories, and affects, is a prime example of a situation dominated by shame affect but bearing no resemblance to what we call the shame family of emotions. There is a good deal of distress affect in this seasonal sadness, mostly because it simply won't go away—this steady-state discomfort triggers distress. But the impediment to positive affect triggers shame affect, and that is what makes some people so miserable around the holidays.

LOVE, DISSMELL, AND DISGUST

The countervailing force that mitigates the abject state of isolation associated with social shame is the sense of communion inherent in love. (*Abject* is derived from roots that mean "to throw down." It is a synonym for *downcast*, and of nearly identical origin. Both words describe the physical actions associated with shame affect.) Earlier I suggested that the adult experiences of shame and pride could best be understood as poles of a shame/pride axis—that nearness to one always meant distance from the other. Now I ask you to accept the idea that adult life places us within a social matrix, the poles of which are defined by nearness to love or to social shame. Why is it easier to speak in terms of the polarity of love and hate than that of love and shame?

This circuitry is capable of further analysis. A few pages back I suggested that the word *hate* itself actually derives from the drive auxiliary of disgust; that (in common language) to hate someone means to wish that person destroyed or in some other way driven from our system. When a small child says, "I hate spinach," she means that this innocuous vegetable triggers disgust. Exile, excommunication, and disgrace are understandable within the spectrum of shame but by no means fully explained by it unless we add the concepts of dissmell and disgust. Just as the child comes to understand the innately scripted feelings associated with dissmell and disgust and learns that an offending foodstuff can voluntarily be avoided when it smells bad or expelled when it tastes bad, the child generalizes from these experiences of food-centered repulsion to form a system of interpersonal distancing and rejection based on dissmell and disgust.

When another person defines me as bad or offensive, exposes me as having qualities found dissmelling or disgusting by that other, I experience the peculiar triune assemblage of negative affects to which we referred earlier. Since the other person has defined me as a bad-self, I now experience self-dissmell, self-disgust, and (as I, too, look at me) self-shame. No matter how solid my self-image before this moment of shame, what is now revealed will be those elements of my character the "significance" of which I had avoided.

Here again is one of the central aspects of the adult emotional experience of shame. Whatever portion of us is revealed during a shame experience causes the unfolding of a process that brings from their hiding places a host of other hidden memories. Our ability to group memories, to order our experience so that it may be handled in some intelligent manner, this very facility that allows us to organize our internal world becomes the source of the very images we would most like to forget. Shame can be triggered by exposure of the self to the view of others. But it triggers further exposure of the self to the self, maintaining and amplifying shame, creating shame-filled moments or even shame-dominated moods. When it is in the presence of another person that we have been shamed, it is to that other person that we attribute the pain of shame and against that person that we must defend ourselves.

In order to deal with the experience of social shame, we must develop scripts for the detoxification of this assemblage. Although the fantasy of perfect isolation from the shaming others remains the most sturdy emotional defense against shame, it becomes less and less possible as we grow up. In the chapters that remain, we will discuss all of the ways that people defend themselves against this noxious interpersonal experience. We will address the effect of shame on our entire culture.

Yet before we can discuss such matters there is one more facet of shame to take up. Have you noticed that so far I have ignored the one aspect of shame most often associated with it? Certainly no book on shame can be complete without some reference to the relation between embarrassment and sexuality. I have taken great pains to distinguish among the many faces of shame so that they might be evaluated independent of each other. So much attention has been given to sexual shame and the ways we handle sexuality that, for some, sex and shame are practically synonymous.

By now, of course, it should be quite clear that the sexual drive is but one of the life forces capable of assembly with shame affect, just as it can be linked with excitement, or fear, or anger. Intuitively, we can guess that anything so capable of engendering excitement and enjoyment is likely to be associated with the affect that amplifies impediment to those affects. The revolution in our understanding of child development has affected our understanding of much that has to do with sexuality, and it is to this stream of data that we now turn our attention.

19

THE GENERATIVE SYSTEM

Did you ever notice that all those books purporting to be about "the joy of" something or other are really attempts at reducing shame? The first, of course, was Irma S. Rombauer's now-classic cookbook, *The Joy of Cooking*. In 1931, when the first edition came out, many women in our culture felt utterly restricted to the kitchen, shackled to a role in life that allowed them to be little more than what some called "baby farmers" and "unpaid chefs." The very act of cooking was, for some, a symbol of feminine repression and shame. But there is joy in cooking, said Mrs. Rombauer. There is the competence pleasure that comes from knowing how to think out, shop for, and prepare a delicious meal; joy from the knowledge that those who love you are well fed.

In volume 1 of *Affect/Imagery/Consciousness* Tomkins devoted a whole chapter to the dynamic interplay between individual affects, the way one affect is likely to follow another. He noted that excitement must follow the incomplete resolution of shame, and that we experience joy at the complete relief of shame. The bowed head of the oppressed citizen is whisked upward when the source of shame is removed. Anybody who had the opportunity to watch the television coverage of the long-suffering peoples of Eastern Europe as they celebrated their release from domination by their communist governments could note the shift between the energy of excitement and the relaxation of joy, as well as the tears that well up when we are overwhelmed by the sheer density of emotion. But Mrs. Rombauer understood this dynamism before all of us. She anticipated by a quarter of a century Tomkins's recognition of the relation between shame and joy, and by half a century my circuit diagram for pride.

Recently I bought a copy of Leo Rosten's 1968 book *The Joys of Yiddish*. I remember the fears and terrors of the Second World War, when no one knew whether the Nazi forces would win and turn America, too, into a vast network of concentration camps eradicating Jews with the impersonal and implacable efficiency that characterized Hitler's Germany. "If the Nazis come," said my mother in 1944 with the sort of hazy logic we accept in wartime, "go straight to the Unitarian church on the corner." During the 1950s, when I went through the bulk of my formal higher education, we Jews were vaguely embarrassed to look Jewish or even to be Jewish. Synagogues—little buildings full of strange bearded men with black skullcaps and fringed shawls—were replaced by big, beautiful community centers dominated by squash courts and theaters. Nobody wanted to be labeled as "different." Nobody spoke Yiddish. We wanted to be Main Street America.

Although written in Hebrew letters, Yiddish as a language is more German than Hebrew. It is the language of assimilation, the *patois* of a people who have traveled through one country after another since the twelve tribes were dispersed a few thousand years ago. Now it contains lots of words from English.

But the parents and grandparents of my childhood "knew" that we would be marked as "different" if we spoke Yiddish and used it among themselves only as their "secret" language—the one in which they said things we were not meant to understand. We were to bring pride to our parents by looking like, behaving like, learning and (above all) speaking the unaccented language of, our Christian neighbors. No Yiddish for us.

Today those same Jewish community centers teach courses in Yiddish, which is in danger of becoming a lost language; occasionally I hear that some college or other has a formal course in this shameful language of my past. But Leo Rosten has it just right when he flips the axis of shame and pride and offers all of us an opportunity to sample this rich heritage.

Right in the spirit of Irma Rombauer and Leo Rosten, and hard on the heels of the cultural revolution of the 1960s, came Alex Comfort's 1972 book, *The Joy of Sex*. It is one of the most popular books ever published, for it treats sex as a normal, healthy, commonplace part of life. No mystery, no big thing. Just the friendly interpersonal activity of sexually active adults. It is a refreshing, homey, sensible, friendly book, beautifully written, marvelously illustrated, and one of the best antidotes to sexual shame ever composed. So much shame was attached to sexuality in the America for which *The Joy of Sex* was written that the illustrated edition had to be printed in Holland and shipped here in relative obscurity.

Before Comfort was Krafft-Ebing, whose *Psychopathia Sexualis* was replete with clinical anecdotes that were as likely as not to begin with such statements as, "This 20-year-old confessed masturbator was brought to the clinic complaining of . . ." Alternatives to Krafft-Ebing? "Marriage manuals" by equally Germanic prose stylists whose objective clinical description of "lovemaking" sounded more like the instructions packed with the kit for an outdoor gas barbecue grill purchased from the neighborhood hardware store. Or the neighborhood porn shop with shelf after shelf of poorly written "novels" designed only to allow us to resonate with the scenes depicted, then to masturbate or wander out aimlessly or angrily in search of a partner who would do with us what we had just read.

There was so much shame associated with everything about sex in the 1950s, when I was growing into manhood. We boys were embarrassed to talk about sex with any degree of frankness—wherever possible we even referred to specific acts and techniques by code names. The thought of a partner who both wanted sexual pleasure and took delight in our pleasure seemed not only remote but bizarre. That consenting couples might even use their mouths to bring genital pleasure, each to the other, was called "69" because the shape of the numbers resembled that of people in the act itself. No word, no phrase was more likely to reap gales of embarrassed laughter than "69." Even to mention such a thing in "mixed" or "polite company" was a guarantee of social disgrace. Surely, I thought 'way back there in the '50s, so deadly was the shame associated with the number itself that 1969 would be a national year of mortification.

Yet so much was changed by the cultural revolution of the '60s that by the time 1969 rolled around nobody noticed or remarked about the sexual reference. Alex Comfort treated the issue with characteristic aplomb, saying that "good hand and mouth work practically guarantee a good partner" (34). During a recent psychotherapy session, a 20-year-old woman mentioned with amusement something that had happened during lovemaking, and I commented about the recent history of that sexual practice. She had never heard of "69" and asked me to explain the history of the term. "We don't have a name for it," she said. "We just do it." Other things about sex might embarrass her, but not that.

The Joy of Sex was not the first book to use drawings to illustrate parts of the body or the positions in which people shared each other. But it was the only book in our culture to show those people with friendly facial expressions. No guilt, no shame, no anger, none of the bored neutrality you see in most of the Persian miniatures and Japanese prints that graced the literature of those cultures. None of the smarmy anatomism of the once ubiquitous turn-of-the-century "French postcards." Just the facial displays associated with interest, excitement, pleasure, and joy.

Comfort's book represented one form of breakthrough in the path away from our cultural tendency to see sex within an obligatory system of shame. Only two years earlier we had seen the publication of Masters and Johnson's landmark work, *Human Sexual Response,* in which these sober and gifted scientists described the results of their studies on the sexual nature of man. Working with hundreds of volunteers, they were able to observe the *sexual response cycle*—what actually happens to the sexual organs before, during, and after the act of intercourse. What previously had been only the stuff of locker-room talk, course material of the college of the street, now was transformed into direct observations capable of scientific analysis. What previously had been known only from speculation based on the psychoanalytic exploration of individual adults in treatment for emotional disturbance now could be understood from the open scrutiny of healthy, happy, satisfied men and women. Suddenly we were in an era of change; sex itself moved from the shadows onto its own stage.

There is so much that can be said about sex. Although the word itself makes us think first about the act of sexual intercourse, that particular set of deeds makes up only a tiny portion of what we know to be sexual. Its energy infuses life in every way, influencing everything from fashion to drama, assisting the advertiser or the recruiter, drawing fire from pulpit and pundit. For most of us, it is important to know that we are sexually attractive or sexually competent. There is perhaps no aspect of adult life as securely linked to shame and pride as our relation to sex.

If by now I have convinced you that each of us holds a vastly different personal definition of shame, one determined by our life experience, perhaps it will be somewhat easier for us to arrive at a mutually acceptable understanding of sex. My goal in these next few chapters is merely to indicate some of the linkages between the affect shame, which is the declared subject of this book, and the sexual forces that influence us with such power and intensity. Yet in order to do this we must first figure out what we mean when we use the word sex.

Even the very word brings immediate confusion. Sometimes we use it to refer to matters of gender—masculine, feminine. This takes on even more significance in European languages than in English, for ours is one of the few tongues that legislates no attributes of maleness and femaleness to the various classes of objects. Aristotle claims that it was Pythagoras who (25 centuries ago) brought his sense of geometric precision to language and demanded that all things be classified according to gender. Doubtless this dichotomy was useful then; it is restrictive and perhaps obnoxious in our current era of sexual egalitarianism. What must go on in the minds of the French academician who declares or defends that the words *force, cuisine, ville* (city), *tête* (head), *lettre* (letter), and such are "feminine" and preceded by *la* or *une?* Why should *village* be masculine, especially when *ville* is feminine? Why are the words for train, tea, voyage, wolf, and lesson all masculine?

These are not trivial questions. That such (any) nouns might be labeled male or female indicates not merely a judgment of the feeling they evoke in the grammarian but also an inherent judgment about the difference between men and women. And I doubt that these perceived or attributed or declared dissimilarities are either kind to women or made by women. Involved here is an inherent system of shame and pride based on qualities attributed to gender. Whatever reason we determine for the relation between sex and shame must take into account the existence of such a system.

Much as we might decry the noxious implications of this artificial attribution of gender, true gender identity forms a major part of our sense of self. We know ourselves first as "baby." Only later do we state with authority that we are a boy or a girl; once achieved, we retain this new chunk of identity throughout life. Gender identity dictates our mode of dress, our role in society, which locker room and which bathroom we use, and with whom we will form kindred groups.

Despite how alike are men and women, how equal their potential to do so many tasks, they differ in many ways. Often I have joked in lectures that "what are known on this planet as men and women are descendants of two distinct life forms first found on far separated star systems by a race of interstellar explorers who put them together on Earth in an experiment that failed."

But just as most life forms can be divided into groups by their gender, mature individuals tend to form couples because of these sexual differences. Inherent in the system that causes us to be different on the basis of gender is also the force that creates attraction. Even in our language we search constantly for paired opposites that can be used as metaphors to express the sexual force that tends to unite: north and south poles of a magnet, up and down, yin and yang, fire and ice. Sex refers to the passionate attraction between opposites, to the active process that begins as the coupling of male and female, unites them in sexual intercourse, and results in procreation and the maintenance of the species.

Look, for a moment, at the sheer variety and range of themes attached to sex. Gender itself seems to be genetic, controlled by scripts written in the germ plasm, mechanisms that make the body itself into something male or female. The parts of the body that differ only on the basis of gender, the sexual equipment, seem to be affected or even controlled by programs that need neither conscious awareness nor social training. From earliest infancy, males experience erections during the dreaming phase of sleep; from puberty through the menopause women experience the complex series of events associated with the menstrual cycle. Gender identity (knowing one's gender) involves *awareness* of the fact that one has been assigned by biology to one or the other gender. And gender identity also requires awareness of how that gender assignment is viewed in one's social milieu.

Some of sexuality is body, some is programmed activity, and much is learned; we are dealing once again with hardware, firmware, and software. Over the centuries that our species has paid attention to itself there has been little quarrel about the nature of the hardware. It is undeniable that women provide eggs which are fertilized by sperm provided by men; no one doubts that only women can become pregnant and be delivered of babies. Much debate has raged about the difference between firmware and software. By custom, women in our culture are more likely to rear babies than men; yet both are equally capable of this task. Anyone who says that "women belong in the home" and that "only men can fight" has linked gender to social role—a confusion between what is learned as software and what (like the menstrual cycle) has been carved into the firmware by evolution.

One of the peculiarities of the scientific world is that a lot of people begin to study the same problem at the same time—there are themes and vogues in science just as there are in any other realm of human endeavor. Most of the books that revolutionized our understanding of sexuality came out about the same time as *The Joy of Sex* and *Human Sexual Response*. Dr. John Money, a researcher who has devoted his long and enormously fruitful career to the study of gender and gender identity, joined with his colleague Dr. Anke Ehrhardt in 1972 to write *Man and Woman, Boy and Girl*. Just as it is unlikely that anyone will ever need to repeat all the work done by Masters and Johnson, which allowed us to understand how the various organs of the body are affected during sexual activity, it would be difficult to imagine anyone making a significant improvement on Money and Ehrhardt's meticulous study of the relation between sexual biology and sexual behavior.

From the standpoint of my own interest in the scripts and programs that influence human emotion, it is fascinating to read their description of the mechanisms that produce human sexuality. Here, for once, is a complex group of scripts known to be stored in one readily studied library, the X and Y chromosomes that make us female or male. Money and Ehrhardt point out that these chromosomes control maleness and femaleness at three levels.

From the moment that egg and sperm unite to initiate the process of fetal development, all body systems unfold toward their eventual mature form. At each stage in development, all embryos are pretty much the same. Only in the area of sexual development are they different—the X and Y chromosomes differentiate human embryos into two quite specific shapes. Money and Ehrhardt refer to this difference as *sexual dimorphism*, two separate morphologies (body shapes) distinguished only by factors that have to do with sexuality. The library for femaleness is contained in the X chromosome, and the library for maleness is contained in the Y chromosome.

Actually, the basic plan of the human embryo is female. We all started out in life with a urogenital region made up of little buds of tissue that are quite female in appearance. Left to themselves, these embryonic structures would go on to make everybody female. But when a Y chromosome is present, under its command the primitive undifferentiated gonad of the fetus becomes a testicle rather than an ovary. Speedily, other programs are set in motion by the testicle, which produces the male hormone called *testosterone*. The structures that in the female would become the *labia minora* (the inner lips of the vagina) now alter their path and grow to enclose the clitoral bud and the *urethra* (the tube channeling urine from the bladder) to form the penis. The *labia majora* join at the midline to form the scrotum, and the ligaments that would have held the ovaries within the pelvis now contract to draw the testicles into it. In the male, all of the structures capable of erotic response have been moved outside the pelvis.

In those rare cases when the primitive undifferentiated gonad fails to appear, there can be no testicle; even though the organism may be genetically male it continues to develop as a female. From the standpoint of embryology, the book of Genesis is in error—maleness is created from the basic plan of femaleness.

This effect on our hardware is the first realm of action demonstrated by the scripts contained in the sex chromosomes. The second realm of action is equally important, but much more subtle and difficult to demonstrate. There appears to be a real difference between the brain of the male and of the female, a divergence produced by the presence or absence of testicular secretions.

One portion of this gender difference of neural pathways is easy to understand. Each of the structures made sexually dimorphic by the relative balance of male and female sex hormones, each of the urogenital organs, develops along with its own distinct supply of blood vessels and nerves. The circulatory system evolved much earlier (and remains far simpler and more primitive) than the central nervous system. The heart does not need to know how the vessels are mapped out to enable blood to course through these pipes to and from the center. But each nerve that develops in the periphery must have some exact representation at the center of the nervous system. It must be registered in the brain. As testosterone converts the body of the fetus from its basic female pattern to biological maleness, it forces the brain itself to register this now-masculine pattern.

There is good reason to believe that more is changed during fetal development than the mere representation of peripheral pathways. The balance, the relative amount of male and female sex hormones coursing through the embryonic brain, controls certain patterns of organization. Especially does this seem to affect the hypothalamus, the region of the brain containing much of the firmware that controls gender-related behavior. Examples of this sort of firmware include the programs that make little boys so much more avid for rough-and-tumble play than girls and that cause erections during dreams. Often (but not always) it can be proven that some little girls who are quite masculine in their energy level and preference for rough-and-tumble play, but otherwise very normally feminine, have been exposed to an unusual amount of testosterone during fetal development.

Of course I know that some women are stronger than some men and that some women can fight better than some men. But by and large, the urge to fight and the need to fight seem to be part of maleness. No matter how we try to limit professional boxing, the heavyweight championship fight remains the essence of one aspect of masculine sexuality. Our culture has recently become enamored of the Asian martial arts; thus the fight scenes which enliven our feature films now utilize karate and kung fu as well as traditional fisticuffs. Yet men have since time immemorial jousted, wrestled, and boxed; they pummel each other in rugby, football, and other sports. Boys and men can be trained to be gentle, but this is an outgrowth of our growing interest in empathic relatedness rather than any alteration in sexual dimorphism.

Girls can (and should) be encouraged to participate in sports, even rough-and-tumble sports; their exclusion from such activity has been a noxious social aspect of sexual dimorphism grafted onto femininity by a culture that needed to suppress certain realms of feminine potential. But part of the system of innate preference for certain forms of activity is scripted by the X and Y chromosomes.

So the sex chromosomes contain maps for the mechanisms that later produce the firmware for some portion of gender-related activity. Money and Ehrhardt comment that there is a third realm of characteristics orchestrated by these script libraries, an effect on the social milieu into which the infant is born. All over the world, people pay attention to pregnant women, wondering whether the baby hidden within will be a boy or a girl. From the instant the baby emerges from the birth canal, how it is treated by the world into which it has arrived will largely be determined by that society's reaction to the baby's externally visible genitals. Babies with penis and scrotum will be treated as boys with whom people will tussle, and babies with vaginas will be treated as girls to cuddle.

Boys learn to identify with the men around them, just as girls learn to identify with the women in their surround. But men and women understand the difference between boys and girls and treat them quite differently. Men react to girls in line with their understanding of femininity, women react to boys in line with their understanding of masculinity. Thus, by the process Money and Ehrhardt call *complementarity*, each gender tends to perpetuate its cultural understanding of both sexual roles. From the moment of birth, children are taught that they are either boys or girls and encouraged to behave accordingly.

Whereas it is no doubt better for a child to be reared with both parents available, women in general do not raise boys to be feminine and men do not raise girls to be masculine. Even when children are raised from infancy by a pair of homosexual men or a pair of lesbian women, there is only a slight increase in the likelihood that their gender identity will be disturbed. (Lesbian women and homosexual men still see themselves as women and men. The alteration is in sexual object choice, not gender identity.) The growing child draws a blueprint of what it means to "be" a member of either sex from data provided by everybody in his or her milieu.

Sexual dimorphism is much more than the superficial difference between boys and girls, than even the secondary sexual characteristics of men and women. The two genders differ in many more ways, all characteristic of a system that has evolved to guarantee the maintenance of the species through sexual reproduction. Easily observed in pet dogs is the characteristic prowling behavior of the male, whose nose is ever attentive for signs of femaleness; more likely than not a female dog will accept patiently the male's need to inspect her before he is available for other forms of play. Men, too, are generally more preoccupied with mating behavior than women, while they have far less involvement with pregnancy and early child-rearing. The basic differences dictated by the scripts stored in the X and Y chromosomes affect behavior throughout life.

THE GENERATIVE SYSTEM

It is possible to study the development of gender identity, the nature of courtship, sexual intercourse, the sequences involved in pregnancy and delivery, or any one of the many other processes linked to human reproduction, without recognizing how they are linked. I prefer to view each of these important and complex systems of behavior as subroutines of a far more complex overarching program that I call the *generative system.* In this regard I suggest that it functions in a manner analogous to the affect system, with sites of action located all over the body, structural effectors running from the central nervous system throughout the body, chemical mediators manufactured at locations such as the endocrine glands and within the brain itself, and organizers of innate programs that are responsible for conduct known to us as specifically sexual, which are stored in the hypothalamus.

Thus, the menstrual cycle would be seen as a specific form of organized innate program, the script for which is stored within the hypothalamus, utilizing hormonal messengers manufactured there and in the ovaries, causing effects at such widely separated sites of action as the lining of the uterus, the breasts, and the gastrointestinal system. The cyclic process by which, from infancy through senescence, erections are triggered during the cerebral activity associated with dreams is the result of another innate program. Further examples of such subroutines include the processes of pregnancy and nursing, in which specific bodily sites are transformed from their normal state of quiet preparedness into the active loci of the work for which they have evolved.

The affect system evolved much more recently than the generative system and differs from it in several aspects. The nine innate affects are each triggered by a specific stimulus, and each affect is an analogue of that stimulus. An affect is an analogue that acts to amplify this stimulus and bring it into consciousness with what becomes a characteristic sort of urgency. In contrast to the affect system, the subroutines of the generative system appear to be set in motion not by analogic triggers but by built-in biological clocks. All of the functions associated with sexual reproduction seem to be derived from mechanisms that have an inherent time constant. Unless intentionally initiated, all the generative programs start and stop under the control of their own timekeepers.

The menstrual cycle provides for the female a regular routine by which the system is guaranteed one fresh egg every month and provides for that egg a freshly made bed of uterine lining. Thus, a biological clock makes women fertile for a couple of days each month. But the generative system also makes sure that the male is always ready with a supply of freshly made sperm. Soon after puberty, when the male reproductive system moves into high gear, innate programs organize the manufacture of sperm, seminal fluid, and all the other components that eventually will be needed to guarantee male fertility. These fluids and cellular components are produced at such a pace that they must be expelled at a frequency determined by that rate of production. Initially this tidal flow of male sexual elements appears as a nocturnal emission, an ejaculation that, like the erection cycle, occurs during the dreaming phase of sleep.

Each woman will release no more than 3 to 400 eggs during her three decades or so of fertility; each ejaculate contains millions of sperm. That these two processes are different is clear. They are similar in that both are run by biological firmware activated and maintained by internal clock mechanisms. Money and Ehrhardt refer to such innately programmed cycles of activity as the "rehearsals" of the sexual system.

There are other examples of this rehearsal process clearly visible and available for study both in humans and in other life forms. Anyone who has ever owned a dog knows a lot about the process of rehearsal. Male dogs who have never seen their elders in the act of sexual intercourse will practice some sexual behaviors very much as if they are living out a script. When approximately two years old, our Gordon Setter began to mount any visiting dog (and even the occasional placid and confused small child) who happened into his territory. Each time, he would reach with his forepaws over the back of his playmate and initiate a series of powerful pelvic thrusts into the space between them. This is precisely the sort of behavior that must be called into play when needed for the purpose of procreation.

That this behavior was scripted seemed clear, for the humping movements he made occurred at no other time and bore no relation to behavior otherwise normal for him; the power with which he grasped his partner was uncharacteristic of this otherwise gentle animal. But it was also clear that he had no idea of its purpose, for he grabbed at and humped the front, side, and rear of these "sexual objects" with equal frequency.

His regular playmate is our other dog, a neutered female Border Collie of extraordinary intelligence and energy. One of her characteristic modes of play involves a game in which she bends forward on her right shoulder, ducks her head under her chest, and presents her rump. A female in heat is scripted by mechanisms that encourage her to offer a male the part of her body that makes his motions more useful. Our Border Collie has never been in heat. We have never observed any coordination of these scripts; at no time has the mounting behavior of the Gordon Setter occurred when his playmate has experimented with "presenting" behavior.

Money and Ehrhardt note that juvenile male animals of many species—including man—will rehearse mounting behavior long before they are capable of producing sperm, even though they have never seen their elders in the act of intercourse. And juvenile female animals of many species—including man—will rehearse presenting behavior long before they are capable of maintaining a pregnancy, even though they have never seen their elders in the act of intercourse.

So the generative system ensures that we humans are divided into two groups on the basis of our body shape or form, that the organs which make us different are under the control of firmware programs capable of making them work in specifically sexual modes, and that these programs operate under the control of clocks that guarantee optimal function. Wherever these mechanisms utilize systems that are also capable of being used under conscious control, we can learn or decide to use them for our own purposes.

In this way the generative system resembles many other intrinsic systems. The organism will be prompted to eat by the hunger drive when certain physiological conditions are fulfilled, but it can decide to eat when it is not hungry. Without intending to do so, we experience the innate affects when they are triggered by stimuli for which we are prepared by firmware programs. But we are capable of having or imitating any emotion any time that we want.

So it is for sex. We learn to make use of the innate programs, to place under our conscious control the sexual behaviors that can also be run by firmware programs. Basic to adult sexual practice is some sort of interplay between the intrinsically scripted and the intentionally scripted forms of bodily activity; it is necessary to appreciate both to explain human sexuality.

Notice another realm of resemblance to the affect system: Tomkins has pointed out that the first observable intentional acts performed by the infant involve the autosimulation of behavior initially triggered by the drives and the affects. Just as soon as the infant begins to suck at breast or bottle, it is capable of making sucking motions on purpose—even when it is not hungry. Just as soon as the infant experiences its body being taken over by the affect programs, it begins to experiment with the intentional production of those same behaviors.

Here, in the generative system, are a series of behavioral patterns initially scripted by firmware programs under the control of internal clocks. Unlike the affect programs, which are available to the organism from birth, the subroutines of the generative system do not come on line until much later in development. Some of these subroutines utilize muscles that are normally under voluntary control, so it is easy for the organism to simulate intentionally any series of actions that had previously been only "automatic." Even though mounting and presenting behavior can be set in motion and run by innately scripted programs, we humans take pride in the fact that we can perform these actions under our own control, at the time and place of our choosing, and with the partner we prefer above others. Even though ejaculation can be set in motion and run by innately scripted programs, we tend to take it over and make it intentional.

Already we have a great deal of information suggesting why sexuality is so profoundly linked to matters of shame and pride. Since the genetically determined characteristic of sexual dimorphism divides humans into two distinct shapes, and since our genital appearance determines so much of how we are seen and treated by those around us, a significant part of our identity is associated with gender. Shame and pride, the two most self-related emotions, must become involved with that part of self-definition that results from gender assignment. Furthermore, any pattern of activity that can be performed intentionally is capable of becoming associated with either pride or shame. This understanding must figure in any attempt to determine how shame and pride have become so deeply involved in sexual life.

True and important as this may be, it still falls far short of the mark. There is much more about sexuality and sexual arousal that connects them to the emotional life of humans. And this will be the subject of the next chapter.

20

A New Theory of Sexuality

Pause, for a moment, and consider again why it is so important that sexual reproduction be assisted by firmware programs and not left merely to the wish and whim of adult organisms. The generative system exists in its present, highly intrusive form in order that it handle one specific part of the evolutionary process. What we call the sex drive is a response to the increasing mobility of life forms.

No rooted organism has a sex drive. When pollen can be wafted from stamen to pistil by a breath of wind, or carried from one flower to another by bees, there is no need for the organism to force into consciousness the process of reproduction. *The sex drive evolved to solve the problems created for life forms that are both sexually dimorphic and capable of leaving their moorings, as well as advanced enough to analyze their world or achieve conscious control of their behavior.* The more advanced organism is able to pay attention to whatever garners its interest. Life forms with the greatest powers of cognition are the most likely to remain involved with whatever is the subject of their current interest. Only because man is the most conscious of organisms is it necessary that the sex drive evolve to intrude so powerfully into consciousness. With the evolution of consciousness came the need for the generative process to take it over.

Tomkins has suggested that consciousness itself evolved in tandem with our increasing mobility. Whereas it is possible for the homeostatic mechanisms of the body to be programmed for a great many possibilities, as life forms became more mobile they grew to encounter situations that could not be predicted. Thus, consciousness evolved as a way of allowing the organism to use its newly developed cognitive skills toward the solution of novel problems in living. With the appearance of these cognitive skills came an increase in the organism's capacity to store and retrieve both the conditions for the once-novel problem and the solution achieved.

The pheromone secreted by the female gypsy moth will call to her any male gypsy moth of the same species. I have read that only one lone molecule of this marvelous substance is needed to affect all moths in a space measuring 50,000 cubic yards! For organisms as primitive as the gypsy moth, only the pheromone is needed to draw male to female for the purpose of sexual reproduction. The generative system is merely one of the many homeostatic systems when there is no need to access consciousness.

Whereas in the stickleback fish it is the male who initiates the dance that attracts to him the female, in the gypsy moth it is the female who must attract the male. Wherever the male and female elements can be separated by physical distance, they must be drawn together by the generative system. Only to the extent that it is difficult to distract the organism from its other pursuits will the generative system be required to use "nonsexual" bodily functions to help it take over behavior.

Thus, a bitch in heat will, by her pheromonal broadcast, cause the wailing and howling of male dogs over a radius of many blocks. The moth merely flies in the direction of the pheromone; the moth is unlikely either to "know" or to "care" that it is now on the path toward a sexual meeting. The more advanced central nervous system of the dog makes it far more capable of knowing or caring about its actions. It is the greater independence and freedom of the dog, the degree to which the dog is more free than the moth to choose its course of action, that makes it necessary for the pheromone to activate so many more systems. Yes, the pheromone does create a path along which the male travels toward the female; and yes, the pheromone "gets the attention" of the dog, distracts him from whatever he had been doing only a moment ago. But other systems cooperate to serve the generative function. Merely to resist the power of the pheromone activates the affect of distress, which brings into consciousness the constant pressure created by the sexual stimulus and makes it urgent, lending the urgency of distress affect to the urgency normally associated with the sexual drive.

I have defined the generative system as that which provides for the maintenance of the species through reproduction and suggested that the generative system has become increasingly intrusive as life forms have evolved into highly conscious beings capable of living as they intend rather than as they are urged by homeostatic mechanisms. It remains to demonstrate how the generative system enters into consciousness and by what means sexuality achieves the degree of urgency by which we know it.

All of the subroutines of the generative system mentioned so far have but scant influence on consciousness. Men have little awareness of the erections that take place during sleep, and, unless ovulation is accompanied by pain, women are normally unaware that an egg has left the ovary to begin its passage through the Fallopian tubes to the uterus. What does garner our attention is the complex group of waking experiences called *sexual arousal*. Like the affects and the other drives, it involves devices that can be run on "automatic pilot" when taken over by innate programs, but that can be controlled, modulated, or otherwise altered by training and skill.

One of the fallacies of adult life is the belief that sexual arousal exists primarily in the organs of intercourse, the penis and vagina. Prior to the work of Masters and Johnson there was only anecdotal evidence that arousal involved sites of action throughout the body. A novelist, like André Malraux, might describe a lover's hope that "the pleasure of the senses would imprint [passion] on Valérie's face," and Valérie herself might note that "a familiar warmth seized her, mounted along her body to the tips of her breasts, to her lips, which she guessed by [his] look were imperceptibly swelling" (126). But we lacked a scientific explanation of these observations until the publication of *Human Sexual Response*.

Like the affect system, much of sexual arousal involves the circulatory system. First noticed and earliest studied was the penis, which contains three cylindrical bodies of erectile tissue—the paired *corpora cavernosa*, which flank the urethra, and the *corpus spongiosum*, which lies beneath it. Under the control of nerve impulses sent along the *parasympathetic* trunks, microscopic valves in the arterioles and veins of the penis alter blood flow so that these normally empty structures fill with blood and become rigid pontoons.

Here, as elsewhere in the body, the action of the parasympathetic nerves is opposed by the *sympathetic* group; nerve impulses sent along sympathetic trunks will cause rapid subsidence of the penile erection. Both, of course, are controlled by higher brain centers. (How interesting, how convenient for evolution that the sites of action for fear–terror involve the sympathetic nerves; fear is an intrinsic off-switch for sexual arousal.) Autonomic nerve flow affects other structures—some of what the male experiences as sexual tension is due to the contraction of specialized groups of muscles located throughout the urogenital system.

For the male, then, the local effect of sexual arousal involves vasocongestion and muscular tension. The penis, scrotum, and rectum are thus made infinitely more sensitive to touch. Sexual arousal does not create local sexual sensitivity—it merely amplifies it.

In the female, parasympathetic nerve flow also produces alterations of the microcirculation, but the effect is quite different. Here there are no pontoons to create their dramatic alteration in surface anatomy, but rather a vaginal area that, when suffused with blood under pressure higher than usual, begins to allow the transudation of a glistening, mucoid material that acts as a lubricant. Just as the penis may spring rapidly into full erection, the vagina is capable of responding to sexual excitement by becoming fully lubricated in a matter of seconds. Other pelvic structures are affected by sexual arousal, all of them involving a combination of muscular tension and vasocongestion.

Yet it is in the study of female sexuality that we become aware that these circulatory changes occur at sites of action all over the body. As noted by the novelist in the quotation above, female arousal also involves the skin of the entire upper part of the body—especially the breasts and face. For a man, it is the penis that calls to attention or confirms the degree of lust being experienced. For a woman, the changes in the vagina are noticed well after she has come to appreciate the sensual transformation of her lips and breasts, bodily structures made infinitely more sensitive when engorged with blood. Kissing is sexual, perhaps somewhat more so for women then for men, because it involves the receptors for this transformation.

All this, of course, is part of sexual dimorphism. Men and women are built differently and experience sexual arousal differently. Each of the organs or regions affected by sexual arousal has its own group of receptors that must be represented within the higher centers of the brain. To the extent that men and women differ in their anatomy, they will differ in their experience of sexual arousal. And, within any group of men and women, one will find a wide range of patterns of arousal. Our experience of sexual arousal involves such varied parts of our makeup as the sexual anatomy, the neocortical structures responsible for awareness, memory, and fantasy, and the affect system. It also seems likely that some portion of our emotional experience of this arousal is independent of the affect system, involving brain centers that evolved much earlier.

Any attempt to analyze the nature of sexual arousal brings one back to the question of the relation between firmware and software. I think that psychotherapists know more about this than anyone else, for, since the days when Freud first blazed the trail we follow, we have been trained to listen impartially to the world of adult sexuality. So intensely are humans affected by sexual excitement that, throughout life, we attempt to control and modulate the power of the sexual drive by a host of maneuvers that become an important part of both our individual personalities and our culture. The range of what we must consider normal is extraordinary.

I have interviewed women who began to masturbate to orgasm when five years old and who (when involved in a relationship they felt appropriate) enjoy intercourse several times a day. I have spoken at length with women who felt no urge to masturbate or to participate in intercourse until their early twenties, after which they entered a phase of adult sexuality indistinguishable from that of women whose sexual history had been quite different. All of these patterns of sexual activity are "normal." On the other hand, I have worked in therapy with many women whose ability to enjoy their sexual nature had been impaired by early emotional experiences, but who assumed full control of their engines when therapy had been successful.

Similarly, I have spoken with men who evinced no interest in sexual activity until late adolescence, and others who felt they were deeply involved in sexual fantasy accompanied by masturbation from earliest childhood. One 30-year-old man of my acquaintance is happily capable of intercourse or masturbation to ejaculation three times a day, but, after a recent psychotherapy session which stimulated a group of intense erotic fantasies, saw his level of interest double. Other men his age tell me they find intercourse or masturbation similarly pleasurable, but at a frequency approaching once or twice in a month. And for men, just as for women, sexual function can be distorted by emotional illness.

Without citing the host of references that support my opinion, I suspect that each of us differs somewhat in our sexual makeup, that the sexual drive demands attention over a wide range of activity. Just as each of us must learn how to make do with the physical equipment given us by our genetic makeup (just as we vary, for instance, in our muscularity and our avidity for athletic play), we learn to accommodate to the type of sexual drive pattern given us by a similar set of biological scripts. As mature adults, we are capable of adjusting to the sexual needs of our partners, despite the fact that each of us has our own individual sexual rhythm set by some internal biological clock system.

It is pretty easy to identify the workings of the generative system and its sexual drive when you look at adults, just as it is rather easy to discuss adult emotion. Things change when you know about the innate affects and begin to trace the pathways along which these physiological mechanisms travel as we grow from infancy into adulthood. It is important that we find the earliest manifestations of the sexual drive so that we can figure out how it comes to be assembled with so many psychological matters.

Before Freud, it was taken for granted that humans did not become sexual until adolescence. Using the archaeologic model, digging backward into the past history of each patient who came to him, he found that most four- to

six-year-old children go through a phase of sexual ideation that seemed to
dominate that era of their development. There were three phenomena in need
of explanation: (1) Why was there no evidence of sexual fantasy before this
period? (2) Why, shortly after this critical period, was there a clear decrease in
the importance of sexual ideation, at least until the beginning of adolescence?
(3) Where did it come from? Why, suddenly, at age four, did a child become
involved with its sexual nature?

Although now known to be incorrect, his answer has become a part of our
culture itself, one of the building blocks of our current world-view. He suggested that we differ from other life forms in that our machine is infused with
libido, a special force that makes us uniquely human. At birth, said Freud, libido
guarantees that we explore with our mouths the world into which we have
emerged; a year later the realm of our interest will be the region of the rectum;
still later we become interested in our genitals as libido alters in focus. At four,
the libido coalesces into a purely sexual force and makes us lust for a parent of
the opposite gender. Over the next two years we go through a highly complex sequence of interpersonal interactions through which we decide that it is
not yet time to be fully sexual, and that we had better go about the job of
being children before we try to be adults. At adolescence, when we are much
better able to handle sexuality, libido gains in force and pushes us into adulthood. All this is libido theory.

Libido theory works only in terms of the three questions noted above. If we
can find evidence that children have sexual ideation long before the oedipal
phase of development, and that not all children renounce their sexuality immediately after it, the significance of the theory is reduced. Such evidence exists in
profusion, and is quite important to our understanding of the entire generative
system. None of it was available to Freud.

In a remarkable book published in 1985, the psychoanalytic psychologist
Johanna Krout Tabin summarized her life work with patients who had come to
her for help with the eating disorders called *bulimia* and *anorexia nervosa*. In her
analytic treatment of these patients Tabin noted something perplexing: Significant parts of their inner life, the style and substance of their fantasies, could
only be explained by the experience of sexual fantasy at an age well before
that accepted in the theoretical system of her training. Indeed, her own archaeologic study suggested that they had been occupied by truly sexual feelings
and ideas when only 18 or 24 months old!

Tabin was stuck with the kind of problem that afflicts only the honest and
sober clinician. People with eating disorders, often declared nearly untreatable
by other practitioners, seemed to get well when she worked with them. And

central to her treatment was Tabin's acceptance of infantile sexuality at an age that could not fit into the classical Freudian theory that was the core of her professional life. One does not take such matters lightly.

Her solution was highly individual. Had she decided to publish her own few cases, most of us would have ignored her work, saying that she simply misunderstood her patients and that she certainly did not understand libido theory. Instead, Tabin went to the library, where she found hundreds of case descriptions indicating the existence of sexual fantasy at the age important in her own patients. Some of these cases, like her own, involved work with adults. But the overwhelming majority of the published studies she reviewed were from child therapists—competent observers who reported exactly what these toddlers did, what they said, and how their parents responded to these clearly sexual interactions.

It now appears that toddlers can indeed feel sexual, and that they attempt to explain these sexual feelings in terms of the logic available to them at that age. Tabin suggests, with great good sense, that children try to explain everything that happens to them. When a toddler becomes sexually excited, that little person must try to explain these pesky feelings. It is during the toddler era that children stop identifying themselves as "a baby," and begin to add gender to their identity. A two-year-old says, "I'm not a baby! I'm a boy!" or "I'm a girl!" Such a realization, says Tabin, may be the result of a process of discovery initiated to explain sexual arousal. Certainly much of our gender identity is formed as the result of identification and complementarity, of how babies are treated by the adults in their milieu. But we do not suddenly, in the toddler era, start telling our offspring that they are boys or girls. From the moment of their birth we have made this distinction in their presence.

It was only after I read Tabin's work and began to correspond with her that I recognized how often I had ignored certain information confided by my patients. Often I had heard mothers describe what sounds like clearly sexual behavior on the part of their infants and toddlers and had not known how to understand it. Three mothers have described scenes in which a six- or seven-month-old boy, lying naked on the changing table, looked directly at her, grinned, and then developed an erection. Prior to this current interest in the nature of the sexual drive and its relation to the generative system, most of us would have assumed that the report was faulty, or that the mother was guilty of sexual stimulation of an infant, or that the infant's erection bore no relation to the events she described.

My own conclusion is quite different. I believe that the sexual drive, like all the other drive functions, is operative from birth. Unlike the other drives, which are fully formed when the infant emerges from the birth canal, sexuality cannot take its adult form until the organism has reached full biological maturity. The sexual drive affects us in different ways at different times in development. Looking at the individual over time, one might say that the drive itself emerges in waves.

From the moment of birth every human is sexual. The erection that occurs during the excitement phase of dreaming sleep is but one subroutine of the program. Boys will have erections any time they are excited—all day long they go through periods of penile tumescence and relaxation, covered from birth by diapers. I suspect little girls go through an analogous process kept invisible by their anatomy. In each era of development, each child must try to explain the part of the sexual drive that is unfolding at that time; the explanation will be entirely dependent on that child's understanding of itself and of its world.

We humans are the only life form that attempts to have sexual intercourse while facing each other. In all other organisms that are fitted up with a sexual drive, this powerful mechanism ensures that the fertile female will present her vagina to the aroused male as efficiently as possible. Sexual intercourse is accomplished rapidly, rear to front, and repeated as often as the male is able to perform. In the female, sexual arousal produces the need to be touched, to be entered; in the male, sexual arousal produces the need to be propulsive. I know of no life form other than the human that attempts to use procreation as a form of recreation.

Such might be the case for the human species had not we evolved both an affect system and the group of brain mechanisms allowing the formation of empathic relatedness. Recall (as we discussed in Chapter 18) the Greek division of love into the three categories of *eros*, *filios*, and *agape*. Mature erotic love involves both the circuitry for love as sketched earlier and the circuitry for sexuality being developed here. One of the peculiarities of *homo sapiens* is our attempt to merge the twin themes of a sexual drive system that pushes us together for the purpose of procreation and the affect-based system of empathic relatedness that pushes us together for the purpose of mutual nurturance. At every stage in child development we can see evidence of the process through which these themes are linked.

The oedipal phase of development is nothing more than a child's attempt to explain its experience of lust in terms of what it has already learned about human relatedness. The lust is created by a drive program that has evolved to guarantee attention, to take over the consciousness of a mobile organism. Lust is experienced as the desire to touch and to be touched in special places, to find a partner with whom this touching can be accomplished. It produces a powerful need to make a special form of contact with others. The oedipal-era child must decide how to explain its sexual feelings, and it does this through the creation of a script or story designed to handle all aspects of its sexual experience.

This is yet another example of the interaction between hardware, firmware, and software. Earlier I mentioned that an adult who has taken too much of the nasal decongestant *pseudoephedrine* will complain of anxiety. The experience created by the presence of a chemical substance introduced from outside the body can only be explained as if it had been produced by an affect program. This is why such people say that they are anxious "about" something, or that they have been made nervous "by" some event or situation in their lives.

Any novel idea or experience will trigger the affect interest–excitement; I believe that the reason manic patients are so full of ideas is that a distortion of the normal balance of neurotransmitters has suffused the individual with what it defines as an affect—one that can only be explained as if it had been produced by a flow of ideas. And it is the experience of this excitement that leads a manic person to search with excitement for ideas and to behave as if it had been the ideas that had triggered the excitement.

Similarly, I believe that the only way we humans, whether infant, toddler, child, adolescent, or adult, can come to understand the effect on us of the sexual drive is to explain it within a system of fantasized and actual human relationships. The biological drive produces feelings that must be explained; we attempt to explain it as conscious intent rather than the effect of a prewritten firmware program. That these fantasized relationships will have been based on our life history of affective interaction is self-evident. Each wave of increase in the sexual drive comes to be understood in terms of our relational history. Each wave of sexual increase produces turmoil until it has been integrated into the self of the individual, after which we go on about the business of living with this new, upgraded self system.

I don't know how the six-month-old boy understands the sort of sexual interaction described above. Each of the three mothers who described to me this scene reacted with mild amazement and embarrassment ("Why that little scamp!" "My son the sex maniac!" "OH! I was soooo embarrassed! I told him, 'Hey! You cut that out!'"). Recently I discussed some of this material at a scholarly conference, where a Puerto Rican psychiatrist told me how such a scene would be handled in his culture: "Either the mother or father, whoever saw the erection, would smile and laugh, point right back at it with the index finger, even touch it, and say something happy like 'Look at the little man!'"

Where one culture reacts with shame to infantile sexuality, another responds with pride. At how many levels might we be able to trace such examples of cultural divergence in the modulation of sexual drive function?

Most likely Tabin is correct when she asks us to understand that toddlers must find explanations for their own experience of sexual arousal. The classical oedipal phase of development is, as Money and Ehrhardt have commented, only one of the rehearsals provided by what I now call the generative system. If neonatal arousal is the first wave of sexual drive function, toddler sexuality is the second, oedipal phase sexuality the third, and adolescence a fourth.

Recently a man reported that he had been called from his weekly poker game by the housekeeper, who had been alarmed by something that had happened to his 10-year-old son. While bathing, the boy had experienced profound swelling of the penis, which prevented him from urinating and frightened him enough to ask her help. Physicians were called. The domestic worker was African-American, and the doctor unaware that the child in her charge was Caucasian. The presumptive diagnosis of sickle cell crisis was relinquished only as more data came to the fore. Eventually it was determined that this was the young man's first "real" erection—the moment that the fourth wave of sexual drive increase had chosen to assert its action.

There are lots of other such waves of increase, each with its own amplitude and frequency. It is not unusual for women in our culture to note a surge in sexual interest and sexual pleasure in their early thirties. Many women describe two periods of increased sexual arousal paralleling the menstrual cycle—one when they are most fertile and another immediately before menstruation. Money and Ehrhardt (1972) describe a number of studies that suggest specific dream and waking imagery accompanying each of these peaks of arousal—a wish to be pleasured passively during mid-cycle and an urge to be aggressively sexual in the premenstrual phase. Each of these recurring sequences of drive-mediated personal experience must be integrated into one's self-concept.

It is characteristic of the sexual drive itself to increase in surges. Each surge, of course, provides a new form of self-experience, a new way the individual must come to understand himself or herself. For a while, this increase in sexuality is a disturbing alteration in the self we have known to date. Eventually, when we get used to each new level of sexuality, we enter into a period of relative calm. It is not that the sexual drive system calms down—it will remain relatively constant at the new level now achieved—but that we are no longer troubled by the alteration in self-experience and no longer disturbed by the scenarios we create to explain it.

Just as we now know that the drive causes arousal in children long before the classical oedipal period, we can understand that there is no such thing as a period of sexual latency following it. All that has happened is that the child has come to an acceptance of its sexual nature—one appropriate for its age and stage of development—and no longer experiences turmoil. Most children are full of sexual ideas and fantasies throughout the period Freud called "latency." Such thoughts disturb the child much less then they did during the beginning of the oedipal phase. This is because they have been explained satisfactorily, placed within a relational scheme, and modulated by techniques analogous to those through which we learn to handle innate affect.

The big surge, of course, the one so huge that it often places human life at risk, is the wave of increase in sexual drive function that takes place during adolescence. For both sexes, the hormonal explosion of puberty brings with it a radical amplification of all activity, one that may be considered an analogue of the earlier-appearing sexually dimorphic rough-and-tumble behavior. Whoever one has become, whatever the self that has developed from the combination of factors operating until the moment of puberty, that "package" is what will now be turned on to its maximum.

Sexual arousal produces a need for the tissues involved to be touched. Male arousal focuses attention on the organs of intercourse; male imagery explains this arousal on the basis of fantasized experiences in which those organs figure prominently. Given the geometry of the male genital organs, which form a peninsula, the greatest percentage of stimulated tissue can be touched when the penis is entirely contained. This containment can be offered by a hand, a wish that can be achieved without the cooperation of another person. Insertion in the mouth, vagina, or rectum of a sexual partner will also produce the desired effect.

In boys, drive-based arousal is experienced as visual imagery, explicitly sexual scenes peopled by a cast of characters drawn from every realm of their experience. With the increasing sophistication born of exposure to the sexual scenes depicted in the literature, anecdotes, and visual aids available to him, a boy will grow into manhood with a library of sexual ideas and fantasies that he will try to live out with real partners.

His urge to do this derives not from any active seduction or suggestion planted by the women in his milieu, but from the physiological arousal produced by sexual drive programs operating out of awareness. Later in his experience, of course, he will be exposed to women in varying states of arousal, and their arousal will trigger, augment, or amplify his own. But initially, the theater of his imagination plays only the drama of his drives. Men learn to gratify through masturbation the needs created by arousal, to initiate and complete this process with a sense of urgency and dispatch. Male sexual theater tends toward fantasies of brief encounters in which the partner accepts his arousal with ease and offers speedy gratification.

In women, the vasocongestion and muscular tension associated with sexual arousal are experienced at sites scattered throughout the body. Female imagery must explain and satisfy the needs created by this pattern of arousal. Thus, women are likely to fantasize about men who kiss them on the lips and neck, who are unhurried in their approach, and whose arousal increases at a pace matching their own—in other words, men who understand, or behave in accordance with, the nature of female arousal. This pattern of arousal favors the emergence of romantic fantasy that differs in many respects from that created by men.

When this arousal has spread to the genital region, it produces a need to be touched there. In the absence of interfering negative affect, every region of aroused (engorged) tissue that it is touched will contribute to the pleasurable feeling we call gratification. It is, of course, true that an educated and sensitive sexual partner may, by hand and mouth work, touch an aroused woman in ways that are more precisely attuned to her moment-to-moment needs than can be achieved with any penis. Such sexual attention is the result of extensive training involving neocortical cognition and in no way programmed by firmware mechanisms. The geometry of the female sexual apparatus does, however, provide that a great surface area of tissue will be touched or stretched by vaginal penetration and penile excursion. Obedience to firmware, to drive-based instructions, leads to sexual intercourse.

Yet we humans do not grow up in the sort of "state of nature" that might predispose adults to obey such firmware programs with impunity. The decision to accept actual penetration is quite complex, involving recognition of a fully sexual self that may place a woman in emotional conflict for a variety of reasons.

One way for a woman to short-circuit the process of analysis necessary for full acceptance of intercourse is to fantasize about rape, which (in this specific form of imagery) involves penetration without the affects that accompany decision. The fantasy of rape is an excuse to permit intercourse in the context of massive sexual arousal that is complicated by a host of emotional issues; actual rape involves the penetration of a woman who is not only unaroused but who is in a state of terror precluding arousal.

This vast difference between male and female rape imagery serves to illustrate a gentler point: Sexual dimorphism produces two patterns of arousal that

become widely divergent blueprints for the architecture of sexual relationships. No part of his own sexual growth and development prepares a boy for
the sexual fantasy life of women, who are equally ignorant of the nature of
male arousal and the fantasy life it encourages. Men and women must teach
each other how to understand and accept the nature of their sexual systems.
Our ability to develop healthy and fulfilling sexual relationships will depend
largely on the history of our attempts at empathic relatedness. The tensions of
this struggle produce the energy that powers much of the drama that infuses
our lives; painters, writers, poets, dancers, and all the other creative people of
each era translate these tensions into art.

THE RESONANCE OF AROUSAL

There is more that must be said about sexual arousal. It is peculiarly, marvelously capable of transmission from one person to another. Partly this is because of the affects with which it comes to be associated, but arousal can
communicate without any accompanying affect. It is not unusual for a man to
be informed by his penis that the woman with whom he is conversing is in a
state of mild arousal. It is not unusual for a woman to feel in her breasts and
face the mild stirrings of arousal when she is in the presence of an aroused male
companion or to react with surprise when she recognizes an unexpected degree of vaginal wetness.

How, and why, does this occur? The questions are those I raised for the
affect system. What is the mechanism through which we let others know about
our arousal—the mode of data transmission—and what is the mechanism for
its reception?

Most of the evidence points to three factors, all inherent to the biological
nature of sexual arousal. For many of the less complicated life forms we can
isolate a pheromone and show that it is responsible for the transmission and
reception of information about arousal and availability. In the human, the tufts
of pubic and axillary hair, known as "secondary sexual characteristics," are
thought to be involved in this process. The armpit and the genital region are
covered by relatively small areas of skin known to contain scent glands; but
the area available for the evaporation of pheromones is multiplied greatly
when one takes into account the surface of the hairs themselves. Pheromonal
transmission may be involved in human sexuality.

If pheromones are a significant part of the system through which others
become involved in our own, personal arousal, it is interesting to speculate
about the timing of pheromonal release. Are these scent-borne messenger

molecules wafted into the air about us during the early phases of arousal, when we may have made no decision about availability? Or might this occur only late in the process, when we are deeply committed to our arousal and thus driven to need a partner? My intuition favors the latter view. Couples dancing in public seem involved only with each other, despite how easy it is for us as bystanders to see the degree of their sexual arousal. Although it is true that powerful social rules may be in force, rarely do others in their vicinity seem equally aroused. If mildly aroused humans were powerful sources of phero-mones I would expect us to be a species in which group sex was common (either historically or in the present), rather than the rarity it seems to be.

The second factor, of course, and the one to which I have devoted the most attention so far, is local vasocongestion and muscular activity. Through most of our cultural history this particular set of bodily reactions was held as what Schneider called one of the "central privacies" of human life. Yet today, the half-lowered lids, slackened jaw, puffed-out lips, and thickened speech of arousal are the sexual icons of our civilization. We are bombarded by the information available in still photographs, from the tiny but-mobile representa-tions of people seen on television, from the data to be studied on the 30-foot-high images projected on our motion picture screens. Today, the display of sexual arousal is ubiquitous. Like the display of innate affect, the display of sexual arousal can be simulated either for the purpose of initiating the feeling in ourselves or in order to produce in the unwary other the contagious effect of true arousal.

And, just as for innate affect, there are two possible circuits for this conta-gion: On the one hand, we might imitate the facial display of the aroused other, thus triggering our own arousal by mechanisms similar to one of the circuits for empathy. It is my belief, however, that there is a supplemental path for this resonance that has evolved as part of the sexual drive system itself. The existence of such a built-in pathway for resonance would conform exactly to my basic theory for the sexual drive—something that provides a way for sexual arousal to guarantee communication. An optimally effective sexual drive would garner the attention (enter into the consciousness) of both the organism to be driven and of a host of possible partners. Facial display (and the other alterations in normal function produced by vasocongestion and muscular contraction) might suit some of these requirements.

But facial display is more a factor in female arousal than in male. More easily observed in men, but equally present in women, is a peculiar sort of agitation that I see as the third mode of biologically based sexual signaling. This agita-tion is one of the special qualities of the sexual drive mechanism.

Intrinsic to the concept of a drive system is the idea that each drive produces its own form of discontent, a discomfort that can be satisfied only at specific bodily sites. Think again of the intrinsic system that makes us hungry: We experience the annoyance called hunger as a desire to put food in the mouth. Should the body need specific foodstuffs, the drive mechanism is so complex, variable, and adaptable that it can make us crave whatever might satisfy that particular need. Other parts of the innate program for the drive guarantee that the ingestion of food will not only reduce the specific discomfort that triggered hunger, but also produce the sort of pleasure specific for that drive. This pleasure is independent of the affects with which the drive may be joined. Although it is affect that lends urgency to the drive, and affect that amplifies the pleasure that accompanies the reduction in the drive-based need, the particular form of pleasure experienced in that situation is specific to the drive.

The sexual drive, too, is a source of discomfort. It produces the specific sort of discomfort that is often likened to "an itch that wants to be scratched," a need for the touch that relieves but then continues to stimulate toward further pleasure. Sexuality differs from other drive mechanisms in that the discomfort associated with it does not decrease in intensity during the process of satisfaction. Thirst is slaked long before imbibed water has been distributed to the tissues responsible for the message that triggered it. Even one who had been famished before beginning to eat will feel the beginnings of satiation long before the needed nutrients have arrived at the tissues in need of them. But sexual arousal makes us long for the touch that both relieves the need to be touched, gives pleasure specific for that need, and also produces an increase in the need to be touched. This is a very annoying drive.

When all the conditions for its satisfaction have been met, the annoyance subsides after the explosion we call an orgasm, which, as Tomkins has suggested, can best be understood as a powerfully amplified analogue of the pleasurable discomfort itself. Here, too, the difference between the sexual drive system of men and women becomes evident. Male arousal occurs rapidly and is focused in the genitals; stimulation of the affected tissues produces rapid relief of the discomfort in the form of an ejaculation. Female arousal occurs slowly, spreading over large sections of the body, and is increased at a rate so slow relative to that found in men that it is often almost inconceivable to men. Sexual dimorphism requires men and women to teach each other a great deal—the software of adult sexuality necessitates long periods of mutual training.

But it is the firmware of sexuality that produces sexual arousal, even though we learn to trigger the system for reasons unrelated to the biological need for procreation. I think that the annoyance of sexual arousal produces its own form of agitation, one that men and women recognize and learn to accept as a form of sexual signaling. And it seems likely that this agitation is as capable of achieving resonance as any other part of sexual display.

Were sexual arousal only a matter of annoyance and discomfort, there is little likelihood it would achieve such prominence in human experience. We come to know our sexual nature not just from the annoyance of the drive and the pleasure of its gratification, but also from the affects it triggers. From our own life experience we know that "normal" sexual arousal involves excitement and that orgasm is followed by the calm and contentment associated with the affect enjoyment–joy. Wherever there is intense positive affect we may be sure to find shame as its auxiliary; there is shame aplenty in normal sexuality.

Interest, enjoyment, and shame are but three of the nine innate affects. Their link to sexuality has been honored for centuries. Yet there is a tendency to overlook the fact that sexual arousal can be assembled with fear, distress, anger, surprise, dissmell, and disgust. Sex claims no affect as its specific domain.

I have defined the generative system as the hardware, firmware, and software responsible for the maintenance of the species through reproduction. It is a system that has evolved to arouse us, to engage us with each other for the purposes of procreation, to provide a womb for the fetus that develops as the result of the union of generative elements, and to nurture the infant after it emerges from the birth canal. In the next chapter we will discuss some of the ways the generative system becomes intertwined with affect, concentrating on the worlds of shame and pride.

21

SHAME, PRIDE, AND SEX

"The ultimate development of mature sexual intercourse," said a senior colleague, "is for sex to become play. Sex," he continued, "at its best, is play for grownups, the adult version of two little kids rolling down the hill together." Early in a relationship, sex is about excitement; later it is more about contentment. A good sexual relationship, that all-too-rarely achieved goal toward which we are supposed to strive, involves a variable and dynamic alliance. It requires mutual positive regard, a remarkable degree of interpersonal tolerance, and great unselfishness. Nevertheless, for many couples, sex works best when a relationship is new and each can afford to believe that the other really does meet the criteria for specialness that so often lend spice to the mix. With mutual knowledge, unfortunately, often come boredom and contempt, which operate to impede arousal, excitement, and enjoyment. Sexual activity is a highly variable experience, many things to each of us.

The life work of psychoanalyst Robert J. Stoller was to study sex as it is lived, sex as it appears in real life rather than in theory, the sexual lives of those individuals who were willing to share with him their most private thoughts. Stoller traveled all over the planet, interviewing people in far-flung societies as well as probing the sexual psyche of patients in psychoanalysis.

From his research—thousands of hours spent asking questions most of us are far too shy to frame—emerges one sturdy conclusion: Central to the experience of sexual arousal are thoughts related to shame. All of us, he has said in *Sexual Excitement*, each time we contemplate a sexual event, think about those moments in our lives when we have been traumatized by shame. Man or woman, the process of anticipating a sexual interchange involves the visualization of such scenes and adding to them new scenes that will provide retribution against those who have humiliated us in the past. Pornography, he has written, can best be understood as a group of daydreams designed to cure humiliation (1987). In Stoller's meticulous and painstaking research it turns out that sexual fantasy (the thoughts that accompany sexual arousal) is one of the ways we try to undo shame, to reverse our life experiences of shame at the hands of others.

I visited him in Los Angeles not long ago so we might discuss in person my attempt to develop this completely new rationale for sexuality and to demonstrate the linkage between sex and shame. Patiently, quietly, this courteous gentleman (whose scholarship in the area of sexual fantasy has made him for more than a generation the unquestioned leader in his field) explained an aspect of his work I had not known. Despite the popularity of sexual excitement as a theme in film and novel, no one really wants to face up to Stoller's conclusion that sex and shame are intimately connected. His books and papers have reached an enormous audience within the psychotherapy profession. Huge numbers of nonprofessionals have read his books for the lay public; an even larger audience has read about him in the major newsweeklies. Yet almost never does any member of this enormous audience refer to Stoller's work in public. Psychoanalysts (whose steadfast refusal to discuss shame is the shame of their profession) rarely mention Stoller's theories when writing about the sexual aspects of their cases. It is almost as if our population were too embarrassed to discuss this relation between shame and sexuality.

We are excited by sexual arousal and calmed when released by orgasm from that arousal. Every aspect of sexuality is capable of triggering intense experiences of the positive affects interest–excitement and enjoyment–joy. Sexual arousal is accompanied by fantasy, by images of scenes in which our sexual wishes will be gratified. To the extent that we can get others to become players in these scenes, we will share with them both our excitement and our release. Sexual success, for man or woman, brings pride.

Yet the human is so constructed that whenever that other person falters for so much as a moment in his or her willingness to resonate with our arousal and its accompanying positive affect, we will experience shame. No matter how sensitive our sexual partner may be, no matter how precisely attuned to the nuances of our arousal, it is impossible for any two aroused and excited individuals to match perfectly each other's patterns of arousal. Always, inevitably, invariably, our experience of sexual arousal must meet with some sort or degree of impediment. Shame affect, the painfully amplified analogue of this impediment, is as much an accompaniment of sexuality as the positive affect by which we prefer to know it better. And, as I have shown throughout this book, wherever there is a stable and recurring trigger for shame there will form a category of shame-related thoughts capable of intruding into consciousness whenever we are embarrassed for any reason.

Here are three from the infinitude of sexual shames confided by others, observed directly, or experienced personally:

"Is that all he wanted?" exclaimed a young woman who felt suddenly foolish when she realized that the attentions of a lover had represented more his quest for sexual satisfaction than a search for love. Her pain is shame affect triggered by a blow to her sense of safety within a relationship—a reaction to the experience of betrayal. For the moment, at least, she continues to find him interesting, continues to anticipate enjoyment–joy. His perfidy triggers shame–humiliation because it is an impediment to ongoing positive affect, the hoped-for good feelings she cannot yet relinquish. She feels "taken," used, cheapened. A sexual interaction has caused an acute reduction in her self-esteem.

Returning home late from work, exhausted and drained, a 35-year-old attorney shucked her work clothes and snuggled close to her husband. After a little while they became aroused. "Would you mind . . .?" he asked. It is his preference that they have intercourse by candlelight and with a musical accompaniment. Quickly, so as not to lose the mood of the moment, and hesitantly, for the moment is always ephemeral, she complied by lighting the candles and turning on the record player. On her return to bed she found him reading a magazine. I asked how that made her feel. "I was so hurt," she said, gesturing to the center of her abdomen. The name of that pain, too, is shame affect—triggered by the sudden impediment to positive affect in a situation where there also remained adequate and continuing reason to maintain that positive affect of excitement.

My mother contributed this anecdote from the elderly widow and widower retirement culture of Miami Beach in the 1970s: "Mr. Rabinowitz walks over to Mrs. Goldstein at the swimming pool. 'Mrs. Goldstein,' he says, 'I'm thinking that maybe you would be willing to join me for a cocktail here at the pool before dinner. And I'm thinking that maybe after we have a couple of cocktails you would be willing to join me for dinner. Then, I'm thinking, maybe we could go out for a little dancing. After that, I'm thinking, I could go back with you to your apartment. . . .' 'Please, Mr. Rabinowitz,' interrupts Mrs. Goldstein. 'Everybody can see what you're thinking!' "

From infancy to senescence, male arousal is as visible as female arousal is private. Women are allowed by nature to hold sexual fantasy in privacy, a privilege denied to men. For men, shame always hovers around the borders of sexual arousal. Until he learns the skills that will let him control his erections, every boy risks humiliation every time he becomes even mildly aroused within eyeshot of others. It is incomprehensible to me how three generations of psychoanalysts could maintain Freud's misconception that shame is more important in women than in men. Didn't Freud have erections? Was he never an adolescent?

As we grow to maturity and learn the interpersonal skills that make us sexually interactive beings, we pass through stages of development characterized by varying responses to sexual arousal and the affects associated with it. We are organisms programmed to experience arousal long before we are capable of achieving the release of orgasm, and long, long before we are able to manage that arousal within a stable and intimate interpersonal relationship. As Tomkins has said, shame will appear wherever desire outruns fulfillment. Given the order in which the various subroutines of the generative system are brought on line, we grow to maturity knowing far more about the impediments to arousal than the enjoyment of its release. (Masturbation to orgasm is a late acquisition.) Any attempt to appreciate the affective climate of sexuality demands an understanding of sexual shame and the myriad of mechanisms by which we defend against it. Conversely, any attempt to understand shame demands study of its relation to sexuality.

There may be no human activity that so opens us to the scrutiny of another, nothing we do that exposes so much of what is normally private. We are embarrassed, or made capable of embarrassment, by nearly everything associated with sexual performance. We worry whether our partner will laugh at us for making too much (or too little) noise during intercourse, for the size of our erection or the degree of our wetness and the size of our breasts. Early on, perhaps until we have become jaded by experience, we are torn apart by fears that a partner has enjoyed our sexual encounter to a degree much lesser than he or she has told us. Shame teaches each of us special lessons about the safety of privacy and the role of love as protection from shame. Sex without love requires disavowal of shame.

Sexual intercourse provides one of the few situations in which we are allowed (or even expected) to give up the fundamental rule of human sociality, the cultural insistence on modulation of affective display. Everywhere else we are required to match our affective display to the reference standards defined by convention as adult or mature. True, we are allowed to scream, yell, and gesticulate our approval or disapproval at sporting events. But there, too, our behavior is choreographed, held within limits made clear by the behavior of those around us, stylized by conventions and trends legislating our actions.

We can choose to go with the crowd or to withdraw from it. Sexual intercourse holds us within a crowd of two, and the moment-to-moment reactions of our partner matter all the more because intimacy offers no place for naked people to hide.

Oftentimes, even the shield of intimacy allows inadequate protection from shame. When love is new, and lovers new enough to each other that interest is linked mostly to novelty, directly proportional to the degree of that interest will be our anticipation of shame. Lovers are well-matched when they enjoy the range and style of affective expression with which they are each comfortable during sexual play.

Not long ago, a young woman called the radio station where I was discussing shame on an interview show. A lover had broken off their relationship, saying that he could no longer tolerate one part of her sexual behavior, even though he had seemed to enjoy it earlier. Furthermore, he left her with the impression that she, too, would have abjured such behavior had she any proper sense of shame. I told her that I considered dating the process by which we screen applicants for the job of best friend; that he had made the short list but withdrawn as unable to handle the job; and that she was all the more fortunate for his withdrawal. Better to know now about this incompatibility than later, when the process of idealization had drawn her more deeply into love.

Gingerly, for I had no way of knowing whether one of them had actually exceeded the norms accepted in our culture, I asked whether she would be willing to divulge the nature of her supposed transgression. Involved (she confided to me and to the listening audience) was only what she had thought their mutual pleasure at arousing each other during telephone conversations. Neither of them, of course, can be considered "wrong." His discomfort with the self he saw exposed during their sexual intimacy created too much shame to be contained within the fabric of the relationship and so he withdrew to prevent further pain.

Each of the firmware programs produces its own highly specific type of recurrent experience. The nine innate affects produce nine forms of affective experience, all of which must be integrated into the umbrella concept we call the self. I must come to know the angry me over a range from pique through rage, just as I must learn the joyous or content me over a range from the merest hint of a pleased smile to the guffaws of belly laughter. The hunger drive allows me to know myself over a range from the urge to nibble through the voraciousness of starvation. And I cannot be considered either complete or mature until I have come to understand my sexual self over a range from mild to full arousal, whether alone or in the company of another.

We start out in life with innate affects that operate on an all-or-none basis; they are silent until triggered, and operate at full blast when turned on. Growth and maturity require modulation of these occasionally raucous mechanisms. Our need to eat, breathe, drink, defecate, or urinate does not change a whit as we move through time; only the force of the affects with which each of these drives is assembled will change as we mature.

Alone of the firmware programs, the sexual drive mechanism of the generative system does not operate at its fullest level when we are young. It increases in power as we grow toward the child-bearing years. Doubtless this has great evolutionary significance, for no life form could survive were it able to bear young before it had learned to take care of itself.

It is like looking at a graph with lines diverging in opposite directions. On the one hand, we are learning to modulate our innate affects and their coassemblies with the drives, learning to handle and control and accept the workings of our firmware programs. In these areas of life, the roiling forces that afflict the infant are increasingly subdued through growth and development. All the while we are doing this, the sexual drive is stepping up in power and intensity, increasing its capacity to take us over. By adolescence, when we are otherwise prepared to be useful citizens, the sexual drive assumes such power that we are rendered functionally useless to society until it, too, can be tamed within acceptable limits.

SEXUALITY AND AFFECT

At any age, no matter when it is engaged, sexual arousal does not hit us suddenly, at full force. It starts as a murmur and rises in intensity—at first gradually, then with increasing rapidity. Were it the kind of mechanism that when switched on was at its maximum, we might expect it to trigger surprise–startle or fear–terror, the affects of suddenness and overmuch. But we have evolved as creatures perfectly designed to link sex with excitement. The slope of the curve—the rate of rise of sexual arousal—seems just right for something that might work best if associated with positive affect.

Just as with any other psychobiological system, the drive and the affect influence each other in a recursive fashion. The more we are excited by this arousal, the more we become aroused. The addition of positive affect makes the thrilling annoyance of arousal into something even more pleasant; the increase in arousal produced by further stimulation of the affected areas triggers even more excitement, leading to even more arousal until the arousal is

terminated by orgasm, its genetically programmed terminal analogic amplification. Orgasm is cherished all the more because it triggers the affect enjoyment–joy, which is pleasant in direct proportion to the amount of stimulus it
reduces and the rapidity with which that stimulus is decreased. "Good sex" is a
paradigm of efficacy experienced in the context of positive affect; a good
sexual experience brings pride and a host of thoughts about our best possible
self. Repeated sequences of this relation between arousal, excitement, and the
calming release of orgasm function as a teacher—one can look forward to
sexual arousal with great avidity.

But this logic also helps explain why sexual arousal is so fragile a mechanism, so capable of being turned off even when all the conditions for its
amplification seem present. Anything that can interfere with the rising tide of
interest–excitement is likely to trigger shame affect. Where sexual arousal will
make us turgid, erect, alive, and "up," shame affect will cause a sudden droop-
ing, a loss of posture, a slump, a turning-away of gaze (and therefore a reduction in our ability to interact with another person), a cognitive shock that
renders us momentarily unable to think clearly, then an avalanche of shame-
related cognitions that force us to think about our worst and most damaged
self.

I guess it is possible to theorize about an upbringing in which interest was
never daunted, in which excitement led always to discovery unimpeded by
resistance from internal or external sources—a life historically devoid of shame
affect. (We have some sort of analogue for this in the medical marvel of
children born without an immune system and reared within the controlled
environment of a laboratory bubble. What to us might be only an antigen for
which we would produce a counterbalancing antibody, to them would be a
deadly poison. Thus they must be protected from experiences we find only
normal, and from which we draw strength.) Perhaps it is possible to devise a
hypothetical human with no life experience of shame, and to imagine that
person engaged in sexual interplay with a partner whose history formed an
exact match. Arousal could lead to excitement without fear of shame; this
couple could make love in full sunlight while gazing at each other unabash-
edly.

Actually, most of the life forms that evolved prior to the human do seem to
prefer sex by day rather than by night. They are enabled by prewritten mechanisms to find each other, built to enjoy sexual interaction, and destined to
forget about it as soon as it has been completed. It is the further evolution of
memory that has fostered our human ability to turn the brief reaction patterns
of the affect system into complex ideoaffective linkages. And it is the very

nature of sexual emotionality that has made our species so shy in the realm of generative play.

Through most of our history we have used the cover of darkness to shield our sexual activity from the scrutiny of a shaming world and thus from the possibility of shame. So attuned are we to the merest alteration in the way we are regarded by the other that we dare not look into his or her eyes lest a change in that regard produce shame. So secret are our thoughts during the moments we are sexually excited that we avoid the eyes even of our beloved lest the world of associations created within us by that excitement leak to that other and provide an impediment to the mutuality of our pleasure. Wherever there is secrecy we will find the potential for shame.

Yet a secret hatched by an adult carries with it a different affective charge than a secret kept by a small child. The earlier we can trace the link between sexual arousal and shame, the more clearly can we come to understand the unique character and intensity of sexual shame. I am sure you will accept without question the significance for adult life of embarrassment that begins in adolescence. What if I can uncover evidence that sexual shame can begin before puberty? Or in the toddler? Or in the infant? Each era of development is characterized by its own rich and complex style of thought. The most brilliant insight of a seven-year-old, the genius of a conclusion drawn by a toddler, the primitive linkage assembled by the baby—each of these will influence all subsequent understanding of the issues involved. It matters a great deal how early we begin to see both shame and sexuality. All of the early experiences of sexual arousal discussed in the previous chapter are more likely to produce shame than satisfaction.

We began this chapter with the comment that consenting adults can use their sexuality as play. Yet on the way to such an enlightened maturity one finds a host of impediments. Let us examine what might prevent men and women from free and uninhibited enjoyment of sexual arousal.

MEN

No matter what else it may be, the penis is a source of great embarrassment throughout development. Partly because its proclivity for sticking out and becoming noticeable is in itself a trigger for shame, little boys begin to think that someone is going to cut it off. Some of the fantasy elaborations of this ideoaffective complex lead to what is called "castration anxiety." Such themes become important when the oedipal phase is made more difficult by other problems in development and can lead to a complex assortment of interferences with adult sexuality. Understandably, every boy must somehow come to terms with the fact that he develops erections at the most unexpected of moments.

A significant portion of male behavior and attitudes is based on avoidance of this embarrassment. Each wave of increase in sexual drive function places the growing boy at greater risk of shame in the presence of others. By the middle of the adolescent phase, when the drive has reached its peak, boys grow increasingly likely to risk some form of interaction with girls. Throughout this early period of experimentation with dating behavior, a boy will live with the constant fear of being laughed at for the visibility of an uncontrollable erection or the far worse horror of an ejaculation that stains his pants for all to see.

In order to contemplate a sexual liaison, a man must anticipate the reaction of a girl to his penis—its size as well as his skill in controlling it. As a diversion from this realm of terrifying humiliation, boys become concerned about the entirety of their bodies. This is one of the reasons boys "work out" to develop whatever physique is currently popular and stare at themselves in the mirror in order to analyze the good and bad features that may bring pride or shame. If he has been raised in an atmosphere of love and acceptance, a boy is most likely to expect that his early sexual experiences will be colored by that affective climate. To the extent that he has been rejected, scorned, or humiliated by his parents, family, and milieu, he will anticipate sexual experience that matches his knowledge of interpersonal danger. It is this latter population of men who search intuitively for partners they can dominate.

To the best of my knowledge, no one has ever tried to catalogue the sequence of shame and its relief during the learning period of dating. Dancing slowly with his partner, she held close to him by the conventions of the dance form, a boy is forced to learn how girls react to his erections. Naturally, a boy who is terrified of shame will either avoid dancing or try to regulate the distance separating him from his partner in order to minimize the possibility of discovery. Each girl's reaction to his tumescent penis will provoke volumes of excited and frightening fantasies, all of which must be integrated into his rapidly changing self-concept.

It is interesting to note that in this current era, "slow dancing" has been replaced by more theatrical dance forms in which the partners avoid steady pelvic contact, although the participants learn the skills of sexual intercourse much earlier than ever before. I suspect that this represents a move away from intimacy toward the use of sexual experience for its druglike properties. The shame associated with sexual arousal makes intimacy so much more difficult that many people try to keep sex and love as separate as possible. The macho style allows shame to be countered by excitement and anger; it reduces the shame of early sexual interchange at the expense of intimacy.

Directly proportional to the degree and intensity of shame experienced by a man (regardless of its source) will be his tendency to blame others for it. This is one of the reasons some men are so apt to blame women for their own arousal ("She did it to me") and thereby to excuse behavior for which they might otherwise be ashamed or guilty. But those men who are fortunate enough to learn about sex in the context of an affectionate relationship come to find out a great deal about the inner nature of women and are far less likely to misinterpret their partners' feelings.

Imagine what it must be like for a boy to incorporate into his concept of self a penis that grows to what seems to be an enormous size, and that demands attention as never before. Scant wonder that many men never quite solve this mystery and treat the penis as if it were another person who happens to live with them. Some even give it a name, like "my John Henry."

The period during which a boy and his penis get to know each other is characterized by an interplay of arousal, excitement, and shame. His early efforts at masturbation will be colored both by the cultural attitudes within which he has been raised and by the counter-shaming fantasies he uses as inspiration. There may be no antidote for shame so potent or so transient as the pride to be derived from masturbation; for some there may be no shame so great as the fact that one has been forced to achieve it through masturbation. Imagine the sheer volume of psychological material associated merely with any man's life experience of masturbation! Yet it is precisely this load of fantasy, this burden of shame explored, risked, savored, endured, and feared, that a man brings to any attempt at intercourse.

There is more. As we have discussed, the experience of shame is really just a physiological affect, unconnected to any particular source or trigger. Intense excitement predisposes us to intense shame, and intense shame is capable of dredging up from memory any and all of our worst memories of humiliations past. The more we are aroused and excited, so much more are we liable to experience shame at a density for which we are ill-prepared. In order to offer ourselves to a sexual partner, we must overcome all these terrors of possible shame and convert them to excitement and enjoyment.

Perhaps you recall Woody Allen's aphorism, "Masturbation is sex with someone who loves me." Love implies acceptance within a relationship; such relational stability provides a hedge against shame. Masturbation fosters such fantasies as the illusion that there can be a perfect partner who understands us perfectly, desires nothing more than our perfect satisfaction in an atmosphere of maximal arousal, and who experiences our release as a source of joy. Masturbation, therefore, is damn poor preparation for the real thing. Men approach sexual intercourse with great fear that their sexual organs are inadequate, of failing to satisfy their partner, of somehow being found foolish. One of my patients was the sole sibling in an Irish Catholic family who did not become a priest. Referring to the omnipresence of God in his household, he explained his reason for never attempting masturbation by asking, "Could you masturbate with your father watching?" How much more humiliation might he have risked in intercourse?

Women

The extraordinary visibility of male arousal has no counterpart in the lives of women. Arousal is interior, internal, secret. A woman may feel her lips become engorged, appreciate the sensation of vascular change in breasts and vagina, find herself overwhelmed by sexual ideation appearing as if from nowhere— and all this will yet remain a private experience. Triggered by this slow and steady increase in stimulus gradient will be a certain degree of accompanying excitement. And, as we have seen in so many realms of human functioning, whatever impedes the elaboration of that excitement will therefore trigger shame, which will be regarded as purely sexual. To grow up female is to learn that you will be embarrassed at moments when nobody knows why you are uncomfortable.

The hair-trigger response of men to broadcast arousal provides for women another sort of problem. So clearly does arousal broadcast from one person to another that female arousal is in itself a powerful stimulus to male arousal. Although secret in that no one but she knows the extent to which any woman is aroused, masculine response is intrinsically embarrassing to a woman unprepared for it. Women must learn how to handle the effect they make on men lest that effect cause confusion, embarrassment, and anger. Many women will later develop the skills that allow the use of this knowledge in a program of allure, but only after they have taken control of a system otherwise capable of producing shame.

Whereas for men it is the arousal phase of the sexual program that produces the greatest degree of embarrassment, women are discomfited in areas about which men know little. For many girls, the vagina first calls attention to itself by leaking some sort of discharge. Stained underpants call to mind the shame of urinary dyscontrol and all the frailty of early childhood; the fear that one has contracted some deadly disease may follow in rapid succession. As Gail Paster has commented, women often think of themselves as "leaky vessels" that spill whatever liquids are entrusted to them. Menstrual blood, male ejaculatory fluids, even the secretions accompanying sexual arousal, place women at risk of exposure and shame. With the leakage of fluid also comes odor—thus a woman is subject to both self-dissmell and self-disgust merely because she is female. These affects, of course, keep company with shame.

The interplay of affects around the issue of women's breasts is one of the most complex in Western society. No other part of the body has ever been the source of so much public attention; whole industries have sprung up to capitalize on this dynamic tension. Mammary development is, of course, part of sexual dimorphism. Breasts, which for most of a woman's life form part of her cosmetic array, are built to supply milk for nursing infants. Like so many other components of the generative system, they have been taken over for far different purposes.

Prepubescent girls compare themselves to adult women and wonder what their own breasts will look like. Not to have breasts means that one is a child; to have breasts implies readiness to compete in the world of women. During the period of breast development, girls compare themselves to each other constantly and relentlessly. Every day offers an opportunity for pride, shame, excitement, or fear. Exposure in school locker rooms becomes for some girls a source of overwhelming shame; the move from "training bra" to real brassiere is marked by relief (the affect enjoyment–joy) and/or excitement (the inevitable responses to any decrease in shame). Almost all clothing is selected in terms of its relation to the display of breast size and shape. Breasts change with age, during pregnancy, as the result of surgical procedures. Every possible alteration in her breasts will be viewed by a woman in terms of the shame/pride axis.

Female dress is a dialectic between hidden and shown. But it is not from women that breasts are hidden, for all of this affect is generated in terms of male fascination. There is no better way to guarantee interest than to hide something—that girls cover their breasts and giggle among themselves helps set boys on fire. However a girl may feel about her size and physical power relative to the boys who interest her, she has power over them simply because she has breasts that will remain hidden from them as long as she wishes. No matter how much a girl learns from friends and feature films about the power conferred by breasts, nothing equals the thrill of personal experience. Even now, when women appear at the beach in bathing costumes that expose all but a symbolic area of breast surface, the female breast is treated as if it were invisible. Men and women can touch the male chest in conversation or athletic play; neither will touch the female breast.

Think, then, about the woman who has by some fluke of nature been denied the development of mature breasts. She will experience some degree of shame relative to other women, some lessening of her power over men, and significant interference with her ability to admire herself. It is this shame that fuels much of the specialty of plastic surgery; women can purchase what they have not been given. And, should a woman grow to maturity in a milieu that denies her the feeling of full acceptance and love, she may attribute the shame associated with that loss of face to some perceived problem with her body. The breast is a magnet for excitement, pride, and shame.

The foregoing passages are meant only to suggest the wide range of issues that link shame with female sexuality. I omit such book-length topics as the intense pride and shame associated with pregnancy wanted, unwanted, or unattainable. Some of them are intrinsic to the physiological mechanisms involved, others are purely social. Yet men and women differ on the basis of their history of shame associated with the generative system, and this difference must be kept in our awareness if we are to understand the full range of the shame experience.

SHAME AND THE HOMOSEXUAL WORLD

One of the great contributions of Kinsey's early work on sexual behavior was his patient and understanding approach to homosexuality. Most contemporary investigators agree that very few adults are "totally" heterosexual—we believe that the sexual interests of most people lie on some sort of continuum. My own opinion, based only on a lifetime of clinical experience rather than formal psychological studies, is that most of us are restrained from homosexual experimentation only by the affect disgust.

Somehow, early in development, well-nigh all male children are instilled with disgust at the idea of homosexual activity and with excitement at the idea of heterosexual behavior. Man or woman, it has been my experience that whoever experiments with partners of the same gender has placed a lessened significance on disgust. Much of male homosexual play, as well as heterosexual fetishism, involves excretory function normally kept secret by dissmell, disgust, and shame. Indeed, on the several occasions that men have sought my counsel for the discomfort felt after a first homosexual encounter, it is the displeasure of self-disgust that has forced them into therapy.

I think this is one of the reasons we see so many men experiment with homosexual behavior when they reach 40.* It is at this age that a man has achieved some comfort with his ability to accumulate and handle whatever degree of power he will be allowed; usually he will have been married and had access to heterosexual intercourse with some degree of ease. The general dissatisfaction that permeates his life, notwithstanding its deeper roots, is linked tentatively to an unfulfilled yearning to try this form of sexual behavior. He does so at a time when he is more free from shame than any other.

Yet, in our society, few groups are so closely identified with shame as the male homosexual. Imagine that you, as a small boy, find yourself daydreaming not about sexual liaisons with girls, but about the opportunity to cuddle with another boy. Pretend that you have no real interest in the opposite gender but find members of your own fascinating. Then try to imagine what would happen were you to communicate this interest to your peers. Their disgust and aversion would create in you profound shame in the immediate situation because of the sudden impediment to mutuality (what Kaufman calls "the interpersonal bridge") and shame at yourself for being wrong, defective, disgusting.

Stoller and Professor Gilbert H. Herdt once studied the Sambia of Papua, New Guinea (Stoller, 1985, 104–34). In this "primitive" tribe, tribal lore states that no boy can become fully male until he has drunk a great deal of semen. All seven- to-ten-year-old boys are brought through a period of obligatory homosexual interaction with their pubertal elders. Following this period of sexual initiation, they go through a further ritual that prepares them for adult heterosexual behavior by making them semen donors for the younger boys. When a wife has been found for the post-pubertal boy he will immediately cease all homosexual activity and become fully heterosexual. Even in this society those few men who remain homosexual are thought of as unusual, defective, or weird; they bear the name "rubbish man." Stoller forces us to focus on the difference between gender roles (what it means to be male) and erotic behavior (the form of sexual expression one enjoys).

What if I take the position that "pure" homosexuality is only a variant of normal sexuality, representing either some poorly understood program of the generative system or one that fosters the induction of disgust toward the opposite gender? We now understand the obsessive-compulsive disorder to be the result of innate circuits released from suppression by other brain centers. Might not the phenomenon of homosexual interest exclusive from infancy be

*Richard C. Friedman (1988, 1989) has written with exceptional sensitivity and good sense about a wide range of such matters involving male homosexuality.

an example of such a circumstance? Elsewhere (Nathanson, 1990) I have suggested a third possibility—that the degree of homosexuality found in any man (or woman) may be the result of varying patterns of cerebral lateralization (formation of actual hypothalamic structures) produced during intrauterine development by certain shifts in maternal sex hormone levels. These neurophysiological variants would then be altered still further by family- and culture-based scripts.

My theoretical opinion still does not help the large fraction of our male population that is destined to grow up as identified homosexuals. Each and every one of them will be subjected to taunts, shaming assaults, physical attack and abuse, neglect and outright abuse by the legal system, ostracism, and rejection on a massive scale. Merely to act tenderly toward a beloved companion sets up so much disgust and dissmell in the average heterosexual onlooker that the homosexual world has always been one of secrecy and isolation. "Gay pride" is shame denied, warded off, reversed, occasionally transcended. No one should be forced to defend his right to be sexual with a consenting partner. We know far more about the homosexual world than about the disgust and dissmell in "homophobic" mainstream society. We know very, very little about the bisexual world of men who seem both emotionally healthy and comfortable with partners of either gender.

Listen to your homosexual colleagues and friends; sit in with them at barroom or dinner table. Encoded in the banter of this entire group you will hear wit that is specifically counter-shaming, precisely tuned to the shame, self-disgust, and self-dissmell experienced in everyday life. Within homosexual society, within the personal interactions that characterize individual relationships, are a host of sources and triggers for shame both specific to same-gender sex and common to all adults. The patterns of arousal and excitement choreographed by any group will lead to constellations of shame and pride unique to it. There is yet another group for whom any experience of sexuality seems connected to shame—the officially celibate clergy. A. W. Richard Sipe (1990) discusses this secret world and its reservoir of pain.

The world of female homosexuality is even more secret than that of men. We take it for granted that women (partly because our society pays them less than men) will share living quarters, but rarely do we suspect that the arrangement suggests any sexual connotation. Here, too, shame is associated with the very idea of being "different." Some segment of the lesbian population has been so since early childhood, while another group enters this life after a series of failures in the heterosexual world or out of a decision to sample what has always been secretly desired. And the patterns of arousal and excitement choreographed within this small society lead to a limited pattern of triggers for shame unknown in heterosexual society, as well as many common to both.

Sexual Interaction

Sexual arousal exposes us to the scrutiny of another person at a moment when we are ready to let ourselves be taken by forces that overwhelm us. In the moment of sensuous excitement we must handle some combination of arousal and affect—even though we have spent a lifetime trying to control ourselves. Sex is a period of dyscontrol. This loss of control over our feelings and our functions and our ability to think must be experienced in the company of another person whose acceptance of us is critical to our self-esteem. We must believe that this person is capable of accepting everything about us that will be opened to the view of self and other by the experience of arousal. Shame hovers everywhere in the bed of lust.

Small wonder, then, that we rehearse in the private theater of masturbation or search for partners with whom a particular scene can be enacted. If the search for intimacy is difficult, then it is that much more difficult for people to be both intimate and sexual. Usually we lie to ourselves and the other about the degree of intimacy involved in our interaction in order to experiment with the thrilling and rewarding sexual arousal. We bribe each other to avoid shame.

Yet directly proportional to the amount of disavowal that allowed one to get into the game will be the self-disgust, self-dissmell, and shame that follow the act. Many people are literally unable to bear the sight, smell, or touch of the other after sexual intercourse. So diverse are the realms of thought released and amplified during intercourse, so much revealed to the self that usually is held in a hidden state, that often some sedative action is sought to calm the mind. It is for this reason that some will smoke a cigarette, for nicotine soothes while the smoke clears the sensorium of sexual smells.

But we may also be disgusted with self or other after intercourse because the sudden decrease in arousal and excitement that follows orgasm leaves us with no fascination for each other. It takes fascination to overcome the impediment of shame, and now there is no arousal-based interest. Couples have to be pretty friendly to tolerate the period of exposure that follows intercourse.

Each experience of sexual involvement with others teaches us something about the relation between sex and interpersonal life. Occasionally we feel "screwed" or violated; that represents one realm of experience. Alternatively, we can feel glorious, triumphant, full of pride that we have made a partner so happy, and proud of our own pleasure. A good sexual experience need not change us—despite what the gratified other may say, we can maintain our preexisting belief in the nature of our relatedness by becoming paranoid and attributing to the other our worst fears. This parallels the disavowal that had gotten us into the liaison in the first place, and operates to maintain the level of shame with which we entered the interaction. Indeed, the links between sex and shame are so many and varied that it is small wonder that we have until now taken for granted that there is an intrinsic connection between them.

UNDERSTANDING ADULT SEXUALITY

Do you own an automobile? It can be used equally well to take a child to the hospital, to assist a bank robbery, or as an instrument of attack. It is merely a vehicle; only as we use it does it become defined as an ambulance, a getaway car, or a murder weapon. So it is for sexual arousal. The generative system provides us with equipment that needs to operate only once in order to maintain the species. All other applications of the apparatus are to be considered either as some form of rehearsal for the procreative event or as recreational uses. The system is there for us to enjoy to the extent that we are able to integrate all of its power within the self. Adult sexuality is learned behavior that makes use of preexisting biological mechanisms in whatever fashion suits one's mood of the moment.

Anything with so much power is likely to get out of control. Few of our biological attributes create so much havoc as sexual arousal. With its built-in affinity for excitement and enjoyment, sexual arousal must always bring us in proximity to shame. Both sex and shame involve the infinite variety of possible interactions, of links between self and other. To know sex is to know shame, just as is true that to know shame one must understand sex.

These first three sections of the book complete our survey of what I believe to be the full range of situations in which an individual is likely to experience shame affect. Everything described so far forms the memory bank to which we turn any time shame—humiliation is triggered. In the next section we will see what happens as we try to react, to respond to the combination of triggering source, physiological affect mechanism, and the host of memories laid down by our life experience of shame affect. It is time to learn about the compass of shame.

IV

THE COMPASS OF SHAME

22

THE COMPASS OF SHAME

So here we are. We have learned a lot about the nature of affect itself and concentrated on the operation of shame affect. We have a new theory for the nature of sexuality that explains why there is such a bond of union between sex and shame. All of the drives, including the sexual drive programs of the generative system, and all of the affects cause recurrent experiences that form the nidus of the self. We can see how affect and sex are linked to the birth of the self.

What we have discussed amounts to a survey of the major situations in which an individual will experience shame affect throughout life. These experiences become the library through which, as an adult, each of us will browse when attempting to think about any current situation in which shame affect has been triggered. We have shown how shame and pride are tied to matters of size, shape, dexterity, skill, dependence and independence, love, and sex, as well as the very idea of an individual self. It is affect that makes things matter, and shame affect that makes these particular things matter in the manner described.

Each of the drives creates a need which, when satisfied, brings pleasure, just as the mitigation of any negative affect becomes a positive experience. But there is more to pleasure than the satisfaction of drives or the release from discomfort. Every activity we find both pleasant and urgent has been made so or assisted by the positive affects of interest–excitement and enjoyment–joy. These particular affects lie at the heart of sociality and conviviality. They animate and enliven most of what we enjoy in life. Notwithstanding their immense power as motivators, both of the positive affects are capable of being interrupted by a host of stimuli that can act as impediments.

At all times it is important to remember that shame affect is triggered any time interest or enjoyment is impeded, and that relatively few of these many such situations are known to us as members of the shame family of named emotions. Reconsider the example of the young woman whose husband interrupted their sex play to ask that she yield to his demand for the ritual of candlelight and music as an accompaniment to intercourse. We have every reason to believe that the painful "hurt feelings" she experienced (on returning to their bed from the requested tasks to find him reading a magazine) were caused by shame affect. To her, this was an episode of "hurt," which became the emotional experience of "rejection" only after she had "thought about it for a few moments."

A generation ago, working without the concept of innate affect, Helen Block Lewis referred to such incidents as examples of "bypassed shame," characterized by a "wince" or a "jolt" to the system. Like most of the previous investigators of shame, Lewis felt that there was a proper way to express or experience shame; the many variants she described were seen as defenses against "true shame." She described "bypassed shame" as if the triggering incident had evaded some brain center in the path toward recognition; to her it was a form of shame in which we do not acknowledge the emotion because awareness would lead to bad feelings about the self. Nevertheless, she points out that "bypassed shame" is usually accompanied by the thought that another person holds us in disrepute.

Today, in the language for shame I have introduced, this would be considered just another script for shame affect. Rather than being bypassed, the affect has shown up in an assembly of trigger and response that does not appear in our library of experiences already labeled by the shame family of words. Nevertheless, what we experience as the "wince" or "jolt" she describes is the characteristic cognitive shock associated with the physiological phase of shame. In each case, it is easy to demonstrate that it had been preceded by an impediment to positive affect; the thoughts that follow it are typical of the cognitive phase of shame emotion.

To complicate matters, as we go through life we learn to attach shame to situations that might not have triggered it innately. (Only if society attaches importance to fashion will style be linked to shame.) The number of situations in which the innate affect shame–humiliation can be triggered is immense and constantly growing.

Yet it is improbable that every time any affect is triggered we are required to scroll through all our memories of similar situations and bring them into current awareness. It appears most likely that similar situations are grouped and stored as a bundle, and that a current experience of affect is compared to the bundles themselves. The existence of such bundles, which Tomkins calls scripts, allows us to bypass the full review that would be required by their absence. Such a script involves both a compression and a condensation of all previous episodes, summated as an experiential pattern. The death of a friend does not trigger a review of every shared experience. What we call mourning is actually a review of the scripts, the bundles of affect-laden experiences that involve us with that now-departed other.

Whenever we are aware of our affective reactions (in other words, should we happen to have a feeling), we are capable of forming an emotion by recalling previous instances of that affect. Thus, each time shame affect is triggered, we are drawn backwards in time to experience some representation of our lifetime of similar or related shames, whether or not we recognize the incident as typical of shame.

Providentially, the phenomenology of recall does far more than this, for such a use of memory might have led to the evolution of mechanisms for forgetting far more powerful than those now in place! Stored along with our reminiscences of shames past are our recollections of all the ways we have made ourselves feel better when hurt. To have lived until this moment, each of us has accumulated a library of defenses against painful experiences. The stacks of our library are loaded with entire scenes in which we, or others we have observed, have handled the noxious experience of shame affect in a tremendous variety of styles. Intimately associated with the affect is our history of reaction to it.

Until this point I have used the definition of emotion introduced by Basch in 1976—an assemblage consisting of an affect and our associations to previous experience of that affect. From the work presented so far, it seems clear that we must alter this definition to take into account both the trigger to affect and our reaction to it. Every emotion actually consists of a four-part experience initiated by some stimulus, which then triggers an affect, after which we recall previous experiences of this affect, and then, finally, react to the stimulus in some manner influenced by that affective history.

There are, then, four explicitly different phases of the shame experience. Each of the innumerable forms of shame is ushered in by some clearly discernible triggering event. Usually this will be some easily defined impediment to whatever positive affect had just then been in progress. Yet to be discussed are other, learned triggers to shame, some of which can be set off even when we are already in the throes of a negative affect—shame can take us from bad to worse. But always there is a trigger, some event that ushers in the unpleasant flow of events we call shame.

Second in this sequence, of course, is the innately scripted action of the affect itself, a series of physiological events occurring at sites of action all over the body. During this phase, whatever positive affect we had been experiencing is impeded painfully by a programmed mechanism that pulls our eyes away from whatever had been the object of our attention, dilates blood vessels in the face to make us blush, causes our neck and shoulders to slump, and brings about a momentary lapse in our ability to think.

Yet this cognitive shock, this transient inability to think, lasts but a moment before it is replaced by a flood of new thoughts as, quickly, we become aware that we have been "hit" by an affect. As if in swift compensation for its brief failure, our cognitive apparatus now makes access to its script library to find and organize all information relevant to shame affect; one attempts to see what script this new experience fits, or whether a script must be changed. Such is the cognitive phase of shame, the period during which feeling begins to blend into emotion. By and large, it is the history of our prior experiences of shame and the importance to us of these painful moments that will determine the duration and intensity of our embarrassment.

Notice that I did not suggest that the cognitive phase of the shame experience involves review of the individual memories, the discrete occurrences of shame which have until now occupied our attention. *What we review in this brief period is the group of shame-related scripts.* Each script is the equivalent of a computer chip—a miniaturized integrated circuit from which all relevant prior shame experiences can be retrieved, reconstituted, revived into full affective power. And each of these collections of memories has been grouped in such a way that the collection itself achieves further urgency by assembly with affect in the manner we defined earlier as affective magnification. It is the script (rather than the individual memories) that contains the real power.

There is a fourth and final phase of the shame experience, composed of our repertoire of responses to the felt quality of these scripts. Among the great variety of responses we note those that fall loosely into two major groups— patterns of *acceptance* or *defense.* Were we humans more creatures of assent than justification and preservation, I doubt there would be much need for books such as this. It is our avoidance of the lessons to be learned from shame that causes us the most trouble. Occasionally, however, we do examine the impediment and learn from it. Recognizing both the affect and our historical experience of it, we may decide to use this particular moment of shame as the spur to personal change—an unexpected opportunity to make ourselves different.

Say, for a moment, that I have fancied myself a trim and youngish individual, the dashing and debonair creature of my post-adolescent dreams. Now somebody produces a poolside photograph that reveals me as a paunchy, graying, middle-aged physician. I react, of course, with a degree of embarrassment directly proportional to the "importance" to me of my prior misconception of self. But what if I study the offending image, turn to my wife, and announce, "Look at this. You were right. I have gained a lot of weight. Time to diet." Exposure has triggered shame but led me to work in order that I might approach more closely my idealized self-image. A year later I will smile tolerantly at the memory of that photograph and credit it as the stimulus that made me work toward a healthier, more modish figure.

All of us know that such a reaction is rare indeed. I am much more likely to respond defensively, to do something that mitigates the pain of shame but requires no alteration in my being. The moment of shame, this combination of physiological and cognitive factors to which we have devoted so much attention, always leads us to a psychological crossroads. Which way we turn, how we handle this moment, what we do next, turns out to be a major factor in the architecture of our character structure, our entire personality.

The reactive phase of shame involves all the habits, defenses, tricks, strategies, tactics, excuses, protections, buffers, apologies, justifications, arguments, and rejoinders that we have devised, witnessed, or stored over the highly personal series of events we know as our lifetime. So swiftly do we shift from affect to response that often the triggering stimulus is linked in our awareness neither with the intervening feeling of shame itself nor with the complex assortment of thoughts that follow it, but with the angry or tearful or humorous style of reaction that comes to define us as individuals.

Often these reactions are situational, linked directly to some feature of the triggering event. Take, for instance, the example of a man who has been involved in an extramarital liaison. Denounced in church by his religious leader, our miscreant is likely to bow his head in deference. Yet the same allegation, made by his wife in the privacy of their home, might lead to angry denial; made by barroom cronies, a host of amusing stories; and if by an enemy, a physical altercation. In each case, exposure has triggered shame affect that in its turn has called forth some series of remembered scenes. These four scenarios differ both in the style of reaction—the reactive phase of the shame experience—and the social milieu of the otherwise similar triggering event.

Remembered at all by our philandering protagonist, each of these would be recalled not in terms of shame, but as four completely different experiences. I do not mean to suggest that these experiences are devoid of reference to shame, but that certain mental mechanisms operate to shift his attention away from shame toward something else. For the experience in church he might use the term "disgrace"; by his wife he has been "unfairly" accused. He might think of the interaction with his friends as an opportunity to make a couple of good jokes; certainly he would see his reaction to an "insult" as reasonable and proper.

All of his life experiences of disgrace will be grouped to form a script—sequences linked by specific affects. These sequences of actions and affects must, of course, differ somewhat each time they are set in motion, but the important feature is that they tend to recur with regularity. Similarly might he form scripts that group his experiences of the avoidance of shame through denial or disavowal, or his use of self-deprecating humor to minimize the toxicity of shame, or the use of anger to turn the tables on whomever has caused him shame.

Tomkins's use of the term derives from our experience of scripts in the theater, where an author sets down rules for the behavior of others. Psychological scripts are formed when we assemble a set of related scenes for the purpose of generating responses that will thereafter control and direct the outcome of such scenes. Scripts are how we realize that life events are apt to fall into predictable sequences and that our responses to both the events and the sequences tend to be predictable. Since many of these scripts contain rules for the handling of powerful affective experiences, we develop affective responses to the scripts themselves. So complex and pervasive are the habits and skills of script formation that we adults come to live more within these personal scripts for the modulation and detoxification of affect than in a world of innate affect. So it is that we adults "understand" or experience our emotions differently and find the very concept of innate affect so difficult to grasp.

If you share my fascination with the long history of theories about the nature of emotion, then this is the point at which you will exclaim "Aha!!" Now we know why nearly all of the competing theories have been at least partially correct. The definition of a mature emotion that I am promoting here takes into account the display noted by Darwin and the visceral changes so important to James and Lange, as well as the perceptions essential to their theory. In the chapters that follow you will see ample justification for DeRivera's observation that mature emotion causes us to move toward or away from self, toward or away from other. Ideas and memories stored within the unconscious can also magnify affect-related scripts—Sartre, Freud, Jung, Hillman, and many other theorists are also partially right. And the neurobiologists are also correct when they demonstrate the existence of so many circuits that produce subroutines important in normal and abnormal emotion, and that can be triggered by aberrations in the chemistry and structure or the brain. Linking all is the concept that mature emotion depends on hardware, firmware, and software.

You will remember that each affect is both an analogue and an amplifier of its stimulus conditions—that is why we keep referring to shame affect as a painful analogic amplification of any impediment to positive affect. If the function of a defensive script is to reduce the toxicity of a particular affect, the very fact that the script reduces a negative affect makes it (as a whole) a positive experience and a source of positive affect. Alternatively, imagine that we group as a script some assortment of sequences that we find repulsive. Our sense of disgust at the entire sequence, at the script itself, will tend to color everything within that script with disgust affect. It is this *coloration* to which Tomkins refers as affective magnification. Scripts take on their own affective climate, which, in turn, magnifies all of the affect contained within the scenes themselves.

When an event occurs, we analyze it to see if it fits into a script; we try to interpret it as one of a series of events that has been analyzed before. We are capable of having an affective response to an imagined outcome or to a set of possible outcomes. It is to this set of *possibilities* that we now generate affect; since this new affect will influence everything within the set, we call the mode of influence *magnification* rather than *amplification* to distinguish between the higher and the lower orders of influence.

Affective magnification is affect multiplied by affect. If the affect contained within the scripts is the same as our affective reaction to those scripts, then the process of magnification produces something like "affect squared." In the process of magnification, affect amplifies something that is already being amplified, conferring on it a new and far more intense quality of experience. It occurs when many scenes are grouped together into a script on the basis of their similarity, and when these scripts take on a life of their own because they have been made "more so" by affective magnification. You will recall that Demos explained innate affect as a mechanism that converted quantitative information into a qualitative experience. Now we add the idea that affective magnification causes both a quantitative and a qualitative increase in the intensity of that experience.

When something occurs that fits into a script, it is experienced with a degree and intensity of affect far exceeding what one might have expected on the basis of its action as a trigger to ordinary innate affect. This is akin to what I suggested as the rationale for the formation of normal mood—each remembered scene is capable of acting as a stimulus to further affect, accounting for the duration of mood. Mood, therefore, can result from a script that controls the time span of triggered affect more than its intensity. And, of course, there are loads of scripts in which affect rises in intensity, as when we become increasingly angry at something the more we think about it.

For many of us, almost any affect feels better than shame. If we are to convert the experience of shame into something less punishing, we must develop some group of defensive scripts that foster such a transition. All that is interesting or calming in life can be impeded; each experience of impediment will trigger shame. Great vigilance is needed to monitor life for the possibility of shame, to prevent it wherever possible, and to limit its toxicity when it cannot be prevented.

In the case of shame, our defensive scripts fall into four major patterns, which I have organized as *the compass of shame*. For the adult, depending on just what had triggered interest–excitement or enjoyment–joy and the "who, what, why, when, and where" of the source of the impediment that triggered shame affect, we will choose a defensive strategy that best fits these particular circumstances. In any such given sequence of events we will fly to one of the four points of this compass:

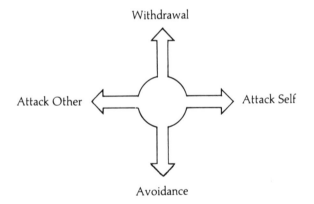

Each of these categories represents an entire system of affect management, a set of strategies by which an individual has learned to handle shame affect. They are characterized by widely divergent assortments of values. In each, shame affect is experienced differently—the *purpose* of the strategy is to make it feel different. All of us, from time to time, use the techniques and strategies of all four systems. Nevertheless, to the extent that we can be said to have a personal style (a group of attitudes and actions by which we are known to ourselves and others), we tend to favor one or another of these systems of defense. Essential to the birth of the self is the development of the reactive phase of the shame experience.

The four poles of the compass contrast and compare in many respects. Those who withdraw are the most willing to experience all of the physiological manifestations of shame and all of the thoughts that flood us during the cognitive phase. For them, the physiological qualities of the affect provide escape from an intolerable situation. Escape, in the language of *withdrawal*, is swift and occasionally total.

Raised in different families, in different circumstances, some people find the experience of shame so toxic that they must prevent it at all costs. Flocking to the *avoidance* pole of the compass, they engage in a number of strategies to reduce, minimize, shake off, or limit shame affect. It is at this locus of our compass that we will find most of those who abuse chemical substances, engage in defensively hedonistic activity, purchase the services of the plastic surgeon, and go out of their way to distract our attention away from what might bring them shame. Indeed, as a patient pointed out to me the other day, those who suffer the most from chronic shame are the most likely to be seen as "narcissistic" because of their constant attention to anything and everything that might produce even more shame.

Withdrawal and *avoidance* scripts have a peculiar relation to the idea of time—the former is a rapid, the latter a slow and deliberate movement away from an uncomfortable situation. As we will see later, in both script families one can react with different degrees of remoteness. Mild withdrawal and mild avoidance are considered quite normal, while those whose reactions to shame induce the greatest degree of remoteness or self-aggrandizement are considered truly ill.

Those who find intolerable the helplessness and isolation characteristic of shame-induced withdrawal will tend to take over the experience of shame, to place it under their own control within the system of behavior I call *attack self*. They are willing to experience shame as long as we understand that they have done so voluntarily and with the intention of fostering their relationship with us.

In the remaining quadrant of the compass we find the community of those who experience as most unbearable that part of the cognitive phase of shame which discloses information about their inferiority. "Someone must be made lower than I," says the denizen of the *attack other* pole. Every incident of domestic violence, of graffiti, of public vandalism, of schoolyard fighting, of put-down, ridicule, contempt, and intentional public humiliation can be traced to activity around this locus of reaction to shame affect.

Just as the *withdrawal* and *avoidance* poles bear some special relation to the signifier of time, the *attack self* and *attack other* poles house scripts that focus on an object in space. These latter scripts *recast* our relationship to others in some way that reduces the toxicity of shame.

The four poles of the compass of shame function as libraries that house some of the most important affect management scripts in our repertoire. At each pole we will find a different assembly of auxiliary affects brought in to shore up its defenses: *withdrawal* is likely to be accompanied by distress and fear; *attack self* by self-disgust and self-dissmell; *avoidance* by excitement, fear, and enjoyment; and *attack other* by anger. Of all the drives, the one most closely identified with the sense of self is the sexual drive mechanism of the generative system. At the locus of *withdrawal* we will tend to find sexual abstinence, impotence, and frigidity; *attack self* will be characterized by sexual masochism; the *avoidance* pole by sexual machismo; and the *attack other* pole is likely to be rife with sexual sadism.

Poets, novelists, psychologists, playwrights, and all the other commentators on the human condition have forever been telling us there are vast differences in the ways men and women express and experience shame, some of which were easily explained in the previous chapters when we discussed gender dimorphism. Yet it is in the scripts formed by the reactive phase of shame that we will find the remainder of the reasons for these observations. Finally, each of these defensive systems operates over a wide range, from the most mild, useful, acceptable, and benign to behavioral systems that are clearly pathological.

In the pages that follow I will explain the features of the compass of shame, delineating for each pole all the mechanisms to which I have alluded in the paragraphs above. Viewing the adult experience of shame in this manner, it is easy to develop new ways of mitigating the toxicity of shame. From this schema will emerge a logical approach to the psychotherapy of shame-related problems. Too often, writers on shame confine their attention to behavior and feelings that represent only a small part of the full picture of shame. It is my hope that the very concept of a compass of shame will make clear the full range of shame-related experiences. Let us start with what my colleague Léon Wurmser calls *shame simpliciter*—shame itself, shame as withdrawal.

23

WITHDRAWAL

Sandy and I are well into the initial history, that group of sessions during which a therapist should be the most intrusive. At forty, she has a graduate degree that allows her to make a good living, but is otherwise unhappy with her life. What she wants out of therapy is clear: "I want confidence—believing in yourself. I am so afraid of intimacy that I am afraid if I meet the right person I won't know what to do." Near the end of our first meeting she touched her cheek fleetingly as if to check its temperature, then breathed a sigh of relief and said, "At least I didn't say 'I'm sorry' every five minutes like I used to."

Married right out of high school, Sandy divorced a year later, worked as a commercial artist, a bartender, an artist's model, and at various secretarial jobs. Dipping her head slightly and turning a little to the side, she told me, "I did all that while I got my head together enough to finish college and get into graduate school." We have agreed that, in order for us to learn what lies beneath her symptoms, I will be permitted to ask several deeply personal questions. She is talking about elementary school:

I did very poorly in second grade because my eyesight was so bad. One day the teacher moved me from the back of the room to the front—to the first seat in a row right in front of her. She made the whole class stand up and then she switched me and another girl. Then she said to the class, 'You can see why we've moved Sandy. She flunked because she can't see.' I cried all the way home that day. My mom got me glasses, which I hated; now I wear contact lenses. I never opened my mouth again. If I was asked a question I would be terrified. Every move I made I was self-conscious. If anyone even looked at me I would run and hide.

No matter what the cause, the activation of shame affect alters our interaction with others: The sudden loss of tonus in the neck and shoulders makes the head droop; if we are involved with another person our eyes drop from contact and all sense of mutuality is lost. Interaffectivity and affective resonance are impossible. It is at moments like these that we wish for a hole to open up and swallow us, to remove us from the eyes of the other. Right at the moment when we might hope for invisibility, we realize, from the sudden incandescence of our cheeks, that a blush has made our shame even more conspicuous. For all of these reasons, shame produces a sundering of what Gershen Kaufman refers to as "the interpersonal bridge."

Certainly shame affect itself is capable of pulling us away from our social milieu. Nonetheless, what Sandy has described is a series of powerful and important reactions to shame, rather than the affect itself. Some progression of experiences has made her extremely sensitive to shame—the early stages of therapy will most likely hover around this issue—but her reactions are something more than the affect itself. One place to look for clues to the nature of our reaction to shame is in the thoughts that follow the physiological phase. Between affect and reaction is the cognitive phase, which is summarized in Table 5.

Each of these eight categories is in itself a library of scripts involving shame; each contains subdirectories of scenes and a host of cross-references to the other categories. The cryptic descriptors listed in the table are offered as highly condensed summary statements meant to evoke the spirit of the entire chapters from which each was derived.

As you might expect, initially we tend to focus our attention on the group of memories most clearly associated with the triggering incident. In linguistic terms, we might view these memories as *cognates*—they are all more or less similar or equivalent to the triggering incident. Thus, when I learn that a friend has told to others something I entrusted as a secret, this mishap is reviewed in the context of my life experience of betrayal. (Anything that breaks the interpersonal bridge will trigger shame and therefore produce an analogous—and highly amplified—further break in the interpersonal bridge.) Defeated in an election, first to spring to mind is likely to be the history of one's previous losses in competition.

But now, let's expand that last scene. There are lots of reasons anyone might covet elected office, ranging from an altruistic desire to perform the duties of that job with dignity and grace to the wish for an increase in social status or the power to punish those who had earlier caused one negative affect. A victory may bring pride simply because it is an efficacy experience, but it may also bring the extra increment of positive affect we call triumph because it decreases or dispels shame from some other form of defeat. Although the first

---

Table 5
THE COGNITIVE PHASE OF SHAME

Search of memory for previous similar experiences.
Layered associations to

A. **Matters of personal size, strength, ability, skill**

("I am weak, incompetent, stupid.")

B. **Dependence/independence**

(Sense of helplessness.)

C. **Competition**

("I am a loser.")

D. **Sense of self**

("I am unique only to the extent that I am defective.")

E. **Personal attractiveness**

("I am ugly or deformed. The blush stains my features and
makes me even more of a target of contempt.")

F. **Sexuality**

("There is something wrong with me sexually.")

G. **Issues of seeing and being seen**

The urge to escape from the eyes before which we have been exposed.
The wish for a hole to open and swallow me.

H. **Wishes and fears about closeness**

The sense of being shorn from all humanity. A feeling that one is
unlovable. The wish to be left alone forever.

---

layer of associations to the combination of incident and affect might well be that of the cognates, following immediately will be a group of associations linked to the *metaphorical* importance of elected office. Assembled alongside the scripts representing our bundled memories of defeat may be the archives of our humiliations by more powerful others, the sting of shame caused by one's relative powerlessness in society, the feeling of overall inferiority, or the haunting misery of a snub by a much-desired lover. Each of these realms of remembered shame will operate as a metaphor for the triggering incident and add its own particular seasoning to the stew.

To each of these memories we are likely to have further associations, all uncomfortable or unpleasant. For a moment, then, we may wish to be alone with our discomfort. It is at this point that we may elect to accept the hint given us by the physiological phase of shame and withdraw further into ourselves. Withdrawal allows us to ponder everything that has just flooded into consciousness, to contemplate it in the privacy of our inner world. Withdrawal allows us to be overwhelmed.

Under most circumstances, this removal will provide respite from the worst of the shame experience. Each of the affects, after all, has its own temporal contour. Affects begin when triggered but, unless constantly restimulated, eventually they end. Left to our own devices, we heal pretty well. Should we have the luck to be born into a family that understands the pain of shame and sees no need to augment so searing an experience, we may find ourselves readily welcomed back into the fold once we have recovered enough to meet the gaze of the loving other.

The duration and the intensity of this withdrawal are quite variable and depend on a number of factors. If, through the history of one's development, shame has occurred sporadically and then only as a relatively minor component of interpersonal life, then each shame event is likely to be self-limited and of relatively slight toxicity. But for those to whom shame is the climate of their lives, whose expectation of shame is constant, each new humiliation adds its flavor to a huge and growing cauldron of stew. (One greets rain quite differently in Painted Desert, New Mexico, and Seattle, Washington.) In a loving family characterized by good empathic relatedness and a healthy sense of mutual respect, failure or incompetence or loss will produce shame soon to be mitigated by love. In a family whose very style of operation involves the use of shame for each to achieve dominion over the intimate other, and in which there is no habit of solace for an injured other, the wounds of shame demand withdrawal to some deeply private space where they can be licked until the pain has decreased enough to permit reentry into the ever-dangerous social milieu.

Accompanying withdrawal, of course, is a certain amount of safety from the immediate increase in shame that might occur should one remain in the view of those before whom one has been shamed. In our society, withdrawal is considered a proper response to shame. Who among us has not witnessed the abject humiliation of one who could not escape the taunts of a far more powerful other? Each of us knows a myriad of such horror stories; no season of feature films goes by without some such spectacle gracing the screens of our theaters. Indeed, the intentional use of humiliation to achieve social control is properly considered a form of torture—witnessing such a scene we tend to avert our own gaze and cry out our wish that the protagonist be shielded from view.

One of the most painful parts of the psychotherapist's job is the responsibility to hear and to respond properly to such stories. I remember particularly my own sense of helplessness, when, as a beginner, a patient told me this story: In order to explain how thoroughly her grandfather dominated their family, this young woman recounted the legend of what he did to her mother, when, at 18, she had asked to attend a school dance. They were a farming family in a region becoming increasingly gentrified, increasingly sophisticated. "That Saturday night, while everybody she knew was at the dance, he made her walk the family cow through the entire town, right in front of the place where the dance was being held. She never asked him for anything again." Then, 20-odd years ago, I could do no more than wince. Today I might have a bit more to say.

Crucifixion is one epitome of public humiliation. The famous witch trials of colonial Salem, the public stocks of colonial Williamsburg, arrest, trial and imprisonment of any sort, public spanking or reprimand, any form of punishment by exposure to public censure—all these are but the merest hint of the catalogue of punishments made all the worse because the culprit is denied the recourse of privacy. Shame teaches us the value of privacy: the privacy that protects us from shame, and the private place to which we must repair when humiliated. Just as shame follows the exposure of whatever we wished to keep private, the wish to withdraw provides a reasonable compensatory stratagem.

The more you think about the relation between shame and privacy, about the natural tendency toward withdrawal associated with shame, the more you are forced to reconsider the nature of psychotherapy. As E. James Anthony has said, all of the uncovering therapies produce an "arena of shame." Best known of the uncovering therapies are those based on psychoanalytic or psychodynamic principles, in which the therapist assists the patient by promoting the process through which current malaise is linked to past experience. Each revelation—each clump of memory brought into the open from the place where it had been hidden—must bring with it a sudden burst of shame. Memories are hidden for good reason!

The skillful therapist must recognize the inevitability of this discomfort and provide for the patient the type of relational safety that fosters both the emergence of whatever must be disclosed and the healing balm of love that soothes the inevitable pain associated with disclosure. It is fascinating to note that most of the great teachers of therapy have stressed this point without ever mentioning shame. When Carl Rogers taught us to treat the patient within an atmosphere of "unconditional positive regard," he was creating a counter-shaming attitude. All of the great psychoanalytic masters stressed the need to treat patients with infinite respect. All of the regulations about the nature of "privileged communication" are veiled references to the importance of shame within the therapeutic encounter.

The psychotherapist takes the position that disclosure, despite the pain of shame that attends the move from withdrawal to revelation, will ultimately be of benefit to the patient. Yet there are many situations in which our tendency to defend against shame by withdrawal is treated with much less respect. The enquiring reporter takes the position that, notwithstanding the pain it will cause for the one so exposed, disclosure serves the public interest. Journalism thrives on the energy that links shame to withdrawal.

There are other motives behind our cultural preoccupation with journalistic exposure. The scripts that characterize the cognitive phase of shame reference our most uncomfortable memories—there is not a good moment in the lot. To the extent that we can see somebody else suffering from the pain of exposure, we can feel at least a little better than somebody else. Whereas Freud taught that all spying and prying derived from our curiosity about sex, it now seems clear that sex is only one of several realms of human life held in privacy for the sake of shame. Whoever is impelled to ferret out the secrets of others in disavowal of the meaning of withdrawal bears some special relation to shame.

Were it not for our affective history and the dynamic relation between the innate affects themselves, none of this would be important. That which was revealed in each of these situations would stimulate only the response normally accorded the appearance of new information. If I am a scientist searching the forest for new plants, then whatever new plant I see will be entered into my log book and studied in its turn. Yet to be a scientist of the self fills one with the pain of shame because of our history of shame. People cannot be truly open to self-scrutiny until their archives of shame have been examined and understood. For most of us, this is the role of psychotherapy—a guided tour of the self in the company of a trusted other whose professionalism guarantees that the shame of self-discovery will be minimized.

Often I wonder just what goes on in people during the period of withdrawal in response to shame affect. Just as our modern electrophysiological studies have demonstrated that sleep is an active phase of mental life, rather than "down time" for a machine that has been switched off, I suspect that it is during the periods of withdrawal that we make a lot of decisions about our nature. Certainly this is a period of time when many of the thoughts listed in Table 5 gain even more magnification, rise even more in significance.

Because nearly everything associated with shame goes into the category we call "hidden," these cognitions (and indeed the entire process of such thinking) tend also to be hidden from consciousness. Tomkins views consciousness as that portion of mental life which has garnered enough affective amplification to take center stage; that which remains active but not so amplified might be what Freud called "preconscious" life. It is beyond question that shame is the primary affect in our resistance to releasing material from its hiding place in the unconscious. If shame, with all the force of its amplification and urgency, is what keeps things hidden, then might it not be one of the major forces that helps create that layer of mental life we call the dynamic unconscious? In some of his earliest work, Freud spoke of disgust, shame, and the moral ideals derivative of these affects as the primary forces that create repression. This intuition was later ignored as he shifted the focus of his attention from shame to guilt. Not only is the withdrawal phase of reaction to shame a natural response, but it may be one that is essential to the formation of a normal personality.

Notice that there are degrees of withdrawal just as there are degrees of shame. Normally we drop our eyes for a moment on unintentionally meeting the gaze of another—perhaps the briefest example of this mode of reaction to shame affect. Should it be noted at all, this form of shame is called *politeness.* More vivid, but still well within the limits of a healthy and normal response to shame, is the behavior of a small child who ducks behind mother when caught inspecting the face of a stranger, or who might run and hide when embarrassed. In each of these examples, the subject has experienced shame affect, then run through some version of the thought process listed above, reacted by withdrawal, and returned to society when the affect has waned and the coast seems clear.

Often, as adults, we demonstrate this mild degree of shame as withdrawal by small, economical gestures—putting a hand to our lips as if to prevent our very mouth from leaking unacceptable words, briefly biting the lower lip while glancing down and away, or stuttering for a moment while looking clearly uncomfortable. In some cultures, a woman will indicate sexual interest by returning a man's gaze and lowering her eyes briefly, as if embarrassed by her own arousal. Nietzsche, among many others, described his own feeling of pleasure when a woman exhibited such apparent embarrassment.

At the other end of the spectrum, I have met patients afflicted with biological disorders that produced paralyzing degrees of shame, who have described the period of their depression as one in which they became "like a hermit." One woman told me that in the four years of this illness she did not leave her home for fear of meeting the eyes of any person outside her family. The withdrawal accompanying severe biological depression is not specific to the disease but rather a learned defense against intense and enduring shame affect that has been produced by a defect in neurotransmitter mechanisms. It is an example of the most severe form of withdrawal reactions to shame.

This helps explain the effect on depression of the various forms of psychotherapy. Most often, clarity and relief are obtained when we can identify the experiences from the past that were used to construct one's personal categories of shame cognition. Some patients, however, are little helped by discussion of the apparent historical roots of their shame or guilt. Despite how real it feels, their emotion has not resulted from the thoughts and memories brought into the therapeutic encounter. These, of course, represent the cognitive phase of the shame experience, even though in this case shame has been triggered by chemical misinformation. Medication that corrects the neurotransmitter imbalance will reduce or remove the inappropriate and unreasonable amount of shame, allowing both a return to society and a remarkable decrease in attention to the thoughts that previously seemed to cause so much distress. On the other hand, cognitive–behavioral therapy, by altering the thought patterns associated with the biological shame state or by setting up conditions that force the patient to give up the withdrawal reaction, can also produce a remarkable improvement in the patient's outlook. In the more malignant forms of depression, both chemical and behavioral manipulations are usually needed.

Momentary gaze avoidance and hermit-like depression represent two extremes of the withdrawal reaction to shame affect; they help define this spectrum of responses to shame. Between them lie an infinite number of forms and types of withdrawal, each capable of analysis in the manner I have suggested here. There are two realms of benefit conferred by the system of withdrawal. However long it may last, the period of isolation can allow an individual to regroup and recover self-esteem so that emergence into the world of others is facilitated or enhanced. But while secluded, we are relatively immune to further shaming incidents—withdrawal can protect from injury as well as foster healing. Withdrawal can become part of an affect-reduction script or an affect-avoidance script; in either case the action involved is undertaken in order to minimize the experience of shame.

On several occasions I have mentioned the condition currently known as *atypical depression,* a persistent form of mood disturbance characterized by "rejection sensitivity," "social phobia," and "applause hunger." This, too, presents over a wide spectrum of severity, for in some patients we see these symptoms in the absence of discernible depression, while in others the associated affects of distress and disgust (self-loathing) predominate and cause a morbid, paralytic, self-deprecating withdrawal.

We know that this illness is best treated by the use of medications that make more of the neurotransmitter *serotonin* available to certain groups of neurons. Most of these symptoms dwindle or disappear when the patient is given one of the monoamine oxidase inhibitor antidepressants (Parnate, Nardil) or *fluoxe-*

tine (Prozac), for these two classes of medication are (at this writing) the best we have to reduce biologically induced shame. Nevertheless, the actual symptom complex may be understood as one in which a biochemical illness produces an inordinate amount of shame affect against which the patient defends by strategies linked almost purely to withdrawal. All of the patients with this illness seem to have used the withdrawal system of shame management long before there was any evidence of an illness; when they did become ill, the way was prepared for their method of handling it.

I do not mean to imply that biologically induced or maintained shame states produce reactive scripts involving only the *withdrawal* pole of the compass of shame. Biochemically triggered shame can evoke responses from any of the four poles of the compass; when treated with proper medication, the behavior associated with that script library tends to diminish significantly. *Fluoxetine* (and, I suspect, the newer drug *paroxetine*) helps lots of people whose shame syndromes involve the other quadrants of the compass. But most of what my colleagues recognize as "atypical depression" involves the *withdrawal* pole.

Always of special interest is the relation between shame and sexuality, which is uniquely sensitive to the reactive phase of shame. Wurmser has commented that we are embarrassed to be seen naked unless the viewing other is held under what he described as the spell called "fascination." This is easy to understand if we accept that when fascinated one is in the throes of an *irresistibly* attractive influence. In such a situation there is (almost by definition) little or no likelihood that anything can act as an impediment to rapt interest or cause a breach in the interpersonal bridge; the one who is disrobing can feel safe, free from the anticipation of shame.

To the extent that one does not feel such safety within a relationship, withdrawal presents an ever more attractive alternative. Reticence and modesty form the mature and healthy end of the spectrum; they are attitudes or systems of behavior that require of the viewing other either permission to reveal or some sort of safeguard from humiliation. Directly proportional to our expectation of shame in any encounter will be the degree of anticipatory protective withdrawal.

Thus, the effect on sexual arousal and excitement of the *withdrawal* system of reaction to shame will range from normal modesty to complete impotence and frigidity. The more one expects or actually experiences shame as an impediment to the excitement accompanying sexual arousal, so much will one withdraw from sexual interaction as protection from this particular discomfort.

Although shame is rarely if ever discussed within any of the modern systems of sexual counseling, much of the therapy itself seems directed at its reduction. The use of tasteful illustrations, anatomical models, and well-directed films to demonstrate the range of normal anatomy and normal sexual behavior serves to reduce shame significantly. Even the decision to request treatment implies that one is ready to trade the shame of chronic sexual failure for that accompanying exposure to professional counselors.

Often the withdrawal defense is accompanied by other affects which serve to promote the sense of alienation, resignation, and retreat associated with some forms of shame. When withdrawn, some people weep in distress, while others look frightened. Distress, an analogic amplifier of a steady-state noxious stimulus, stretches out shame and helps to make it a steady experience. Fear, another sort of analogic amplifier of overmuch, worsens the experience of shame by adding the discomfort of overmuch to the pain of impediment to positive affect. To the extent that both of these affects are coassembled with shame that is reacted against by withdrawal, we will interpret the entire package as "classical depression," with its stigmata of guilt, foreboding, gloom, sadness, tears, and agitation.

Since both disgust and dissmell motivate us to stay at a distance from whatever has triggered them, both affects may be brought into the picture to augment withdrawal. Thus, a withdrawn, depressed patient may see him- or herself as a loathsome object worthy only of our scorn and rejection. The balance between self-disgust and self-dissmell can easily be determined by attention to the individual's reasons for (cognitive explanations of) this particular feature of the self.

The *withdrawal* system of adaptation to shame is perhaps the easiest to treat in psychotherapy. Essential is a basic empathic stance that shows you know and feel the other person's pain. This must be verbalized in a distinctive manner that indicates some sort of joining with the patient. Central to treatment is the understanding that the patient, stuck alone in the shame experience, is unable to return to normal interpersonal interaction unaided. The empathic therapist is able to enter the patient's pain at this deeply personal level, join with it, and then pull both out of the humiliation.

The therapist must be willing to teach the definition of a shame experience. I try to use the situation of the moment to identify as much as possible about what it feels like to be humiliated. The purpose here is to drive home the concept that the basic feature of any period of shame is an innate affect, a brief, scripted, physiological experience common to all humans, one that has a temporal contour.

It is useful to focus the patient on the temporal aspects of the episode. Even though these moments tend to feel endless, eventually they pass. The very fact that patient and therapist continue to talk, continue to maintain some form of empathic link, disproves or undoes one of the cardinal elements of the shame experience—the sundering of the interpersonal bridge. Whenever possible, I try to catalogue (and get the patient to agree to the existence of) the good features of the self that remain. This helps reduce the dominance of the bad self that was depicted during the cognitive phase of shame.

In summary, treatment of the *withdrawal* reaction to shame requires that the therapist enter the other person's system in an empathic manner, identify the shame experience, and define it in a way that demonstrates a conviction that recovery is as certain as is the remainder of the experience. *Therapeutic passivity—the decision to remain silent in the face of a humiliated, withdrawn patient—will always magnify shame because it confirms the patient's affect-driven belief that isolation is justified.* In a manner of speaking, one might say that such a mode of treatment encourages the patient to switch from defense by withdrawal to defense by self-attack, the system that will occupy us in the next chapter.

Look once more at the issues listed in Table 5. Might there be one or more categories of discomfort most important to those who use *withdrawal* strategies? I think that it is the last two categories that matter most here: Issues of seeing and being seen; and wishes and fears about closeness. Wurmser said once that the eye is the organ of shame *par excellence*. When we withdraw, we escape the eyes of the other, the eyes before which we have been shamed. Morrison has pointed out that much of shame involves the viewing eye turned inward, shame as we face ourselves, as we see what we wish to hide from ourselves. But withdrawal works pretty well as a metaphor for escape, especially in terms of those two specific categories from the cognitive phase of the shame sequence. Other defenses work better for people more occupied by the rest of what we see in Table 5. It is to these script libraries that we will now turn our attention.

24

ATTACK SELF

A small boy does something really stupid in class, something that makes everybody laugh at him. How he handles this loss of face will depend a great deal on his previous life experience. If he is "one of the boys," a "regular guy," someone everybody likes and respects, his gaffe will be excused as a mere blip on an otherwise smooth curve. He will continue to see himself as a competent person, and those around him will only like him more. When he looks to his fellows as a mirror for his own personality, he will see little change, except that everybody seems to have had a good time. His "stupidity" has presented the class with a pleasant moment of enjoyment—joy and the relaxation that accompanies this affect. Sometimes it is a relief to know that even one of the best can make a fool of himself. To err is human, to forgive is divine.

For anybody who cares to draw a lesson from happenstance, here, in a nutshell, is the art of clowning. In this example, let's suppose that the boy recognizes immediately their laughter as benign and friendly—indeed, as a potential source of power. Inspired by the moment, he proceeds to doff an invisible hat and bow to the audience, after which the class laughs even more and cheers him. By this gesture he has effectively taken control of what had, only a moment ago, been something unintentional and "stupid." A brief and quite bearable moment of personal embarrassment has brought pleasure and comfort to an entire group that now views the "jokester" with increased respect. Even if shame did cause him a moment of discomfort and unpleasant isolation, his rueful willingness to accept the laughter of his friends fashioned an even stronger connection to them.

We grow through life with a myriad of such experiences, all capable of teaching us that there are bargains to be achieved from the open acceptance of shame. One of the central tenets of our society is the balance between sin and repentance. The dictionary tells us that the components of *rue* include sorrow, repentance, distress, and regret, all leading to *contrition*. The Latin root of the word contrition contains the idea of bruising or grinding something until it achieves another form. This steady, grinding quality is an analogue of the innate affect distress. Central to the concept of rue is the idea that something about one's inner nature is grindingly inescapable.

The whole issue of rue and contrition involves a fascinating study of the relation among three affects: *shame* triggered by awareness (both of the nature of one's actions and the nature of the self who committed them); *fear* of punishment for what one has done; and *distress* produced by the constancy of one's shame. There is a continuum, a spectrum of possible responses to self-awareness. At one end sit those who show no discernible signs of conscience, who trample ruthlessly on the lives of others, while at the other end are those so involved with questions of right and wrong that they are paralyzed into inaction. As citizens we require our leaders always to be capable of action, but at the same time do not want their actions to be uninformed by shame.

Conventional, "normal" morality implies a healthy awareness of shame— not too much, not too little. In order to feel comfortable with powerful people, we need to know that they are capable of looking at themselves, that they are willing to accept the shame that accompanies negative self-evaluation, and that they are able to move forward after experiencing shame.

Robert F. Kennedy, attorney general during the brief presidential administration of his brother, John F. Kennedy, made a special effort to disentangle the complex involvement of organized crime in the major national labor unions. One of his special targets was Jimmy Hoffa, president of the Teamster's Union, who retaliated against the attorney general by calling him ruthless. So successful was Hoffa's public relations campaign that Kennedy was able to reap gales of laughter and applause when, in a public speech, he quipped, "I guess I've got to learn how to be more ruthful."

In a 1985 motion picture called *The Terminator*, Arnold Schwarzenegger played the role of an android, an invincible metal-framed robot cloaked in human flesh, animated by a computer programmed only to kill those defined as enemies of its creators. Incapable of emotion, the terminator showed neither enmity toward its targets nor satisfaction at their execution. Contrasted with this central character were the extremely human and attractive young man and woman for whose death it had been designed. During this immensely popular film, Schwarzenegger killed an enormous number of people using a wide range of techniques. Whereas many films of equal violence arouse public outcry for their callous indifference to human sensibility, most viewers described the killings as more like ballet than carnage.

In a number of discussions with people who enjoyed *The Terminator*, I found that everybody had accepted the idea that this android was constitutionally incapable of anger, hatred, disgust, or fear. The terminator's actions and its inability to express or experience shame, remorse, guilt, or sorrow were understandable and even excusable because of its constitutional deficiency. An implacable human, however, is an even more terrifying monster because of our intrinsic belief that everybody is capable of empathic response. The film allowed us to think about remorseless, ruthless, implacable humans by focusing our attention on a nonhuman substitute.

The public image of an adult is softened or humanized by the expression of a full range of affect. When a powerful individual like Robert Kennedy is willing to moderate his or her intensity by showing some degree of mild, amused embarrassment, he will usually be viewed with affection. Such a person is not so ruthless and powerful as to ignore the feelings of the masses and of us as individuals within the horde. When those in authority refuse to let the public know that they are capable of feeling shame and distress, they create an aura of fear. We, their subjects, feel safer with someone who is capable of shame.

There is, of course, an enigma here. Look again at the table of shameful ruminations presented in the previous chapter. There's not a happy thought in the bunch. We need to protect ourselves from these uncomfortable reflections just as much as we need to know that others experience them as well. Shame produces a wondrous double standard in which we want everybody else to express freely what we wish to keep hidden. The paradox is that we may feel a certain kinship or affiliation with one who has been embarrassed, while that other person feels estranged, isolated, extruded, rejected, alone, and unlovable. Anyone who understands this paradox has learned a valuable lesson about living in the real world.

Used with care, the intentional display of shame can make people feel kindly toward us. Overused, pushed beyond the limits of good taste, self-abnegation provokes disgust in the observer. Here we are looking at the range between attentiveness and servility, between appropriately deferential respect and slavish docility. One is reminded of the cartoon in which a waiter, while presenting the check, bows to the diner and says, "I hope I have been successful in treading the fine line between excellent service and fawning obsequiousness." In the character of Uriah Heep, Charles Dickens created a model of the oily, fawning, spineless, groveling, subservient person for whose otherwise excellent services we can have no respect.

So much depends on the relative importance to us of the categories of shame summarized as Table 5. Those who handle shame by acceptance are willing to admit into consciousness any and all of the thoughts listed in the table. No matter what is revealed by the moment of shame, no matter what defect or incompetence is detected, it will become the stimulus to some form of work on the self. Those who react by withdrawal have also chosen to accept the feeling of shame, but with no way of using it as a source of information for such a commitment. They withdraw in order to evade the eyes before which they have been exposed, to leave the society from which they feel shorn.

Most of us some of the time, and some of us all of the time, actually function in a quite different manner. To a great number of people, the worst part of the shame experience is summarized as category B, the group of thoughts associated with dependence and independence. In Chapter 12 it was noted that we are usually proud to be independent and ashamed of our dependence on others. Furthermore, we came to recognize that any time the child is confronted with a situation in which painful affect is linked with interpersonal distance, the affects dissmell and disgust may become involved as auxiliaries. So for many people, nearly any moment of shame is likely to bring with it thoughts both of utter dependence on others and of the helplessness we might feel were we to be utterly rejected as dissmelling or disgusting objects. For them, there is great relief to be obtained from any strategy that helps avoid this terrifying sense of helplessness and the deadly fear of abandonment.

It is to this group of scripts that I refer as the *attack self* mode of reaction to shame. Involved is the universe of systems by which we vary the biblical injunction to read instead, "Do unto yourself what you fear others may do to you." What is it that happens when, intentionally, we put ourselves down in a conversation with others, ridicule ourselves, describe our own actions with disgust, refer to ourselves with dissmell, or exhibit anger toward our own self? Simply stated, such a maneuver permits us to accept a moment of shame during which we anticipate that all of those other affects and ideas will be totally under our own control. We have, for instance, avoided the possibility that others *really* view us with dissmell or disgust because *we* gave them the idea in the first place. The much-feared unpleasant affects still exist in the interpersonal interaction, but they have been reduced vastly in significance.

SHYNESS

Is not shyness a form of shame avoidance by which we accept one portion of the shame experience in order to prevent the emergence of the whole? Shyness is a complex system that includes some measure of prophylactic withdrawal. It is a way of keeping a profile so low that no one can reduce it. It says to a world we see as probably shaming that we aspire to no height from which we can be dropped. Shy is timid, bashful, wary, slight of stature, willing to live at a level to which shame might decrease one rather than risk the sudden diminishment that accompanies acute, unexpected shame. In marketing terms, it is a "loss leader," a way of getting customers into the store by accepting one loss while hoping for a gain in other areas of commerce. Shyness is shame instructed by fear.

The shy person may hold a secret view of the self far in excess of that which is broadcast—shyness need not imply a perceived decrease in personal worth. It says that there is no need to reduce me because I am already lower than you, despite that I have not shown you a fraction of my real self. It enhances privacy (which reduces shame) by advertising that one has nothing to advertise. I live willingly with the shame of being lesser than you, but I have guaranteed that you are unlikely to attack me and will not reject me. Shyness is a form of shame that produces affiliation rather than rejection. Central to shyness is often a disavowal of interest in hopes of decreasing the significance of any impediment to it.

DEFERENCE AND CONFORMITY

As the sociologist Thomas J. Scheff has observed, much of our social system depends on the fact that each of us makes a myriad of careful observations of ourselves and of others that allow us to maximize pride and minimize shame. In our attempt to enjoy whatever degree of power is allowed us while avoiding humiliation as much as possible, most of us develop some sort of balance between arrogance and deference. Scheff describes a system of deference and conformity based on his understanding of shame; unfortunately, however, he ignores the role of positive affect in the formation of social systems and as the precondition for shame.

Sometimes, of course, deference and conformity are legislated, as in the military. If both men are buck privates in the army, it does not matter to their superior officers that Bill is bigger, stronger, wealthier, and from a higher social stratum than John. Their equality is defined by the sameness of their uniform and their rank; they will be ordered about with equal ease. And should John achieve higher rank than Bill, he will command Bill. The man who was once lesser and therefore deferential by conventional standards will now have power over and command deference from him who was previously more powerful.

One of the reasons the military system works is that it provides an easily understandable hierarchy. Merely to remain within the system guarantees sequential elevation in rank, which increases the number of people who will be deferential to you and reduces the number of people to whom you must be deferential. Small wonder, then, that pride and shame in the name of power are matters of central interest to the military. Often in history they have been used as the excuse for war.

Part of the process called "basic training" in the military includes instruction in the rituals of deference. Just as one who has grown up in any large city knows the proper way to address a police officer—including the limits to which one may go in disagreeing with this authority—a new recruit must be taught what now constitutes appropriate respect. The deal is simple: The successful trainee gives up his or her lifetime accumulation of pride and power from such sources as beautiful hair, physical strength, sexiness, or such, in trade for the sense of affiliation derived from the feeling of being part of a powerful group. Those who cannot accept the shame inherent in this new system are removed from it in one way or another; they become defined as proper objects of dissmell and disgust and live in shame until their departure.

Cultural anthropologists often discuss the myriad of ways that systems of deference can clash. In many areas of the rural South, it was common for African-American men to be brought into the local hospital emergency rooms for treatment of scalp lacerations inflicted by the truncheons of the very policemen who had brought them there. In each case, when addressed initially by the officer, the subject had dropped his gaze from the policeman's face in apparent inattention, started to shuffle his feet, and begun to giggle. In our society, such behavior might easily be taken as some pattern of insubordination and disrespect, and perhaps understandable as the trigger to punitive rage on the part of the arresting officer.

Nonetheless, there was a subtext to this script. Anthropological investigation revealed that, in the region of Africa from which the forebears of these particular people had been ripped more than a century earlier, deference to authority had always been expressed by the gestures of polite gaze aversion, the giggle of helpless immaturity, and the shuffle of incoordination. Casual review of Southern literature during the era of slavery reveals innumerable references to similar incidents between slaves and masters. What read out only as arrogance and disrespect in the culture of the policeman had earlier been ingrained within the root culture of the people involved as a measure of intentional acceptance of shame through the system of *attack self*.

Such stories serve to illustrate the range of situations in which this mode of shame avoidance may be used. *Attack self* appears as the good humor of the pleasantly self-effacing adult, the friendly little laugh that uses enjoyment–joy to mitigate the significance of an aggressive move, the kind of joke we call "my most embarrassing moment," and the comedic art of the clown. People of my generation still chuckle at the vaudeville routines of Jack Benny, who pretended to play the violin very badly but constantly offered to give benefit concerts for worthy causes. His feigned surprise at the refusal of those organizations was understood by everybody as a humorous attack on his own broadcast image, and we loved him for it.

The process of getting through adolescence is made immeasurably easier by the adoption of some of these techniques. One must have a certain degree of self-esteem to tolerate the *attack self* system, for it is difficult to give away anything when one has nothing. Yet the happiest teen-agers I know all seem to be able to tolerate banter, the give-and-take of normal adolescent conversation. They learn to trade compliments and put-downs with equal facility.

MASOCHISM

Yet there is a dark side to the system of *attack self*, for some people are so willing to accept shame in order to guarantee the stability of their link to others that they become quite masochistic. The conventional view of masochism represents it as a system of interpersonal activity in which one person seems to take delight in being dominated by another, even to the extent of pain or cruelty.* I know of no episode of masochistic behavior that is free of shame; indeed, among those of us who have written on shame, Wurmser is the most eloquent in his description of masochism as the theater of shame. What passes for delight in the suffering of the masochist is the anticipatory positive affect masking the pain experienced during an activity that is intended to assure bonding.

In sexuality, of course, *attack self* is seen over an astonishingly wide range of behavior and inner experience. As we discussed earlier, Stoller feels that most of what we fantasize during sexual excitement are scenes designed to repair previous humiliations. Whereas there is no obligatory link between the sexual drive mechanism of the generative system and any particular ideoaffective blend, it certainly does seem as if Stoller's empirical data from the psychoanalytic study of adults are correct. In our culture, sexual fantasy—especially the

*Glick and Meyers (1988) edited an excellent review of the classical psychoanalytic views of masochism.

ideation that accompanies sexual arousal—seems to be one of the favored realms within which we seek repair or revenge against those before whom we have been embarrassed. It is instructive to look briefly at the masochistic side of this equation.

At the mildest end of the spectrum lie those fantasies in which we experience ourselves as powerful merely because the much-desired other shares our sexual excitement. Either participant may see deference and submission as the ticket allowing entry to the game—a move as innocent and as choreographed as a dance step. Courtship rituals, in which a man brings flowers, goes to varying degrees of expense to woo his partner, pledges undying interest, and guarantees his fidelity, may be understood both within the system of idealization leading to love and as symbols of deference that allow a woman to feel some sense of triumph despite the fact that they may have been offered more in the spirit of seduction. That a sturdy and athletic young woman will dress for a date in a manner that suggests frailty is one example of the female version of this interplay.

Nearer the midrange are those scripts in which we triumph over hidden and past adversaries while treating with respect and affection the partner with whom we can enjoy these secrets. And at the farthest reaches of behavior are the *Grand Guignol* of sexual madness, the horror show of masochism beyond the imagination of most adults. At each level of severity, these fantasies take the form of scenes within which people visualize themselves playing with or working through some form of deference and submission. No matter what the level or intensity of shame being detoxified within these scripts, masochistic sexuality draws together and bonds partners whose intolerance of shame is high and who will reward each other accordingly.

One of the reasons that masochism is so difficult to treat in a clinical setting is that it represents the end result of a complex and long-standing attempt to reduce deep and painful shame. The people involved in such activities are far less concerned about the pain brought by their masochism than about the profoundly secret shame that causes them even more distress. Furthermore, the *attack self* mode of defense is undertaken in order to prevent the helplessness of abandonment and isolation. Any action taken by the therapist that tends to reduce behavior that is really meant to guarantee safety will be viewed with suspicion by the patient.

Great relief is obtained by the masochistic patient when therapy is aimed initially at the demonstration of the relation between the *attack self* system and the general nature of shame. I try to explain that what now appears to be a significant degree of psychopathology started out as a creative solution for an as-yet-unidentified problem. Together, the patient and I learn how the process of attacking self has come to feel better than the experience of having somebody else do it. Each time we find another example of hidden shame the patient is likely to be mortified or guilty, so much patience and perseverence are required of both.

Over time, we learn to identify this as a consistent pattern, usually one that began in childhood. Even the therapeutic relationship will appear to take on aspects of the earliest parent-child relationship that cannot be verbalized easily. This, of course, is an example of transference within therapy and comes to be interpreted as such. Nevertheless, each time we find an example of this pattern of behavior, we handle it as a clever developmental acquisition—the brilliant intuition of a child—rather than a black mark on the patient's record.

Central to this therapeutic work is the attempt to determine the nature of the relationships within which the patient learned the definition of self that is so connected with shame. Giving up chronic masochism means giving up the shaming parent, which implies abandonment unless the patient feels safe within the therapeutic relationship. All efforts at therapy will cause initial pain because the therapist is asking the patient to give up a defensive system that prevents, or at least mitigates, the experience of shame. Yet this must be done in order to find and heal the pain that lurks beneath the surface.

Another problem that makes the masochistic personality so difficult to treat in psychotherapy is the degree to which the core problem with shame is complicated by the addition of auxiliary affect mechanisms. Admixtures of distress and fear will produce the clinical picture of depression. Unfortunately, unless the underlying shame sensitivity is dealt with as such, these patients tend to experience more disabling side effects from medication than any other I have treated. Indeed, to the extent that self-disgust and self-dissmell are fused with shame, these patients often feel that they should not get better—that their illness is richly deserved.

The masochistic patient seems to operate in a topsy-turvy frame of reference, where it is good to feel bad. Nowhere in human existence is it as important to understand how shame figures into the birth of the self, and how our system of good and bad is formed. The system of reaction to shame that I have called *attack self* is usually a benign mode of defense leading to friendly forms of affiliation. But in certain family systems it can achieve malignant magnification, leading to deadly configurations far beyond what is amenable to the systems of treatment currently known.

The *attack self* system offers a hedge against shame in which one bargains with the devil. It works pretty well, even though one can learn too many variations on the theme and too many ways of attacking oneself in the name of bonding with others. There are many who refuse even to consider it as a reasonable alternative to unintentional, uncontrolled shame, which they try to prevent by a number of techniques. It is to these systems of *avoidance* that we now turn our attention.

25

AVOIDANCE

Perhaps I best remember the day Margaret spilled the coffee because of the color of my beautiful carpet. Real wool, tightly woven, and a little too costly for my first very own office, it achieved its overall soft green look by blending reddish-brown lines against a light green background to make a pattern of miniature checks. Although situated in a center-city medical building, my waiting and consultation areas are set up as if they are rooms in our home, with almost no trace of traditional medical formality. The decor reflects my need for it to be a place where peers and equals gather to discuss matters of mutual interest. Clearly the sort of carpet one might purchase for a fine home rather than a commercial site, it provided the desired final touch. Not unlike a small boy threatened with humiliating censure for failing to take care of an expensive present, I had resolved to guard it carefully.

A couple of steps away from the chairs in which we sit is a tray with the makings for whatever warm beverages might suit a guest. In the first session or two I make and pour the instant decaffeinated coffee or tea for my companion. After the introduction to the system, it is expected that each of us will feel free to use it at will.

And so, that afternoon 20 years ago, Margaret was standing at the tray, talking animatedly while mixing and pouring her coffee. All of a sudden, she lurched, spilling a glop of liquid. Quite used to so normal an occurrence, and geared in my response to such spills like a volunteer fire company, I leaned forward to initiate my coffee-blotting drill. But to my surprise Margaret paid no attention to the accident and continued to talk as if nothing had happened. No guilt, no embarrassment, no morsel of responsibility.

"Excuse me," I said. "What?" "Look at the carpet. You just spilled the coffee." Right heel planted squarely on the floor, she pivoted sharply so the quarter-sized café-au-lait spot was covered completely by her foot. "Where?" she said. "There, under your foot." Margaret lifted her left foot. "I don't see anything." "The other foot." "Oh!" she said in some surprise. "Huh. Look at that!" I proceeded to erase the spot. It was clear that there was no way she would ever be willing to discuss or even remember that incident, which was never mentioned again. Instinctively I knew that the 35-year-old social worker who had entered my office that day suddenly had been replaced by a guilty little girl, and that I was better off paying attention to the frightened child than the sophisticated adult.

But it is interesting for us to enquire where the spot went between the moment it was created and when she agreed to notice it. How does the mind manage to repudiate reality? Obviously, we do not pay attention to everything equally all the time—there must be some hierarchy of values in life. We can easily conceive of crisis situations (like fire, earthquake, or war) in which the act of spilling coffee would be quite trivial in the context of the truly dangerous and terrifying reality. In such a situation the affect triggered by the spill would not compete with the overwhelming affect already in process. But Margaret gave no evidence that she was so engulfed. Her avoidance of the spill was of another sort.

My field uses words in its own particular way, and we reserve the term *denial* for the group of situations in which a defense mechanism interferes with our perception of something. The word itself is derived from roots indicating its relation to the idea of saying "no." Denial implies refusal of anything asked for or desired, the assertion that something is untrue, the contradiction of the existence or the reality of a thing. The form of repudiation utilized by Margaret is known as *disavowal*, a more specific term that indicates one's inability to comprehend information that remains unwanted because it triggers unwanted affect.[*]

In our culture, the most famous example of disavowal appears at the end of the classic film *Gone with the Wind*. Rhett Butler has just rejected a final insincere plea of Scarlett O'Hara, indicating that she is self-centered, greedy, immature, and unable to sustain an adult relationship. Immediately on his departure, Scarlett first recoils in disbelief, acknowledging the importance of his remarks, and then says "I can't think about it now. I'll go crazy. I'll think about it tomorrow." We, the audience, know that what he has said may never

---

[*]This distinction between *denial* and *disavowal* is discussed at length by Basch (1983b). See also Edelstein et al. (1989) for a thorough review of these concepts.

cross her mind again, and certainly will never act as information that might help her grow into a better person.

In this episode, Scarlett remains aware of the incident itself—there is no interference with perception. Nevertheless, she has repudiated the emotional meaning of his rejection, which removes it from consciousness as effectively as if it had not been perceived. Rhett Butler's decision brings her no feeling of rejection; it does not break the interpersonal bridge; it does not achieve meaning because she has prevented it from triggering shame. Stripped of its affective accompaniment, his comments lack urgency for her. Other matters are free to engage her attention.

Disavowal is a major force in human life. All of the psychological defense mechanisms described by Freud, the investigation of which forms such an important part of psychoanalytic therapy, are really strategies through which we attempt to avoid unwanted or uncomfortable affect. They are scripts that operate out of our awareness, in the realm of unconscious life. Psychoanalytic scholars, like Wurmser and Basch, believe that each of them is brought into play only after the decision to disavow.

In a way, disavowal is like lying to the self. Lying, blaming, and the many other ways we avoid responsibility are ubiquitous precautions against shame. "One day," said Rachel, "when I was six years old, I was playing around with my mother's sewing machine and got the needle stuck in my finger. Somehow I got my finger out, but it hurt something awful and it was still bleeding so I had to get her so she would help. So I ran to her and said, 'Mommy! The sewing machine just jumped up and bit me.' " The little fib, so obvious to an adult, is clearly an attempt to shift her mother's anger away from Rachel toward the suddenly animated mechanical device. The feared reprisal, so central to the experience we call guilt, is deflected from the self. It is doubtful that Rachel really believed her own story, which is why we cannot regard it as disavowal.

I do not mean to leave the impression that disavowal is intrinsically *bad*, for life quite often presents us with conditions in which no good is served by continual preoccupation with something that must, by its nature, trigger negative affect. The ability to disavow can be something like having an ace up your sleeve during a big poker game. There are lots of ways of handling unpleasant affect, all of which work pretty well. Occasionally, in a situation where nothing else seems likely to manage or prevent discomfort, we can protect ourselves by pretending that the trigger to it never occurred.

Consider the case of a man who is riddled with cancer, disfigured both by the disease and by antineoplastic treatment, but who disavows the terrible implications of his illness so that he may enjoy whatever time remains him. Ours is a culture that tends to regard with disfavor anything that fails to confront, so some people might say that he is wrong to avoid this knowledge. Surely, however, it would be arch and insincere of us to say that such a person would be more "emotionally healthy" were he to give up this disavowal and think more deeply about his illness! There are a number of foundations that minister to the needs of terminally ill children by granting some long-cherished wish, such as the opportunity to meet a movie star or to visit some famous landmark. By infusing excitement and joy into the lives of those who have been living with fear, pain, and distress, by distracting them to this new focus of attention, these organizations bring the grace of temporary disavowal.

STRATEGIES FOR AVOIDANCE

Shame, for many people the most unpleasant of the affects, is by far the leading reason for disavowal. The strategies through which we humans attempt to avoid, disguise, prevent, elude, or circumvent embarrassment and guilt form an assortment of scripts that I have grouped at the *avoidance* pole of the compass of shame. Included here are all the ways one can say no to shame.

In the matter of shame avoidance there are two masters to be served. For each of us, some portion of our experienced shame comes from our own assessment of ourselves, while another portion follows exposure to others. It is for this reason that Wurmser (1989) refers to the process of disavowal as "blinding the eye of the mind." At the *avoidance* pole are some scripts that fool others, some by which we fool ourselves, and a few in which both are fooled. It is very much like the song from *The King and I* in which Anna describes the awkward embarrassment she feels when anybody knows she is frightened: "Whenever I feel afraid, I whistle a happy tune. . . . And when I fool the people I fear, I fool myself as well." Her display of positive affect—designed to charm and distract the attention of the viewing other—serves equally well as a disavowal of her own discomfort.

For that segment of shame which derives from discovery there are three basic tactical approaches: We can protect ourselves by guarding the perimeters of our personal world; by making sure there is nothing within them that will embarrass us; or by distracting people so that they will forget that they were interested in what may lie within. At the healthy end of the spectrum lie openness and modesty. To ensure those qualities in some forums, there is the group of "sunshine laws" that preserve the rights of citizens to witness what goes on during the meetings of legislative committees. When nothing need be hidden, we are less likely to be suspicious of our leaders. So much do we become inured to the way "normal" adults protect themselves from scrutiny that we describe those who live without any perceived need for such protection as "refreshingly open."

The habit of *modesty* is defined by our dictionary as the quality of having a moderate opinion of oneself; a reserve springing from an unexaggerated estimate of one's qualities; freedom from presumption, ostentation, arrogance, or impudence. It implies the existence of a certain reserve or sense of shame proceeding from instinctive aversion to anything that another person might view as shameful. To be modest one must have a pretty good idea of one's real qualities and have no need to exaggerate those qualities. This requires an accurate evaluation of our place relative to others, as well as no need to be seen as other than we really are. Healthy modesty is summed up by the protagonist in the Lerner and Loewe musical play *Paint Your Wagon*, who sings of his abilities and accomplishments, "I'm more than a lot are, I'm less than some. I'm in between." Such an attitude would constitute an ideal method for the avoidance of shame.

The Sense of a Defective Self

But few of us feel entirely comfortable with ourselves, feel ready, willing, and able to accept what may be seen either by the viewing eye of the other or by our own eye turned inward. How we protect ourselves from shame may be understood easily by returning to Table 5. Everybody is made uncomfortable by failure or shortcomings in each of these eight categories, even though the degree to which we are discomfited may vary from one division to another. As we saw in the previous chapter, those for whom the ideas of helplessness and abandonment loom largest are most likely to use *attack self* scripts to modulate shame by guaranteeing affiliation through the willing acceptance of controlled amounts of shame. Yet other categories achieve greater significance for some people.

Many of us feel generally unloved and unacceptable to others. Naturally, such a feeling may be based on fact, for a number of us have grown up in families that seem unable to love, while quite a few have lived within subcultures that made them feel like aliens. Few children can be so dispassionate as to develop much real understanding of their environment; most use various strategies of denial or disavowal in order to avoid such "knowledge." The child is faced with two contrasting alternatives: a frightening awareness that these parents are incapable of love, implying that they actually might not provide protection from danger; or the creative but false theory that his or her parents are really okay and that their unpleasant behavior is the reasonable response of good people to a bad or defective child.

Clearly, logic most often commands the second choice, which offers far greater emotional safety than the harsher reality. Children will adopt a sense of themselves as being personally defective in order to explain away parental failure. Indeed, so tenacious can be this decision to disavow that often it functions as a core delusion—a fixed, false belief, central to the personality of an individual, unassailable by logic and held in place by a variety of powerfully magnified affects. To grow up in a dangerous home implies nearness to death and an atmosphere of terror, while to grow up believing one is a defective child in a good home implies a life of shame rather than peril.

This compromise works pretty well in childhood, when we are totally dependent on parental protection. The adoption of a sense of personal defect allows the child to trade unbearable fear—the terror of abandonment and death—for merely uncomfortable shame. Yet when we have achieved adult size and adult power, this compromise seems a little less advantageous. As adults, we have far less to fear, while with advancement in years the discomfort produced by shame mounts continually, requiring us to develop strategies for its minimization. If my generalized sense of shame stems from a childhood decision to accept the overarching concept of a defective self, then I can reduce this self-inflicted noxious feeling only by improving myself. Adults who grew up in an unloving, unempathic home often mount a relentless search for specific personal defects that can be overcome as if the achievement of perfection in the present might erase the bad old days of the past.

I have always been mystified, astonished, by the disavowal required in the adage "Sticks and stones may break your bones, but names can never harm you." Bones heal. Names stick with you forever. The shaming taunts and epithets used by those we love often come to invade our sense of self and reduce our self-esteem. Attacked for a real weakness or some fancifully declared inferiority, we tend to attribute to that deficit all the shame in our lives. Not surprisingly, we grow up attaching to that insufficiency a degree of significance directly proportional to the amount that we feel unloved and unlovable. So it is that a huge segment of our population finds shame unbearable and spends much of its time and energy attempting to increase self-esteem through techniques of accumulation and repair.

It is category D, the sense of a defective self, and category H, the idea that one is denied personal closeness because one is at core unlovable, that cause the most pain to those who have elected to use the system of shame avoidance. It is this section of the populace that Kaufman has described as living with *internalized shame* (1985, 33–69). One can do little or nothing to reduce the history of feeling unloved, the reality of parental neglect and exploitation. But anyone can arrange to be a winner at something, or exercise to become bigger and stronger, purchase goods and services leading to a presentation of self that conveys the image of beauty, or become extremely independent, or develop remarkable sexual prowess, or move into the public eye as an object of positive regard. Anyone who has a sense of personal defect, the feeling that he or she is unloved because of something that really cannot be altered, can work to distract our attention away from that supposed defect so that we will concentrate on that of which the individual is proud. And the device chosen, the system through which that person will attempt to turn us away from awareness of such a central defect, will always involve one of the six categories *other* than D and H.

Of course, such preoccupations are independent of any "real" defect, disturbance in the bodily plan, or failure in biological development that might make others better equipped than us. One may grow up blind in a loving environment and become a Helen Keller. Crippled at birth by cerebral palsy, a person might, like Christy Brown, become a celebrated writer; Franklin Delano Roosevelt transcended the paralysis of poliomyelitis to become a world leader. When defect is "merely" another way of being different, when a family refuses to allow a child to feel like a defective person for fault in a bodily system, there is little shame associated with imperfection. And when a real disability can be conquered, the increase in self-esteem so achieved remains with one for life.

CONVENIENT IMPERFECTIONS

The defects and imperfections to which I refer are more subtle. They involve matters such as the minor imperfections that make us individual, the variations in facial or bodily contour that have little meaning unless or until one is searching for something on which to pin one's feelings of inadequacy. Conferring no true debility, they provide rather some sort of psychological relief because they allow us to shift from a general sense of inadequacy to an idea of a discrete and limited failing.

This can construct a topsy-turvy world, as I learned many years ago while interviewing the parents of a 19-year-old recently admitted to the hospital for an acute schizophrenic episode. At 13 she had insisted that a plastic surgeon give her a "better" nose. I asked her mother why the family had encouraged this procedure. "Because we thought it would make her love us more," she answered.

Each era of civilization favors its own system for the remediation of this realm of personal defect; each culture chooses the domains within which we are encouraged to perfect ourselves. A hundred years ago one might exercise with "Indian clubs," which resembled elongated weighted bowling pins, while in my youth Charles Atlas advertised a weight-lifting program that promised to turn a "98-pound weakling" into a "real" man. Later, the Marines offered to "make a man out of you." With each advance in technology we see more and more efficient systems of body development. My local magazine store displays rack upon rack of journals emblazoned with photographs of strikingly muscular men and women, the equipment they used to achieve such brawn, and the disciplines to which they subjected themselves. Some portion of our societal obsession with physical fitness derives from the nearly universal wish to use the development of bulging muscles to diminish the shame that comes from invisible defects.

Are you afraid of personal attack not because we live in an era of physical danger but because you have been brought up to feel like a weak person? Study one of the martial arts—judo, karate, aikido, or boxing. Do you fear exposure of what you feel is a meager intellect? Read any of the books that promises a better vocabulary in 30 days so that you may talk like a more intelligent person. Has the acquisition of wealth, and consequent entry into another realm of society, left you all the more embarrassed about the size or shape of your nose, breasts, buttocks, or chin; the wrinkles rewarding your struggle; a mole or a blemish of any sort? Cosmetic surgery can tailor a new surface for you to show the world.

The search for mastery of any martial art can be rewarding in and of itself; our understanding of the world may indeed be directly proportional to the number of its words we understand; and there is nothing intrinsically wrong with beauty. It is not the goal but the purpose of such quests that must be questioned here. Most of those who undertake the journeys so implied do so with the expectation that the increment in skill, competence, or personal qualities so achieved will produce a happier self. Nearly anybody can learn enough karate to earn some degree of recognition—the problem here is that it may achieve significance only when we seek and find physical danger. Even the act of absorbing a thesaurus often fails to teach us about the world it describes. And plastic surgeons take meticulous before-and-after photographs to prove that the patient did obtain the sought-for physical change, even when the hoped-for emotional lift did not occur.

Children live more in the here-and-now than adults, forgetting in moments of failure their history of success; they need trophies, diplomas, and plaques as palpable evidence of the milestones and triumphs by which they define their ever-changing selves. Most adults live without any need to inform others of their accomplishments—imagine our world were each of us to wear on our sleeve an entire *curriculum vitae*, much as a soldier's dress uniform displays medals and the signs of rank!

Come to think of it, these days literally anything can be printed on a T-shirt. Consider an industry offering to provide clothing that displayed truthfully your name, date of birth, where you went to school, how you did at each grade level, your job history, and the archives of your romantic ventures. In our culture, such an image would be considered bizarre, for it is through such conventions as mode of dress, accent, choice of home and automobile, and type of occupation that normally we make conscious and intentional public definition of ourselves. Most of us want total control over our broadcast image. The intentional exaggeration illuminates my point. The healthiest adults display only themselves and allow us to form our own conclusions about them.

Yet what are we to think of one who lives with a huge cabinet of trophies earned for some activity, or a wall of framed awards, or who leaves all over the living room copies of magazines in which he or she has been featured? Past a certain age or station in life, why is it necessary for some to remind us constantly that they attended one of the most prestigious educational institutions? I do not mean to gainsay anyone the right to be proud of any accomplishment. But no one goes to the trouble and expense of advertisement unless there is something to sell, unless one feels certain that the viewing other might otherwise remain unaware of the self defined by the attribute being exhibited. Frequently, the purpose of such display is to distract the attention of the viewing other toward certain features of the self; the display itself gives much evidence of shame hidden elsewhere.

Often I have worked in therapy with brilliant, successful men and women who were raised in simply terrible, oppressive homes where parental selfishness and cruelty had been embedded in a culture of poverty. In each case there was an instinctive push on the part of my patient to achieve wealth in order to purchase items of quality that defined status—art, antiques, rugs, automobiles, clothing, jewelry, and even a personal jet airplane. Whereas each purchase provided the dollop of pride for which it had been designed, nothing really reduced the immensity of the shame always lurking beneath the carefully presented surface. Eternally shame-sensitive, ever on the alert for any potential slur, any allegation that might reveal the fragility of their self-esteem, they were, as adults, just as brittle and cautious as they had been as children. Such a dependence on the establishment of status through the visibility of wealth has always been called *nouveau riche*. Few people raised in abject humiliation ever learn to step aside from their history and to see their chronic shame in proper perspective.

There are, then, two styles of shame avoidance related to these observations—the acquisition and display of trophies that define a wished-for self and that call to the attention of everybody this new gestalt; and the pressured pursuit of new levels of ability, competence, and wealth in order to prevent recognition of some deeply felt internal defect visible only to the struggling individual. Display and competition can become strategies undertaken to distract both the viewing other and the inner judge.

Were these methods more successful in defining a new self, in eradicating all the shame residing within one who had grown to adult status as an unloved child, one might expect that they would, after a time, simply cease. Tomkins said it well: The incomplete reduction of chronic and enduring shame brings excitement, while the complete reduction brings contentment and surcease (1962, 293). It is the deficiency, the incompleteness, the relative poverty of these techniques for shame avoidance that maintain the individual's affect system in a state of excitement and require ever more costly trophies and quests. Complete relief, the sense of being a loved and whole person, has little to do with such struggle.

Again, I am suggesting more that these time-honored methods of solution for the problems caused by internalized shame are inadequate than that they are unsuccessful. No matter how a man gets to be king, absolute power now makes him beyond shaming censure. (Thus the aphorism "Power corrupts. Absolute power corrupts absolutely.") With enough wealth to build a citadel within which you may be isolated from all but those who salute your excellence, you have evaded shame. What is regarded as deficiency, immaturity, "neurosis," weirdness, instability, or weakness in an "ordinary" person is labeled "eccentricity" and tolerated with grace in the very, very wealthy and powerful.

IDENTIFICATION AND NARCISSISM

Most of us have neither the equipment nor the opportunity to become rich, beautiful, strong, extraordinarily competent at something, to become as independent as a mountain man, or to develop some skill that takes us into the approving eye of the public. It is fascinating to observe that such accidents of fate need not remove us from the ranks of those who can use these techniques of shame avoidance. Identification and narcissism provide two additional routes on our map, two methods by which we wander further and further away from sober acceptance of personal reality. So common are these scripts that we take them for granted as stable forces within society, often overlooking their relation to shame.

What we cannot attain on our own may be admired in distant others with whom we form the peculiar sort of relationship called *identification.* Unable to build into myself certain attributes and powers, I may adopt the self-enhancing fantasy that I share the traits of a cherished idol. As a small child, I may wear the clothing of Superman, Rambo, GI Joe, or Wonder Woman and imagine myself with the wondrous powers and public esteem of that ideal role model. One of the reasons we adults love to read about the great and famous is that the more we know about them, the more we can imagine ourselves living in their world. The deficiencies of our personal identity are somewhat reduced by a fantasized immersion in the identity of someone without those particular defects.

The comic books of my youth told of the crippled newsboy Billy Batson, who could say the magic word *Shazzam!* and turn into the invincible Captain Marvel. Clark Kent is the quintessential nebbish until he reveals himself as the Man of Steel who flies. In an earlier era, when sexual promiscuity ran unchallenged by the current crop of deadly venereal diseases, the James Bond films provided men with a model whose brawn, stealth, courage, sophistication, competitive skill, personal attractiveness, and certainty of his right to be loved and admired were combined with a willingness to accept sexual stimulation as a form of recreation quite free of guilt and shame. The greatest fictional heroes are inversions of the defective self that lies within each of us.

To a large extent, the advertising industry depends on the intensity of the pain caused by chronic shame and our avidity for anything that might make us feel better about ourselves. In its simplest form, the testimonial lets us know that somebody we admire or respect has found some product or service useful and better than its competitors. The use of that entity is therefore linked to the esteemed person. One way we can make ourselves at least a little bit like this valued other is to take on that piece of behavior. In the act of imitation we get to imagine that we share our hero's competence, glory, beauty, or power. Often the advertisement says this quite clearly: "Do what I do and you can be like me," or "You can share this feeling by imitating me."

Transient or temporary identifications of this sort may serve a useful purpose in allowing us to pre-experience some station in life quite capable of attainment; this is one way we prepare ourselves for the future. A young lawyer imagines the kind of boat she will buy when elected a full partner in the firm. Another woman writes over and over again the new name she will bear when marrying her intended. In both cases, anticipation of the event allows easier integration into the new identity. An adolescent boy reviews again and again scenes from the films in which his hero asks a girl for a date, then practices in front of a mirror until the required language and skill become his own.

But what is going on when someone previsualizes what can never occur, pretends to live in a dream that can never be actualized, sees him- or herself as having attributes that do not and plainly cannot exist? Occasionally some child dies jumping from a window ledge in hopeless imitation of Superman. We shake our heads silently at such a misfortune, but "know" with certainty that no adult could do this. Yet some people behave as if they were wealthy when they are not, act as if they were beautiful when they are not, pretend to skills they will neither demonstrate nor attain. To the extent that the altered image is bound to one's identity as a whole and maintained with great urgency, we call this sort of distortion delusional.

If beauty can be bought or mimed and rank assumed by an impostor for the sake of shame, if anyone can lie or whistle care away and thus demolish guilt, if for wounded pride one can attempt any style of sexual performance, and if a publicist can for hire compose a beacon of fame for the most retiring self, then how can disavowal and delusion assist whoever lives in pain for deficiency of love? Shorn by shame from any opportunity to experiment with intimacy, prevented by fear of shame from the risk of love refused, one can pretend to self and others that love exists but far from view. Such is the puzzle presented by certain chronically shy, withdrawn adults who dream secretly that they are loved by the great and famous, but who come to our attention only when some event forces into the clear what previously had been hidden from view.

Called variously *erotomania* or *de Clérambault's syndrome*, and known since antiquity, each of the reported cases I have reviewed suggests the pattern of a chronically shame-bound adult whose inner world is warmed by the secret fires of a thoroughly delusional love. So central to the personality lies the need to be loved, and so deep and intense the shame that is softened by the compensatory delusion, that those so afflicted rarely tolerate the process of relevation, the uncovering normal to psychotherapeutic investigation. Not surprisingly, since attention to shame itself has within my field until quite recently been sporadic and chronically insufficient, none of these patients has ever been treated with specific attention to shame as such. Here is another of the illnesses for which a new approach may be devised in terms of affect theory.

It is interesting that most of those who have discussed erotomania in the psychiatric literature make the observation that it has something to do with narcissism; they mention nothing about shame. No matter how broadly one tries to expand the concept of narcissism, it always bears the faint aroma of self-pampering, of conceit, self-love, and vanity—none of which speaks very well to the type and intensity of affect seen in such a delusional state. In terms of the work presented so far in this chapter, I propose a limited definition: narcissism is the system through which personal attributes are exaggerated in order to avoid shame.

As you know, Freud adopted the Greek legend of Narcissus as the basis for his concept of narcissism. In the original story, this handsome boy grew so infatuated with the image of his face reflected in a pool of water that he became unable to hear the voice of the lovely nymph Echo by his side and wasted away into death while immersed in self-regard. Her name now describes the situation in which we utter sounds that are reflected back to us without interpretation or understanding. In an interpersonal relationship, one cannot have an Echo without a Narcissus. Normal people respond to our utterances, while the narcissistic person seems unable to "take in" the significance of what we have said.

A simple error made by Freud has resulted in a century of confusion about narcissism. Unaware that infant and mother communicate through the language of innate affect, he saw the inability of the newborn to comprehend adult language as analogous to the seeming inability of the narcissist to accept messages from the outside world. This misunderstanding of infants and of the interaction between babies and their caregivers led him and his followers to believe that the infant enters life immersed in something that resembles self-regard. If we recognize that the normal infant is never narcissistic, it becomes clear that adult narcissism is only and always a protection against shame. Narcissism is the name we give to the broad array of scripts through which people prevent themselves from "knowing" about anything that might increase an already unbearable amount of shame.

When we say that someone is narcissistic, we imply the presence of beliefs about the self that cannot be substantiated, broadcasts of information that cannot be confirmed. Each of these convictions contains some kernel of truth, each has something to do with the eight categories of thought listed in Table 5. In order for an individual to be labeled narcissistic, however, the false, embroidered, exaggerated, disproportionately embellished ideas, the "fish stories" involved, must serve the function of drawing attention away from a centrally damaged self-concept. Narcissism is a term that must be reserved for that part of our self-image that would be relinquished were we to accept shame. It is an ill-fitting mask or a badly made toupee (indeed, a mask or toupee of any sort), a girdle or corset designed to show us as we wish to be rather than as we are, a swagger meant to disguise the slump of disgrace, a house full of imitation fine art and fake jewelry, a phony accent, anything we do to call attention to the self we wish to assume rather than the person we are.

Does narcissism imply freedom from shame? Of course not. Humiliation always lies immediately beneath the surface of deceit. Like the towns built for western movies, it is all front and no depth, a situation constructed to give the appearance of normality with little or nothing behind it. It does no good to poke at narcissism unless for some kind of sadistic sport. This is not a minor defense erected against mild distress. Freud spoke of the "stone wall of narcissism." So protected is the individual from the possibility of shame that great segments of reality may be kept from consciousness.

No one can relinquish the apparent power conferred by a false self-image until something within the self has changed, until one experiences real love. Therapists who speak of "confronting narcissistic overevaluation of the self" know little about shame. People do not give up a single narcissistic boast until someone else has built a scaffolding around the structure of their being, conferring upon them enough power through empathic understanding that the false safety of an artificial surface becomes unnecessary.

The sheer extent of the means through which individual attributes can be exaggerated boggles the mind. Nowhere is the creative spirit so wondrously expressed as in our societal search for modes of personal magnification. The fashion industry provides us with ways we can "look our best" and declare our right to some desired level of social status. Whenever we act in a manner designed to impress somebody else, we are attempting to shift attention from something that brings us shame to something that can evoke pride. Automobiles, homes and home furnishing, jewelry, art, even the choice of pets can be used to alter one's place on the shame/pride axis. Upward mobility is often a system of shame avoidance more than an attempt to reach one's true potential. All of these constitute what I have defined here as narcissistic defenses against chronic shame, against the feeling that we can never be loved for ourselves. They are expensive, high-energy compromises for something that cannot be faced.

THE FALSE SELF

Little Rachel lied to her mother by claiming that the sewing machine had suddenly come to life and attacked her. Her lie was simple and obvious. Most of us shade the truth in order to look better to others. I have evaluated a great many scholarly articles about lying and been disappointed to find little or no reference to shame. Since lying usually involves an action that violates social laws, and therefore places one at risk of punishment, it is likely to trigger the form of shame we call guilt. We can lie about minor and trivial matters, just as we can lie to protect friends from unnecessary discomfort. Yet, in my experience, some coassembly of shame is the most frequent precursor to intentional misrepresentation of fact.

There are, however, people whose very identity is a lie, who live with a concept of self so false that they may be seen as impostors. These are the people Ibsen described as existing within a "life lie." Often, too, I am asked to discuss sociopathy, another extreme of apparent shamelessness. How does one get to be a confidence man, a swindler, a seducer, a crook, the kind of person we used to call a psychopath? How can one so thoroughly defeat the representatives of conscience as to live "without shame"? How is it that some people seem so immune to shame that they can do whatever they want without fear of the pain that afflicts the rest of us?

Over the years that I have been in the clinical practice of psychiatry, I have worked in therapy with several such patients. Some have spent time in prison, others in bankruptcy, most (if not all) have been chronically unable to sustain any form of authentically intimate relationship. Those who see these people as free from shame do not know how to look for shame. In each case I have been impressed by the roaring fires of shame that live at the core of the self. For such people, lies provided more solace than had ever been received from their falsely nurturant childhood milieu. It is true that most of these patients were relatively free from the stigmata of fear, of conventional anxiety. But they lived with so much shame that it had become the center of their lives. The personality, the adopted role they showed the outside world, existed only as a thin veneer pasted over a sickly core.

So far as I can determine, the sociopath uses an *avoidance* script as if it were a model for life itself. Yet even a veneer of sophistication pasted over a core of shame is better than nothing; avoidance has its rewards. Not, though, from uncovering psychotherapy. Sometimes an individual simply cannot imagine dealing with the pain of inner looking, of self-examination, of entry into the "arena of shame" described by Anthony as the therapeutic environment. This synthetic character structure does not wear well. Those who use this dodge cannot sustain intimacy because they cannot allow anyone to peek beneath their cover; any revelation, any opening into the core, places them at risk.

What risk? You and I, when exposed or revealed or put down, suffer from shame triggered by the memories contained in Table 5 as they are organized into the scripts of the compass of shame. Difficult as that may be, it does not even begin to bear comparison to the highly magnified shame-based memories of the sociopath. Earlier, I described the "borderline" patient as one for whom shame had become a destructive force quite early in development. Working in therapy with a sociopath is very much like therapy with a "borderline" patient or someone with a dissociative illness like multiple personality disorder. In all of these conditions shame has magnified the danger of inner looking, made it easier for the patient to run and hide than to sit and ponder.

There are others who live with a core of shame covered over with the veneer of sophistication. Many of the most successful men and women in our society fulfill my criteria for this diagnosis. Often we call them "workaholics" or say that they are "driven to succeed." Scratch the surface of the desperately driven business tycoon, the philandering politician, the relentlessly busy surgeon who cannot afford to slow down for a moment, the empire builder, the famous lawyer known as well for his adulterous lifestyle as for his flamboyant courtroom tactics, the religious leader who seems more interested in his image than his message—drill an exploratory hole into the inner lives of any of these icons of our culture and you are likely to tap a gusher of shame handled by *avoidance.* "Look at me," they say, "but look only where I tell you to look."

COMPARISON AND COMPETITION

Since so much of our self-concept is derived from comparison with others, and since it is through the medium of competition that we set up purposeful systems of comparison, it stands to reason that shame stemming from some perceived but irremediable deficiency of the self can be mitigated by shifting attention toward the pride and status achieved when one wins at something. Directly proportional to the amount of energy devoted to competition is always the degree of chronic shame linked to a persistently lowered self-image.

It is obvious, of course, that there are people whose athletic gifts confer on them the special ability to excel in areas where we ordinary mortals struggle, to soar where we trudge. And it might be suggested that for them competition has little or nothing to do with activity around the shame/pride axis, that victory produces triumph that has no meaning outside the specific contest in which it was achieved, and that losing is viewed only as a learning experience—a pleasant encounter with someone of superior ability. Such people, the theory might state, play games only for the joy of feeling their bodies work at peak performance, see their opponents as equals and friends, and look forward to each encounter with joyful anticipation of good, clean fun. This, I maintain, is sheer nonsense.

No one with such an attitude would bother to play games very much. All the "fun" of games, the interplay of affects that makes sports worthwhile or even exciting, is dependent on the oscillation between negative and positive affect. I hold a capitalist or entrepreneurial view of athleticism. If losing produces no negative affect, if winning does not provide exultation over that negative affect, then there is no urgency, no affective magnification capable of making competition rewarding. Few people engage in hard work without any expectation of a reward.

Haven't we always said that people constantly involved in competition are "trying to prove something"? Winning defines a new sense of self that is to a great degree temporary simply because victory is declared by an outer judge, while the inner judge is more interested in the big issue—"Why am I not loved?" Yet the good feeling that comes from winning is a powerful painkiller, one that attracts the attention of huge masses of people.

The employees of most large corporations organize clubs for athletic competition—bowling, softball, judo, arm wrestling, tennis, and whatever else catches the fancy of a group. These clubs become affinity groups that purchase clothing that links together their members and advertises that they are part of a loving family; teams have "home courts," travel in groups to "away" games, and meet regularly for practice. Associations like country clubs, private skating clubs, racquet clubs, karate dojos, and a wide variety of others all provide opportunities for personal competition befitting a wide range of social classes and customs.

Here in Philadelphia there are dozens of neighborhood clubs that expend enormous amounts of time and money to compete in the annual Mummer's Day Parade. Many of these have been in existence for over a century; membership is a cherished right handed down in families. And no matter what the function of a social organization, within the group itself will be much jockeying for positions of leadership. There may be no realm of our society without several analogous opportunities for competition. Our individual, personal involvement in such combat is sanctioned or legitimized by the ubiquity of the opportunities to compete.

Listen carefully to what is said during any of these competitions and you will learn a great deal about pride and shame. Play, in the sense of carefree abandon, has no place in these games. The participants are clearly involved in a leisure-time activity with tremendous urgency of purpose. One of the nice things about games is that they have distinct beginnings and endings, that they provide the possibility of shame or pride at predictable times. Whereas the feeling of being loved cannot be scheduled, bureaucratic systems see to it that our sporting matches conform to the needs of all the businesses and people involved.

More evidence that competition can be an attempt to avoid shame, a distraction from perceived inner weakness, an analogue of narcissism? Why else do so many people hire coaches, pay for lessons, read books and magazines that purport to improve their record in competition, rent or buy training films and videotapes? What else might excuse an extraordinary level of expenditure on sporting clothes? What about all the people who are so determined to win that they cheat at games, rig sporting events, pay bribes to gain public office, or fix elections? Competition means a great deal to those who use it as a system for the verification of competence.

BORROWED PRIDE

Nevertheless, to the extent that we are unable by our own efforts to demonstrate our competence, thus giving ourselves a sense of healthy pride, or to fake efficacy and achieve false pride, what we seem to do is borrow pride and prestige through some sort of identification with others whose efficacy we admire. Nowhere in contemporary Western society is the preoccupation with shame and pride to be as easily seen or studied as in our preoccupation with public sporting spectacles.

The overwhelming majority of the population, unable to participate in competitive sports and certainly unable to feel like winners, must satisfy its need to win through the vicarious experience of competition. Those of us who cannot or dare not compete on our own can hire others to fight or play or contend in our stead. The fabled kings of old, whose absolute power commanded the actions of their subjects, might find it entertaining to order into mortal combat one or another of their knights. Today it is the immense wealth of powerful businessmen or groups of investors working in concert that addresses and outfits the armies of our professional teams. It is by our purchase of tickets or through our patronage of those whose advertisements pay for television coverage of our favorite teams that we become personally involved in their exploits. Commercial sports events have taken hold of the public imagination to the extent that media coverage of them can make up the majority of our weekend reading and viewing.

What motivates such extraordinary expenditure of time, money, and energy on the public display of sports as entertainment? Even the television crews who broadcast the games have become interested in the audience, for the audience itself has become a participant in the overall spectacle. More and more people attend games that will be telecast in the hope that viewers will see them in the audience; to maximize the possibility of being noticed they wear theatrical costumes, make banners and signs, organize cheering sections and devise stunts—all to catch the attention of the television crew. It would seem that the average person feels so invisible, so fungible, that merely being seen on television is an efficacy experience.

When the relatively new and inexperienced local franchise of the professional hockey association won its first championship, two million people formed a conga line dancing through the streets of our city screaming its joy in victory. Whatever sense of inadequacy relative to any other person in our lives (or relative to any other city, or anything which creates in us a sense of lowered self-esteem and therefore chronic enduring shame) will be turned to joy in victory, the intensity of the joy directly proportional to the intensity and duration of the preceding chronic shame.

Yet it is not our own individual self-esteem that has been raised, but only our estimation of ourselves as we identify with our gladiators. Failing in our lifelong quest for the experience of efficacy in the context of interest–excitement or enjoyment–joy, we borrow pride from those we hire. Strangers, paid to perform in competition for teams whose aggregate skill is kept within precise limits by bureaucratic organizations, become regular household figures for the legion of those who dare not compete for fear of being ranked or who feel themselves so much the loser in competition that they must identify with a winner. By far the most important reason people invest so heavily in public displays of athletic endeavor is the role of such activity in allowing outward displacement of tension deriving from activity along the shame/pride axis.

STRATEGIES TO REDUCE SHAME

This really happened to me: I was 19, working on a research project in experimental embryology at the Marine Biological Laboratory in Woods Hole, Massachusetts. In retrospect, it was a summer of triumph for a terribly shy adolescent—my first published scientific paper, a leading role in the local summer stock production of Noel Coward's *Hay Fever*, and the winner's trophy at the regional Ping-Pong tournament. But if you asked what affected me most I would probably turn beet red and tell you about Elissa.

She was blond, lovely, attentive, fascinated by my research, and able to turn me from Earth's most incompetent dancer into someone quite willing to take a turn around the floor. We spent a wonderful amount of time together. This was the early 1950s, well before the sexual revolution, and kissing represented the epitome of our amorous activities. But kiss we did, and for me it was an incredible experience. Even Martin, two years older, taller, better looking, more "experienced," and the proprietor of a larger laboratory and a bigger grant, was forced to acknowledge my good fortune at finding so lovely a companion.

Leaving my laboratory late one night, I spotted a desk light in Martin's office and walked over to confer with him about some now long-forgotten idea. There I found him locked in passionate embrace with my Elissa. His was a reaction of mild guilt and evident triumph, while she hid her head in shock and shame. As for me, I was barely able to breathe for the pain that suffused every fiber of my being.

For the first time in my life, I walked immediately to the neighborhood tavern, where I took an unaccustomed seat at the bar and stared wordlessly at the bartender. I have no idea what he saw in my face, but without any further clue he placed before me a double shot of bourbon, which I swallowed in a gulp. Once again he filled my glass, once again I downed my medicine. Feeling immensely better and not a whit inebriated, I paid up and left without talking to anyone.

The obvious questions: Does massive humiliation have its own special facial expression, one best known to bartenders? How did he know that I "needed a drink"? Why did it help? Why didn't I feel drunk after an amount of alcohol that might have leveled me at any other time?

The answers are less interesting than the questions. If you walk into a bar, the chances are that you have already decided that you need or want a drink. Bartenders are like auctioneers—the latter interpret your nonverbal gestures as meaning "bid" or "no bid", the former interpret them as "drink" or "no drink." Why it helped is quite another matter.

The relation between shame and alcohol has been known since antiquity. (I have heard it said that, save for two isolated aboriginal cultures, every society on the planet has spontaneously found caffeine, nicotine, and alcohol. It seems as if the biological nature of the affect system leaves us vulnerable to certain recurrent noxious experiences that are ameliorated by these chemicals.) The

Latin proverb, *in vino veritas* (in wine there is truth), indicates both that shame affect can teach us to hold our tongue and that alcohol can unleash it. Booze is forever "allowing" us to say what we "shouldn't."

It is in the cultures that are the most afflicted by shame that we see the greatest amount of personality change with alcohol. The rules of Japanese society require absolute control over affective display lest any leak of feeling cause loss of face and therefore great shame. Yet, when drunk, Japanese are effusive.

Léon Wurmser once commented to me that "in Sweden there is a kind of great resentment about those who reach above mediocrity. Ingrained in the popular consciousness of many European democracies is an intense emphasis on equality, an attitude which is enemy to competition. In Europe one is really ashamed if one tries to win, if one does win." Dr. Wurmser described a Swedish novel about the people of a "narrow, petty, bourgeois town where everybody who refused to accept the views of the majority would be ostracized, where any deviation from the norm might produce envy and resentment against the one who is better. In such a society, to exceed the norm produces shame." And, in such a society, the risk of alcoholism is equally great.

Physiologists say that alcohol has a "disinhibiting effect," that it acts as a "releaser" of emotion or of action. People are more likely to get angry when drunk, more likely to fight, to speak with feeling. It seems reasonable to assume that one of the primary actions of alcohol is to release us from the bonds of shame, that it is a "shamolytic" agent. We can take courage from a bottle because whatever reticence prevents us from action will be reduced by booze. Perhaps, to some degree, fear also is soluble in alcohol. But to the greatest extent, it is the shame-based painful inhibition of action that is soothed by alcohol.

That probably helps answer the last of the questions I raised a moment ago—why I didn't feel drunk after a dose of alcohol far in excess of my normal limit. Within certain limits, alcohol works pretty well to reduce the pain of shame, and we need the medicine in direct proportion to the amount of pain. Obviously, when the source of the pain disappears, we can start to feel how much we have drunk; then, too, we can overestimate the amount of alcohol needed and drink past the medicinal level of effectiveness.

So one of the ways people can decrease the occasional acute bout of shame is to use alcohol. It doesn't work as well for chronic enduring shame, as any member of Alcoholics Anonymous will be glad to explain. But, to an extent, most of us will, on occasion, drown our sorrows in alcohol. It reduces a variety of nonspecific tensions quite well, although I suspect that the majority of them are related to shame anyway.

Take, for instance, the ubiquitous social gathering called "a party." Most of us are at least a little shy, afraid to talk with strangers (even, occasionally, with friends) at first. Alcohol is served as an "ice breaker." (The affect fear–terror makes us cold.) Our use of metaphors like "cold" and "warm" indicates the extent to which anticipated, feared embarrassment interferes with the warm, pleasant interchange afforded by mutual interest–excitement and enjoyment–joy. Here, too, we drink to reduce shame.

But have you ever taken a couple of drinks in one of those rare moments when you were in a really good mood, when nothing was bothering you, when you actually felt calm? Then alcohol only makes us dog tired, unpleasantly unable to function. Unless there is a negative affect in need of control, alcohol is a sedating agent, one that reduces our ability to function in any situation that requires critical thinking. It is like most medicines in that it works when we are sick and produces little more than side effects when we are not.

For this reason, there is a lot of confusion about the nature of "fun." The moral philosophy of *hedonism* suggests that it is okay to pursue anything that feels good. Every few years or so a new drug is released, its inventors promising that it can take us from boredom to ecstasy in moments without risk of danger. What most people do not understand is that these drugs only "work" if one starts out in a really bad mood. All of them make you feel simply terrible if you start out feeling good. Hedonism, then, is usually a way of decreasing chronic shame and distress, rather than a search for pleasure. It represents an attempt to avoid whatever might be learned from introspective study of the lessons to be learned from shame.

There are other ways to substitute hedonism for shame. Joy-rides, thrill-seeking, dangerous pastimes of any sort, and a host of other activities form the macho system of defense in which excitement and anger substitute for shame. In many respects, the use of certain drugs, like cocaine and the amphetamines, can represent an attempt to escape shame through the pharmacologic instigation of excitement. Sometimes this excitement is used for its own sake, occasionally to power some suddenly interesting activity, and often it is used for the pharmacological enhancement of sexuality. Sexual arousal, so deeply enmeshed in the world of affect, provides an excellent way to avoid shame.

SEXUAL SCRIPTS FOR THE AVOIDANCE OF SHAME

Return, once again, to Table 5 and look at category F, the part of shame that has to do with sexuality. So much shame and pride are associated with sex. A man or woman with a new lover often walks with lilting step, head raised high, eyes twinkling, interested in everything around, ready to find pleasure every-where, broadcasting to the world a newly confirmed certainty of sexual competence. Much more is involved than pure sexuality, for approval in this critical area of the self can generalize, can spread from the exclusively sexual to other areas of the person. In short, sexual competence can either make us forget about other areas of inadequacy or at least make them seem less important for the moment.

This is a perfect situation for those whose sense of self has been wounded in ways that cannot be repaired easily. So it is that many people will broadcast sexual availability and interest as a distraction (for self and other) from more deeply internalized shame. There are many trades available here. Should a young woman be willing to dress, walk, talk, dance, and gesture in an overtly sexual manner, she will swap her "reputation" for power with men. She can tolerate the "bad names" she is called because this behavior is under her own control—this particular type of shame is far easier to accept than what she has felt within her nuclear family. Her sexual partner is likely to be a young man who makes clear that his interest in a woman has only to do with her sexual availability and that he is but marginally interested in her as a fellow human with whom he might commune as an equal. What he gains in sexual experience he will lose in the realm of empathic relatedness.

Yet those who engage in these transactions are usually people who have already been so injured in the area of self-esteem that they see their conduct only as a victory over the shame of seeming undesirable. This is the world of machismo, in which fear of being unloved or unlovable leads women to become teasing, histrionic, flirtatious, seductive, or "sexy" in an attempt to guarantee attention rather than provide introduction to a lasting relationship. It is male machismo, the world of bravery for the sake of attention, danger for notoriety, sexual advertisement for the purpose of creating an aura of generalized competence and personal pride.

The best place to study the processes involved is not the consultation room of a psychiatrist but the racks of your neighborhood magazine store. One after another, the covers of these slick publications show beautiful women scantily and alluringly dressed for seductions that they have engineered from scripts laid out for them in the accompanying text. These are training manuals for female machismo. Accompanying them are the equivalent journals for men, which feature the clothing, facial attitudes, language, and behavior necessary for masculine involvement in the culture of machismo.

CAN PEOPLE CHANGE?

Nobody uses these systems of *avoidance* unless they prevent or reduce pain so noxious that there seems no other way of handling it. Unless you are one of those who believes that shame is good for people, don't merely confront someone who uses these devices. In the main, you are dealing with people who have been exposed to so much shame at critical points in early development that their entire expectational set for intimacy includes the idea of rupture. If you try to explain that they are using self-defeating tricks to avoid shame, they are likely to prevent further interaction with you.

When I work with those whose methods of handling shame fall into this group of scripts, it seems essential to define the nature of shame with great care, describing in miniature what we have worked so long in this book to develop. Usually they are glad to know that others find shame painful as well. It is important to explain that, given their particular history, it really is easy to understand why they might try too hard to avoid shame. Also is it helpful to explain that each of us suffers shame, that it is not something known only to "sick people," and that they do not need to feel inferior to the apparently calm, apparently superior therapist.

One final group of scripts remains. We must now turn our attention to those who handle shame by attacking others through the techniques of putdown, ridicule, contempt, and character assassination. These are the people in our society most of us find truly dangerous, for no one can really avoid shame successfully, and we live at risk of their wrath. Those who must attack rather than withdraw make our common turf into a terrain of danger.

26

ATTACK OTHER

Join me at the movies for a while. Here is actor Clint Eastwood, a handsome, athletic man famous for two signature characteristics—the impassive face that accompanies his emotionless delivery, and the off-repeated line ("Go ahead. Make my day.") that precedes his explosions into deadly violence. On another screen we see Charles Bronson, whose best-known roles show him as a mild-mannered and courteous gentleman who bears with grace the insults of a marauding world until some critical point is reached and he bursts into a murderous rampage. More recently, such actors as Arnold Schwarzenegger, Sylvester Stallone, and Chuck Norris have established stable characterizations of protagonists whose superb physical conditioning and skill at the martial arts allow them to erupt into savage fury to protect themselves and others from indignity. Milder examples? Pause, for a moment, over the scene in the film *Network,* in which Peter Finch plays television personality Howard Beale, who cracks under the strains of life and exhorts the members of his wide, unseen audience to open their windows and shout, "I'm as mad as hell and I'm not going to take this anymore."

For men only? "Hell hath no fury like a woman scorned," reads the old adage. Despite that men will kill for reasons other than revenge or the remediation of humiliation, films rarely show a woman committing murder for any other motive. Occasionally brutal toward physical inferiors, like children or slaves, and sadistic toward those who are bound to them by other ties, women in the cinema are likely to be portrayed as exhibiting cruelty only when shame has driven them mad. (Indeed, one of our cultural gender stereo-types defines violent conduct as normal for men and abnormal for women.) Although Bette Davis was famous for her scorn, no actress, to my knowledge, has been willing to limit her career to roles in which she explodes with deadly force. Yet there is a broad range of situations in which women attack with other weapons. In *Dangerous Liaisons*, for example, Glenn Close won the Oscar as best actress for her portrayal of a marquise who engineered the death and destruction of many as revenge against a man whose withdrawal from their relationship caused her unbearable humiliation.

Turn your attention from films to sports: A "bad loser" is someone who gets angry after competitive failure. Golfers often throw or break clubs after a bad shot; undisciplined table tennis players will smash their paddles against the edge of the table (ruining both paddle and table) when particularly humiliated by failure; the fights that break out between professional hockey and football players are so commonplace that we think of them as part of the game itself. Such behavior is only rarely restrained—famed coach Vince Lombardi said, "Show me a good loser and I'll show you a loser."

Am I asking that the reader develop tunnel vision and see only shame? At first glance one might say that there is much more here than the association between shame and anger. Everyone who has ever watched a toddler knows that children learn quite early that anger can be used as an instrument for the accomplishment of goals unreachable during milder moments. Isn't the anger of athletes merely "frustration"? Don't bad people "deserve" to be attacked by their victims? Notwithstanding the power of such long-standing truisms, when you really study the wide range of interpersonal situations in which we see anger erupt, shame seems to figure in almost all of them.

Miscellaneous associations: An old Chinese proverb suggests that "he who lands the first blow was the first to run out of arguments." In the Old West, a gun was called an "equalizer"; only the shame associated with physical inferiority can explain such a use of language. A fleeting scene from a nameless movie remembered only for this interaction: The chronicle of an adolescent girl emerging from terrible shyness into normal interaction, it showed her at a high school dance, able to feel whole and alive for the first time. "Do you put your hair up at night?" she asked the most popular girl in the school while whirling past her in some complex dance routine. "Of course," came the reply. Our newly confident young woman responded "Better put it up higher. It looks like the dog got at it!" With this gesture, our heroine actually defined her new self by stating that she felt able to compete with the leader of the pack. The movie is teaching its viewers that we are not mature until we can attack others, until we are capable of increasing our own self-esteem at the expense of others.

Yet few of us go through life doing nothing but diminishing others. Most of us are reluctant to belittle, disparage, deprecate, threaten, or actually injure people unless and until some intensely private point of no return has been reached and passed. It is the myriad of scripts that spell out for each of us this system of reaction to shame that I group under the classification *attack other*, and that will occupy our attention in this chapter. There are three areas of enquiry: What sort of stimuli act as triggers to attack, and what are the conditions for its release? What is the range of reactions involved? How do these reactions alter our inner and our outer world?

TRIGGERS AND CONDITIONS

Those who are able to accept all the uncomfortable thoughts listed in Table 5 withdraw into some private space so that shame can run its course. When we agree to accept shame within relationships that demand deference it is because we most fear isolation or abandonment. And when no portion of the shame experience is tolerable, we use the strategies of *avoidance* to prevent or attenuate the affect. On what portion of our list must we focus to understand the scripts and politics of attack?

Look again at category A. For many people, it is when we feel most brittle about the adequacy of what classical psychoanalysis calls the "body ego" that we favor the use of *attack other* scripts. The earliest ways we come to know ourselves, these are primitive matters, clearly related to core issues of personal identity associated with our physical and mental equipment. They are the concerns that define us in relation to others on the basis of size, strength, ability, and skill—concerns about whether we feel large or small, strong or weak, proficient or incompetent, articulate or dumb. These are the realms of self-definition most associated with real danger to life and limb.

In the chapters on the nature of the self and the relation between shame affect and the sense of self, I pointed out that shame quite early becomes linked with the idea of an incompetent self. Further, I presented the idea that the earlier in development one could trace the link between shame and a particular personal attribute, the more primitive and unmodulated was our affective reaction likely to be. If something happens that makes us feel like a child in danger, as adults we react to this threat with all the power and skill developed since childhood.

When called into play, the compensatory mechanism usually involves what Wurmser (1981) calls "turning the tables" on the other person. These are the reactions that best conform to the idea of "talionic law." Have we have been made to feel small? The other will be made to feel even smaller. Have we been made the butt of a joke, laughed at by others? Then the rebuttal will reduce our tormentor even further. Is it a matter of wit or strength? The ensuing repartee will be characterized by barbs or blows tossed with increasing fervor until someone cries "uncle!" Has life itself been placed in seeming jeopardy? Then death must come to whomever has threatened us.

In Act 5, Scene 8 of *Macbeth*, Macduff and Macbeth are trading insults during swordplay. Macbeth says:

> I will not yield,
> To kiss the ground before young Malcolm's feet,
> And to be baited with the rabble's curse. . . .
> . . . Before my body
> I throw my warlike shield. Lay on, Macduff,
> And damn'd be him that first cries, "Hold, enough!"

Not too many years ago, "The Incredible Hulk," a popular comic book, was turned into a television series. The premise underlying both is elegant and simple: David Banner, a mild-mannered physician, had narrowly escaped death in an automobile accident. His beloved wife, however, was trapped inside the car and killed; Banner's normal human strength was not sufficient to allow him to rescue her before it burst into flames and exploded. Dr. Banner's helpless, impotent rage was piteous, even more so because, as a physician, he has a special relation with life and death. Shortly afterwards, in a laboratory accident, Banner received a dose of radiation that changed his metabolism so that, each time he becomes angry, he turns into a hulking green monster. The Hulk can rip the door from a car as easily as he can toss a tree or bend a rod of steel.

Yet Dr. Banner remains mild-mannered, save for the rare moments when someone tries to intimidate or humiliate him and he becomes angry. Then he is temporarily transformed into an immensely powerful humanoid creature with the emotional and intellectual maturity of an infant. ("Don't make me angry," he says to an obnoxious, persistent, enquiring reporter who suspects he is the Hulk. "You wouldn't like me if I got angry.") It is as if David Banner is given the choice between witless power and powerless wit. Like so many highly successful fictional characters, the Incredible Hulk is all of us who have ever writhed in silent rage at our inability to demolish a persecuting enemy or chafed at the injustices to which we are forced to submit.

Rarely has there been so clear a statement of the transition to the set of scripts housed at the attack other pole of the compass of shame as that made by the heartless television producer Diane Christianson in the opening scenes of the film *Network*. In the speech that prepares the audience to accept Howard Beale's aforementioned exhortation for the visible demonstration of disgust and rage, she tells her staff about the shift in public attitudes she has predicted:

> The American people are turning sulky. They've been clobbered on all sides by Viet Nam, Watergate, the inflation, the depression. They've turned off, shot up, and they've fucked themselves limp, and nothing's helped. This concept analysis concludes the American people want someone to articulate their rage for them.

The shift from shame to rage carries a significant degree of risk. Notwithstanding our wish for power, we are all afraid of the Hulk within us. Earlier, when we discussed *The Terminator*, it was clear that this murderous metal-framed robot was incapable of emotion, even though it had been given intelligence and strength of the highest order. Yet the Terminator attacked only those targets for which it had been programmed; the more primitive Hulk has little control over its actions.

In the normal adult, strength has developed in tandem with intelligence, both tempered by the presence of an affect system. Shame usually prevents, protects us from, rage because the affect comes to form such coassemblies as reticence, anticipatory guilt, remorse, and the understanding that public awareness of our rage-filled misdeeds might lead to rejection. Rage triggered by shame, then, is a paradoxical formation.

We are looking for the chain of events (a sequence stored within a script) that can undo the normal social training responsible for this inhibition. Any switch into the *attack other* mode of functioning can occur only after such a string has acted like the combination of digits that opens a lock. The trigger is learned, rather than innate. As I indicated above, it is something that makes us feel like a child in danger, one who cannot expect protection from a loving other, and one who must mount a solitary defense against increasing peril.

It is, of course, only when we feel unloved that the presence of a defect becomes a matter of concern. When narcissism allows us to employ the face-saving formulas of self-deception, or when other methods of *avoidance* permit us to remain functionally ignorant of our defects or to distract others from what might in different circumstances bring us shame, we can live in relative comfort within the larger world—even though we are still defective. But occasionally some accident of life will deny us the privilege of avoidance, or a ruthless foe may strip from us the layers of covering that provide solace. Then we are left both bare and unloved, suddenly endangered and in need of forceful protection.

Look again at our table of shame cognitions. In the situations we are discussing, the thoughts that cause the most pain are those of weakness, smallness, incompetence, clumsiness, and stupidity. If all else pales in significance alongside those issues, then any strategy that attenuates these painful thoughts will be acceptable, even if it risks the acceptance of ideas that belong to the other categories. In a burst of rage we prove our power, competence, and size, even though the previously intimate other may be forced to reel away from us. The alienating rage that repairs one form of shame is likely to leave us alone and unloved, shorn of personal companionship, highly visible, ugly, and cursed with a form of sexuality in which we experience no mutuality. In short, rage cures one part of shame while it magnifies most of the problems associated with the remainder of it.

Clearly, then, category A must contain scripts in which the noxious quality of shame is highly magnified—so much so that one is willing to suffer loss in other aspects of life in order to reduce this toxicity. The vicissitudes of life ensure that some portions of our self-image are more important than others.

Think, for a moment, about what might be going on inside the mind of a person who is being subjected to a humiliating encounter. A recent Stan Hunt cartoon from *The New Yorker* suggests this process: In the foreground we see two balding, middle-aged, well-dressed businessmen engaged in an incongruous fist fight; on the floor lie their cocktail glasses, their spectacles, and a table lamp. Around and behind them are the other guests, gowned and dressed for a posh party, all standing by in various attitudes of polite disbelief. The caption is spoken by one of the observers to another: "Well, they started exchanging wisecracks, then good-natured barbs, then openly hostile barbs, and then blows." Why? As one taunt follows another, layer upon layer of self-esteem is ripped away until something shifts.

On the basis of the interactions I have studied, it seems to me that the decision to enter the realm of *attack other* scripts and to advance from one form of attack to another depends at least partially on our assessment of the interpersonal relationship involved. If the all-powerful king calls me a stupid idiot, a worthless clod devoid of intellect, an impotent sexless castrate, an ugly defective loser, and a traitor worthy only of exile, I may have no choice other than to defer to his judgment. ("Surely Your Serene Highness, although always accurate in his analysis, is having a bad day.") My ability to sense and test the reality of my existence declares the uselessness of protest and the essential need for submission.

Should a similar opinion be voiced by someone whose inferiority to me is a condition of his or her existence, like one of lower military rank or a prisoner over whom I stand guard, the range of choices is wider. The shaming other may be acting from a truly masochistic script, within which I am expected to provide further reduction by "putting him in his place." Alternatively, this other person may be so far below me in power that I may overlook the attempted reduction, as if to say that the insult is too trivial to bear notice. This "good-natured" and tolerant attitude toward the taunts and boasts children throw at their elders is considered part of normal kindness.

But should these insults be delivered by an authentic rival, I am likely to respond with more energy, especially when I cannot afford any shift in the balance of power between us. In order to attack that particular other I must have decided that his or her actions alter our relationship to such an extent that different rules now obtain. The shift produced by these actions may even remove someone from the category of those with whom I have an intimate tie. This person has proved not only to be dangerous, but to be no longer truly loyal, or worthy of my trust, or for me, or operating in my best interests, and therefore can and must be attacked. Often the purpose of the attack is to return this person to a more "normal" identity, both to him- or herself and relative to me.

In short, then, for someone to shift into the *attack other* mode of functioning the following conditions must be met: (1) The individual must feel endangered by the depths to which his or her self-esteem has been reduced; (2) this danger, regardless of the realm of the self in which it was initiated, must then be viewed as if it really derived from one of the items in category A, the body-ego; (3) the person must have grown up in a family system or some sort of environment that permits or encourages the use of attack to handle such forms of danger; and finally (4) the value and the importance of whatever interpersonal relationship had existed previously are critically reduced by the actions of the other.

RANGE OF REACTIONS

Think of all the mean things you have ever heard about all the ways people have hurt the feelings, body, career, public image, and relationships of others. Anything capable of bringing discomfort can be used to reduce one's personal experience of shame by forcing it on someone else. The concept of discomfort can stretch from mischief and malaise to mayhem and murder. The choice of weapons and the degree of meanness involved are a measure of the perpetrator's preexisting pain. Shame induced is directly proportional to shame feared and detested.

You may attack another person with an army, with a couple of hired thugs, with a gun, a baseball bat, your bare fists or fingernails, a slap in the face, a communicable illness, a curse, an insult, a contemptuous sneer, a barely raised eyebrow, by refusing to acknowledge a friendly greeting, by cutting that person from your social circle, or by requiring of one's friends that they, too, snub or shun your enemy. Each of these gestures can be experienced as an attack. It is the range and style of attack that concern us here.

Casual inspection reveals that any attribute, power, or ability may be used as a source, technique, or vehicle for attack. Neocortical cognition can allow us to conceive in the mind any number of plots against another person. The subcortical affect system can be used to treat that person with anger, disgust, or dissmell to produce distress, fear, or shame. We can kick, hit with fist or elbow, butt, or wrestle into submission the object of our anger; if our power over the other person is great enough we can show contempt by urinating on or smearing with feces whoever must be reduced to the status of an execrable thing.

The happiest use of the generative system involves the mutualization of arousal, excitement, and contentment in sexual activity; yet sex can be used as a weapon over a range from mild hostility to outright rape. The habit of cruelty to a dependent other is known as sadism. Rarely limited in practice to the sexual behavior described first in the novels of the Marquis de Sade, this form of attack is designed both to maintain connection with a chosen partner and to demonstrate the degree to which the perpetrator remains ascendent over the victim.

Do you wish to study the *attack other* form of reaction to shame? You have only to spend the evening watching television. On one show after another you will see people attacking each other in all of the ways described above. Words by which you might describe these attacks include, but are by no means limited to: Bully, blackmail, slander, put-down, ridicule, disdain, sarcasm, scorn, derision, mockery, satire, burlesque, haughtiness, criticism, censure, supercil-iousness, scoffing, sneering, slurs, vituperation, caustic, asperity, venom, viru-lence, viciousness, spite, petulance, cynicism, scathing, harsh, malevolent, ma-lignant, hateful, insulting, excoriating, abusive, corroding, surly, and contemptuous. Each of these terms describes a process by which some aspect of another person is reduced, abraded, diminished, abased, abashed, destroyed, hurt, dashed, daunted, dispirited, lessened, depreciated, belittled, disparaged, discredited, defamed, weakened, blunted, lessened, devalued, blemished, tar-nished, injured, punished, or inconvenienced. The study of the *attack other* mode is an exercise through which we come to appreciate the extraordinary range of human creativity.

When the purpose of attack is to induce in the other the affects of shame, dissmell, and disgust, the methods used can be marvelously subtle or terribly broad. They can gratify the needs of the attacker by their delicacy or by their intensity. The factors that govern both style and intensity of attack are related to highly personal scripts operating far from the conscious mind of the subject.*

To live in the world and to interact with others always brings risk of shame, from the momentary twinge of embarrassment at the most minor of slips to the mortification that accompanies massive public failure. We ourselves will continue to experience shame in some degree as long as we draw breath; one of the tasks of living involves the need to handle our own personal shame over its immense and varied range of presentation. But of even more importance here is the fact that wherever we go in life we are forced to be in the presence of others whose response to their own private pangs of shame may well be in the *attack other* mode. Maturity and safety in the world at large demand that we learn some degree of restraint in our response to the taunts and slurs offered by those whose personal shame had nothing to do with us until we entered their orbit.

These are the moments when a telephone operator addresses our complaint by uttering a string of curses and cutting us off; when someone bumps into us in the street for no apparent reason; when a driver cuts you off or makes a sudden move that demonstrates the power and handling capability of his or her car but waves to you with upraised middle finger; when a clerk suddenly and unaccountably tells you to "go to hell" and simply stomps off. It is garbage dumped down the elevator shaft of an apartment house, graffiti on public buildings, cyanide placed in food or medicine to be purchased by the innocent, the incessant battle of the haves and the have-nots. It is about power used to erase the sting of weakness and disgrace—the "burn, baby, burn" of Watts rather than "build, baby, build." It is the leavening influence of envy that seeks to find some null state of entropy in which we are all equally disadvantaged.

Sometimes it is easier to study the trivial than the extreme examples of a process. Here is a minor, everyday scene that I witnessed just the other day. Its very unimportance makes it ideal for our purposes, for the study of shaming interaction.

In a commercial district not far from my office, I observed two men arguing in a parking lot, their voices rising in volume but remaining below the level of

---

*I have discussed these "shaming systems in couples, families, and institutions" in an earlier contribution (1987b).

shouting, the tone of their conversation ranging between truculent and sneering. The customer was upset that the attendant had refused to park his brand-new, shiny, expensive automobile in the most protected part of the lot and made known to the attendant his displeasure:

ATTENDANT: I don't give a good fuck where you want to park that mother-fucking car. It goes where I fucking say it does.
CUSTOMER: What, is it too long for you?
ATTENDANT: You want to know what long is?
CUSTOMER: I know what long is. I got long. You wouldn't know how to handle long. Park my fucking car by the fucking wall so nobody hits it! And if there's one fucking scratch on that car I'm going to have your fucking ass.
ATTENDANT: That'd be the only ass you ever got except for the ass you put behind the wheel.

Other customers, both men and women, wait tolerantly for this conversation to end. Judging from their faces, you would say that they are studiously pleasant and perhaps occupied by internal concerns. In order to avoid being drawn into the argument, these unwilling spectators take care not to smile to the degree they are amused by the interchange or to exhibit disgust at the language used. All of us have heard conversations like this all our lives. Everybody knows that these men are using sexual language to argue over matters of power and dominance.

There are lots of reasons for someone to buy a new car, few of them automotive. New cars make us feel good about ourselves to the degree that they allow us to move up on the shame/pride axis. So the customer's request for special treatment was at least partially a demand for recognition of his recently elevated, fragile sense of self. Involved here is the unspoken demand that we salute the success of the technique by which he has tried to avoid some moiety of personal shame. If our actions reduce the effectiveness of this *avoidance* script, he must shift to another quadrant of the compass of shame.

It is unlikely that someone who works in a parking lot can afford such a car. Poor people who work comfortably among the rich either accept social stratification or handle it by the mechanism of disavowal. The exchange described above represents one of those moments when this attendant's protective mechanism broke down. For some reason, this particular demand by this particular customer on this particular afternoon made the attendant feel suddenly that the customer saw him as an inferior, throwing the attendant into an *attack other* script.

He reacted, as we all do, by jumping to the layer of the shame/pride axis where he felt most comfortable, creating an argument at another level of comparison and competition. Although the attendant certainly would have lost face in an argument characterized by claims about financial net worth, he felt quite comfortable in the realm of sexual comparison. Furthermore, by introducing "dirty words" into a public forum where they will be heard by everybody, the attendant has removed one aspect of the social distance between him and his customer.

Immediately the conversation becomes clear. The attendant uses the word "fuck" three times in his opening statement, indicating the new battleground. The customer takes the bait and agrees to equate financial worth and genital size. Although the dispute remains one of power and dominance (which the attendant cannot win without placing his job at risk), he has been able to reduce the gap between himself and the customer. Neither of them can prove his allegations about sexual prowess or genital size; bragging statements exist within their own domain and are not meant to be taken literally. If the interchange is successful for both men, the driver will retain the sense of dominion bundled in with his automotive purchase and the attendant will feel he has held his own with someone who tried to humiliate him. Neither man was forced to resort to physical violence; both experienced the interchange as some combination of victory and defeat.

ALTERATIONS OF THE SELF

If an attitude of *withdrawal* makes one appear somewhat depressed; if *attack self* tends to support deference and masochism; and if *avoidance* tends to favor narcissism; then *attack other* halts any tendency to look within the self and thus fosters systems of externalization, blame, and paranoia. A great deal happens to us when we decide to enter the world of attack other.

One of the central themes underlying Sullivan's interpersonal psychiatry was the idea that those who are born into a family capable of empathic connection tend to grow up with a feeling of power in interpersonal relationships. Empathy allows us to experience ourselves as having power *with* others. But to the extent that our parents do not seem to hear, see, appreciate, or understand us, said Sullivan, we grow up looking for ways to have power *over* others.

Like most of the great innovators in psychiatry prior to the development of affect theory, Sullivan did not distinguish among the many forms of shame we are now able to describe; neither did he have a scientific basis for the concept of empathy. Today we describe the unempathic parent somewhat more precisely as one who is not able to enter into affective resonance with a child. The lack of empathic connectedness and the consequent need for power can always be traced to failures in the communication of affect. My concept of the *attack other* system may be thought of as a refinement of his "power over" theme. I chose not to retain the older term simply because the thrust of this reactive system is more to reduce the other than to have authentic power that can be used for other purposes. Imagine, though, what it is like to go through life so destabilized by shame that you spend a significant part of your time looking for ways to diminish others. Whatever can produce such an effect becomes a potential weapon.

There are three affects that produce a state of inferiority, powerlessness, or estrangement from others: (1) We tend to become fearful when the intimate other is angry; the affect fear–terror can be a component of the shameful states of powerlessness, frailty, weakness, and impotence. (When we describe someone as attacking with a "cold, dissecting anger," we know that the recipient has experienced shame as layer after layer of the protections expected in normal social life has been carved away by one who wished to bring pain to the other.) (2) Nearly all of us use some form of soap or deodorant to reduce the possibility that we will chase others away because we smell bad; when we produce the affect dissmell in others we are therefore shamefully reduced in status. (3) Anything we find disgusting must be kept at a distance; whoever triggers disgust in the other is therefore incapable of achieving intimacy or maintaining social position. So powerful are these affects in producing the sense of diminishment that they can become stable parts of the character structure of those who suffer from chronic shame and powerful weapons in the hands of those who wish to create shame in others.

At the beginning of this chapter I mentioned the cinematic work of actor Clint Eastwood, celebrated for his portrayal of impassive but explosive eccentrics. It really isn't correct to say that he is impassive, however, for always flickering over his face are the unmistakable displays of both disgust and dissmell. You can see this without effort in any of his classic rough-and-tough films; the attitude that characterizes him is one that defines the other person as dissmelling until proved otherwise or disgusting after making the wrong move. In moments of danger it is therefore easy for him to shift into an *attack other* mode because the enemy is viewed as unappetizing and somehow less than human. Even in one of his few romantic roles, that of "Partner" in the film version of *Paint Your Wagon*, this tendency to let his lips quiver in dissmell and disgust can be seen whenever the camera lingers on his face.

Eastwood is rarely angry in his films, which makes his explosions into violence all the more frightening. One might even translate his famous signature line to read, "I do not enjoy this no-man's-land midway between shame and violence. If you will be kind enough to do anything that I might interpret as shaming, I can shift into the *attack other* mode, which I vastly prefer to shameful inaction."

One way that anger, dissmell, and disgust come to be fused in some people is the display of emotion we call contempt, in which one corner of the lip is raised, the other lowered, and rest of the face held in angry tension. The general effect of contempt is to place the other person in a state of actual or potential shame and fear. Although this may be a perfect result for anyone in the *attack other* mode, it does require immense alterations in personal style for the sake of shame. The personality of the chronically contemptuous adult is limited to a narrow range of affective expression.

The bully uses the techniques of physical intimidation to maintain the other person in an inferior status. Bullying confers power, of course, but at the cost of tenderness and empathy. Coercion, the act of restraining or demanding compliance by the application of superior force, is another way of diminishing the self-respect of another person. Throughout the business community we find examples of people who use each elevation in rank as an excuse to treat increasing numbers of people as inferiors; similarly do we see power misused in the academic, religious, military, political, and artistic communities. Each of these subcultures legitimizes some characteristic form of the shame/pride axis; in each we find individuals who look on those below them as their immediate inferiors.

Wherever there is inequality of physical strength we are likely to see groupings of people based on the need of the weaker to be protected and the need of the stronger to feel important. Many marriages are based on the willingness of an abused wife to accept contempt, physical battering, and sexual slavery because she salutes or otherwise accepts the power and strength of her husband. Many people seem puzzled by sado-masochistic relationships, asking why anyone would enter such a system or accept the treatment it demands. Sadistic behavior requires masochistic surrender.

Yet the secret lies not in the picture we see when such relationships have reached the final form that explodes into our awareness, but in their early beginnings as the pairing of individuals with radically different but finely meshing attitudes toward shame. It is only a person with a characteristic stance of *attack self* who can form a stable link with one whose approach to life favors the scripts of *attack other*. And it is obvious that one who lives within the code of *attack other* would be lonely indeed were it not for the ubiquity of people who agree to accept a somewhat reduced status in order to prevent insecurity or abandonment. In none of Clint Eastwood's films do we see him involved in a stable, intimate relationship; if he does end up with a female companion it is only because she becomes emotionally bound to him when his heroic behavior has saved her from death or the kind of sexual degradation and shame we call "a fate worse than death."*

THE SEXUAL POLITICS OF ATTACK

There is perhaps no area of human endeavor as likely to be enlisted in the service of the defense against shame as sexuality. First in our daydreams, then in our rapt attention to the versions of *attack self* and *attack other* scripts provided by the entertainment industry, and finally in the experiments with others known as "dating," we move from the absolute secrecy of inner life into interpersonal passion.

In the chapter on *attack self* I called attention to the work of psychoanalyst Robert J. Stoller, whose lifetime of attention to sexuality has brought us a rich harvest of descriptive and theoretical contributions. As I mentioned there, anybody who has read his work understands the association between shame and sexual excitement. When sexually aroused, or when imagining scenes that contain sexual arousal, our thoughts hover about humiliations past and present, injustices experienced and feared, disgrace, failure, loss, ignominy, dishonor, put-downs, and ridicule endured—all recast in the language of sexuality.

In the *attack self* scripts we are likely to overcome these emotional traumas by some act of personal sacrifice. Stoller suggests that the romance novels favored by millions of women are a thinly veiled form of pornography in which, by softness and sexual availability, any woman can see herself turn a pirate king (or soldier of fortune or captain of industry or football hero) from the dangerous, tautly muscled, erect figure of a man he represents initially into a limp, harmless, relaxed, and unintimidating companion. Men, too, use this sort of script when they plan scenes of courtly deference as predecessor to seduction. As Stoller points out, an infinitude of variations on such themes enlivens the sexual fantasy life of our civilization. Where he is more likely to

*Melvin R. Lansky (1987) has advanced our understanding of what Piers and Singer (1953) referred to as shame/guilt cycles and Helen Block Lewis (1971) called humiliated fury. Lansky brought entire families into a hospital unit in order to observe the relation between shame and violence.

see humiliation as an obligatory part of sexual excitement, as intrinsic to the nature of sexuality, it will be clear to the reader that I understand the link between sex and shame as the result of a far more complicated process.

All our lives, the sexual drive programs of the generative system have been intruding into our consciousness, making us first feel the stirrings of sexuality and then try to make sense of these feelings by placing them into some kind of story. Sexual arousal, as we have discussed, operates at first from innate scripts that are controlled by subcortical centers and triggered according to internal timeclocks that respect no social code. The sexual drive makes us want each other, draws men and women together for the purpose of procreation. Yet the way we grow into our drives produces a predictable range of problems.

Sexual dimorphism is a fact of life; male and female humans experience the sexual drive differently. From birth to death, male arousal is inherently public simply because the penis is an external organ and engorgement moves it from quiescence to highly visible prominence. Female arousal is internal and inherently private. For a man to be sexual he must learn to convert the inherent embarrassment of arousal into social scripts through which he interacts with partners who accept his arousal. I do not believe there is anything intrinsically embarrassing about female sexual arousal, any real equivalent for women. Women may be embarrassed by the odor and sight of their menstrual flow (which are capable of triggering dissmell and disgust both in themselves and in others), but in the matter of arousal they experience shame only when taught to do so by social conditioning and, at that, quite late in development. Most women grow quite used to the early forms of sexual arousal long before they begin to menstruate.

This gender-based dimorphism directs the design and performance of scripts that influence all human society. Initially, boys and men learn to think privately about the problems caused them by sexual arousal, which become grouped with all the other sources of shame in their development. Soon enough, they talk among themselves about these particular mixed experiences of bodily pleasure and social discomfort. As I indicated earlier, I suspect that this difference in embarrassment scripts based on predictable and unavoidable drive-related experiences is a prime reason boys and girls segregate early into gender alliances. Even though other things are going on at the time, this is the period during which they must learn from each other how to handle arousal.

Look again at the compass of shame. When embarrassed, one may withdraw, become deferential; ignore, avoid, or distract from the issue; or make it a problem for someone else. Nowhere is this more clearly demonstrated than in our gender-differentiated attitude toward sexual arousal. Quite early on, boys learn that the normative male approach to drive-based sexual arousal is to blame it on women. Depending both on the degree of courage instilled in them by parental conditioning and peer sanction and on the attitude toward shame resulting from their individual experience as registered in Table 5, boys learn to approach girls. In our society, the normative masculine solution for the embarrassment caused by sexual arousal requires the formation of *attack other* scripts that come to be thoroughly intermingled and confused with the sexual drive itself. Indeed, it is this tendency to blame women for men's arousal that makes it so much more likely that men will grow up with the *attack other* system and women within the scripts of *attack self.*

The early attempts at heterosexual interaction made by boys may be viewed as experiments in which they try to figure out what to do with these girl creatures who are now deemed to be the cause of their arousal. ("Boys," said the 19-year-old daughter of a friend, "are okay until they reach adolescence and get testosterone poisoning.") The wide range of masculine approaches to this problem creates, for women, one of the great puzzles of their lives. A significant part of what is considered normal female sexual development is actually the formulation of scripts devised to handle male sexual and counter-shaming approach. Later, of course, women do learn to control their sexual engines and do intentionally (as well as unintentionally) produce sexual arousal in men. But initially they are blamed for what is really a process going on within boys, who experience arousal whether or not there are women around. The very nature of gender dimorphism and its peculiar relation to shame forces women to develop their sexual identities in the context of masculine counter-shaming behavior.

If all this seems difficult and complex, imagine the problem faced by a boy who is heading for a homosexual orientation, whose sexual arousal is localized in the penis, just like that of his heterosexual companions, but who tends to blame these feelings on other male figures! Think, too, about the girl whose imagination persists in conjuring up scenes of romantic involvement with women every time she feels aroused. In both cases, some approach to conventional heterosexual behavior must be designed, and some compromise with embarrassment must be sought.

If we are lucky, we learn to accept the positive affects of interest–excitement and enjoyment–joy as they can so naturally become associated with sexual arousal. Sexuality can become intensely rewarding, both in the solitary experience of masturbation and in the interpersonal experience of intercourse or its equivalents. There are significant rewards to be derived from the integration of sexuality into interpersonal life. But in order to do this, one must learn to deal with shame. To complicate matters, just as sexual arousal is likely to attract shame, shame from other sources will become mingled into our attitude toward sexuality. It is rare, or perhaps unlikely, that anybody can enjoy sexuality as an island of normal function in a sea of shame.

As will easily be deduced from what has just been reviewed, sexual daydreams must, by their nature, include scenes in which humiliation is faced. Stoller suggests that the function of these flights of fancy is to allow us to dream up, in the theater of the mind, methods by which we can convert the defeats, rejections, slights, slurs, and failures of our past into the sexual successes of the future. Men and women alike, we are novelists and movie directors of wondrous ability, who design sturdy plots through which we satisfy needs created by the central issues of shame that come to haunt the lives of each of us.

Donald Mosher, working in concert with Tomkins, has made an extensive study of the group of scripts known as the *macho personality* or *machismo*. The macho man thinks of the negative affects distress, shame, and fear as uniquely feminine emotions synonymous with weakness. He develops a personal style that, by a process of education and experience, converts fear and distress into excitement and anger, and utilizes aggressive sexuality in order to prevent shame. In the macho script sexual success tends more toward rape than mutuality, for sexual arousal is allowed to work only in the service of *attack other*.

It is for this reason that the words used for sexual intercourse ("screwing" or "fucking") have a positive connotation when used in the active sense ("I fucked him/her good," or "I really screwed him") and a negative connotation ("I've been fucked!") when used in the passive. Notice that such a use of sexual action verbs conveys no suggestion of pleasure or contentment except as it produces shame in the recipient. Machismo has become a behavioral standard for a huge segment of our population, which is moving rapidly from a cultural psychology of courtly deference to one of contemptuous attack.

The foregoing is by no means intended to represent a thorough survey of the *attack other* mode of defense against shame. Rather, it is my intent to suggest that the principles involved here may apply to a wide variety of human actions not heretofore thought involved with shame. The compass of shame suggests the extraordinary range and complexity of our methods for the detoxification of the intrinsically painful affect Tomkins calls shame–humiliation. The concept should lend itself to further elaboration in a number of areas.

One final observation before we move on to the next section. It is interesting to note that, as I have commented on many occasions, Wurmser sees shame as a layered emotion (1981, p. 27–28). The six categories of shame-related thoughts that he is able to bring into consciousness with the use of psychoanalytic technique (see p. 144) are quite similar to what I have called the cognitive phase of shame (Table 5). He is able to detect most or all of these layers in the analysis of any shame situation.

Yet when we are in the middle of a shame experience we are unlikely to be aware of such thoughts—what we do recall is some combination of triggering source and an action that fits within the compass of shame. In contrast to Basch's definition of emotion as the combination of an affect and our association to previous experiences of that affect, I have added the dimension of scripted reaction. Once a script is brought into the picture, discrete memories in response to a triggered affect are both unnecessary and unavailable. Only through analytic enquiry can the microcircuitry of a script be evaluated; only then do we begin to learn why certain reaction patterns are likely to occur in certain contexts.

Let us move on in a lighter vein. Our dour and often heartless attitude toward sexuality is not mirrored in other cultures. The Eskimo culture (a happy one until destroyed by our introduction of alcohol) calls sexual intercourse by the same word they use for laughter. It is possible for adults to be both playful and safe with each other. Yet in order to do this they must develop an attitude toward shame quite different from those sketched in the preceding chapters. It is to the phenomenology of *acceptance* and openness that I wish now to turn, the ways and means through which we learn to laugh at ourselves and thus to accept the lessons to be taught by shame.

27

BUDDY HACKETT AND THE
COMEDY OF ACCEPTANCE

Here's a problem for you: You are a wise, all-powerful, gentle, good, and kind public health official charged with the responsibility of solving a broad range of social, cultural, and psychological problems for the citizens of this era. You want people to see and accept, rather than hide, defend, or attack; you want a population comfortable with self-knowledge. You decide that too many people suffer from emotional discomfort related to the general area of shame. You wish to decrease the tendency of people to be upset about the shape, odor, and the very nature of their bodies, to be embarrassed about issues related to the toilet, around matters of gender identity, sexual prowess, and sexual intimacy, and to be unduly sensitive over the small cluster of words relating to all of these functions and attributes. How do you approach this problem?

Should you call a White House Conference on Shame? Produce a list of books and articles on shame to be distributed by the Superintendent of Documents? Convince one of the cable television systems to produce a documentary mini-series on the ubiquity of embarrassment? Hire an evangelist to start a quasi-religious movement based on the toxicity of shame? Schedule a World Conference on the Reduction of the Pain of Shame?

Nope. All you have to do is invent Buddy Hackett.

Wherever I go to lecture about shame I carry a videotape of one or another Buddy Hackett show. In the professional conferences where we therapists congregate to trade ideas, the very thought of presenting material by a professional comedian always raises a few scholarly eyebrows. Hackett, I am informed, is "so vulgar." "Why does he always use such dirty language?"

I asked him about that once. "War is dirty," he said. "Hunger is dirty. Those other things are just words. The real question is why people get so upset about certain words."

Let me start from the beginning. I am going to ask you to join me in a study of a man considered one of the great comedic artists of our time. We tend to dismiss comedians, as if anything that makes us laugh is not worthy of interest. If you study shame you start to take comics very seriously. If love is the balm that heals the pain of individuals, comedy is solace, consolation, and relief for entire tribes.

For us as individuals, each moment of emotional pain is caused by a specific interaction. In order to help one person, the empathic healer must understand something about the particular sequence of events that preceded the painful affective reaction. To relieve the pain of an entire culture, one must be deeply aware of the ways these singular moments of pain are grouped by that society into affect management scripts. It is only because shame is managed by the techniques I have described as the compass of shame, by scripts stored within the four major libraries described in the preceding chapters, that the comedian can affect so many people with a single joke.

Right now, at the time I am writing this book, Buddy Hackett is "king of the hill," top banana, the kind of performer who fills night clubs at record fees. He is everywhere—appearing on late night interview programs, in cameo roles for major films, as the voice of a cartoon character in the Disney film *The Little Mermaid*, even as Santa Claus in Macy's Thanksgiving Day Parade down Fifth Avenue in New York. A loyal following trades anecdotes about his antics with all the energy of collectors on the trail of precious objects. Often reviled because of the "obscene" language with which he peppers his shows, this performer inspires deep love in a legion of admirers spanning a wide range of ages.

"Look at these," he said to me one evening. A packet of fan mail had been awaiting his arrival at the resort where we had met to discuss the relation between comedy and shame. Opening one at random, I learned that a recently divorced young lawyer had recovered her emotional balance by the simple expedient of watching nightly the very same Hackett videotape that I first used in my lectures. "There is so much love in you," she wrote. "Your warmth and your willingness to be openly loving stand in stark contrast to the harsh world around us." Yet always in the audience of my own lectures and courses is one or another detractor, who approaches me with gritted teeth and the face of contempt to say, "How dare you turn Hackett into a god! That man is disgusting and has nothing to teach us."

There is no question about the fact that the polite and affectionate Buddy Hackett makes jokes about matters that are usually forbidden in "polite company." He flies in face of social convention by discussing a wide range of subjects that are considered taboo in our culture. Although each individual joke and routine stems from material he has thought about and worked over for years, Hackett's comedy depends on direct, personal interaction with that fraction of the audience which has chosen to sit in the first few rows of the theater. His is less the work of an actor reading lines prepared in the safety of a private space than it is the craft of an improvisational jazz artist who takes the risk of generating ideas in public.

In a recent night club show I saw him first compliment a 75-year-old woman on her considerable beauty and then speak the mind of the audience by saying, "Look at the jugs on that broad! Ain't she got a great body?" Later that evening he discussed the universal male problem of unexpected erections, a host of embarrassing situations related to normal bowel and bladder function, the discomfort anybody might feel during a barium enema, and the alterations in sexual function following prostate surgery. He found a couple of women who were unable to use any "four-letter words" and made them recognize the innocence of such language.

Videotapes of Hackett performances focus a great deal of attention on the audience. Nobody looks angry, nobody looks disgusted, nobody looks distressed. Most people seem to exhibit three affects. Easily seen is the oscillation between rapt fascination and vivid displays of embarrassment, both punctuated by sustained bursts of hilarity. Nobody seems uncomfortable—they look for all the world like people having a good time. Why they are there and what they get out of being there are the twin subjects of this chapter.

Even though my own personal affection for the man and his work is a matter of record, it really isn't important whether or not you and I think Hackett is funny, whether we think his work is artful or tasteless, whether we see him as vulgar or profound. Of the greatest importance for our study of shame and pride is the fact that millions of people go out of their way to watch his performances on television, pay to see his movies, and wait on line to attend his night club performances. It is his success that we must explain—the affection he inspires in a wide and still-growing audience. I am, of course, suggesting that the central theme in Hackett's work is an awareness of the pain inherent in shame—especially the shame associated with the avoidance pole of the compass of shame—and the degree of relief from this pain offered by comedy. First, however, I must define comedy in some way that conforms to the understanding of affect presented so far.

THE NATURE AND ART OF COMEDY

Pleasant or unpleasant, most of the affect we encounter is the more-or-less-unexpected accompaniment of life—affect amplifying whatever else is happening. Normally, we do not attend school in order to experience affect; we do not go to work for the sake of affect. Even though our hunger may be made more urgent because affect told us so, we eat to satisfy the call of a drive. Sometimes our actions, thoughts, or experiences trigger one or another of the six negative affects, sometimes we are startled briefly, and often we meet up with the positive affects of interest–excitement and enjoyment–joy. The affect is important, the affect produces urgency, the affect operates in all the ways we have discussed so far. Notwithstanding the significance of affect, always it is triggered because something else is happening. The script formed by an event, its triggered affect, and our response are what we recall as our emotional memory of that event.

Yet we come to learn that, just as food makes us feel better when we are hungry, sometimes it can make us feel better even when our distress stems from other sources. Equally well can the thrill of excitement (or the rapt attention required by a puzzling situation or any experience of laughter) dissipate a bad mood that has been caused by situations completely unrelated to whatever triggered this new excitement. Sequences of experience that end with a positive affect, occurring naturally throughout life, can be induced intentionally in order to improve the mood of the moment.

Every culture offers or sanctions a wide range of activities designed for no purpose other than to produce the remediation of unpleasant affect. In our examination of the *attack other* pole of the compass of shame we recognized that the discomfort of shame and distress can be reduced or even dissipated by the induction of excitement or anger. Here we are interested in the relation between negative affect and laughter.

We have defined the affect enjoyment–joy as that which is triggered by any decrease in stimulus density; a slow decrease produces the mild experience of pleasure and a slight smile, while a sudden decrease fosters the release of the affect program as laughter. Literally anything that causes a rapid reduction in whatever is going on in the central nervous system will cause laughter! All of the theories for humor devised prior to Tomkins's affect theory depend on the content of whatever preceded the laughter.* This one explains why we laugh

---

*There is a centuries-long tradition of books attempting to explain humor on the basis of content. J. C. Gregory (1924) provides a representative example of this genre, linking it to physiological relief produced by either specific biological triggers or learned mechanisms.

at moments that seem, on the whole, distinctly unpleasant.

In a family album I found a photograph that brought to mind such an experience. Taken during World War II, it shows me as a toddler being tossed from one to another of my father's younger brothers, all of them dressed in uniform. Instantly and powerfully I recalled the scene. I was terrified when Uncle Marty picked me up and tossed me high in the air. Yet, despite my terror, I remember the guffaw I let out when I landed safely in the arms of Uncle Arnold. Each subsequent throw and catch produced the same sequence of fear and relief, each moment of relief accompanied by a similar burst of laughter. I suspect that they read my laughter as a sign that this was an altogether enjoyable activity. Trust me: There was nothing funny in the situation, which I found terrifying and still remember with distaste.

Earlier, I called attention to the fact that we are likely to laugh during horror movies when there is any sudden decrease in the degree of terror being induced. (Why else do we laugh when the protagonist bravely opens a closet, expecting to find whoever has butchered her family, and encounters a bunny rabbit calmly munching on a carrot?) Real laughter will occur whenever the conditions of rapid stimulus decrease have been met.

Although the comedy of life presents a myriad of situations that we find funny, the comedic arts are characterized by the intentional simulation of such happenstance. Choreographers often describe a similar process through which they integrate into a dance some sequence of movements made by ordinary people. Comedians, who are among the most astute observers in our culture, can make us laugh about nearly anything—as long as they satisfy Tomkins's criteria for the induction of enjoyment—joy. What they notice, what they find interesting and worthy of comedic exaggeration, is always dependent on their own personal way of seeing the world around them. As I mentioned in the opening section of this book, some are artists of shame, while others paint comedic pictures while working from a palette of fear, disgust, dissmell, anger, or distress.

Let us imagine, for the moment, that all artists were born with equal skill and technical virtuosity. (The modern camera can allow nearly anyone to take pictures that are sharply focused and properly exposed.) The range between the triviality and greatness of an artistic product is a function of the subject chosen and the importance to us of the scripts in which it is embedded. Da Vinci's *Mona Lisa* achieves its mystical quality by virtue of the meaning we attribute to it—the way it fits into our own lives, the complexity of the scripts involved and the density of the affect magnified within them. The great artist chooses to immerse him- or herself in scripts that have great commonality and carry the highest degree of magnification, invoking our reaction to the deeply personal aspects of the scenes picked for expression. And since artists, like all of us, vary tremendously across the spectra of intelligence, skill, wisdom, courage, and depth, their productions will affect us in relation to all those factors.

Comedic artists differ from their creative peers only in the medium of expression chosen, in the vehicle through which they choose to analyze and compare scripts. The "Little Tramp" of Charlie Chaplin, Jackie Gleason's innocently narcissistic Ralph Cramden, Lucille Ball's artfully "stupid" housewife, Woody Allen's embarrassed adolescent, and Emmett Kelly's sad clown all allowed us to laugh about issues and memories contained in scripts of the highest affective magnification. Only mediocre entertainment is judged by the number of laughs produced per unit of time; great comedy is appreciated at a far deeper level, even though it makes us laugh.

Minor art produces momentary pleasure because the scripts in which it is embedded have a minor place in our library. Great art brings pleasure while also fostering change in internal scripts that carry with them the deepest and most powerful levels of affect. Minor art soothes or nettles slightly; great art wrenches us in ways that alter central scripts. "Psychotherapists," said my own great therapist and teacher, Bob Pottash, "are minor artists in the only field where creativity requires two people. Our canvas is the ephemeral thing called a 'session'; if we are really lucky and really good at what we do, our partner will be changed by our work and not remember that we did anything at all. At best they may recall it as a vaguely positive experience." As I have indicated, this chapter represents my efforts to call attention to the kind of art and therapy offered by Buddy Hackett.

COMEDIC SCRIPTS

We might characterize any study of human endeavor as some form of script analysis. The mechanics of script formation explain what we do in our day-by-day attempts to manage experience. Although Tomkins has described many specific types of scripts, so far we have focused on those developed to manage and control affective experience. There are many others, all of which involve various types of affective magnification, but which serve a wide range of additional purposes.

Among these are scripts through which we handle loss or gain, those by which we manage to recreate and maintain the ambience of our childhood home throughout our adult lives, some which foster the development of addiction, and others that might lead us to fight and even die for our beliefs. Most of those described in the previous section on the compass of shame are properly considered affect remediation scripts because they are constructed to modulate or somehow handle the experience of shame affect.*

Comedy may be understood as a separate library of affect remediation scripts in which the unit of analysis is the particular kind of script called the *joke*, the purpose of which is to create laughter. In most jokes, the action takes place purely in the mind. A *practical joke* is neither practical nor impractical, but a script through which an operator forces the subject to perform a series of actions that must cause enough embarrassment that we may laugh at that person's expense. The term derives from *praxis*, the Greek word for action or doing.

Like all scripts, a successful joke must follow certain rules. In general, the operator begins by giving the audience the minimal amount of information necessary for the mental construction of a scene. Then the scene is manipulated in such a way that it is transformed into one with a different cluster of affects. Usually this is accomplished by *exaggeration*, which stretches our sense of the adequacy of fit of the initial script. The resultant shift causes a rapid decrease in stimulus density, which triggers laughter.

Incidentally, this helps explain one of the peculiar phenomena associated with shame and pride: As Annibale Pocaterra said in 1592, praise makes us uncomfortable because it is couched in the same language as ridicule. Anything that is exaggerated, including the data from which our self-image is derived, is capable of being used in a joke. Discomfort with praise is directly proportional to our propensity to shame; it is a measure of our expectation that someone might make a joke at our expense.

It is a tribute to the art of the comedian that it takes more words to explain a joke than to make one. The condensation, amplification, magnification, and associative range embodied in all script formation make it one of the great wonders of neocortical function.

A famous example of this process is Henny Youngman's "shortest joke in the English language." In it, the comedian addresses his audience and says, "Take my wife. Please." The opening statement, which prepares us for the usual litany of marital complaints, sets the scene. ("Take my wife, for instance. You know how she goes shopping? She writes out a list of what's needed in the house . . .") The second statement, "Please," indicates that the operator meant the verb "take" not in its sense of *to apprehend mentally, to comprehend*,

*See Tomkins (1987b) for the most complete list of affect-related scripts.

but in the alternate meaning of *seize, grip, catch,* or *remove.*

By shifting his command from *comprehend* to *remove,* Youngman alters the scripts conjured initially from those of marital discord within a comfortable style of bonding to those which involve enough acrimony that marital dissolution may be considered. The very fact that we are listening to a professional comedian ensures that we are not meant to "take him seriously" and actually remove his wife. The rapidity with which we drop our investment in the initial group of scripts, with all the affective magnification they may carry for us as individuals, is a competent trigger for laughter. Most people, when told this joke for the first time, actually "do a double take" and laugh again a few seconds later as they consider and then drop the scripts involved in the fantasy of "wife removal."

A similar process is involved in our reaction to the *pun.* Here the substitution of a word sounding like the one expected, but actually quite different from it, produces a rapid oscillation between the scripts invoked by each. Thus, in the example cited by Freud in his book on jokes, a well-known wit said that he had driven *tête-à-bête* with a friend. We expected the phrase *tête-à-tête,* which implies intimacy and all the sequences of positive affect associated with it. But what we hear is that the supposedly intimate other is little more than a *bête,* a dumb beast worthy only of contempt. The shift from one set of scripts to another produces enough alteration in stimulus density to trigger mild laughter—again followed by "second thoughts" related to the matter contained in the scripts invoked. Any mental content that is dropped quickly is likely to trigger laughter, notwithstanding its content or the content of what follows next.

Mild laughter is one thing, but what about the belly laugh, or the phenomenon called "roaring with laughter," or laughing until the density of the affect itself is so great that tears come to our eyes? Our recognition of the innate mechanisms involved helps us understand that where we see affect of high density the preexisting situation must have been characterized by stimuli of great intensity and/or duration. The lysis of chronic and enduring distress, shame, terror, or anger produces joy far exceeding that triggered by the removal of mild and comparatively recent negative affect. Great comedians have the ability to conjure scenes that involve scripts with the highest degree of affective magnification, to gauge correctly the length of time we are allowed to react on the basis of those scripts, and to remove us from them at the greatest speed.

The trigger to release is called the *punch line* because, no matter how gracefully it is delivered, the audience experiences it as swift and sudden, like a blow leveled by a boxer. When comedians themselves speak about their peers, it is to their ability to read the degree of immersion in a script best suited a particular audience and to know when to administer the punch line that they pay most attention; this is called *timing*. The importance of exaggeration as a major tool of script manipulation may be determined by any conversation with one or more comedians. Every possible embellishment, extravagance, or elaboration is tested for its utility in a joke. This is why they are often accused of "never having a straight conversation" and one of the reasons they are (by most reports) "difficult" companions.

When a comedian links one joke after another in some sort of sequence, each building on the emotions of the one before, this is called a *routine*. Even though the individual jokes contained within a routine are all scripts, the sequence itself is a higher-order script because each joke magnifies the affects contained in its predecessors, thus evolving a central theme. Audiences are rarely able to remember individual jokes from a successful routine because the effect of the whole progression has been to evoke matters of such an intensely personal nature that the triggering stimulus is of relatively little importance.

Many comedians have demonstrated their ability to "make a joke about anything," even to the point where they will ask the audience to choose the topic. We can be made to laugh about any subject that can be incorporated in an affect script, about anything that can be amplified by affect. Naturally, this is easiest with subjects that can be linked to themes containing high-density affect. The affect management techniques characterized as the compass of shame offer some of the most popular such vehicles in our culture.

Drawn from the *withdrawal* pole of the compass are jokes about our moments of weakness, stupidity, incompetence. The *attack self* pole may in itself actually be considered a form of joke script, for it houses a library of methods through which we get people to like us by reducing our own self-esteem under conscious control. It is the way we tell jokes about ourselves. From the *avoidance* pole come jokes about narcissism, about the ways all of us try to make ourselves look better by exaggerating some of our personal characteristics or accomplishments. And the litany of hate jokes and racial slurs—remarks and comments that define the speaker as superior to the one being reduced—all of these use the *attack other* pole as the source of their material. In each script library are themes of love and abandonment, of victory and defeat, of sex and hunger, of wealth and poverty—all viewed in terms of shame and pride.

Such jokes are staples in the larder of comedy. Any student of the art could fill entire books with examples of each. Every time we laugh at one we reinforce the script from which it is drawn. And since most people tell jokes in order to decrease their own tension, the presence of a constant comedic theme is a telling sign of internal concern. Comedians live inside out, showing publicly what the audience must keep most private.

It will be clear from the foregoing that the comedians whose work we prize most are those who have elected to live at the greatest risk, to work in the realms of the most intense negative affect. These artists are, as I have suggested, like solo improvisational jazz musicians, who prosper in direct proportion not just to their skill and creativity, but also to the depth of character and feeling conveyed in their music.

BUDDY HACKETT

In a way, I wish the reader could have been there in the hotel room where I interviewed him. I don't know who was more nervous at the beginning—the entertainer who has worked rooms all over the world or the psychiatrist who spends his life interviewing people. Yet for Buddy, even though I had sent him a draft of the introduction to this book and some of my earlier work in the area, there still was the chance that I was going to be like so many other interviewers who were unable to focus on anything other than his use of "dirty words."

There is that other problem, of course, one faced by anybody in our culture. I am a psychiatrist. Maybe I was going to tell him something terrible about himself that he didn't want to know. Then, too, he said, even though he had a measured IQ of 148, impressive by anybody's standards, he'd gone no further than high school. Well read, much more scholarly than anyone in his audience might guess, he suffered from the same anticipation of embarrassment that all of us experience when confronted by someone with special training.

Me? Nearly all the people I interview are relative strangers, about whom I have no preexisting emotions. I had known and loved Buddy's work for perhaps 30 years. My head was full of ideas, memories, and feelings all triggered by the scenes evoked in his routines. And this was a world-famous entertainer! Surely he is used to meeting people far more important and intelligent than I! Nervously, each anticipating embarrassment at the hands of the other, we broke the ice by talking about ourselves, by telling those safe stories one has tested on others.

We talked about our children, about the rigors of travel, about our experiences of marriage. Once or twice we got into areas so deeply personal that he asked me to turn off the tape recorder. (There are some things to be entrusted to a friend but not to a tape cassette that might someday escape into the public domain.) But what had been scheduled for one hour stretched into many. My assessment of him as a deeply loving man of extraordinary intelligence had turned out to be accurate; his hope for me, too, was validated.

Haltingly, I started to talk about his work in terms of shame. It seemed, I said, that he liked to expose the fact that most people are afraid of exposure. Buddy recalled a lecture he had attended in Los Angeles some years ago, fact and exaggeration swirling together:

"Are we talking the Johari Window here? One of the great tools of psychiatry. Picture a window cut in four. It's about you. A psychological autopsy, almost. The first window is what I know about you and what you know about you, me being the rest of the world. The second piece of the window is what I know about you that you don't know about you. The third part of the window is what you know about you that I don't know about you, and the fourth part of the window is what we both don't know about you. The point of adjustment is when that last window gets very small. That's Johari. I think he was a Japanese psychiatrist."

We discussed the implications of this concept—that knowledge is better than ignorance. He remembered Johari as having stressed the importance of the compartment representing what is unknown to both parties. Nevertheless, the Hackett style of comedy seems to concentrate on those who believe that they hold secrets when the information really is evident to all. There are lots of people who act as if the third part of the window were under their own control. I told him, "You seem to work in the area where people are hiding things from themselves more than from others. You expose things that people don't want to know about themselves. And you do it in such a way that, instead of producing terrible embarrassment, they realize you are a loving person and they laugh."

He responded, "Let me change a little about what you just said. They know about it, they know those things about themselves. They don't want to admit to another person that they know about these things and that they are indeed guilty in the performance thereof or in the recognition of it. So they suppress that a little bit, because 'It's bad enough I know it, they shouldn't know it.' And I'm saying to you, 'Yeah, it's bad enough that I know it and you know it and we all know it. But we got to stop feeling bad about it because that's the way it is.' If you're going to talk about things that are undignified, and you understand the indignity of death . . . once you've got death, what the hell is everything else?"

I realized, all at once, that we were talking on the occasion of his 65th birthday. Not only was his own mortality a matter of concern, but his network of friends had been threatened by illness and reduced by death. He paused here, in an apparent digression about what happens to us after we die. He pointed out that we no longer have any control when we are dead and that much of our attention to death rituals is an attempt to control what we would be better off ignoring anyway because we're gone. I tried to return him to my subject: "So death is a transition for which one cannot prepare. When you compare dying to the moderate revelation . . ."

He interrupted: "Of pissing in your pants—huh!—Nothing." I continued: "But shame seems to be an emotion that terrifies people. You take an attractive woman from the audience and, in effect, you say to her, 'I know you think about penises, I know you think about erections.' Everybody knows that everybody thinks about such things, but you're the only person who says them aloud. That's astonishing. There's people who copy you, but you started it. You take the real, the fundamental, the basic things about human nature, and you say them out loud. When did you start to do that?"

"When I was a little bitty boy. Well, I remember this. Why I did it I don't know." He frowns here, searching the memories of his boyhood in Brooklyn for the clue that might let him place this moment more precisely. "We moved from 56th Street to 54th Street, and I got there when I was ten, on 54th Street. In order for this to have happened, I had to have been under ten—and it might have been as young as seven or eight, or even six. I remember sitting with my back against the building, with four or five boys, on the ground, on 16th Avenue between 56th and 57th Street, sitting in a circle. And a woman comes by and says, 'What are you boys doing?' 'We're telling dirty jokes,' I said. And she gave us a big lecture. That was okay. I'd heard lots of lectures from grown-ups. But as she gave the lecture, she got more and more involved in her lecture, and angry." He paused here, for this had been on his mind nearly all his life. "After a while, I realized that I could smell something from her. And I guess it was fear.

"I thought about that many times. And I know that that grown-up—I could then make the distinction that some grown-ups are only old and not grown up at all—there was something wrong with her, something terribly wrong with her. Almost 60 years ago that happened, and I have thought about it a great deal. What could be so bad in the kind of jokes little boys tell each other? What concerns little boys? Things like shitting, and pissing, and penises."

There is an odor associated with terror, I commented. Some observers have called it *caproic,* named for the way goats smell. We tossed around our ideas about why she might have been so afraid of words relating to excretion or genitality. "Yeah, I can see that it has something to do with her own shame. But I didn't know anything about that at the time. All I knew is that something was terribly wrong with her. To me, the true shame could come if you hurt somebody. The people who are amoral, they don't feel that pain. If you could start early enough making people learn that. . . . My emotion at that moment was that I am very different. And the minute, the times in my life I have tried to hide that difference, and be like everybody else, at that point I was unhappy and I was dysfunctional."

I pressed a little: "So at eight, nine, ten you already saw the difference between a fake person and a real person." "But I didn't know that, I couldn't have said it like that right then." "So you felt strange." "Yeah, I was the outsider. Growing up in my family I always felt wrong."

Anybody who has studied the lives and work of comedians knows a great deal about what he means here. The factors that go into the making of a major talent are as complex as those producing any other form of success or greatness. There is no simple explanation for something that has so many levels of causation. Yet if you read their autobiographies and study the case reports written about people in the joke business, it appears that most, if not all, grew up in homes characterized by high and relatively constant levels of negative affect. The future comedian learns early the value of anything that might reduce the general level of tension. For Buddy Hackett, this affective environment seems to have produced a sense of estrangement, which itself (as we discussed in a earlier chapter) is a profound shame experience. Awkwardly, I asked what he could tell me about this:

"When did you decide that the difference was so great; when did you start doing comedy; when did you start telling jokes?"

"When I was a little bitty boy. My uncle came to see me, and I was four. And he says, 'I can't shake hands until you take your gloves off.' I said, 'What gloves?' My mother said, 'He wants you to wash your hands.' So I washed one hand because I was only going to shake hands with one hand. And everyone thought that was hilarious—and I thought it was practical. See, I didn't do it to be funny. I knew my hands were going to get dirty again anyway, so I just took a cloth and wiped that hand off and shook his hand. I thought if he's so idiotic that it means any difference to him. . . . I humored him. Years later, he came to see me at the Bradford Hotel in Boston and stole the towels and they put it on my bill. When my mother died, he went to the apartment, being her brother, brought a second-hand dealer, and sold everything. Huh! Heh, heh! The great . . . he's the guy told me to keep my hands clean!"

We talked a bit about his family. His father, an upholsterer, was an unpredictable parent: at times loving and intimate; at other times distant; occasionally ill-tempered and perhaps violent. Here, indeed, was evidence of the affective climate I had expected, one that he had learned to ameliorate by inducing laughter.

If you are a professional psychotherapist, you know the dilemma facing me at this point. The door to further exploration was open. Yet were I to probe more deeply, I would risk injuring my host by setting up the illusion of a therapeutic relationship with an entertainer who must, for professional reasons, live as a nomad. Wurmser once defined tact as the ability to understand the other person's nearness to shame. I know of few actions so tactless and self-serving as the induction of intimacy that cannot be sustained. Prostitutes don't kiss. Interviewers must keep a respectful distance. I shifted back to the purpose for which I had requested this interview.

"So hypocrisy, and chicanery, these things are all around us." "Yeah, but I don't judge it." "What you do is you just expose it, you demonstrate it, you show it." Somewhat testily, he replied: "I don't know what I do with it. You're giving me credit for being a lot smarter than I am, or deeper than I am, or something than I am. This is as natural to me as some guys throwing a baseball harder than another guy."

We talked a little bit about his use of personal disclosure. Anyone who has watched one of his shows knows about his marriage to Sherry, about his children, about his love of skiing. Two things happen when an audience is privileged to learn such intimate details of a performer's life. His willingness to expose what normally is kept private or secret propels us into a state of mutuality, trust, and openness. We are less likely to worry about our own secrets with such a man—and that, of course, is the major thrust of his art.

But the cost is that millions of people come to believe that they have a real, truly personal relationship with him. On several occasions, when I have referred to Hackett's work in my own lectures, men have sought me out afterwards to tell me how they knew him in grade school, in high school, from the ski slope. Each of them quoted some highly specific interaction. I collected all of these on one sheet of paper and read them aloud during this interview. Nearly all turned out to be innocent fabrications through which the authors had attempted to make more real their profound emotional connection to this professional entertainer.

An interesting analogue of this process may be seen in the public response to actors we watch in romantic scenes on film. As I mentioned in an earlier chapter, in our culture one is embarrassed to be seen naked unless the viewing other is held either by fascination or within the bonds of real intimacy. We tend to have a "special" feeling of intimacy with people we have seen unclothed, especially when we identify with the romantic partner with whom we saw him or her involved. It is for this reason that most professional entertainers are forced to live in far more privacy than they might like. They become prisoners of their success, of the way the characters they play become involved in our personal scripts.

Often the successful comedian is almost terrified of the public unless held under his control the way he has them in the theater. People must be kept at a distance. He recounted this story: "I'm backstage at the Sahara Hotel years ago, in my dressing room, and my son is with me. A woman comes in and she says, 'I'm Mrs. So-and-So from Des Moines, Iowa.' So I says, 'Hello.' She says, 'Well, you act like you don't know who I am.' 'Well, I don't know who you are.' 'Well, I'm the woman where your son has dinner every Wednesday.' I said, 'He does?' 'He goes to the university there.' I said, 'Well, I don't have a son in Des Moines, Iowa. This is my son, right here.' 'Oh, no,' she says, 'that's not your son.' It's bad enough some people think they know you when they don't. Some guy in Iowa owes me a lot of money because he's getting fed regularly!" The comedian who does so much to foster intimacy by reducing shame lives at constant risk of personal invasion.

Again, we talked about the work itself.

"Relief is built into the way I think. Maybe it'll help if I tell you what I think humor is. There are two kinds of pain. Physical and psychological. Any time I do something that releases you from that pain, I create laughter. The laughter is a feeling of relief, of release and relief. When you go *ha ha ha ha*, whatever's hurting you in your head or in your knee, you don't feel either one of those things. And that's the whole story of laughter. Release from pain. And that's the whole story of what I do. What's the difference what method I use if my feeling underneath is for you not to be in pain?"

"And now, to be skillful enough to use taboo things and still make the people not get pain from me, 'cause 'I'm not supposed to hear this,' or 'I don't want to hear this, I've been preached against what he's saying here,' and then say it, and they say, 'Well, wait a minute, that wasn't so bad.' So I'm allowed to think it the way I've been thinking it, and it's okay for it to slip in and out of my mind just as easy as I can think 'no cream, no sugar.' I go by the principle that two bodies can't occupy the same space at the same time. A joke is not a dirty joke. It's either a joke or it's dirty. It's either funny or dirty. Hunger is dirty. Hunger is a real terror."

Although most of us tell jokes from time to time, some people seem able to do little else; the pursuit of humor, for them, is a constant preoccupation. As a psychiatrist I have worked in therapy with a number of minor comedians, both amateur and professional. The more one is tied to telling jokes or being witty as a way of life, the greater the inner reservoir of tension about the area of shame. The witty person, the one who is constantly telling jokes, is often more interested in the laugh than in the underlying subject. Other people tell jokes that hover around some consistent motif—in therapy these are as useful as dreams in searching for areas of unconscious conflict.

Two basic themes emerged from this therapeutic work: The comedic talent, like so many other special gifts, seems to exist as an independent mental ability, much like the capacity to compose music or to sketch; it is not derivative of emotional illness. But the decision to make comedy a way of life is impelled in direct proportion to the amount of magnification produced by shame or the degree to which shame interferes with life. This latter observation fits well with the large number of studies that demonstrate the role of "depression" in the life of a comedian; one wishes the authors of those books and papers had access to this new language for affect.

As I mentioned earlier, the greatness of an artist is measured by the complexity and importance of the scripts involved in the artistic product. Hackett has spent his life trying to find the essential comedic center of an idea. "First of all, abundant material is so scarce. Most comedians only touch the edge. When Henny Youngman does the one-liner, like his 'small room jokes,' he takes a good idea but drops it too quickly." He pauses for a moment and starts on his friend's material: " 'The room was so small, I closed the door, the knob got in bed with me.' Then he goes on and says: 'The room was so small you had to go out in the hall to change your mind. I kept taking aspirin 'cause the guy in the next room had a headache.' Each one is a new joke."

"What I'm saying is, take any one of those jokes . . . that if you say, 'I closed the door, the knob got in bed with me,' then take it from there: 'I looked at the knob. In the middle was a lock with a hole. It said 'Segal.' I said, 'What could be bad, a Jewish knob. Even though we don't know each other.' Okay. 'The knob felt cold. What the hell, I was married.' See, I'm peeling the onion. Start again with the other one: 'You had to go out in the hall to change your mind. Locked myself out, didn't have the key, didn't know which room it was because I already changed my mind.' "

It isn't enough to tell a joke, he says. The important thing is to see how deep it can go. Perhaps the most famous story associated with Buddy Hackett took place 30 years ago while he was playing golf with three friends. Hackett hit a ball into the woods, went after it, and disappeared from view. After what seemed an unbearable amount of time, just as the others were beginning to worry whether something had happened to him, Buddy ran from the woods onto the fairway, stark naked, yelling at the top of his voice, "Help! Help! Locusts are upon us!"

I suggested that a lot of people might have wanted to take off some piece of clothing on a hot day and that maybe a couple of people might actually have taken something off. He explained that the temperature was unbearable on the fairway; it was 15 degrees cooler in the woods. So he stripped off his shirt. It felt wonderful. So wonderful that he took off his pants, and then decided to take off his shoes, socks, and underclothes.

I asked, "But what's different about you that, in an era when everybody else was too embarrassed to go naked in public, you decided to step forward?" "Peeling the onion. Searching for the specific. The joke never ends. That's a joke, standing there naked in the woods. But why should it end there? If you take one more thin onion skin off, you do something else with it. Suddenly you say, them guys should know that I'm standing here naked in the woods. What am I going to say? 'Come on, you want to see me naked in the woods?' 'Come on, hit the ball, willya?' But 'Help, Help!!!' and they come running."

Hackett has published one book of doggerel verse, and another on golf. I wondered whether he had written any serious fiction. He explained, "When you write, you have to leave a lot of stuff out. What I write is about my own personal experience; some things might hurt somebody's feelings, so I'd rather not write anything." Clearly, he has no wish to produce embarrassment for other than comedic reasons or in situations out of his immediate control.

Comedy, which careens so often close to the edge of shame, and which in the hands of some is a powerful vehicle for humiliation, can become one of the most profound weapons for the reduction of the pain associated with embarrassment. All of us who spend our lives doing psychotherapy have watched with pleasure when a patient learns to laugh gently about some once-hidden subject, something that once caused searing pain. There is a laughter of love, a laughter that shows the sudden pleasure of self accompanying healthy new self-recognition. Anybody who seeks consciously to reduce the pain of others is a healer, a therapist.

We joked about this, the comedian and the psychiatrist. "We do the same kind of work," I said. "I just work smaller rooms." "Yeah," he responded. "But if you do a bad session, only one patient knows about it. And he's gonna come back anyway. If I work a room with a thousand people, and I'm no good that night, then maybe two or three hundred come the next night, and maybe the management doesn't ask me back again. Every single night I am on the line. But yeah, I do therapy. Anyone who sits through 90 minutes of my show is going to walk out of here feeling better, and maybe a little less worried about the things I talk about."

Buddy and I were sipping drinks, trading anecdotes about our own marriages, children, friends. We had long ago finished our formal interview, the tape recorder turned off and returned to its case. Just as we made ready to part, he whirled around and said, "Wait a minute. You turn that thing back on." He spoke directly into it with great intensity, recording something he had always wanted to say, another dimension of the humor responsible for his devoted following.

"If I have any kind of credo or feeling, it's this. I was a poor kid, and I liked to read. I bought, two or three cents, I think, for a used magazine, and there was a story there called the Hawk, or The Hawk's Nest. There was a man called the Hawk, and he lived in an aerie, a hawk's nest. I don't remember the story. But the description of the Hawk was, 'Nobody ever came into his life that didn't leave a little richer and a little wiser.'

"And right then that was my thought of power—not conquering countries, not owning audiences, not having. . . . Imagine someone meets you and leaves a little richer and a little wiser. . . . And underneath every motivating thing I do, if you could leave me a little richer and a little wiser, then I own a little piece of you and I own a little piece of this and a little piece of that, and then, you could be anywhere on this earth and say, 'Oh, that's a friend of mine.' 'Cause you know, they don't even remember your name anymore, but you did something to make their life a little bit better. And that's, I think, my basic feeling when I'm working. There's no malice, 'Hey look what I can get away with!' Wrong. Pay attention to me. What I'm doing here is not to get away with anything. What I'm doing here is to say, 'It's all right, take my hand.' "

THE RAVAGES OF SHAME

It would surprise no one were I to mention that (whether or not you enjoy his work) people like Buddy Hackett are rare. The tendency to increase the toxicity of shame is far more common than the wish to reduce it. Everywhere we see evidence that the *attack other* style of reaction to shame is ubiquitous—less a defense than a skill, an essential component of normal adult emotional paraphernalia. Hackett's sensitivity to the ravages of shame and the scripts he has devised to counter them are part of an intensely personal script of his own. Among the reasons he is both popular to most and equally disagreeable to others is that there are many people whose "life work" seems to be a matter more of the magnification of shame than its diminishment.

We live in a society dominated by issues of pride and shame, in which the have-nots suffer indignity at the hands of the haves and look always for someone weaker or lesser on whom they can turn the tables. Whereas in Chapter 26 I derived a logic for the *attack other* quadrant of the compass of shame, little attention was paid to those who live as recipients of such emotional attack. It is accurate but not sufficient to say that true adult competence requires that we be able to handle each of the negative affects, for there are degrees and intensities of shame that far exceed anything for which the human system seems to have evolved.

But even to consider this sort of cultural anthropology, this method of exploring our current civilization, presents another problem. We suffer the risk of reductionism, of assigning to one affect far too much significance. If we are to understand the real nature of shame, the emotion at all levels of intensity, we must first examine what happens when any affect is pushed beyond reasonable limits. If we are to consider what it is like to exist in an atmosphere contaminated by shame, in a family or a subculture characterized by the constant magnification of shame-related troubles, we must first learn about the outer reaches of affect itself.

V

From Moment
to Madness

28

THE REALM OF VERY DENSE

AFFECT:

MECHANISMS OF INCREASE

Item: "You dance like a faggot," said one high school senior to another at the prom. Whirling suddenly, the boy pulled a knife and killed his jeering classmate. The event occurred 30 years ago, but was told me by a patient in therapy for whom it remains a terrifying example of the relation between shame and rage.

Item: A lawyer discusses a client who raped repeatedly his 14-year-old daughter and threatened to beat her senseless unless she then cooked his dinner.

Item: On 13 March 1964, 28-year old Kitty Genovese parked her car and began to walk toward her apartment, at which point she was stabbed by an assailant. She screamed, "He stabbed me!" A neighbor looked out his window and said to the attacker, "Let that girl alone." The assailant looked up, shrugged, and walked to his car. No one called the police, and while his victim was struggling to get to her apartment he returned and stabbed her again. "I'm dying!" she shrieked. Thirty-eight neighbors heard her scream, but none called the police. The killer returned a third time and then stabbed her fatally. Now one neighbor did call the police—well after she had died. Her death has formed the basis of a cautionary tale designed to shame those who are too cowardly to act with even a minimal sense of civic or human responsibility. Surely (we are told) someone could have done something to distract, dissuade, or limit the severity of his attack. Yet I have never heard anyone enquire what might have been going on in the mind of the perpetrator to power so *prolonged* and persistent a murderous attack.

Item: Last year a stranger entered a neighborhood tavern in my city and for several hours held its customers at gunpoint. Selecting one 18-year-old man as his special victim, the perpetrator forced him to strip naked and dance before them on a pool table, after which he killed him.

Item: A recent trial laid bare the story of a man who killed the chronically schizophrenic daughter who had made his life a living hell by her constant and unpredictable attacks with knives and clubs. Interviewed later, the jurors thought that these extenuating circumstances might have led to his exoneration had he not then proceeded to chop into her body small chunks, which he then cooked. How can someone remain so angry at his victim that he continues to cut, chop, saw, and cook her body for hours—long after the actual moment of her death and his consequent release from the danger she had presented?

Item: Joy, too, can be of prolonged duration and great intensity. When any of the professional sports franchises achieves transient dominion by winning a championship game, entire cities have been known to revel in the streets for hours. Of interest, too, is the fact that police officers line the route of revelry, containing it within limits determined by bureaucratic decision. As any student of history can attest, for more than 25 centuries such victory celebrations have been choreographed by civic decree. And redemption from the terror of wartime is even more dramatic a source of prolonged joy. I was ten years old when World War II ended; nobody then alive can forget the extended nationwide sense of relief, release, and joy that accompanied the signing of the armistice agreement. There is plenty of newsreel footage available to anyone who wishes to confirm my observations of that sustained societal outpouring of love.

It is very easy to accept the occasional burst of joy or violence. Why, how, affect can be maintained at such high intensity for so long a period of time is less apparent. We prefer to think about disquieting themes only when we wish, often treating criminal activity as a macabre source of entertainment. Actually, I suspect that the immense popularity of gangster movies and the entire genre of film violence is largely dependent on our fascination with the prolonged display of affect. As far as I have been able to determine, *attack other* scripts are a way of life in the criminal world—what we see in the movies is little more than a dramatic version of this approach to life. Real criminal activity requires a blend of highly magnified affect (for which we seek societal controls rather than understanding) and some sort of entrepreneurial skill (which is, indeed, capable of limitation by law). The equation of crime and punishment does act as a deterrent, but only in those situations where affective magnification is much lower than in the incidents cited here. There has been very little work done on the affective roots of violence

Always there is some popular theory offering an easy explanation for such phenomena. An earlier, more righteous era thought such "excesses" possible only in cases of moral failure, with shame and guilt acting to prevent wrong-doing. Today, however, it is fashionable to say that violent or cruel behavior is both abusive and based in shame. Therapists, teachers, preachers, and politicians who declaim about "abuse" (whether of spouses or children, by pain or sexuality, or of oneself with any number of drugs or activities) are avoiding the task of figuring out what really is going on. The word itself is a clue to its failure to explain anything—to *abuse* means "to use improperly." No child, no spouse, no employee, is meant to be used. Most of the experts involved in this sort of work speak as if once we stop ab-using people we can use them properly!

The literature of "abuse" is awash in moral judgment and condign punishment. Abuse has become a code word for any behavior that is to be treated or managed or distanced with dissmell and disgust in order to produce shame and guilt in the perpetrator, thus justifying some form of "cleansing anger." It should be obvious that these tactics merely shift people toward the *attack other* pole of the compass of shame and away from the *attack self, avoidance,* or *withdrawal* poles. Rather than a valid explanation of the mechanisms involved, such systems are actually part of the current cultural drift toward machismo. What they really do is declare machismo as normative, place the accused in the category of reviled things, and shuck any responsibility for study. Needed is an approach that allows a deeper understanding.

I think we can do a bit better. We can figure out how people get this way.

THE ROOTS OF MADNESS

There is a cultural stereotype, a sturdy myth around which we build our false understanding of childhood. According to this widely believed fiction, parents accord special treatment to their children, giving them the benefit of kindness and sensitivity they would not show to strangers, competitors, or enemies. The story line includes subtexts about mother love, paternal protectiveness, and the sanctity of the family. But to whom is this narrative applied? From what "central casting" reservoir are these actors drawn? What is the raw material from which parents and families are constructed?

We are taught from earliest childhood to compete, to be "number one" at all costs, to cheat, take, trick, push, strive, connive, to reduce anyone whose success brings us shame, to win, enlarge ourselves, build an image, resist any effort to reduce us in any way. Life is complex, demanding, sometimes pleasant, often harsh. All of us live with our own library of scripts, each of which has been devised to manage scenes both wonderful and terrible.

Some of us marry when we have "won" at courtship, often competing for love and striving for social success in climates characterized by the entire range of negative affect. Many others consider marriage and its constellation of responsibilities to be a "trap." For them, to marry is to lose, rather than to win.

But as if a switch had been thrown, in the moment of marriage two individuals who had been living and competing in such a noisy world are expected to change suddenly into warm, sensitive, caring, stable, and empathic adults. For better or worse, those who enter into the state of marriage are seen from without as part of a culturally defined romance. Notwithstanding whatever adjustments to each other were made during the courtship, throughout the first phase of marriage the new partners must learn to merge their lives.

While it is true that each of us brings to marriage some stock of idealized scripts, of roles we hope to play with the consenting adult of our choice, our ability to live within these sets of expectation is limited by many factors. We who become parents were once children born with our own roiling symphony of innate affects and wordless drives. No one emerges from the birth canal with the slightest idea about the modulation of anything—and we cannot teach what we have not learned. Almost everything we know about soothing, calming, relaxing, consoling, comforting, satisfying, cheering, or loving others has been learned from someone else and adapted for our own use within highly personal affect modulation scripts.

We need to discuss what happens when the world of the infant is not soothing, not calming, not relaxing, not consoling, not comforting, not satisfying or cheering or loving. Several questions emerge: What happens when those who are responsible for the nurturance of children fail at the task of teaching the attenuation and modulation of affect? What happens if the general effect of parental attention is an increase in the density of affect? How much intensification of affect can one handle? To what stratagems do we turn in order to handle the higher realms of emotion, mood at the maximum?

There is a subtle and wrenching problem that bothers everybody who has ever tried to approach these questions. All of us tend to get angry at parents who mistreat their children. Our own morality is deeply offended when we learn about intentional cruelty or living conditions that terrify us. Disgust, dissmell, and fear coalesce to produce a sense of revulsion and horror as we approach this subject. The distancing emotions interfere with science, too.

And there are other, frankly personal reasons for our discomfort. Notwithstanding how sincerely we loved our parents and felt loved by them, nor how much happiness we assign our memories of childhood, not one of us grew up free of discomfort. Though the reader be of cheery disposition and wondrous calm, perhaps the beneficiary of optimal psychotherapy by a true master, yet there remain feelings and memories with which any of us may be loath to deal. Whatever disavowal of memory has been used to protect us from affective response to our own history will be undone by this material.

Empathy and identification are not always pleasant. The normal, healthy adult feels the pain and suffering of any child who is being beaten and humiliated. Often we lose our neutrality and think only of punishing the perpetrator of a crime. Here, however, we must suspend these judgments in order to study the actual flow of events involved.

You have to start somewhere. From the outset, I have focused on innate mechanisms and the effect on development of their modulation by external forces. I take for granted the realities of actual existence and the natural imperfection of parents. The entire psychotherapy movement can be viewed as a loving attempt to undo the effects of such imperfection and to offer individuals the chance to become someone from a more optimal history. Although everything presented in this book can be used to form a more effective system of therapy, my purpose here is the elucidation of the processes that make it necessary.

TEMPERAMENT

A good place to begin is with the concept of *baseline*. Think of it as a matter of architecture: Visualize a huge group of tall buildings interconnected at many levels. If you have enough space on each "floor" so that one could run from building to building without ever going up or down, the concept of "ground floor" changes dramatically. Many people might live, work, and play only on the twelfth floor, taking it as their shared world—the locus of their existence. Another population lives, works, and plays on the second, yet another on the fourth below ground. (If the cluster of buildings gets so large as to become the crust of the earth, then the concept of true ground level is lost forever.) In the course of normal life, all denizens get to travel one or two planes above and below their normal locus of activity. This latter vertical motion represents their normal range of affective experience. Each group tends to accept its horizontal reality as the baseline, the norm, the zero point from which all reckoning is made.

People seem to cluster on the basis of their inherent, or constitutional, activity level, which is sometimes described as *temperament.* There is a wide range of "normal" temperament. Some of us quite naturally work 18 hours a day, enjoying the free and unhampered use of our talents and abilities. Others feel it an imposition to engage in effortful activity for more than a couple of hours at a time, after which they tune in to some form of passive entertainment. Most presidential candidates and chief executive officers of huge corporations, for another example, seem to need and prefer five or less hours of sleep each day. Certain jobs seem to attract specific types of temperament.

We humans are born with a wide range of possible levels of inner nature or temper. Often I have heard the mother of an extraordinarily intense and successful adult describe this offspring as having been more active than her other children even when in the womb!

Yet such an activity level is neither necessary nor sufficient for the achievement of success in life. Temperament is only one of the innate characteristics that goes into the mix—just like size, intelligence, physical strength, degree of beauty, and talent. An interesting aspect of my work as a clinician has been the observation that those who benefit most from successful therapy seem to find their own level. An enlightened adult lives and works in terms of his or her true complement of attributes. Most people have grown up living on the wrong floor of my metaphorical building.

Temperament seems to be an innate set point, the net result or gestalt of perhaps dozens of biological factors. No matter what level of activity is normal for any of us, it provides the zero point from which we then experience positive and negative affect. The woman who enjoys practicing law 14 hours a day, playing squash or swimming daily, and writing for a couple of hours in the evening is brought by enjoyment–joy to a different null point than one who feels it unnatural and an imposition to work more than a couple of hours at a time. To each, the affect itself will be experienced as contentment and solace; what each does or thinks as the result of that moment of peace will be dramatically different. Both constitutions, of course, are normal and healthy.

If you have ever played in a band or orchestra, you know the difference between the way music is written for the various instruments. For the piano, the five lines that make up the G and D clefs form an invariable semantic structure; notes are always where you expect them to be, and the key is indicated by the presence of sharp and flat signs at the beginning of the line. But clarinet music is different. The same five lines represent entirely different parts of the scale depending on the key chosen. So it is for temperament. We are born at some place on a scale decided outside of our understanding and control, designed to live within a structure not of our devising. And it is from the null point of our own particular scale that each of us is moved by affect.

It was Tomkins who established the concept of an affective baseline around which is sketched our experience of good and bad feelings. Our task here is to build a logic for those situations when affect is pushed, or magnified, to levels of density beyond anything for which we possess skills or even equipment for modulation. How many floors can the human be made to travel before reaching some critical end-point? When do we get nosebleeds from the height and earaches from the depths of affective excursion?

The problem falls naturally into distinct categories: What biological and psychological mechanisms increase the density of affect? How do we experience affect of high density and high intensity? By what systems do we attempt to handle such assemblages of affect? How is personality influenced by such emotion and our characteristic ways of handling it? We need a special kind of map for our housing project—one that shows not only who lives where, but how people differ on the basis of their internal and external affective environment.

THE MECHANISMS OF INCREASE

Biochemical

In this current sociocultural environment it is fashionable to suggest that any violent action was triggered by, or made possible only by, drugs. "Everybody" knows that excesses of emotion can be "caused" by drugs. Naturally, since normal affect is dependent on neurotransmitters and the family of substances I have called mediators of innate affect, all emotion is in some way chemical. Here we are talking about affect that is initiated solely by one of these chemicals, not the situation when the chemical has been released at its normal point in the chain of reactions.

Although it has been fashionable to say that drugs act as a "releasing agent," in Chapter 1 I explained that exogenous chemicals can produce somatic effects that feel nearly identical to those produced by ordinary innate affect because they mimic the effect of the normal chemical mediators. A single cup of coffee or glass of wine can cause a surge of excitement or contentment; these affective excursions, or movements from the baseline, are of brief duration and limited extent.

Our reaction to brief bouts of chemically induced affect is dictated by our way of handling affects that have been triggered by their normal programs—as if the induced mood had come from an affect script. Imagine what would happen were we to arrange for a steady infusion of some mediator substance. Since chemically induced affect tends to last as long as the substance in question is active, this would produce a prolonged and intense emotional state. *Any affect that is supported by such a constant chemical presence becomes the baseline, the temperament of an individual.* Rather than being experienced as an innate affect with a known and predictable temporal contour, it becomes something more like a mood. When such a mood is the more-or-less-permanent atmosphere of one's inner life, it becomes part of the self, a piece of an identity. In the language of script theory, any time our biochemical environment allows an affect to become a constant presence, that affect comes to magnify all other psychological functions. All of our scripts are formed with this strange affective experience as a constant magnifying force!

To me, the best model for this sort of chemically induced mood state is the regular and patterned shift between mania and depression seen in bipolar, or manic-depressive, illness. During a manic episode, for instance, the chemicals that cause the astonishing increase in interest–excitement are responsible for the magnification of every psychological function. Mania can push any affect, any drive, any form of thinking, to such a degree that it can become toxic for the organism.

Similarly, depressed people have been known to remain frozen in inaction, unable even to think effectively for long periods of time because of the profound interference produced by that phase of the illness. ("I didn't leave my house for four years," said one patient.) Anybody who is afflicted by a chemical lassitude or by a chemically produced and maintained state of increased excitement, must somehow come to terms with this emotional environment. The prolonged and relatively constant chemical aberration controls the floor on which one lives. The person not afflicted by this illness might consider it merely an alteration of normal biology, an oddity of nature; for the bipolar patient it produces "reality."

This effect on overall mood and general functioning, which we might think of as a biochemical alteration of the affective set point, can be either endogenous or exogenous, depending on the source of the chemical. Among the endogenous factors would be the level of thyroid, adrenal, pituitary, and sexual hormones, as well as the neurotransmitters involved in bipolar illness; among the exogenous would be a host of substances taken into the body for the explicit purpose of altering mood. For instance, the culture of medical

machismo normative in my youth required house officers to work like machines with 36 hours of activity and 12 hours of rest. In such an environment
one drinks strong coffee all day and all night; temperament was maintained by
caffeine.

The weariness and torpor produced by failure of the thyroid gland come
from two realms of causation: Not only does the general reduction in biological functioning seen in hypothyroidism drop one to a lower floor of our
building, but the hormone itself seems to be a factor in the biochemical circuitry for interest–excitement and anger–rage. All of the life-management
scripts devised by a hypothyroid patient are colored by this biological reduction in set-point.

Similarly, consider the patient whose chronic asthma is being treated by the
more-or-less constant use of medication that mimics the effects of adrenalin.
This person, too, must devise life-management scripts that take into account
whatever limitations are presented by the basic respiratory illness, as well as
the constant sense of rush or hurry brought by medicine. Most of us have on
one occasion or another ingested some substance like this; most over-the-
counter drugs for nasal stuffiness include such compounds. In addition to their
expected effect on respiration, they produce a rush of excitement quite welcome when our activity level has been reduced by a minor virus. But can you
imagine living day by day with the degree of affective magnification produced
by this kind of adrenergic drug? Inescapable and immutable, this sense of hurry
must be incorporated into the patient's self system as the new baseline.

Obviously, when our general level of functioning is held down by some
biological interference with the normal range of affective expression, as in
certain forms of depression, optimal treatment requires ingestion of a chemical
that neutralizes the abnormal biology. But what about people who end up
using caffeinated beverages all day long in order to fight off normal weariness,
or cocaine to increase the general level of excitement and arousal, or tranquilizers to reduce constant fear? All of these substances might be considered acceptable under certain circumstances; when they become constant companions, regular or stable components of one's life, they come to govern the floor
on which we live. This association between the (natural or artificial) chemical
environment and baseline temperament is a reality of existence—neither good
nor bad.

It is difficult not to be deeply moved when watching the emotional growth
of an adult whose affective set point has been stabilized by the use of lithium
salts or an antidepressant. Patients whose chronically low self-esteem, fear of
rejection, and nearness to shame are due to some malfunction in neurotrans-

mitter mechanisms become different people when given the opportunity to take proper medication. Chemically induced shame can become such a dominant part of one's life that all action is impeded by shame magnification.

It would take a shelf of books to describe in detail all the possible interactions involving chemical substances, the affect system, and temperament. Important here is only the idea that the chronic experience of an aberrant biochemical mediator, or of a normal mediator pushed to an abnormal level, can alter the affective set point. The emotional development of a child who has grown up with a chemical aberration, or in the care of a parent with some sort of biological alteration of temperament, will be influenced powerfully by these factors.

Neocortical

It was Basch who suggested to me that the much-vaunted neocortex, that part of the brain which is responsible for most of what people call "thinking" or "cognition," had evolved to enable the modulation of innate affect. "Look at it," he said. "It wraps around the rest of the brain like a cap." One at a time, little structures must have developed, each allowing a bit more opportunity to evaluate, understand, manage, control, and respond to innate affect, as well as the situations in which it had been triggered. Any increase in the potential for affective modulation might have conferred on the organism an increase in the potential for survival. True enough, the network formed by the interconnections between these new brain systems has turned out to confer other benefits. But Basch may be right to suggest this concept for its origin. The thinking of the new brain may have evolved to alter the thinking of the old.

If you watch any experienced mother deal with any ordinary crying baby, you can get a pretty good idea of the ways affect is attenuated. There is no better example of the interconnection between subcortical and neocortical activity. First, she seems to tune in on the display of affect itself, perhaps mimicking it briefly. This momentary joining, or linking, is what we call affective resonance; it is the beginning of empathy. Next, this caregiver attempts to find out which of the most common stimuli to affect has acted as trigger. If the child is hungry, food will be indicated; if in pain, then attention to its source is warranted. Concomitant with her efforts to answer the affect-triggering message will be a decrease in the amount of affect generated.

But if none of these simple remedies seems applicable or available, something must be done about the affect being expressed—affect must be modulated for its own sake. Now she calls on her own repertoire of calming techniques. First, as caregiver she must check her own control of the affect she has begun to experience through resonance; next will she demonstrate for her child how this control is accomplished. In order to reduce crying, she may hold the baby to her chest and rock side-to-side. Also might she make rhythmic noises at a volume precisely attuned to that of the baby—louder when the baby's cries are more strident, softer and cooing to merge with its quiet sobs. At other times she will simply take over the infant's affect by merging with it for a moment and then switching to another of her own choosing. Done well, this can be a fine way to distract a child; done without regard for the moment-to-moment response produced, it can have the opposite effect and push the child into a far greater degree of negative affect. Successful techniques include nuzzling and stroking.

Sometimes all we need is a brief period of freedom from an affect that is not being maintained by its original triggering stimulus but has begun to recycle itself through the recursive process of internal contagion. Bright lights and jangling bells can distract attention for a moment, just as a pistol shot or handclap can cause a momentary break in the flow of affective expression by triggering surprise–startle. "BOO!" is such a resetting stimulus.

In an older child we can suggest a strategy more dependent on higher cortical function, like counting to ten, reciting the letters of the alphabet, or naming the 50 states and their capital cities. As adults we can disperse the mood of our everyday lives by attending any public entertainment, taking a vacation, or going for a drive in the countryside. Usually we return refreshed, or at least in a somewhat different "frame of mind" from when we left. Each of these methods works by providing a new source for affect, which then takes over the central assembly and keeps us focused on this new source long enough for the original (noxious) mood to wane.

So there is a wide range of actions capable of reducing or "down-regulating" affect. Of perhaps equal importance is the rarely discussed fact that there is a wide range of actions capable of increasing or "up-regulating" innate affect. So important to the very concept of innate affect is this idea that affect is experienced in degrees of intensity that Tomkins gave all of them paired names indicating the range over which each might be expressed. (It would have been easy enough to call one "dissmell–shunning" and the other "disgust–revulsion." "By giving dissmell and disgust single-word names," Tomkins told me, "I meant to drive home the point that they were highly complex auxiliaries to a drive, rather than true affects.") Anything capable of triggering anger can be pushed further, leading to rage; similar observations can be made for all affects.

Extending Basch's above-mentioned idea and extrapolating it in a direction he never intended, I suspect we can approach this aspect of the realm of very dense affect by calling attention to the same neocortical mechanisms that may have evolved to modulate affect. It is my opinion that *any faculty capable of down-regulating affect can be used in a perverse fashion to increase it to levels that may be toxic for the organism.* One of the penalties exacted by the inexorable process of evolution has been the emergence of affective magnification far in excess of anything that is good or useful for the species.

Whatever emotional waters can be calmed by music can be roiled by music; involved is one's reaction to music. Sudden bursts of sound can startle; soft music can soothe; loud music can irritate. A slow rhythm can provide a stimulus profile analogous to enjoyment–joy, while an intense, fast beat can mimic and therefore trigger excitement, fear, distress, or anger. The child who can be calmed by counting privately to ten can be made more agitated by a parent who fires questions at a rate sufficient to increase agitation; the same neocortical mechanism is responsible in each case.

Note, too, that there are ways of preconditioning the organism so that an affect is likely to be expressed at the higher, rather than the lower, end of its spectrum. One does not have to be at the baseline, at the null state of no affect, when a new stimulus for affect begins. The alterations in gradient or density responsible for affect can be initiated from any level of preexisting stimulation. Certain stimuli can accumulate—when I am hungry or exhausted any increase in my load is likely to make me shift from distress to anger. Even birds, who have no affect system, show an exaggerated startle reaction when "potentiated" to do so by chronic fear. (It is unfortunate that few, if any, of those psychologists and neurophysiologists who have studied such additive effects have also taken into account the nature of the human affect system.)

We like to think of the caregiver as one who calms the fears of the young— explaining away the confusions of childhood, removing or deciphering whatever mystery might frighten. But imagine, for a moment, a child being reared in an atmosphere of parent-inspired terror—danger everywhere, solace nowhere to be found, love unimaginable. There really are parents who do more than warn their children about the bogey man or Sweeney Todd; they seek out and call attention to anything that might produce fear. I mean to suggest that some mothers and fathers have less interest in solace than control. (The power to create dependency through fear is seductive. It binds the frightened to the giver of fear and provides a system of behavioral control.) In such an environment one lives on guard rather than at rest.

Then, too, there are kinder parents who have no choice of climate and must raise their offspring to handle a terrifying, uncompromising reality. Such children grow to maturity within a mood state of chronic fear. The hovering, omnipresent affect fear–terror will magnify every scene so that even the most banal and simple stimulus is likely to be viewed as frightening simply because it has been encountered in the context of fear.

Were we born without a neocortex, without the ability to store, link, group, assemble, retrieve, or associate memory, such a degree of magnification would not occur. The seeds of this process may be seen in the work on fear-potentiated startle in pigeons. But this is minor compared to the intensity of magnification made possible by the new brain. However, affective magnification is not dependent only on neocortical thinking. Magnification is assisted by data coming from the feedback provided by affect receptors located all over the body, from the contour of events made to occur at far-flung sites of action. Yet it is our very ability to learn that makes magnified affect both bearable and unbearable.

Try another affect: Imagine someone who grows up in a city where so much is happening at the same time that the dominant affect is distress–anguish. Momentary joy, which moves the healthy infant from bad to good, can move the troubled adult only from worse to bad. Contrast the most ghastly districts of Manhattan, Los Angeles, or Chicago with rural Maine. An event that would perhaps earn only a quizzical glance in one locale, might cause tempers to flare in the other. The very density of some cities makes them tinderboxes simply because so many people are forced to live at a high level of stimulation; in this context solace provides only brief respite before one returns to the baseline distress. I have read many studies of experimental situations in which animals like laboratory rats were bred to population densities that produced horrific changes in normal behavior. Imagine reinterpreting such work in terms of the human affect system and our potential for script formation!

More? Anybody who has the ability to tune in to the affective experience of another person is said to be empathic—and that is supposed to be a worthy talent. Yet what of individuals (and they are legion) who use this empathic skill to achieve affective resonance and then proceed to make worse whatever was going on in the other? Call it cruelty, or sadism, if you will. But no matter how such behavior is viewed within the moral system important to you, the "technical aspects," the mechanism for its effectiveness, are worthy of study.

For better or worse, the overwhelming majority of our populace really doesn't give a hoot about the inner experience of others. Most of the time, if someone (infant or adult) is expressing affect in a manner or at an intensity we find unpleasant, we do something about it for our own sake. We dislike the contagious quality of affect unless it entertains us; in fact, the social rules require everybody to mute the display of affect. Usually we simply ask people to stop shouting, or crying, or laughing too loudly. But when these appeals fail, we resort to more restrictive techniques, which themselves produce a peculiar constellation of emotional effects. Every non-empathic interpersonal experience increases the amount of negative affect floating around. Every recurrent non-empathic interpersonal experience must be handled by some sort of affect management script, which then becomes part of the repertoire we think of as our personality.

Asked to summarize the concept of an affect-management script, most readers would describe the methods and techniques through which adults calm or diminish the noxious experience of negative affect. Yet only a tiny fraction of such scripts involves the induction of calm. Take, for instance, the entire library of scripts described as the *attack other* mode of reaction to shame. Shame (shifted, interpreted, and experienced as the idea of personal inferiority) becomes anger, put-down, calumny, ridicule, torture, abuse, rape. Hardly a calming experience in the lot.

Every one of us has attempted to improve the mood of the moment by substituting one affect for another. There are times when it feels just great to yell and scream at the ludicrous theater of professional wrestling, to feel terribly frightened at a horror movie, or to savor the strange combination of excitement and fear we call "being thrilled" while watching others take mortal risks. These dynamic shifts from one affect to another provide an excellent form of distraction from discomfort. Yet sometimes we get stuck in the distraction, which threatens to take us over in ways for which we are unprepared. Intending to avoid or escape shame and distress, we can get involved in behavior that itself magnifies affect and becomes life-threatening. Anything can be pushed to and beyond the limits of tolerance.

So many and varied are the strategies for increasing affect that any summary tends to trivialize the process. The subject is one that must be approached in meticulous detail elsewhere; it is far beyond the scope of this present book. Here I wish only to point out that life tends to augment rather than damp our ambient load of affect. Partly responsible is the wondrous neocortex, the giver of complexity and calculation, of modern memory and mimesis. The batch of equipment that may indeed have evolved to modulate affect can also be used to push affect to ever-higher limits.

Forgive an interpolation important to one of my generation. If there remains any psychoanalytically trained reader who has not long ago thrown down in disgust this treatise on the nature of emotion, there is yet another stake to be placed in the heart of Freud's theory. Freud maintained that all psychic energy came from the drives, which were expressed as the *id* and seen most clearly in the roiling affective expression of the infant. Since, to him, all emotion was derived from drive forces, it is by definition impossible for any adult emotion to be more intense, more powerful, than that seen in the infant. Yet there is no infantile analogue, nothing in the repertoire of the infant, that resembles the prolonged and intense displays of emotion described at the beginning of this chapter. Psychoanalytic theory contains no provision for the unlimited magnification of affect by affect.

I have deliberately avoided discussing what happens when shame is magnified to toxic proportions. Shame affect involves a painful analogic amplification of any impediment to positive affect. No matter when and how triggered, shame damps and impedes and reduces and makes painful everything with which it is coassembled. Yet, before we can consider the specific problem of an atmosphere of shame, replete with reactive systems organized at the furthest extension of the scripts found in the compass of shame, we must extend our survey of madness. In the next chapter I will sketch some of the ways affect— affect in general—is handled when it goes beyond our limits of tolerance.

29

OVERLOAD: AFFECT BEYOND THE LIMITS OF TOLERANCE

Need we be surprised at the idea that a certain density of affect can be "too much" for the system? All bodily systems have limits. Take, for instance, the outer reaches of athletic ability.

We devote a great deal of attention to the exploits of our finest athletes, who spend their lives attempting to perform certain tasks at peak levels of effectiveness. There was a time when everybody wondered whether it was possible to run a mile in less than four minutes. Working in the physiology laboratory and studying his own oxygen utilization, the young English physician Roger Bannister devised a strategy that allowed him to increase his already remarkable efficiency to the point where he became the first to break through that particular barrier. Every year another great champion shaves a few tenths of a second off that record; indeed, today's best runners rarely fail to equal Bannister's achievement.

Yet the human machine seems incapable of running this distance in significantly less time—no one talks of a "three-minute mile" or a "two-minute mile." The concept of a four-minute mile remains an excellent approximation of optimal human performance. Even though we like to think of our species as capable of continuous and limitless improvement, we do seem to have certain boundaries.

Our culture calls the upper range of affective experience by the simple name "stress," thus ignoring the whole problem of identifying its components. Sometimes we are taken over by affect of tornadic intensity, when the "mood of the moment" creates a din so loud that we cannot hear anything else. Affect at this level is so intense (many together, one amplifying the other, producing sequences of terrible vehemence) that we lose much of our ability to give it a specific name.

In this chapter I will discuss what happens when normal distractions cannot work simply because they are incapable of garnering enough attention to take over a central assembly locked to a more powerful stimulus. (I am unlikely to be distracted from a hurricane by the tinkling of a harpsichord.) Just as it takes dynamite to loosen a log jam, the mechanisms capable of giving us freedom from dense affect have evolved to handle other stimuli of great intensity.

THE PARADIGM OF PAIN

There are well-defined limits to the conditions under which we can appreciate certain stimuli and to the intensity of stimulation that the body can handle. Our experience of pain provides an excellent illustration. As we discussed earlier, pain itself may be described as an analogue of injury in that the sensation itself bears some felt resemblance to what caused it. Pain enters consciousness—calls attention to injury—by providing information that is at once localizing and motivating. When something hurts we know not only where the damage has occurred but that urgent attention must be paid to the source of this discomfort. It is for this reason that Tomkins considers pain as a *system* to lie somewhere between drive (an information source) and affect (an amplifier). It has features of both. Pure somatic pain achieves meaning and significance based on these properties.

Although pain and affect are neuropsychological events produced by quite different mechanisms, there is a significant relation between them. All of the negative affects are experienced as intrinsically painful, even though the discomforts of fear, dissmell, disgust, anger, distress, and shame are qualitatively different both from each other and from the type of sensation experienced when one of the pain receptors is stimulated. And, on the other hand, the duration, intensity, and stimulus contour of pain can trigger any of the negative affects as an accompaniment.

Pain, then, has evolved as a signal that tends to enter consciousness and motivate us to remove its cause so that the message can be turned off. The two parts of the pain message—localization in space and motivation—can be separated. This is why the tooth hurts until you call the dentist—once the message has been heard, it no longer need be urgent.

The ability of pain to distract us is limited by many factors. In the heat of battle soldiers often are aware of but not hurt by wounds that might at other times produce agony. One's ability to survive on the battlefield requires attention to a wide variety of percepts unrelated to the self. It is these other sources which therefore gain urgency through affective amplification, emphasis far in excess of that produced by pain, thus guaranteeing them preferential entry into the central assembly.

Simply stated, sometimes an otherwise competent signal is lost in the noise of other, "louder" information. Affect is one of the bulletins that can overwhelm and replace pain. Something like this is going on when hypnosis is used to control pain. Hypnosis involves a contract between operator and subject in which some sort of affect mutualization is achieved by the techniques of hypnotic induction, after which attention is shifted to another focus.*

Notice that pain is unlike affect in that it is neither a contagious nor a recursive stimulus. Because it is initiated by highly specific receptors, pain does not maintain itself or trigger more pain; nor is my pain likely to cause pain in an empathic other. Each affect, however, is triggered by some stimulus that forms a profile, and it is this contour that is duplicated as the innate affect. We should not be surprised that affect itself triggers more affect, because the system has no way of detecting differences in sources. Pain, on the other hand, is so specific to the site that has been irritated that its message is intrinsically specific.

Like the drives, then, pain provides information about a highly specific source; affect amplifies any information and is intrinsically general. The hypnotic device of shifting attention from pain to affect, and then to some other focus, allows one to pretend that the source of discomfort is far afield from the actual tissue that has been injured. It can do this simply because heed has been shifted from a system with only one possible source to another system capable of being triggered by a nearly infinite number of sources.

It is interesting to consider our response to torture, which may be defined as *the perverse use of pain to motivate rather than inform.* When the operator produces pain of an order and intensity beyond what can be tolerated by the subject, the central assembly switches into the circuit we call unconsciousness. As well as providing a remarkable degree of anesthesia, this mechanism turns off all contact with the tormenting outside world. So, at least in the case of pain, the body is wired to release us from stimuli outside the range it can utilize.

I live by a stream that meanders through a suburban neighborhood crossed by roads. In their infinite wisdom, the civic officials of an earlier era elected not

---

*I have discussed this mechanism at some length in Nathanson (1988).

to build bridges, but to save money by channeling the stream into large pipes over which they laid roadways. This system works well until we have a major downpour, when the sheer volume of water far exceeds what can possibly flow through conduits of that size. Rainwater, unable to go in its usual direction, backs up in the form of a flood.

In physics, this is referred to as a "bandwidth" phenomenon, involving the relation between anything that must be transported and the means available for its movement. A traffic jam, with motorists searching for all possible alternative routes, is an automotive flood; gridlock and logjams are bandwidth problems. So may we use the language of physics to describe the loss of consciousness in response to overwhelming pain. Stimulus overload triggers a shunt to another system.

The affect system has some similar limiting features. The nine genetically determined, prewired mechanisms described by Tomkins govern our range of normal emotional responses. The enormous range of possible emotions is a function of the permutations and combinations of these nine programs assembled with the immense variety of actual human experiences to form higher-order scripts. It is for this reason that moods tend to cluster into certain predictable groups. Emotional expression, for all its complexity, is limited to what can be done with the tools at hand. The variety is great, but not infinite.

Then what about our ability to handle densely packed affect? What does it mean to be flooded or overwhelmed with emotion? The process of magnification can produce an emotional state so extraordinary, so strained, stinging, extreme, or radical, that it must be managed by techniques that have little or nothing to do with affect. The extremes of emotional excess and explosion that we call psychopathology are based on normal and otherwise healthy psychological mechanisms that have been called into play to handle situations for which they did not evolve.

One model involves the history of the mechanism called "fainting." Historically, we know that it was once fashionable for women to faint when confronted by certain situations, especially those involving shame. Indeed, like so many poorly examined phenomena, this used to be considered a normal ingredient of feminine physiology. Nevertheless, men and women are equally likely to faint in anticipation of severe pain, when given an injection, or when blood is drawn. Such a response may be considered analogous to the loss of consciousness seen in torture.

Sometimes the operative affect is fear–terror, sometimes shame–humiliation; with a bit of investigation one can usually figure out just which is involved. But central to the symptom is the avoidance of affect, a technique of sidestepping—moving away from it into something else. The general name for all mechanisms of this sort is *dissociation*, in which the central assembly causes a shift from one form of consciousness to another. Most likely we should drop this term, which comes from an era when it was thought that the symptoms observed resulted from an interruption in the flow of information from one neural center to another. The actual mechanism for the sort of shutdown seen in dissociation is more likely to involve turning down the nonspecific amplification of the reticular activation system. We know now that nothing really becomes dissociated—only a finely tuned, correctly operating neurological system can produce such an effect.

Today, someone who faints in public is more likely to be teased than comforted—shame has come to prevent, rather than cause, fainting. But the very fact that women rarely swoon in public these days suggests both that there is a volitional component involved—a choice of response patterns—and that (as a biological mechanism) it remains available. These clinical anecdotes hint that we humans can switch to our huge repertoire of devices for the management of pain when intense and densely packed affect cannot be reduced by techniques drawn from our repertoire for affect modulation. It is only when an intense affect has gone on for a long period of time that it becomes what we think of as too dense.

There is a wondrous logic to such a shift. Whereas affect can be triggered by a myriad of sources, pain normally is focal. When someone is overwhelmed by negative affect due to any of the causes described in the previous chapter, the act of pretending that the discomfort is due to somatic pain allows one to mitigate the noxious affective experience by techniques that work for pain. Anything that has ever worked to reduce pain has been used to detoxify devastating degrees of affect.

The transformation from affect to pain is something like hypnotic pain control in reverse. I had a personal experience of this conversion of symptoms early in my medical career, one that may serve as an example of the process. It was during my residency in internal medicine that I entered a formal psychoanalysis, hoping to find the sources of my personal discomfort. A month or so into the process I developed a three-millimeter red lump on the tip of my tongue; initially merely uncomfortable, it soon became intensely painful. Careful inspection of the swelling revealed nothing alarming, and the steady, boring pain went away when I put ice chips on it. I learned to walk around the hospital carrying a little paper cup full of ice chips. Despite this inventive solution, the pain only intensified; now I began to use a topical anesthetic. Only because this local anesthetic tasted horrible did I mention the situation in an analytic session.

To my surprise, this localized steady pain was of great interest to my analyst, and we spent a number of sessions trying to link it to some part of my emotional life. In desperation, for there was no way I was going to get the picture unaided, eventually he asked, "Something raw and painful on the tip of your tongue? Don't people often comment that they have something right on the tip of their tongue but can't say it?" Literally within minutes of my realization that I was angry, very angry at someone, both the steady pain and the red lump vanished.

Psychotherapy works. Only one other time in my life was I forced to endure that steadily painful lesion on my tongue, which reappeared in the context of a romantic involvement. Forced by neurosis to disavow any anger at my then beloved, instead I suffered the distressing or angry pain of psycho-somatic illness. Nowadays this sore appears only when I disavow my need for sleep and work past any rational level of tolerance. Fatigue, too, is a constant-density stimulus quite analogous to the steady, boring pain of my private and idiosyncratic internal signal.

The scripts that had blocked both the expression and the awareness of my anger are too complex and personal to warrant mention here; my purpose is only to suggest that the monotonously painful lesion functioned as an ana-logue of the affect anger–rage. I do not know how such things come to happen, even though as a psychotherapist I have seen dozens of similar cases. (Surely we can admire what we do not completely understand.) What I have come to accept is that a steady, intensely noxious emotional stimulus, ignored and disavowed in its more usual form of distress and anger, was converted into something that I would not ignore. That it could be partially blocked by the use of "painkillers" is evidence for the efficacy of the shunting mechanism.

Most, if not all, nonmedical narcotic use works in this manner. These drugs seem to diminish the experience of pain by altering consciousness at many levels of brain function, although more gradually than the on/off switch of fainting. Taken in excess, they certainly will knock one out; used when nothing hurts and one is in a state of pleasant calm, they produce an uncomfortable loss of critical awareness. The majority of our population makes occasional use of alcohol, nicotine, caffeine, marijuana, and a host of other substances in order to ameliorate intense noxious affect.

Once, in 1970, I discussed with philosopher Alan Watts our societal use of drugs. He commented that "chemicals certainly can be a doorway into another realm of consciousness. Unfortunately, for some people the drugs become a revolving door in which they get stuck." Since street drugs offer only a tran-sient and (at best) a partial solution for the problems caused by otherwise intolerable levels of affect, many people attempt to surmount this obstacle by

increasing both the dose of their chosen substance and the frequency at which
they use it. The scripts and predicaments of addiction are quite another matter,
well beyond the scope of this current book.

There are many other systems of affect avoidance based on the model of
dissociation and pain. One, just now receiving the degree of scrutiny it deserves, is the problem of those who have been exposed to so much terror,
humiliation, and sexual arousal that they are forced to call upon even more
psychological systems. The large group of dissociative disorders, including the
florid syndrome called *multiple personality disorder*, is characterized by alteration in the sense of self as a device for the amelioration of unbearable affect.
Essentially, the central assembly decides that, although it can do nothing about
the immediate overwhelming situation, it can trick us into believing that it is
happening to someone else. Only those who disavow the whole idea of
affective overload deny the ubiquity and importance of these terrifying illnesses. Excellent work in this area may be found in the writings of Richard P.
Kluft and Frank Putnam.

Other dissociative defenses against intense and enduring affect include immersion in physical activity. Most of us know at least one adult who seems
addicted to jogging or some other solitary form of exercise. The simple regularity of the discipline itself acts to induce trance, while the exertion itself is
usually maintained at the border of pain. ("No pain, no gain.") Certainly there
are many whose interest in physical fitness is reasonable and healthy. Yet in
this current era I suspect that the triad of "sporting goods" stores, exercise
facilities, and "sports medicine" clinics offers mute testimony to the lure of
physical exercise as an affect-modulation script. When used to reduce intense
and abiding shame, these scripts for dissociation form a significant part of the
avoidance pole of the compass of shame.

Often we see a macabre reversal of this process, when successful dissociation produces a kind of anesthesia called *depersonalization*, itself lasting so long
that it acts as a trigger for distress and then fear. So painful is the resulting
magnification product that people will do literally anything to escape. It has
been my experience that patients who injure themselves with repetitive gestures (like cutting their skin with knives or broken glass or burning themselves
with cigarettes) do so in an attempt to undo the dissociative state. They cut or
burn or pick at themselves until they can feel again, after which they rest or
begin to react to the overwhelming affective complex which they had so
recently handled by depersonalization. In general, most people seem to prefer
physical pain to affect at the level of density we are discussing here.

Let me summarize this section: There are a number of life situations in which affects are piled one on the other, magnifying and intensifying each other, forcing the hapless human to experience emotion at a density, an intensity, and over a duration for which we were not designed. Shame, distress, dissmell, disgust, fear, or anger, magnified to this extent, can be handled like somatic pain. Extrinsic agents and a wide range of psychological systems that alter consciousness are prime among the ways we control affect in the name of pain.

THE PARADIGM OF HUNGER

Whereas the affects are a group of nonspecific amplifiers, capable of adding urgency to anything with which they have been coassembled, the drives are a group of highly specific information sources, each involved with a different bodily need but providing no motivation for its satisfaction. The true function of a drive is to inform the central assembly that some substance is needed or must be transported. Only when the drive garners affective amplification will it become urgent enough that we are motivated to do something about it.

The fact that certain drives most often become associated with one or another affect led previous investigators to assume that the affect "belonged" to or was a derivative of the drive. Hungry babies cry, sexually aroused adults seem excited, wounded animals roar angrily. Yet we can cry for reasons quite unrelated to hunger, just as we become excited for reasons other than sexual arousal and angry when we are not in pain. It is the steadiness of hunger pangs that makes that drive most likely to trigger distress. Likewise, the optimally rising stimulus profile of sexual arousal quite naturally triggers interest–excitement. Chronic pain, because it is often both a steady and an intense noxious stimulus, can trigger affective responses ranging between distress and anger. These three linkages occur with regularity simply because of the mechanisms involved.

Until this moment we have focused entirely on the separateness of drives and affects, ignoring exactly the sort of combinations with which we are most familiar. Until one understands the plasticity of the affect system, and its utter lack of obligatory association with any other bodily function, the old way of seeing emotion tends to pull us away from the more biological view presented here. Nevertheless, there is much to be gained from the study of what happens most often, now that it can be surveyed from this new vantage point.

Take, for instance, the situation that obtains when hunger is quelled by food. Mild degrees of hunger require only small amounts of food, while intense hunger usually reflects a more serious nutritional deficit. Drives are activated by need; yet, despite the mass of food actually needed, the flow of information we call hunger is turned off when the process of satisfying that need has begun. Both the drive and the affect it had triggered are turned off long before the actual deficit has been remedied. Just as the hunger of a small child is turned off by the initiation of consummatory activity, so is the accompanying (amplifying) affect of excitement, distress, or rage. With experience comes knowledge: Food is both relief from hunger and a modulator of distress. We learn from earliest childhood that food is a calming substance, a sedative.

Naturally, the caregiver cannot always guess the cause of the infant's negative affect; on occasion the child will be offered food when tears have been provoked by stimuli other than hunger. And, on occasion, this proffered food will serve not as satisfaction of a drive-based need, but as an adequate distraction from the actual trigger for distress. Thus it is that we learn to eat when we are not hungry. Whenever consummatory behavior is used in an attempt to wipe away intense and dense affect, it has been engaged to handle affect as if it were drive.

Even though we can be mollified by candy, ice cream, pizza, or junk food of any sort, this approach to the modulation of negative affect contains some inherent defects. Normal hunger, simply because it is triggered by a drive-based program, turns off when consummatory behavior has begun—that is the nature of a drive. But the eating we do when we are not hungry does not have such a protective mechanism. It wasn't real hunger anyway, and it isn't turned off until some other switch is activated. For most of us, that button is the feeling of fullness.

Eating behavior is influenced dramatically by its accompanying affects. Newborn babies demonstrate pure drive response. Usually they make known their hunger, suck for a moment or two, then either drop off to sleep or become interested in something else. Not so the adult whose discomfort stems from other causes, and who continues with great intensity to eat until sated. This, of course, is the reason most "reducing diets" fail to make us more than temporarily slim. Intense, distressed people eat intensely, diet intensely, and then return to their normal level of intake without ever learning anything about the affect modulation scripts responsible for their inappropriate hunger.

Enduring distress is not the only affect likely to be handled in this manner. We can overeat, or snack, or gorge for the sake of any negative affect. When frightened at the movies we may reach for the solace of popcorn or candy; consequently, theater owners often rate films in terms of their likelihood to provoke sales of food. It is easy to tell when people are eating out of anger, for the correlative property of innate affect makes them ask for and take food angrily, chew angrily, and end their meals angrily; they are more likely than most to "chew out" a hapless underling.

The trick of eating to diminish intense affect is usually taught as part of a family system of affect modulation scripts; this is another reason it is so difficult to help adults alter their pattern of daily food intake. Often you will see families use shame as a tool for the accomplishment of this goal. It is easy enough to embarrass someone into eating by threatening ostracism, which produces conformity in the *attack self* mode. One patient, whose bouts of "compulsive eating" proved untreatable until a similar link to shame was uncovered, described the nightly ritual of family dinner: "If you looked up and met anybody's eyes there was so much shame in the other guy that you would be the immediate target of abuse. So you learned to keep your head down as much as possible and finish your plate. The two of my brothers who are overweight, like me, are the two who are the least likely ever to say anything bad about anybody. And the two of them who are thin are scornful toward everybody; they look around for people to make fun of."

Shame of great intensity and prolonged duration can trigger distress, just as chronic distress can produce a feeling of helplessness and chronic shame. These two affects commonly form a reciprocating pair, one mangifying the other. If the conditions are right for the addition of fear, which makes us experience shame in the form known as guilt, most of us will define this assemblage as "depression." This particular combination of affects is seen in the type of depressed patient who seems compelled to eat into oblivion. These people do not eat "because" they are in the throes of shame, guilt, fear, or depression, but because they know no other way of handling affect of such density.

Using the language of his script theory, Tomkins has introduced a new way of explaining such behavior. Simply stated, Tomkins sees some people as developing what he calls *deprivation affect*, a complex and highly magnified affective state which the individual attributes to the absence of whatever substance or activity has come to bring solace. He gives the name *sedative scripts* to the actions through which one attempts to reduce the deprivation affect by which the absence of this substance or activity has been made to appear dangerous.

Not infrequently, people become quite upset at the idea that something might interfere with a sedative script. These are times when we worry that we might run out of cigarettes, alcohol, or anything chosen to relieve or reduce deprivation affect. Tomkins calls the affect that accompanies such ideas *addictive affect*. An *addictive act* is one taken to prevent or limit addictive affect; this is when we light more than one cigarette at a time so there is no possibility of being without one, drink in order to avoid the way we might feel if we needed a drink and couldn't find one, horde or earn money to ward off the danger of poverty we will therefore never feel, engineer sexual release so we will not get the kind of nervousness calmed by an orgasm. In the true sedative act, once is enough because the psychological device really works to make us feel better. In addiction, however, one never really achieves sedation because what is being ameliorated is only the dense and terrible affect associated with the idea that we might not have access to our sedative script when we really need it!

When circumstance demands chronic and enduring shame, steady and stable humiliation that must for the sake of some relationship be maintained in the *attack self* mode, a certain constancy of internal mortification may be produced by self-dissmell and self-disgust. Although you might think that dissmell and disgust would prevent hunger, for this certainly is their physiological function, I have worked with a number of patients who force themselves to eat in order to overcome the noxious experience of these affects. The difference, of course, is that these latter individuals are experiencing something other than innate affect as such. Rather, they are forced into torrential levels of emotion by conditions well beyond their control, by scripts written when they did not have the power of choice and by distortions of neurobiology of which they have no concept.

Again and again in my study of affect I am drawn to the conclusion that all sciences follow some common rules. Affect at its highest realms of magnification is nothing like innate affect. The heat of a nuclear fusion engine, the core of the sun, plasma energy—such forces bear only slight resemblance to the flames with which we heat the kettle for our morning coffee. In like manner, when affect is piled on affect, one magnifying the other continuously, all in the context of a social or interpersonal situation forbidding surcease or solace relevant to the affects really involved, the resulting affect density can be unbearable. Small wonder that the search for relief in the context of such torture leads to consummatory behavior.

More is involved here than the use of foodstuffs. Just as we learn from infancy that food relieves distress as well as hunger, we come to know the pleasure of rewards. It feels good to be given a present, to win a prize, or to feel the power and freedom conferred by earned income. Reward itself can be a shorthand term for healthy pride or for anything that alters the negative affect in a scene by bringing contentment. Any sequence capable of producing a shift from one affect to another can be incorporated into a script. The library of scripts I have characterized as the *avoidance* pole of the compass of shame contains many systems for the reduction of shame through the induction of pride.

Evidence for the ubiquity of the link between *avoidance* and consummation may be accumulated from many fields of enquiry. For many years, the American economy has been held at an artificially robust level by consumer debt. The average person purchases goods and services in amounts disproportionate to earned income, enabled by a banking system geared to finance this hunger on the basis of future earnings. Encouraged to disavow the danger of steadily mounting debt, the consumer piles one responsibility on another. An astonishing number of adults work at two jobs in order to maintain a relatively exorbitant style of living made necessary by the decision to purchase what they cannot really afford.

Think, for a moment, about what happens when one or both parents work at this pace. Family, rather than being the locus of our solace—the place where we commune one with the other and allow each other the right to decompress, to reduce affect—becomes merely a pit stop on an endless loop of striving. The economy may be buoyed up by the concept of "fly now, pay later," but the human lives better in a system of "work now, fly later." Ignorant of the realities involved in the constant magnification of innate affect, encouraged by market forces to disavow the spiraling cost of debt against which we must mortgage our future, all of us tend to seek out and find devices that provide only brief respite from our understandable discomfort and bind us to an ever-worsening load of affect. Small wonder that ours is a world of tranquilizing substances, objects, and entertainments for which we hunger without understanding.

THE PARADIGM OF SEXUAL AROUSAL

One of the most interesting aspects of the sexual drive program of the generative system is that it provides a script that works unlike anything else in our lives. Most of our innate mechanisms are designed for brief temporal contours—they call us to action, after which their signal is diminished. But sexual action is an analogue of arousal—it is meant to be increased.

In practical terms, once aroused we are unlikely to become comfortable until arousal has been increased to its built-in breaking point. From kindling to explosion to contentment, the events involved in sexuality offer a form of tranquilization equaled by few other human experiences. Sexual activity, whether solitary in the form of masturbation or in some pattern of interpersonal behavior, can provide a wonderfully effective way of distracting us from negative affect. Although for moral reasons we prefer to discuss sexuality in its idealized context of love, marriage, and procreation, in the normatively socialized human the overwhelming majority of individual sexual encounters has more to do with affect modulation.

Initially, of course, the drive itself provokes us to touch what has become inflamed. A glowing ember that we learn to fan into a roaring fire, increasing sexual arousal provides sensory data of steadily rising gradient—capable therefore of triggering either excitement or fear. In this current era of graphic sexual imagery and universal discussion, few children grow into adolescence ignorant of the connection between stimulation and orgasm. Yet I suspect that in an earlier, more private and reserved epoch, boys were frightened of their first ejaculations, and girls often apprehensive about the rising tide of arousal as well as the overwhelming experience of orgasm. Most of us, however, do learn about our sexual system and take control of it for our own pleasure.

Shame affect, the painful analogic amplifier of any impediment to ongoing pleasure, is more likely to humble sexual arousal than is any other psychological function. Embedded in moral philosophy, shame has for centuries been used to reduce our proclivity toward free access to sexuality. One might think, therefore, that shame is only associated with reductions in sexuality. Actually, sexual ardor is cut down by shame affect only when bundled into the *withdrawal* scripts of the compass of shame. Shame as deference, submission, or masochism characterizes the *attack self* pole of the compass; as rape and the sexual exploitation of children it powers a significant part of the *attack other* pole; also does it power a significant fraction of scripts in the *avoidance* library. In each circumstance, orgiastic behavior is used in sedative or addictive scripts to blow away whatever noxious affect had previously held sway.

Just as the built-in systems that have evolved for pain and hunger give us imperfect but useful hedges against intense and enduring negative affect, sexual arousal, too, can make us feel good when everything else is simply awful. In this, of course, it is more like a painkiller than anything else. Remember that we are describing people (ourselves, some of the time; some people most of the time) whose affective baseline has been pushed far above the theoretical null point that we would call the neutral state of no affect.

These are adults whose inner lives are the screaming face of an Edvard Munch painting, the hell of Picasso's *Guernica*, the nightmarish agitation of Leonard Bernstein's *Age of Anxiety*. These are the tortured men who sought surcease in the bath houses that served as homosexual brothels but died horribly of AIDS. This is the doomed heroine of the film *Looking for Mr. Goodbar*, whose last masochistic sexual fling brings her death at the hands of an equally overloaded marauding lover. Whoever among us who has not resorted to sexual intercourse or masturbation for the simple goal of tension reduction is more than likely afflicted with crippling shame or some biological anomaly. Not to try, not to test the system, is foolish; to live as though there were no other route to solace is deadly.

Simply because we have had until now little or no language for intense emotional experience, many otherwise sober clinicians have begun to express their desperation at the breadth and severity of the individual and societal problems created by this use of sexuality in sedative or addictive affect control scripts. Resorting to a technique based on dissmell and disgust, placing the sexual paradigm in a special category of self- and other-abuse, they have attempted to limit such behavior through attitudes redolent of 19th-century moral suasion. I have interviewed quite a number of patients treated in this manner. Each told me that he or she suffered from some form of sexual disorder caused by shame; in each all sexual behavior had been restricted intentionally by therapist-induced shame, self-disgust, self-dissmell, and guilt. At no time was attention paid to the nature of their internal emotional state; that sex was being used for a nonsexual purpose came to each as a not-unpleasant surprise. To inform someone that he or she is a "sexual addict" is merely shaming and frightening unless addiction has been defined in terms of affect modulation.

Just as the mechanism of dissociation can be used when there is no physical pain, and the system of consummation allow us to purchase inedible objects when there is no hunger, the sexual drive program can be mimicked by gestures that have nothing at all to do with the sex organs. The sexual paradigm for the modulation of intense and enduring affect is at work whenever people pick a fight in order to "clear the air" or make things worse in hope that they will get better afterwards. The sequence of events—intense negative affect, intentional magnification until the trigger for some action program is reached, an explosion of violent behavior, and quietus—is itself an analogue of sexual expression.

Such analogues of sexual release are so common in our society that this system of affect modulation deserves elaboration at book length rather than the sketchy treatment I can afford it here. Explosive relief is built into much of our system of public entertainment, which has always functioned as a modulator of civil "tension."

It is for this reason that gangster movies, with all their conventions of cruelty, sadism, violence, and antisocial behavior, have been popular for so long. Every few years another form of filmic explosion is developed, all part of the genre known as "sex and violence." One of the conventions of filmland requires that the underlying affective state of the protagonist be left as mysterious as possible. We, as audience, neither know nor care why the protagonist is explosive. This makes it easier for us to identify with the character's hedonistic, violent, explosive, or destructive actions, as well as the incorporation of these acts into sedative and addictive scripts.

Whereas once the world of athletic competition favored the attributes of endurance, discipline, and skill, now attention and praise are heaped on those who are most likely to explode. Watch the television theater of professional wrestling. The announcers are truculent and explosive, the performers violent and frankly contemptuous of their opponents. Whips, chains, masks, costumes suggestive of extreme dangerousness—all this is commonplace and expected. The audience participates by screaming its pleasure and displeasure, an integral part of this choreographed explosion.

Television commercials, popular songs, and video performances also promote the system of affective magnification leading toward explosive behavior. When was the last time you saw a movie chase scene that did not cause at least one accident? The culture of machismo (characterized by the downgrading of shame, distress, and fear in favor of excitement and anger) requires ever-new and different forms of explosion in order to produce its mild and momentary decreases in an already intolerably magnified affective state.

Much recent attention has been paid the group of affect management scripts called "eating disorders." Those who suffer from anorexia nervosa limit their intake of food, in part to avoid the roundness they associate with somehow humiliating sexual maturity. Others will act as if ravenously hungry—forcing themselves to eat until they feel so stuffed that not another morsel could fit inside them—after which they induce vomiting; this latter pattern is known as bulimia. Anorexia may be understood as a method of affect management in which distress and shame are handled by techniques learned in the management of hunger, while the explosive quality of bulimia more resembles the calm-inducing system I characterize as sexual explosiveness. Forced vomiting produces shame, self-disgust, and self-dissmell, which may be one of the reasons that those who use bulimia as a sedative or an addictive script tend to withdraw afterwards. These concepts have proved quite useful in the treatment of those whose use of such scripts brings them to medical attention.

There are other problems associated with our chronic disavowal of dense and enduring affect. We live in a world that requires ever more intense attention to detail, vigilance while driving our automobiles lest the other guy use us as an excuse for explosion, harder and harder work over longer and longer hours in order to meet the payments for purchases meant as anodynes for our chronic mental pain. And we do come to need painkillers. Fatigued and drained, the more we live at the upper reaches of affective experience, the more we are forced to experience the physical aspects of affect. Not only does high-density affect cause "emotional" imbalance, but it causes so much activity at the sites of action from which we come to know affect that we begin to experience it as a somatic event. Worse yet, we fool ourselves into believing that the next round of affect triggered in this recursive process is a "reasonable" response to somatic illness rather than a manifestation of a much larger system.

Often it is precisely those people who suffer the most from "panic disorder," "cardiac neurosis," "depression," or psychosomatic gastrointestinal disorders like "irritable bowel syndrome" and "spastic colitis" who know the least about their emotions. Shame, at this level of intensity, often is experienced as bodily weakness, fatigue, dullness of thought, depression. Experiencing only persistent and highly magnified symptoms at the varied sites of action we understand as signs of affect, such patients come to us for relief of what they fear are deadly somatic diseases. Not infrequently they use caffeine, alcohol, chocolate, nicotine, headache remedies, fad diets, and any available nostrum in order to achieve some degree of relief.

ON COMPLEXITY

Every few years some expert comes along, presenting experimental data from which is derived a new theory for all human woe. Suddenly fashionable, this idea is found appealing by an audience hungry for simplicity; the perpetrator is lionized by the broadcast and print media, while envious colleagues grab headlines by suggesting or denying that the theory merits prizes of great financial and social value. Immense numbers of people are exposed to the treatments implied by the new theory; many of them actually prosper. Yet very few of those who profit from the new approach experience anything so dramatic as the cures promised by the early enthusiasm surrounding its initial presentation.

Always in our civilization there has been a persistent split between the mind of the alchemist and the attitude of the philosopher. Popular through the Middle Ages well into the 16th century, alchemy refers to "the pursuit of the transmutation of baser metals into gold, which (with the search for the alkahest or universal solvent, and the panacea or universal remedy) constituted the chief practical object of early chemistry."* Science (and journalism, too) is peopled by humans with their own affect modulation scripts. One of the most seductive scripts involves the wish for simplicity. Despite the evidence presented by a lifetime of immersion in an increasingly complex world, we still hunger for simple and clear-cut rules that will make everything different by

*Oxford English Dictionary

removing both uncertainty and negative affect. Instinctively we shun the philosopher who shows us the truth of complexity.

Like it or not, the human condition is multideterminate. The impatient
swordsman offering to cut rather than unravel the Gordian Knot threatens us
with the immense power of his weapon.

In this chapter I have attempted to show that extraordinarily dense human
affect is by nature immutably complex, far more complex than can be accepted
by most of those who study it. Directly proportional to the density of affect
seen in an individual will be the complexity of the scripts that have produced
it. Social forces are important, but they are not the one true key to understanding. Neurotransmitters, drives, affects, and prewritten habit patterns are important, but we are more than the sum of our parts. Neocortical cognition is
important, but, notwithstanding the yearning of 19th-century rationalism, it
too is biological and cannot be separated from the biological field from which
it evolved. Whoever wishes to help guide humans along their best paths
toward their highest goals must learn all of these systems.

30

A BRIEF HISTORY OF SHAME

"In olden days a glimpse of stocking was simply shocking. Now, goodness knows, anything goes." Written in the 1930s, the song says loudly and clearly that shame changes over time. What acts as a source or a trigger for shame affect differs from one era to another.

Glance at a pictorial survey of bathing costumes in our culture. Adorning the beach, fashionable men and women ushered in this century covered in fabric from wrist to ankle, with ruffles and other devices concealing the outline of breasts and genitals. In stark contrast to this standard of public modesty, aquatic nudity—emphasized by smidgens of cleverly placed cloth—has become more rule than exception in our current era. Bodily beauty has always been celebrated; it is the rules of display that have changed. A presentation of self so revealing and devoid of subtlety that it once was a source for shame is now a source of pride.

This observation is not so trivial as it might appear at first glance. We know that there are both learned and innate triggers to every affect. Always will shame be triggered by something that interferes with ongoing positive affect; although certain experiences must inevitably cause such an impediment, others become impediments only because we are so taught. At the most superficial level it is apparent that currently there is little risk an adult will be embarrassed by the intentional public display of nakedness. One impediment to positive affect has been canceled.

Wurmser said it best. Only when the viewing other is held under the spell of fascination are we comfortable being seen naked. For a long time, this kind of interpersonal transaction was universally accepted as the most private of matters. In order for public aquatic nudity to become acceptable there had to be a shift in both the observer and the observed. Now all of us are encouraged by social forces not to turn away but to look at and admire public nakedness. Now the adult observer risks no personal shame for being interested in the public display of nudity. Another impediment to ongoing positive affect has been canceled.

Always there is a partnership, an oscillation between the beholder and the beheld. It is not just the wearer of the bathing suit who has changed—there are more layers to this evolutionary process. If the observer is male, he has been forced to change his understanding of the sexual significance of female nudity. Where once such display implied the imminence of sexual involvement, now it means nothing more than an opportunity for mutual positive regard. Lest he be embarrassed for conspicuous misunderstanding, the attentive male has had to learn yet another set of rules for the control of sexual arousal and the visibility of his erections. Men have not gone lightly into that new world. Manly anger, resentment, sexual slurs, and outraged attempts at seduction—all manifestations of the *attack other* library of scripts in reaction to shame—have greeted those women pioneering this new frontier of display.

Imagine a graph depicting these changes over time in the relation between shame and public nakedness. I wish to focus your attention on three points of the curve: 1900, when bathing costumes were at their most chaste; 1970, an interim period during which the rules had clearly begun to change; and 1990, when bared bodies were normative and commonplace. A child, growing up in each of these eras, would learn quite different standards. Witnessing a modern beach scene, shock, amazement, revulsion, scorn, the urge to censure, and a wish for civil punishment would flood the mind of one raised in 1900. Confusion and anger would bother our second time traveler, while a contemporary observer might have no negative affect in response to this tableau.

All this is simple enough and really quite obvious. What anybody experiences as the emotion of shame is a complex assemblage of source, physiological phase, a brief cognitive phase brought up in reaction to the affect, and a reactive phase based on some script found in the compass of shame. It is to a far deeper implication that I wish to call your attention.

As long as there have been humans I believe there has been no significant alteration in the pattern of physiological reactions that Tomkins calls the innate affect shame–humiliation. Yet if the sources for shame can change, then the cognitive phase (which is entirely dependent on the history of our own personal experience of the affect) can change and has changed throughout history, and the individual scripts within the reaction patterns I group as the compass of shame must also have undergone constant alteration. Along with their triggers, the styles of withdrawal, deference, avoidance, and contemptuous attack have varied over time. Therefore, the experience of shame—what people actually feel and think and do when embarrassed—has been in a constant state of flux.

Throughout this book I have made the observation that in order for two people to enter into the contract we call psychotherapy they must learn each other's language for affective experience. Although all of us were born with pretty much the same hardware and firmware, we develop such different forms of software that the resultant complex ideoaffective assemblages veer far away from innate affect. Despite the immense range of our similarities, in the matter of these scripts we are all quite different. The initial phases of any therapeutic enterprise require us to construct a lexicon for affect so we understand each other's language.

Now I ask you to recognize that the very word shame has represented quite different *inner experiences* over time. If it is difficult to know exactly what one of our contemporaries means when using emotion labels, it is even more difficult to know what those labels meant in an era characterized by a vastly different realm of daily experience and accumulated history. Affect scripts themselves have history. Just as it is impossible to know the inner world of another person without learning something about the unique experiences that brought that individual to the shared present, it is impossible to understand a script without some regard for its path through time.

The archaeologist of affect faces challenges not unlike any those of other diggers. Lost to us is the technique of interviewing, for our subjects are long dead and buried. Yet entombed with them are scraps of evidence that can be sifted and evaluated for our purposes. From the layout of their homes we can see how people slept; from their recovered costumes we can see how they dressed; and from their writings we can learn how they expressed themselves. From its graphic arts we can see the faces and bodies of a culture and learn something about its habits. All of these shards can be dusted off and assembled to tell us something about the history of shame.

Rather than a sparse harvest, actually we are surfeited with information so fascinating that it could fill several monographs this size. Assisting our search, for instance, is a marvelous work of European learning, a lavishly illustrated four-volume text called *A History of Private Life*, written originally in French and published in English translation by the Belknap Press of Harvard University. Certainly the group of scholars who compiled data from so many sources were not primarily interested in shame. Yet, as Wurmser (1981, 1987) and Schneider (1977, 1987) have demonstrated so well, it is shame that guards the boundary between public and private. The French study of privacy offers an opportunity to make a number of observations about shame and about pride from the days of Rome and Byzantium, through the Middle Ages, the Renaissance, and from the French Revolution to the beginning of the First World War.

Much as I would like to describe in detail everything I have learned about the history of shame from this and other sources, that is a task better left to the professional historian. I suspect that an adequate rendering of the subject would require a life's work or several doctoral dissertations. Perhaps this current book will intrigue some young mind enough to power such a project. Here, in these closing chapters of my own book on the nature of shame and pride, I can do no more than sketch what I have gleaned.

Of all the themes that can be traced over a 2500-year span, easiest to study is the cultural attitude toward the naked human body. Greek and Roman statuary, as well as the decorations painted on pottery, often depict men and women unclothed. I know of no large painted vessel (no *krater* or *amphora*) from which we can detect evidence that in these cultures embarrassment accompanied the exposure of breasts or the male genital.* There are woodcuts from the Middle Ages showing happy families running naked together through the streets on their way to the communal bath house; the eldest male does, however, wear a loincloth. And, when fully dressed, the 16th-century male would cover his genitals with a codpiece that resembled an erect penis.

With the Renaissance arrives a new sense of modesty, for now the male genital is more likely to be covered and hidden, the female draped to distract attention from her genital region. Medieval ivory carvings show the Christ child fully naked, genitals exposed; from the 17th century on he wears a loincloth. During the 18th century we see an increasing tendency to cover the female breast; over the next hundred or so years any tendency toward nakedness was considered increasingly risqué. Indeed, as civilization moved away from an open and unabashed appreciation of the human body as a source of visual beauty, nakedness came more and more to represent sexuality.

What about sexual intercourse itself? In pagan days people huddled together in close proximity; couples enjoyed intercourse in full view of those who shared their living space. The excavations at Pompeii brought a brothel to light—there would have been no need for it to have been enclosed within walls unless some forms of sex then required privacy. More privacy seems to

---

*Otto Kiefer's book *Sexual Life in Ancient Rome* (1934) provides an excellent source of such information, despite whatever bias was natural to his own era.

have been required during Roman days, less during the Middle Ages (when it was not uncommon for couples to couple publicly). Drawings and woodcuts of the latter period show people equally unconcerned about the public nature of human and animal sexual embrace. With the Renaissance came the requirement for more privacy, and an ever-increasing linkage between sex and shame.

Other affects have changed in significance over time. The relation between shame, anger, and dissmell that we identified as part of the *attack other* script provides another example. In classic Greece or Rome, an insult based on dissmell (designed to produce interpersonal distance and shame) might be tolerated and responded to in kind, rather than taken as a stimulus to anger and fighting. Arguments that raged in the Roman Senate were rarely taken into the streets as deadly combat. A millennium or so later, merely to bump into someone in the medieval town square might occasion a fight to the death. The civil or cultural attitude toward dueling as redress for humiliation has also undergone constant revision over the centuries.

In Table 6 I have noted how each of the eight categories associated with the cognitive phase of shame seems to have been experienced in four eras: classic, medieval, Renaissance, and modern. By no means an authoritative historical survey, it is presented only as an early approximation of what I hope others will flesh out in the future. Casual inspection of this table reveals marked differences in the pattern, the mosaic formed by the elements in each column. I believe that these cultural differences are responsible for the varying expressions of shame known to have occurred during each era. Nevertheless, it is to the more recent evolution of shame that I will later call the most attention.

Table 6
TRACING AN AFFECT THROUGH TIME

The relative value of each attribute during the era in question:

Attribute	Classic	Medieval	Renaissance	Modern
A. *Size, strength, ability, skill*	crucial dimension of life	crucial dimension; rules life	state looms over individual	technology as equalizer
B. *Dependence/ independence*	fact of life	fact of life	state dominant over individual	all social forces favor independence

Table 6 (Continued)

Attribute	Classic	Medieval	Renaissance	Modern
C. *Competition:* The nature and importance of interpersonal strife	deadly	deadly	begins to be more playful	symbolic, displaced, universal
D. *Sense of self:* What do I define as *me*? How clearly does an individual define his or her identity?	partial, incomplete	group rather than individual	increasing sense of individual identity	life in a full-length mirror
E. *Personal attractiveness:* How am I seen by others?	dependent on class	related to class and power	power through beauty increasingly available to all	universal availability of techniques for improvement
F. *Sexuality:* How seen in the culture; how integrated into everyday life	male domination taken for granted	public, open	increasingly linked with mystery and hiding	intensely private, movement toward gender equality
G. *Seeing and being seen:* The degree of concern with how one is seen by others	discretion important	broad and bawdy display	increasing control over appearance	criticial issue
H. *Closeness:* The role of intimacy; the degree to which people developed what we might call a real emotional link	minor concern; banishment commonplace	minor concern; wandering nomad common	begins to achieve importance; forced isolation to be feared; personal privacy begins to appear	major concern; banishment inconceivable, expatriate status extraordinary

The Recent History of Shame

The Revolution of 1530

All of us who study shame owe much to the work of the Swiss sociologist Norbert Elias, whose masterpiece *The History of Manners* was completed in 1939 but unavailable in English translation until 1978. As you might expect, his influence has been greatest on European thinkers, whose access to it was not limited by the fact that Elias wrote in German. For an English-speaking audience it is even now new and startling.

Elias was concerned with the evolution of social control, of the ways human behavior is controlled in and by groups, the refinement of control by governments, and the complex system he calls "the civilizing process." Starting with the patterns of life known to have existed during the Middle Ages, he demonstrates a steady increase in the societal requirement for affect modulation and a lowering of the threshold for shame and delicacy (115). As more and more pieces of previously normal behavior were declared and taught to be triggers for shame, and/or dissmell, and/or disgust, Western civilization moved inexorably to its present form. It was to courtly society that Europeans looked for social leadership; our word "courtesy" reflects this historical train of thought. Thus government, which in feudal days had been based on power and strength amplified by the affect fear, shifted to a system of respect and awe amplified by shame.

Much can be learned, said Elias, by studying books on manners. Ignored by most scholars, they form for him a valuable resource from which to observe this instruction toward delicacy. You will recall my observation that humor travels poorly in both time and space—sometimes we have no idea why people of a particular culture laughed. A corollary of this may be seen in our response to ancient books on manners, for we are so many centuries away from the shifts in morality produced by them that often we are repulsed by the instructions themselves.

From 13th century sources Elias quotes the following injunctions: "When your companions anger you, my son, see that you are not so hot-tempered that you regret it afterwards." "A man of refinement should not slurp with his spoon in company; this is the way people in court behave who often indulge in unrefined conduct." "Some people bite a slice and then dunk it in the (communal) dish in a coarse way; refined people reject such bad manners." "A number of people gnaw a bone and then put it back in the dish—this is a serious offense." "A man who clears his throat when he eats and one who blows his nose in the tablecloth are both ill-bred, I assure you." "If a man wipes his nose on his hand at table because he knows no better, then he is a fool, believe me." People used their hands to take food from the common dish, thus, "It is not decent to poke your fingers into your ears or eyes, as some people do, or to pick your nose while eating. These three habits are bad. (63–64)."

Some years ago a colleague told me that the intellectual discoveries of classical civilization are routinely made by contemporary three-year-olds, that the discoveries we associate with medieval thinking are the spontaneous inventions of the modern seven-year-old, and that the average adolescent of today brings up in class ideas first expressed during the Renaissance. Clearly written for an adult population desirous of bettering its social standing, these 13th-century directives are today nothing more than what any mother now teaches her toddler. This, too, is evidence of a "civilizing process."

Yet all of these instructions are but a prologue to the real shift. The concept of civility, of modern polite behavior, can be traced with extraordinary precision to a short treatise published in the second quarter of the 16th century.

Written by Erasmus of Rotterdam, first released in 1530 under the title *De Civilitate Morum Puerilium* (On Civility in Children), it achieved enormous popularity. In the first six years after its publication there were more than 30 reprints. Elias tells us that more than 130 editions may be counted, 13 as late as the 18th century. Two years after its initial publication the first English translation appeared, followed immediately by German, Czech, and French versions. A 1558 Italian adaptation, the *Galatea* of Giovanni della Casa, Archbishop of Benevento, is even today taught in some American parochial schools. The typeface in which the French adaptation was first issued came to be known as *civilité*, and all French versions of Erasmus were printed in civilité type until the end of the 18th century. To an extent perhaps unimaginable in our era, this little book literally controlled public behavior for nearly 200 years. And all this for a monograph its author considered the most minor of his works.

Erasmus had grasped the wind of change like a hawk catching a thermal. *De Civilitate* answered a need it helped create.

Don't stare, he said. It would be best for you to demonstrate by your look and demeanor that you have "a calm mind and a respectful amiability." "Not by chance do the ancients say: the seat of the soul is in the eyes." Elias explains:

> Bodily carriage, gestures, dress, facial expressions—this "outward" behavior with which the treatise concerns itself is the expression of the inner, the whole man. Erasmus knows this and on occasion states it explicitly: "Although this outward bodily propriety proceeds from a well-composed mind, nevertheless we sometimes

find that, for want of instruction, such grace is lacking in excellent and learned men." (p. 55–6)

From what behavior did Erasmus make these deductions? Elias summarizes some of these injunctions: There should be no snot on the nostrils, he says somewhat later. "A peasant wipes his nose on his cap and coat, a sausage maker on his arm and elbow. It does not show much propriety to use one's hand and then wipe it on one's clothing. It is more decent to take up the snot in a cloth, preferably while turning away. If when blowing the nose with two fingers something falls to the ground, it must be immediately trodden away with the foot. The same applies to spittle" (p. 56). For most of his contemporaries, Erasmus had declared a new threshold for disgust.

If someone offers you liquid from a communal tankard, wipe your mouth before tasting. Food, in this era, is served from communal bowls; plates are rarely found and the fork was unknown. (Look at paintings from this period. Dining tables hold little more than a bowl of food, a saltcellar, a goblet or two, and perhaps a knife. Art copies life.) Make sure, says Erasmus, that your hands are clean when you take meat from the bowl, and place it on a slab of bread. "In good society one does not put both hands into the dish. It is most refined to use only three fingers of the hand. This is one of the distinctions between the upper and lower classes" (p. 57).

Yet Erasmus rejects behavioral controls that are contrary to the realities of biology. Nature requires that the alimentary canal expel its gaseous contents; to withhold a fart, says Erasmus, can lead to illness. Do not be afraid of vomiting if you must; "for it is not vomiting but holding the vomit in your throat that is foul" (58).

A message begins to emerge as one reads Erasmus from our modern perspective. Where once eating was a communal affair, now it moved slowly and steadily to the realm of privacy. Schneider, whose 1976 book *Shame, Exposure, and Privacy* I have mentioned on several occasions, calls eating one of the central privacies. Today's diner, whether at restaurant or home, assumes a capsule of perfect privacy into which no one dare intrude without risking censure. (Thus the choreography of waiting table, the elegance of proper food service.) We are bred to eat without bothering others and to allow others the right to dine without interference. All this was unknown before Erasmus.

It is more than eating behavior that is involved here. Erasmus requires precise control of affective expression; indeed, it is this little book that first defines lack of affect modulation as shameworthy. Bump into a medieval citizen in the town square and expect an explosion of affect; "excuse me" became meaningful only after the revolution started by Erasmus.

All communality begins with the free interchange of affect, is mediated by affective resonance, and monitored by the empathic wall. Erasmus pointed out that our true inner affective state can be deduced from our behavior. By codifying, legislating a requirement for the control of affect, by linking dyscontrol to shame, Erasmus creates or at least requires the separateness, the isolation, the insularity, the invisible wall that now exists between one person and another. It seems likely that Greek and Roman society, at its highest, also required affect modulation and also fostered this isolation of one person from another. But somewhere it got lost. As far as Western society is concerned, at least for this current cycle, *De Civilitate* was the fulcrum around which the change pivoted.

The sharp edges of innate affect, so easily distinguished in infancy but increasingly blurred or rounded during development, are similarly obscured by contamination and admixture with other affects in the course of cultural history. Civility is the glue of society partly because it reduces the clarity, the specificity of display for all affect. Pure, perfect, unadulterated affect is tolerated only in infants. Certainly some version of the empathic wall existed before 1530, some sort of "personal space" associated with the ability to screen out the affect of others. All societies require their members to limit the free expression of affect. But our current view of the relation between affective expression and privacy began with Erasmus. Even the empathic wall changed after 1530.

There is more. Elias points out that Erasmus regarded clothing as "the body of the body. From it we can deduce the attitude of the soul. And then Erasmus gives examples of what manner of dress corresponds to this or that spiritual condition. This is the beginning of the mode of observation that will at a later stage be termed 'psychological.' " (78). "The increased tendency of people to observe themselves and others is one sign of how the whole question of behavior is now taking on a different character: people mold themselves and others more deliberately than in the Middle Ages (79)."

A line of development becomes clear. As courtly behavior drifts into the public at large we see a constant decrease in the threshold for embarrassment. Everywhere this change is called "refinement" or "civilization." But the affect giving it power and urgency is that of shame informed by dissmell and disgust. Over periods of, say, 50 or 100 years, Elias can show that what was by this process linked to shame next was viewed as merely rational, after which it was considered "hygiene" or sanitary science.

One of the most fascinating examples of this "civilizing process" may be seen in our use of cooked meat. In the Middle Ages the consumption of meat was directly proportional to one's wealth. The nobility might eat two pounds per person per day because for them the supply of domesticated animals was unlimited; the peasant ate only what could be poached. Elias again:

> Another change can be documented more exactly. The manner in which meat is served changes considerably from the Middle Ages to modern times. The curve of this change is very instructive. In the upper class of medieval society, the dead animal or large parts of it are often brought whole to the table. Not only whole fish and whole birds (sometimes with their feathers) but also whole rabbits, lambs, and quarters of veal appear on the table, not to mention the larger venison or the pigs and oxen roasted on the spit.
>
> The animal is carved on the table. This is why the books on manners repeat, up to the seventeenth and sometimes even the eighteenth century, how important it is for a well-bred man to be good at carving meat. (118–19)

Yet by the end of the 17th century it no longer is necessary for an upper-class Frenchman to know how to carve; within a hundred years fashion has changed and only selected joints of meat are carved at the table. Soon it is considered distasteful to bring to the table any piece of meat that evokes the image of what has been killed. What once was a source of visual pleasure now has become a source of disgust. By the 19th century English books of manners discourage the use of the knife, asking polite people to peel an orange with a spoon and wherever possible cut food with the fork. Today, stored out of sight in museums, nearly unsalable either at auction or in art galleries, is the entire genre of "after the hunt" paintings with their vivid and realistic depiction of pheasant, rabbit, deer, and other game strung up to demonstrate the prowess of the hunter.

Elias, writing half a century ago, predicted that this curve of change would continue to a point where increasing numbers of people would eschew meat itself. I suspect he would have been amused that our modern medical science keeps finding increasingly convincing "reasons" to avoid meat. It is no longer considered unusual for someone to renounce the eating of flesh in any form and declare as a vegetarian. The rise in popularity of macrobiotic cooking and other regimens considered by some to be "fad diets" is an exact reflection of the "civilizing process." And this current era has witnessed an enormous increase in the number of people who are diagnosed as having "eating disorders" because they avoid food of one sort or another or because they evince disgust at their need to eat. Vigilante groups now monitor the use of experimental animals in scientific laboratories, and even as I write there is an increasing outcry against the killing of animals for their fur.

All this is part of a developmental line stretching from the Renaissance to modern times. It involves a radical shift in the nature and importance of shame, with disgust and dissmell acting as increasingly significant triggers and validators of shame. Yet there are more data to scan before we can comprehend the recent evolution of shame. The river of change tries many paths before finding its true bed.

In all of Shakespeare the word "shame" appears in 178 passages; there are 33 uses of "ashamed," 15 of "shamed," 15 of "shameful." "Shun" appears in 20 speeches. The words "embarrassment," "mortification," and "humiliation" are nowhere in the writing of the Bard of Avon.* The relation between competition and shame is well described, for Shakespeare often uses the word "sport" to indicate both rivalry and ridicule. In *A Winter's Tale*, Paulina states that to shun another will cause a feeling like death.

I am unable to find any Shakespearean reference to shame that implies the terrible degree of isolation we take for granted today. In nearly every situation where shame appears, he uses it to indicate embarrassment in the presence of another, rather than a cause for withdrawal. On occasion, one character may *suggest* that another withdraw in order to heal after a moment of embarrassment. Even the sense of shame as an internal withdrawal, a movement inward into the self, is barely intimated. It is as if people of his era were locked together in a communal embrace, shame operating only to make that embrace uncomfortable.

There are hints of the shift yet to come. Look at this passage from Act 3, Scene 2 of *Troilus and Cressida*:

CRESSIDA: My lord, I do beseech you, pardon me;
   'Twas not my purpose, thus to beg a kiss:
   I am ashamed. O heavens! what have I done?
   For this time will I take my leave, my lord.
TROILUS: Your leave, sweet Cressid! . . . What offends you, lady?
CRESSIDA: Sir, mine own company.
TROILUS: You cannot shun
   Yourself.
CRESSIDA: Let me go and try:

*This information is provided by the search modality of the CD ROM version of the *Complete Works* of Shakespeare (1989). Other Shakespeare sources give slightly different numbers.

I have a kind of self resides with you;
But an unkind self, that itself will leave,
To be another's fool. I would be gone:
Where is my wit? I know not what I speak.

Here is the confusion that accompanies shame, described so well by Darwin. This passage offers one of those rare examples of an adult shame experience that contains only the innate affect described by Tomkins with no other affects blended in. This is shame as a monitor of love, truly painful amplification of an impediment to positive affect, an impediment to good feelings which continue to be triggered. It is clear that Cressida would have far less pain were she less in love with Troilus. Here, too, is the sense of a split self so normal today in shame—the very idea of "splitting" that has confused a generation of psycho-analysts into thinking that it is a defense mechanism seen only in "borderline" patients. All this shame has been triggered by the exposure of love, a source no less important then than now. I have presented this passage to demonstrate that Cressida, in the throes of shame affect, must *ask* her beloved Troilus for permission to withdraw in order to compose herself. There are no more than one or two other instances in all of Shakespeare where shame is linked to withdrawal and the experience of personal isolation. The revolution started by Erasmus had not yet reached its peak.

The Road Not Taken

There was another Renaissance genius who wrote about shame. The story of Annibale Pocaterra and his brilliant book *Due Dialogi della Vergogna* (Two Dialogues on Shame) is one of the most peculiar in literary history. Born in 1562, Pocaterra was appointed professor of medicine at the University of Ferrara at 23. Tasso and Montecatini describe him as one of the best poets of the late 16th century; Luzzasco Luzzaschi and Alfonso Fontanelli set to music some of his work as madrigals that were considered masterpieces of this genre. At 30 he wrote the first book on shame, the only scholarly work on shame until that of Darwin nearly 300 years later. A few months later he was dead, this treasure ignored and forgotten.

Only 38 copies of his book are known to exist. One came to me because antiquarian bookseller James Hinz, proprietor of F. Thomas Heller Inc., wrote after reading a newspaper account of my attempt to study every aspect of shame. With the help of Werner Gundersheimer, director of the Folger Shake-speare Library, I was able to find Piero Alongi, whose lyrical translation has

proved so useful to this work. Using the unequaled resources of the Folger
Library along with his own encyclopedic knowledge of the period, Dr. Gundersheimer has established the facts of Pocaterra's life and placed this discourse
in proper context. We have arranged for the publication of the resulting
annotated translation so that others may enjoy the work of this remarkable
man.

Right away, in the dedication to his patron, Pocaterra tells us that "in the
end, shame is an honest thing" (2)* a reality of everyday existence and quite
worthy of study. A lover's blush introduces the relation between shame and
exposure; as a physician, Pocaterra knew that this required some connection
between mind and body. Required by convention to use the language of
Aristotle, he debates whether shame is a virtue or a passion. We learn that
shame makes us timorous, humble, and contrite, but also causes outrage
against the self. Pocaterra hints that shame keeps constant company with all
the negative affects.

But when men are attacked by shame, observes Pocaterra, they "would like
nothing better than to run and hide from themselves and from the eyes of the
world, even if they had to burrow underground to do so" (16). Shame is also
described as "fear of infamy" (17), which can lead men to attack their enemy
with passion—so it is capable of causing both cowardice and bravery:

> Let me repeat once again that nature draws a veil of blood over the face of the
> ashamed. And let me add to this that, to my knowledge, shame is always accompa-
> nied by ire, and that this ire increases the intensity of the fire already burning within
> man. The ashamed becomes angry at himself in the manner that a man can feel
> anger against his own self, but also becomes enraged against those who are aware
> of his faults—even though, under other circumstances, he may love and respect
> them. This happens because the love we feel for ourselves is more powerful than
> any other kind of love, the spring from which all other loves, like rivers, run. (34)

Pocaterra sees emotion much as will Tomkins some 350 years later: "Insofar
as our feelings are naturally planted within our souls, and insofar as they are
among the things which are given us by nature, then, by common agreement,
we can neither praise nor fault them" (44). Feelings "are like swords; they are
only as good or evil as the end to which they are used" (44). There is an innate
and a learned component to all emotion, says this man of the Renaissance.

*All quotations are from the Alongi translation manuscript, which is as yet unpublished. I have
given page numbers that refer to this typescript and which will be of only relative use to future
readers of the final publication.

"There must be two shames. One natural and free from awareness; and the other acquired, moved by reason, and led by understanding" (93).

Shame is a teacher because we can learn to avoid what will produce it; shame can therefore protect us from evil. "The shame of children is like a seed which, having sprouted, becomes a small plant in the years of youth, and, at a mature age, it produces the ripe fruits of virtue" (96). Yet "solitude and darkness make man audacious and daring. . . . It is for this reason some say Love should be represented as blind because it makes lovers brazen" (80–81).

Self-love, says Pocaterra, is essential to life—too much shame can interfere with healthy self-love. But "praise often resembles ridicule" (70), and "one who is praised feels shame because he fears that others might believe that he invites this praise and takes too much pleasure in it . . . and thus accuse him of arrogance" (70). He splits shame yet another way:

> I think there are two shames, one of which it seems appropriate to term internal and the other external. I call internal shame that confusion and remorse of conscience which usually attack a soul guilty of error even when hidden from the eyes of the world. This shame can be with us even in the deepest woods . . . Those who run from the presence of other people . . . can say along with the poet, "I feel shame with myself of myself." . . . And then there are many who, having hidden their defects from the eyes of others, believe themselves to be innocent and alone, not knowing that they have their own selves with themselves.
>
> I say that in addition to internal shame, there is external shame which is that whose signs appear on our face, and which is inseparably united to a flash of fire. (76–77)

No one is immune to stage fright, for "we have seen the heat of shame dry up the most plentiful fountains of eloquence" (157). Pocaterra asks "divine shame" to "illuminate with your lantern the darkness of our errors," to "purge the fog of human defects," to "spur and push the mind on the road to glory." "If shame left me, which good thing could remain with me?" (108) "To one who has fallen, feeling shame is a sign of recognition and of a good desire to regain sanity" (122–23). In 1975 Helen Block Lewis claimed that the blush was a signal informing the shaming other that we recognize the error of our ways and wish to be readmitted to society. Nearly 400 years earlier, Annibale Pocaterra said that "blushing can make anyone worthy of pardon" (123).

I try to imagine the course of Western philosophy and culture had not Pocaterra died so young, had he been given the opportunity to write the many books that would have burst forth from his fountain. What if *Due Dialogi della Vergogna* had gone through as many editions as the *De Civilitate Morum*

Puerilium of Erasmus or the *Galatea* of della Casa? What if shame had been understood, accepted, respected, rather than increasingly secret and shameful? What would psychoanalysis and the entire mental health movement be today had Freud grown up with an awareness of shame as sophisticated as that of Pocaterra?

But it didn't work that way. Some accident of fate threw the switch that sent our train rumbling over quite another track. The editor of *A History of Private Life* sums it up for us:

> Between 1500 and 1800 people developed new attitudes toward their own bodies and toward the bodies of others. Where earlier literature on civility emphasized, say, the proper way for a young man to serve food at table, later treatises stress the impropriety of touching or looking at other diners, thereby creating a protected zone around the body. People stopped embracing with wide-open arms; they no longer kissed the hand or foot of a woman they wished to honor, and men stopped prostrating themselves before their ladies. These histrionic demonstrations gave way to discreet, understated gestures. People no longer attempted to cut a figure, to create an appearance, to assert themselves; they behaved properly in order to discourage attention, to pass almost unnoticed. A new modesty emerged, a new concern with hiding certain parts of the body and certain acts. "Cover this breast, which I do not like to see," says Tartuffe. . . . Newlyweds were no longer put to bed by a crowd of onlookers who returned to greet them the following morning. (Vol. 3, 4–5)

Notice the increasing link between shame and the visible. The affect itself turns our eyes away from whatever source had only a moment ago engaged us for the sake of interest or enjoyment. Pocaterra tried to move us to an understanding of shame that focused on inner experience. The rest of society was moving toward better and better control of what could be seen and evaluated by others.

The Development of the Individual Psyche

Our world, the Western world that was Europe and England and became North America, this culture from which we emerged, grew increasingly private and afraid of shame. Rather than only gossip with friends, people began to keep personal diaries. In the past it was thought unsuitable for a man of quality to be alone, except for prayer; by the end of the 17th century a taste for solitude had developed. Woods and parks took on some aspects of what Rousseau would later salute as "nature."

The rise in importance of solitude, itself a secondary effect of the growing requirement for affect control, brought with it an increasing interest in the development of a personal life. Now people became so fond of being alone that they wished to share their solitude with a dear friend, a teacher, relative, servant, or neighbor—a second self. Thus the modern concept of friendship evolved, and, with it, slowly, a change in our concept of marriage. Only to the extent that one develops an inner life does one wish to share it with an intimate other.

The increasing interest in intimacy and personal relatedness augured the end of arranged marriages. We can accept an assigned companion when there is no expectation of intimacy. The proverb "A rolling stone gathers no moss" indicates that true intimacy appears only in the context of long and meaningful personal association.

Read any competent historical survey of the social institution we call marriage. Medieval society took it for granted that coupling was based on transient attraction. G. Rattray Taylor informs us that Tenth-century ordinances in England stipulated a seven-year period of trial marriage, and that a one-year trial marriage existed in Scotland until the Protestant Reformation of the mid-16th century. Exactly paralleling the development of the individual psyche was the shift toward our contemporary insistence on mutuality and personal fulfillment within marriage. I teach that dating and courtship are the ways we interview candidates for the job of best friend. This is as much a truism today as it would have been an embarrassingly ludicrous statement only a century ago.

The pattern may be seen throughout Western society. Look at Kipling's oft-quoted but little-examined 19th century injunction, "If you can keep your head when all about you are losing theirs and blaming it on you . . . you'll be a Man, my son." Even today, the macho character will apologize for any high-level display of very dense affect by saying, "I lost it." Shame began to loom everywhere as a major force operating to control the display of affect. Couples became increasingly private as individuals, increasingly involved as a marital unit, and increasingly sequestered in their sexual behavior. What we take for granted as the generational boundary between parents and children was magnified as parents moved into the private space of their own bedroom, from which children were increasingly excluded. In one era it was taken for granted that children might witness parental intercourse just as they might view the coupling of barnyard animals. By the beginning of the 20th century Freud would state with accuracy that "exposure to the primal scene" was a major psychic trauma capable of producing neurosis.

Family Life

Elias observes that by the mid-17th century it was no longer acceptable for parents to send their children into the world uneducated to its social mores. Worldly education, the job of socialization itself, moved from the larger community into the family. He suggests that what we take for granted as the nuclear family seems to have developed as the result of this wish to avoid shame and to protect children from shame, dissmell, and disgust. Mother may always have been the primary teacher—but from the 17th century on there was a massive increase in the curricular responsibilities assigned her.

Evidence for the process abounds. Among its other requirements, each time some new source of shame was legislated by custom, it became the responsibility of the family to protect children from the ever-growing opportunities for public embarrassment. Home became the first place where we learned how to live in the world—what to hide and what to show, how much of self to reveal and in what manner.

Humor

So much did we become a society of shame and of affect control mandated through shame that tension around this locus rose constantly. Any historical study of humor, of what was deemed funny in each era, shows the shifting patterns of subjects that came to be viewed as embarrassing. I am a fan of the humorist James Thurber, and a lifelong admirer of his friend E. B. White, famed writer for *The New Yorker* and one of the great prose stylists of the century. Yet in their astonishingly successful 1929 book *Is Sex Necessary?*, I can find no single joke that a modern reader would consider funny. Indeed, I suspect that it is full of comments no longer recognizable as jokes because they represent an attempt to integrate into polite intellectual society the then novel, upsetting, and embarrassing theories of Freud that had moved sexuality to the foreground.

The developmental line is clear: First some piece of human activity is declared shameworthy and a source of dissmell or disgust, the population at large approving only slowly of this new source for discomfort. Next, as the behavior comes to be controlled more and more by shame, it is a fit subject for humor. And when society has accepted completely the new balance of shame, exposure, and privacy, there is neither tension nor humor associated with it.

The mid-19th-century rivals Gladstone and Disraeli, always feuding, always attacking each other's convictions, met once in the lobby of a London theater.

"You will die of a pox, sir, or upon the gallows!" said Gladstone. "That depends," answered Disraeli, "on whether I embrace your mistress or your principles." A century later, Hollywood screen- and songwriter Sylvia Fine is spied on the street shortly after the surgical procedure that had adjusted the shape of her nose. A rival (attacking her both for being Jewish and for the "narcissism" implied by cosmetic surgery) snaps, "Sylvia, darling, I see you have cut off your nose to spite your race." "Yes," came the swift answer. "Now I am a thing of beauty and a goy forever." The two interactions are much the same in form. Only the sources of shame have changed. Shame, the affect of cutting down, becomes a weapon as it is embedded in a complex of ideas and other affects that change its meaning. Directly proportional to the importance of shame in our culture has always been the sheer volume of comedic produce.

The Technological Revolution

There are animals that crawl on the surface of the earth, some that burrow beneath it, others that fly above, and still others that swim. It has been said that until the human, all life forms evolved in the manner called "adaptive radiation," plants and animals emerging to occupy every ecological niche. Alone of all creatures, we have adapted to these special environments through our technology. It is our inventions that allow us to run faster on the surface, to tunnel underneath, to fly, to sail.

We claim that it is necessity that powers our search for invention. Yet no need creates urgency unless it triggers an affect; the inventions of man and woman always involve affect. By the time of the Industrial Revolution Western culture was deeply involved in two themes involving affect—the control of affective expression and the growing importance of shame. Many (certainly not all) inventions, despite whatever else powered them, came to be evaluated for their worth in these two realms. It turns out that the industries and inventions which appeared after 1800 changed not only the way we live but the way we experience shame. The revolution we associate with Erasmus of Rotterdam was opposed and perhaps ended by the Industrial Revolution.

Two developmental lines may be discerned. On the one hand, shame continued to increase, conquering more and more territory. During the 19th century, those who identified with the ruling classes became proper, prudish, fastidious, and prissy. Our code name for this process was taken from its presentation in England during the reign of Queen Victoria. There was, nevertheless, a Victorian Europe and a Victorian America, lands where the good queen herself did not rule but where social custom was governed by the relation to shame-as-propriety she came to symbolize.

True, there would always be a counter-revolutionary segment of the population that resisted fashion and refused to acknowledge the latest fad in sources for shame. But even these wicked and daring people were children of their environment, full of shames they took for granted. The other line of development was ushered in by technology, and it ripped an ever-widening hole in the fabric of this shame-controlled society.

Consider, as only one example, the phenomenology of lighting the home. Most of us now use candlesticks as decoration. Candles adorn birthday cakes; their warm glow lends special charm to romantic dinners. But the lamps and candles of the past are to the illumination of this current era as a bicycle is to an interstellar rocket. It has been estimated that the cost of illuminating a room with candles to the level we now require of our electric devices would be a thousandfold greater than what it costs today—hundreds of dollars per hour. Progress has turned night into cheap day.

The fear that makes us illuminate our night-time environment to reduce the dangers that can be hidden by the dark has also taken away the sky. Modern children grow up with no sense of the richness and beauty available on a dark night. Inside or outside our homes, the same electricity that put an end to dark corners and vanquished the shadows also destroyed the little nooks of privacy that had only a century or so ago become so important. Shame and privacy always dance together; when one is changed, so must the other follow in step. Privacy, so recently established as a norm, now required more effort.

But no technological advance affected shame and privacy as did the rapidly developing science of photography. Look what the camera did to the concept of the self and to the language of shame. By the middle of the 19th century there was a rapid progression in technique from primitive daguerreotypes that were locked to copper plates, to negatives made on glass that could be transferred and reproduced as paper prints. Before photography, only the wealthy were able to commission portraits, which allowed them to see themselves and to be seen by others. Now the camera offered everybody the ability to study self and others at will.

This matter of being able to observe the self is much more significant than you might realize. It was not until the latter part of the 19th century that full-length mirrors were available at all, and much, much later that their cost decreased to a range that made them universally accessible. As with every other "advance," the full-length mirror brought with it a new relation to shame. First a luxury, then a statement of vanity, and finally a clearly defined necessity, the mirror allowed everybody greater power and freedom in the presentation of self. But before the mirror was the photograph:

An aid to memory, photographs changed the nature of nostalgia. For the first time a majority of people were able to look at images of dead ancestors and unknown relatives. It became possible to see the youth of people with whom one rubbed elbows daily. The hallmarks of family memory also changed. Symbolic possession of loved ones channeled the emotions. Visual contact became more important than physical contact. The psychological consequences of absence changed. Photographs of the dead attenuated the anguish of loss and alleviated remorse.

The ability to put photographs on postcards improved the distribution of personal images. The millions of photographic portraits shot and religiously preserved in albums established new norms that completely transformed the private scene. They taught people to look at the body, and in particular the hands, in a new way.

Finally, the new technology multiplied images of nudity, now easier to behold than ever before. As early as 1850 a law was passed prohibiting the sale of obscene photos on public streets. After 1880 amateur photographers were able to cut out the professional middleman. Thereafter poses became less elaborate, and all of private life was laid open to the lens, whose appetite for intimate scenes was unlimited. (*A History of Private Life*, vol. 4, 465)

Where shame had created a new culture of privacy, the camera ripped it asunder. Indeed, as privacy grew more and more important, and as more and more of our society came to be controlled by forces operating behind closed doors, an intense pressure developed around the seen and the unseen.

Ignore, for a moment, the rapid advances in the production and distribution of the printed word that accompanied the Industrial Revolution. Books, newspapers, pamphlets, posters—all of these fostered the immediate distribution of ideas. Ignore, too, the world of radio, which disseminated the written word in its own way and shifted words back to spoken language. (Did you know that until the time of Erasmus people read aloud? Only as shame came to control all expression did it become important to make the written word a synonym for the silent thought.) For most people, words are only a poor substitute for seeing. One picture is worth a thousand words when they are your words and my picture. What I see, I can evaluate myself. Words can be used to hide the truth. We trust what we can see far more than what we read. What you see is what you get.

I believe that photography has done more to change shame than any other force in the history of our society. Again, I have introduced an area of scholarship far too vast for this space. Perhaps it is worthy of study by some future colleague. But at least let me sketch some of the issues involved.

The economic success of photochemistry revitalized the world of optics, as new lenses were developed that allowed us to see and photograph at ever-greater distances. The merger of telescope and camera revolutionized astronomy but also caused a drastic reduction of our terrestrial privacy. Distance alone no longer guaranteed concealment. Even darkness gave way to the flashbulb and then to films and lenses capable of revealing fine detail where the human eye is blind. The speed with which the modern shutter can open and close allows the camera to capture moments so brief that for all practical purposes they did not exist before we could study them at leisure. And a wide range of photomicroscopes allows us to peer into the heart of things so small that they had once "escaped detection."

Also did we learn to take photographs in rapid sequence, and then to present them in ways that mimicked life itself. The motion picture offered a new level of intrusion because it allowed us to show real life in greater detail than ever before. As film entertainment, it opens door after door as we become an audience seeking ever more "fascinating" secrets.

All movies have two plots—the human interactions we call the "story" and the private world within which that story unfolds. Films take us with equal ease into boardroom, boudoir, or the engine room of a submarine. They show us the terror of trenches and the wastage of war, allow us to spy on the working conferences of master criminals, the inner world of a prison, the bloody tension of an operating room, the very bed where sexual arousal is turned into sexual activity. Films take us where we do not belong and show us what we want to see simply because someone has closed us out or said that we do not belong there. They search for tension that has been created around the issue of what is hidden.

Nevertheless, the motion picture is an extension of the portrait camera. It requires exquisitely careful preparation before the action is to take place, followed by extensive and expensive laboratory work to produce the completed images. None of this is true for television, the next phototechnical development. It has become possible for us to look at nearly anything with a minimum of difficulty—shamelessly.

The movie theater involved the trade of place and privacy for magnification. As long as you were willing to travel to the theater and join a crowd of other observers, you would be able to peep at life enlarged on a 40-foot screen. Every gesture, every nuance of facial expression, was magnified as large as a hillside. Television, however, traded size for access and privacy. With the advent of cable systems and video recording/playback equipment, the small screen can show the same picture over and over until every aspect of it has been engrained on our memory. Where the still photograph allowed children to study some aspects of individuals, television permits them to observe in safety the small details of life previously available only through personal trial and error. No generation in history has ever known as much about the larger world into which it will emerge as that of today's children.

This technological trail has led to a permanent change in the nature of the shame experience. The photographic techniques pioneered in the 19th century allowed us to study any aspect of ourselves or others capable of being impressed on film in a fraction of a second. We were enabled to look in privacy at the face, the hands, the naked body of anybody who could be photographed. Yet the still camera did not capture the feeling of life as it is lived, life in motion, life with all the movements and sounds that convey so much data about the inner world of another person.

The Australian sociologists Fred and Merrelyn Emery have pointed out that with television any of us can look squarely into the face of another person without flinching. It was the delicacy of affective expression and the nuance of personal revelation hovering around the locus of the face that led Tomkins to comment that shared interocular contact is the most intimate of human activities. Now we can look at the face of another who is there but who is not there to respond to our gaze; this is unilateral "shared" interocular contact! Information previously available only from intimacy is now accessible without the risk of shame.

Honing its skills at home, a generation has grown into adulthood with no fear of visual confrontation, with no sense of shame about staring. Our modern population expects to look at everything, complains when anything is hidden from our view, rewards handsomely its most intrusive and shaming investigative reporters. Much that was once taught by shame is now ignored.

And as we grew more accustomed to seeing people in the movies, on television, and in magazines, we tended to imitate those who were now held up for us as exemplars. Anyone can strive for the muscular body of the trained athlete or the lithe animality of the professional model. Every force in our competitive society urges us to work toward the attainment of goals previously seen as shameworthy. Magazines, books, instructional videotapes, therapists, tutors, all offer courses of study allowing us to be beautiful, seductive, overtly and publicly sexual—all now as matters of pride rather than shame.

"Are you embarrassed to be seen naked on the screen?" I asked an intelligent, gifted actress whose roles usually involve some sort of sexual activity. Laughing softly, sardonically, she replied, "No. You worry more when the producers stop asking." The simulation of intimacy is this woman's work, and her personal relation to shame differs from that which we might have found in any other era. Her job is to pretend that neither we nor the camera that has allowed us to spy on her are triggers to shame.

My survey of the relation between shame and technology has concentrated on the revolution in pictorial imagery. Available for study and comment, but ignored for reasons of space, are other changes. Take, for instance, the matter of personal strength and fighting ability. The handgun changed the nature of self-defense by permitting a short, weak, ungainly man to kill someone who might otherwise have demolished him in a fight. Less shame was therefore associated with physical weakness because power might devolve from another source. Here it is the *instrumentation* for the *attack other* script that has changed, promoting a shift to scripts within the macho system.

The instrumentation of medicine has changed—the physician invades everything, discusses everything, writes articles about everything. The machines of transport allow us to peer at people anywhere—no matter how remote may be a culture, it is no longer a stranger to us. I could have focused my entire discussion on systems for dissemination of the printed word, which from the moment of its invention allowed the publication of what individuals had seen and thought. The list is endless and nowhere trivial.

I ask you, then, to accept that the rapid advance of technology has been associated with a major change in the nature and significance of shame and of the affects and ideas within which it is embedded. Is it merely a coincidence that Freud introduced psychoanalysis, the art and science of personal revelation, just at the moment in Western history characterized by the greatest tension between the hidden and the shown? Shame itself is an auxiliary to the positive affects that power all sociality. In Cressida's world, it is a loving affect; as it is embedded today, shame is involved with anger and danger. It is time to turn our attention to the effect of this change on society and on the individuals within it. What happened to Western culture when shame was rendered ineffective as a modulator of affect?

31

THE RANGE OF SHAME

Shame

by Vern Rutsala

This is the shame of the woman whose hand hides
her smile because her teeth are so bad, not the grand
self-hate that leads some to razors or pills
or swan dives off beautiful bridges however
tragic that is. This is the shame of being yourself,
of being ashamed of where you live and what
your father's paycheck lets you eat and wear.
This is the shame of the fat and the bald,
the unbearable blush of acne, the shame of having
no lunch money and pretending you're not hungry.
This is the shame of concealed sickness—diseases
too expensive to afford that offer only their cold
one-way ticket out. This is the shame of being ashamed,
the self-disgust of the cheap wine drunk, the lassitude
that makes junk accumulate, the shame that tells
you there is another way to live but you are
too dumb to find it. This is the real shame, the damned
shame, the crying shame, the shame that's criminal,
the shame of knowing words like "glory" are not
in your vocabulary though they litter the Bibles
you're still paying for. This is the shame of not
knowing how to read and pretending you do. This is
the shame that makes you afraid to leave your house,
the shame of food stamps at the supermarket when
the clerk shows impatience as you fumble with the change.

This is the shame of dirty underwear, the shame
of pretending your father works in an office
as God intended all men to do. This is the shame
of asking friends to let you off in front of the one
nice house in the neighborhood and waiting
in the shadows until they drive away before walking
to the gloom of your house. This is the shame
at the end of the mania for owning things, the shame
of no heat in winter, the shame of eating cat food,
the unholy shame of dreaming of a new house and car
and the shame of knowing how cheap such dreams are.

From *The Bluest Eye*
by Toni Morrison

. . . The sofa, for example. It had been purchased new, but the fabric had split straight across the back by the time it was delivered. The store would not take the responsibility . . .

"Looka here, buddy, It was O.K. when I put it on the truck. The store can't do anything about it once it's on the truck. . . ." Listerine and Lucky Strike breath.

"But I don't want no tore couch if'n it's bought new." Pleading eyes and tightened testicles.

"Tough shit, buddy. Your tough shit. . . ."

You could hate a sofa, of course—that is, if you could hate a sofa. But it didn't matter. You still had to get together $4.80 a month. If you had to pay $4.80 a month for a sofa that started off split, no good, and humiliating—you couldn't take any joy in owning it.   (32)

Each night, without fail, she prayed for blue eyes. Fervently, for a year she had prayed. Although somewhat discouraged, she was not without hope. To have something as wonderful as that happen would take a long, long, time.

Thrown, in this way, into the blinding conviction that only a miracle could relieve her, she would never know her beauty. She would see only what there was to see: the eyes of other people.   (40)

Pecola stood a little apart from us, her eyes hinged in the direction in which Maureen had fled. She seemed to fold into herself, like a pleated wing. Her pain antagonized me. I wanted to open her up, crisp her edges, ram a stick down that hunched and curved spine, force her to stand erect and spit the misery out on the streets. But she held it in where it could lap up into her eyes.   (61)

Now we must deal with the problem of chronic shame. It is the complex emotional picture represented by the poem of Vern Rutsala and the novels of Toni Morrison. It is life itself for so many of us—lives of unreached goals, unmet expectations, chronically and repetitively and recurrently and constantly dashed hopes. It is a world where wish itself becomes only predecessor to humiliation. To the extent that we cannot augment our experience of self, to the degree that we are unable by our actions to have an experience of efficacy that can elevate us in our own self-esteem, to the limits (often apparently limitless) that life prevents us from achievement, we can develop a shame-based personality.

Make no mistake about it. This is about a life of pain, the constant pain that afflicts, to one degree or another, the overwhelming majority of any population that has been raised without hope. What does one do to diminish the pain of such a life?

Simple. We can, for instance, become jealous of whoever is loved more than us, or we can through greed marshal our efforts to acquire superficial but highly visible evidence of achievement, or we can through envy seek to destroy the self-esteem of anyone who seems to have some personal competence or sense of self-confidence. To the extent that we are unable to reduce our own steady sense of pain, we can share it with others. We can share our own harvest of shame with those whose more conventional crops we covet.

By vandalism and graffiti we can deface the public structures that represent the affluence and pride of a society and which therefore can come to represent the poverty and degradation of an individual whose life is the reciprocal of the visible norm. If enough of our fellows share our pain and accept our creative urge, we can roam out in groups attacking, frightening, dispiriting, discouraging those who have become emblems of our discontent. (What must happen for a section of society to accept, legitimize, sanction, cheer, or otherwise amplify graffiti? Who makes the first gesture, and what powers the split of cultures into such widely divergent styles of display?) Vandalism and graffiti are statements, messages, instructions about shame.

Once, driving to work in my precisely tuned state-of-the-art foreign car, traveling from my beautifully landscaped upper-middle-class suburb to the center of our city and the enclave of tony offices where I have practiced medicine for so long, passing through one of those sections you can find in any American city—once bustling and white middle-class, now slum and black and full of the danger that lurks in any cluster of the disadvantaged—I realized that the smooth brick side of a large old home had become the medium of display for that particular slum, the vehicle through which the most articulate of its inhabitants had learned to gain access to the consciousness of those who saw this route as nothing more than a convenient access to the city. "Free Huey Newton," it cried for a while. Later, in sequence, the wall saw each mayor skewered verbally by the precise language of this ghetto. No slogan lasted very long before it was painted out and replaced by the cry of its day.

I watched the neighborhood change, saw the buildings crumble and the shoulders of its people slump into chronic helplessness. A large blank space appeared on this billboard of discontent, and I waited to see what would replace the now routine display of complaint. It was an interesting slogan, one which remained there for many years, untouched by later editors. Only when the neighborhood had rehabilitated itself, had spruced up the faces of its buildings and tidied up its gardens, when the general level of local affluence had improved just enough for the commercial advertisers to recognize that this was a neighborhood now with enough money to purchase more expensive brands of liquor or cigarettes or hair goo, that the more conventional billboards were again suitable for assignment to one or another of these products, did anybody dare to replace or deface this particular slogan.

There have been no graffiti on that building since that neighborhood rose in status. For some years now its bricks have been clean and russet, the mortar pointed and pretty. But I still see what is no longer there, the message of another day. It had stared at us for too long to be forgotten, stared at its neighborhood for nearly a decade, demanding change. Neatly written, in Palmer penmanship script better formed than I can write at my best, its very neatness in stark contrast to the ugly violence of the other spray-painted messages that came to frame it as a wooden gilt molding outlines a painting, it told us that "the name of the game is shame."

Did the sign change anything? Yes, I think it did. I draw significance from the fact that for years no one altered or defaced or removed or supplanted this slogan. It hit home, reached its target, maybe even awakened people to the idea that they lived in shame. Nobody had to tell them that they lived with anger. When shame is identified as shame there can be change, however subtle and slow.

Faced with societal discontent, whole nations have been urged on courses of action designed by their leaders to reduce chronic shame. Is the public hungry for evidence of personal competence? A war might be just the thing. "No one can humiliate us," announced Saddam Hussein as a massive array of multinational troops and matériel began to assemble in response to his invasion of Kuwait. "We will pluck out the eye of the invaders." As individuals we can feel bigger when our nation annexes territory, humbles an enemy, develops a weapon that can destroy more people and lay waste more territory than ever before.

Take, for instance, the situation where everybody is more or less equal, where misery and comfort are distributed along a gradient understood and accepted by all. What happens when somebody emerges from this culture, becomes differentiated on the basis of innate excellence? I refer to the special light of genius, the prodigious strength of a Samson, the talents of a Pele or a Pavarotti or a Picasso or a Paul Newman, the goodness of a saint, the business creativity of a tycoon, the luminous beauty of a star. We hear about these special people when their ability has been nurtured, when their cultural milieu provides a platform from which their careers can be launched. By definition, we do not hear about those whose light is snuffed by a cultural milieu that cannot tolerate anyone who might place it in danger of invidious comparison. That is the stuff of novels.

All too often it is the stuff of case histories, a world to which we can gain real entry only through the door of empathic understanding, where we can create change only by therapeutic techniques based in empathic relatedness. You cannot treat such people by remaining safely remote. In order to be helpful you must have the courage to live their pain as it hovers and buzzes around your own empathic wall, the strength and self-confidence to wrest yourself from their pain by the techniques of decentering, and the wit and skill to offer new ways of understanding, new safety within the therapeutic relationship that allows the formation of a new inner world. But first you must learn about shame as affect and the compass of shame as our assemblage of responses to it.

It is all around you, this shame. Rarely is shame presented to us, available for study as shame affect in the pure state introduced to us by Tomkins. What we see is shame bundled with the affects of dissmell and disgust—the other inborn mechanisms of interpersonal distance—as well as shame embedded in anger, distress, and fear. Often what we encounter is shame affect experienced not even as anything we might call shame but as a reaction pattern determined by the point on the compass of shame made natural by the way each of us has traveled through time to develop our attitude toward shame affect.

Yet always associated with the moment of shame will be certain inviolable characteristics. Normally, things have to be pretty good for shame to happen, for shame affect provides an innate limitation to the pleasant experiences of interest or contentment. There will have been a source—something that triggered the affect—something that interfered, even for a moment, with the flow of the initial positive affect that otherwise would have been sustained. But shame can be induced in situations that are already awful. It can be made to take us from bad to worse, for we can be humiliated when we are already in the throes of a negative affect. The triad of shame, dissmell, and disgust make for a powerful weapon in the arsenal of misery.

Once triggered, shame affect proceeds along its prewritten path, pulling eyes and face from communion with others, recarving the upper body into a slump, attacking higher cognitive functions to produce a cognitive shock within which we are incapable of clear thought. Shame makes us stammer, hesitate, halt. Suddenly this moment of shame affect forces from memory into awareness a host of scripts, of situations within which we had experienced shame. Unbidden, unwanted memories of shames past course through consciousness, adding to our discomfort.

Now we have a choice. Up to now there had been no choice. Source has triggered affect because that is the way we are built. Affect has unfolded as it has evolved to unfold. Memory has been triggered as it had been laid down, scripts assembled from clustered memories. Until this moment, no part of this sequence of actions is capable of alteration. But now that it has brought us to this point, we can choose to reflect on what we have been shown by shame—and we can agree to learn from it. Shame can teach, can reinforce our best intentions to learn from error and failure.

It is this pattern of acceptance that so often characterizes an attitude of personal enlightenment. I think that the facial display seen on anyone who has achieved personal mastery is the affective disposition of one to whom shame is no worse or no more powerful a message than any other source of information provided by the human instrument. It is possible for an enlightened adult to enjoy a moment of stupidity as an opportunity to learn, to relish a moment of incompetence because with it will come a welcome lesson that can lead to further exploration of human ability. The sometimes puzzling face of the Zen master reflects an attitude of joy toward all learning.

Most of us are less masters of self than slaves to shame. Unable, unready to accept what can be taught by shame, we barely pause when given this moment of choice by the cognitive phase of shame. Instantly we move into some characteristic pattern of reaction dictated by the scripts stored as the compass of shame. We withdraw, submit, disguise, or attack as seems most appropriate to the moment. Rarely do we "know" that we have been in the throes of shame affect; even less frequently are we aware that the actions of another person have been dictated by shame.

SHIFTING PATTERNS OF REACTION

One recent evening, stopped at a light during my drive home, in my usual end-of-day trance, I was shocked into frightened alertness by a sudden thumping noise. Standing next to me, pounding on the side of my car, was a tall, angry man of African descent shouting obscenities. I had cut him off at an intersection, he raged. "Where, how?" I asked. I had no idea what had provoked his anger. From among his threats and imprecations I dissected the following statistics: Half a mile back we had been driving two abreast, he to my left. At a point where we crossed a major thoroughfare, he paused, apparently in preparation for a left turn. I moved into the lane he had now made available and continued in that direction. But he had paused for other reasons and saw my action as endangering and humiliating him.

His was certainly an *attack other* script! As he strode back to his car I was left to muse about the changes in our society that might make a relatively trivial driving incident into something that could have ended with real danger to my person. Something has happened to encourage a large and growing segment of our population to extend the radius of its response to shame. People now go to greater lengths to redress humiliation than ever before in my lifetime.

There have always been a number of people who carry firearms in their cars—witness the number of roadside signs used as targets for the game of "Dot the i, center the o." But now it is increasingly common to hear that guns have been used to terminate the common highway altercation. Cut off at an intersection, "beaten out" at a traffic light, motorists on occasion will reach for their trusty sidearm and shoot the driver now defined as a tormentor. Affronted at barroom or pool hall, men are likely to leave, only to return with a gang of friends determined to heap severe injury upon whomever has delivered the initial insult. This era is witness to a radical escalation of the techniques, the severity of response, deemed appropriate for the *attack other* script. There may be no better example of the *attack other* script than vigilante action.

One rule seems applicable to all of these situations, these explosions of civic violence as part of an *attack other* script. In each case I have studied, the perpetrator was one whose otherwise normal use of attacking scripts had earlier been further restrained by social shame. It was the societal approval for release from that specific variety of shame that had given permission to launch an actual attack. And the extraordinary intensity of the ensuing attack was directly proportional both to the length of time this response had previously been inhibited and to the importance-to-the-self of the original insult.

Meyer Kahane, a rabbi born in New York City, was so inflamed with rage at the injustice done the Jews during the Holocaust that he organized the Jewish Defense League and insisted that its members learn karate. Kahane knew that the Italian word *ghetto* referred to the sections of Rome within which Jewish merchants had been confined; indeed, that they were merchants and moneylenders only as a function of restrictive laws forbidding them to own land because they were Jewish. What in biblical times had been a tribe of warriors was forced to live in shame as a legion of otherwise powerless businessmen, artists, and scholars. It is not surprising that Kahane's JDL operated under the slogan "Never again!" And it is not surprising that Kahane was eventually assassinated by Middle Eastern forces ill-disposed toward the concept of outspoken Jewish warriors.

A similar process, less easily impeded by the death of a leader, may be seen in the plight of the African-American population. Brought as slaves to the land of the free, African tribesmen and women were removed from their own vigorous culture and turned into little more than beasts of burden and creatures designed to fulfill the fantasy needs of fellow humans who now claimed to be their owners. Can there be a greater source of chronic and ongoing shame than to be declared so much less than human that one is only a piece of property? Richard L. Rubenstein, in *The Cunning of History*, notes the succession of legal maneuvers through which Nazi Germany was able to orchestrate the wholesale extermination of the Jews: Jews first were declared non-Aryan, not truly German. Next, those who were not truly German were declared not true citizens; soon they were defined as a lesser species of human; then not truly human and therefore worthy of treatment more suited to animals designated as a source of food or pelt. But this was done with German efficiency and a truly German sense of legal nicety.

The slave trade incorporated none of this artful system of legal redefinition, for it was not neighbors and doctors and artists resembling us who were being redefined, but scantily clad men and women with bones in their hair and rings in their noses who could quite easily be treated as some life form intermediary between the more powerful (armed) Caucasians and the beasts of burden then used for farm work. In the 19th century there was much debate about whether Negroes were capable of blushing, for it was thought that only humans could feel shame and that slavery was an acceptable economic pattern only if those enslaved were not truly human. Whatever the social stratification of African tribal life prior to capture and translocation, slave life in America was based in a system of shame and terror.

Throughout history we have studied examples of the processes through which whole cultures emerge from slavery. For 40 years Moses kept his tribe of Egyptian Jews wandering through a region the size of Rhode Island, only to "find" the Promised Land immediately on the death of the last individual born in slavery and not trained by him. No one with a slave mentality would be permitted entry into the new world.

No such period of retraining was made available to the African-American slaves, to whom legal freedom and apparent equality were conferred by the

Emancipation Proclamation and made more real by the Civil War. After a century of slavery, this large group of Americans was intellectually and emotionally incapable of full assimilation as equal members of the larger culture. Denied the education necessary for acculturation and reared to accept definition as inferior individuals or members of an inferior segment of humanity, this group of Americans lived for another century as a nation within a nation.

Whatever differences can be detected between newcomers and the established majority will be magnified as "reasons" for exclusion. Skin color, hair, language, remnants of tribal custom, and lack of relevant formal education formed continuing barriers to acceptance, excuses for the maintenance of this vigorous citizenry in the status of a dissmelling subculture. Person or group, whoever is exposed to chronic dissmell will adopt an attitude of self-dissmell and shame-of-the-self; merely to be of African descent meant that one was born into shame.

Read (if you can bear such prolonged immersion in the world of shame, dissmell, and disgust) Toni Morrison's 1970 novel *The Bluest Eye*. Young Pecola grows into adolescence surrounded by, immersed in a literal sea of, parental contempt, from which she derives a self-image of terrible ugliness that she attributes to her negritude. If only her eyes were blue (like those of her pretty blonde classmate), then certainly Pecola would be less dissmelling and perhaps even acceptable to her chronically angry and shaming parents. Nothing slows or modulates the constant onrush of degradation to which she is exposed. She is steadily and steadfastly beaten by her mother, then raped and impregnated by her father. A trusted adviser leads her to kill a dog—the only creature with whom she has some sort of kinship—by giving him poisoned meat that will make him vomit to death. Pecola is allowed no solace save psychosis. Peace comes to her only with the delusion that she is beautiful, that she now has the bluest eyes ever to be seen, that finally she is worthy of love.

What makes Morrison's novel so extraordinary is the apparent ease with which she makes us understand that such mistreatment of individuals within a family is a metaphor for our societal treatment of an entire population. Pecola's parents treat her much as they themselves have been managed by the host culture that so clearly defines them as dissmelling and shameworthy aliens. One is reminded of the young Polish boy in Jerzy Kosinski's novel *The Painted Bird*, who becomes mute when tortured by immersion in a vat of human excrement, then forced to duck his head below the surface of this foul milieu rather than risk physical injury. Shame bundled with self-disgust and self-dissmell can destroy self-esteem with a ferocity unequaled in human experience.

Why do we—all of us—do such things to people? Examine the 1972 *New Yorker* cartoon by Stan Hunt, in which one businessman refers proudly to another as his "immediate inferior." It seems that nearly everybody needs an inferior. Life assaults as often as it beckons with opportunity. If we have through study or religious discipline or psychotherapy achieved an attitude of enlightenment that turns each failure or defeat or rebuff into a welcome lesson, such incident then adds no degree of toxicity to our own personal well of shame. But where study has been inadequate for this purpose, or religion designed for other intents, or therapy ignorant of these issues, the *attack other* form of reaction to shame asks for vehicles of detoxification. Good masochists are hard to find. Masochist submission from within an *attack self* script legitimizes an *attack other* script; it requires a partner whose shame must be handled by the accumulation of power over others. When there are too few masochists to go around, we need inferiors. It is through the creation of legions of inferiors that entire cultures spend their accumulated and perhaps nearly inevitable shame.

The poem of Emma Lazarus assures each wave of immigrants that the Statue of Liberty holds her lamp beside the golden door so that she can welcome "your tired, your poor, your huddled masses yearning to breathe free." Yet each member of those tempest toss'd huddled masses experiences America as a land hungry for new inferiors. The Irish of the 19th century East Coast, the Chinese of the West Coast, the freed slaves of the Reconstruction, the displaced persons of war-ravaged 20th-century Europe, boat people, Cubans, Thai, Laotians, Puerto Ricans—the list is endless and always capable of increase by whatever new group is willing to trade the discomforts of an unbearable homeland for the ignominy of immigrant status. All nations seem to hunger for inferiors capable of doing work "unfit" for their "betters."

Slavery afforded every southern Caucasian the opportunity to be far more powerful than every African. The entire population of slaves was kept under control by terror mediated by whips, chains, forced concubinage, lynching, ritual murder, castration, branding, and public humiliations of unimaginable variety. Poverty, denial of voting rights, exclusion from educational opportunity, and the brilliantly designed structure of the Ku Klux Klan (which mimicked African tribal ritual in a calculated campaign of terror and humiliation)—all operated to maintain this citizenry as virtual if not actual slaves. Such politically sanctioned and maintained systems of behavior served to protect the southern economy from any loss of cheap labor. But at the emotional level, the system kept alive contrasting ideas of white supremacy and black inferiority. For the white majority, shame (notwithstanding its actual source) could always be mitigated by an *attack other* action taken against its African sub-population. To be called "black" in America meant to live in a state of shame; negritude implied helpless submission to overwhelming force.

Note, too, that the scripts available in the reactive phase of the shame sequence were quite different for the two cultures. Whites were permitted to attack both whites and non-whites; African-Americans were permitted only to attack their own people. (Discussing rape as an act of insurrection, Eldridge Cleaver wrote that he perfected his skills in the ghetto before bringing them into enemy territory.) A culture inhibited from redressing wrongs perpetrated against it (especially wrongs committed by those pledged to uphold a legal system promising, guaranteeing equality for all) will store and accumulate and build up a powerful arsenal of resentment. The forces of the majority preferred that its African populace express shame as *withdrawal;* as "Step'n'fetchit" *attack self* scripts; as *avoidance* scripts expressed as shiny new Buicks in front of and expensive television sets within the shacks of successful workers who had been denied any opportunity to buy better homes; and *attack other* scripts restricted to the boundaries of clearly established ghettos. Fear and shame work wonderfully well to prevent the expression of anger within the *attack other* script. They also foster the magnification of self-disgust and self-dissmell.

All of this worked until the cultural explosion of the 1960s, when, under the banner called "freedom of expression," legions marched protected by a new understanding of constitutional guarantees of civil rights. Suddenly free to attend any school in the land—indeed, urged to do so by a majority populace now ashamed of its history of repression—African-Americans entered the mainstream of contemporary culture. Now our doctors, lawyers, politicians, engineers, and bankers might derive from the racial and ethnic minorities so long excluded from such privilege. A more affluent African-American minority became a new source of income to an entire economy; advertisers and the entertainments they used as a medium of display began to feature models drawn from the society at whom the advertising was aimed. The newly released African-American population provided a significant portion of the energy, the excitement that drove the '70s and the '80s.

But, on the other hand, something had to happen to the mountains of shame, self-disgust, and self-dissmell heaped up within this population. The scripts through which this newly released community expressed its response to shame old and shame new shifted toward the *attack other* system once fear and shame no longer limited the expression toward others of anger, disgust, and dissmell. The problem of urban or civic violence, the cultural need to "shove it to whitey" within shame-reversing *attack other* scripts, public bravado expressed as growing insolence toward authority figures historically associated with the repression of both positive and negative affect, machismo, redress of previous wrongs, and magnification of cultural methods of active attack all devolved from this relatively "abrupt" but long-overdue removal of external control over affect expression.

This subculture would now be causing major change in society simply because of the gifts it brings to it—the absence of these gifts has made our world poorer for far too long. But more has happened. Major social change had to occur also because shame and fear no longer operated as culturally sanctioned impediments to the attack other script. Unfortunately, a sizable fraction of the African-American community now has come to equate all modulation and control with shame, which has made for a terrible problem in shared living.

Were this a cohort in psychotherapy we would describe such behavior as part of the process through which one achieves freedom from depression. Therapists (and the families of their patients) have long come to accept that people released from clinical depression tend to be effusive and uncontrolled. But nothing so simple has happened here. Release from control by shame and fear has come to operate like an antidepressant drug spread over an entire city by a department of public health. And there is no kindly and trusted psychotherapist with whom the patient can discuss what it feels like to be so suddenly empowered.

When you add to the mix the tragedy that the psychoactive drugs of the street have become normative accoutrements of ghetto life, and that these drugs generally act to amplify the same excitement and anger that power the macho defense against shame, the current pattern of public violence and explosiveness becomes increasingly understandable. Death by gunshot is four times more common in the African-American than in the Caucasian-American population. The *attack other* script has no inherent object of attack; whoever is handy when the mood strikes will be struck down.

Such a radical shift in the way one group interacts with others must force a commensurately fierce reaction in what was once the dominant society. Two styles of response may be noted: One stresses the need for us as a society to accept this change and all the tension it brings, simply because we are the descendants of those who caused the problem. The other seeks to return the world to its previous level of comfort for the dominant group by interfering with the ability of African-Americans and other minority groups to reap the benefits of political change. The tension between these two sociopolitical systems can be made more understandable in the language of script theory and the differential magnification of innate affect.

In the name of "affirmative action," it is the first path that has been taken by many colleges, universities, foundations, and other institutions. For some years, they have taken the position that inter-group violence is a direct result of our long-standing policy of inequality. Needed, they say, is a reverse prejudice through which members of previously suppressed minority groups are assisted toward prominence throughout the educational establishment. Critics from the second group complain that the scholars and teachers made newly powerful by these political decisions are "poorly qualified" for their grafted-on eminence. They worry publicly about possible declines in teaching standards, quality of research, fluency with language. Affirmative action implies that the hypothesized but unproved period of decrease in quality of education would be but a small price to pay for the rich rewards to be reaped by a society exposed to such a broadened base of cultural knowledge and attitudes. Defending such a position is a host of novel educational and philosophical theories that aim to reduce the significance of the very values and training in which minority scholars are thought to be deficient.

This latter, "politically correct" belief (that traditional values must be scrapped to produce a new world order) has been given considerable power through its use of shame psychology. Anyone who dares suggest that the old values have intrinsic validity is accused of unconscious or inherent bigotry, of standing in the way of the new, counter-shaming philosophy. Academic violators of this new set of rules have been isolated, humiliated, stripped of their local political power, threatened with loss of research grants and access to graduate students, and "exposed" before the student body as perpetrators of foul and incorrect ideas. The very movement that seeks to redress the wrongs done to minority groups through a century or more of chronic humiliation now uses the tactics and techniques of the oppressors it disavows! Spirals of sophistry are being wound around the compass of shame.

Not unexpectedly, an inevitable backlash has gained power and momentum; this is the second path mentioned above. Seen on a college campus recently and reported by Dinesh D'Souza, was the sign, "A mind is a terrible thing to waste—especially on a nigger." This macabre, dissmelling assault on the hallowed slogan of the American Negro College Fund is emblematic of the anger now being expressed by those who feel their rights are being ignored in favor of the previously suppressed African-Americans. Muttering in the wings is the huge crowd of those whose self-esteem depended on their ability to feel better than the hated (dissmelling, disgusting, shameworthy) designated inferiors.

Read *God and General Longstreet—The Lost Cause and the Southern Mind.* Thomas L. Connelly and Barbara L. Bellows follow an array of issues—the consistent theme of sadness in southern songs and ballads, a cultural sense of inefficacy and incompetence relative to the "northern establishment," the need to prove cultural superiority to "the Negro race"—and attribute them to defeat in the Civil War and the forced termination of slavery. A group shorn of its designated inferiors will be destabilized just as much as the group that has been freed from the status of inferiors. The renewed contemporary attacks on African-Americans have been launched by powerful forces whose purpose is to restore the early 19th-century balance of power that gave every southern white a feeling of superiority over every "black" man and woman. No *attack other* script works unless someone can be found to receive the attack.

It is very difficult to redress the wounds created by shame unless one understands shame. I plead for an understanding of the affective roots of prejudice, and for systems of release from forced inferiority that take into account the compass of shame.

WOMAN IN AN ERA OF MADNESS

But no society has ever had to go outside its boundaries to find a band of designated inferiors. For the greater part of recorded history, Western civilization has taken for granted the "right" of men to control women. Men have been able to victimize, seduce, rape, impregnate, enslave, humiliate, entrap, and otherwise use women simply because men are, on the whole, larger and stronger than women. And it is true that the more advanced a life form, the more time is spent by the female of the species on matters related to childbearing and childrearing. Women, therefore, can be rendered noncompetitive with men by insemination.

None of this is to say that women are without power over men. Women have been able to victimize, seduce, enslave, humiliate, entrap, and otherwise use men. They do not, however, have the *same* sort of power available to men, an asymmetry that creates its own tension around the issues of shame and pride, as well as its own cluster of scripts stored within the compass of shame. Humankind is by nature split into groups on the basis of gender, each group debating its worth relative to the other. Always do we compare ourselves to others in our own set, while for different reasons we contrast ourselves to members of the other. Wherever there are significant differences between clusters of traits there will be the opportunity for attribution of both shame and pride. I mean only to indicate with the most casual of brushstrokes that the war between the genders is eternal—and unavoidable as long as people remain uneducated about the complex nature and history of shame.

"What fools men are!" say a multitude of knowledgeable women. "Aren't women so damn stupid!" say a horde of apparently well-informed men. Issues of shame and pride hover constantly about the interface between the genders.

Although for obvious reasons men and women exist in approximately equal numbers, it has become fashionable to refer to women as members of a minority group simply because our societal treatment of women resembles our behavior with groups whose powerlessness devolves from their numerical inferiority. Again, this classification by analogy would be unnecessary were the connection to shame affect of inferiority, helplessness, weakness, and dependence understood better. Yet the assignment to minority psychology of gender-based problems has encouraged the use of sociopolitical maneuvers directly analogous to those used to reverse discrimination against African-Americans. The changes? Everywhere we see women who are more sure of themselves, more free to compete in a male-dominated marketplace, more comfortable with their sexuality. And everywhere we see evidence of trouble among those men for whom the shaming of women formed so large a part of their own security system.

Motion pictures model and suggest the new woman; she is athletic, comfortable with her body, often scantily dressed, freely and comfortably sexual, wise and energetic in business, skilled in the arts of self-defense, and ready to fight back against anyone who endangers her. It is not unusual to see a woman in the movies using the advantage conferred by anatomy to disable an attacker by kicking or kneeing him in the groin. Nor is it unusual to see film images of women who are far more powerful than their men, occasionally subjecting them to torture and humiliation. These films cater to the long-suppressed desire of women to reach out and kick someone in an *attack other* script.

Yet crimes against women are increasing at an alarming rate; it is no longer unusual to see movies in which women are treated with savage brutality and to read in the daily paper of similar attacks on our own friends and neighbors. Perhaps in some bizarre spirit of equality we now see men treat women just as they treat men—by hitting them full-force with a fist in jaw or midgut.

I scanned a group of "violence" films recently. Yes, most of them still show the interplay of good and evil; resolution of the central conflict (the story line) allows good to triumph and evil to be punished. One subtext involves the idea that prolonged study of the martial arts under the aegis of a master leads to power that can only be used in the service of good; the new hero has achieved affect modulation through mastery of violence. This, too, is a shame theme: Confidence conferred by physical superiority is a powerful antidote for shame. Every little boy longs for the day he is safe from taunts and malevolence.

But there is another subtext that speaks to another audience. The bad guys in the movies are different these days. These are vigilante films in which the climactic horrific and disgusting execution of the villain, rendered as never before permitted on film, is excused on the basis of Talionic law. They are designed less to show the moral superiority of the enlightened hero than to demonstrate for the great mass of macho men these new trends in cruelty. What they do to women is more humiliating, more deadly, more violent, and more graphically rendered than at any time in our history. I do not believe that the economic success of this genre depends a whit on a societal interest in the triumph of good over evil.

And, as part of this process, real women are being mauled, slashed, disfigured, raped, kidnapped, and murdered in numbers and to a degree previously unimaginable in our history. Once we clucked over the idea of a "Jack the Ripper" who murdered and dissected prostitutes in London. Now he is everywhere, and the target of his attack is the innocent woman whose only crime is her enjoyment of her femininity.

A PLEA FOR EDUCATION AND MODULATION

Our societal attitude toward homosexuality provides another example of this process—the emergence of a disease seemingly specific for this group of men (seen often as dissmelling and disgusting) was taken by some as the operation of moral justice. There were many who felt that the autoimmune deficiency syndrome should not have received so much expensive research attention because this fatal disease "only" affected homosexuals. These angry citizens seem to view as a shame-reducing personal efficacy experience the extermination of what to them is a dissmelling and disgusting tribe.

Next examine the police riot at the 1968 Chicago Democratic National Convention. One group of radical activists decided to diminish our faith in the police. Taunting "the men in blue" by calling them "mother-fuckers," dropping on their heads balloons filled with excrement, intentionally violating every possible standard of commonly accepted behavior designed to limit dissmell, disgust, and shame, they provided a stimulus for which these officers of the law were completely unprepared. Reacting with violence in classic *attack other* scripts, the police clubbed, beat, humiliated, jailed, and terrorized large numbers of their tormentors—producing a reduction in their own public image that will not be repaired in our lifetime.

The rising tide of "civil disobedience" (more precisely, of shaming gestures toward those in authority) has made the police as a body increasingly helpless and increasingly apt to use main force in an *attack other* mode—itself producing more shame and rage in citizens exposed to police rage. In reaction to this shift in behavior on the part of those they are supposed to protect, many law enforcement officials complain that "these people are being allowed to get away with murder." At the same time, more and more documented instances of police brutality are brought to light. In one recent, celebrated case, an innocent motorist was beaten by four officers while other policemen stood by in mute permission. Their attack was recorded on videotape and shown publicly on TV throughout the country. Registered on the police computer was a communiqué issued by one of the policemen, stating that the incident felt good because he hadn't beaten up an African-American citizen in a long time. As the populace grows increasingly explosive so does the police force, making the problem worse because now the issues appear focal (the result of special, local conditions) rather than diffuse and culture-wide.

The story is the same everywhere we look. Sociopolitical manipulation undertaken without a clear understanding of the psychological forces involved will always keep the war alive. Few if any of the pundits recommending social change seem to have any interest in decreasing the affective tension associated with it.

Earlier we established that Renaissance sensibility brought about what Elias called a change in the threshold for shame and delicacy, along with a growing requirement for the modulation of affective expression. For hundreds of years, Western civilization has told us that it is better to control one's output of affect than to be undisciplined and therefore humiliated. Anticipation of shame served well to modulate affect. For the first time in centuries, shame and affect dyscontrol have been unlinked and allowed to travel along separate paths. Since it was partially for the sake of shame that Western civilization learned to control affect itself, it was to be expected that widespread release from domination by shame would foster an explosion of negative affect.

Essential to solving this problem are cross-cultural studies of the relation between shame and cultural types. Have you ever watched television coverage of a sporting event held in Japan? In this most successful of the modern shame cultures, it is considered improper to cheer or jeer unless instructed to do so. Many popular Japanese "game shows" provide an exactly countervailing opportunity to witness the humiliation of contestants and to express contempt by mocking, taunting, and yelling. There are many other examples of public affect management scripts of this sort: Roman rulers encouraged the presentation of "circuses" at which spectators might see gladiators fight to the death or prisoners mauled by carnivores. Such entertainments were consciously de-

signed as antidotes to societal discontent, spectacles allowing culturally sanctioned expression of shame-based rage. More? I suspect that the vigor of both
French and German productivity was lowest during eras of "shamelessness"
and "sexual licentiousness" and greatest during periods of political repression.

In a former era the models for behavior most available to us were religious
and political leaders, doctors, lawyers, all of whom were known to us either
through our own interactions with them or what we were allowed to read in
magazines or in the press. Radio brought more, television still more of their
presence and style. But most of these exemplars achieved prominence through
study that demanded affect modulation. Now we have the phenomenon of
massive television and movie exposure of sports figures and rock stars, most of
whom are well-trained, but whose work celebrates explosive behavior. The
majority of what is available as televised diversion each weekend is sports
entertainment, often characterized by savage effort in the name of competition, and passionate response to it on the part of the audience. The population
watches events that teach affect dyscontrol.

We are moving more and more into a culture of explosion, as a huge and
growing segment of our society has adopted the macho script, within which
shame is converted to anger and fear to excitement. Civil disobedience, crime,
vandalism, an elaborate disregard for the simple rules that allow all of us to
share an increasingly cramped space—all this involves disavowal of shame.
Violation of the law has become an efficacy experience—a moment of competence engineered to produce pride and reduce chronic shame. More and more
people ignore traffic lights because there simply aren't enough police to catch
them; some walk the crowded streets with immense audio systems that literally take over our sonic environment and deny us privacy. All of these are
shaming gestures from the macho division of the *attack other* script library.
And they are part of a steadily rising tide of affect dyscontrol that is sweeping
our civilization.

War movies have been a staple commodity since the introduction of filmed
entertainment. But now we as audience are exposed close-up to battle scenes
more gory than the surgical operating room, and from which we were previously screened by the mechanism of disgust—Elias's concept of delicacy. In
other contemporary films, under the guise of "realism," murder victims (usually
female) are exposed naked, bloody, and horrifically defaced. Directors compete
with each other to see who can "get away with" the most graphic depiction of
carnage. And the modern attitude, shifting the balance of favor between shame
and exposure, has shamed the motion picture industry into withdrawing from
the business of monitoring its product on the basis of any arbitrary standard of

"taste." I am fully aware that we Americans have a constitutional right to see anything we want, and that the current shift in moral values can be seen as a healthy reaction to the previous century of stultifying repression. But this current relaxation of "rules" against anything that once brought shame, dis-smell, and disgust has been used to witless advantage by a highly competitive industry directed more by market forces than by any sense of responsibility or morality. Perhaps some social good is served by the cable television programs that demonstrate the latest in surgical technique. We medical students worked hard to curb our revulsion at the bloodless dissection of cadavers, and later at the gory spectacle of surgery. No educational system protects the itinerant viewer who happens on these programs and remains transfixed by horror and curiosity unprotected by the years of study that help diminish the affective experience of such exposure.

War, garish movies, police brutality, gender turf, academic squabbles—is this shame? We have come a long way from our initial study of clowns and comedians. The study of shame affect illuminates matters far afield from such workaday experiences as embarrassment and shyness. I believe that Western civilization is poised on the brink of a precipice to which it has been driven by forces incapable of comprehension until the new era of psychological sophisti-cation made possible by affect theory. Great hordes of people are rendered effectively dysfunctional by addiction to chemical substances; these drugs are ingested to modulate affect of unimaginable density. They alter affective expe-rience in ways for which none of us is really prepared. Some of the pain so treated happens to involve shame affect. But at the root of the problem is the change in the socialization of shame, the release of an entire culture from the constraints once imposed by shame.

Even our religions have split into groups that increase affect and those that damp it. Traditional Judaeo-Christian worship incorporates the modulation of affect into a system of moral values. Our behavior during services is highly modulated—we chant quietly in concert with our fellows, sing politely, listen politely to the more professional choir, cantor, or soloist, worship in hushed tones. Those members of the macho culture who do attend church are likely to choose one in which group activity is loud and demonstrative, in which the leader orates with a wide dynamic range of affective expression, and where the musical accompaniment raises, rather than lowers, the general level of affect in the room. In both systems one may find the solace of moral suasion. It is to the affective tone that I call attention.

Our Hope for the Future

What are the moderating forces available to assist our recovery from this crisis? In times of disaster, some return to organized religion in order to hear about a power higher than those now destabilizing life. This involves the form of shame Schneider described as awe, setting into operation the program of affect modulation with which the population is most secure. Recognizing the benefits to be achieved from internalized religious discipline, many have tried to enforce religious study. The civil rights movement had earlier legislated removal of such modulating influences as school prayer, first on the grounds that it violated constitutional separation of church and state, and later for the reason that it "forced" on all children some type of submission to nondenominational Protestant Christianity. Now there is a reactive movement seeking to reestablish this particular moderating influence within our schools, a "fundamentalist" trend looking to "return America to her roots" in Christian theology.

It is likely that the pendulum of social change will move in just that direction, for our country has always swung back and forth from a system of humanistic freedom to a psychology directed by strictly enforced codes of behavior. These two groups, into which our entire population seems to be split, have been studied extensively by Tomkins, who found them to differ on the basis of certain affect scripts. The *humanist* is more likely to smile, to enjoy the mutualization of positive affect, to experience more often the impediment of shame, and to tolerate or accept the affect of distress. The *normative* is far less likely to smile in public, will not tolerate shame (which is converted to dissmell and disgust toward others), and uses anger as a stable force in interpersonal relationships. Anyone can confirm these experimental data by inspecting photographs taken of people massed in rallies both for and against abortion. The pro-choice ranks are likely to be smiling, while the faces of the anti-abortion group will demonstrate dissmell, disgust, and anger. Powerful affect modulation scripts always underlie deep divisions in systems of belief.

Unfortunately, it is for precisely these reasons that a shift toward "fundamentalist values" cannot produce a significant reduction in public turmoil. Notwithstanding its highest motives, normative psychology seeks control through shame and fear. Ours is an era that simply will not tolerate or accept control through shame, therefore forcing the normative leaders to resort increasingly to fear through violence and oppressive civil control. Such a maneuver, even if temporarily successful, will only sow the seeds of the next (and more violent) swing of the pendulum. The risk of this program includes cycles in which violence and dyscontrol rise steadily in amplitude and ferocity until the forces of law and order take over again, reintroducing a guilt psychology that eventually enfeebles the normative leaders and opens the way for equally uninformed humanist control.

Needed is a change in our entire cultural attitude toward affect; a shift from this use of shame to control toward the definition of each affect as such; and instruction in techniques for modulation. We simply must study both innate affect and affect management scripts. Even the world of psychotherapy must adapt to this new language.

Our methods and approaches to psychotherapy need revision in terms of this new understanding of affect. Early in my career we were taught that depression would lift when the patient learned how to accept and express anger. People learned how to hit each other with foam rubber baseball bats, to utter the "primal scream." But depression itself is changing in our era. Whereas an earlier generation of therapists might correctly characterize it as "anger turned inward," now there is little shame at the expression of anger and little benefit to be achieved by encouraging its release. I suspect that few therapists raised in this new culture of dyscontrol now concentrate on "the lifting of repression." It is shame, self-dissmell, and self-disgust (poorly defined, inadequately conceptualized, until now little understood) that lie at the heart of the modern clinical complaint of depression. All of us therapists must be reeducated in the language of affect theory.

When affective expression seems blocked we tend to look for a medical reason, a hardware error preventing release. In this current era of concentration on brain mechanisms it is important to recognize that each aberration of neurotransmitter function, each new drug, each newly understood neural circuit, must be evaluated for its relation to the affect system. Individuals who are forbidden by their software from expressing affect often develop somatic illnesses. Few, if any, psychosomatic illnesses have ever been studied for their relation to the neurochemistry of any specific innate affect. We must learn to shift back and forth between our habitual focus on affect as a personal experience and affect as expressed on a societal or cultural level. No study of interpersonal conflict—indeed, of interpersonal relatedness—can be valid without attention to affective resonance and its modulation by the empathic wall.

Charmed by the myriad of fascinating themes and memories encoded within our dreams, Sigmund Freud called the analysis of nocturnal imagery "the royal road to the unconscious." The inner life is far too complex a territory to be served by only one major thoroughfare. It has been my intent to introduce the reader to the affect theory of Silvan Tomkins, a system of thought capable of providing an entirely new map. I understand the affect system as a democratic system, with no royal road.

This group of nine actors—who put on the plays that make up our entire affective life—becomes an internal repertory theater. The study of any affect can lead us to a new understanding of the human condition. The study of shame forces us to reconsider everything we ever knew about the nature of self and other. Such an enquiry cannot end simply because we have reached the end of a book. It is the future history of affect that must now be written.

BIBLIOGRAPHY

Ainsworth, Mary D. (1979). Attachment as related to mother-infant interaction. In J. B. Rosenblatt, R. A. Hinde, C. Beer, & M. Bushel (Eds.), *Advances in the study of behavior* (pp. 1–51). New York: Academic.

Amsterdam, B., & Levitt, M. (1980). Consciousness of self and painful self-consciousness. *Psychoanalytic Study of the Child* 35: 85–90.

Anthony, Elwyn James (1981). Shame, guilt, and the feminine self in psychoanalysis. In Sol Tuttman, Carol Kaye, & Muriel Zimmerman (Eds.), *Object and self: A developmental approach (pp. 191–234). New York: International Universities Press.*

Anthony, Elwyn James (1984). *On the development of shame in childhood and adolescence.* Paper presented at symposium, Shame: New Clinical and Theoretical Aspects. American Psychiatric Association, Los Angeles.

Ariès, Philippe, & Duby, Georges (Eds.); Arthur Goldhammer (Tr.). (1990). *A history of private life.* Vol. 1, *From Pagan Rome to Byzantium* (Paul Veyne, Ed.); vol. 2, *Revelations of the medieval world* (Georges Duby, Ed.); vol. 3, *Passions of the Renaissance* (Roger Chartier, Ed.); vol. 4, *From the fires of revolution to the Great War* (Michelle Perrot, Ed.). Cambridge, Mass.: The Belknap Press of Harvard University Press.

Basch, Michael Franz (1975a). Toward a theory that encompasses depression: A revision of existing causal hypotheses in psychoanalysis. In E. J. Anthony and T. Benedek (Eds.), *Depression and human existence* (pp. 485–534). Boston: Little, Brown.

Basch, Michael Franz (1975b). Perception, consciousness, and Freud's project. *Annual of Psychoanalysis* 3:3–19.

Basch, Michael Franz (1976). The concept of affect: A re-examination. *Journal of the American Psychoanalytic Association* 24:759–57.

Basch, Michael Franz (1980). *Doing psychotherapy.* New York: Basic Books.

Basch, Michael Franz (1983a). Empathic understanding: A review of the concept and some theoretical considerations. *Journal of the American Psychoanalytic Association* 31:101–26.

Basch, Michael Franz (1983b). The perception of reality and the disavowal of meaning. *Annual of Psychoanalysis* 11:125–54.

Basch, Michael Franz (1984). Selfobjects and selfobject transference: Theoretical implications. In P. E. Stepansky & A. Goldberg (Eds.), *Kohut's legacy* (pp. 21–41). Hillsdale, N. J.: Analytic Press.

Basch, Michael Franz (1988). *Understanding psychotherapy: The science behind the art.* New York: Basic Books.

Beach, Frank A. & Levinson, Gilbert (1950). Effects of androgen on the glans penis and mating behavior of castrated male rats. *Journal of Experimental Zoology* 114:159–71.

Beck, Aaron T. (1976). *Cognitive therapy and the emotional disorders.* New York: International Universities Press.

Beebe, Beatrice, & Gerstman, Louis (1984). A method of defining "packages" of maternal stimulation and their functional significance for the infant with mother and stranger. *International Journal of Behavioral Development* 7:423–40.

Beebe, Beatrice, & Lachmann, Frank M. (1988). Mother-infant mutual influence and precursors of psychic structure. In A. Goldberg (Ed.), *Frontiers in self psychology: progress in self psychology,* vol. 3, pp. 3–25. Hillsdale, N. J.: Analytic Press.

Bliss, Eugene L. (1986). *Multiple personality, allied disorders, and hypnosis.* New York: Oxford University Press.

Bowlby, John (1982). *Attachment and loss.* Vol. 1, *Attachment* (2d Ed.). New York: Basic Books.

Bowlby, John (1987). Attachment theory: new directions. ACP–Psychiatric Update Audiotape. Port Washington, N. Y.: Medical Information Systems.

Brenner, Charles (1955). *An elementary textbook of psychoanalysis.* New York: International Universities Press.

Broucek, Francis J. (1979). Efficacy in infancy. *International Journal of Psychoanalysis* 60:311–16.

Broucek, Francis J. (1982). Shame and its relationship to early narcissistic developments. *International Journal of Psychoanalysis* 63:369–78.

Buck, Ross (1984). *The communication of emotion.* New York: Guilford.

Cleaver, Eldridge (1968). *Soul on ice.* New York: Dell.

Comfort, Alex (1972). *The joy of sex: A gourmet guide to lovemaking* (Illustrated Edition) New York: Crown.

Connelly, Thomas L., & Bellows, Barbara L. (1982). *God and General Longstreet: The lost cause and the southern mind.* Baton Rouge: Louisiana State University Press.

Cook, David R. (1987). Measuring shame: The internalized shame scale. *Alcoholism Treatment Quarterly* 4:197–215.

Cook, David R. Shame, attachment, and developmental psychopathology: A review with research and clinical implications. Paper in preparation.

Crile, George W. (1915). *The origin and nature of the emotions.* Philadelphia: W. B. Saunders.

Darwin, Charles (1872). *The expressions of the emotions in man and animals.* Reprint. New York: St. Martin's Press, 1979.

Della Casa, Giovanni (1558). *Galateo.* Reprint. Konrad Eisenbichler and Kenneth R. Bartlett, Trs. Ottawa, Canada: Dovehouse Press, 1990.

Demos, E. Virginia (1983). A perspective from infant research on affect and self-esteem. In J. Mack and S. Ablon (Eds.), *The development and sustaining of self-esteem in childhood* (pp. 45–78). New York: International Universities Press.

Demos, E. Virginia (1988) Affect and the development of the self: A new frontier. In A. Goldberg (Ed.), *Frontiers in self psychology,* vol. 3, pp. 27–53.

De Rivera, Joseph (1977). *A structural theory of the emotions.* New York: International Universities Press.

diCicco, Dennis (1991). The great eclipse of 1991. *Sky and Telescope,* 82:589–595.

Donovan, Martin (1990). Garlic bliss. *Science News,* vol. 138, 20 October 1990. Letter to editor.

D'Souza, Dinesh (1991). Illiberal education. *Atlantic Monthly* 267:51–79.

Edelstein, Eli L., Nathanson, Donald L., & Stone, Andrew M. (1989). *Denial: A clarification of concepts and research.* New York: Plenum.

Ekman, Paul (1972). Universals and cultural differences in facial expressions of emotion. In J. Cole (ed.), *Nebraska symposium on motivation 1971.* Lincoln, Neb.: University of Nebraska Press.

Ekman, Paul (Ed.). (1973). *Darwin and facial expression: A century of research in review.* New York: Academic Press.

Ekman, Paul (1980). *The face of man: expressions of universal emotions in a New Guinea village.* New York: Garland STPM Press.

Ekman, Paul, & Friesen, Wallace V. (1975). *Unmasking the face: A guide to recognizing emotions from facial expressions.* Palo Alto, Cal.: Consulting Psychologists Press.

Ekman, Paul, & Friesen, Wallace V. (1978). *Manual for the facial affect coding system.* Palo Alto, Cal.: Consulting Psychologists Press.

Ekman, P., Levenson, R. W., & Friesen, W. V. (1983). Autonomic nervous system activity distinguishes among emotions. *Science* 221: 1208–10.

Elias, Norbert (1939). *The civilizing process.* vol. 1, *The history of manners.* (Edmund Jephcott, Tr.) New York: Pantheon, 1982.

Emery, Fred, & Emery, Merrelyn (1976). *A choice of futures* Leiden: Martinus Nijhoff Social Sciences Division.

Freud, Sigmund (1915). Instincts and their vicissitudes. In *The standard edition of the complete psychological works of Sigmund Freud.* (James Strachey, Tr.) Vol. 12, pp. 159–204. New York: Norton.

Freud, Sigmund (1905). Jokes and their relation to the unconscious. In *The Standard edition of the complete psychological works of Sigmund Freud.* (James Strachey, Tr.) New York: Norton.

Friedman, Richard C. (1988). *Male homosexuality.* New Haven: Yale University Press.

Friedman, Richard C. (1989). Denial in the development of homosexual men. In E. L. Edelstein, D. L. Nathanson, & A. M. Stone (Eds.), *Denial: A clarification of concepts and research* (pp. 219–30). New York: Plenum.

Fromm, Erich (1956). *The art of loving: An enquiry into the nature of love.* New York: Harper & Row.

Glick, Robert A., & Meyers, Donald I. (1988). *Masochism: Current psychoanalytic perspectives.* Hillsdale, N. J.: Analytic Press.

Gregory, J. C. (1924). *The nature of laughter.* London: Kegan Paul, Trench, Trubner & Co., Ltd.

Gundersheimer, Werner L. (1991). *Renaissance concepts of shame and Pocaterra's "Dialoghi della Vergogna."* Paper presented at Renaissance Society of America Conference, 12 April 1991, Durham, N.C.

Harlow, Harry F. (1959). Love in infant monkeys. *Scientific American,* June 1959. In S. Coopersmith (Ed.), *Readings from Scientific American: Frontiers of psychological research* (pp. 92–98). San Francisco: W. H. Freeman.

Hess, Ekhard H. (1958). "Imprinting" in animals. *Scientific American,* March 1958. Reprinted in S. Coopersmith (Ed.), *Readings from Scientific American* (pp. 13–17).

Hillman, James (1961). *Emotion.* Evanston, Ill.: Northwestern University Press.

Izard, Carroll E. (1971). *The face of emotion.* New York: Appleton-Century-Crofts.

Izard, Carroll E. (1977). *Human emotions.* New York: Plenum.

James, William (1884). What is an emotion? *Mind* 9:188–205. Reprinted in M. Arnold (Ed.), *The nature of emotion.* Baltimore: Penguin, 1968.

James, William (1890). *Principles of psychology.* Vols. 1 and 2. New York: Holt.

Jenike, Michael A. (1984). A case report of successful treatment of dysmorphophobia with tranylcypromine. *American Journal of Psychiatry* 141:1463–64.

Jung, Carl G. (1923). *Psychological types.* New York: Harcourt, Brace.

Kaufman, Gershen (1985). *Shame: The power of caring* (2d ed.). Cambridge, Mass.: Schenkman Books.

Kaufman, Gershen (1989). *The psychology of shame: Theory and treatment of shame-based syndromes.* New York: Springer.

Kernberg, Otto F. (1975). *Borderline conditions and pathological narcissism*. New York: Aronson.

Kernberg, Otto F. (1990). New perspectives in psychoanalytic affect theory. In R. Plutchik and H. Kellerman (Eds.), *Emotion: Theory, research, and experience*, vol. 5 (pp. 115–31). New York: Academic Press.

Kiefer, Otto (1934). *Sexual life in ancient Rome*. London: Abbey Press.

Kinsey, A. C., Pomeroy, W. B., & Martin, C. E. (1948). *Sexual behavior in the human male*. Philadelphia: Saunders.

Kinsey, A. C., Pomeroy, W. B., Martin, C. E., & Gebhard, P. H. (1953). *Sexual behavior in the human female*. Philadelphia: Saunders.

Kluft, Richard P. (1984a). An introduction to multiple personality disorder. *Psychiatric Annals*: 14:19–24.

Kluft, Richard P. (1984b). Treatment of multiple personality disorder: A study of 33 cases. *Psychiatric Clinics of North America* 7:9–29.

Kohut, Heinz (1971). *The analysis of the self* New York: International Universities Press.

Kohut, Heinz (1972). Thoughts on narcissism and narcissistic rage. *Psychoanalytic Study of the Child* 27: 360–99.

Kohut, Heinz (1977). *The restoration of the self* New York: International Universities Press.

Kosinski, Jerzy (1965). *The painted bird*. Boston: Houghton Mifflin.

Krafft-Ebing, Richard von (1906). *Psychopathia sexualis*. Brooklyn: Physicians & Surgeons Book Company, 1932.

Krogh, August (1948). The language of the bees. *Scientific American*, August 1948. In S. Coopersmith, (Ed.), *Readings from Scientific American* (pp. 4–7).

Lange, Carl Georg (1887). *Uber Gemutsbewegunguen*. Leipsig.

Lansky, Melvin R. (1987). Shame and domestic violence. In D. L. Nathanson, (Ed.), *The many faces of shame* (pp. 335–62). New York: Guilford.

Leites, Edmund (1986). *The puritan conscience and modern sexuality*. New Haven: Yale University Press.

Levine, Seymour (1960). Stimulation in infancy. *Scientific American*, May 1960. In S. Coopersmith (Ed.), *Readings from Scientific American* (pp. 100–106).

Lewis, Helen Block (1971). *Shame and guilt in neurosis*. New York: International Universities Press.

Lewis, Helen Block (1981). Shame and Guilt in Human Nature. In S. Tuttman, C. Kaye, & M. Zimmerman (eds.), *Object and self: A developmental approach* (pp. 235–65).

Lewis, Helen Block (1987). Shame and the narcissistic personality. In D. L. Nathanson (Ed.), *The many faces of shame* (pp. 93–132).

Lewis, Michael (1989). Presentation at Institute of Pennsylvania Hospital.

Lichtenberg, Joseph D. (1983). *Psychoanalysis and infant research*. Hillsdale, N. J.: Analytic Press.

Liebowitz, Michael R., Gorman, Jack M., Fyer, Abby J., & Klein, Donald F. (1985). Social phobia: Review of a neglected anxiety disorder. *Archives of General Psychiatry* 42:729–36.

MacLean, Paul D. (1975). On the evolution of three mentalities. *Man-Environment Systems* 5:312–24.

Mahler, Margaret, Pine, Fred, & Bergman, Annie (1975). *The psychological birth of the human infant*. New York: Basic Books.

Malatesta, Carol Z. (1990). The role of emotions in the development and organization of personality. In R. A. Thompson (Ed.), *Socioemotional development: Nebraska symposium on motivation* (1988) 36:1–56. Lincoln, Neb.: University of Nebraska Press.

Malatesta, Carol A. & Wilson, A. (1988). Emotion cognition interaction in personality development: A discrete emotions, functionalist analysis. *British Journal of Social Psychology* 27:91–112.

Malraux, André (1934). *Man's fate*. New York: Random House (The Modern Library).

Masters, William H., & Johnson, Virginia E. (1966). *Human sexual response* Boston: Little, Brown.

Masters, William H., & Johnson, Virginia E. (1970). *Human sexual inadequacy* Boston: Little, Brown.

Money, John, & Ehrhardt, Anke A. (1972). *Man & woman, boy & girl: The differentiation and dimorphism of gender identity from conception to maturity*. Baltimore: The Johns Hopkins University Press.

Money, John (1986). *Venuses penuses*. Buffalo, N. Y.: Prometheus Books.

Morrison, Andrew P. (1983). Shame, ideal self, and narcissism. *Contemporary Psychoanalysis* 19:295–318.

Morrison, Andrew P. (1987). The eye turned inward: Shame and the self. In D. L. Nathanson (ed.), *The many faces of shame* (pp. 271–91).

Morrison, Andrew P. (1989). *Shame: The underside of narcissism*. Hillsdale, N. J.: Analytic Press.

Morrison, Toni (1970). *The bluest eye*. New York: Holt, Rinehart and Winston.

Mosher, Donald L. & Sirkin, Mark (1984). Measuring a macho personality constellation. *Journal of Research in Personality* 18:150–63.

Mosher, Donald L. & Tomkins, Silvan S. (1988). Scripting the macho man: Hypermasculine socialization and enculturation. *Journal of Sex Research* 25:60–84.

Murray, Henry A. (1981) American Icarus. In Edwin S. Schniedman (ed.), *Endeavors in psychology: Selections from the personology of Henry A. Murray*. New York: Harper & Row (pp. 535–56).

Nathanson, Donald L. (1984). *Shame: New Clinical and Theoretical Aspects.* Symposium 9 May 1984 (Los Angeles) meeting of the American Psychiatric Association, co-sponsored by the American Psychoanalytic Association. Panelists included E. James Anthony, Otto Will, Carl Schneider and Léon Wurmser.

Nathanson, Donald L. (1986). The empathic wall and the ecology of affect. *Psychoanalytic Study of the Child* 41:171–87.

Nathanson, Donald L. (1987a). A timetable for shame. In D. L. Nathanson (Ed.), *The many faces of shame* (pp. 1–62).

Nathanson, Donald L. (1987b). Shaming systems in couples, families, and institutions. In D. L. Nathanson (Ed.), *The many faces of shame* (pp. 246–70).

Nathanson, Donald L. (1987c) The shame/pride axis. In H. B. Lewis (Ed.), *The role of shame in symptom formation.* Hillsdale, N.J.: Lawrence Erlbaum Associates.

Nathanson, Donald L. (1988). Affect, affective resonance, and a new theory for hypnosis. *Psychopathology* 21:126–37.

Nathanson, Donald L. (1989). Denial, projection, and the empathic wall. In E. L. Edelstein, D. L. Nathanson, & A. M. Stone (Eds.), *Denial: A clarification of concepts and research* (pp. 37–55).

Nathanson, Donald L. (1990). Project for the study of emotion. In R. A. Glick & S. Bone (Eds.), *Pleasure beyond the pleasure principle: The role of affect in motivation, development, and adaptation* (pp. 81–110). New Haven: Yale University Press.

Nathanson, Donald L. (1991). *What might the world be like if Pocaterra had not been ignored?* Paper presented at Renaissance Society of America Conference, 12 April 1991, Durham, N.C.

Nemiah, John C., Freyberger, H., & Sifneos, Peter E. (1976). Alexithymia: A view of the psychosomatic process. In O. W. Hill (Ed.), *Psychosomatic medicine,* vol. 3, pp. 430–39. London and Boston: Butterworths.

Oxford English Dictionary (1933) on Compact Disc. Oxford: Oxford University Press. (CDROM version published 1987 by Tri Star Publishing, International Computaprint Corporation, Ft. Washington, Pa.)

Papoušek, H. & Papoušek, M. (1975). Cognitive aspects of preverbal social interaction between human infants and adults. Ciba Foundation Symposium. *Parent-Infant Interaction.* New York: Association of Scientific Publications.

Paster, Gail Kern (1987). Leaky vessels: The incontinent women of city comedy. *Renaissance Drama* 18:43–65.

Piaget, Jean (1968). *Six psychological studies.* New York: Random House, Vintage.

Piers, Gerhart and Singer, Milton B. (1953) *Shame and guilt: A psychoanalytic and a cultural study.* Springfield, Ill.: Charles C. Thomas. Reprint. New York: Norton, 1971.

Pocaterra, Annibale (1592). *Due diologhia della vergogna.* Ferrara, Italy. Translated by Piero Alongi and Werner L. Gundersheimer (1990). *Two dialogues on shame,* edited and annotated translation by Donald L. Nathanson and Werner L. Gundersheimer. In preparation.

Pribram, Karl H. (1970). Feelings as monitors. In M. B. Arnold (Ed.), *Feelings and emotions*. New York: Academic Press.

Pribram, Karl H. and Melges, F. T. (1969). Physiological basis of emotion. In P. J. Vinken & G. W. Brunyn (Eds.), Amsterdam: North-Holland. *Handbook of clinical neurology* (pp. 316–42).

Proal, Louis (1901). *Passion and criminality in France: A legal and literary study* Paris: Charles Carrington.

Putnam, Frank W. (1984). The psychophysiologic investigation of multiple personality disorder: A review. *Psychiatric Clinics of North America* 7:31–50.

Rapoport, Judith L. (1989). *The boy who couldn't stop washing: The experience and treatment of obsessive-compulsive syndrome*. New York: Dutton.

Rodale, J. I. (1947). *The word finder*. Emmaus, Pa.: Rodale Books, Inc.

Rogers, Carl R. (1951). *Client-centered therapy*. Boston: Houghton-Mifflin.

Rombauer, Irma S. (1931). *The joy of cooking*. Indianapolis: Bobbs-Merrill.

Rosten, Leo (1968). *The joys of Yiddish*. New York: McGraw-Hill.

Rozin, Paul & Fallon, April E. (1987). A perspective on disgust. *Psychological Review* 94:23–41.

Rubenstein, Richard L. (1978). *The cunning of history*. New York: Harper, Colophon.

Rutsala, Vern (1988). Shame. *The American Scholar*. Autumn 1988, vol. 57 no. 4:574.

Rycroft, C. (1968). *A critical dictionary of psychoanalysis*. New York: Basic Books.

Saint Augustine. *The confessions of Saint Augustine*. (R. S. Pine-Coffin, Tr.). New York: Viking Penguin, 1961.

Sartre, Jean-Paul (1948). *The emotions: Outline of a theory*. New York: Philosophical Library.

Sartre, Jean-Paul (1956). *Being and nothingness: An essay on phenomenological ontology*. (H. E. Barnes, Tr.) New York: Philosophical Library.

Scheff, Thomas J. (1988). Shame and conformity: The deference–emotion system. *American Sociological Review* 53:395–406.

Scheler, Max (1954). *The nature of sympathy* (Peter Heath, Tr.) London: Routledge & Kegan Paul.

Schneider, Carl D. (1977). *Shame, exposure and privacy*. Boston: Beacon.

Schneider, Carl D. (1987). A mature sense of shame. In D. L. Nathanson (ed.), *The many faces of shame* (pp. 194–213).

Shakespeare, William. *Shakespeare on Disc!* Portland, Ore.: CMC ReSearch, Inc. (CDROM version), 1989.

Shaw, George Bernard (1903). *Man and superman*. Baltimore: Penguin, 1952.

Sipe, A. W. Richard (1990). *A secret world: Sexuality and the search for celibacy*. New York: Bruner/Mazel.

Spitz, René (1965). *The first year of life*. New York: International Universities Press.

Sroufe, L. A. (1979). The coherence of individual development: Early care, attachment, and subsequent developmental issues. *American Psychologist* 34:834–41.

Stern, Daniel N. (1985). *The interpersonal world of the infant: A view from psychoanalysis and developmental psychology*. New York: Basic Books.

Stoller, Robert J. (1968). *Sex and gender: On the development of masculinity and femininity*. New York: Science House.

Stoller, Robert J. (1979). *Sexual excitement*. New York: Pantheon.

Stoller, Robert J. (1985) *Observing the erotic imagination*. New Haven: Yale University Press.

Stoller, Robert J. (1987). Pornography: Daydreams to cure humiliation. In D. L. Nathanson (ed.), *The many faces of shame* (pp. 292–307).

Sullivan, Harry Stack (1953a). *Conceptions of modern psychiatry*. New York: Norton.

Sullivan, Harry Stack (1953b). *The interpersonal theory of psychiatry*. New York: Norton.

Sullivan, Harry Stack (1954). *The psychiatric interview* (Helen Swick Perry and Mary Ladd Gawel, Eds.) New York: Norton.

Tabin, Johanna Krout (1985). *On the way to self: Ego and early oedipal development*. New York: Columbia University Press.

Taylor, G. Rattray (1953). *Sex in history*. Reprint. New York: Vanguard Press, 1970.

Thurber, James, and White, E. B. (1929). *Is sex necessary? Or: Why you feel the way you do*. New York: Harper.

Tinbergen, Nicholas (1952). The curious behavior of the stickleback. *Scientific American*, Dec. 1952. In S. Coopersmith (Ed.), *Readings from Scientific American* (pp. 8–12.)

Tomkins, Silvan S. (1962). *Affect/imagery/consciousness*. Vol. 1: *The positive affects*. New York: Springer.

Tomkins, Silvan S. (1963). *Affect/imagery/consciousness*. Vol. 2: *The negative affects*. New York: Springer.

Tomkins, Silvan S. (1965) Affect and the psychology of knowledge. In S. S. Tomkins and C. Izard (Eds.), *Affect, cognition, and personality*. New York: Springer.

Tomkins, Silvan S. (1979). Script theory: Differential magnification of affects. In H. E. Howe and R. A. Dienstbier (Eds.), *Nebraska symposium on motivation*, vol. 26, 201–36.

Tomkins, Silvan S. (1981). The quest for primary motives: Biography and autobiography of an idea. *Personality and Social Psychology* 41:306–29.

Tomkins, Silvan S. (1982). Affect theory. In: P. Ekman (Ed.), *Emotion in the human face* (2d ed.), (pp. 353–95). New York: Cambridge University Press.

Tomkins, Silvan S. (1987a). Shame. In D. L. Nathanson (Ed.), *The many faces of shame* (pp. 133–61).

Tomkins, Silvan S. (1987b). Script theory. In J. Aronoff, A. I. Rabin, & R. A. Zucker (Eds.), *The emergence of personality*. New York: Springer.

Tomkins, Silvan S. (1991). *Affect/imagery/consciousness*. Vol. 3: *The negative affects: anger and fear*. New York: Springer.

Wurmser, Léon (1981). *The mask of shame*. Baltimore: Johns Hopkins University Press.

Wurmser, Léon (1987). Shame: The veiled companion to narcissism. In D. L. Nathanson (Ed.), *The many faces of shame* pp. 64–92.

Wurmser, Léon (1989). Blinding the eye of the mind: Denial, impulsive action, and split identity. In E. L. Edelstein, D. L. Nathanson, & A. M. Stone (Eds.), *Denial: A clarification of concepts and research* (pp. 175–201).

INDEX

Page numbers in *italics* refer to illustrations.

empathic failure is abandonment